JEFFREY WOLF GREEN EVOLUTI

NEPTUNE

WHISPERS FROM ETERNITY

Jeffrey Wolf Green

Edited by Linda Jonson

and the School of Evolutionary Astrology

Swami Sri Yukteswar and Paramahansa Yogananda

A child is born on that day and at that hour when the celestial rays
are in mathematical harmony with his or her individual karma.
The resulting horoscope is a challenging portrait revealing
his or her unalterable past, and its probable future result.
But the natal chart can be rightly interpreted only by
women and men of intuitive wisdom:
these are few.

SWAMI SRI YUKTESWAR
GURU OF THE GREAT PARAMAHANSA YOGANANDA

ABOUT THE AUTHOR

Jeffrey Wolf Green has been called the founder of Evolutionary Astrology because he first started to lecture on the revolutionary astrological paradigm in 1977 after receiving a dream from the spiritual master Swami Sri Yukteswar, Paramahansa Yogananda's guru. In that dream the entire paradigm of Evolutionary Astrology was conveyed to Jeffrey. This was the first time in astrology's long history that a specific paradigm was realized that allowed for an understanding of the evolutionary progression of a Soul from life to life. Jeffrey lectured all over the world on Evolutionary Astrology from 1977 to 2001. He established Evolutionary Astrology schools in a number of countries and wrote three books on Evolutionary Astrology.

The first of these, *Pluto: The Evolutionary Journey of the Soul, Volume I* was published in 1984. It has been in continuous print ever since and has become one of the all-time best selling astrology books. Translations have been made into French, German, Dutch, Chinese, Bulgarian, Spanish, Portuguese, and other languages. Volume II, *Pluto: The Soul's Evolution through Relationships* was published in 1998 and has been in continuous print. A third volume, *Essays in Evolutionary Astrology: The Evolutionary Journey of the Soul*, was published in 2010. *Essays* was compiled by his daughter Deva Green from transcriptions of workshops Jeffrey gave over the years. It covers topics that are part of Jeffrey's Evolutionary Astrology paradigm that were either not covered in depth or in some cases at all in his original two volumes.

Since starting his original Pluto School in 1994, Jeffrey had many EA students, a number of whom are now professional EA astrologers. He personally counseled over 30,000 clients in his lengthy career. This exposure to so many Souls from so many different backgrounds and orientations allowed him to come to the deepest possible understandings of the nature of the Soul. He communicated these insights through all of his teachings. In 2008 his daughter Deva Green, took over her father's work. She established the Jeffrey Wolf Green School of Evolutionary Astrology website, and created the EA School's Evolutionary Astrology Council who assist Deva with the School's mission of disseminating Jeffrey's original work around the planet.

www.schoolofevolutionaryastrology.com/school/

CONTRIBUTORS

Catharine J. Anderson (Cat)

Patrick Chehab (Skywalker)

Kristin Fontana

Linda Jonson

Ari Moshe Wolfe

Rad Zecko

and

Members of the School of
Evolutionary Astrology message board

TABLE OF CONTENTS

Foreword by Deva Green

FOREWORD

Neptune: Whispers From Eternity has been compiled from a variety of my Father's materials that include his message boards, transcribed lectures, and various pieces of paper in which he would write down many of his thoughts that correlate with Neptune, Pisces, and the 12th House.

This book includes the Neptune thread on our existing message board that is also full of ideas and, especially, the practice charts of the wonderful contributors who have given us such wonderful, practical, examples of the various archetypes that have been discussed. We have purposefully chosen to include these practice charts because each one is like a 'hands on' that supplies the Evolutionary Astrology reasoning for the statements that are being made. If you really desire to understand how to apply Evolutionary Astrology these examples will help make that so for you.

This then gives you, the reader, a great feel for how Evolutionary Astrology as developed by my father, Jeffrey Wolf Green, is meant to be understood, and practiced. Our contributors range from being relative beginners to advanced in the development of being Evolutionary Astrologers. Thus, as you read these example charts you hopefully can also become inspired to either learn Evolutionary Astrology, or deepen your existing understanding and abilities.

To my knowledge there has never been a book written on Neptune like the one you are about to read. It is breathtaking in its scope, breathtaking in its ability to *PRACTICALLY* apply all the archetypes covered into the life of yourself, your dear ones, and your clients if you are a practicing astrologer.

This book would not have been possible without the great efforts of its editor, Linda Jonson; Rad Zecko, as the moderator for our current message board; as well as the staff at the School of Evolutionary Astrology.

God Bless, Deva Green
Ashland, Oregon
April 16th, 2014

CHAPTER ONE

NEPTUNE: THE CONSCIOUSNESS OF THE SOUL

Introduction

Consciousness: all Souls have it. Consciousness permeates the manifest Creation. It is very interesting to consider the fact that not all the empirical sciences can explain what consciousness is at all: it cannot be measured in any of their ways. Yet, of course, it exists. In the same way, these sciences cannot measure or explain what humans call 'God' either. Yet intuitively the consciousness in the human form knows that 'something' has to be the source of the Manifest Creation. So here we have a situation where both consciousness and what is called 'God' cannot be empirically known by any science on Earth. Yet both exists. Within consciousness is the natural law of intelligence. Souls that are in human form thus share consciousness and intelligence, which is what Jung called the collective consciousness.

Yet each human form with a Soul in it is then an individualized Soul with its own consciousness and intelligence. Consciousness can be fully consciousness or it can be minimally conscious. This natural law can be illustrated by using the example of a light bulb that has the total capacity to be illuminated, say, by 100 volts of electricity. If I attach a dimmer switch to this light bulb, I can then control the degree of electricity that illuminates it from the most minimal amount of electricity, voltage, to the maximum degree of electricity that would then be reflected in the degree of brightness within the bulb.

In the very same way the degree of electricity that is within an individual's Soul's consciousness correlates to how conscious it is, how bright, that itself is a function of its intelligence. Intelligence is a function of evolution: the totality of intelligence versus minimal intelligence.

Consciousness is defined by form where form is the determinant of consciousness. If I put water in a cup, where water correlates to consciousness, then that water is defined by the form of the cup. In the same way, consciousness is defined by the human form. All Souls in human form thus correlates to the collective consciousness. Yet, again, each human has its own individual consciousness that is a function of the structural nature of its consciousness. The structural nature of its consciousness is reflected in the ongoing evolutionary nature of it that is determined by desire. Thus, desires become the determinant of the dynamics within consciousness, and those dynamics then are the determinants of the structural nature, form, of its consciousness.

Thus, what any given Soul is conscious of by way of the degree of its evolution: how much voltage or electricity is present within it. This is then reflected in the four natural evolutionary states. It is critical to know this from an evolutionary astrology point of view. For example, many Souls will have the same or similar birth charts. Yet it is the degree of evolution of any given Soul that then determines the degree of self-awareness or how conscious it is of itself as well as how conscious it is relative to the totality of the Creation: the very Origin of itself.

As you at this very moment are reading these words you are experiencing the 'world' around you as it is: all the events going on in the world, your country, your region, your city, your group or tribe of like-minded Souls, and your own individual Soul reality within all of this.

THIS IS YOUR LIVING EXPERIENCE OF NEPTUNE! THIS IS NEPTUNE'S CONSCIOUSNESS. RIGHT NOW, AND IN EVERY OTHER MOMENT IN TIME. THIS IS THE NATURAL TRIAD OF CONSCIOUSNESS SYMBOLIZED BY THE MOON, YOUR EGO; PLUTO, YOUR SOUL; AND NEPTUNE ITSELF: YOUR INDIVIDUALIZED CONSCIOUSNESS RELATIVE TO THE COLLECTIVE CONSCIOUSNESS OF ALL HUMANS.

The Structural Nature of the Soul and the Consciousness within it

The Soul has its own unique identity as created by the Source, or God. As such, it has its own ego that creates an image in the Soul of that unique identity. The awareness of that unique Soul identity is a function of evolution itself which finally leads to being self-aware, and has the evolved capacity, at some point, to objectify itself. The South and North Nodes of Pluto correlate to this ongoing evolutionary development of the Soul from within itself. The natal position of the current life Pluto simultaneously correlates to what the desires have been within the Soul for its own development, thus where it left off in those lives that have led to the current life, and the evolutionary intent for the current life for its evolution to proceed: the natural polarity point of that natal Pluto.

The South Node of Pluto, by its own house and sign location, aspects to it from other planets, and aspects to its natural planetary ruler all correlates to archetypes and dynamics that the Soul has used to develop itself, evolve itself, relative the its core desires for its evolution that is symbolized in the natal position of Pluto itself. The North Node of Pluto correlates to how and why the Soul evolves itself from within itself: what it needs to continue in its evolution. Other planets that aspect this North Node are archetypes that correlate to this ongoing evolution of the Soul within itself.

In order for all these internal dynamics within the Soul itself that correlate to its own ongoing evolution it must project or externalize itself through the creation of forms: the human form. This natural law or principle is the same as of what we call the Source Of All Things, or God, projecting and externalizing itself in the form of what we call CREATION. What we call God does this in order to know itself in all of these forms in the totality of Creation. So too with the individual Soul. The Soul needs to project or externalize itself in order to know itself, to objectify itself.

Therefore, the Soul projects and externalizes itself form life to life in the form of the lifetimes that it lives that are all finite. The Soul itself is infinite just as God itself is infinite. Each finite life that the Soul projects from within itself, just as God projects each individualized Soul from within itself, reflects and symbolizes the core desires from within the Soul that reflect its own ongoing evolutionary desires to evolve. As a result of this projection from life to life we then have the birth charts for each of those lives that reflect the finite forms that the Soul creates in order to affect its ongoing evolution. In each of these finite forms that the Soul creates, it thus creates a consciousness that has its own subjective self-awareness that we call the ego or 'I'. And of course, that subjective ego, the egocentric structure, is a projection from the Soul itself in order to know itself relative to the finite form it has created in each life that reflects its ongoing evolutionary needs and requirements.

The subjective 'I' or ego that is created in each life by the Soul of course is the archetype of the Moon. The evolutionary journey of the Soul through time is thus symbolized through all the different finite forms or lives that it creates that are determined by its evolutionary needs and desires. And it is each of these finite lives that the Soul creates that the birth chart correlates to. And in each of those lives the finite ego does indeed 'die,' just as the body dies. Yet the memories of each life are sustained and live on within the Soul itself. And it is these ongoing evolutionary experiences from life to life that are the ongoing determinant and cause for yet another life.

Questions and Answers

(Q) Why does Pluto represent the Soul's evolutionary desires from previous lives whereas all the other planets, assuming they are not in aspect to any Node (or Pluto), do not innately imply past lives?

(A) Because Pluto correlates to the Soul itself, and within that, the natural law of evolution. It correlates to what the desires of the Soul have been that have led to the current life, and the desires that correlate to its ongoing evolutionary needs. This is contained with Pluto, the Soul, itself. All the other planets in a current life birth chart are thus created by the Soul for its ongoing evolutionary needs that are reflected in its desires. The current life birth planets do have their own North and South Nodes. It is the South Nodes of these planets that correlate to the past life dynamics that the Soul has created for itself that have led to the current life, and the position of whatever planet IN THIS LIFE that symbolizes the current life's evolutionary needs.

The current life position brings the past forwards through it: the South Node coming through the current position of the planet itself. The North Node of the planet in turn correlates to the ongoing evolutionary journey of the Soul as it continues to evolve through each of the archetypes of all the planets. The cause of that evolution is the Soul, not any of the other planets themselves. The natural polarity point of the natal Pluto is the bottom line evolutionary intent for the Soul in each life. It is the primary cause that causes the North Nodes of all the other planets to actualize according to that primary evolutionary intention. The natal planet in the current life birth chart serves to integrate the past and the future in each moment FOR THE ENTIRE LIFE.

(Q) Okay, so within the EA paradigm, in general how much 'weight' should we put on the South and North Nodes of the planets when working with a chart? Obviously, we put a lot of weight (or emphasis) on the North and South Nodes of the Moon. How much, then, to give to the Nodes of Pluto itself, and how much to give to the rest of the planets?

If some planets are highlighted in the chart for various reasons, i.e. on an angle, part of a tight aspect pattern, or a Moon Node ruler, or in aspect to Pluto etc., would that mean the Nodes of these planets become more important in chart analysis?

(A) Pluto and its Nodes, their planetary rulers, and aspects to these from other planets, correlate to the root structure within any birth chart. From that root, all else, the South/North Nodes of the Moon, their planetary rulers, and aspects to these points, are 'birthed' from that root. It's like a tree that has branches where the root produces the trunk of the tree, and the trunk then produces branches with leaves. This core root and its branches within the birth chart is treated EQUALLY for it is the very structure of the chart itself. If we understand this root structure within the birth chart and relate it to the natural law of cause and effect then we can understand that core structure within the birth chart at once. It will, of itself, induce inductive logic. And from there we can then understand the origins and causes of all the specific leaves manifesting from the branches, i.e. why is this Mars in Gemini squaring Mercury in Pisces.

(Q) Thanks for that foundation perspective; it clarifies the whole bottom line of the chart. To clarify I understand correctly, this then means that:

- Pluto (sign/house)
- Pluto's nodes (sign/house)
- Pluto's nodal rulers (sign/house)
- aspects from all of the above to other planets (and their signs/houses – and if more information is required, also their Nodes)

… are the fundamental root of any chart. From there, the sign/house of the Moon's nodes, Moon's nodal rulers, and Pluto's polarity point are brought in. Then aspects from all these to other planets (and their signs/houses). Also at this level, a planet's nodes can be examined if more information was required. Then progression to examination of any other part of the chart that thus becomes implicated out of this. (Realizing of course that every part of the chart has a part in the whole person/event and so eventually needs to be included in a totally complete analysis.) Please correct me if I haven't got any or all of this right.

One question I have is: Pluto's polarity point shows the Soul's current evolutionary intentions for this life (unless Pluto is conjunct the Moon's North Node in which case there is no polarity point for Pluto). So how does Pluto's polarity point (PPP) differ to Pluto's North Node in this regard?

(A)   Yes, you have summarized it correctly.

(Q)   So how does PPP differ to Pluto's North Node in this regard?

(A)   The North Node of Pluto reflects the ongoing evolutionary development of the Soul from within itself that is then actualized through the creation, projection, externalization of itself via the finite form it creates in each life. This is symbolized by the polarity point of Pluto in the current life birth chart. The Soul, from within itself, of course contains all the previous identities, singular life/finite forms, that it has ever lived. It also contains within itself all the different possibilities, future life/finite forms that could occur. That which can occur is dependent on what the Soul, within itself, DESIRES. Those desires have been the prior life causes of what has already taken place. And in each of those lives the Soul created the necessity of subjective egocentric identities, finite life forms, for the desires to be actualized which of course has led to yet more desires to evolve that have led to yet another life.

In each of these lives the Soul, from within itself has had a North Node that has symbolized those ongoing evolutionary developmental desires. And in each life, those desires are then actualized by way of the polarity point of Pluto in each life, the individual birth chart. It's like, from within the Soul itself, it says: I need or desire to evolve in the following way: North Node; and in order to do this, I will actualize it like this: the polarity point of Pluto in the individual life that the Soul creates in each life.

The Nodes of Pluto stay in signs, i.e. Cancer/Capricorn, or whatever signs, about 2,000 years. Most Souls of course will have more than one life within a span of 2,000 years. So the core evolutionary desires from within the Soul exist beyond the singularity of one finite life. In each of those singular lives, the Soul continues to desire to evolve in this core archetypal way that is then actualized through each of the specific singular/finite lives that it lives. And in each of those singular lives that core evolutionary intent within the Soul is actualized by the polarity point of Pluto in those lives: the birth chart that symbolizes this entire process.

Let's make a simple example of these dynamics. Let's say person X has in their current birth chart a 9th House Pluto in Leo, the South Node of Pluto being in Capricorn in the 2nd, which is ruled by Saturn in Leo in the 9th. The North Node of Pluto would be in Cancer in the 8th, and Pluto's polarity point would be in Aquarius in the 3rd. The Pluto in the 9th in Leo would correlate to a Soul that has desired to understand and actualize itself by way of understanding the nature of the cosmos, and the Natural Laws of Creation. It has spent many, many lives in relative isolation, the South Node of Pluto in Capricorn in the 2nd, in order to inwardly contemplate that nature of Creation in order to realize by way of that isolated contemplation the nature of these Natural Laws, which thus become the very basis of the Soul's inner relationship to itself: the 2nd House. This, in turn would constitute the Soul's core sense of meaning for existence, of that which held the core meaning for life itself.

The ruler of that South Node is also in Leo in the 9th. This would restate the Soul actualizing these core desires within the context of Nature, living and being within Nature in order to inwardly know all the Natural Laws that are responsible for Creation, Leo, itself. In relation to the South Node being in the 2nd, these symbols put together correlate to a natural loner who has realized what it has desired in essential isolation in this way.

Yet, in this way, the Soul has reached an evolutionary limit, and needs to continue to evolve. The Soul, from within itself, realizes this which is then symbolized by its North Node being in Cancer in the 8th House: the desire and need to jump out of the well of its own isolation, and to then engage and help other Souls on their own evolutionary journey. In so doing the Soul will then necessarily interact with other Souls and THEIR REALITIES: the interaction of the South and North Nodes of Pluto where Capricorn correlates to the archetype of reality, the realities of Earth itself. In this interaction with others, it thus causes the Soul from within itself to confront its own evolutionary limitations that then creates the ongoing awareness of what it needs to continue to evolve itself. This confrontation can then cause the Soul to feel insecure from within itself as it is required to evolve beyond where it was by way of its own understandings of the nature of reality on this Earth that are reflections of the Natural Laws of Creation. These confrontations are intended so that the Soul can evolve beyond where it has already been.

In order for these core Soul intentions to evolve it then creates a singular or finite life in which the polarity point of the natal Pluto is in Aquarius in the 3rd. This will manifest, in the context of the example we are using, by creating a life in which the very opposite of where it has been: living alone in relative isolation within Nature. The Soul now will create a life in which it will be totally involved with others who are living within the world, in their cities, wherever whole groups of people exist: Aquarius in the 3rd. And, in this way, purposefully engage the realities of countless others who have all kinds of ideas, opinions, points of view, ideas, and philosophies from A to Z, so to speak. And all of this will then of course impact on the Soul's current state of understanding the nature of reality that it has already realized in its past. The Soul then has another choice to make: it can retreat back to where it has been in order to remain secure from within itself, or make a choice to continue to grow from within itself due to the confrontations to that existing reality through the diversity of ideas manifesting within these groups of people, other individuals.

If it makes the choice to proceed in this way, it will then of course continue to evolve which reflects the intention of Pluto's North Node in Cancer in the 8th. That North Node of Cancer of course will be ruled by the current life Moon, its egocentric structure created in the current life. So the underlying dynamics within the Soul that we have been discussing will then be focused, like a lens in a movie projector that creates images on a screen, into a current life identity, the 'I' of the current life. This is the natural law of how a Soul externalizes or projects itself from life to life by creating an 'image' of itself that correlates to the entire 'movie' of that life.

(Q) Fascinating! – showing the cause of the PPP and the wider context for any chart's bottom line. Thanks a lot for that.

As it happens, I have a friend who has almost the same signature as the one you used for your example, everything in the same signs and houses (except Saturn is in Virgo not Leo). And interestingly enough the Moon (the ruler of Pluto North Node in Cancer) is back in the 9th (!) in Virgo (but not conjunct Pluto or Saturn).

Guess that's possibly a subtle version of keeping "one arm waving free" (but at a core Soul level), reflecting a bit of residual ambivalence (which would then manifest on an ego/personality level) about following through on their intention in this lifetime of getting fully involved in discussions etc. with others in urban/group situations, as indicated by the PPP (3rd house Aquarius). Would that be right?

Seeing that subtle paradox in that chart, it then occurred to me that one of the things that's really useful about this wider understanding of Pluto's evolutionary intentions in a chart, is how the intentions of the Soul (known from within itself) become implemented in a natal chart as the PPP, via the Moon and its nodes and their rulers. And also how the Moon and its nodes and their rulers relate back to Pluto's nodes and their rulers.

To try and show what I mean by that, I'll use another example – an actual chart with some interesting paradoxes (and also see how well I go!):

This chart has Pluto in Leo in 4th, Pluto's polarity point (PPP) in Aquarius in 10th, Pluto's South Node in Capricorn in 9th, ruler Saturn in Sagittarius 8th (and conjuncting the Moon's North Node there too), Pluto North Node in Cancer in 2nd, ruler Moon in Gemini 2nd (and conjuncting the Moon's South Node there too).

This would correlate to a Soul that has embarked on a new evolutionary cycle, desiring to actualize itself through the development of internal security. In a nutshell, this would be achieved by attaining emotional maturity, creatively establishing its own individuality through its own efforts, and uniting the anima and animus within itself (Pluto Leo 4th). It would have done this in the context of having spent many lives traveling in different lands, experiencing different cultures, and expanding its understanding of natural laws and nature itself (Pluto South Node in 9th).

With Pluto South Node ruler, Saturn, being in the 8th house in Sagittarius, within each society that was lived in, it would have been involved in a 'hands on' way. It would correlate to someone who would learn by getting deeply involved in situations with other people (8th). For a Soul at consensus reality level, as an example, perhaps setting up business (Saturn) of an entrepreneurial kind (Sagittarius), or becoming involved in the political or judicial structure of that society at a local or national government level. Alternatively, if the Soul was at the individuated reality stage, they may have formed close associations with powerful people, outsiders to society, for the purposes of occult study (8th, Sagittarius), operation of black markets (Saturn, 8th) etc. If in the spiritual stage, they may have joined spiritual groups for experiments with alchemy, study of scriptures etc. (Saturn, Sagittarius 8th).

As the Soul experienced the limits of itself, it would have desired to evolve beyond them, symbolized by Pluto North Node in Cancer in 2nd. This would represent a need to become less entangled in the affairs of any society and the individuals so involved, and a need to stop traveling around and to settle down more, gravitating to the relative isolation of living in just one place in order to develop a more personal self-sufficiency and self-reliance. To establish its own set of values that made sense to just itself, instead of all the time incorporating the needs of other people it had attached to, into its sense of what was important. Taking care of the needs of its own self and immediate family members only.

In so doing external confrontations would occur as it withdrew from relationships of a societal and dependent nature, and internal confrontations via the insecurity it felt in then not being able to draw upon others for resources, advantage and as symbols of power, a sense of loss of power and powerlessness would accompany the transition.

So, stemming from these inner evolutionary desires and thus needs of the Soul, which are to move towards Cancer in 2nd house experiences (Pluto North Node) and in turn doing that via Gemini in 2nd house experiences (Pluto North Node ruler), a new life would be created to implement these core intentions, and in this case it is one where the PPP is in Aquarius in 10th.

And, as an extension of that, the Moon South Node in Gemini 2nd, and Moon North Node in Sagittarius 8th. However, the Soul has also manifested in this new life the Moon conjuncting the Moon South Node, and Saturn conjuncting the Moon North Node. Here's where the paradoxes lie: the Soul's (Pluto's) nodal rulers, Saturn and Moon, are now each conjuncting one of the Moon's nodes in the new life!

With the Soul's (Pluto's) South Node ruler in Sagittarius in 8th, in theory the Soul has finished with that as a way of realizing its South Node (Capricorn in 9th) intentions and is desiring to move towards Cancer in 2nd shown by Pluto North Node, via 2nd house Gemini experiences shown by the placement of Pluto North Node ruler, the Moon.

Where it's aiming for in its new life form is to realize the Aquarius 10th house archetype shown by PPP in the chart of the new life. And by doing this the Soul will be effecting its evolutionary desire symbolized by Cancer in the 2nd house.

The life implied by the PPP is one where the Soul will move again in society but in a different way to before. The intense, and possibly heavy, involvements of the 8th house from past lives give way to the more open (Aquarius) and contributory manner of the 10th. Thus the person will be bringing everything they learned (Sagittarius), experienced (9th), and osmosed (8th) from past lives into a form (10th) that can be used in a much larger and more objective (Aquarius) way in society. In other words, the test will be: can they put their knowledge (Sagittarius learning from past lives) to good use (10th) in this life in a way that benefits many people, not just themselves or others they are intimately entangled with (Pluto South Node ruler and Moon North Node, Saturn in 8th).

Additionally they will be associating with groups of others of like-mind based on broad human interests, innovative explorations and networking (Aquarius) rather than the secretive and murky kinds of associations they may have involved themselves in the past (Pluto South Node ruler in 8th) and may still do (Moon North Node in 8th). All the while, building on the Soul's core singular evolutionary intention and progress to date (Pluto in 4th), and a major part of its intentions for the future as well (Cancer in 2nd): actualizing internal security.

This will be effected in the current life by a fair amount of reliving the past (paradox) as the Moon is conjunct the Moon's South Node in Gemini, and Saturn is conjunct the Moon's North Node in Sagittarius.

The Moon's South Node indicates the lessons the Soul has been learning before as part of actualizing internal security, and being in Gemini this would have involved dynamics and the circumstances they created relating to, among other things, communications, thinking, study and commerce (Mercury ruling the Moon's South Node). This indicates that the Soul's previous intense involvements from many lifetimes ago (Pluto South Node ruler Saturn in 8th) had morphed into a lighter and less focused way of relating to people in recent past lives, and that the Soul has been learning how to relate to much more diverse, and perhaps more common elements of society. This may have actually been a necessary preparatory step towards the future desire of withdrawing more from society (Pluto North Node in Cancer 2nd) in that it may have afforded the Soul more choice in those lives, which would have been helpful on the way to coming closer to the self-reliance and self-sufficiency of the 2nd house. Also the Moon's South Node being in the 2nd house shows that the Soul has in recent lives already started learning the lessons it needs to, indicated by the Pluto's North Node (2nd house).

The Soul desires to move towards realization of the Cancer in 2nd archetype (Pluto North Node) with its ruler the Moon being instrumental in this – this is the Soul's future. But with the Moon conjuncting the Moon's South Node in the current life this future process is now partially brought forward, hastened, due to the fact that experiences related to the Moon will be relived or fruited in some way (Moon conjunct Moon's South Node).

The Moon's North Node indicates the new way for the Soul to operate, new lessons to learn in this current (new) life that will help the Soul realize the PPP in this life, i.e. to actualize self-determination, discipline, social responsibility and to establish their individuality and authority within society. The lessons that will help the Soul achieve this will seem very familiar for this Soul, as they are shown by the Moon's North Node in Sagittarius in 8th which it has experienced before (Pluto South Node ruler territory) and thus will remember on a Soul level.

Since Saturn is conjuncting the Moon's North Node and Saturn is also Pluto's South Node ruler, the Soul has done all of this before in previous lives (as described above). Here again there will be a lot of reliving as a result, but being at the North Node there will be the chance to do the same things in new or better ways, to make different choices when faced with circumstances, situations and dynamics that the Soul has experienced in (perhaps quite recent) past lives.

Obviously Jupiter (Moon's North Node in Sagittarius ruler) will be a key factor in what these choices will be. As examples of the extremes of the situation, if it was in the 4th or 2nd house, it would strengthen the likelihood that the Soul would make choices in line with its own core inner intentions (Pluto North Node in Cancer in 2nd), whereas if it was in the 10th or the 9th house it may gravitate to old ways (Pluto South Node in Capricorn in 9th) of dealing with similar situations encountered freshly in the new current life.

So in summary, while this Soul is embarking on a new evolutionary cycle (Pluto in 4th) its new current life that it has manifested is still intricately connected to relatively recent previous lives, and it will use material from those lives as part of its efforts to further its evolutionary intentions.

By realizing its PPP it will be establishing its own individuality on a much more tangible basis than previously (PPP 10th house is more immediate than Pluto South Node Capricorn), in a much more open way (PPP Aquarius compared to Moon's South Node in 2nd, Pluto South Node ruler in 8th). This in turn will prepare the Soul to come closer to its future desire (Pluto North Node in Cancer in 2nd) as it will have completed a major involvement in society in a number of varying ways, and achieved a significant amount of understanding of natural and metaphysical laws and principles. Thus, it will be able to withdraw largely on its own terms, which is a primary requisite for realizing the 2nd house archetype of self-sufficiency and reliance.

During the current life, the person may feel that their future and past are often intertwined, with a strong feeling of déjà-vu at times. It may seem they are repeating things they feel they have finished with long ago, and even in the current life may restart things that they had thought they'd put behind them long before – Soul's (Pluto's) nodal rulers conjunct this life's (Moon's) nodes.

By the end of this current life, the various kinds of involvement with people that this Soul will have had via its 8th (Pluto South Node ruler, Moon North Node) and 4th (Pluto) houses, plus Gemini (Moon South Node) and Moon (conjunct Moon South Node) will have taught it some very fundamental and also very varied things about people and relationships with them. This will be preparing it for a more simple Cancer orientated involvement with people in the future (Pluto North Node in Cancer).

I do not know what you'll make of that! It came in a burst of inspiration, but I would really like to know if it's any good. It's pretty long winded and may not be appropriate. In a way, I feel as if I'm going way ahead of myself here, as I always felt I haven't really grasped working with just the Pluto house, and Moon's nodes and rulers yet, let alone diving into things at this level. However, I've done it now. If it's off the mark, I'd really appreciate to know that.

(A) You are demonstrating a very fine and keen intuitive ability to use and apply the reasoning inherent to the EA paradigm. What seemed to have just burst through you is VERY ACCURATE in what you have covered. There are of course other dimensions within all those archetypes but what you have covered thus far is very, very well-reasoned and accurate. Bravo!!

(Q) I am trying to integrate this material about the nodes of Pluto in my understanding. I am not sure if it is correct to consider the Pluto SN and its ruler as correlating to older chapters in the Soul's journey, these older chapters coming through the past symbolized by Pluto.

Let's say a Soul with Pluto in the 2nd House Virgo, Pluto SN in the 7th Capricorn, ruler Saturn in the 10th Taurus, trine Pluto and trine Pluto SN. Pluto NN in Cancer in the 1st House, ruler the Moon in the 2nd House Virgo conjunct Pluto. With Pluto in the 2nd House Virgo, the Soul has passed many lives in relative isolation and relating to himself in order to discover its own sense of value, relating to himself in critical ways.

The SN of Pluto in the 7th would then indicate that the Soul had prior desires to have its sense of identity created through relationships with others. Through patriarchal conditioning (Pluto SN in Capricorn), its patterns of relatedness to others (7th House) become overly defined by responsibility and authority. Thus, this Soul attempted to have its sense of identity created through relationships with others, which were, then, defined by responsibility and by a sense of authority, which was dependent on being acknowledged by others.

With the planetary ruler of Pluto SN being Saturn in the 10th House Taurus, the Soul gravitated towards positions of relative social authority. With this Saturn being trine to Pluto SN in the 7th Capricorn, and trine Pluto in the 2nd Virgo, not only the Soul's patterns of relatedness with others and sense of identity obtained through relationships (7th House, Capricorn), but also its own sense of value (2nd House) were defined by dynamics of authority.

The Soul would have desired to be acknowledged by its social role, and would have also been increasingly relating to others being in authority positions within society. Its own sense of values would have become dependent on social validation and/or validation by other social authorities (the trine between Saturn and Pluto). This would have created very fixed and narrow patterns of self-identity in relationships to others and to himself. This would have also set the scenario for the Soul's downfall from any positions of social authority.

If the Pluto SN correlates to older chapters in the Soul's evolution coming through the past symbolized by Pluto, it would be these dynamics that created the conditions for the Soul's need to go deeper within itself (2nd House Pluto in Virgo) to critically find out from within what its real value and values were, regardless of validation by others and by society. The trine between Pluto and Saturn (Pluto's SN ruler) would indicate also that in some lives others put the Soul in situations of confinement and isolation. There would also be guilt because of the Soul's prior submission to socially defined values and authorities and how this submission defined its patterns of relationships, versus creating its own value associations.

Upon a large series of lifetimes in this condition, the Soul would now require to go out of isolation in order to confront others and gain through confrontation an increasing awareness of what his values and resources are and how he can relate to others and serve others in a new way, a way not to be excessively dependent on the validation of others from a consensus point of view.

The NN of Pluto in the 1st House Cancer would correlate to the Soul's need to create a new series of experiences for himself, i.e. not dependent on relationships with others. The Pluto NN being in Cancer would correlate to the need of de-conditioning itself from patriarchal set of values and approaches which had defined the Soul, through a search of meaning from within, by means of emotional self-relatedness.

The ruler of Pluto NN being the Moon in the 2nd House Virgo would indicate that this new set of experiences and searches of emotional nature would have the purpose for the Soul to go deeper into itself though further experiences of relative isolation and withdrawal, in order to gain increasing self-sufficiency and reformulate its self-image from within. Thus, the Soul would need to keep confronting others in order to face its limitations in value associations (PPP in the 8th) thus creating new emotional experiences (Pluto NN in the 1st Cancer) leading to further isolation though, now intending to gain self-reliance and deeper knowledge of its value and resources, this fueling the purpose to keep on going toward others despite the feedback received.

There would be a theme of repetition and reviewing of the past life experiences of isolation, though, given the Moon rulership of the Pluto NN, the need would be to integrate these experiences in a new way, this allowing in the long run not to perpetuate this isolated condition but to keep on seeking confrontation with a transformed self-image and greater self-reliance.

Is the above analysis correct? Your feedback is most desired and appreciated.

(A)   In the symbols you used it would be more accurate to understand that this Soul, from within itself, has desired positions of authority within a social context, a society, a tribe, a group of people, in which the Soul was responsible for supplying the needs of that group of people because of its social position. This was reflecting the Soul's desire to be of service to a larger whole: Pluto in Virgo in relationship to its South Node in the 7th in Capricorn, ruled by the Saturn in Taurus in the 10th.

Combined with the desire to be of service to a larger whole through the positions of social authority also reflects the Soul's desire to give to others what they have needed in order to survive: South Node in Capricorn in the 7th, ruled by Saturn in Taurus in the 10th.

The nature of the grand trine between his natal Pluto in Virgo in the 2nd, South Node in the 7th, and Saturn in the 10th would mean that the Soul desired from within itself to learn how to listen to the needs of others in such a way as to attune itself to those needs. In so doing, the Soul then desired to give to others exactly what they needed in order to survive. Thus, the Soul would choose time frames and places to incarnate in which this underlying theme of survival was the consensus state of reality of those times. In actualizing itself in this way the Soul thus felt fulfilled and satisfied that it was able to help others based on their needs.

Over many lifetimes, the Soul then began to feel inwardly empty: Pluto in Virgo, which is the current life birth symbol for the Soul. It has come to a point of evolutionary limitation in these prior desires, and the way that they manifested. Pluto in Virgo in the 2nd House. Emptiness, feeling empty, is the archetype of Virgo. With the North Node of Pluto in Cancer in the 1st House the Soul is desiring within itself to begin a brand new cycle of its own evolutionary development that starts with accessing its own emotional needs to BE GIVEN TO: The South Node interacting with the North Node of Pluto in this context. In essence, the Soul has emptied itself in those lifetimes of giving to others in which survival of the whole group was on the line. It has reached a place of Soul exhaustion because of Pluto's South Node in Capricorn compounded by its ruler being in Taurus in the natural Capricorn house.

As a result, the Soul is desiring personal renewal by beginning a brand new cycle in its ongoing evolution: Pluto's North Node in Cancer in the 1st House. With Pluto in Virgo in the 2nd in relation to its North Node, it would have begun the process of ISOLATING itself from the overall environment in order to begin the process of inner renewal. In the current life it thus creates a egocentric structure, the Moon in Virgo in the 2nd, in which the Soul's need to withdraw, based on where it has been, is simultaneously reflected in the Pluto in Virgo itself, where it had just left off previous to the current life, but remains to be a need of the Soul as manifested through the current life egocentric structure of itself manifesting as the Moon in Virgo in that 2nd House.

This is where, when we begin to fill in the whole picture, to add the North and South Nodes of the Moon itself. The Soul, Pluto in Virgo in this case, is in the 2nd which of course correlates to where the Soul has been, and why, and where it has left off just previous to the current life. By establishing what has been going on within the Soul itself, Pluto and its Nodes, their planetary rulers, the South Node of the Moon will then correlate to specific lifetimes and the egocentric structures that the Soul has created to actualize the desires within it. The location of its planetary ruler, aspects to it, aspects to the South Node of the Moon, the location by House and Sign, all fill in what these past life, finite, lives have been. And all of this, in turn, of course establishes the individual context in which to understand the North Node of Pluto by House and Sign, the natal position of Pluto, the current life Moon, and its North Node.

Given that context of the past, it thus establishes the reasons that the Soul needs to isolate itself. It's as if the Soul in this isolation will be rebuilding and renewing itself from within itself. It will be discovering new capacities and different dimensions of itself in this way. It will be giving to itself in this way, and it will attract others who are natural givers because the Soul desires to be given to based on where it has been. The prior context establishes this need from within the Soul, the interaction and evolution of the North/South Nodes of Pluto.

These others will then be natural listeners who are able to evaluate what this Soul needs on a personal emotional basis in order to renew itself. Instead of being the server to others, which it has done for many lives, it will desire to be served in this way: Pluto and the Moon being in Virgo in the 2nd. These others will also symbolize and reflect the specific life that the Soul is living by way of the 2nd House Pluto's polarity point into Pisces in the 8th. That Pisces polarity point trines the North Node of Pluto itself. This means these types will be deeply and naturally psychological in nature. They will desire to penetrate to the core of themselves, as well as the core of this Soul. As a result, they will know what this Soul needs emotionally and psychologically in order to evolve from where they have been. The natural planetary ruler of that Pisces polarity point would be Neptune. And that would then be in Scorpio in the 4th House of this chart. This reinforces the North Node of Pluto being in Cancer, and the Soul's desire/need to renew itself from within via its emotional body.

The Soul will orientate to activities that all have the intent of leading to personal Soul renewal, and discovery. Through natural evolutionary progression, given this context, the Soul will begin to emerge from this purposeful cocoon and once again begin to find new ways of integrating itself back into the world, the group, the tribe, with new roles that reflect its ongoing desires to serve and to give to others what they need.

(Q) I am wondering what relevance the ruler of Pluto's sign has, if any, with regard to understanding Pluto.

(A) First, the sign that Pluto is in, i.e. Leo, Virgo, etc., CONTAINS within itself the archetype of the planet that rules that sign and, thus, how the Soul desires to actualize itself. The actual House and Sign of that planet that is the ruler of the Sign that the Soul is in acts like a tributary stream that feeds the main river of the Soul. The river itself is Pluto by House and Sign location, and its North and South Nodes with their respective planetary rulers. The tributary streams that flow into that river are the aspects by other planets to these Nodes, their planetary rulers, and Pluto itself.

(Q) I'm not quite getting this – do not quite have the feel for it yet. Where I think I'm stuck is my habit of always looking at the ruler of a planet. I understand that Pluto is the main factor – the river itself. But say Pluto is in Sagittarius in the 8th. SN Taurus in 1st. Jupiter in Scorpio in the 7th. Say 3rd stage Individuated. So maybe they've done some pretty deep psychological explorations to discover who they are within themselves and to get feedback so they can really nail down who they are (I'm not sure I'm interpreting the symbolism correctly). Wouldn't the fact that Jupiter is in the 7th house be relevant, i.e. that this exploration would have been done in the context of relationship? Also, Scorpio would suggest intensity in these relationships and perhaps manipulation?

(A) The Pluto in Sagittarius in the 8th, the river of the Soul, has desired to understand the WHY'S of life itself, the causes and effects of anything, human psychology in its fullest dimensions, its own psychology and the causes of it, and Natural Laws of Creation itself, how people in general interpret the phenomena of life in all of its forms and dimensions, what motivates people and why, and the sexual realities and the reasons for those realities in human nature, and so on. One of the tributary streams that feeds this Soul river, with Jupiter in Scorpio in the 7th, would correlate with the cultural anthropology of humans in diverse cultures, tribes, and societies that the Soul would contemplate in order to understand the core desires as manifesting in the 8th House Pluto. This contemplation would be fueled by reading a variety of materials, traveling to many places, and observing the diversity of peoples.

The South Node being in Taurus in the 1st, creates and egocentric structure in which the Soul keeps itself distant and independent from people in general. This symbolism correlates to a banyan tree that remains rooted in one place for thousands of years while the panorama of time passes it by. The banyan tree, the egocentric structure, thus is secure within its own inner isolation as it observes and learns by all that which passes it by. On a very selective basis the Soul through its 1st House Taurus egocentric structure would engage others in relationship, the tributary stream of the Jupiter in Scorpio in the 7th relative to Pluto in Sagittarius in the 8th House, who were inwardly evaluated to be of use by the Soul for its evolutionary intentions: needs. In turn, this would set in motion very intense and deep philosophical and psychological type discussions in which the core desires of the Soul were being met.

In your example, this would then place the evolving egocentric structure, one of the core evolutionary intentions, in the 7th House: North Node in the 7th in Scorpio. This would then mean, that as a next step in the Soul's evolution, that it now must learn how to jump out of its cocoon of self-isolation: South Node in Taurus in the 1st. Rather than observing in such isolation in the ways that it has before, it must now learn how to FULLY ENGAGE, emotionally and psychologically, others. The Soul intends to learn how to be in relationships with others in general in this way, and learn how to commit to being with a partner on a one to one basis. It is thus learning how to unite a core psychological and emotional paradox, the core paradox manifesting from the Soul. And that is the paradox of needing total independence and freedom relative to committing to others in general, and a partner specifically.

(Q) I think I am getting this but I want to be sure. In my example, I had Jupiter (ruler of Pluto's sign) in the same house as the NN and in Scorpio, Pluto's natural sign rulership. If it were, instead, say, in the 5th house in Virgo, would the search (Jupiter) regarding the 'why's' being asked by Pluto in Sagittarius in the 8th be focused more on understanding the psychology of feelings of profound emptiness due to a sense of lack in terms of one's life purpose? Would that now be one of the tributaries? There would still be the need to jump out of the cocoon (SN Taurus 1st/NN Libra 7th). But would Jupiter/Virgo/5th color the nature of that cocoon (SN) simply because it rules the sign that Pluto is in? Does this make sense?

(A) In the 3rd Stage individuated, as per your example, the answer would be yes. The nature of the cocoon would be colored by whatever House and Sign the Jupiter would be in as that tributary flows into the river of the Soul itself. In your example this would also include within the Soul a very critical self-analysis of any over-identification with the egocentric word 'I' which is reinforced through the specific egocentric structure the Soul has created via the South Node in Taurus in the 1st House, the natural ARIES House. As a result, the Soul would also then be very critical of all others who were parading their egos around in a peacock like fashion. Within this, the Soul would be critically examining the very purpose of life itself: the 5th House of course being Sun ruled – purpose. And, thus, be inwardly focused on determining its own specific life's purpose, its reason for incarnating in the first place.

Relative to the river, the 8th House Pluto in Sagittarius, the tributary stream symbolized in Jupiter in Virgo in the 5th, that purpose would be linked with naturally desiring to help other Souls fulfill their own life purposes, their reasons for being. As a result, there would be a natural attraction to the helping professions. Within all of this, the tributary stream feeding the river of the Soul is one wherein the Soul will constantly be desiring to improve itself, to focus on all of its perceived shortcomings, and doing something about that. In turn, the Soul will naturally have this focus towards others in general, and intimate others specifically. This is just some of the stuff that this tributary stream creates within the Soul itself.

(Q) Your 'readings' are so eloquent and make such tremendous sense. If the person were, say, 3rd stage Consensus instead of 3rd stage Individuated, are you saying that Jupiter's rulership of Pluto's sign would NOT be relevant? Or would it be that it would manifest differently, i.e. as religion (identifying one's ego with religion, as an example)? So, regardless of evolutionary state, it would still be a tributary, but feed in differently to a river that itself was manifesting differently?

(A) Yes. This is why it is so critical to understand the specific evolutionary state of any given Soul. The evolutionary state conditions the entire EA paradigm, and thus the orientation of the archetypes.

The Consciousness of the Soul and the Four Natural Evolutionary States

A very, very important principle to review concerns the four natural evolutionary conditions, or stages, of a Soul's evolution.

One of the great problems of 'modern' astrology is a total ignorance of this natural law. As a result, much if not most of astrological understanding correlates with the 'one size fits all' approach. Of itself, this approach does a total disservice not only to astrology in general, but to the very people it attempts to help.

This approach flies in the face of common sense, not to mention life itself. It's like saying if I have a Venus square Pluto then the 'meaning' of that astrological pairing would be the same for all. This approach never takes into account the INDIVIDUAL CONTEXT of anything.

Let us remember a core truth about astrology: it only works relative to observed context. If the 'one size fits all' approach were in fact true, then for example, when Uranus transited Pisces in the 1920's, the same social themes would have existed all over the planet. In reality, they did not because of individual context. In Germany and their context, for example, following World War I, it manifested as an almost total breakdown in the social order where literally one had to haul wheelbarrows full of money just to buy a loaf of bread. Yet at the same time, in the United States it manifested as the 'roaring 20's' because of the individual context of America at that time. This was in essence fueled by the 'invention' of the non-secured credit card.

Again, the evolution of the Soul is based on the progressive elimination of all separating desires, to the exclusion of the only desire that can remain: to return 'home' to that which is the Origin of all Souls in the first place. Based on this natural law, there are four natural evolutionary conditions, with three subdivisions in each, that correlate to the Soul's evolutionary journey. And, again, if you doubt this, simply stand back in a Uranian (i.e. detached) way from any society, country, culture, or tribe, and observe it. Upon observation, any detached observer will then be able to notice these four natural evolutionary conditions. The four conditions are:

(1) The 'Dimly Evolved' State Roughly three to four percent of all Souls are in what I have previously called the 'dimly evolved' state. This means one of two things. Either Souls that are evolving into human consciousness from other forms of life such as animals and plants. Or Souls that are 'de-evolving' backwards into this condition due to 'karmic' causes.

(2) The 'Consensus' State Souls that have evolved into what can be called the 'consensus' state of evolution, which comprises roughly seventy percent of all Souls on the planet at this time.

(3) The 'Individuated' State of evolution, where individuated is used in the Jungian sense of the word. This comprises roughly twenty percent of all Souls.

(4) The 'Spiritual' State of evolution that comprises roughly four to six percent of all Souls on the planet.

It is extremely important to understand no astrologer can determine which evolutionary condition exists for any Soul by simply looking at the birth chart alone. The astrologer must observe and interact with the client in order for this determination to be made.

A good way to do this in a counseling situation where a client has come to the astrologer is to simply ask the client why there are there, and what questions do they have. Generally, the very nature of the questions that the client has will clue the astrologer as to what evolutionary condition exists for that client. For example, if one client asks, "When can I expect enlightenment," and another asks, "When will I have my new BMW," there clearly is an observed difference reflecting the level of evolutionary progression of the Soul.

The Dimly Evolved State

Souls that are evolving into human consciousness from other forms of life, typically animal and plant (animals and plants essentially have the same 'emotional' and 'nervous' systems as humans) are characterized by a very limited sense of self-awareness. This self-awareness is typically limited to the time and space that they personally occupy. When one looks into such Souls' eyes they typically express a 'density' within the pupils, like a film effect within the pupils. These Souls are typically very joyous; very, very innocent; and can bring great love to those who are close to them. Modern terminology that reflects these types of Souls are words like cretinism, very low IQ's, mongolism, mental retardation, and the like.

The root desire within this evolutionary stage or state is the desire to be 'normal,' where normal means to be like most other people: the consensus state.

Conversely, it can occur, due to 'karmic' causes, that Souls can be de-evolved; which means that such Souls are forced back into this state. This then becomes very problematic for such Souls, because they had previously evolved beyond this stage. Thus, such Soul now experience great and humiliating 'limitations' because of the de-evolution. As a result, these Souls are very, very angry, and some can go about creating great disturbances for other people. These souls can also be 'classified' through the modern terminology as above. But the great difference is that when one looks into the pupil of these Souls' eyes, one will notice a great white light manifesting from the pupil: piercing like. And within that light, one will inwardly experience the intense anger within such a Soul.

STAGES OF EVOLUTION		
CONSENSUS	**INDIVIDUATED**	**SPIRITUAL**
1st stage Consensus	**1st stage Individuated**	**1st stage Spiritual**
– beginning – established – culminating	– beginning – established – culminating	– beginning – established – culminating
2nd stage Consensus	**2nd stage Individuated**	**2nd stage Spiritual**
– beginning – established – culminating	– beginning – established – culminating	– beginning – established – culminating
3rd stage Consensus	**3rd stage Individuated**	**3rd stage Spiritual**
– beginning – established – culminating	– beginning – established – culminating	– beginning – established – final liberation

The Consensus State

Astrologically speaking, this state correlates to *Saturn*, because of the underlying desire to conform to the consensus of any society, culture, tribe or country. Thus such Souls' entire orientation to reality, including their values, the sense of meaning for life, moralities, customs, norms, taboos, what is right and wrong, and so on, are simply an extension of the prevailing consensus of whatever society they are born into.

In essence, 'reality' for such Souls is merely an extension of the external conditioning that any consensus group of people provides. They cannot step out of the box, so to speak. For example, if a scientist claims that 'astrology is bogus,' then all those within the consensus state will have the same opinion.

Within the consensus state, like all the other states, there are three subdivisions that we must account for, where each subdivision reflects the ongoing evolution of a Soul through the entire evolutionary state, which then leads to the next evolutionary state with its three subdivisions, until the final 'liberation' of a Soul occurs, relative to exhaustion of all separating desires, ultimately reflected in the third subdivision of the Spiritual State of evolution.

The way that evolution occurs through each state is by exhausting all the desires that are intrinsic to the nature of that evolutionary state or condition. Within the consensus state, the root desire that propels the evolution of the Soul forward, from the first subdivision through the third, is characterized by the desire to 'get ahead,' to get ahead of the 'system,' which of course means the consensus society that they belong to.

1st Subdivision of the Consensus State

Souls within the first subdivision of the consensus state are characterized by a limited sense of self-awareness, essentially limited to the time and space that they occupy; a limited awareness of the dynamics of the community that they inhabit; an even more limited awareness of the dynamics of the country that they live within. And yet they are incredibly self-righteous relative to the values, moralities, consensus religion of the existing society of birth, how life is 'interpreted' according to those beliefs, the judgments issued because of those beliefs, and so on.

There simply is no ability to separate themselves from any of this. It is as if they are like social automatons. An apt analogy for these Souls is the worker bees in a bee hive. Typically, they are in the lowest social strata of the society of birth.

2nd Subdivision of the Consensus State

As evolution proceeds for these Souls, relative to the desire to 'get ahead,' it will lead them into the second subdivision of the consensus state, because that root desire means that they will want more from society than simply remaining in its lower strata. These Souls of course perceive from the point of view of the lower strata that there are others who have more than they have.

This perception is more or less limited to others having more possessions of a grander nature than they have, social positions within society that they do not have, thus more social 'freedom' than they have, and so on. Yet that limited perception fuels the root desire to get ahead and have more. In order for this desire to be realized, they must learn ever more how society and its dynamics work. It requires an expansion of their personal awareness for this learning to take place. It is the very fact of the evolutionary necessity to expand their awareness that propels the evolution of the Soul into the second consensus state subdivision.

There it becomes necessary for the Soul to learn ever more about the nature of society, to use the social system to its own evolutionary advantage – to get ahead. The 'reality' for such Souls is still totally defined by the consensus of society: its values, moralities, religions, judgments, right and wrongs, and so on. Yet by desiring to get ahead, the Soul must expand its personal awareness of the nature of the dynamics of how the society it is a part of is put together: its rules, regulations, what is required for this or that ambition to be actualized, and so on.

The Soul thus becomes ever more aware of 'others,' of the community that it is part of, and the country that it lives within. This expanding awareness also includes the beginning of becoming aware of other countries and the differences in values, moralities, religions, and so on, as reflected in other countries and societies. Thus, personal awareness – self-awareness – expands, because of the heightened awareness of 'others' relative to the Soul's desire to get ahead. This evolutionary stage correlates to the 'middle strata' within the social order of any given society.

3rd Subdivision of the Consensus State

As the Soul evolves through this state it increasingly becomes aware of the *upper strata* of society, of those that are in positions of power and leadership, of those that have great material abundance, and, as result, the desire to get ahead fuels the ongoing evolution of the Soul into the third subdivision within the consensus state.

For the Soul to evolve into the third subdivision within the consensus state, an ever increasing awareness of how society 'works' in total is demanded. Because of this, personal awareness expands through evolutionary necessity, in order for the Soul's desires (defined by ambitions to get ahead) to be realized.

The Soul's personal awareness has now expanded to the point that it is now very aware of the totality of the community and society that it belongs to, and of the country that it lives within. This also includes a progressive awareness of other countries, other cultures, and of the relativity of moralities, values, religions, and so on, as reflected in other countries and cultures.

Even though this awareness progressively expands, it does not mean the Soul in this third subdivision considers other countries, values, beliefs, and religions equal to its own society and country of birth. In fact, within this third subdivision, the self-righteousness born out of conformity (the underlying hallmark of the consensus state in total) is sustained: we are right, and they are wrong. In total, the consensus state correlates to what is called 'nationalism.'

In this final subdivision within the consensus state the Soul desires to be 'on top' of society; to have positions of social importance and relative power, prestige, and material abundance – the politicians, CEO's of corporations, important positions in the business world, mainstream religious leaders, and so on. As a result, these Souls constitute the 'upper strata' of society.

As the Soul evolves through this last subdivision, it will finally exhaust all the desires that are inherent within the consensus state. As a result, the meaning of life itself will be progressively be lost, as those desires no longer hold any meaning. At the very end of the journey through this state, the Soul will finally ask the question, "There must be more to life than this."

This very question implies an awakening alienation from the consensus, from 'normal' life as defined by the consensus. It is this awakening alienation from normalcy as defined by the consensus of any society that now triggers the beginning of a new desire that will propel the Soul into the individuated evolutionary state: the desire to liberate from all external conditioning that has previously defined the Soul's sense of reality in general, and its sense of personal identity, or individuality, specifically.

The Individuated State

Astrologically speaking, the individuated state correlates to *Uranus,* because the Soul now desires to *liberate* or *rebel against* the consensus state from which it is now evolving away from. Instead of the Soul being defined by the consensus to shape its sense of reality in general, and its personal identity specifically, the Soul now desires to discover whom and what it is, independent of such conditioning.

Earlier it was stated that if a Soul were in the consensus state and the scientist said, "Astrology is bogus," this would then be the automatic belief of those Souls who are within the consensus state. If that same scientist said this to a Soul within the individuated state, the response would be something like, "No thank you, I will think for myself."

Souls in this evolutionary state inwardly feel 'different:' different than the majority of the society and country of birth. Because of the desire to liberate from the consensus, the awareness of Souls in this state progressively expands to include ever-larger wholes, or frames of reference.

This expansion of awareness begins because the Soul no longer can identify with the consensus of the society of birth. As a result, the Soul now feels a progressive *detachment* from society: like standing on the outside and looking in. This then allows the Soul to 'objectify' itself, relative to personal awareness and self-perception. Rebelling against consensus beliefs, values, moralities, what constitutes 'meaning' for life itself, and so on, the Soul now begins to question the assumptions that most people hold dear to their heart that correlate to what 'reality' is and is not.

As a result, this Soul now begins to 'experiment,' by investigating other ways of looking at and understanding the nature of life itself. This is a reflection of the independent thinking that characterizes this evolutionary state. And it is through this independent thinking and investigating all kinds of different ways of understanding life, including ideas, beliefs, and philosophies from other lands and cultures, that allows for an ever-increasing expansion of their consciousness, and thus, their sense of personal awareness. As a result of this, such Souls no longer feel at 'home' in their own land, in their country of birth.

1st Subdivision of the Individuated State

The Soul will typically try to 'compensate' for this inner feeling of being different, of not belonging to the consensus, and the inner sense of alienation, by trying to appear normal. This compensation then causes the Soul to structure their outer reality much as Souls do in the consensus state: normal kinds of work, normal kinds of friends, normal appearance, and so on.

Yet inwardly they feel and know that they can no longer personally identify with that compensatory reality that they attempt to sustain. This compensation manifests in this subdivision because, after all, the consensus is where the Soul has just been. Thus, it constitutes a sense of security, relative to the inner feeling of being detached and different. We must remember that for most people, the sense of security in life is a function of constancy, self-consistency. And self-consistency is a function of the past. As a result, the compensation manifests as a reaction to this increasingly new feeling of being different, of not belonging anymore to the consensus. This feeling creates a sense of insecurity in this first subdivision because is it brand new. The Soul has not been here before. Yet this act of compensation creates a very real state of 'living a lie.'

Even as this compensatory behavior occurs, the Soul will nonetheless be questioning *everything,* deep within themselves, in the privacy of their inner life. Typically, they will read all kinds of books that contain ideas that go way beyond the 'norm' as it is defined by the consensus. Many, depending on cultural possibilities, will take classes or workshops that have these themes or intentions. Some will seek out 'alternative' environments to find and bond with others of like mind – others who feel as they do.

This compensatory behavior will progressively give way, involute, as the Soul evolves further in this subdivision. The Soul will progressively distance itself from the consensus and begin to form relationships with other alienated Souls just like itself. Because of the necessity of work or a job, most of these Souls will either do any kind of work just to get by, without identifying with such work in any way, or they will actualize a work that is individualistic and symbolic of their own individuality.

2nd Subdivision of the Individuated State

The underlying archetype of Uranus as it correlates to rebellion is at its highest. This rebellion is so extreme that the Soul has now 'thrown off' almost any idea or philosophy that has come before, at any level of reality. Such Souls end up in a kind of existential void, and typically hang out with other such alienated Souls, which has the effect of reinforcing the total state of rebellion from all of reality other than the reality they have now defined through the existential void.

These Souls will exhibit a deep fear of integrating into society in any kind of way, for the fear suggests to them that if they do, that somehow that very same society or reality will absorb their hard won (at least to them) individuality, which is *defined* through the act of rebellion, in this stage.

As a result, these Souls typically hang out in the avant-garde of society, hurling critical atom bombs at society, so as to reinforce their sense of personal righteousness, defined by their alienation from the consensus. Because of the natural law of evolution (which is always preceded by an involution), these people at some point will realize that their fear of integrating into reality, into society, is just that: a fear only. Once this is realized, they then begin to make the effort to integrate back into society, but with their individuality intact. Once this is realized, the Soul will then evolve into the third subdivision.

3rd Subdivision of the Individuated State

The Soul will then begin to manifest within society or reality as a truly unique and gifted person, from the viewpoint of the consensus.

This means that such Souls will have in some way a unique gift, or capacity, to help the consensus itself evolve, through integrating that capacity or gift within the consensus. Yet these people will not inwardly feel identified with the consensus: they stand inwardly very distant from it. The consciousness of these Souls has progressively expanded through the individuated state in such a way that they are aware of the entire world and the relativity of beliefs, values, moralities, and so on. As a result, they will feel within themselves to be 'world citizens' much more than being a singular citizen of the country of birth.

The inner pondering of the very nature of existence, the nature of Creation, the nature of who they 'really' are, essentially defines the nature of their consciousness. Progressively, these people begin to really open up their consciousness to the universal, the cosmos, to God/ess. Not the God/ess defined through consensus religions, but the real or natural God/ess. A perfect example in recent history of such a Soul is Albert Einstein. Another would be Howard Hughes.

The Spiritual State

Astrologically speaking, this evolutionary state correlates to *Neptune* because now the root desire becomes to consciously KNOW, not just believe in, but to know and unite with the Source Of All Things: the universal, God/ess. Because of this root desire, the consciousness now progressively expands into the universal, the cosmos, in such a way that the very nature of the interior consciousness within the Soul becomes conscious of the living universe within: the wave within the ocean, and the ocean within the wave.

Progressively, in this spiritual state of evolution, the very center of gravity within the Soul's consciousness shifts from the subjective *ego* to the Soul itself. Once the center of gravity shifts to the Soul, then in the context of any given life the Soul is then able to experience simultaneously its specific individuality as reflected in the ego, while at the same time experiencing being centered in the Soul – the ocean that is aware of the waves that it manifests.

The Soul contains within itself all the prior life memories from every life it has ever lived. And the Soul has its own 'identity,' or ego. This identity or 'ego' is not the same as the ego that the Soul creates in any given life on places like Earth. The ego of the Soul is one's 'eternal' identity.

An easy way for any of us to understand this occurs when we dream. Obviously when we dream, we are not identified with our subjective ego. After all, we are 'asleep.' The subjective ego has temporarily 'dissolved' back into the Soul when we sleep. So the question becomes, "Who and what is doing the dreaming?" Obviously, it can only be the Soul, with its own ego that thus allows the Soul to know itself as a Soul that is eternal.

Another way to validate the same thing occurs when we sometimes wake up from sleeping and cannot immediately 'remember' who we are: the current subjective ego, the 'I,' of this life. It takes some effort to actually remember the subjective 'I' when this occurs. So, again, the question becomes, "Who and what must make the effort to remember the subjective 'I' of the current life?" Obviously, it can only be our Soul.

So, again, as evolution proceeds in this spiritual state, there is a progressive shift in the center of gravity within the Soul's consciousness. When this shift firmly takes hold, then the Soul, in any given life, is simultaneously experiencing its eternal 'self' or ego, while at the same time experiencing the subjective ego, and the individuality attendant to it, that it has created for its own ongoing evolutionary reasons and intentions.

This is very similar to when we stand at the beach when the Sun goes down and at that moment when the Sun is equally half above and below the horizon. In this state of consciousness, the Soul is aware from within itself of all the prior lives that it has lived, and at the same time aware of the specific life, ego, that it is currently living.

Progressively, as evolution proceeds in the spiritual state of evolution, the Soul also becomes consciously aware of the Source Of All Things. This occurs as the consciousness of the Soul becomes truly universal: the inner experience of the entire universe within one's own consciousness. This state of 'cosmic consciousness' allows one to actually experience the very point of the manifested Creation itself: the interface between the un-manifested and the manifested. As this occurs, the Soul then also becomes aware of all the natural laws that govern and correlate to the very nature of Creation itself.

In the most advanced states of evolution, the Soul, now being completely identified with these natural laws of Creation, is then able to harmonize with those laws in such a way as to use those laws at will in conjunction with the Will Of All Things: that which is the very origin of those natural laws.

1st Subdivision of the Spiritual State

The Soul progressively becomes aware of just how 'small' it is, because of the increasing universal dimensions that are occurring within its consciousness. This is vastly different from being the center of one's own universe, as reflected in the consensus state for example. Of itself, this has a naturally humbling effect on the Soul, and thus the current subjective ego, Moon, that it has created. It is exactly this naturally humbling archetype that progressively allows the center of gravity to shift within the Soul's consciousness from the subjective ego to the Soul itself, and ultimately to a conscious union with the Source Of All Things.

As a result, the Soul desires to progressively commit itself to the desire to reunite with the Source. As this occurs, the Soul will progressively commit itself to devotional types of spiritual practice in this subdivision. Within this, the Soul desires to commit itself to various forms of work that all correlate to being of service to the larger whole, of service to others in some way.

Many will naturally want to orient to various forms of the healing arts or to start 'centers' in which the healing arts in some way are the focus. The core issue here is that the Soul desires to do a work *on behalf of* the Source Of All Things, and to use the work as a vehicle through which the Source can be inwardly experienced because of the nature of the work. In the East, this is called Karma Yoga.

In this first subdivision, the Soul becomes progressively aware of all that it needs to *improve upon* within itself. A heightened state of awareness occurs that makes the Soul aware of all its imperfections and, as a result, the Soul can now become highly self-critical. Even though this is natural, it also creates a potential danger or trap to the Soul in that this heightened state of critical self-awareness can cause the Soul to not feel 'good enough' or 'ready' to do the task, or work, that it is being inwardly directed to do. This then sets in motion all kinds of excuse making, always manifesting as perfectly rational arguments, of why the Soul will not do what it should do when it should do it. The way out of this trap is to realize that the path to 'perfection' occurs by taking *one step at a time*.

As evolution progresses through this first subdivision, the Soul will increasingly have direct perception of the 'single eye,' or the third eye, which is inherent to consciousness. As a result, this perception allows the Soul to merge with that single eye in such a way that various types and states of cosmic consciousness will occur, which will lead into the second subdivision within the spiritual state.

2nd Subdivision of the Spiritual State

As the Soul evolves into this subdivision, it has already had various kinds of inner cosmic or universal kinds of experiences within its consciousness. Yet in this state the final shift in the center of gravity within consciousness from the subjective ego to the Soul itself has yet to occur. In this state, the shift manifests more like a rubber band, wherein the gravity point keeps going back and forth from the subjective ego to the Soul.

The problem that this generates is that the progressive inner experiences within consciousness of the universal, the cosmic, the Source, fuels the subjective ego in such a way that the Soul feels more evolved than it actually is. This can then set in motion in varying degrees of intensity 'spiritual delusions of grandeur' from an egocentric and Soul point of view. When this occurs, such Souls will then feel that they have a spiritual 'mission' to fulfill on behalf of others, of the world itself. It is important to remember in trying to understand this subdivision that as the Soul gets ever closer to the Source, The Light, that whatever egocentric impurities remain within the Soul must be *purged*. As a result, as the Soul draws closer to re-uniting with its own Origin, these impurities will manifest through the current life subjective ego that the Soul's own ego contains.

These impurities can be many things, depending on the specific nature of each Soul, but all Souls in this subdivision will share one common impurity: the 'ego' of the Soul that is still identifying itself as somehow 'separate' from that which has created it. This ongoing delusion is thus reflected in the subjective ego that the Soul creates.

This common impurity will then be exhibited in specific psychological behaviors that essentially boil down to such Souls pointing the way to *themselves* as the vehicle of 'salvation,' or to know God/ess; while at the same time, pretending that they are not. In other words, they are extremely good salespeople who peddle God/ess as the hook, in order to have themselves revered as the way to actually know God/ess. There is always a hidden or secret egocentric agenda within these Souls that is masked by the overlay of whatever spiritual or religious teaching they are representing. Examples of this, in recent modern history, would be Bhagwan Rajneesh (Osho), Claire Prophet, JZ Knight (Ramtha), Da Free John, Rasputin, and the like.

As the Soul evolves through this subdivision, it finally realizes the nature of this root impurity. As a result, it experiences a 'natural' guilt. This guilt is then used by the Soul to create its own *downfall*, in order to 'atone' for that guilt. The downfall can occur in many different ways, depending on the specific nature of the circumstantial life that the Soul has generated. This downfall, caused by guilt and the need to atone for that guilt, thus serves as the final evolutionary development that allows the Soul to evolve into the third subdivision within the spiritual state.

3rd Subdivision of the Spiritual State

In the final subdivision within the spiritual state, the Soul is now finally and firmly identified with that which has created it: the Source Of All Things. The center of gravity within consciousness has finally centered within the Soul, not on the subjective ego created by the Soul.

At this point in the evolution of the Soul, all subsequent evolution through this final subdivision will be focused on the elimination of any separating desires that the Soul still has. Because of this final shift within consciousness to the Soul itself, the Soul is inwardly attuned to the Source Of All Things in such a way that it perceives itself as but a singular manifestation of the Source. Simultaneously, the Soul perceives all others, all of Creation, as manifestations of that Source.

Thus the Soul's inner and outer responses to life itself, how life is understood and interpreted, how it comes to understand the nature of the life it is currently living, how it understands the purpose for the current life, and how it comes to make decisions relative to the life being lived, are all based on this inner attunement and alignment with that which has Created it. As evolution begins in this final subdivision, the Soul inwardly feels and knows that it is here to serve The Source in some way. It knows that it cannot just live for itself. It knows that it has some kind of work to do on behalf of the Source. The consciousness of the Soul at this point is entirely structured to give to others, and to give purely without any ulterior agenda or motive involved. The nature of the work will always involve the theme of teaching or healing in some way.

Because the Soul is now consciously identified with the Source, the very nature of the Soul's own vibration radiates in such a way that many others are drawn to it like a magnet. Many other Souls are drawn magnetically to these Souls, because they also reflect and radiate a fundamental wisdom of life, of a deep compassion at the 'human condition.' This occurs because, after all, these Souls have traveled a very long evolutionary journey, which has taken them through almost every kind of life experience imaginable.

Such Souls are naturally very unassuming, naturally humble, and have no desire whatsoever for any kind of acclaim to their ego. Quite the opposite: they shy away from such things and always remind anyone who tries to give them acclaim of any kind for that which they do, that all things come from God, or the Source. They only point the way 'Home,' and never to themselves.

Conversely, these Souls can also attract to themselves others who *project* onto them all manner of judgments, projection of motives, intentions, of 'who they really are,' and wholesale persecution. The reason this occurs is because the very nature of these Souls is fundamentally pure, and full of the inner Light of the Source. As a result, their own inner light has the effect of 'exposing' the impurities in others, of the actual reality of others, versus the persona created by others; of others actual intentions and motives for anything. Accordingly, those who do this kind of projection and so on feel threatened by these types of Souls, for they know they themselves are fundamentally dishonest, and that they are invested in having others believe in the persona they are creating to hide their actual reality/agendas. Feeling threatened thus causes these types of people to manifest this type of behavior (projections) with these Souls.

In the beginning of this third subdivision, the nature of the work that the Soul does, the number of people it is destined to help in some way through the vehicle of teaching or healing is relatively small and limited to the immediate area of the community in which they live. Progressively this evolves from a limited application to increasingly larger circles, in which the nature of the work on behalf of the Source increases.

In the end, this increasing circle will include the entire world. And at the very end of evolution in this subdivision, the Soul will be remembered by countless others long after the physical life of the Soul is over – the nature of their life, and the teachings they represented. Examples of these types of Souls are 'individuals' like Jesus, Yogananda, Lao-Tzu, Buddha, Mohammed, Saint Teresa, and so on.

It is important to remember, again, that these are the natural evolutionary conditions that reflect the current reality of all peoples on Earth. For those who wish to use evolutionary astrology, it is essential that you make the necessary observations of any given person to determine their evolutionary state, and then to orient yourself to their natal chart accordingly. Again, one size does not fit all.

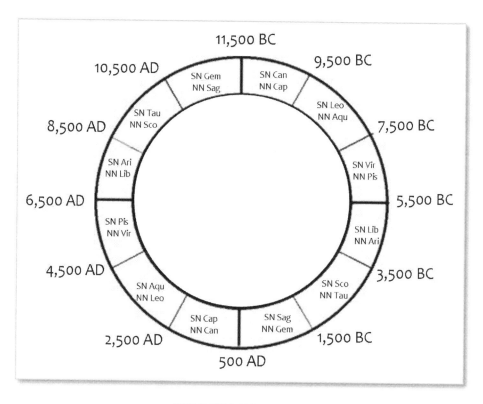

THE PLUTO NODE CYCLE

CHAPTER TWO

NEPTUNE AND THE PROJECTION OF ULTIMATE MEANING

Introduction

Time and space correlates to transitory meanings wherein timelessness correlates to ultimate meaning. This is reflected in the dual desire nature of the Soul that is the essence of Evolutionary Astrology. Time and space correlates to the natural laws of cause and effect that correlates to the natural law of duality or polarity.

Timelessness correlates to the absolute or oneness that reflects the first or ultimate cause of the manifest creation. This simple natural law can be understood by all Souls as reflected in the inhaling and exhaling breath for the body that the Soul inhabits where inhale and exhale correlates to cause and effect, duality. Yet, between the inhale and exhale breath, there is an interval. It is this interval that correlates with timelessness, the absolute, and the ultimate Source Of All Things. When the breath is still, the consciousness of the Soul naturally expands within itself that leads to the ultimate inner perception of the manifested creation: the manifested and the un-manifested.

Thus, Neptune correlates to the ultimate desire in all Souls for that absolute meaning upon which, once realized, all other meanings that have been projected onto its various lived becomes relatively meaningless. The natal placement of Neptune by house, sign, and aspects to it can thus correlate to where any given Soul projects an ultimate sense of meaning into the dynamics, or archetypes, that correlate with those houses, signs, and aspects to other planets. Sometimes this projected ultimate meaning is so absolute by a Soul that it can do anything to defeat or negate any inner or outer cause that attempts to oppose or undermine that projection in any way. Thus, this causes the dynamic and archetype of fanaticism to manifest.

In trying to understand what constitutes ultimate meaning for a given Soul, or groups of Souls, relative to Neptune's South Node in Aquarius, we need to consider that this is really about the nature of beliefs. Pisces, the 12th House, and Neptune are part of a mutable grand cross involving Gemini, the 3rd House, and Mercury; the 6th House, Virgo, and Mercury; and the 9th House, Sagittarius, and Jupiter.

It is the 9th House, Jupiter, and Sagittarius that specifically correlates with the archetype of beliefs, and has a natural square to Pisces, the 12th House, and Neptune. If one steps back, detaches, from one's own life, or the entire life of all humans on the planet, it should be sadly clear that all humans define their lives, their sense of meaning, including ultimate meaning, according to that which they believe.

As a result, we have on our planet seven billion Souls who believe whatever it is that they believe. And, of course, one group, one individual, can have vastly different or completely oppositional beliefs from another individual, or groups of individuals. Whole countries can believe in something that other countries do not believe. Within the archetype of beliefs, we also have religions of all different types and kinds.

As a result of all this, we end up in a world, now, and since the time when humans shifted from being nomadic in nature to living as groups of people in one place by way of cultivating food sources and raising animals, where the perversion of the natural laws of giving, sharing, and inclusion manifested as self-interest and exclusion. This has led to whole groups of humans fighting and competing with other groups of humans, of individuals fighting other individuals, of countries fighting other countries, of one religion fighting with other religions in such a way that could very well lead to the extinction of the human species itself.

And in all these competing groups, individuals, countries, and religions, all feel justified in that which they do because of the NATURE OF THEIR BELIEFS where the very nature of whatever beliefs constitute a sense of ultimate meaning for all of them.

When a Soul projects an ultimate sense of meaning upon that which is temporal by its very nature this will lead, at some point, to the experience of disillusionment. Disillusionment can be one of the most bitter of psychological experiences for any Soul. To be disillusioned re-orientates the Soul to actual reality. Disillusionment will occur to any Soul that manifests for one of two reasons:

(1)   The Soul has created for itself something that is utterly delusional in nature that has no actual reality or truth whatsoever. A simple example of this could be a Soul who is projecting that the Earth is in fact flat.

(2)   The Soul has projected a sense of ultimate meaning into something that is real yet is, in fact, not the ultimate meaning when ultimate meaning is understood to be a function of the Soul inwardly realizing its relationship to that which has Created it in the first place: The Source Of All Things.

In either case, the experience of being disillusioned is to re-orientate the Soul to actual reality.

Questions and Answers

(Q) If the consensus Soul essentially goes to sleep until its next incarnation, what would it mean for the individuated and spiritual state Souls? The more advanced a Soul is, would that then equal being 'awake' longer to take in further teachings?

(A) Being 'awake' yes.

(Q) Would it also mean that only the very advanced Souls, as in 3rd stage spiritual, would help out, for example, here on Earth or anywhere else while out of the body? I am asking this because I know that Wolf shared that his Soul would be used in sleep (Neptune) to help others. His Neptune in the 11th (astral plane) in Libra is exactly trine the North Node in Gemini in the 7th.

(A) Yes.

(Q) You wrote, "When a Soul dies in an existing human form it then goes to the relevant dimension that reflects its own degree of evolution." So if Souls in different stages of evolution travel in different astral dimensions – I remember Wolf calling the different astral places and spaces similar to a honeycomb – does that mean that a Soul will not necessarily see their loved ones if they are in a different stage of evolution once they cross over?

(A) No. They can meet for a relatively short period of time if the evolutionary/karmic degrees of evolution are different. After that short period of time then, in general, there will be a parting.

(Q) To reach human form, have we evolved from the most basic life forms such as cells and then progressed from there to bacteria, plant life, animals then humans?

(A) Yes, the humanoid life form has evolved in this way.

(Q) Does despair correlate to Neptune?

(A) No, despair as an archetype correlates with Saturn, Capricorn, and the 10th House.

(Q) People who are in deep despair that even 'paradise' (or any good condition in life) doesn't interest them, totally lose hope, and just want to disappear. What is the cause of that level of despair? Is there a way out? I am thinking it's about stopping acting like a victim?

(A) A state of absolute futility that interfaces with the psychology of total defeat, self-defeat, is the cause of this. These are Saturn, Capricorn, and 10th House archetypes/dynamics. The causes of this type of psychology can be many, many things, not just one thing. The feeling of wanting to disappear, however, is indeed Neptune, Pisces, and 12th House: the desire to be invisible. The way out is a self-determined effort to take charge of whatever the situations are/is that has caused this psychology to manifest, and to understand, as hard as it may be in specific types of circumstances, that we are all responsible for that which we create. Taking charge in some way relative to the specific nature of the circumstances is the key issue that then eliminates being a victim to what the situations are.

(Q) The guilt caused by such a condition of despair (refusing to be saved) – is that natural guilt?

(A) Yes.

(Q) I need clarification on the collective-individuated and conscious-unconscious correlations. So far, this is what I understand:

Neptune – collective unconscious AND conscious
Uranus – individuated unconscious
Mars – individuated conscious

Is this correct?

(A) The individuated conscious is actually the Moon because it correlates with the egocentric structure of each Soul.

Neptune – collective unconscious and conscious
Uranus – individuated unconscious
Moon – individuated conscious

Coming into human form, the Soul will manifest what is known as the ego. The ego correlates astrologically to the Moon. The ego, too, is pure energy. We cannot open the brain and find it.

Unlike the energy of the Soul, which is sustained from life to life until the final merging with The Source occurs, the energy of the ego in any life is dissolved after that physical life ends.

The analogy of the wave and the ocean again serves to illustrate this point. The ocean can be equated with the Soul, and the wave can be equated with the ego. Of course, the ocean (Soul) is manifesting the waves (ego), life after life. And just as the waves can rise and fall in any given life that the Soul creates, the ocean is sustained.

In other words, the egos that the Soul manifests in each life rise from birth, but finally dissolve back into the ocean (Soul) upon the completion of that life. Its energy is not destroyed, but simply absorbed back into the energy that created it in the first place. The ego created by the Soul thus allows for the individualizing aspect of the Soul in each life.

The Ego as a Vehicle of Evolution

In each life the ego is created by the Soul in such a way as to serve as the vehicle through which the evolutionary intentions of the Soul in that life can occur. Each ego that the Soul creates is oriented to reality in such a way that the very nature of the orientation serves as the vehicle through which the life lessons can occur and be understood by the Soul. In each life, the ego allows for a self-image of the Soul to occur, relative to the individualizing aspect of the Soul.

An analogy to a movie projector will illustrate the point. If I have a movie projector loaded with a reel of film, and a screen in front of the projector, and I turn on the machine, generating light from it, I will have no distinct image on the screen unless I also have a lens in the projector. Without the lens, what manifests from the projector is simply diffuse light. Thus, the lens serves as a *vehicle,* through which the images on the film can be focused and given distinct shape and form.

In the very same way, the ego that the Soul generates in each life allows for a vehicle, or lens, through which the inherent images that exist with the Soul can take form. This natural law of consciousness is thus the cause that allows for individual self-perception and the word "I" itself.

The Soul, Pluto, also correlates to the genetic code – RNA and DNA, chromosomes, and enzymes. In each life, the Soul **IS THE DETERMINANT FOR THE ENTIRE GENETIC CODE OF THE LIFE, HUMAN FORM, THAT IT IS BEING BORN INTO**. Each life that the Soul chooses is a continuation of that which has come before, where each new life taken correlates to the ongoing evolutionary lessons or intentions of that Soul. Thus, the body type, which includes which race to be born into; the appearance of it; the culture to be born into; the parents of origin; the specific and individual nature of the emotions, feelings, psychology, desires, and so on, correlate to the Soul's intentions, reflected in the genetic code in total, in each life.

This is all then given individual form in each life via the egocentric structure (Moon) that the Soul creates in that life. Thus, any person can then say things like, "This is who I am," "This is what I need," "This is what I am feeling," "This is what I am trying to learn," and so on: the individualizing aspect of the ego that the Soul creates in each life.

The Astral Plane

When 'death' occurs in any given life, as stated earlier, the ego that the Soul has created for a life then dissolves back into its origin: the Soul. Since both are energy, and energy cannot be destroyed, where does the Soul go upon the physical death of the body? In other words, where is it on an energetic level?

Most of us have heard the words 'the astral plane,' or heaven and hell. Obviously, what these types of words refer to are other realities or planes of existence. There are in fact other energetic realities or planes of existence.

Simply speaking, the astral plane is an energetic plane of existence that all Souls go to after the completion of a physical life on places like Earth. Energetically, this plane of existence is much less materially dense than places like Earth.

After physical death the Soul 'goes to' the astral plane, in order to review the life that has just been lived, and to prepare for yet another birth on places like Earth. Upon the completion of a life on Earth, the 'ego' dissolves back into the Soul in such a way that the center of gravity within the consciousness, within the astral plane, is the Soul itself.

For most folks living lives in the material plane we call Earth, the center of gravity of consciousness is the ego itself. This is why the vast majority of people living feel within themselves that they are 'separate' from everything else, the center of gravity being the egocentric 'I.' In the astral plane the center of gravity shifts to the Soul itself so that when death occurs in any given life the 'memory' of the ego of that life is sustained.

Lives to Come

This memory of the ego is necessary for the Soul, for it is the memory of the ego that allows the Soul to not only review the life that has just been lived, but also serves as the basis for the next life to be lived, relative to the continuing evolution of the Soul itself. In each life we all pick up where we left off before. Thus, this memory of the ego in each life serves as the causative factor of what type of egocentric structure the Soul needs to create in the next life.

In essence, it is the memory of the ego that the Soul draws upon, the 'images' contained therein, that serve as the basis of the next ego that the Soul needs to generate in each successive life to promote its ongoing evolution. Astrologically speaking, this is symbolized by Pluto (the Soul), and the South and North Nodes of the Moon.

The South Node of the Moon correlates to the Soul's prior egocentric 'memories,' which determine the natal placement of the Moon in each life – the current ego.

The North Node of the Moon correlates to the evolving ego of the Soul – the nature and types of inner and outer experiences that the Soul needs, desires, in order to facilitate its ongoing evolution. In turn, this will then constitute the 'new' egocentric memories, images, that the Soul will draw upon when a life has been lived and terminated at physical 'death.'

Most of us are aware that the Moon also correlates to one's family of origin in any given life. It should be clear then that upon the 'death' of the physical body, the Soul 'goes to' the astral plane, and meets again important family members and others close to the Soul. This is also why, for many Souls, we continue to meet again those family members upon rebirth into yet another physical life on places like Earth. It is the memory of the ego now combined with the memory of family that is the determinant in this phenomenon. And this phenomenon is sustained until there is no longer any evolutionary or karmic need to sustain such relationships.

So we can now see the natural trinity, archetype, of consciousness not only at a collective level, Neptune, that is also expressed in the individualized structure of the Soul, Pluto, that in turn creates an egocentric structure in each life, Moon. The function of the egocentric structure of the Soul at an individual level, is the Moon. Mars would then correlate with the desires emanating from the Soul that are consciously acted upon relative to the ongoing evolutionary journey of the individualized Soul.

(Q) Is the 1-2 meditation the Hong Sau, or a derivative of, the Hong Sau meditation?

(A) Yes, the 1-2 meditation is that which is in fact natural to consciousness without any other conditioning being added to it by way of religions, etc. Thus, no added names such as Hong Sau. Just 1 and 2 will do.

(Q) Did JWG speak only of peyote as a natural visionary experience through which one may quickly see through the veils? Did he comment on Ayahuasca?

(A) He spoke about different natural plants that had/have inherent chemicals that affect the physiology of the brain when ingested and that naturally induce expanded states of consciousness. These expanded states induced in this natural way, he said, are permanent: they are sustained. He contrasted that with artificial man-made drugs, chemicals, like LSD, that do indeed alter one's consciousness in all sorts of ways but that those altered states do not remain once the drug wears off. He personally was initiated into the peyote way by a traditional Navajo Indian for a period of time in which he lived in the high chaparral of northeast New Mexico.

(Q) I feel like I heard/read somewhere in EA that the structure of consciousness correlates to Capricorn, Saturn, 10th?

(A) Yes, Saturn correlates to forms as reflected in the natural law of gravity. Gravity is thus the determinant of form. Form then correlates to functions: the structural nature of form is determined by necessary functions relative to an organized whole. Consciousness, Neptune, that manifests from Pluto, the Soul, that manifests through the form of the humanoid is thus limited by the nature of that form as defined by the inherent functions of that form. From an evolutionary point of view, this then correlates to the limits of any form that requires the changing of form for the evolution of consciousness to proceed.

Saturn correlates to the structural nature of consciousness that the Soul determines from life to life because the specific structural nature of consciousness will then be orientated to 'reality' in such a way that it then reflects the ongoing evolutionary needs and requirements of the Soul itself. Thus, by house, sign, and aspects to the natal Saturn, the sign on the 10th house cusp, any planets in the 10th with their own aspects to the planets, will all correlate to this structure.

The South Node of Saturn, which all humans on the planet share during this epic, correlates to the transition from natural times, the matriarchy, to the patriarchy: South Node of Saturn being in Capricorn. Individually, the South Node of Saturn by house, and the aspects to it from other planets, correlate to the prior life structural nature of the consciousness of the Soul that applies to the current life ongoing evolutionary needs and requirements of the Soul.

Saturn correlates to the nature of the 'conditions' that the Soul chooses to be born into that reflect the evolutionary needs of the Soul, and how this conditioning reflects those intentions. The nature of this conditioning reflects the totality of the society or culture, country, and regions with countries that impacts on the Soul in this way.

One of those conditionings is reflected in the fact that humans live together as structured groups: societies, tribes, countries and, as such, correlates to the social role that all humans have on behalf of that society: thus the role that Soul choses in any given life that reflects its evolutionary needs and intentions. That role on behalf of society, and on behalf of the individual context of each Soul, correlates to the work or 'career' that the Soul uses relative to facilitating its ongoing evolutionary needs.

This then correlates to the formation of goals or ambitions of the Soul relative to its individual station within the context of the whole of the group, and the means necessary to actualize those goals and ambitions. Each country or society has its own socially accepted norms and customs that the consensus of the society or country has established that then correlates to whatever means must be used, as prescribed by society, to actualize the individual goals and ambitions reflected in the choices that the Soul makes for itself: its career, work, or role within the context of the country or society of birth.

In turn, this then correlates to the interfacing between the role of authority, as defined by society, parents, and the authority of the Soul itself, and how the Soul responds or reacts to these external authorities.

Because Saturn correlates to the nature of laws, customs, norms and taboos that any group of people create in order to live together as an organized whole that then becomes the basis of judgments made by the individual or the group: or judgments made by the individual within itself. The issue then becomes one wherein the judgments being made are a function of man-made beliefs with all the attending moralities, ethics, rights and wrongs, etc. or judgments that emanate from natural laws. Judgments are necessary and a part of natural consciousness in human form. It is one of the natural ways that correlates to self-knowledge, and knowledge upon the nature of anything.

Saturn correlates with the very nature of time itself. Time is nothing more than that motion itself where motion equals time. One of the functions of time, motion, is aging. This natural aging as defined by motion, time, naturally leads to crystallization wherein the nature of whatever forms exist no longer reflect the evolutionary imperatives of the whole, or the individual. This then leads to the necessity of change, of evolving new forms and structures. As a natural function of time leading to necessary evolutionary change, the consciousness of the Soul in human form creates reflection. Reflection is thus natural to consciousness for it leads to the awareness of that which is crystallized that needs to change in order for evolution to proceed. Reflection also allows consciousness to learn through the vehicle of hindsight.

Because reflection infers the evolutionary necessity to change in order to evolve, this then directly correlates to a consciousness feeling limited or blocked by the very nature of its existing conditions, within itself, and external to itself, which can then lead to depression within the consciousness of the Soul. This is intentional from the point of view of Natural Laws, the laws set in motion by the Creator Of All Things, in order for the Soul to make the changes necessary for its evolution to proceed.

Saturn also correlates to gender assignment as defined either by the nature of the culture, society, or tribe of birth and/or natural laws. Thus gender conditioning either through artificial conditioning as a reflection of norms, customs, and taboos that are made by men as a function of beliefs versus conditioning relative to natural laws: natural male or female.

(Q) Can you clarify what you meant when you said that time is nothing more than motion itself where motion equals time, and one of the functions of time, motion, is aging?

(A) If we have a starting point, and then an ending point, we have motion between those two points where motion is a function of velocity. Velocity within motion, no matter what the rate of that velocity is, creates time: the time it takes to get from point A to point B. Motion is also the determinant of gravity when combined with mass: Saturn. Thus, the center of gravity within consciousness where consciousness is then defined by the nature of the form, Saturn, that is within. Form correlates then with boundaries that correlate within consciousness to the natural boundary between conscious awareness that is determined by the egocentric structure within consciousness that is created by the Soul in any given life. The totality of consciousness of the Soul includes the subconscious or unconsciousness that is created by this natural boundary of Saturn between the egocentric awareness that is symbolized by the Moon, the natural polarity to Saturn, and the subconscious or unconsciousness of the Soul.

(Q) Since very advanced Souls like Jesus or Sri Yukteswar do not need to incarnate anymore to continue with their evolution, does this mean that this is the end of the line for all humans, that this is the most evolved life form we all will incarnate into and then can stay in the higher dimensions?

(A) Yukteswar and Jesus and many like them, continue their Soul's evolution within the seven vibrational planes of existence that all Souls, and the consciousness within them, evolve within. The human life form is but one form that consciousness, of itself, can manifest in. The individualizing aspect of consciousness is that which correlates with a Soul. The Soul by way of individuated consciousness can thus find itself in many different forms of life: not just the humanoid life form.

(Q) I have experienced a level of awareness for a short period of time with 'help' where anything I desired to experience could be directly experienced without any limitation whatsoever. I have read that this is the Fifth dimension, where anything can be experienced instantly. Is that true and where we are all heading, or is that just our natural un-incarnate state?

(A) I am not familiar with the term 'fifth dimension.' There is a vibrational plane of existence wherein the Soul, relative to its evolutionary progression and thus capacity, can inhabit that is a casual universe in which all that is desired can be manifested instantly. An individualized Soul to naturally evolve to this type of universe, or vibrational plane of existence, takes a fairly long period of time when time itself, Saturn, is measured from this Earth. This is indeed the plane of existence that both the Souls of Jesus and Yukteswar are currently within.

(Q) Could you briefly describe the seven planes of existence or point me/others interested in this, to a website/body of knowledge that can accurately describe them?

(A) Briefly three of these planes of existence are rooted in time/space dimensions: three are rooted in timeless dimensions, and one is transitional between these three, the interface portal, if you will. The best source of this knowledge in fact is a book by Yukteswar called *The Holly Science*. Everything in that book is in fact true: actual knowledge.

(Q) Please explain why a Soul would come into a life, be persecuted, crucified and die, then be liberated through trauma and suffering? It does not make evolutionary sense, to be liberated through suffering. Unless one were Catholic. It would seem to make sense that there would be a need to be reincarnated to resolve that horrible trauma. Also, do you receive your knowledge through books and teachers or actual experience?

(A) The causes for anything are many, as well as the resolutions of those causes.

So let us now work with some example charts and focus on the archetype of Neptune, and how it can project its ultimate sense of meaning for the consciousness of the Soul.

EXAMPLE CHART A

Neptune and the Projection of Ultimate Meaning
Neptune in Scorpio in the 8th House

by Linda

Because of the 'fixed' nature of Scorpio and the 8th house archetype, the projected ultimate meaning is doubly intensified. The dynamics have been fixed for a long time. The Soul contains a lot of resistance to change. This could mean any false ideas about what Spirituality really IS would be up for transformation. The Soul wishes to remain where it feels a sense of security and familiarity. It does not want to change, yet, due to the transformative nature of the Scorpio archetype, the need for the Soul to grow beyond its own limitations and sense of powerlessness, there can be both a deep resistance to letting go and surrendering to the process as well as a deep desire to grow and transform. The Soul can manipulate everything on an inner and outer level in order to maintain the fixed dynamics around what it has created that gives it a sense of projected ultimate meaning.

> Every human being is essentially a Soul, covered with a veil of maya. Through evolution and self-effort, each human makes a little hole in the veil; in time, one makes the hole bigger and bigger. As the opening enlarges, the consciousness expands; the Soul becomes more manifest. When the veil is completely torn away, the Soul is fully manifest in him/her. That woman/man has become a master – master of their self and of maya. (Paramahansa Yogananda)

Since the role of Neptune is to realize the full potential of consciousness, the Soul experiences lack that reflects a desire to return to Divinity. The stage of evolution and the level of awareness of the Soul will depend upon how much the center of gravity has shifted from the ego to the Soul. As more and more illusions are dissolved, the Soul evolves further into the potential of expanded consciousness in human form.

In the 1st stage Spiritual, the Soul has a natural empathy that allows it to give to others what they actually need. It understands the illusory nature of many of its and others' egocentric desires as well as the psychology of 'why.' The Soul is aware that God is not perfect. It understands that various religions had always conceived God to be perfect, thereby generating all the 'SPIRITUAL SHOULDS' and moral teachings of man-made spiritual systems. This kind of shadow still lurks in the Souls of many who are coming out of the Sub-Age of Virgo in the Age of Pisces (guilt and atonement for not being perfect enough). These 'spiritual should be's' are actually a violation of Natural Law and pertain to extreme delusion in many Souls. However, there is a natural goodness that expresses as the Soul moves along in the Spiritual stages. This natural goodness is an impulse coming from the Natural Goddess, and another way it expresses is by always putting others first.

The Soul has an intense need to 'spiritualize' by way of targeting any illusions that are keeping it separate from Divinity. Depending upon the desire nature of the Soul, in this process it can make all kinds of emotional assumptions that emanate from the natural psychological purity or innocence of the Neptune archetype. The Soul can assume that other Souls are not bad or harmful. (An example of this is Anne Frank during WW2 who believed that 'everyone is good.' This belief led to severe disillusionment when it turned out to be horribly wrong. She eventually died in the concentration camp at the hands of evil men in her spiritual fight against evil – Asteroid Lucifer Pisces 8th, Neptune Leo 2nd.) Disillusionment is one of the hardest experiences a Soul can have.

With Neptune in Scorpio in the 8th house there is a strong compulsion, addiction or repetition of the desires within the Soul. The compulsive attraction to 'whatever' is a desire that is actually coming from the Soul, making the desired object a 'de-facto God or Goddess' that will give the Soul a sense of (projected) ultimate meaning – but failing to recognize it as false. Thus, delusional beliefs and experiences can be repeated over and over. Reaching a limit, a point where that falseness cannot be tolerated, the Soul becomes ready to be transformed through the internal journey into its own psychological dynamics. For this to happen, the Soul can create experiences of the proverbial 'rug being pulled out from' underneath it.' These experiences expose the dynamics within the Soul, as well as identifying the 'outer' dynamics that are playing a part in the Soul's lessons. The Soul can experience great shock but also great relief at this point because not only has it been able to pierce through some of the veil, it can also see how and WHY it created particular egocentric circumstances. Natural Law is restored that little bit more making for a natural and true inner knowing or psychology of itself and others. Thus, the Soul is able to 'spiritualize' through a pure desire to merge with the Truth or the Absolute itself.

An example of a delusion that the Soul with Neptune in Scorpio in the 8th house can create can be in the area of commitment or marriage to an intimate partner. The Soul and the karmic partner enter this relationship on a SOUL level. The unconscious desire nature is at the forefront of the relationship dynamics correlating directly to the evolutionary intentions. Part of the unconscious desire nature could be the instinctual sexual act that ties the Souls together even more. The Soul wishes to grow beyond limitations and chooses a partner who symbolizes becoming more powerful than the Soul was before by merging together and osmosing qualities and capacities that have been lacking. The compulsive need for the other originates on an UNCONSCIOUS level and can lead to manipulating the other because of the incredible need for the Soul for this particular relationship that symbolizes a lack and a need to grow beyond it.

Motivations and intentions – short of being perfect – could lead to betrayal, abandonment, loss and violation of trust, and of course to disillusionment. The way to grow and evolve is by exposing and transforming the old dynamics within the Soul, therefore there is no room for untruth since both are seeing each other with an 'eagle's eye' that exposes mutual weaknesses, fears, wounds, traumas, taboos, and phobias that unleash SEETHING EMOTIONS. These dynamics bring a bird's eye view of the penetration into the depths of each other's Souls.

It is possible that the partner is put up on a pedestal because he or she is perceived to have 'spiritual' qualities that the Soul wishes for itself. The Soul may feel it has found the 'PERFECT PARTNER.' At some point, the delusions that the Soul has created out of the other – such as de-facto God or Goddess, Soul mate, perfect sexual partner, always being together, will be together forever – need to be exposed. During the course of the relationship, a natural truth that can be revealed is that the couple each have good and bad qualities. Once the Soul feels there is nothing more to gain from the relationship, it can bring it to an end. If both are evolved to the 1st stage Spiritual, the relationship could be one of mutual growth as each see THE TRUTH as well as the truth of each other, and both consciously cooperate with the evolutionary intentions.

The overwhelming intensity, possessiveness and need for the partner needs to be balanced with the 2nd house Taurus polarity by separating from each other for a time in order to look within. This necessary separation then allows the Soul to identify who it is apart from the other and the osmosis effect of sexuality. The Soul can be transformed through discovering the core of itself and growing through self-sufficiency, non-dependency, non-manipulation and non-compulsion. The Soul will be able to heal past life karma by unconditionally accepting the other for their 'imperfections' … removing yet another veil that reveals the natural wisdom and knowledge bestowed by the Divine.

One reason two Souls can come together again in the current life is to simply forgive each other for past life traumas: with Scorpio's penchant for revenge, forgiveness is the last spiritual hurdle. Neptune in Scorpio in the 8th house is a double-water signature making evolution possible through really feeling the emotions that have the effect of cleansing and healing the Soul, expanding consciousness and promoting evolution. The Soul is able to pick future partners in this life and the next with whom it resonates with on a Soul level.

EXAMPLE CHART B

Neptune and the Projection of Ultimate Meaning
Neptune in the 12th House

by Cat

Neptune correlates to the ultimate desire in all Souls for that absolute meaning upon which, once realized, all other meanings that have been projected onto its various lives becomes relatively meaningless. The natal placement of Neptune by house, sign, and aspects to it can thus correlate to where any given Soul projects an ultimate sense of meaning into the dynamics, or archetypes, that correlate with those houses, sign, and aspects to other planets. Sometimes this projected ultimate meaning is so absolute by a Soul that it can do anything to defeat or negate any inner or outer cause that attempts to oppose or undermine that projection in any way. Thus, this causes the dynamic and archetype of fanaticism to manifest. (Rad)

Neptune in the 12th House, which it rules, can manifest in a variety of ways depending on the evolutionary state of the Soul and the life experiences and conditioning of the individual. In a more evolved Soul whose focus is more spiritual and less focused upon worldly desires, having Neptune in the 12th house can provide for a very positive Neptunian experience. Those who are less evolved and/or focused on ego gratification and pleasure seeking addictions are more likely to experience the darker side of the Neptune archetype.

With Neptune in the 12th House, there is a need and desire to dissolve any and all boundaries and limitations that are preventing a direct relationship with the Source no matter what evolutionary stage the Soul is in. These limitations and boundaries are self-created and are based upon illusions that the Soul believes to be reality and projects upon the external world.

Once the Soul recognizes these illusions for what they are, he or she is one-step closer to transcending the ego and merging with the Source. Until such time, the Soul will progressively experience states of disillusionment that serve to dissolve these self-created boundaries and limitations through events and circumstances that lead to sorrow, disappointment and suffering of one degree or another. Only in this way does the Soul come to realize that everything that it has desired and sought after is ultimately meaningless, and that true meaning can only be found with the Source.

An individual with Neptune in the 12th House usually has reclusive tendencies and enjoys being alone. He or she has a deep appreciation of solitude even though he or she is very likely to be aware on some level of the collective and the greater whole. He or she is likely to be very sensitive and compassionate with highly developed intuitive faculties.

An individual with Neptune in the 12th House is naturally attracted to otherworldly and spiritual practices, topics or beliefs. This is one area where a 12th House Neptune may potentially project his or her illusions out upon the world. He or she may believe that ultimate meaning can be found in some transcendent religion, new age philosophy, or 'the occult.' If he or she becomes involved in any such practice or belief system, he or she will eventually become disillusioned with it and move on to yet another and another until he or she becomes conscious that it cannot provide the meaning he or she is seeking.

An individual with Neptune in the 12th House may search for a sense of meaning through the arts and music. Others may attempt to find it through escapist and self-destructive activities such as indulging in drugs and alcohol. No matter what the focus, there is often a desire to escape the 'reality' of the external world and create and develop a rich inner life.

Being that real meaning can only be found through a direct relationship with the Source, an individual with Neptune in the 12th House is likely to experience significant suffering and/or loss, or a sense of isolation, loneliness or abandonment at some point, or throughout, his or her life. These experiences are meant to bring about a state of disillusionment in order to dissolve the illusionary limitations and boundaries the Soul has created for itself.

Once the individual with Neptune in the 12th experiences disillusionment, he or she will either choose some form of escapist activity and/or self-destructive behavior in order to cope, or will choose a spiritual path that allows for an inner relationship with the Source to develop and flourish. He or she may be drawn to sacrifice his or her own desires and serve others in some way. Should an individual go down this path, care must be taken not to allow the ego to develop martyr tendencies as the process of disillusionment will occur once again. No matter how the individual chooses to serve, he or she must remember that he or she is an agent of the Source and that the Source is the actual doer. Should the individual forget this, he or she will face further experiences resulting in disillusionment.

When Neptune is in the 12th House, the potential to actualize the transcendent impulse is very strong and the individual is very likely to feel uncomfortable in the external world and prefer his or her inner world and/or the company of spiritually minded-people. There is a strong tendency and desire to retreat within oneself and engage in some form of meditation or to indulge in an escapist world of dreams and fantasy.

Ultimately, the individual with Neptune in the 12th house has a strong desire to surrender him or herself to a higher source. The danger here is that he or she is likely to project this desire onto someone or something other than The Source. He or she may idealize another person or group. He or she may idealize the mystical state and anyone associated with mysticism. It is also possible that he or she may simply idealize anything that is mysterious and otherworldly. In all cases, except that in which The Source itself is the object of idealization, the Soul will once again become disillusioned.

EXAMPLE CHART C

Neptune and the Projection of Ultimate Meaning
Neptune in the 9th House

by Kristin

This 9th house Neptune placement reflects Souls who project ultimate meaning onto the search for truth and cosmological understanding. Souls' projected ultimate meaning is linked in many cases with the nature of their beliefs. All Souls have a need to feel secure and will do whatever is necessary to prevent a threat to this relative security connected to whatever beliefs are in place. With Neptune in the 9th, the Soul may create a belief system surrounding God (Neptune) and a faith that creates a safety net to support this ultimate fear of the great unknown. This of course will manifest in various ways depending on the Soul's stage of evolution. Ultimately it comes down to a choice with this house placement, as Jeffrey writes, ". . . boiling down to whether you want to do this in a natural way or a patriarchal way."

An example of this is in the Neptune article where Jeffrey speaks about the Gnostics, where this would represent someone following that natural intuitive current within, waking up to real truths while interfacing with the consensus reality of beliefs. This need for freedom to KNOW actual truth came with severe consequences.

> To illustrate the point I'm trying to make, in the tenth century, there was a whole movement within Christianity whose focus and intent was to know God. They were called the Gnostics. And the Christian church--the Vatican at that point--because that was the time of the Inquisition, and all that, in fact, killed these people. Every single one was rounded up over three hundred years and destroyed. Now what does that tell you about your Roman Catholic Church? People

actually wanted to know God in a Christian way and yet they were killed. Now I will ask you again the question: Do you think that's an intention from God? People who want to know God were then killed. Do you think that's an intention from God? That's an example of free choice: political issues, authoritarian issues.

(Jeffrey Wolf Green)

One way Neptune in the 9th manifests is in the following of false teachers, man-created religions that are preaching teachings that create a belief in the perfect God, that God will save, forgive or protect us, i.e. in mainstream Catholic religion, if I simply go to confession, all will be purified, cleared and forgiven. In the consensus state, this can be known as the Billy Graham archetype, someone who is following religious teachings in search of someone or something to 'save' them, a refuge or a need to be 'rescued' from the sea of sin. This is on offer if only you 'accept Jesus into your heart.' There really becomes little responsibility for actions, as these beliefs involve an opportunity to be forgiven and thereby dismiss the wrong doings of their past. You reap what you sow, karma, as in the law of cause and effect and evolutionary necessity is not part of the equation.

Many of the charismatics and even those in high positions in a religious order or in politics are famous for hiding (Neptune) behind God. They use God as their reasons for doing, choosing, what they do, projecting their own conjured-up versions of the truth to rationalize whatever choices they make, all in the name of God, including bloodshed and war. Also within many religions, there is this delusional indoctrination with the attitude that 'we are right and you are wrong,' an 'us versus them' mentality that only breeds intolerance between people. The disillusionment occurs when the results of violent opposition linked to these beliefs take the lives of loved ones or watching your country be bludgeoned and bombed. All in the name of God? In addition, this can reflect a Soul being born into a culture that chooses to interpret a certain set of beliefs that fits their model of security and in many cases the leaders follow these man-created belief systems to gain control over the people, i.e. the followers therefore becoming prisoners (the other side of Neptune) of faith, bound by its teachings. This also occurred in the time of Joan of Arc when they were threatened by her lens and her capacity to connect with God where these so-called 'men of God' could not. As a result, she was burned to death.

The idea and belief of the perfect God, also the judging God as in the man on the throne, would be prevalent at this stage, and God would be someone or something outside itself. This can also connect with Souls that feel that if they pray that their prayers will always be heard and answered, that this male God on the throne will always take care of all things. The disillusionment occurs when the worst case scenario happens, the unthinkable, and then the question becomes, "Where was God?"

As we progress into the individuated state, this can be a Soul whose boundaries of these beliefs are dissolving into something more seamless and in some cases this can be someone who feels so lost and uncertain that they throw the whole system of mainstream faith and religion out the window and demand the freedom to explore and pursue paths that embrace more natural ways to spiritualize. This Pisces question would repeatedly begin to surface as one deepens into the individuated state and would begin to haunt this searching Soul, "Is God really perfect?" and if so, "How can a perfect anything make an imperfect anything?" It is not possible, so the Soul learns that clearly God is an evolving force.

Many of these Souls may have traveled far and wide for lifetimes in search for truth, projecting ultimate meaning upon this search, where nothing can get in the way of this pursuit. So the search for truth, believing that ultimate meaning will be found in this quest, crossing borders and boundaries of different international cultures and lands to find their version of the truth. This projection of ultimate meaning can occur within this search for higher learning and higher wisdom inwardly trusting that the truth will ultimately be found and that God or the Source Of All Things can be understood and experienced. "This search for truth can play out physically by traveling to many states or countries, intellectually through reading literature or books on philosophy and it can be experienced by drifting." (JWG)

Neptune in the 9th can also create total uncertainty, or a spiritual fog linked with what is true and not true, so in the individuated state, especially the 2nd stage, the Soul may feel like such an alien that nothing makes sense and there are many at this stage that may believe that there is no God at all. Their projected sense of ultimate meaning may simply be in having the freedom to drift and to disappear. The disillusionment along these lines occurs when none of those truth-seeking questions can be answered. This can inevitably lead to a crisis in faith.

Just because a Soul evolves does not mean that the tendency to follow false teachers lessens. There is still this risk, as with Neptune in the 9th, for people to take in teachings that are totally delusional yet create some fantasy reality that feels good, gives them a way out, or a way in, as seen with the spiritual 'woo woo's' of this world. They can be seen acting like they are living a spiritual life, creating altars, going to kirtans, living intentional communities with the appearance of the spiritual walk, but Souls may not inwardly be walking the talk. This can represent the illusion of the enlightened one; they may even believe for themselves that they have a heightened sense of elevation or evolution that is not real at all. But at some point the unresolved past will catch up with any Soul. No amount of meditating or positive thinking will erase whatever the Soul has karmically collected. The spiritual 'high' may be replaced with an inner chaos and hysteria.

This may represent a Soul well into the individuated state as well as into the early spiritual state who is into seeking refuge in spiritual quests such as spiritual retreats, silent meditations etc., in essence taking in teachings that fit some belief system that allows them to still escape or hide, from who they actually are, their natural way of being in the world, in some cases avoiding their emotional body and just 'going to God.' When the Soul is not honoring its actual nature, this at some point will lead to an inner emptiness, a void that cannot be filled by any form of faith or participating in spiritual workshops.

Rajneesh and community

Neptune in the 9th could equal someone not only following a spiritual teacher in the search for truth but the desire to be a spiritual icon as well. For example, I just spoke to a client who is still quite young, in her 20's, who has this signature including strong Aquarian aspects and has always wanted to be a Unitarian minister. Take the Rajneesh's of this world, who are in the 2nd stage spiritual, motivated by delusions of grandeur that lead to a form of spiritual fanaticism. He criticized institutional religions and was against any kind of commandment. His teachings emphasized the importance of meditation, awareness, love, celebration, courage, creativity and humor, qualities that he viewed as suppressed by adherence to static belief systems, religious tradition and socialization. He also had very loose limits around sexuality that earned him the name 'sex guru.' Nevertheless, the followers 'believed' what he was pedaling, because it 'felt good,' 'no rules,' and they came out in droves.

In essence, this can represent Souls taking in perceived truths that are in fact lies or made up realities that only create a further separation from actual truth. An example when Neptune is in Scorpio in the 9th can be a Soul with very little discernment and no filter, innocently taking in whatever is being voiced. The disillusionment comes when a Soul puts another up on a spiritual pedestal, making them a saint or a prophet and then the truth about their actual motivations and capacities become apparent.

This lack of discernment at times with Neptune in the 9th can reflect a Soul innocently believing that what someone is saying is true, the Soul falling for the 'silver tongue' as Jeffrey used to call it, as in the man seducing his prey with words to hook the woman. So someone who has loose borders and boundaries concerning what is taken in, they will easily trust, projecting the highest of intention of what is being spoken. They project ultimate meaning into a version of the truth, hearing what they want to hear because it fulfills some fantasy or ideal.

A true expression of Neptune in the 9th in the highest sense would be a Soul who is projecting ultimate meaning into their spiritual practice, one who can actualize the truth of God consciousness through natural means of spirituality, i.e. Hong Sau meditation and the like, a Soul who has the natural capacity to go directly to the Source for truth and to find their own natural means there, either to find God in nature or through other forms of natural spiritualizing. This would be where ultimate meaning is found.

Paramahansa Yogananda

Neptune in the 9th not only connects to spiritual beliefs but any beliefs that represent some form of security. For example, a recent study came out stating that 46% of Americans believe that the world is only 6,000 years old dismissing evidence to the contrary, these beliefs manifesting so it fits their model of security, and undoubtedly this will also fit in to their religious model. At the end of the day, this Neptune placement may represent that whatever is being pedaled and how a Soul chooses to interpret the truth may not hold water, Neptune in the 9th.

Another way this might manifest is in the world of sports. The 9th house/Sagittarius connects with sports and Neptune here can connect to projecting ultimate meaning into either the sports icon or the desire to become a sports icon. You can see this with athletes who pour everything they have into their sport, project ultimate meaning into their role within it. When they retire, these athletes often fall into a deep depression and, in the worst cases, attempted or successful suicide, because their ultimate sense of meaning is lost, gone.

EXAMPLE CHART D

Neptune and the Projection of Ultimate Meaning
through the Houses

by Skywalker

Neptune in the 1st House or Aries can project the ultimate meaning of their existence upon their potential to achieve anything they desire to accomplish. To pioneer and be first and the best at whatever they do. Neptune in the 1st will project ultimate meaning upon their freedom of action. This freedom is necessary since Neptune in the 1st can feel they have a special destiny to fulfill on behalf of society or the universe. The ultimate meaning of their freedom to act will be projected upon their family members, intimate partners and society as a whole in the form of expected support to fulfill this special destiny.

Neptune in the 1st can become disillusioned when others are not supportive of their desire to achieve the high potential they believe they have. When this potential is blocked and they are forced to act with consideration for others. When they realize that others are as special/important or unimportant as themselves. When they do not have the energy to act, or lose their freedom to achieve what they sense is possible from their point of view. When their actions do not produce the desired or projected results or when they lose in a competition, they can be disillusioned as a result.

Neptune in the 2nd House or Taurus can project ultimate meaning on their ability to survive and generate resources, or on their personal value and ultimately the value of life itself. In the 2nd, ultimate meaning can be projected upon their ability to generate income and their resources/possessions if in modern society. In a tribal context, to survive by their ability to hunt for food, through agriculture or fishing or their ability to build their shelter. In a tribal context, they can also project ultimate meaning upon their physical strength, the land that they inhabit and to Mother Earth that sustains them. In the second they can also project ultimate meaning on their sexuality and sensuality.

Neptune in the 2nd can be disillusioned when they themselves lose personal value/self-esteem or life itself loses meaning. When their ability to survive is undermined in some way and they are obliged to depend on another. When what they value most proves to be nothing more than a possession that loses meaning to them or when they outright lose their possessions or ability to generate income. For some, when they lose their libido and sexual drive as they feel they are not useful if they cannot reproduce. In a tribal context, they can be disillusioned when things go wrong with their crops or their hunting does not suffice for them or the tribe to ensure sustainability. Also, when nature is not supportive of their survival and comfort or natural disasters happen and undermine their ability to survive thus disillusioning them relative to Mother Earth and life in general.

Neptune in the 3rd House or Gemini can project ultimate meaning on their own intelligence and ability to relate through communication. In the 3rd house, there can be ultimate meaning projected upon their wits and mental ability, their education and ability to understand/transmit information to and from others. They can project ultimate meaning on their ability to be understood and to understand others since they can sense the inter-connectedness between all things. On their ability to be mobile and go from one place to another. On their mental abilities.

They can be disillusioned when they fail to understand others or are limited by language barriers and are thus unable to communicate or understand others in a logical way. When they fail to empirically explain to themselves or others whatever they feel on the inside. When they realize their information is superficial or incorrect or limited in some way. When they feel less intelligent than someone else feels or are unable to secure their education or when the information they acquired through education is rendered obsolete by some new form of information. When they are limited and confined without the ability to move around from one place to another.

Neptune in the 4th House or Cancer can project ultimate meaning on their ability to be nurtured and nurture others in an emotional way that leads to a sense of inner security and self-consistency. This can take the form of desiring to care for their parents or humanity and all living things and the desire to be cared for in the same way. The desire to feed and nurture others and be appreciated for that and, in turn be nurtured in whichever ways the individual feels necessary. They may also project ultimate meaning on their family of origin, one or more members in the family or someone in the home environment that made them feel secure and cared for. They may project ultimate meaning on their home environment, their country and/or the planet itself. Ultimate meaning may be projected upon emotional empathy for the other and the ability to express emotions.

Disillusionment can come once they realize that others do not care about them the way they do or when they are taken advantage of for their giving nature. When they themselves are unable to give the necessary care and nurturing to others or even to themselves. Disillusionment may be experienced when realizing one of the parents is less than ideal or when someone in their family environment is impure. When their national leaders are corrupt and this is revealed or when they discover the world at large is not as caring as they believed and can in fact be a hostile place. When they are unable to show emotional empathy or others show no empathy towards them.

Neptune in the 5th House or Leo can project ultimate meaning on their own creative abilities, their own ability to shine and attract others, their own egocentric sense of purpose and specialness and their children as a vicarious extension of themselves. They may project ultimate meaning on whatever they do actually, as it reflects them and their specialness or superiority… to themselves at least. They may project ultimate meaning on the respect others have for them and the attention others give them. On their own importance and special abilities whether real or imagined. On their power and authority to lead and, their youth, vitality and beauty.

Neptune in the 5th may be disillusioned when they discover that they are not as special as they thought they were, when they are forced to face the fact that they have much to learn and are in fact many times under developed. When they come to terms with what is really going on, which is really a need to be loved and acknowledged. They may be disillusioned when their children turn out to be less than perfect or when their children do not relate to them or vice-versa. When their creative projects are not appreciated by others or when they themselves are not recognized for their special abilities, imagined superiority and special sense of purpose in life. When they are faced with others who are in fact better than they are in some area where they would like to be the ultimate source of inspiration or, for some, when they realize they are only human and as limited as all other humans on the planet.

Neptune in the 6th House or Virgo may project ultimate meaning on the purity of those they interact with or their own selves. They can project ultimate meaning on the importance of their work as a form of service to the whole or on the ones they serve such as employers or animals or just regular people. Neptune in the 6th can idealize him or herself as the savior who desires to be of service to others in a self-sacrificial way as a way of avoiding their own shortcomings. They may project ultimate meaning on their ability to heal themselves or develop their own technical abilities. Virgo is the sign of practice and improvement, the sign that desires things to be pure or as perfect as possible, and ultimate meaning may be projected upon their own ability to perform a certain task or duty to perfection. To be impeccable.

Disillusionment may be experienced when their ability to help or serve is undermined or limited in some way. When their health fails them or their services are inadequate. When they fail to achieve the ideal of perfection and purity they projected upon whatever it was they were trying to achieve or accomplish. When the ones they try to serve or help do not want to be helped or do not manage to heal. When their efforts are shown to be useless compared to what they imagined and are not the saviors they had dreamt of being. When they discover perfection does not exist or is relative and they realize they are not as clean/impeccable as idealized.

Neptune in the 7th House or Libra can project ultimate meaning on their partners and others whom they relate to. They can project ultimate meaning on their marriage partner and the relationship itself, the quality of the relationship, of that which is given and received within the relationship and the direction it is heading in. Their own ability to please and give that which others need. Neptune in the 7th House can project ultimate meaning on balance and fairness within personal relationships of all kinds, especially intimate ones. Thus, they project ultimate meaning on justice, what is graceful, fair and equal.

Neptune in the 7th House may be disillusioned when their partners don't measure up to their projected expectations of perfection, purity, beauty and godliness. When they realize their partners are only human just as they are. When they realize their relationships are mundane and just like everyone else's, without the beauty, justice and grace they desired. When their partners are unable to understand their needs and satisfy them or when they are unable to satisfy the needs of those with whom they relate. When they realize they are not in love any more as they realize the person they loved was in fact an illusion or idealization and not a real person. Neptune in Libra or the 7th House may be disillusioned with how others treat them or others in general as they have a natural desire for beauty and fairness. They may be disillusioned when suddenly left by a partner and discover the partner doesn't care about them in the way they expected and realize that they are always alone in a sense.

Neptune in the 8th House or Scorpio can project ultimate meaning on evolution itself and their ability or power to evolve as they desire. As a result, this can then be projected subconsciously onto anything that equals evolution for them, ranging from sexual experiences that have the effect of empowering them through merging with another and assimilating their strength, to acquiring power over others in any way imaginable or financial wealth as a form of power and security. Some may desire to penetrate and merge with the very source of all power, God. Or, in the negative sense, to merge with evil forces that can empower them. They may wish to develop magic abilities and project ultimate meaning on those abilities and the hope to be invincible. They can also project ultimate meaning on those whom they trust and open up to emotionally. Some may project ultimate meaning on the purity of their intentions and the intentions of those they trust or admire.

Disillusionment may be experienced when those in whom they invested their trust and faith betray them in some way. They may be disillusioned when they are in a situation of powerlessness, where they are disillusioned with themselves and their own limitations or with their relationship to forces more powerful than they are, such as God or evil entities. They may be disillusioned with those that they once supported were not there for them when they needed support. They may be disillusioned when their intentions are shown to be less than pure or the intentions of others they respected are not pure. Disillusionment may be experienced when they are shown to be vulnerable and not invincible, as they had hoped to be.

Neptune in the 9th House or Sagittarius may project ultimate meaning on whatever constitutes truth for them, on their belief system and whatever connects them to their belief system such as their religion or spiritual teachers or for many in the consensus, their sports teams and icons which can represent or substitute their religion. They may project ultimate meaning on a system of knowledge and those who pass the knowledge to them or on their own ability and freedom to acquire this knowledge for themselves. Some may project ultimate meaning on their freedom to travel in this world or in their own minds/other worlds as this is linked with their desire to expand their awareness through discovering new horizons. They may project ultimate meaning on nature, natural law and their connection to nature as a great teacher. On their own marksmanship, hunting abilities and ability to hit the target as in sports.

Neptune in the 9th House or Sagittarius may be disillusioned when what they believed to be true does not pan out the way they had expected, when their religious beliefs are shown to be limited or wrong and when those they admired and respected for their knowledge or abilities turn out to be dishonest or simply limited in their knowledge with the result of being wrong or ignorant, especially relative to their spiritual/philosophical/religious beliefs. They can be disillusioned when they realize that their own knowledge and beliefs are proved wrong or limited or when others are dishonest with them, and when they themselves are dishonest and others turn away from them because of this. They may also be disillusioned if the places they desired to travel, inner or outer, do not measure up to the experience they had envisioned or when the body of knowledge they invested themselves in fails to satisfy their desire for unlimited growth and expansion. Their sports teams when they discover results can be fixed and icons when they discover they are less than what they imagined or use drugs to boost performance. In this world, they may also be disillusioned with the huge lack of honesty that permeates most of the people inhabiting the world and the destruction of nature. They may be disillusioned with human's lack of respect for nature and natural law and the distortions that this creates in their lives and the lives of all affected by these distortions.

Neptune in the 10th House or Capricorn may project ultimate meaning on the structure of the society that they live in and the laws and regulations that govern the world at large. Some may project ultimate meaning on the inherent rights and wrongs, including those of a spiritual nature therefore projecting upon morals. Neptune in the 10th may project ultimate meaning on authority figures and the very system itself or the very rules/laws that govern the universe. They may also project ultimate meaning on their culture, their parents or their own role as responsible parents. They can also project ultimate meaning on their ability to lead or execute and complete a task to a desired goal. On their role or profession within the society they live in and their status, authority, or importance. They may project ultimate meaning on values of the past and how things were done back in the olden days. On their time and how it is spent.

They can be disillusioned when they discover that those who are in charge of their world are corrupt or dishonest, and when they themselves have an unsatisfactory role within the society they live in. When their parents turn out to be 'rule breakers' and immoral. When their parents are just ordinary people with no real position or status in the world. When their own parenting is questionable by society at large. When their own authority is undermined by others or their profession does not bring the status and recognition they had hoped for. They can be disillusioned when their sense of right and wrong is in fact limited or obsolete in some way or when they themselves fail to act accordingly with their own code of morals and end up being judged by themselves or others. They may be disillusioned when their sense of what is real is suddenly not dependable anymore and therefore leaving them drifting and not knowing what is real. When reality turns out to be less than ideal and is actually ugly and repressive. When those whom they admired as correct, professional, moral etc. turn out to be tyrannical or corrupt. They may be disillusioned by the fact that they have a limited time here on earth and their bodies will decay and die. They may also be disillusioned when values from past epochs and values relative to their culture do not fit into current times anymore or when their culture is being lost due to globalization or other reasons.

Neptune in the 11th House or Aquarius may project ultimate meaning on their own individual uniqueness and that which makes them different. They may project ultimate meaning on their ability to be objective and different from those they consider to be obsolete or stagnant. They may project ultimate meaning on their freedom and those they relate to of like-mind, their friends and their shared ideals. They may also project ultimate meaning on humanity and humanitarianism, desiring fairness and equal rights for all people around the globe. They may project ultimate meaning on their hopes for the human race for the future and where we are all headed, on science and technology and how we use it to connect to each other, on the power of the mind itself. On humans ability to share and act as a brotherhood.

Neptune in the 11th House can be disillusioned when they realize that life isn't fair, that there are social and racial groups and differences and that people are not all treated as equals, at least not in this world. They may be disillusioned when they realize that the world does not care about them or their high ideals for humanity or that their own ideals cannot be implemented even if they are for the good of all. They can be disillusioned when they discover their friends do not actually share the same values and ideals as they do or when their faith in humanity is shattered as they realize not all humans see them as a 'brother.' They can be disillusioned when humans treat others as commodities or when there are things such as wars and famine to the benefit of some. They can be disillusioned when they realize they are not appreciated for their uniqueness and are actually treated as strange or a freak by those they valued and respected, or when no matter how much of a rebel and objective or different they are, they are still in the same boat as everyone else and don't manage to make much of a difference.

Neptune in the 12th House or Pisces can project ultimate meaning on virtually anything it interfaces with, consciously or unconsciously, as it perceives the underlying connectedness and unity between all things on a subconscious level. Therefore, Neptune in the 12th can be disillusioned on a constant basis, as the person interfaces with human selfishness and individual desires of a separating nature, while he/she sees unity in all things.

EXAMPLE CHART E

Neptune and the Projection of Ultimate Meaning
Neptune in the 4th House

by Ari Moshe

The 4th House corresponds to the energetic experience of home. It describes the emotional body, how the Soul creates a context of security for itself to embrace the constant flow of change in life. On the most basic level of understanding, the 4th House corresponds to the nature of the ego: the sense of identity that in virtue of being an identity, serves as a filter through which all experiences are given personal subjective context. The identity that the Soul creates for itself however is never fixed – the ego is always a reflection of the inner reality of the Soul itself and thus the sense of self is in a constant process of re-definition.

The ego is also something that is necessarily shaped and limited within the structural conditions of the human incarnation, and thus develops within time and context. An example of this is simply the reality of all Souls, as they come into human form, being in a state of such utter vulnerability that their identity is not even consciously formed – they just need to be taken care of. Such care implies a total and profound receptivity to the nurturing forces that exist outside of oneself that one is completely dependent on. Examples of this would be things like being fed and being held.

On another level the 4th House archetype also corresponds to the natural phases of human identity development which corresponds to an actual physiological development as well as a development within the human brain which correlates psychologically to how each human will begin to adopt to its environment and shape its own self-image at different stages of life (4th House relative to the 10th). The astrological cycles simply exemplify this: Mars return equaling the initiation of conscious desires and will within the individual, Saturn cycles equaling the gradual maturation and adaptation of the individual within its current social reality, etc.

The 4th House corresponds in part to the early emotional imprinting from the current life which may describe the nature of the Soul's mother (or at least the Soul's relationship to their mother/source of human nurturing) and on the other hand it also points to the way each Soul is ever developing their own sense of self within the world; the kind of home and family the Soul will orient towards and the karmic needs surrounding that. It represents how the Soul will nurture others and provide nurturing for themselves, which includes knowing how to create safe and supportive environments that will allow for growth in a healthy and safe way. The nature of the environments the Soul creates for itself brings necessary changes as the Soul adopts more to understanding themselves in a broader context. Example: living in a room in the parent's home as a child with stuffed animals, versus creating a more 'mature' living environment later on in life. The similarity that weaves them together is that

57

both contexts represent a safe container, or at least a container that Houses the Soul's growth through the human experience that is relevant for the Soul at that time.

Last preliminary thought on the 4th House: the underlying reality of being a human being is that basic needs aren't always met. The child isn't always given what they inherently need. Thus the adult human doesn't always know how to provide for their own selves (and thus for others) what they inherently need. This sets the stage for all kinds of karmic circumstances to unfold.

Neptune represents the way in which the Soul will spiritualize their life: how they will come to know their direct and inherent relationship with God. Relative to the 4th House archetype, this is about knowing God as a source of ultimate nurturing; that all Souls no matter what the age or form are like children of the ultimate Source, and are sustained by and provided by that Source. Thus, one's inherent relationship to God is like a baby's inseparable relationship to the mother through the umbilical cord. The mother provides the womb, the food, everything on every level that the unborn baby needs. Then when the baby is born the mother still provides all the basic needs. (However even this is an imperfect analogy as even while in the womb the possibility for neglect is there. This is even more possible once the baby is born. I'll speak more to that later on.)

God is ultimately experienced as the source of all nourishment: thus the divine will is for all Soul's to be safe and protected and provided for on the most fundamental human emotional levels. However, from the point of view of delusion, a Soul with this signature may naively expect one of two things:

(1) All beings are safe and taken care of. This expectation can easily be misplaced onto mother or family, or to other beings. The expectation that life is inherently nurturing and that everyone will be 'held' metaphorically and literally, whenever and however he or she needs. The reality of things of course can be totally disillusioning in the sense that it seems that there are many people who are in fact not 'held' by reality. The Soul may react to this in one of two ways:

(a) The Soul may create and project false stories about people who are starving or without a home, or who have been abandoned. The Soul may completely deny the actual reality of such things and paint over that reality an alternative reality that hides the actual reality from being acknowledged. The Soul will become disillusioned when they realize that the reality they created isn't true. This realization can happen in many ways such as when they witness actual violence or trauma that is energetically stronger than their illusions, or when they themselves are in a situation without basic needs and are dependent upon others to take care of them only to ultimately realize that they are alone and abandoned, and not cared for.

(b) They will position themselves in such a way as to nurture and heal all those who are needing it. Whenever they see another in some form of suffering, they will in essence 'take them home' literally or metaphorically and provide for them. They will be adapting to the emotional reality of another as to make others feel more safe and comfortable. The issue here is that this is being done with no discrimination as to whether the others are essentially wanting this, or if this is actually helping them. In this process, the Soul is essentially martyring their own self on behalf of 'saving' others. The need to help others is coming from a fundamental vulnerability and insecurity with the reality of life that very often appears NOT to be nurturing and supportive to all beings. This can be applied especially to one's mother. This eventually leads to exhaustion and a deep feeling that one's own basic needs are not being met: perpetually living in 'someone else's home' on an energetic level.

(2) One's own self is always safe and taken care of. The Soul, however, may experience total neglect. From the point of view of a child, when basic needs aren't met – needs which are expected and assumed to be met – this creates the need for the child to form an identity structure to somehow make sense out of the lack of basic needs. Thus, this can lead to a fantasy life wherein the Soul does one of two things:

(a) Convinces themselves of an alternate reality that they can escape into wherein all of their needs are essentially met and they are totally taken care of. This alternate reality may be a place the Soul escapes to within their own imagination, or they may actually project that onto the actual reality as a way of ignoring what is. This leads to disillusionment, similar to above, when essential needs are so fully ignored and they find themselves grossly undernourished on a physical or emotional level.

(b) Project onto their mother, or others who are close to them (such as family or close relationships) a reality that reflects the false expectation that these individuals are essentially like God: that everything they do is perfect. This can also express by way of projecting onto these people that they need the Soul in some way to take care of them. In the case of one's mother, the Soul may picture their own mother as perfect and that they are always doing the best for them. Or, on the other end, to deal with the possibility of the mother being completely absent (literally or emotionally), the Soul may place themselves in the role of being a savior to the mother who may herself be out of touch with reality. What is hidden to the Soul is that their need to either project some absolute higher meaning onto others as an ultimate provider, or to save and be the ultimate provider for others, is ultimately a reflection of how they are trying to find ways to stay safe within their own day-to-day experience.

Disillusionment occurs when the Soul realizes that the unshakable sources of nourishment and love that it thought were real are in fact not. That in fact mother or anyone else is just on his or her own evolutionary journey and that the Soul cannot depend on them to be the provider. It is also realized that in nurturing others and making everyone 'feel safe' and taken care of, the Soul is not always going to be supported in kind, and furthermore others may not actually be saved in the end. Ultimately this can lead a Soul to feel incredibly alone and vulnerable, never at home, overwhelmed by other people's needs. Basic human needs for touch or nourishment through food may be neglected which may lead to a weakness in the emotional and physical bodies.

As I reflect upon this, I feel a core projection of ultimate meaning with this signature is the assumption that human beings and beings in general will want to take care of one another. This leads to disillusionment when it's revealed that that simply isn't the case.

One false projection that can occur: projecting an illusory emotional reality onto something that holds some sort of sentiment to the individual whether this something is an inanimate object or an illusory home that does not exist. An example of this would be care taking for a doll and projecting actual emotions onto that doll. These projections create a relationship between the individual and the doll that provides a sense of caring for another that vicariously makes one feel cared for and also allows the individual to displace and externally project their own unrecognized emotional needs onto something outside of itself, thus providing for the Soul a sense of control and safety.

Another false projection that can occur is to recognize an individual's need for home and nourishment and then to elect oneself the position to care for them to the point of lacking healthy discrimination. In the mind of the Soul with this signature, the individual being cared for is looked upon as the 'abandoned child' that just needs to be taken care of and nurtured. Every emotion from that individual that the Soul senses will trigger the Soul to somehow sooth and care for that individual.

Another basic theme that is worthy to mention: abandoning one's own family for the sake of a higher calling; escaping from one's human needs by drawing upon a higher, spiritualized (or universalized) sense of identity. This can then lead the Soul to project all kinds of ideas as to what having a family must be like: that it is antithetical to one's spirituality. Human emotions in one's self and in others will then be ignored, unaddressed, escaped from in whatever way the Soul knows how to do so. This can be disillusioning once the Soul finds themselves, by chance, with a family and with children... or housesitting for a pack of dogs!

CHAPTER THREE

NEPTUNE: WHISPERS FROM ETERNITY

Introduction

We have just focused on how the Neptune, Pisces, and the 12th House can correlate to where a Soul can project its ultimate sense of meaning for life with the resulting disillusionment that will come when that projection is anything other than the desire to know the Ultimate Source Of All Things.

One of the archetypal dimensions of the Neptune archetype, because it is about the Ultimate Source Of All Things is rooted in the fact that that Source can inwardly induce within the consciousness of the individual Soul impulses manifesting as thoughts that leads to desires to act upon, actualize, those impulses. These impulses are linked with the ongoing evolutionary journey of each Soul, and these impulses, if acted upon, are one of the ways that a Soul can 'spiritualize' their lives.

This spiritualization occurs OF ITSELF if acted upon. In other words, any given Soul may not even have the language of the Source Of All Things, a religion or philosophy, within their consciousness. Yet, if acted upon, because these impulses are being ignited by the Source a NATURAL spiritualization process will occur. Thus, this can manifest in any of the four natural evolutionary states of the Soul.

These impulses will be linked with the natal placement of Neptune by house and sign, and its aspects to other planets: the archetypes of those planets and houses. These impulses will also manifest via the 12th House, and the location of the sign Pisces in the birth chart which then refers back to the natal house location of Neptune: the natural planetary ruler of Pisces.

These impulses, anatomically speaking, manifest from the pineal gland deep within the brain by way of a hormone called melatonin. The neurotransmitters within the brain carries these impulses to the right and left-brain hemispheres that originally manifest as a deep inner 'whisper' within the consciousness of the individualized Soul, whispers that reflect and contain the 'messages' of the impulses themselves. These whispers, at first, manifest within the right-brain, kind of like a big sign way in the distance that will progressively become ever closer IF the Soul pays attention to it. On that sign will be some sort of message, like on a billboard, that symbolizes the very nature of the original impulses themselves.

So, for example, on the billboard there could be a sign that symbolizes movies. In time, that sign will manifest as messages by way of the left-brain that would then translate, for example, into the IDEA of being a filmmaker. The left-brain will then begin to analyze and figure out how to make that idea a reality: from A to Z, so to speak.

If the Soul does indeed desire to act upon these original impulses of Neptune, etc., in this natural way, then a natural spiritualization of the Soul's consciousness will occur because, after all, these impulses are being induced by the Source Of All Things. So to act upon them is to move in the direction of that Source in ways that are natural to each Soul.

Questions and Answers

(Q) Does the Sun also possibly correlate with the individualized consciousness along with the Moon?

(A) The Sun gives purpose to that individualized consciousness that correlates with the Moon, and how that individualized consciousness, relative to the entire EA paradigm, is integrated relative to that purpose throughout the current life of a Soul.

(Q) Regarding your quote: "The desire of the Soul, at this stage of evolution [3rd stage Individuated], would be just the opposite: direct inner perception of that Source by way of expanding the interior of the consciousness itself." Could you please show me an example of how 'expanding the interior of consciousness itself' manifests in a 3rd stage Individuated Soul?

(A) As the Soul evolves from the consensus to the 3rd stage spiritual, there is a NATURAL expansion of consciousness that is rooted in the ever increasing awareness within a Soul of the increasing concentric circles of the Universe itself. Relative to this natural expansion in any given Soul at the last stages, this can take on various forms within the individual consciousness of the Soul. So, for example, Einstein. For him, this natural expansion involved the universe of mathematics. For his Soul, mathematics were of course symbols of very large natural processes within the Manifested Creation. In that mathematical universe, this finally arrives at the number ZERO. This number originates from the 3rd century in India and the mathematics there at that time. And this number then correlates, naturally, to 'out of nothing there is something': the un-manifested/manifested. In this way, for Einstein who was a Pisces, he intuitively concluded that this ZERO is the 'evidence' of God Itself.

(Q) Does this mean that the Soul approaching the end of 3rd Individuated would see the impulse or whisper from Source as coming from ITSELF, and not coming from Source, in effect being atheistic?

(A) This would depend on the individual Soul itself depending on the underlying philosophy that it has chosen for guiding principles of its life.

(Q) If an atheistic 3rd Individuated Soul does not believe in or 'know' God, yet God IS whispering to that person, then WHAT is that person inspired by? Himself OR God?

(A) Again, it depends on the underlying philosophy that any given Soul has chosen for its guiding principles of life: how life is philosophically understood which then correlates to how the Soul is 'interpreting' the phenomena of life itself.

(Q) Once the Soul starts to understand, realize and truly 'know' that the inspirations coming to him/her 'internally' ARE the Whisper of God, would that indicate that the Soul is in fact moving into 1st stage Spiritual?

(A) Yes.

(Q) Would a spiritual statement such as this relate more to 1st stage Spiritual than the preceding Individuated stage?

"The kingdom of God is within you" (Jesus)

(A) Yes.

(Q) What about this quote from Ramana Maharshi: "Happiness is your nature. It is not wrong to desire it. What is wrong is seeking it outside when it is inside"?

(A) This statement really has nothing to do with the natural spiritualization of consciousness.

(Q) Is it implied in your response here that the true nature of each Soul is different because each Soul is in their own process of evolution? And the perspective that Ramana Maharishi is speaking from is a generalization from his perspective that is imposing a one size fits all mentality on every Soul? Which is the problem with man-made forms of spirituality to begin with; to say that the impulses and whispers we are receiving from within are somehow NOT the messages from the Soul itself, causing people to turn and look to something outside themselves? Which sets up the cycle for more disillusionment?

(A) His statement is actually ridiculous because all Souls, all of life, live within the natural laws of duality. Happiness of course occurs in all of us, yet it is as fleeting as any other emotion including its polarity: sadness. By issuing this statement it can also cause a Soul to feel that there is something wrong with it because, somehow, it has not arrived at a place of perpetual 'happiness.' The true nature of all Souls is that they have been Created by the Source Of All Things which then means to realize this within. The natural process of the expanding consciousness within the Soul will arrive at the place of knowledge that is rooted in PERCEPTION. This is universal. And in that state of perception the Soul perceives, the ultimate state of consciousness that can be evolved into in human FORM, the interface between the un-manifested and manifested. In that state, while in it, the EMOTION of WONDER or RAPTURE is that which is experienced by all Souls. Yet that state of expanded consciousness cannot be sustained indefinitely. At some point the consciousness of the Soul, like a rubber band, is pulled back into the 'normal' state of consciousness that all humans share which is one rooted in the natural law of duality: happy, sad, and so on.

So the bottom line is very simple in this: when anyone including the 'teachings' of Souls like Ramana Maharshi are not rooted in all the Natural Laws of the Manifest Creation, this will lead to many Souls who 'believe' in those teachings to a state of disillusionment at some point because such teachings are of course delusional: necessarily so. And that must happen in order to realign the Soul with that which is Natural, thus real, and that which is not.

The whispers deep within the consciousness of the Soul can in fact either be caused by what we call God/ess, or those whispers can in fact be messages from the Soul to itself that if acted upon move the Soul closer back to its Source. What we have tried to discriminate is the difference between these, and also the critical understanding of when a Soul claims or states that such whispers are coming from God when they are not. Maharshi's words are a perfect example of just that.

(Q) So, in effect, the REALIZATION of the happiness that a Soul seeks that is its True Nature, would indicate that the Soul is moving into 1st stage Spiritual?

(A) No, because the underlying assumption about the true nature of the Soul is rooted in happiness is simply wrong in the first place.

(Q) I was studying Pluto Vol. 2 because the Soul I am analyzing has Neptune in Libra and one of its main desires is to evolve through relationships. Pertaining to my analysis of the 12th house cusp as well as 5th house cusp being Pisces, for a couple in the Individuated Stage, for Pluto in the 12th house or Pisces, JWG says, "They will share a common commitment to some guiding spiritual philosophy, yet apply it in their own individual way." Is it correct that the whisper is coming from Source that guides the couple toward a spiritual philosophy? What does 'spiritual' mean in this case?

(A) Yes, but that does not necessarily mean that that couple is identifying it in this way. Spiritual means, in this case, some 'cosmological' way of defining their individual lives in the context of being together.

(Q) What is the difference between 'evolution,' 'spiritualization' and 'expansion of consciousness?'

(A) In the end, none.

So let us now prepare some example charts that demonstrate how these 'whispers from eternity' manifest.

EXAMPLE CHART A

Whispers From Eternity

Neptune in Scorpio in the 12th House

by Cat

When God whispers in one's ears, the intent is for the Soul to align itself with a transcendental belief system in order to realize the unity of all of Creation and to experience their individuality as an extension of the source of Creation. The message instills a desire to dissolve all of the barriers that are preventing the Soul from merging their power with the collective whole and return to God.

Some resist the pull to surrender to the Source while others embrace it. Those who reject it choose to carry on as before and deny any source outside themselves. In doing so, they become very ego oriented. This in turn causes them to experience states of powerlessness at some point in time in order to correct the situation. These states of powerlessness can manifest in the form of physical disabilities, physical confinement, or being blocked from exercising any power at all. As harsh as it sounds, this occurs in order to inspire them to embrace the collective whole, and the Source of All, rather than the ego.

Others may only respond to these impulses, or whispers from God, only in times of personal crisis. During such times, they will turn to God and pray for help. In general, they will experience periods of meaninglessness, futility, or disillusionment throughout their lives that serve to force them upon the path back to God.

Others respond and react to the whispers of God, allowing their ego created limitations to be dissolved, so they can become channels through which God, or the Source, operates.

Those who respond, or react, to this impulse in this way feel a desire to return to God on a conscious or unconscious level. There is a bit of a paradox here, as the Pisces archetype accepts God and the Soul's ability to return to its source with blind faith, while the Scorpio archetype insists on penetrating to the core of the matter and demands proof that there is a God and that it is possible for the Soul to return to the Source and be as one with God. An individual with Neptune in the 12th House in Scorpio will therefore focus on examining what he or she already believes and knows. He or she needs to experience directly, even though he or she already believes in that which it needs and desires to experience.

The Soul with Neptune in the 12th House in Scorpio will use both his or her intuitive faculties and analytical capabilities in order to carry out this investigation. Over time, he or she will progressively become less self-focused and self-oriented and more oriented towards serving the needs of others, including humanity as a whole, as there is an impulse to make a difference in the world and a desire to follow this calling from God.

The Soul with Neptune in the 12th House in Scorpio desires to live a life of purpose and meaning. He or she will pursue this goal with passion, striving to share his or her God given gifts with the world, while serving others in some way.

On an anatomical level, these impulses, or whispers from God, manifest from the pineal gland via the hormone melatonin. They are received by the right-brain in the form of a feeling that the Neptune in the 12th House in Scorpio Soul feels deeply on an emotional level. It may come telepathically or in the form of a dream or a déjà-vu, or through some type of imaginative or artistic work. No matter how the message is sent, it easily slips into the individual's conscious awareness from the unconscious making itself felt on an emotional level. It is then processed by the left-brain that works towards figuring out what the symbolism impressed upon the right-brain means. The individual will seek quiet time alone in order to analyze his or her dreams and/or the symbolism that springs forth from his or her art and/or unconscious.

This transcendental impulse, or message from God, will cause change to occur in both the individual and in his or her life. The intent is for the Soul to evolve, so this change is necessary. This can lead to cyclic meltdowns as that which is not real, but is an illusion, will dissolve out of the individual's life. This can cause the individual to become disoriented. He or she will start wondering about the meaning of life and may feel as though he or she is losing control. Everything may seem meaningless during these key points in time. This serves to re-enforce the desire to find meaning and purpose in life by identifying with the collective or whole and ultimately return to God.

In the case of the consensus Soul, this desire to make a difference and to live a life of purpose and meaning may influence the individual to do something that benefits his or her community in some way. He or she may be attracted to volunteer work of some type, social work, or pursue a career that allows him or her to reach out and help others. Raising money for charity is one possibility as is counseling people with drug and alcohol problems or working in a hospice. The possibilities are numerous.

The consensus Soul may also be inspired to align him or herself with some kind of transcendent belief system. The individual may feel a need to start going to church as he or she likely believes, or feels, that in order to find God, one must attend church and abide by the dogma of his or her consensus religion. He or she is likely to choose a traditional church that is recognized and accepted by the consensus society or culture of which he or she is a member. More likely than not, he or she will chose one belonging to the denomination that he or she was raised in, or that of his or parents or grandparents.

When the whisper of God is received and welcomed by the Soul with Neptune in the 12th house, the Soul may be inclined to spend much time in prayer or meditation in quiet and seclusion. The consensus Soul is more likely to pray than meditate. The difference being that when one prays, one talks to God, when one meditates, one allows God to speak to them.

Like most people with Neptune in the 12th House in Scorpio, the consensus Soul will enjoy spending time alone. He or she may simply enjoy spending quiet times in a room of his or her own at home or taking walks on a beach or some other natural environment. He or she may decide to create a garden, paint, write poetry or play a musical instrument. In these ways, the consensus Soul begins to learn how to meditate.

Sexual fantasies and themes are also common as the individual with Neptune in the 12th House in Scorpio yearns for a spiritual form of ecstasy on a sexual level. The consensus Soul may express these desires in the form of sexual role-play through which he or she seeks a connection with the divine via his or her sexual partner.

In the case of the individuated Soul, this desire to make a difference and to live a life of purpose and meaning is likely to inspire him or her to do something that benefits others not only in his or her community, but on a grander scale. He or she desires to serve the public at large in some way. Think of the poet or the songwriter with a message for humanity, the Peace Corps volunteer, relief workers in Africa, Green Peace volunteers, animal rights activists, so on and so forth. Some may choose to work as psychics, astrologers, tarot readers, spiritual counselors, visual artists, musicians. Again, the possibilities are many.

Those who are inspired to align themselves with some kind of transcendent belief system may feel a need to explore religions that are very different from those they were brought up in or exposed to early in life. For example, someone brought up as a Catholic, may decide to become a Buddhist or study Hinduism. Some, especially since Neptune is in Scorpio, may delve into the Occult and New Age philosophies.

Some may align themselves with pagan religions. The individuated Soul with Neptune in the 12th House in Scorpio is attracted to religions or spiritual philosophies that are considered 'taboo' relative to those prescribed by, and accepted by, the consensus society or culture that they are rebelling against.

Like most Souls with Neptune in the 12th House in Scorpio, the individuated Soul will also attempt to create a place, or a space, in which he or she can be alone with him or herself in order to explore his or her own innermost self. He or she may take up some form of Yoga and begin to learn how to meditate. At this stage, the Soul is usually attracted to Hatha Yoga at first, and then progressively moves on to other forms as well. It is also possible that an individuated Soul may experiment with mind-altering drugs in an attempt to induce a mystical experience.

The individuated Soul yearns for a spiritual form of ecstasy on a sexual level just as all Souls with Neptune in the 12th House in Scorpio do. The individuated Soul may seek the divine in the form of his or her sexual partner, just as those in the consensus state do. In addition, he or she may experiment with pseudo forms of Tantric Yoga. Although the goal in Tantric Yoga is sacred sex and connecting with the divine through one's partner, those in the individuated state are more likely to focus on the physical aspects of Tantra than experiencing scared sex in its highest form.

In the case of the spiritual stage Soul, this desire to make a difference and to live a life of purpose and meaning involves overcoming his or her own ego and focusing instead on compassion, humility, community service and love for humanity in all aspects of his or her life.

Those who are inspired to follow some kind of transcendent belief system may feel a need to isolate themselves and spend a great deal of time meditating and experiencing God from within. He or she may practice some form of Raja Yoga. The spiritual stage Soul with Neptune in the 12th House may have an intense interest in reading and studying the sacred texts and scriptures of all religions. Although the individual is not very likely to align him or herself with any one religion or spiritual philosophy, he or she is likely to spend time researching and studying them all. He or she is capable of seeing the common thread that underlies them all. He or she also understands that the religions that are based upon these ancient texts have, for the most part, distorted these truths. If he or she felt a need to align him or herself with a spiritual philosophy, it would have to be one that teaches that the answers can only be found within, that the Kingdom of God lies within us, and that we are all but one small part of the greater whole. Gnosticism and Theosophy are good examples of such spiritual philosophies. In any case, those in the spiritual stage seek truth and meaning from within. They meditate in order to allow messages from the Soul, higher self and the Source to speak directly to them. In addition, they adhere to natural law, whether they are conscious of doing so or not.

The spiritual stage Soul yearns for a spiritual form of ecstasy on a sexual level just as all Souls with Neptune in the 12th House in Scorpio do. At this stage, the Soul has an understanding of the unity and oneness of all and is capable of practicing Tantric Yoga in its true form or engaging in sacred sex with his or her partner.

All of these Souls, in each of these states, have chosen to suffer in some way as part of the spiritualization process as, in order to feel empathy and compassion for others, one must first learn what it feels like to feel pain and suffer themselves. In this way, the Neptune in the 12th House in Scorpio Soul can truly understand the emotional realities and needs of others. Empathy leads to a desire to help others and to give to others what they actually need without thought of oneself or expectation of something in return. In doing so, the Soul evolves as its consciousness shifts away from the ego and towards the collective or whole. Those in the spiritual state are capable of feeling the pain and suffering of the collective whole. In any case, the Soul with Neptune in Scorpio is learning to put others first before themselves.

All Neptune in the 12th House in Scorpio Souls process their life experiences through their emotional bodies, as direct experience enables them to fully experience the natural consequences of their choices and desires. In this way, they develop the ability to feel empathy and compassion for others. In addition, this is how they grow and evolve on a spiritual level.

All Souls with Neptune in the 12th House in Scorpio may struggle to find a way in which they can make a meaningful difference in the world. Although the desire to make a difference may be strong, the individual may find him or herself feeling that no matter what he or she does, their power to change anything is limited.

In the case of the consensus individual, he or she may suffer along with the rest of his or her community when a natural disaster strikes, or a young soldier from his or her community is killed in battle in some foreign land, or a neighbor loses a child. Although he or she feels the pain of others, he or she feels helpless as there is nothing in his or her power he or she can do to change what happened.

The individuated Soul may suffer when he or she reads or hears about animal abuse, war, a natural disaster in some distant place, or other events that are more global in nature than just those in his or her everyday life and community. He or she is likely to feel powerless in regard to what he or she can do about such events or situations other than signing petitions or protesting.

The Spiritual Soul may suffer from anything he or she encounters that goes against natural law on any level. He or she feels the collective pain of others no matter who they are or where they are.

In all cases, this suffering cannot be avoided as no one person can change the world. No one is meant to. We are here to change ourselves, not the world. The physical world is merely a place in which we are born in order to learn the lessons that each of us individual Souls need to learn in order to fulfill our divine destiny and return to the Source. We are not here to change this world, but rather to learn from our experiences in it and develop and evolve our Souls.

Anyone who thinks that they can change the world is delusional. The Soul with Neptune in Scorpio in the 12th house will try and they will suffer from feelings of powerlessness and frustration in the process. This will occur until they realize that they can only change themselves and their true role is to help others do the same. In this way, they can serve God by helping others learn to grow, evolve and return to the Source.

EXAMPLE CHART B

Whispers From Eternity

How, What and Where the Impulses and Whispers Originating from Source can Manifest as Messages, Thoughts and Signposts

Neptune in Libra in the 11th House

by Linda

Introduction

The Soul's evolutionary condition is at the end of 3rd stage Individuated. The Source inwardly induces within the consciousness of the Soul an archetypal dimension of Neptune that manifests as impulses and thoughts that lead to desires being acted upon. The desires that are acted upon lead to ways the Soul can naturally 'spiritualize' its life. The impulses, linked with the evolutionary journey of the Soul, manifest from the pineal gland as a deep inner 'whisper' that contains messages within the consciousness of the Soul, like a big sign way or billboard, that symbolizes the original impulses being induced by Source. When the Soul desires to act upon these impulses of Neptune by way of moving in the direction of Source, a natural spiritualization of the Soul's consciousness occurs.

Neptune in Libra in the 11th house is a healing signature for past traumas. The Soul experienced psychic disillusionment and severe trauma in past lives. This could also be a signature of suicide, alcoholism, drug abuse, and any other kind of escapism. Some of these Souls feel they cannot be here anymore because what they have projected Ultimate Meaning onto is being dissolved. Having lost the natural relationship to Source or to Nature through the distortions of the patriarchy, the Soul is on a quest to regain meaning, fulfillment, joy, the natural self, and the natural relationship to Source. It is via the process of disillusionment that the void becomes filled with the Truth of God.

(1) 3rd stage Individuated

The Soul is discovering who it is independent of Consensus conditioning. Feeling different from the majority of people, he is detaching and objectifying himself and reality through independent thinking. Investigating different ways of understanding life progressively expands his consciousness. The Soul has unique gifts and capacities that he is able to offer society yet he will stand apart from it. He is aware of the relativity of beliefs, values and moralities of the world. He is progressively opening his consciousness up to the real or natural God. Since the Individuated stage of evolution correlates to Uranus, having Neptune in the 11th house reveals that this Soul has been very deeply questioning the nature of existence and creation, and his courage and desire to 'individuate' creates an acceleration of the Soul's evolution and spirituality.

(2) Pluto paradigm: the ongoing evolutionary journey of the Soul

From the Pluto paradigm can be ascertained why this Soul has Neptune in Libra in the 11th house. The impulses and whispers induced by Source manifest within the Soul as returning desires. The Soul and every other Soul, no matter what evolutionary stage, are evolving back to Source. Neptune in a non-stressful sextile to natal Pluto creates the impulse to isolate from the external environment in order to effect self-contemplation and integration of spirituality.

With Uranus coming out of the disseminating phase and approaching a last quarter square aspect with Neptune, the Soul needs to interact socially with periods of isolation. The Soul that has created a separate self from life to life seeks ultimate meaning in something to fill the void. Impulses and whispers from the Source effects evolution through sudden revelations, arousing and mobilizing the Soul to action. It is by the Grace of God that the Soul receives the impulses and whispers of God that allow a natural spiritualization to occur.

(3) Natal Neptune

The Soul has a desire to experience transcendental reality through faith. It is able to tune into the collective unconscious pertaining to the whole human race that alters his perception of reality, and into the collective conscious that is the totality of thoughts and vibrations on a conscious level. Resistance to the dissolution of the ego triggers confusion, disorientation and unconscious fears. Surrender to the impulses and whispers of God allows the distorted aspects of ego to be dissolved. This process brings transformational change, healing, love, loving kindness, empathy, and forgiveness of self and others. The revelation into the dynamics of the ego will lead to the revealing of the true and authentic self.

(4) Natal Neptune in Libra

The Soul desires to learn how to be in relationship by actualizing and developing spiritual desires and needs through relationships with individuals, friends and groups in order to balance the levels of giving and receiving. With others, he will explore ways of relating that are independent of the existing social conventions, such as rebelling against traditional gender assignments, or playing out both male and female principles. Impulses and whispers from Source prompt the Soul to action by carrying out what partners, friends or groups need from him, or what God wants for him regarding sustained efforts that actualize equality and balance. These Divine messages inspire the Soul to psychically attune to the desires, needs and expectations of others. This happens by way of developing the awareness to actually 'listen' objectively to the reality of others, and not just through the filter of his personal reality. Being able to truly love others by giving them what they actually need builds a commitment to a spiritual or philosophical system of thought. He is also able to fulfill a personal vision that correlates with his own sense of unique purpose.

In past lives, there had been psychological and symbiotic enmeshment with others due to excessive proximity and dependency. Feeling so symbiotically tied to others can create a need for freedom, detachment or escape. Because the Soul is sharing and comparing himself with others, this produces the ability to have deep discussions regarding the nature of expectations. Thus, through this process, he is able to understand a larger context, and a different, deeper perspective of the nature of the dynamics and issues of interpersonal relationships. The messages occurring naturally in the Spirit would bring balance to dynamics that have reached extremes of imbalance. The kinds of messages and signposts change to reflect the Soul's ongoing need for further spiritualization, in effect bringing in new relationships, friendships and involvements with progressive groups, thus fulfilling a wider collective need.

Through these impulses and whispers from the Divine, the Soul is able to love unconditionally, not conditionally, with the power to transform his life, the lives of others, and truly forgive others. From here, he is able to progressively dissolve ego barriers that are preventing merging with the Cosmic Whole. The whisper from Source brings to a Soul with Neptune in Libra in the 11th house, through his relationships with others, a capacity for deep healing, wisdom, insight, forgiveness, equality, balance, natural goodness, love of others, and love of self.

What leads to disillusionment in the Soul is a very persistent repetitive belief, need, and projection over many lifetimes that he needs a partner. He may believe that in order to feel completely whole and fulfilled there is a necessity to find a partner, so that he is not alone. In this way, he moves from one relationship to the next, believing that the next partner will be the right one. The whisper from God comes to the Soul by way of a message that nothing outside of himself can bring satisfaction, and that no partner or friend can complete the Soul. At this stage of evolution, the Soul is just beginning to learn that we are made for and compliment God, and not each other.

When the Soul progressively understands and acts upon the spiritual messages, he will understand that only a relationship with God will bring satisfaction. However, these revelations are only just beginning to take place for the Soul in this evolutionary stage, end of 3rd Individuated.

(5) Natal Neptune in the 11th house

The impulse originating from Source during times of self-contemplation occurs through repetitive thought patterns that pertain to the Soul's future. The Soul will receive signposts revealing when to act at the right time. Acting upon these messages enables the Soul to liberate itself from outmoded conditioning patterns that had generated trauma, shock, fragmentation, alienation or hysteria in past lives. Repeating messages direct the Soul to stand back and view reality objectively. The impulse from Source will lead to rebelling from existing conditions of stagnation and non-growth. He may be prompted to join groups, social causes, or humanitarian movements, for a shared or social purpose. These messages may direct him toward altruistic or philanthropic work for others.

A friend in need is a friend indeed!

The Soul may be guided to form an intimate relationship with someone in order that both learn how to see objectively the nature of their reality. Through objectively learning the dynamics of relationships and restoring balance and equality, the Soul is able to effect deep transformational change, and heal past trauma, wounds and phobias. He could be led to form an intimate relationship with someone who had been a friend, or vice-versa, become a friend to someone with whom he is hopelessly enmeshed. Some relationships or friendships will allow the Soul to expand his consciousness through accepting the individual differences and diversity of life so that evolutionary growth progresses.

The Soul may be guided to form a partnership of like-mindedness to fulfill a shared objective or goal of a social context or non-intimate nature. He may find it difficult to differentiate his personal values from group values, or express his own identity because of becoming too fused or devoted to others. Yet the transcendental impulse will allow a letting go or surrender of fixed obsolete values in order that evolution continue. In this way, outmoded patterns in the Soul's individuated unconscious are transformed. A whisper from Source may suddenly allow the Soul to find his courage, to stand up for a social cause, develop spiritual conviction to help or rescue others, or self-sacrifice himself for others, thereby not only expressing uniqueness, strength and individuality, but fulfilling a higher purpose for Source.

The Arousing – Shock and Thunder!
Thunder repeated: the image of SHOCK.
Thus in fear and trembling
The superior man sets his life in order
And examines himself.

The shock of continuing thunder brings fear and trembling. The superior
man is always filled with reverence at the manifestation of God; he sets
his life in order and searches his heart, lest it harbor any secret
opposition to the will of God. Thus, reverence is the
foundation of true culture.
(I-Ching)

The Soul may receive the whisper in the form of shock, astonishment, surprise, or his hair standing on end when a spiritual thought wants to distinguish itself from the ordinary workings of the mind. Another way God's whisper takes place is through synchronicity, confirming that the Soul is on the right path at the right time. In this way, the Soul is led step by step to surrender to the Spirit that gives him free rein. The whisper from Source brings to the Soul with Neptune in the 11th house a capacity for egalitarianism, autonomy, equality, sovereignty, and freedom. God whispers that we are all equal, that no one is any better than anyone else is. Through experiences of sudden spiritual awakening, the bonds of conditioning are broken and past trauma and blocks to liberation are removed.

(6) Aspects to Neptune

Neptune sextile Pluto. Neptune in the 11th house and natural ruler of Pisces inconjunct Pisces on the 5th house cusp. This aspect generates crisis and self-scrutiny. While Pisces symbolizes the Divine, the Timeless, the Absolute, the 5th house symbolizes the Soul's personal will, power, and creative purpose. Through this aspect, the impulse to spiritualize takes place through receiving messages as to what the Soul needs to do to atone, adjust, purify, improve, de-glorify itself, and be of service to others. Messages or signposts could manifest through dreams or waking consciousness with visions such as joining a group (eg health retreat) where the Soul can rehabilitate from past abuse of drugs, alcohol and marijuana. Or, the signpost could appear as the 'next creative venture' through collaboration with like-minded others in the arts, music, or drama. This course leads to taking action through the strength of his will, fulfilling an individual purpose of creative self-actualization as well as a group purpose to be of service to the group.

(7) Sign on the 12th house cusp Libra ruled by Venus

In addition to Neptune being in the sign Libra, the 12th house cusp is ruled by Libra, and Venus will be found somewhere in the chart. Venus ruling the 12th house pertains to creating and projecting a sense of Ultimate Meaning onto relationships that are culminating in some way. The impulse from Source occurs through the imagination, introspection, dream-state, or daydreaming. The Soul is capable of universal, unconditional love being ultra-sensitive to the needs of others, compassionate, sympathetic, and self-sacrificing. The 12th house correlates to the impulse to transcend all that has come before, to withdraw, retreat, or become reclusive, and also to tie up loose ends.

With Pisces on the 5th, and Libra on the 12th, this combination points to Neptune and its higher octave Venus corresponding to the Heart chakra. The Heart and Crown chakras resonate together and manifest unity consciousness. While Neptune correlates to unconditional love that has no expectations attached to it, Venus correlates to conditional love which can stand for expectations and projected needs onto the other. While the lower octave Venus manifests as a function of evolutionary and karmic imperatives, the higher octave Neptune manifests as the universal timeless Natural Law of sharing, caring, and giving to others. The finite plus the Infinite. The octave transformer Juno (sacred marriage) acts as a bridge between the conscious and the unconscious, raising the values of Venus to Neptunian compassion.

When a relationship falls away, what is left? The Self. The Soul, guided by an unseen power, is able to survive the emptiness of being alone, through his ability to detach and objectively observe these dynamics. Slowly the obsessive need diminishes and he is able to let go of the addiction be it to a partner, alcohol, drugs, or other escape mechanism.

The whispers from God helps the Soul to become open, healed and free, to love, care, bond with others, and make a commitment to a philosophical or spiritual system of thought. The Soul will be sent impulses from God that allow him to realize the unity inside the diversity, the Higher Consciousness in which we are all One, and the true reality that is Love. The Soul realizes that his intense need or addiction for friends and relationships gets him entangled in duality, while the whisper of God beckons him toward the Truth, peace, tranquility, unity and pure bliss. He learns that friends and partners merely enhance the Truth of God, and do not replace it.

(8) Location of the sign Pisces on the 5th house cusp

The Soul desires to actualize itself in a way that is symbolic of its own individuality. The impulse or whisper could lead to messages of ways how to actualize himself through relationships, love affairs, creativity, the arts, or music. Signposts that manifest in self-contemplation could be instigating a love affair based on idealization and glamorization of a partner with a desire to put the partner up on a pedestal, and make him or her the center of his universe. With the 5th house being a phallic symbol, the Soul could learn a lesson in equality in giving and receiving when engaging in natural sexuality. The Whisper of God will manifest as sacred sexuality.

The Soul feels pulled towards Love in its many forms from familial, to friendship, to romance, to the Divine. There is a compelling need to gain insight through surrender as the Soul's guidepost. With the Soul approaching the end of 3rd stage Individuated, there is some unrest when he worries, "What about my purpose?" "What will I do now?" Anxiety about what to do next is akin to Divine boredom. The Soul hears a whisper to let his concerns and attachments fall away, bringing him Peace.

EXAMPLE CHART C

Whispers from Eternity

Neptune in the 5th House

1st subdivision of Spiritual

by Skywalker

In this assignment, we will look at how an individual can spiritualize his or her life relative to their Neptune/Pisces/12th house archetypes. Spiritualizing one's life in the sense of returning to the Source or working on behalf of the Source can mean many things for different people. In my understanding, it means doing things that are inherently GOOD, with good intentions, for the benefit of not only ourselves but others as well. In my experience, the Source or God or whatever one desires to call this 'energy' where we come from, is pure unlimited goodness, love, understanding and compassion of the highest kind imaginable. To work on behalf of this energy, in my experience, is to be as good and pure as we possibly can, to do the very best in whatever circumstances we find ourselves in, to live with the desire to perfect ourselves and evolve as we transmute that which is negative or selfish about ourselves.

Where Neptune is placed shows where we can give to others without any personal ulterior motives or desires, in some cases even where we can sacrifice ourselves for others or the whole. Neptune's placement shows where and how we can unite with others and overcome our sense of separateness by simply being in the moment and letting go, by being one with others and our surroundings, by opening up and being receptive to anything and everything and by putting the self or ego in second place for the higher good of all.

So for me, to spiritualize is essentially to evolve in the direction of what is good and right. To move towards the light and eliminate darkness and ignorance (Neptune in Sagittarius). To do this involves making the right choices for ourselves and for others every single day. Good and evil are real and exist in all of our lives but it is our choice and responsibility to know and decide which side to give our energy. That is why we are alive, in my opinion and experience, to evolve towards that loving, understanding and life-giving force. Life itself with all its twists and turns presents perfect opportunities to spiritualize by learning how to adapt to negative/difficult circumstances by making the right choices that lead us each time closer to what Source energy is all about. Neptune is also consciousness, and to spiritualize means to expand our conscious awareness to re-align with that which simply exists and is of its own accord in a natural way. To just be, as opposed to the way we live our lives on this planet in this day and age, full of distorted egocentric needs and desires that are leading to the destruction of many life forms here on earth and potentially even the planet itself.

In the 5th house, Neptune can be inspired to spiritualize via one's inherent creativity and personal self-expression. The person may be inspired by music or the desire to take on certain roles like an actor does and integrate into that role with the purpose of touching the hearts of countless others. Neptune in the 5th can spiritualize via anything that involves artistic or dramatic expression. As a performing musician/DJ, I myself felt the unity between all the people that shared those magical moments in which we were all simply enjoying the unity of the emotions that the music made us feel. The musician or artist can be a channel for good feelings to be shared between people, can send out messages of unity, love and compassion and be a channel for divine feelings or messages to come through him or herself. The performing artist may desire to heal and be healed through such experiences as the unity is felt and cherished as something sacred and transcendental. Something that cannot truly be described with words but only through sensation and experience of the moment as people come together and are united by sound and music. It truly does transcend cultures and religions and beliefs as the people simply feel the connection and togetherness as they experience the music that has the effect of dismantling their individual egos. Neptune here correlates to the collective feeling that is shared at such an event. This unity reminds people we are all one and gives them a sense of togetherness, a sense of potential and belonging that transcends personal differences.

In this sense, someone with Neptune in the 5th can spiritualize and work on behalf of the Source Of All Things as he/she unites people and gives them a sense of belonging to something larger, even if it is only subconsciously perceived or a feeling they cannot really put into words. Neptune in the 5th may touch the hearts of the collective just by letting the Source energy flow through him/her as a creative force that has the effect of expanding the awareness, sensations, feelings and the hearts of others.

As I write this in the coffee place where I´m currently studying, a young man around 20 years old just came up to me and asked me some questions about my computer as he saw it was a Mac. He wanted to get into music production and was told a Mac was better so he asked me some questions. Fortunately, I was able to help him with some technical information and, as he spoke to me, I felt this must be the Source drawing me back into the music world. I told him I wasn't interested in playing at the moment and was done with that world but when he left, he thanked me and said for me to think about playing again. It clearly feels like Source energy sending the message that my music is only on standby and not totally over. The synchronicity of this event is astounding as he came to me as I am writing this assignment on Neptune!

On a personal egocentric level, someone with Neptune in the 5th may go through many humbling lessons until he or she consciously decides to align their willpower and life purpose with Source energy. Neptune and the 5th house together have a natural difficulty in expression until the person aligns their will with higher principles and divine will. Neptune is formless and unselfish while the 5th house is about personal creative expression and our personal life purpose. It is not until there is a conscious desire to express divine energy for the benefit of all, that the individual will truly find ultimate meaning in his or her life. This is also true for the other evolutionary levels but their awareness of Source energy and how to sense it and align with it will be much more limited. They will mostly be humbled by realizing their selfishness and sometimes-ridiculous desire to be acknowledged as special. This humbling will allow them to re-align their personal will with something of collective value that extends beyond their own self-interest.

Another way that Neptune in the 5th house can spiritualize is through children, not only our own children but all children. With this placement, one can have a natural empathy for children and wish to help them in some way. There are many under-cared for, under-educated or under-nourished children in the world and someone with Neptune in the 5th may have the inherent knowledge that children are the future of mankind's destiny. They may see the inherent potential within children and young people and desire to serve as a channel to bring out that potential. This could be by many and any means such as teaching or having an orphanage or working in an NGO that helps children in need. The main core dynamic in my understanding is one of desiring to care for and help these young children to realize their true and highest potential. To help keep them pure and protected from some of life's injustices and to put an end to their needless suffering. Also, for some others, just to bring up a child or stepchild could be a form of dedication and devotion where the person feels they are sacrificing their time and energy for someone else to have the best life possible. This can be a form of service to others as one helps the child realize his or her highest potential with no sense of egocentric desire whatsoever, just the desire to give to the child whatever it needs to be as healthy and happy as possible.

Another form of creative expression for the 5th house can be that of love affairs and passions of all sorts. This may include creative hobbies to simple flirting or anything we do just for fun and games. The 5th house Neptune may spiritualize its life by being a symbol of inspiration for others as he or she actively and passionately plays their destined role to the maximum of their creative and expressive potential. This also includes their passions as they may ignite feelings that are dormant in others or share themselves in ways that inspires others to open up naturally and simply be themselves. In matters of the heart, the 5th house Neptune may spiritualize by having a huge heart that gives freely to others. They may feel special in some way and desire to share their gifts with others so they too can be inspired to find their own creativity and express it in their lives. In matters of the heart, they may wish to touch others in ways that make them feel special and loved and out of the ordinary.

Pisces on the 8th house cusp

Pisces in the 8th house cusp can reflect a Soul whose desire is to confront (8th house) limitations that limit a direct connection to the Source (Pisces). This placement can reflect a Soul who desires to spiritualize by way of dissolving all limiting factors that limit a direct merging with the Source. This placement can correlate to someone who desires to spiritualize through merging with others that, in some way, can promote a sense of personal evolution. The person with Neptune in the 8th or related signatures may be attracted to magic rituals, shamanic rituals or any source of power/knowledge that can promote a dissolving of limitations to his/her spiritual progress. It can mean someone who desires to align with sexual energy in a sacred way and to explore those sacred principles and techniques. It can correlate to someone who takes commitments very seriously and desires to have a committed relationship with someone who is also searching for the same type of evolution towards Source energy, therefore creating a desire to find the Soul mate. It may correlate to someone who desires to use their resources in a way that can benefit others or to manage the resources of others in a way that benefits the people that made the investment, or others such as in charity work.

Neptune in the 8th house or related signatures will desire to have direct experience of Source energy and to feel empowered by it by dissolving all subconscious insecurities and fears that limit experiencing the Source directly. In my experience, Pisces on the 12th or related signatures can mean the Soul will have to make choices as to which energy to really align with, the forces of good or evil. As one is tempted (8th house), one will have to consciously choose and commit to that which is good and right. This will serve as a way of purging the Soul of desires that prevent a direct merging with the Source, as those desires create ongoing karmic lessons until there is only the desire to return home.

Cancer on the 12th house cusp

This can correlate to a Soul who desires and needs to heal the emotional body and dynamics relative to their childhood, parents, home environment, emotional nurturing needs and everything to do with their self-image and sense of security in the physical world as emotional beings. To heal is to come closer to Source energy; as one heals one rids the emotional body of negative emotions that prevent true perception of ultimate reality. Cancer on the 12th can correlate to a Soul who in this life will need to forgive and forget all those who hurt him/her. It will correlate to someone who has a lot to dissolve on an emotional level as there may be many lifetimes of emotional suffering and pain. To come closer to the Source would be to heal the self so one is in a position to do good for others instead of desiring others to care for one's self. It is a position that will teach the person that emotional security can only truly be found by aligning one's sense of security and self-consistency with Source energy in some way.

One with this position will only truly find security in the timeless values and principles that are beyond the scope of one finite life. One will have to turn to the divine for inner security as, in the physical world we live, there is no ultimate security since we will all have to face death someday. Cancer on the 12th house can dissolve the desire for ultimate security in the physical world as the person aligns him/herself with God or the Source as the only real way to be totally secure from within. Cancer on the 12th house can also correlate with someone who can spiritualize by having as little of an ego as possible. By dissolving the ego to the point where there is nothing but what is truly necessary to complete their journey in this life, with as little personal needs or with little to nothing filtering out the Source's light. The ego, as we were taught in EA by JWG, is like a lens that projects the images on a screen. These images are made of light and are distorted by the ego since the ego is not able to see the totality of reality, and filters out or distorts things so that it is able to cope with reality. Cancer on the 12th or related signatures in the spiritual stage of evolution can spiritualize by dissolving as much of the ego as possible so that the personality is aligned with the Source, what is true from a universal and timeless point of view. This will have the effect of leaving the person secure from within as he/she is aligned with truth and has as little personal security needs as possible, thus practically being free from distorted emotional needs.

EXAMPLE CHART D

Whispers from Eternity

The Whisper that, if Acted Upon, Leads to Ways of Spiritualizing Your Life

Neptune in Libra in the 11th House

by Kristin

Regardless of the stage of evolution, when the Soul has Neptune in this placement, the whisper can be experienced as a download from on high, the revelation that comes via some spontaneous idea or brainstorm. In some cases, it may appear like a crazy idea; at least from the mainstream's perspective, this would be true. In essence, it will lead to endeavors involving people of like mind. The 11th house also connects to innovation and trend setting, a Soul drawn to the alternative or the progressive as one advances further along in their evolutionary journey. There is a natural inventiveness and creativity with Neptune in the 11th. In special and unique cases, this could equal the revolutionary, or the genius, for Neptune knows no bounds reflecting no limits with respect to the capacity for ingenuity with immeasurable potential as seen in the case of Albert Einstein and Wolfgang Mozart, who both have Neptune in the 11th.

By adding the archetype Libra, there will be a strong pull toward justice and the need to promote or energize what is fair for all. Being that Neptune is the higher octave of Venus, and Venus is the ruler of Libra, this could also connect to a Soul who feels drawn toward the universal language of music, where no borders or boundaries can limit the Soul's imagination to express their unique individuality. The field of acting and music can play out in many different stages of evolution, much of which depends on intention and content, but Libra reminds me of a tuning fork as well as synthesizing, harmonies and the universal language that we all share and enjoy, the language of music that can serve to help heal heartache, especially when you feel the artist has 'been there,' that you are not alone in your misery. The key for this artist is in their capacity to be relatable, Libra. Neptune in this position can also involve filmmaking, in particular documentary films about the imbalance and lack of justice in the world or films about stories of real people who are victimized by their circumstances as a result of the sub-group of culture within their society that they are a part of. An example of this could be women not given a fair shake, or being raped and used and thrown around like a rag dog in cultures who feel as if they are not revered as equals and only mere objects to be traumatized and abused.

A few movies that come to mind, the first of which Angelina Jolie was the lead is a movie based on a true story called *Changeling*. She is a grief-stricken single mother who takes on the LAPD to her own detriment when it stubbornly tries to pass off an obvious impostor as her missing child, while also refusing to give up hope that she will find him one day. Her fight and total rebellion to their broken system had her tossed into the psyche ward where she joined countless other women who were drugged and given electric shock treatment because of their own rebellion toward men.

Also, a documentary movie that Jolie wrote and directed called *In the Land of Blood and Honey*, a woman in Bosnia at the time of a brutal ethnic conflict with the Serbs. *In the Land of Blood and Honey* tells the story of two people from different sides of a brutal ethnic conflict: Daniel, a soldier fighting for the Serbs, and Ajla, a Bosnian held captive in the camp he oversees, knew each other before the war, and could have found love with each other. But, as the armed conflict takes hold of their lives, their relationship grows darker as Bosnian women, including Ajla were brought to a Serbian barrack to serve the soldiers. The abuse toward women, sexual and otherwise, that occurs at the hands of men during war, also as a result of cultural and religious differences.

Although Jolie does not have Neptune in the 11th, documentary film making is reflected with her South Node in Gemini there with her Sun and the ruler Mercury, and this opposes Neptune in Sagittarius in the 5th; her Pluto in Libra in the 3rd trines this Gemini stellium, documentary films to 'tell the truth' so people can rightfully witness and observe the extremity of injustice, in particular with respect to women. Documentary filmmaking can occur within the consensus, individuated as well as the spiritual stage of evolution, the intent and content will reflect the stage.

Consensus State

In the consensus state, this signature can be reflected in any way that a Soul feels connected to be involved with others of a likeminded nature. Thus it can include any form of mainstream social groups such as church groups, political groups or any other likeminded sub-group in society that may be working together to help others,

Neptune in Libra in the 11th. This might also include groups such as AA. I realize that these Souls could also be further along in their evolution, as in the Individuated state, as there are many cases where Souls have a difficult time on Earth and use drugs and alcohol as a means of escape.

In essence, any group of like mind with the intent to help support one another and to connect with people who understand the feelings of despair linked with this disease that accompanies the feeling of alienation that is usually the root of where this leads. Also like-minded groups who share similar creative pursuits and similar interests. Actors and musicians in the consensus, depending on the content and intention with their work, would also apply here. It would be an opportunity at any stage for the Soul to work through unresolved trauma utilizing imaginary or acted out roles.

Neptune in Libra in the 11th would potentially hear whispers to lead movements for social reform, even within the consensus state. In Pluto Vol. I, Jeffrey writes, "Social change occurs when enough people of like mind band together to enforce change within, and relative to, the outmoded structures in society." An example of how a consensus state Soul with Neptune in the 11th in Libra may play out on a big stage is prior 1st lady, current Secretary of State and democratic candidate for the next presidency, Hillary Clinton, who has Neptune in the 11th, and best known for her diplomacy and ability to see both sides of any situation, and helping people see what is fair and just and right. Her policies are big on bringing people together – we are better together – uniting the world with her diplomatic principles and bigger vision capacity. She is a strong advocate for women's rights and those in the middle and lower classes of society. She is a strong voice for promoting change and bringing greater balance and fairness for all. She is also the first woman who ever ran for president.

Her leadership and courage, including her ability to spearhead projects that have a far-reaching impact on the big stage of life, is seen with the polarity being Neptune in Aries in the 5th house, Pisces on the cusp. Hillary's track record is reflected in this Neptune in Libra in the 11th signature as she embodies the art of transformation, bringing people together of all classes, gender and race to combine and create a stronger society. She may yet still become the first woman as president of the U.S.

Even with the whisper occurring in any stage, with Neptune in the 11th within the consensus and early stage of the individuated, this can reflect someone hiding behind their own unique individuality whereby it may not be seen by others. There may be a fear of unveiling this unique vision for fear people will think you are crazy, Neptune, so a fear of what people might think, and how it will be received, Libra. Obviously, the 11th house connects to a rebellion from the mainstream but in the consensus state this could also have the extreme opposite effect.

In the Pluto book, Jeffrey writes about the three ways the Aquarian/11th archetype manifests. The 3rd type is a total Saturnian approach. There will be some who not only reject the whisper but these people are social dinosaurs who use the "old order as a panacea to correct the perceived ills of the moment rather than allowing themselves to develop a new vision to a changing world." They project an old tired vision onto the future, an illusion of what they feel works, as the cure for the problems of today and inwardly suppress in a desperate way the inner impulses to 'shed skins.' They too will form groups of like mind and anyone not in their camp will be experienced as being different and radical. In essence, they are resisting the call, versus answering the call.

Individuated State

Philanthropic as well as humanitarian pursuits with the intention to help those in need is reflected in the spirit of this global venture to produce change and improve the livelihood of children. My sense is this is an early 1st stage individuated Soul who started the business called *Tom's Shoes*, the owner starting this pursuit as a result of traveling in Argentina and witnessing the hardships for children growing up without shoes. His solution to the problem was simple, yet revolutionary: to create a for-profit business that was sustainable and not reliant on donations.

Tom's Shoes

While I realize for profit businesses are not linked to the 11th house, it is the way in which he used his profits to help others, in particular, the feet of children that makes this a Neptune in Libra, 11th house issue. Also a way of thinking outside the usual box to be able to help more children instead of depending on donations, his motto being, "One for One," with a commitment and a calling to give. "With every product you purchase, TOM'S will help a person in need. One for One." *Tom's Shoes* has given millions of shoes away to children in 60 countries.

His unique idea was to help children, in particular with their feet, and to offer something that to these children, 5th house polarity, would come as a giant blessing and a great surprise. He clearly had a humanitarian call to help and used a marketing approach to also create a good feeling for others that when they bought his shoes they too knew they were helping a child in need. This in and of itself would bring together people of like mind who shared this impulse to give and to share.

Tom's Shoes

Neptune in Libra in the 11th connects to those who feel the impulse to help others who have been traumatized or victimized in some way and could be seen as a Soul who becomes a trauma or flight nurse where they arrive at the scene and victims are air lifted out of any sort of collision or even war. They are Souls who have the ability to detach from the scene whereby their main motivation is to save the suffering and those who have been traumatized in some way. I can see these roles being played in the 3rd stage consensus and 1st stage individuated.

Rock and folk legend Neil young is a great example here a for a 3rd stage individuated Soul with Neptune in Libra in the 11th house. Examples of a few of Young's most popular songs ring true to Neptune in Libra in the 11th: *Only Love can Break your Heart, Bad Fog of Loneliness, Rockin in the Free World*. His music brought people together of like mind with similar alternative beliefs and had a huge following during the hippie era.

Beyond the reach with his deeply personal lyrics through music, he started an organization to raise money for the *Bridge School*: an innovative organization educating children with severe speech and physical impairments through the use of creative approaches to education and communication, augmentative and alternative communication systems and assistive technology, with extensive involvement of families and community. He and his wife were inspired due to one of their son's being born with Cerebral Palsy that is also an 11th house phenomenon. He was an outspoken advocate for environmental issues and the welfare of small farmers using his reach and audience to promote change and to wake people up.

Considering the 11th house connects to the alternative arts, Neptune in the 11th in Libra can also reflect alternative ways of healing and helping to bring the body and Soul back into balance. A healing expression and professions that come to mind are reflexology (feet) and acupuncture that connects to pressure points to correct imbalance of flow of chi, the natural energy life force, through channels known as meridians.

Spiritual State

Music legend Leonard Cohen has Neptune in Virgo in the 11th but it is conjunct Venus as well as Venus ruling his 12th house, so this will manifest similar to Neptune in Libra. He has just come out of the 3rd stage individuated and is in the early stages of the spiritual state. His song lyrics are a great deal about the pain of relationships and the trauma that it creates making him so relatable, Libra, to his audience. Also, he simply being in love with being in love and this love worth all of the pain such as in his song *Dance Me to the End of Love* and *Waiting for the Miracle*. His music has a way of seeping in to those hard places like a balm.

The singer then becomes silent. Cohen retreated to the Mt. Baldy Zen Center near Los Angeles, beginning what became five years of seclusion at the center. Cohen was ordained as a Rinzai Zen Buddhist monk and took the Dharma name Jikan, meaning 'silence.' Also, his lyrics evolved over time, and his surrender to the path that God wanted for him in his tunes, *If It Be Your Will*, *Hallelujah*. Also, lyrics such as "There's a crack in everything, that's how the light gets in":

If it be your will
That I speak no more
And my voice be still
As it was before
I will speak no more
I shall abide until
I am spoken for
If it be your will
If it be your will
That a voice be true
From this broken hill
I will sing to you
From this broken hill
All your praises they shall ring
If it be your will
To let me sing
From this broken hill

All your praises they shall ring
If it be your will
To let me sing

If it be your will
If there is a choice
Let the rivers fill
Let the hills rejoice
Let your mercy spill
On all these burning hearts in hell
If it be your will
To make us well

And draw us near
And bind us tight
All your children here
In their rags of light
In our rags of light
All dressed to kill
And end this night
If it be your will

If it be your will

Early in the spiritual state, Neptune in the 11th in Libra can reflect a Soul drawn to becoming an Evolutionary Astrologer or any form of alternative or progressive metaphysical calling that has a spiritual focus. A Soul can also move through the appearance of earlier stages, for example, earlier in life, say in the early 20's, having interest and fascination with making documentary films with the intention to wake people up, but the Soul, through extension the Source, has perhaps a more intense or potently profound calling, and this could be revealed during key transitions in time such as a Saturn return.

At this stage of evolution, it would require the work to be something that could reach and teach people about natural spiritual teachings that to the herd state would appear radical and yet it will be revolutionary for the planet. The pull to go deeper into its role in helping humanity evolve will be more than a whisper it will be a nudge or a dream, Neptune, with clear instructions. This was the case for the founder of EA, Jeffrey Wolf Green.

In latter stages of evolution, the Soul may set up spiritual centers as JWG did in his earlier years, forming a satellite SRF community that included teaching people how to inwardly experience God for themselves via meditation. In his case, he also used astrology as a vehicle to help people objectify their life and path in order to promote change and to help bring Souls into better natural balance with themselves, his intention being to help the suffering and the traumatized, to help re-awaken people to natural laws and spirituality through teaching and via the Evolutionary Astrology model. His teachings offered an alternative entry point that allowed an objective way for Souls to understand themselves, the ones they love, and evolution itself.

For Jeffrey, these spiritual teachings and instructions were far more than a whisper; the entire Pluto book came to him in Sanskrit through a dream Neptune, from Sri Yukteswar. Jeffrey also taught about natural gender roles and how, as one evolves, the Soul will become more androgynous in nature, Libra, equally male and female, teaching people how to naturally integrate both sides of gender, helping people find that balancing point within themselves, their own natural center of gravity – Saturn as well as Uranus rules Aquarius, 11th house – and this balance being achieved by the Soul accessing and expressing its own unique individuality in the world, being a group of one if necessary, and ultimately actualizing their unique purpose in the world in the way they were designed by God.

CHAPTER FOUR

NEPTUNE: DELUSIONS AND BEING DIRECTED BY 'GOD'

Introduction

We have been learning about how Neptune, Pisces, and the 12th house correlates to projecting ultimate meaning for one's life, the disillusionment that can occur when that projection is anything other than the Ultimate Source Of All Things, and how that Source attempts to naturally spiritualize the consciousness of the Soul through the 'whispers' from within or without that if acted upon naturally leads to a spiritualization of that consciousness.

We will now focus on how the Soul can identify its own desires, for whatever those desires are about, as being directed by, motivated by, the Source Of All Things WHEN IN FACT THEY ARE NOT; in essence, using God/ess as the rationale or justification for those desires. Of course most of us are all familiar with the various 'guru' types like Rajneesh, Clare Prophet, and the like, who use God as the justification for that which they do, these types claiming to be inwardly 'directed' by God to do what they do.

As 'reality' prevails at some point, the total delusions, delusions of grandeur, of such Souls becomes painfully known to those who 'believed' in these delusional characters who were using God to mask the desires of their own Souls: to self-inflate in a delusional way so as to convince themselves, thus others, of how special, wonderful, and Zarathustra-like they are for whatever the inner dynamics are in each of them that has led to this state of affairs.

All Souls have the potential to delude themselves in this way by way of using God to justify or rationalize desires within the Soul that are simply about their own ongoing evolutionary needs. Neptune, Pisces, and the 12th House contain archetypes that can cause a Soul to have personal delusions of grandeur that are inwardly justified by "God is telling me to do . . . x, y, z": to use God as the justification to find an ultimate sense of meaning through some dynamic or role that is larger than the Soul itself; to use God as the justification and rationale for that which is, in fact, not coming from God or the Source at all.

Thus, the archetype of delusions and illusions that are considered by the Soul to be 'real'. And when the necessary disillusionment occurs to realign the Soul with actual reality, that which is real versus that which is not, not only can a psychological state of meaningless occur, confusion, but it can also lead to hysteria in the worst cases when actual reality prevails.

When reality intervenes relative to the Neptune archetype that which is being dissolved through a necessary disillusionment is not IMMEDIATELY replaced with anything. Thus, the Soul can then feel adrift, out at sea in a belt of fog, not knowing what or where to go. Because of this, the Soul will attempt to replace that which has been dissolved with something else in order to replace the lost sense of meaning that it has just experienced. Or, when a Soul has so invested itself into 'believing' the very nature of its own delusions and illusions, it can manifest a resistance to the necessary disillusioning , to actual reality, which can then lead to fanaticism and/or the thought that says, "Well, I just do not believe it" when actual reality prevails. This then reinforces the delusion/illusion itself.

Wherever the natal Neptune is by house and sign, the aspects it is making to the planets, the sign on the 12th house and the location of its planetary ruler by its own house and sign, aspects to it, and the sign Pisces by house which then refers back to the natal placement of Neptune, all correlate to where any given Soul can project God as being the ultimate rationale for the natural Soul desires that emanate from those places in the birth chart.

Thus, all these avenues that can correlate with illusions and delusions that the Soul considers to be 'real' until some sort of circumstance, a circumstance that is created by the Soul itself and/or the actual Source, then has the intended effect of disillusioning the Soul in order to re-orientate it to actual reality.

Questions and Answers

(Q) I have been having some confusion surrounding looking at Neptune in all the stages linked with this specific stage of the assignment, and was wondering if you could give an example beyond Clare Profit or Rajneesh as they are specific to charismatic religious/spiritual examples.

If someone has Neptune in the 7th for example, I can imagine a Soul choosing partners for some religious or patriarchal reason as in God wants me to marry this person but how might that signature play out in other stages individuated and otherwise.

I am feeling limited in my scope as we advance into this topic as I have never looked so deeply into Neptune in this way. I so appreciate the opportunity to understand more clearly how this manifests.

(A)   With Neptune in the 7th there are many different ways where a Soul can be utterly deluded by way of projecting God versus the actual reality at hand. For example, a Soul can delude itself into believing that "'God' is telling me to be with so and so" when the actual reality is not that at all: so and so is simply a person who the Soul desires to be with yet finds the need to project the rationale of 'God' as being the reason to be with so and so. Another example would be for the Soul to project 'God' like qualities onto others in general, intimate others specifically, where no such qualities that are being projected actually exist. Conversely, a Soul could project all kinds of conclusions or judgments upon another(s), very critical ones included, where there is no actual basis, reality, for such conclusions or projections. Neptune in the 7th could also correlate to the projection by a Soul that it is 'God' like, its egocentric self-image, that is utterly deluded by being a special messenger of God, an "agent of God, who is here to 'help'" others in need. And so on.

(Q)   Is contact with agents of God also part of the Neptune archetype or is that in combination with another archetype? I'm thinking of angels, master spirit guides and other metaphysical entities.

(A)   Yes, Jesus, Muhammad, and Krishna, would be examples as well as certain Souls who are indeed true agents of God.

(Q)   Also, what about information, the knowing, we bring back with us from our time in the astral realms before we are born? Does this also fit in the Neptune realm?

(A)   Yes, in combination with Uranus.

(Q)   Would one's capacity to recognize the astral memories or contact with agents of God be limited mainly by evolutionary stage?

(A)   Yes. The reality for the vast majority of all Souls is to have no conscious memory at all of their experiences while in the astral realms between births. Because of this, most Souls cannot consciously 'apply' what they have learned by way of those astral experiences in the next birth. Yet those memories do exist within the memory of the Soul itself. But, as we know, most people are not conscious of their own Souls: the center of gravity is the egocentric structure created by the Soul. As such, the astral memories remain hidden deep within the Soul itself. As a Soul progressively evolves and expands its consciousness, there does come a time in which the center of gravity shifts from the ego to the Soul itself. When that happens then the egocentric structure of the Soul can then reflect all the memories of the Soul including astral ones.

(Q) I've been looking through the EA Glossary trying to find if anyone has stratified types of 'knowing' ... beyond the basic correlations of data/thought/left-brain (Gemini-Mercury), philosophy/beliefs/Natural Law/right-brain (Sagittarius-Jupiter), and flash of insight/objective awareness (Uranus). For example, would ethics and morals be Libra by way of the natural square to Capricorn in contrast to evolved consciousness/direct access to knowing God (Pisces-Neptune)?

(A) Morals, morality, and the ethics that follow what the morality is about manifest from the 9th House, Sagittarius, and Jupiter. Moralities, and their ethics, are a function of what philosophy and/or religion a Soul has orientated to for its own ongoing evolutionary/karmic reasons.

(Q) Rad, your quote:

> He spoke about different natural plants that had/have inherent chemicals that then affect the physiology of the brain when ingested that naturally induce expanded states of consciousness. These expanded states induced in this natural way, he said, are permanent: they are sustained. He contrasted that with artificial man-made drugs, chemicals, like LSD, that do indeed alter one's consciousness in all sorts of ways but that those altered states do not remain once the drug wears off. He personally was initiated into the peyote way by a traditional Navajo Indian for a period of time when he lived in the high chaparral of northeast New Mexico.

So, regarding the tendency to escape one's reality through heavy chemical drug use in a Soul at the height of 2nd stage Individuated, could this be a subconscious desire to return to Source?

(A) Yes, but the key is 'subconscious.' Consciously, many in this state with Neptune in Scorpio in the 3rd would reject the Source outright to the point of using the drugs as a statement to that 'fact.'

(Q) Are these desires to escape reality through drugs purely a means to evolve the Soul's separating desires by breaking through the fabricated egocentric identity?

(A) In the sense that these types of desires, in that EA state of development [height of 2nd stage Individuated], are used by the Soul to realize, at some point, the total delusion it has created by itself by way of all the rationalizations for the drug use in the first place. The disillusionment necessary to arrive at that point of realization can be extremely severe in nature including the loss of its physical life because of the drug use.

(Q) If a Soul is avoiding dealing with life through drugs and drink, yet is finding some satisfaction through a feeling of surrender or letting go, is that state true rapture or revelation, or artificial and even more deluded?

(A) Artificial and even more deluded. Of course, the drugs can create that false sense of rapture or revelation while the consciousness is infused with the drug itself. Once the drugs are removed that false state is realized at some point, and in some way.

(Q) Does the Soul that abuses drugs and drink need to reach some sort of crisis point before it can be healed and aligned with reality? What is one way that crisis can play out?

(A) Yes. It can play out in many, many ways. For example, a person who is using a blowtorch-like fire to create an extract of marijuana or hashish and in the process of so doing the tank containing the propane being used for the torch blows up. The person is now aflame and burning up. They either die or are scarred for life. The intensity of this could then lead to the necessary realizations: or not!

(Q) These kinds of problems seem to take a long time or a whole life time (or more) to work through, with the Soul continually going back to the drug/drink cycle due to the psychological and physical addiction. Does healing for these Souls come about purely through Grace?

(A) It does not come through Grace at all, and at no time. Grace is only directed to a Soul who has made some kind of real effort to change something where the self-determination precedes an act of Grace.

———

So let's go ahead and do some example charts of this archetype.

EXAMPLE CHART A

Neptune: Delusions and Being Directed by 'God'

Neptune in Scorpio in the 3rd House

At the height of 2nd stage Individuated

by Linda

The Soul has been rebelling against the Consensus, the 75% of individuals whose beliefs, values and moralities mirror each other for the sake of maintaining the familiarity and security of the past. The Soul feels detached from society like it is standing on the outside looking in. At the height of 2nd stage Individuated, it can no longer identify with or sustain a compensatory reality and is rebelling in an EXTREME way. The Soul lives in an existential void identifying with other similarly alienated Souls, the extreme rebellion from reality being reinforced. The Soul does NOT want to appear normal because of the inner vibration and desire to rebel against everything external to itself.

Correlating to the Neptune archetype is when a Soul deludes itself to think that its egocentric desire or motivation is coming from Source when in fact it is not. This archetype has its roots in an unconscious fear of losing control of life and a resistance and repulsion to the evolutionary pull to surrender its identity to Source. This results in creating an intensely powerful delusion, illusion, misconception, false impression, false role, or false identity about itself, which it truly believes to be true and REAL. In reality, this unconscious fabrication is a desperate attempt to rationalize its separating desires from Source. Because this created persona is utterly false and deluded, the Soul has a nagging inner sense (either conscious or unconscious) that something is out of order, that this constructed, glamorized, dream-like identity is not really itself. This can mean that others 'do not really trust' the Soul because it does not appear to be genuine, or the play-acting is just too good to be true.

The false identity or role created by the Soul is given tremendous power and has the effect of duping and deceiving not only itself but also others. These dynamics within the Soul naturally create intense cycles of confusion, desperation, doubt, alienation, disintegration and disassociation. Wandering in confusion and doomed to failure, nothing immediately replaces the egocentric aspect that is being dissolved. The Soul feels estranged from others, lives in an existential void, feels separate from the Oneness, is in denial of the truth of God, and is out of touch with reality. The false aspect of itself manifests as a filter through which all areas of life become distorted.

For my example, I am looking at a Soul who identifies with the drug subculture, a group of dispossessed people united by a common bond of the incorporation of drugs into their lives. This group bands together to help each other obtain drugs and avoid arrest. The Soul identifies with the causes and beliefs of this underworld group as a means of identifying itself as an egocentric individual. The specific delusion that the Soul creates is one of denial of its actions, instead believing itself to be free, unrestricted and so revolutionary and powerful that it is above the law and justifies its needs and actions in whatever way it chooses. Living in an existential void, the Soul has lost its ability to care about itself as it indulges in self-destructive tendencies. It can use others for its own self-centered purposes.

The Soul chooses to have a dependence or addiction to an illegal drug, and despite the harm it causes to the body, intensely craves using it. Substance abuse correlating to Neptune gives a false 'high,' and has caused long-term effects including problems with physical and mental health, relationships based on using others, and problems with the law due to stealing. The Soul justifies the continued use of drugs through a delusion that claims that it is God-sent to endow a peaceful state of mind. In the height of rebellion in the 2nd stage Individuated, the Soul has few scruples, will lie and cheat to get the next fix, and will live in denial of its actions. The altered state of consciousness affects the mind of the Soul through empty thoughts and confusion, and in extreme cases psychosis, hallucinations, or brain death. The deluded Soul may experience extremes from fear to euphoria. An extreme resistance to the relationship with the Universal Source can produce insanity or total disintegration and fragmentation. In some Souls, it will manifest as being so totally deluded that the Soul will consider itself to be God.

> Among most uncivilized populations, as among civilized peoples, certain ecstatic conditions are regarded as divine possession or as union with the Divine. These states are induced by means of drugs, by physical excitement, or by psychical means. But, however produced and at whatever level of culture they may be found, they possess certain common features which suggest even to the superficial observer some profound connection. Always described as delightful beyond expression, these awesome ecstatic experiences end commonly in mental quiescence or even in total unconsciousness. (James Leuba)

Psychoactive drugs or chemical substances that pass through the blood disturb brain function, causing changes in awareness, attitude, consciousness, and behavior. In these altered mental states, the Soul with Neptune in Scorpio in the 3rd house may experience mental episodes that induce other kinds of mystical realities. In its deluded condition, the Soul may gain a distorted understanding of existence through a sense of self-authentication, liberation and release from ordinary self-awareness believing that it has understood the ultimate truth or is residing in cosmic unity.

Linked to this background in drug abuse, the Soul with Neptune in the 3rd house makes itself intellectually and emotionally secure through logically ordering its existence in such a way as to maintain the delusion that it has created. The logical superstructure of ideas, no matter how distorted, rationally explains the Soul's relationship to the environment. The Soul keeps resurrecting old patterns of thinking and communication in an attempt to return to the known world because to change the familiar way of relating to self and others threatens to open the door to the unknown. The distortions linked with Neptune in the 3rd house correlate to spiritual delusions, megalomania, problems with mental health, having no mental boundaries, mixed up thinking patterns, telling lies, being in denial, being evasive, bending the truth, deceiving self and others, other-worldly ideas, misrepresentation, fear, paranoia, and a proclivity to daydreams, fantasies and illusions.

The perpetual restlessness and curiosity creates a need to process and release the buildup of energy through interactions or relationships with others, therefore the Soul creates a persona that is extremely attractive, idealistic, charismatic, glamorized, and distorted out of all proportion, in order to be able to cope with daily life. This persona is fabricated as a coping mechanism because the Soul has rejected the natural truth. The Soul can use its sexuality to manipulate others in order to have its own desires and needs met. It can create such an utterly alluring sex-symbol persona that it is irresistible to others. In this way, the Soul attracts key karmic relationships from past lives that lead to dealing with unresolved dynamics such as unconscious memories of abuse, manipulation, betrayal, abandonment and loss. These karmic relationships lead to lessons in disillusionment (Pisces) and discernment (Virgo). Through DENIAL of the evolutionary impulse to identify with Source, the Soul creates one sexual fantasy or illusion after another in order to maintain the egocentric over-identification. Since the drug is desired as the panacea to all its problems, the Soul is able to coerce and capture unsuspecting victims into its web through its silver tongue, telling all manner of lies that appeal to other egocentric identities, in order to use them to satisfy a sexual need (then instantly dump them), to satisfy a need for their resources, or other self-centered reasons.

The tremendous power of false self-belief of the Soul creates specific kinds of desires, a distorted sense of self, a larger-than-life impact upon others, or an icon status in the eyes of others. Through a carefully constructed (albeit unconscious) glamorized social identity, the Soul either captivates the attention, support and loyalty of others, or attracts persecution from those who see through the facade. The Soul has a hard time recognizing the actual basis of its dream reality because it is living its lies through it. The Soul becomes so deluded as to actually believe its own lies. These realities are destined to fail in some way. The Soul will have to face its separating and avoidance oriented desires when the bubble bursts and it is left standing alone without meaning or peace. The fabrications and lies will be exposed – and the rose-colored glasses will break – as the shocking experience of reality illuminates the Light of Truth.

The reasons for escaping reality or denying the spiritualization of God through drugs can be an unwillingness to confront the reality of the environment. This can lead to withdrawal, detachment, a variety of escape mechanisms, and always going back to the drug. Deceiving others may be another coping mechanism because the Soul falsely believes that its natural self is 'not powerful enough' for the world, and finds itself creating a persona that allows it to manage day-to-day life in a larger-than-life fashion. Self-destructive use of drugs may be a method of coping with day-to-day life, or as a means of escaping worldly existence. Since the drug abuse suppresses the natural spiritualization of the Soul, fears, paranoia and confusion that become buried in the subconscious tend to play out as nightmarish day-to-day interactions with others in the environment. Having to face the consequences of its actions, karma, the Soul faces severe disillusionment when it sees the sordid truth of its reality.

EXAMPLE CHART B

Neptune: Delusions and Being Directed by 'God'
Neptune in Various Houses

by Skywalker

Why would a person delude him/herself that God is telling them what to do when it is not the case, in the first place?

- As a form of escaping a subjective reality that is unsatisfactory by creating delusions/fantasies about the self, others in general or one's circumstances.

- Typical Neptunian confusion relative to what is actually real from an ultimate point of view and what is not real.

- A lack of boundaries relative to where the personal egocentric structure ends and others, the Soul and/or God begins.

- A vested interest in maintaining separating desires and a separate identity as the ego and/or Soul fears being dissolved and disappearing, or being reduced to nothing, also a reflection of the fear of change and ultimately death, which are Plutonian dynamics, relative to the dual desire nature of the Soul, to separate and return to the Source of creation.

The concept or notion of God for most of the world we live in and for most people is generally a patriarchal distortion and manmade image of a God that is perfect yet judgmental towards those who sin. It is an external God vs an energy that is within.

If all there is, is the Source, because the Source created everything, then how can there be anything but the Source? Simply put, there cannot be. What there is, is the illusion of self as a separate being from that Source or God or Universal life force. There can be nothing but God if God is the Source of all creation. Therefore, all that separates us from the Source is…us.

It is our free will that separates us from the Source as we use our free will to pursue separating desires. Until we choose to re-align consciously with Source energy, we will continue to create cycles of illusions and disillusionment as we pursue our desires of a personal separating nature until they are totally exhausted and all that is left is the desire to return home.

Neptune in the 2nd House or Taurus can delude itself by projecting the belief that God is the motivating factor behind its desire to sustain itself. In the first subdivision of the Individuated state of evolution, the Soul will be rebelling against consensus/mainstream social values and beliefs unless they directly and truthfully represent their inherent individuality, but they will still feel the need to be accepted by society. They will do their best to 'think freely' but to fit in at the same time, even if that means living a double life relative to their REAL thoughts, ideals, beliefs, and so on. They can literally have very different inner realities than what they show most people. Even their family members and close friends may have no idea of how they really think/feel about things, only those who are of a similar vibration or like mind will be trusted enough in order for them to truly reveal themselves. Relative to resources, in most of the developed world, people see money as the resource that sustains them, and that resource will be highly valued and given immense importance or ultimate meaning.

Neptune in the 2nd house may delude themselves that God is 'telling' them in some way that they should generate and accumulate as much material wealth as possible. They may convince themselves that having as much material resources as possible will allow them to help others in need. Some may use this mentality as a justification towards others and themselves of their dishonest ways of making money. Some may convince themselves that since it is for the higher good, or that is what God wants for or from them, that it is ok to steal, cheat, hoard, be stingy or simply fanatical about money. Of course, when the time comes for them to actually share their resources, they may use God as a justification not to share their resources with another because God wants them to accumulate as much as possible for some other reason of utmost importance; usually only to the benefit of the 2nd house Neptune person since he or she is simply using God to justify their own ulterior agenda.

Sometimes they can and will actually believe in their delusions to the point of convincing themselves and others that their motives are pure and for the benefit of all. Neptune in the 2nd house can use God as an excuse to stay limited to a very basic approach to any situation or life itself, with no need to change things or evolve in any way since 'God created them how they are.' Others can simply value the material and sensual pleasures of life so much, and convince themselves that since they are good people, that God wants them to have as much material comfort as possible, thus justifying distorted behavior relative to material resources, sexual energy, the intake of food, etc.

At key points in their evolutionary journey, Neptune in the 2nd house people can have their true values exposed. This can be through the loss of resources, which when that happens, their emotional reactions will show them and others their real personal/ulterior motives, or through others uncovering and revealing the true nature of their motives. After that, they may choose to have new and deeper values or attempt to re-gain what they lost.

Neptune in the 3rd House or Gemini may delude themselves that they are more intelligent than others for some God given reason. They may delude themselves that God wants them to lie to others for their own benefit, for example, how often the mainstream media lie and distort the truth or many in the Government will lie to the public and say it is for the benefit of all, not to create panic. They may convince themselves that God wants them to study and acquire as much empirical knowledge as possible, thus feeding their desire for continuous growth and expansion of an intellectual nature. That their environment is all-pure and one big thing that is interconnected, therefore fundamentally good or safe. They may delude themselves that they are here to teach others and that they are more intelligent than others, thinking that God made them smarter than others for that very reason.

They may delude themselves that only they know something or that they know better and that it's simply God's will that things turned out that way. They may believe that they have the God given right to share knowledge that they should not, such as secrets that others shared with them or information that can have a detrimental effect on others. They may think they have the God given right to manipulate whatever they feel in their environment or to manipulate the minds of others through false information such as a school teacher or parent who teach falsehoods to a child, all the while thinking they are doing some form of service. They may believe that God wants them to write a book or make a movie that can affect the way others think, and believe that is what God wants from them, when in fact they are attempting to gain support for an idea they may have.

They may believe that God wants them to study endlessly and feel the need to know everything they can about their environment, universe or inner self, with the end result of becoming totally confused and lost with too much information. They may delude themselves that God wants and needs them to assimilate some body of knowledge before they can be ready to act and go in whatever direction they are headed. To assimilate as much information possible without discriminating. To always be open to every possible connection and opportunity to communicate with someone or something and learn about their environment, and what connects what to what, who to who, and so on… turning them into 'human radios' and sometimes idle chatters or gossipers. They might manipulate the realities of others and what others think by manipulating or distorting the flow of information, thus letting others believe whatever they want as long as it serves their own self-interest. On a positive note, they may give a lot of themselves in order to help others get some sort of education or free flow of information, thus really being well intended and serving the Source in that way.

At key points, they will be disillusioned as they are confronted by others who desire to know the real truth, not their opinion or flawed information, giving them the chance to be really honest relative to whatever it is they are not being truthful about.

Neptune in the 5th House or Leo may delude themselves that they are acting on behalf of God or the Source Of All Things by giving themselves unlimited rights to enjoy life in any way they feel like. This can take the form of them getting romantically involved with a very large number of people while deluding themselves that they are in fact helping those people in some way. Some may delude themselves that they are here to 'share' some special quality they personally possess with the people they get involved with. They may delude themselves that God wants them to express divine love to the other when in fact they are using the other to polish their own sense of specialness and importance.

They may use their creative talents in a way that they consider to be for God or for the good of all but in fact is simply a way to gain attention and/or recognition. They may use their gifts to attract others to support their personal agendas while convincing themselves and others that it is for the benefit of all and that is what God wants them to do.

They may wish to educate their children or, if they are in the teaching profession, to educate children in ways that reflect their own core values and desires, all the while convincing themselves and others that it is what God would want or is the very best for the child.

They may delude themselves that no one can perform better than they can, because God wants that for and from them, therefore they may step on others and diminish their value while promoting their own self-importance and value in ways that are pretty delusional. They may believe that God thinks they are special in God's own eyes, and give themselves the right to always be the center of attention, making themselves unbearable to others as a result, just as they may give themselves the right to any form of personal expression they desire.

They may take huge risks and put their families in danger such as in gambling their resources away or even think they have the God given right to waste their family's resources or the resources of others in general. They may think they have a special destiny to fulfill and are special and God will provide for them by a stroke of luck at the casino or by winning the lottery or in some sort of risky business venture.

They may delude themselves that they have a special connection to God and that they themselves are a gift to humanity and to those with whom they interact. They may believe they are doing a creative project on behalf of God, or to spread the word of God through an expressive art form or simply through pure dramatization, when in fact they are not. They may believe that they are God in some cases and act as if they are superior to everyone and everything else in the world.

On a positive note, they may really give all they have when they have a cause and purpose that touches their hearts. At key points they will be disillusioned by finding out their larger than life sense of importance is stemming from a need to be acknowledged as special, and realize they are simply people, just like everyone else and not God's gift to humanity. They may desire then to align with truth and become a true expression of divinity in whatever way the Source directs them to do, or they may attempt to create new rationalizations to maintain their illusions about their specialness.

Neptune in the 6th House or Virgo can delude themselves by thinking they are doing God's work when they help others, even if they are not truly helping others but only themselves. For example, doctors who see themselves as Godly since they 'save people's lives.' Others may think that their new techniques or theories or pharmaceuticals are a gift from God when in fact what they are doing is making some corporation and themselves a lot of money or they are feeding their own egos by believing they are some sort of savior and in some cases think they are God or Godly. Others may stick to petty jobs and delude themselves that it's God's wish for them to serve the whole in that way, as an excuse to not realize their potential and do more than what they are currently doing.

Others may have sadomasochistic behavior and believe it is God's desire for them to suffer since they are impure or sinners in some way as defined by the society they live in. This would be especially true in the consensus and individuated levels of evolution as the mind is still very much influenced and conditioned by the Garden of Eden myth that has effected most of the 'civilized' world today. Because of such myths and similar dynamics operating worldwide today and in the past few thousand years, they can believe that God wants them to punish others for their sins or impurities. They may create the delusion that God wants them to purify others and that it's their job to do so, thinking something in the line of, "It's a dirty job, but someone's got to do it."

Because of their own inner guilt, natural or man-made, and their need to atone for the guilt they feel, they may believe that God wants them to be sick and have bad health or constant crisis as a result. Neptune in the 6th house may also delude themselves that God wants them to sacrifice themselves for others they serve in some way, or if they are an employer or leader, that God has given them the right or responsibility to sacrifice others as they themselves find necessary. On a positive note, they can truly do their very best for others as there can be so much sensitivity with this combination that the person can't bear the overwhelming feedback/criticism from others and self-criticism when they fail in some way.

At key points, they can become aware of their own self-defeating psychology that has led to personal failures and weaknesses. They will have the chance to stop creating crisis for themselves through very honest self-analysis and re-align with truth by allowing themselves to improve one step at a time and move towards Source energy.

Neptune in the 8th House or Scorpio may delude themselves that they are doing God's will when they hurt others by defending themselves or others close to them. They may believe that in order to set things right, they have to 'right the wrongs' done to them or others they love. In effect, they may convince themselves that revenge is what God wants from them and that justice will not be had until they avenge themselves or those they feel have been victimized in some way. They may convince themselves that killing is right and is what God wants them to do. They may convince themselves that they have the right to the resources of others and that God gave them the right to take whatever they desire, no matter whom it may hurt. They may convince themselves that they have a God given right to empower themselves by whatever means they can, especially if they carry deep wounds and have an attitude of victimization. This can take the form of extreme abuses of power over others, to the point of taking a life or sexually abusing someone or just hurting others because they can.

They may believe in a God given right to have the power and freedom to pursue any desire they may have. They may convince themselves that God wants them to fight evil on its behalf thus giving themselves the right to do whatever is necessary to fight those evil forces, no matter how extreme their actions may be. Neptune in the 8th house may use God as an excuse for their own insecure behavior which may lead them to sabotage the efforts of others who threaten them in some way, even if those people are close to them and well-intentioned. Some could commit suicide and convince themselves it is God calling them home. On a positive note, Neptune in Scorpio can make a true and deeply committed effort towards what is right and evolve towards the Source.

At key points in time they can be exposed for their true motives and be disillusioned as a result when they realize they are in fact acting out of a deep sense of insecurity related to feeling totally powerless or due to past violations of trust, thus not being able to trust anyone or anything and living in a state of constant suspicion. By realizing these dynamics, they can desire to find new strength from within, thus minimizing external dependencies that will lead to more personal value, a sense of empowerment, and ultimately to the security of moving in the direction of Source energy.

Neptune in the 9th House or Sagittarius can delude themselves that they are acting on behalf of God when they attempt to convince others of their own subjective beliefs as ultimate truth. In the consensus stage of evolution, I can think of no better example than the religious people of various religions killing others in the name of God. We had some of the Christians who tortured and killed in the name of God throughout history, or recently we had people like George W. Bush using God's name to sell the wars they initiated. At the same time they said they were acting on behalf of God, they were also calling their enemies evil. Whether they believed in what they were saying or not is anyone's guess. What we do know and should all be able to discern is that one of God's commandments in the Bible is "Thou shalt not kill" and yet these leaders are killing people by the tens of thousands or more in the name of that same God. This, to me, is beyond delusional and the fact that people do not question these things is unbelievable and a reflection of the ignorance and inability of the masses to think critically for themselves.

This is the danger with the Sagittarius/Gemini axis as people can convince themselves and others that their beliefs are in fact true, while the Gemini polarity spreads the word like wildfire without any proof (inconjunct to Scorpio) of the information being factual. Virgo discrimination and Pisces simplicity of letting things simply be what they are in essence can help a great deal in avoiding taking action on false beliefs and perpetuating false knowledge/delusions.

Another example of Neptune in Sagittarius/9th house deluding themselves that they are acting on behalf of God is by desiring to convince and convert others to their philosophy or religion. A good example would be the Muslims who believe that unless you are of Muslim faith that you will go to Hell. They delude themselves that God wants them to convert others to Islam and follow up on those beliefs by actively attempting to scare others that they will go to Hell unless they convert. Just like the Jehovah Witnesses who say that, unless one reads the Bible and is part of that particular belief system, that one will not be allowed to enter the kingdom of God. They delude themselves that they are acting on behalf of God by saving others from their ignorance about God and by saving their Souls from eternal suffering in Hell, when in fact they are delusional and ignorant themselves.

Many people will not think consciously it is the Source that is inspiring them or telling them to do something but will think/feel that they are on the 'good side' or right. When polarized, others must be 'the bad guys' or wrong. Therefore, they have a justification for their potentially deluded actions. They will simply assume (Neptune) that they must be 'right,' especially those in the consensus stage of evolution who follow along without much critical thinking, if any at all. For example, I know someone (consensus 3/individuated 1) who had the belief that Jews and Christians were 'the good ones' and all other people from the various religions of the world were 'the bad ones,' especially Muslims. This is what he was taught and led to believe in and, like him, there are many others who assume they are on the 'right side.' These people are grown adults with families and sometimes occupy important leadership positions in society. This particular person has Neptune in the 9th house.

Neptune in the 10th House or Capricorn may delude themselves that they are acting on behalf of God when they use God to justify their ways to achieve their ends or goals. They may delude themselves that they are acting on behalf of God or the good of all people, even those they are harming. They may impose rules on others, including their family members, while saying it is what God desires or what is right from God's point of view. They may decide they have a God given right to lead others and that they are the most efficient person for that role. Neptune in the 10th house may delude themselves that they and only they have the ability to take a responsible leadership role, therefore maintaining control over others at all costs. Neptune in the 10th house may delude themselves that they have the God given right to judge, convict and punish others, thus having the delusion that they have the God given authority over others. On a positive note, Neptune in Capricorn/10th house can be very dedicated and steadfast, a good role model and a rock of support to those who need him or her.

At key points, they can be stripped of their authority/status and be exposed for their desire to maintain control over everything possible in tyrannical ways. This can lead to a new sense of freedom to find constructive ways to build for themselves and others once they surrender to the experience and realign with truth.

Neptune in the 12th House or Pisces can delude themselves into believing that God wants them to suffer as a form of healing themselves and others; that only by sacrificing their own needs and egos can they be saved or save others. They can fall under the delusion that God is directing them to do virtually anything that they feel inspired to do as they may have no sense of healthy boundaries, therefore not knowing who is who and what is what, even within themselves.

They may use drugs, alcohol and other escapist tendencies as a way to feel close to God and convince themselves that it is God's will to use substances as a direct way of connecting with God. They may become addicted to the fleeting ecstasy that drugs make them feel as a substitute for the real ecstasy and wonder/revelation of experiencing Source energy directly. As a result, they may become addicted to drugs and substance abuse. Neptune in the 12th house may also sacrifice themselves for the needy as a way to avoid their own lives and circumstances or suffering, and believe they are doing God's work.

They may totally neglect their needs or the needs of others and lack any form of discrimination as they can think that God will take care of everything in their lives; that personal action is not necessary and all is as it should be and will be taken care of eventually. They may delude themselves that God wants them to suffer, especially in this day and age which has been so conditioned by religious teachings that teach that people were born out of sin or that flesh and spirit are antagonistic or any other distortion that has the effect of distorting what God is, what people are, and everything in between. This creates a subconscious sense of imperfection and impurity deep within the psyche that affects all of us in every moment of our lives.

This distorted dynamic operates and expresses itself through all of the astrological archetypes, especially Virgo and Pisces, but also all the others as their expression is conditioned by the reality humans created and experience on Earth, because of such distortions. Another distortion humankind has created for itself is the distorted belief and way of life that Man is superior and separate from Nature itself. Could this reflect Man's desire to maintain his separate-ness from God? Because of these distorted dynamics and way of life, we all have a deep inner sense of natural guilt and the desire to atone for it whether we are conscious of it or not, and this dynamic can create the delusion that God wants us to suffer for our sins, that God sees us as impure and unworthy of Source's love, and ultimately the illusion that we are separate from the Source itself.

EXAMPLE CHART C

Neptune: Delusions and Being Directed by 'God'
Neptune in Aquarius in the 7th House

by Kristin

Neptune in the 7th house in Aquarius in its most deluded sense would equal a Soul who is not seeing others clearly, projecting realities onto others that are not true or accurate. In some cases, this would be projecting a purer expression onto someone that does not exist, seeing the good and the God in others or being swept away by the spirit of their potential. In other words, the rose-colored glasses phenomenon. Ultimately this could lead to being traumatized, Aquarius, when the reality of other's intentions were witnessed and realized. This could also equal someone who chose to join a group or be a part of a clique who shared certain beliefs that were not true about others. A Soul could project all kinds of conclusions or judgments upon another/others, very critical ones included, where there is no actual basis or reality for such conclusions or projections. This thereby causing trauma for others. This Neptune placement would also include someone who felt they were called to 'save' others, that they were called by God to be a savior for others.

In the most traditional sense, as in the consensus state, this Neptune placement reminds me of the wedding vows spoken that are rooted in man-made religions. This could also equal anyone marrying another because of feeling that God, Neptune, wanted them to marry them, perhaps due to having similar religious imprints. The other belief is surrounding staying married, divorce not being an option, as that is what God would want. There are countless loveless unions where Souls stay in the marriage because of a vow they have made or out of obligation or guilt, feeling if they left the marriage that a judging God, the man on the throne would cast them out. As a result, they are permanently suspended within the relationship, removed and detached. And this is what God would want? Really?

Couples wedding in the Roman Catholic Church essentially make the same pledge to one another. According to the Rite of Marriage, the customary text is:

> I, _____, take you, _____, to be my (husband/wife). I promise to be true to you in good times and in bad, in sickness and in health. I will love you and honor you all the days of my life.

In the United States, Catholic wedding vows may also take the following form:

> I, _____, take you, _____, to be my lawfully wedded(husband/wife), to have and to hold, from this day forward, for better, for worse, for richer, for poorer, in sickness and in health, until death do us part.

The priest will then say aloud:

> You have declared your consent before the Church. May the Lord in his goodness strengthen your consent and fill you both with his blessings. What God has joined, men must not divide. Amen.

Or else?

Consensus State

In the consensus state, a Soul with Neptune in Capricorn in the 7th might believe that God has chosen a certain partner for them. This could include arranged marriages in cultures that are driven and motivated by strict religious rules and keeping the same faith in the same house and keeping the religious bloodlines strong. There are some faiths that believe if you do not follow their way, then you do not go to 'heaven.' The delusion here is that one must marry or partner within the same religion. There are still many cultures in the east where women are totally subservient to the man and in essence a prop, or a slave or an object, a true victim in the partnership. Also, in some cultures, even if a woman is raped, she is sent to exile or locked up or even killed. All in the name of God.

With respect to Souls casting judgments upon others in the name of God, in a recent news story, right wing 'Bible Thumper' Phil Robertson, one of the leads in the popular consensus show TV show *Duck Dynasty* (with 10 million followers in the US) voiced anti-gay commentary and religious beliefs about marriage. Robertson discusses in his GQ.com interview his religious beliefs and about sin, saying, "Start with homosexual behavior, and just morph out from there. Bestiality, sleeping around with this woman and that woman and that woman and those men." Then, the GQ writer paraphrases Corinthians saying:

> Do not be deceived. Neither the adulterers, the idolaters, the male prostitutes, the homosexual offenders, the greedy, the drunkards, the slanderers, the swindlers — they won't inherit the kingdom of God. Do not deceive yourself. It's not right.

For taking these delusions to an extreme, his harsh remarks blasting gays landed him an indefinite suspension from the television series. His wake-up call.

One of my favorite passages in a book on the reincarnation of Anne Boleyn called *Threads* by Nell Gavin is a scene where she has just left her body after being sent to the guillotine by her husband, King Henry. She dies, and the story begins, as her Soul slips into the astral plane and she is greeted by a voice. She learns here that her conditioned 'expectations' and beliefs with respect to what is right and wrong were way off due to what society and her own conditioning, leading to choice making, created. Her understanding about giving and her role in relationships were way off the mark.

I will be harshly accountable for seemingly minor things, forgiven for things I have thought unforgivable, rewarded for small, thoughtless, seemingly unimportant acts of kindness and love, and I see there had been many. Each moment will count in the final tally, which will shape my future as it did my past.

She did have a Pisces Moon in the 7th, and Neptune in Aquarius in the 6th. What she learned at this state was that she had not seen people clearly. She learns here too that, evolutionarily speaking, their beloved servant Rose with crippled hands was far further along in her evolution. Because of her royal rank, she made herself more important than others. This caused trauma for other Souls and she herself was traumatized and ultimately sent to her death by her own husband.

Individuated State

Neptune in Aquarius in the 7th in the individuated state the Soul progressively realizes or experiences the truth that God, that was conjured up in a more consensus reality, is not at all true. Where is God when tragedy strikes? So a progressive rebellion against these old beliefs would occur. The Soul in these stages, in particular the 2nd stage, would experience a complete severing and separation from God. This might be a Soul that calls themselves atheist or agnostic, which is where this disillusionment would lead.

Neptune in the 7th in Aquarius reminds me of the movie *Water*. The film is set in the year 1938, when India was still under British rule. Child marriage was common practice back then. Widows had a diminished position in society, and were expected to spend their lives in poverty and worship God. Widow re-marriages were legalized by the colonial laws, but in practice, they were largely considered taboo. This story was about a 7-year-old girl who was forced from her family to marry. Shortly following, she loses her husband. In keeping with traditions of widowhood, this now 8 year old is dressed in a coarse white sari, her head is shaven and she is deposited in an ashram for Hindu widows to spend the rest of her life in renunciation, in poverty and to worship God. In the movie, 14 widows lived in a small, dilapidated two-story house, sent there to expiate bad karma, as well as to relieve their families of financial and emotional burdens. One of the side businesses girls as children were forced into prostitution to support the ashram. All in the name of God.

It focuses on a relationship between one of the widows, who wants to escape the social restrictions imposed on widows, and a man who is from the highest caste and a follower of Mahatma Gandhi. This movie is a true heart crusher and reflects this disillusionment at its height. For all who hope to fall in love and live the Neptune dream, prepare to be shocked into reality, painfully so. This main character, rebellious at her core, reflects either a later 1st stage individuated moving into the 2nd, or 3rd stage individuated.

Spiritual State – 1st subdivision

A first stage Spiritual state example would be Mother Teresa whose chart reflects the role of Mother Superior in another life. She has Neptune in the 7th in Cancer trine a South Node in Scorpio in the 11th, ruler Pluto in Gemini in the 7th square Mercury in Virgo in the 9th. She had the answers and power over everyone … God told her so, and in a prior life she was beyond strict with her role, rationalizing her actions, in the name of God. In her most recent life, she was the consummate giver, dedicating her life to tending to the sick and the poor. It has been documented that early on in her life, while traveling back to the convent by train from a retreat, that Jesus' astral form materialized in the seat beside her, Neptune in the 7th trining her South Node in Scorpio in the 11th, and told her that her destiny was to leave the convent and dedicate her life to caring for the sick and the poor. After this visit, she never again had a direct experience from God. Mother Teresa writes:

> There is so much contradiction in my Soul. Such deep longing for God – so deep it is painful – a suffering continual – and yet not wanted by God – repulsed – empty – no faith – no love – no zeal. Souls hold no attraction – Heaven means nothing – to me it looks like an empty place – the thought of it means nothing to me and yet this torturing longing for God. Pray for me please that I keep smiling at Him in spite of everything. For I am only His – so He has every right over me. I am perfectly happy to be nobody even to God.

The inner doubt is VERY characteristic of the 1st stage Spiritual from the beginning. It can be cyclically occurring from then until around three-quarters of the way through this 1st stage. Perseverance is a function of desire that can of course manifest in any stage of evolutionary development. And yet there was that inner tension but, because of it, it made her more determined to stay with the Church doctrine anyway. This was because she inwardly felt herself to be a fraud in some ways because of the utter inner darkness that plagued most of her life. And there was a karmic reason for that.

Spiritual State – 2nd subdivision

As Neptune evolves through the Spiritual state, in the 2nd stage a Soul with Neptune in Aquarius in the 7th house may feel from an egocentric place that they are 'holier than thou' and have a special destiny of a Uranian kind, to wake people up, and in some cases this can occur with extremity and cause a collective community trauma as in the people who followed Souls like the Rajneesh's of the world. Someone with Neptune in the 7th in Aquarius in this case would have become totally shocked and shaken by his reality once his actual motivations were exposed although there were many, and still are many, that defend him till the end, that still need to maintain their delusion about him or else their entire belief structure and sense of whatever they have built their life around will fall apart.

Spiritual State – 3rd subdivision

Neptune in the 7th in Aquarius in the most enlightened sense as in a 3rd stage Spiritual would not be free of disillusionment. They may see others as embodying a like-mindedness, others that are in it for the same reasons and a part of their mission or tribe, and then once the Souls following them get what they want from them, and perhaps are even healed by them, they jettison the scene. It may also play out that others with similar 'apparent' intentions, have 'actual' other motivations and delusions that are driving them.

Disillusionment can happen at any stage for any Soul. I remember JWG sharing a story about his pure intention to start a community as a result of the encouragement of others to teach yoga and meditation. He had started by teaching yoga in a formal class and as it turned out all of the students were committed to Yogananda, so this led to continuing to teach yoga as well as meditation on a weekly basis. This progressively grew in numbers as people learned of the class. This group requested that he start an actual Yogananda center because the one already in that town was too formal and filled with old people. JWG was in his 30's and many of the students were this same age or younger with a vibrant vision to set up a spiritual community. One of the students inherited a small sum of money and wanted to dedicate these funds to starting a Yogananda center.

JWG wrote to Self-Realization Fellowship formally requesting that they send up one of their ministers to help them because no one there was trying to play guru, just simple folks needing their help to set up this spiritual center, Neptune in Aquarius in the 7th, and wanting to know the right way to proceed. SRF's response was to excommunicate JWG and send his membership money back. Imagine his disillusionment. (I realize he has Neptune in Libra in the 11th – a reverse signature, but a similar energy.) This then led him to write to Kriyananda, one of Yogananda's well-known disciples asking for his help, which he was more than happy to offer. They ultimately became friends and in the end a center was started which was called *Ananda Seattle* and became a formal Ananda center that is still there to this day.

The organization of SRF had become corrupted long before, as power does tend to corrupt. Kriyananda was SRF's VP in the mid 60's and through Yogananda's empowerment he wanted to act upon one of Yogananda's stated reasons for incarnating: to start 'communities of plain living and high thinking' which just didn't work out in his life, so as VP Kriyananda bought up some land in India to do just that, this became the cause of the projections upon him by 'Daya Mata' who was the head of SRF by that time. They ended up removing Kriyananda from SRF as well, always under the justification of 'God' of course, pretending that 'Yogananda' was giving them these instructions. These projections and his dismissal were cause for great disillusionment for Kriyananda. He has Venus in Aries in the 11th squaring his own Nodes, South Node in 7th in Capricorn, North Node in 1st in Cancer. This became JWG's own experience with his Neptune in the 11th ruled by his Venus is

NEPTUNE: WHISPERS FROM ETERNITY

Scorpio which was conjunct Kriyananda's Saturn in Scorpio, the ruler of his South Node which, again, squares that Venus. Kriyananda had a Neptune/Moon conjunction and JWG a Pisces Moon. You can see the incredible synastry of all this. Yogananda's South Node is in Scorpio in the 3rd conjunct Uranus, these symbols form an inconjunct to the ruler Pluto and Neptune in Gemini in the 10th which are conjunct JWG's North Node, the experience of delusions within communities and organizations, people with power rationalizing their delusional behavior. The result equaling: innocent Souls with pure intentions suffer. In his own words, Yogananda 'hated' organizations of any kind for this very reason but this is exactly what God had him do in setting up SRF, the main objective within it was to unite the Spiritual teachings of the east/west.

EXAMPLE CHART D

Neptune: Delusions and Being Directed by 'God'

Neptune in the 7th House

by Ari Moshe

To summarize what Rad wrote:

(1)   All Souls can delude themselves by using some sort of rationale to use God as the reason for them to pursue the desires they are wanting to pursue.

(2)   When disillusionment does occur, it can lead to an inner state of meaninglessness and loss of faith. In extreme cases, it can lead to hysteria if the nature of the projections were a very extreme diversion from actual reality.

(3)   Relative to an extreme state of insecurity, when meaning is lost, the Soul will often need to find some construct of reality to hold onto so as to feel secure. This can either be the same exact construct that they were believing in – which means they will further their resistance to surrendering to actual reality and become even more extreme or fanatical about their delusion. In such a case, the Soul may develop a strong mechanism of ignoring any evidence that contradicts their construct of reality. Or, the Soul will find some sort of new meaning to replace the old one that doesn't work any longer. In both instances, the actual allowing, inviting of God to reveal the truth, is resisted so that the Soul can continue to deflect responsibility for pursuing its own desires from their own selves and onto God.

One thing to clarify, when I speak of 'God' in this context – this is to imply broadly any conception of reality that points to a higher, ultimate meaning. The specific notion of God is of course not necessary in order for this delusion to occur.

Becoming re-oriented to actual reality is a function of choice. It starts with the willingness to surrender to God – to that which is greater than one already understands and can control through their own version of reality. It is sometimes not possible to even acknowledge that one has the capacity to choose Truth or not when the version of reality a Soul has created is so strong that the Soul truly believes that they are already choosing God. To me what is profoundly beautiful about this is that God itself is still there, 100% available to the Soul. Our delusions cannot touch or affect the only thing that is real.

I'm placing Neptune in the 7th house. The 7th house correlates to the entire realm of relationship: how we meet one another's needs, our expectations and needs that are placed upon others, be they realistic or not. How we learn to get our needs met through relationships, how we learn about our own self and our needs through the experience of contrast, the needs we project upon and fulfill for other people – be it realistic, healthy, or not.

The basic confusion with Neptune in the 7th house is assuming a role that one is being divinely directed to play on behalf of someone else. This can manifest in several ways:

(A) Within an existing relationship the Soul pictures itself as being in relationship with that person to help the other person in some way. There is an inherent inequality here: the Soul is in the role of playing God for the other person and this person is dependent upon the Soul in some way. This Soul will hear the other person's reality, what they are needing and will elect themselves as the one to give it to them. They will think that they were divinely inspired and directed to do this.

(B) Non-specific to any particular relationship, the Soul may picture itself as a universal lover to all kinds of people: available to meet anyone's needs. What happens here is the Soul is projecting a God-like persona that essentially keeps real intimacy and closeness with people at a distance. The Soul will relate to other people's suffering and needs by interjecting onto these people what they think these other people are needing. The Soul may believe it has a divine purpose or role to play.

(C) That they are meant to surrender completely to the reality of the other person. To become a complete vicarious reflection of the reality of the other. This will be based on the belief that they are divinely called to do so; that they are supposed to support this partner, or that the partner is a savior to them and they are meant to trust them completely.

There may be a total lack of awareness of what is actually helpful or not – to one's self or to others. Placing one's self in the position where they are the ultimate provider for others or making others the ultimate provider for oneself and linking that to a divine purpose protects the Soul from taking any responsibility for their own desires.

The disillusionment of reality that occurs here is basically this: if I was supposed to be here, if God directed me to be in this relationship, how do I reconcile for the truth that is revealing itself? [This is a common Neptune delusion. The eternal perfection of each moment, the principle that God is here now, that we are always in the right place – is often misapplied to justify not making the choices that will align the Soul with their own evolutionary needs.]

To recap in a general way, here are three possible responses that a Soul with Neptune in the 7th may have to a disillusioning experience in their relationship relative to their delusion of being in alignment with some sort of higher divine purpose:

(i)   Some sort of justification that amends the original belief, but allows the Soul to stay convinced that they are in fact following a higher divine plan. The justification will essentially allow the Soul to adopt to the new truth that has revealed itself without taking any responsibility for oneself, and thus without actually changing any core behaviors. The same relationship may continue with these new justifications intact.

(ii)   Overwhelmed with the actual reality, the Soul may simply dismiss everything and choose the thoughts, "This doesn't matter to me," or "You do not understand." In extreme cases of denial, the Soul will completely use any excuse to point to God as the source of their own choice making.

(iii) The Soul will gradually come to realize that they do not know the other person. It would be healthy if there were various emotions at this point: anger, confusion, uncertainty, reluctance. That is healthy because it implies that the Soul is beginning to process something that has been so utterly denied. It's necessary to try not to rush this process and replace the lost meaning with something else that can make the Soul feel safe. So often with this signature Souls are disillusioned in a particular relationship and then at a certain point they either 'get back together' with the person they were with, or they just find someone else with whom they can play out the same delusion. What can happen here, if this process is active, is at some point the Soul reaches an emotional empty point wherein the Soul in a moment remembers that there is more they do not understand and that they do not have all the answers. In this moment, the Soul surrenders to God – they let go in some way. At this point grace can come in and new revelations, new ideas, and new insights are possible.

Other expressions of the 7th house Neptune, if we link it with Jupiter, or Sagittarius, would be the belief that one is supposed to speak the truth to someone else on behalf of that someone else. That my purpose is to do so. If we place Capricorn there, to contrast this, the belief that one is meant to go out of their way and "do the right thing" for other people – to play a role in relationship that allows the individual to take some sort of responsibility for others. There may be a total lack of boundaries and capacity to know what 'God' wants me to do versus what I am deluding myself into thinking God wants me to do.

In more subtle ways, I can identify this pattern of linking choices with God when it in fact is coming from within my own self relative to my own inner Soul dynamics. I have a Pisces DC squaring the Nodes. I have often found myself in various relationship dynamics where I have gotten completely lost in the other person's own natural human experience (fears, projections, worries, anxieties, etc.). Without knowing it, I have held the belief that I was supposed to be available for these Souls: to offer counsel, to hold space, to give of myself in some way. I never thought of it as "God wants me to do this," however I have projected that these instances were a sort of spiritual purification for me – that my own inner work in those moments was to be available and present for these Souls – and that there was a reason for why these people were showing up in my life at that moment. Thus, there has been the delusion that there is a higher purpose for me to fulfill within these relationships.

With Neptune ruling my DC in the 4th conjunct the Mercury and Jupiter balsamic – all relative to a balsamic Venus/Pluto in the 2nd, I would engage dialog and essentially invite these people into my inner space – often literally to my own home – to the total negation of my own needs. This would be completely exhausting and lead to great loneliness and deplete my own capacity to focus on the actual service work that wishes to happen here. This has happened in all kinds of relationships – casual as well as more long-term partnerships. Guilt about people's suffering if I am not going to offer myself to them.

What I am learning is to love them, and to take care of myself, however I need to; to be fully nourished and supported in all the ways Source wishes to nurture me (4th house). In so doing, I give myself the healing and nourishment to focus fully on my service in the world in the way that is in alignment with my Soul's own evolutionary needs.

EXAMPLE CHART E

Neptune: Delusions and Being Directed by 'God'
Neptune Rx in Leo in the 6th house
3rd stage Consensus
by Cat

It seemed that no matter what I wrote, I was never satisfied with it. I started with Neptune in Scorpio in the 12th House, coming up with ideas like people having dreams, visions and drug- or alcohol-induced hallucinations causing them to believe that God told them to do such things as become a nun, a priest, or a monk, or commit murder, rape someone, cheat on their taxes, manipulate other people, and other Scorpio and/or Pisces type activities. It made for quite a long list. Something was missing however, and then God spoke to me and told me how he wanted me to do this assignment. (wink)

I decided to write about a 3rd stage consensus Soul who has:

- Neptune Rx in the 6th House in Leo

- Sun in Aries in the 1st House

- Jupiter is conjunct the Ascendant in Pisces

- Neptune, the Sun and the MC (in Sagittarius) form a Grand Trine

- Neptune is square Venus in Taurus in the 3rd House

- Neptune is sextile Mars in Gemini in the 4th House

- Neptune is also bi-quintile Uranus (the ruler of his 12th house cusp) in Aries in the 1st House

As we have learned, these are the main areas in which the Soul can spiritualize his life or experience illusion, delusion and disillusionment. In addition, these are areas in which a Soul can believe that God is telling him or her to do something that is really his or her own personal desire. In order to make things easy, I am going to refer to this Soul as 'Ben' rather than as 'the Soul' or 'the individual.'

Ben is a very religious man who was inspired by a transcendent impulse to serve others through his work in a very big way (Nepune/Leo/6th). He wanted to do something very special that would bring attention and power his way in addition to helping others. He instinctually decided to pursue a career with an institutional religious organization (Neptune/Sun/MC Grand Trine). In addition to his MC in Sagittarius, he also had Saturn in Sagittarius in the 9th House. Early in his career, this placement influenced him to study and then teach theology. If Ben ever thought that it was God's will that he pursue such a career, he was wrong, it was his own personal desire.

Ben entered the Catholic priesthood and became a highly regarded professor of theology. Being that he had Neptune in the 6th House, he was under the illusion that he was doing God's work and helping others understand God. As we know, it was his own personal desire that led him down this path.

Ben was very successful and soon promoted to Vice President of the University and later promoted to the rank of Archbishop. In his early years at the University, he was regarded as a liberal theologian, but as time went on, he adopted conservative views and advocated a return to fundamental Christian values (Saturn in Sagittarius in the 9th). It is possible that he believed that it was God's wish that all Catholics embrace these fundamental values, but it was really his own desire that people do so.

Ben devoted his life to the priesthood and the Catholic Church. With Jupiter, the ruler of his 12th House cusp, conjunct his Pisces Ascendant, he displayed a great deal of self-confidence and had the political skills necessary to succeed and advance to leadership roles in the church. He perceived himself as having the power to carry out 'God's will.' With his Sun in Aries in the 1st House trine his MC in Sagittarius and Neptune in Leo in the 6th House, this was his special creative purpose after all. At least he imagined it to be.

Although the Sagittarius placements in his chart inspired Ben to pursue a religious career focused on theology and Catholic dogma, there was another side of Ben symbolized by all of the Pisces archetypes in his chart. Ben once told an audience, "We need to make time for silence in our lives if we are to pray and listen to God. Silence is the environment that best promotes recollection, listening to God, meditation." These are the words of someone in tune with the Pisces archetype as well as one who believes that God speaks directly to us.

The Catholic Church was rocked by sex scandal after sex scandal during Ben's tenure as a high-ranking Catholic official. He was called upon to investigate these matters. He chose to keep his findings secret and not communicate them to the outside world (Neptune square Venus in Taurus in the 3rd House).

Ben also has Mars in Gemini in the 4th House, Mercury conjunct Jupiter in Pisces along with his 12th House Ruler, Uranus in Aries, in the 1st House. Ben felt empathy and compassion for both the victims and the perpetrators. The priests in question were, after all, a group of like-minded others in terms of belonging to the Catholic family of man. He fought to keep his investigation secret for their sake and could not find it within him to punish them. At the same time, he felt the grief, anguish, sorrow and suffering of the victims and their families. He apologized for the wrong doings of his fellow priests. The manner in which he handled the situation confused and confounded the public and he was criticized for not taking action.

At the high point of his career in the Church, transiting Pluto was conjunct Ben's MC and the transiting North Node conjunct his natal Sun. At this point, he attained a position of power and glory in the Church. He became the powerful leader he was destined to be. The sexual scandals kept pouring in.

After a few short years, Ben may have become disillusioned by it all. It is said, "… although he identifies with the institution of the Church, he is also profoundly spiritual." Dealing with sex scandals probably didn't fit his vision of what God wanted him to be focused upon or his vision of spirituality.

Transiting Neptune entered Ben's 12th House and Ben likely began to feel the transcendent impulse and God 'whispering in his ear.' Before very long, five transiting planets were sitting in, and activating, Ben's 12th house of dreams, fantasy, imagination, illusion, delusion and disillusionment. These five planets were the Sun (purpose), the Moon (ego), Venus (values and relationships with oneself and others), Mars (desires), and Neptune (the transcendent impulse and disillusionment). Is it possible that Ben was becoming disillusioned with it all?

It was not long before Ben made a decision that literally shocked the Catholic world. He decided to resign from his glorious and powerful position in the Church. When he made this decision, he gave very practical and logical sounding reasons for doing so. Afterwards, it was reported that when asked about his motivation for making this particular decision, his answer began with the words, "God told me to . . ."

With five planets, including Neptune, transiting his 12th House, Ben had what he calls 'a mystical experience' through which God inspired within him an 'absolute desire' to retire and devote his life to prayer. Although Ben believes that this is God's will, it is actually his own personal desire.

Having both religious and spiritual archetypes prominent in his natal chart, Ben was likely confused about the difference between the two. With Neptune and Pisces archetypes aspecting each other, there were no boundaries separating the two and he was under the illusion that they are one and the same. In the end, the "Whisper of God" gently pushed him towards focusing on the more mystical side of his nature after a lifetime of devotion to the religious and truth-seeking side if his nature. This may have been a two-fold process in which he first became disillusioned with his role in the Church and then heard God tell him to resign, go into seclusion and spend the rest of his days in prayer. Only he knows for sure. In any case, this was his own desire.

Pope Benedict was the first Pope to resign since Gregory XII in 1415, and the only Pope to have resigned without external pressure since Celestine in 1294. It was reported that:

> Benedict denied he had been visited by an apparition or had heard God's voice, but said he had undergone a 'mystical experience' during which God had inspired in him an 'absolute desire' to dedicate his life to prayer rather than push on as Pope.

> Benedict said his mystical experience had lasted months, building his desire to create a direct and exclusive relationship with God. Now, after witnessing the 'charisma' of his successor, Pope Francis, Benedict said he understood to a greater extent how his stepping aside was the 'will of God.'

CHAPTER FIVE

NEPTUNE AND DECEPTION

Introduction

So we will now continue in our ongoing understanding of Neptune, the 12th House, and Pisces. In this next step, which is intentionally simple, we will examine one of the more sad dimensions of these archetypes: DECEPTION.

Any given Soul can be deceived and/or be the deceiver: or both. Any given Soul can of course also deceive themselves into 'believing' something is either true about themselves that is not, or allow themselves to be deceived because of some underlying need that dictates believing in the deception of another(s).

One of the core reasons that any given Soul can be deceived by another is rooted in what JWG called 'emotional assumptions' emanating from a consciousness that is inwardly defined by Natural Laws wherein there is an expectation that all humans treat one another according to those laws. In Natural Law, there is no need to deceive because all humans are working together, in union, on behalf of the whole of the humans that are interacting among themselves. A simple example of one of those laws is the Natural Law of giving, sharing, and inclusion.

So a Soul that is aligned with those Natural Laws simply assumes THAT ALL OTHERS ARE IN FACT DOING SO WHEN THEY ARE NOT. Such Souls are then shocked when the actual reality of another(s) manifests that is in violation of those Natural Laws: another(s) purposeful deception of this kind of Soul.

Soul's that are not aligned with these Natural Laws, those who have identified with the perversion of those laws, then become the Souls who are able to then deceive others in order to accomplish some sort of agenda that they inwardly feel they could not otherwise actualize. This reflects the perversion of the Natural Law of giving, sharing, and inclusion to one of SELF-INTEREST AND EXCLUSION. This type of Soul can then also attempt to convince itself of its own delusions about itself: that it is not doing what it is actually doing.

Because of the Natural Law of karma wherein an action will have a proportionate reaction, these types of Souls then set themselves up to also be deceived by others.

Yet because of their own deceptions about themselves that manifests as denying their actual reality, they then can feel VICTIMIZED by others who are in fact doing exactly what they themselves are doing.

By creating a consciousness that is now victimized, these Souls then create rationalizations to victimize others by way of their agendas to get back at the others whom they have deceived themselves into believing they have been victimized by.

So, when we look into any given birth chart, we can see where all of these Neptune archetypes of deception can manifest. We can see it by way of the house and sign of the South Node of Neptune and the location by house/sign and aspects to its ruler: Uranus. All Souls on Earth have their collective South Nodes of Neptune in Aquarius, which we will be discussing later on.

The placement of the natal Neptune by its own house and sign, and aspects to it, correlate with any given Soul bringing the past archetypes of deception into the current life consciousness. In other words, the natal house and sign of Neptune in the current life correlates to the vehicles that the Soul is using in the current life that brings forth the past life dynamics of deception in order to deal with them in one way or the other in the context of the current life.

The North Node of Neptune, which of course is in Leo for all Souls, by its own house and sign and the aspects to it, correlates with how the Soul is intending to take charge of these existing dynamics involving deception in order to do what is necessary about them so that, hopefully and intentionally, they are eliminated from the consciousness of the Soul: either by not allowing itself to be deceived by others ever again, or by exposing the inner deceptions the Soul has about itself that then manifests as deceiving others and/or allowing itself to be deceived because of some need that has created that deception in the first place.

In the context of the current life, the sign on the 12th House, the location of its planetary ruler with aspects to it, and where the sign Pisces is on a given house cusp which then of course refers back to the totality of the Neptune archetype, its North and South Nodes, are additional vehicles or doors through which the archetype of deception can manifest.

Questions and Answers

(Q) I get confused (Neptune) about the archetypal distinctions between dishonesty and deception. Dishonesty correlates to Sagittarius, and deception to Pisces. In my brain, these are so synonymous that I'm having trouble distinguishing the two in the exercise. When we're looking at dynamics of deception, are we basically looking at the manner or level dishonesty has been/is applied ... is this the distinction? Also, it occurred to me that perhaps another distinguishing factor between Sagittarian dishonesty and Piscean deception might be the degree to which illusion is actively serving as the vehicle for the dishonesty, i.e. an emphasis on what isn't 'real' (Piscean deception) versus emphasis on what isn't 'true' (Sagittarian dishonesty). If correct, this also ties in the Piscean factor of 'potential,' a common tool used within deception, because until a given potential is actualized in reality, it isn't yet 'real.' Thoughts on this? (I hope these questions aren't redundant!)

(A) First, we need to remember that Pisces, Sagittarius, Virgo, and Gemini, and their planetary rulers, are all part of the mutable grand cross. As such, these archetypes interact within and among themselves. Thus, Sagittarius does correlate to the archetype of lying, being dishonest. To lie and be dishonest has many forms and applications where those various forms, types, and applications are then linked to the other signs, planets, within the mutable grand cross. Those other forms, types, and applications, of course, are all caused by the underlying archetypes of dishonesty or lying.

Deception, as you said, is also linked with the archetypes of illusion or delusion, which, of course, are archetypes that are specific to Pisces, Neptune, and the 12th House. This is why we have already focused upon and discussed those archetypes. And since we have, we can now move on to the archetype of deception because of its link, relatedness, to illusion and delusion. Of course, deception is a form of being dishonest, or to lie.

To contrast this with another form, type, or application that is ROOTED in dishonesty or lying is denial, where denial specifically correlates with Virgo, Mercury, and the 6th House. Or duplicity, where being duplicitous correlates to Gemini, the 3rd House, and also Mercury. Thus, a Soul can be in denial of being duplicit! And then that Soul could convince itself, where convincing as an archetype correlates with Sagittarius, Jupiter, and the 9th house, that it is not in a state of denial relative to being duplicit. In so doing, that Soul is then also deceiving itself relative to being in a state of delusion that is rooted in the underlying dishonesty itself. This is an example of how the mutable cross interacts within itself relative to the archetypes that are specific to each of the signs, and their planetary rulers.

(Q) Does 'deception' principally take place on an 'unconscious' level? In my experience and what I perceive in others, it is mainly coming from the unconscious due to evolutionary intentions, but it can be very conscious too. When it is unconscious, it is self-delusional (self-deception) and unintentional. When it is conscious, it is deception of others and very intentional.

(A) First, we must remember that generally 80% of any given Soul's 'conscious' actions within itself that manifests external to itself are rooted or caused by the individuated unconscious or sub-conscious. It is this dynamic within the totality of the consciousness of the Soul that correlates with Uranus, the 11th House, and Aquarius. This dynamic or component of our total consciousness of the Soul correlates to long-term memories, the memories of the Soul itself coming through time: all of its previous lives. All of these memories thus condition the very nature of how any given Soul thinks, acts, behaves, and what it desires. They condition the very nature of the totality of the emotions of the Soul where emotions are reactive and reflective as to what the Soul has created for itself coming through time manifesting as specific prior lives that are all stored within the Soul that then manifests in its individualized consciousness, unconscious, in each life. Thus, the current life circumstances the Soul creates for itself all serve to 'trigger' all those stored memories and emotions that come with the Soul into the current life in such a way as to 'condition' the Soul response or reactions to those circumstances.

(Q) How do we gauge the level of conscious deception? I'm thinking if the natal Neptune is in a water house, especially the 12th, it could be more unconscious, while if it is in, say, a fire or air house, or in a prominent position, example 1st house or near the MC, it could be more conscious or intentional? What do you think?

(A) Deception, being deceived, deceiving, or both, can occur within the egocentric consciousness of the Soul as well as in its subconscious or individuated unconsciousness. As the Soul naturally evolves through the four natural evolutionary states, the level or degree of what the Soul is conscious of increases, and that which is unconscious or subconscious decreases. Thus, as the Soul evolves, there does come a time in which the Soul is utterly conscious of its own totality in such a way that its consciousness has no boundary between what it is conscious of, and that which it is not. The Soul has liberated, Uranus, itself from this division within consciousness that most Souls have.

So, to understand this question requires an understanding of the evolutionary state of any given Soul. It is not understood by the natal house/sign of Neptune at all. For most, the consensus state, deceiving, being deceived, or both, operates primarily at a subliminal level within their consciousness. When this is so, that subliminal degree of awareness can be 'objectified,' Uranus, either through external confrontations by others who have been deceived by the Soul or through inner confrontations by the Soul to itself that is caused by a desire to understand why it is allowing itself, or attracting to itself, deceptive type circumstances. This is not to say that the archetype of deception cannot be utterly conscious within this consensus state because it can.

As the Soul naturally evolves through the four evolutionary states, again, this correlates to what degree the Soul is consciously aware of anything including deception, and the underlying causes or reasons of why deception is occurring in the first place.

(Q) What is the sign that correlates to 'intention?'

(A) Scorpio, Pluto, and the 8th House.

(Q) And Pisces? Scorpio, because intention is essentially desire, and Pisces, because the 'value' and meaning of whatever we can do, is always in the intention from an ultimate point of view.

Also, I would add that, while the underlying dynamics and bottom line reasons that lead to wanting to deceive, can always be more or less subconscious, depending on the evolutionary condition, until the subconscious has become totally conscious, there would be no reason to want to deceive. However, I would say deception itself, or the specific intention and act of deceiving, can be subconscious, but it can also be totally conscious at any evolutionary stage. Many different legal systems contemplate criminal offenses or felonies, which are based on the conscious intention to deceive. And beyond this, many people go around consciously deceiving others in different ways. In other words, I would add a difference between the deception itself, and the underlying dynamics and desires that lead to wanting to deceive.

Does this make sense to you?

(A) There can be all kinds or reasons for a Soul to deceive, be deceived, or both, whether this is manifesting at a conscious or sub-conscious level, it can manifest in all the natural evolutionary states. Intention, of itself, is specific to Pluto, the 8th House, and Scorpio. When we link Pisces to it in the form of 'ultimacy,' then one can say an ultimate intention. Yet Pisces is not the specific archetype of intentions.

(Q) Is it correct that the more a Soul is evolved and is aware of its own unconscious behavior patterns, that it has more control over itself, and has more power to stop or change the Neptune archetype of deception through conscious action or intention?

(A) Yes.

(Q) Is conscious intention or awareness an 'accelerating' archetype in any evolutionary state?

(A) Of itself, no. When linked to specific types of conscious intentions, it can be. For example, a conscious intention to examine the nature of the Soul's desires in total in order to eliminate that which just is no longer necessary for the Soul's ongoing evolutionary development.

(Q) Would it be through cataclysmic events that a Soul would stop deceiving itself and others?

(A) Generally yes, but not always so and certainly not for those who are psychopaths.

EXAMPLE CHART A

Neptune and Deception
The Deception of Osho Rajneesh
2nd stage Spiritual

by Linda

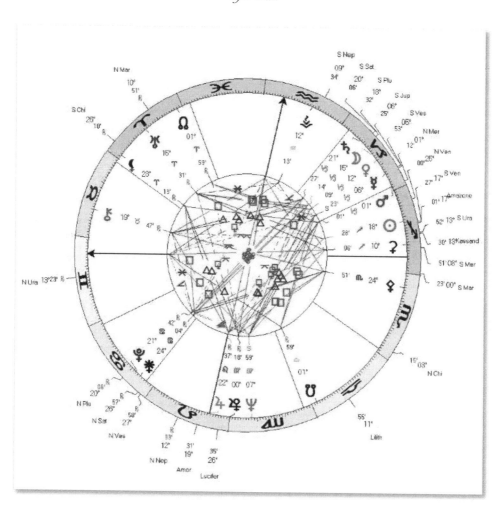

RAJNEESH

Introduction

Rajneesh was born in India the eldest of 11 children. At age 7 (1st Saturn square) he was sent to live with his grandparents. He grew up being a very rebellious child. Receiving full independence and no impositions of education or other restrictions, the lack of boundaries, inattention and the absence of adults around him set in place the early childhood structures and conditioning patterns. Later he associated with Socialism and Indian independence movements, the precursor to setting himself up as a controversial spiritual leader in a community that advocated cooperative management, formulation of meditation techniques, free expression of individuality, and an open attitude toward sexuality. His daily 90-minute discourses were transcribed into books. He taught that you should do as you please because life is both a dream and a joke. He presented himself as a great spiritual teacher while his devotees allowed themselves to be deceived by him due to their own underlying evolutionary needs. Neptune Virgo 4th is ruled by skipped step planet, Mercury Capricorn 7th.

2nd Stage Spiritual – Spiritual Downfall

In the 2nd stage Spiritual, the Soul of Rajneesh has already had various kinds of real inner universal experiences within its consciousness which attracted others, setting in motion intense spiritual delusions of grandeur that led to a desire to fulfill a spiritual mission in the world. Impurities within the current life subjective ego of the Soul had to be purged as he moved closer to the Light. Identifying with the delusion as being separate from Source exhibited in the behavior of a secret egocentric agenda which pointed the way to himself as the vehicle of salvation all the while pretending that this was not so. Beneath a mixture of truth, false humility and a need for idolization was spiritual arrogance. In its evolutionary development, the Soul necessarily experienced natural guilt (Neptune Virgo 4th) to create its own downfall in order to atone for that guilt. The Leo-like explosion of spiritual ego, the fall from grace, and the revelation of his actual reality lead to disillusioning the hopes and dreams of his followers for their own evolutionary reasons.

Soul Structure

The Soul vibration correlating to Pluto Cancer 2nd correlates to fundamental emotional and physical insecurity in the areas of survival, sexuality, resources, and self-esteem, and, as a result, leading to an obsessive need for power and control.

- 5 planets in Capricorn
- Saturn ruling the 8th
- Saturn exactly opposite Pluto
- Saturn exactly conjunct the South Node of Saturn
- Moon conjunct South Node of Pluto
- Pluto conjunct North Node of Pluto

. . . and all of the above placed in the 2nd/8th axis reveal an emotionally disturbed and distorted Soul radiating with dominant sexual energies and instincts (voyeuristic and masturbatory nature) in order to, subconsciously, procreate and survive. The Soul who had lived many lifetimes in the Matriarchy where the application of sexual energy originated, came through the transition to the Patriarchy where a fundamental guilt (Capricorn) was created for being sexual. The natural Matriarchal sexuality of the Soul that, in time, became suppressed and distorted because of judgment patterns, created the evolutionary intentions in the current life – two steps forward one step back (cardinal archetype) – and the necessity to re-live these distortions in order to metamorphose them, and to manifest the original spiritual root.

With the Pluto polarity point conjunct the SN of Pluto, and Pluto conjunct the NN of Pluto, there is a sense of being stuck in the past, or having to revisit the past dynamics in order to change them. The rulers of the 2nd and 8th house, Moon and Saturn, are in balsamic conjunction in Capricorn 8th creating a strong sense of going backwards in order to go forwards in a new way to culminate Patriarchal distortions. Neptune Virgo trining 4 planets in Capricorn would assist the evolutionary intentions through the process of crisis. Uranus (ruler of SN of Neptune) squaring 4 planets in Capricorn would bring liberation from the past. There are many exact and very tight aspects in the chart showing acute intensity between the planets.

During the transition to the Patriarchy, the Soul had two choices: to be a good woman, give birth, and become the property of the man, or become a prostitute with a right to own possessions, property and money (2nd). With Vesta conjunct SN Neptune 9th, it is likely that the Soul became a prostitute (Sacred and/or walking the streets) with her own rights. The Soul's Matriarchal origins, manifesting as the sacred prostitute, are signified by:

- Venus-Moon-Saturn in Capricorn
- Aphrodite conjunct NN Neptune
- Isis 16 deg Libra t-square Venus-Moon-Saturn Capricorn
- Pluto in Cancer
- Planetary South and North Nodes of Pluto-Saturn-Jupiter in Cancer/Capricorn
- Isis exactly opposite Uranus, the ruler of SN Neptune Aquarius 9th
- Eris (trouble/strife) conjunct NN Aries 10th

With Mars-Mercury Capricorn 7th skipped steps, and Resolution Node being South Node Libra 4th, the Soul had to go backwards in order to go forwards, and resolve what was not understood in the past: emotional balance, speaking the truth, equality with others, not domination over others.

Nodes of Neptune

Neptune's function in consciousness is to dissolve the boundaries between the egocentric consciousness, Soul consciousness and the Totality of Consciousness, that is, to spiritualize. The Soul's Neptune Virgo 4th correlates to the Virgo sub-age of the Age of Pisces beginning at 1200 AD where the past life transition between the Matriarchy and Patriarchy became intensified. The Soul vibrated with psychological, emotional and sexual cataclysms. With the planetary North Nodes of Pluto-Saturn-Jupiter in Cancer in the 2nd house, the Soul's unconscious memories of survival due to Patriarchal suppression and judgment progressively caused the Soul to feel guilty with a need to atone for the guilt surrounding its own natural sexuality through Neptune Virgo 4th. The Capricorn distortion of sexuality through suppression caused by guilt created a type of sexual masochism and/or sadism.

The trinity of the planetary nodes paradigm:

- South Node of Neptune Aquarius 9th
- Current life Neptune Virgo 4th
- North Node of Neptune Leo 3rd

. . . symbolizes the Spiritual Law of the trinity of the past, present and future of the Neptune archetype. The rulers of these planetary nodes, Uranus and Sun, show the dynamics through which the current life Neptune is consistently integrated thus releasing the continual state of tension brought in from the past. (Uranus Aries 11th, eccentric/unorthodox, group sex, leader of the group, accelerated evolution; and Sun Sagittarius 7th, purpose, teacher, freedom, extremes of untruth, domination over others.)

South Node of Neptune Aquarius 9th

The function of the South Node of Neptune Aquarius 9th is to dissolve and liberate from past life belief systems that were considered to be the truth. Aquarius acts to break down past conditioning patterns so that new radical paradigms of phenomenal reality can emerge that change the past for good and have the effect of completely changing personal realities. With the South Node of Neptune Aquarius 9th, the Soul vibrated with deep philosophies about the meaning of life. These deep unconscious memories of the Soul, activated throughout the whole of the current life, and made more conscious through the Sun and Uranus, pertained to the Matriarchal Age of Sagittarius and the previous Age of Aquarius where everything was defined and lived through Natural Law. The subsequent Patriarchal transition that suppressed these Natural Laws became the basis of judgment, persecution, distortion and guilt. Women who had been considered the embodiment of the Goddess became suppressed, distorted, abused, controlled and owned as property. Rajneesh who had Vesta conjunct the SN of Neptune in the 9th house had been one of these alienated and hysterical women.

The Soul's spirituality was defined through the Aquarian archetype in past life cultures that used sexual energy and ritual to expand consciousness and access inner Divinity, with these experiences generating knowledge. With the heavy suppression of the natural law of sexuality (Capricorn 8th), the consequences were dire for the Soul of Rajneesh (5 Capricorn planets square Uranus). Uranus correlates to long-term memories relative to the Soul's individuated unconscious, while Sagittarius and the 9th house, connects to the original imprint of Natural Law, intuition and truth. The teachings and lifestyle of Rajneesh were transmitted to and intuited by his group/audiences, impacting them with the 'natural truth' of his words. However, these truths were 'partial-truths' that vibrated, partially, with Natural Laws, and hence where the 'deception' came into the equation. The extreme deception (and outright lie, Mercury skipped step) that he created was that he promised liberation for all through the vehicle of himself. His followers responded because their own Souls had also lived during those times in groups and they sought to re-embrace the origins of their own Souls.

His disciples were easily deceived due to the 'emotional assumptions' that emanated from their consciousness. Surely this great spiritual teacher would satisfy their spiritual dreams and fulfill their expectations that all humans treat one another with love, sharing, caring and inclusion? The deception was created that all were working together, in union, on behalf of the whole community, creating a lifestyle rooted in Natural Laws. Nothing could be further from the truth. However, what was so alluring was that Rajneesh delivered partial-truths stimulating the memories of Natural Law in his devotees.

With Neptune, there was great danger of addiction to a fanatical and extreme form of delusional thinking: that his view of the truth was the only way and the right way. In his spiritual downfall in the 2nd state Spiritual, he mixed truth with untruth. When the truth of his actual reality started being revealed, many of his devotees suffered trauma, shock and disillusionment due to the violation of Natural Laws. For many, this disillusioning experience, the purposeful deception of Rajneesh, brought about a necessary awakening on their evolutionary paths that brought them closer to the true realization or remembrance of Natural Laws and spiritualization.

The Rajneesh community attracted Westerners and people from all over the world. In past lives, too, he had been a spiritual teacher. In the current life, the Soul was able to stand back, observe and objectify the deceitful dynamics that it had created. There would be no more hiding behind the illusion of spiritual teacher since his own Soul, Pluto, would eliminate this falseness through a necessary fall from grace. The belief systems that Rajneesh transmitted to his audiences made them aware of the larger cosmological forces and challenged and revolutionized the obsolete ideologies of the past. The interpretation of his reality communicated to his followers did not come from unconditional love and truth, but from emotional insecurity and fanaticism. Under the deception that he was a spiritual teacher here to help others, he was in fact re-living the past in order to learn discernment, to purify and strengthen the security structures of his egocentric consciousness that were linked with his belief systems, and to learn to feel 'secure' with nothing else but Source energy (Neptune Virgo 4th).

Ruler of South Node Neptune – Uranus Aries 11th

The ruler of the South Node of Neptune, Uranus Aries 11th, shows the dynamics through which the current life Neptune is consistently integrated thus releasing the continual state of tension brought in from the past. While Sagittarius and the 9th house reveals the truth, Neptune dissolves, Pluto eliminates, and Uranus liberates through the realization of the Natural Truth that all humans are co-equal to the totality of creation. Rajneesh's teachings had been fragmented, too radical, and were not able to be integrated into the Saturnian reality (Saturn square Uranus). The patriarchal suppression and perversion of his natural sexuality lead to a need to atone and purify the guilt carried within the Soul due to patriarchal judgments. Atonement linked with guilt and masochism created anger and sadism.

The ruler of his SN Neptune, Uranus Aries 11th, is a symbol of a group experimenting with sexuality based on distorted beliefs that undermined the true nature. With the Lunar North Node at 2 deg Aries conjunct Eris and square Mars Capricorn 7th (paradoxical), Rajneesh was at the very beginning of a new evolutionary forward vibrating with a rebellious me-me-me attitude. Through instruction to devotees not to suppress their desires, there had been experiments into perverted, voyeuristic and detached sexuality rituals, as well as extreme physical activities such as chaotic dance, which allowed a 'release' as devotees got lost in the hypnotic rhythm.

Be happy. I have come to you. Dance. Celebrate. (Rajneesh)

In his community of sannyasins working together, Rajneesh created the deception that he was rooted in the Natural Law of giving, sharing and inclusion. The whole community assumed that all others were aligned with this Natural Law when in fact they were not. Many members of this community of Souls were shocked and traumatized when the actual reality and truth of Rajneesh's purposeful deception manifested in violation of Natural Laws. He was not aligned with these Natural Laws because he and his followers identified with the perversion of those Laws (self-interest and exclusion), thereby deceiving others. Rajneesh and his followers convinced themselves, and were in denial, and some continue to do so today, of their own delusions that they were not doing what they were actually doing.

Neptune Virgo 4th

Neptune Virgo 4th correlates in the current life to the vehicles that the Soul was using to bring forth the past life dynamics of deception in order to deal with them. Rajneesh created a group of people living together (home, community, womb) in an unnatural, distorted fashion, and represented himself as a living messiah during the current Patriarchy. Emotional insecurity did not exist in natural Matriarchal communities, yet the Soul of Rajneesh who was born with Neptune Virgo 4th vibrated with a fundamental insecurity relative to attachment and survival (2nd). It was an evolutionary necessity that he experience many crises relative to his teachings prompting the need to atone and surrender to a Higher Power in order to completely dissolve the egocentric structure or self-image, and bring balance to the distorted dynamics of the past.

The interaction of the SN of Neptune Aquarius 9th with the current Neptune Virgo 4th correlated with compensation for who he naturally was through the psychology of self-defeat, sadomasochism, existential void, and crisis. This stemmed from the patriarchal suppression and perversion of natural sexuality, and the need to atone and purify the guilt carried within the Soul due to patriarchal judgments. With Pluto ruling the 6th house, Mars skipped steps (suppressed anger, sadism), and Eris conjunct North Node 10th (strife), it is clear that atonement linked with guilt and masochism creating anger and sadism, undermined Rajneesh's visions, ideas and realization of truth.

So while there was a need for emotional sustenance from his followers by forming emotional bonds to the community, there was also the distortion of emotional attachment to the spiritual leader. At each morning discourse he inspired others to feel safe and nurtured, that they 'belonged' to a family (4th). In truth, his discourses were a way for his Soul to create a safe womb for HIMSELF. Creating a safe womb for others/the group, was an indirect way of getting in touch with his own emotional problems. He was not relaying the whispers of God, but rather manifesting his own evolutionary intentions.

With a lulling hypnotic voice (Gemini Ascendant), convincing silver tongue, and a discourse made up of a mixture of truth, part-truth and untruth, he was able to lure people in by the thousands (Neptune rules MC), hence his deception reaching the whole world. Neptune makes an astounding 5 trines in the chart to Moon-Mercury-Venus-Mars all in Capricorn in the 7th and 8th houses, and also the SN of Jupiter Capricorn, showing the scale of his ability to deceive others (devotees, intimate partners, society).

Rajneesh was directly responsible for dictatorial slavery and indulgence in the commune. He allowed middle-aged men to have sexual intercourse with underage girls in the name of sexual freedom. On one occasion, he asked a couple to have sex in front of him, which they rejected. This directly correlated to his voyeuristic and masturbatory nature (Pluto Cancer 2nd). He claimed to have third eye powers of telepathy and psychic powers that proved to be false. He squandered millions in hard-earned commune assets on his car collection and expensive jewelry. While disciples worked a 12-hour day in cold and difficult conditions, he enjoyed a private heated indoor pool and watched countless movies on a big screen TV while enjoying his daily supply of drugs. His drug habit devalued himself as a teacher (Chiron Taurus 12th).

There is no doubt that Rajneesh became a hopeless drug addict except in the minds of his passionate followers who did not want to admit the disillusioning truth. It is absurd to think that a realized spiritual teacher would need drugs to get high since enlightenment is a natural state. Rajneesh's teachings were full of intentional lies and falsehoods born out of deception.

North Node of Neptune Leo 3rd

The North Node of Neptune Leo 3rd correlates to how the Soul intends to take charge of existing dynamics involving deception in order to eliminate them from consciousness either by exposing the Soul's own inner deceptions about itself that manifests as deceiving others and/or not allowing itself to be deceived by others ever again. The current life Neptune integrated the NN of Neptune and the SN of Neptune (9th/4th natural inconjunct) through repeated crisis. With the collapse of the Soul's information database causing emotional insecurity, Rajneesh needed to stand strong on his true path without reverting to falseness, duplicity or lies. The North Node of Neptune in Leo is conjunct Jupiter in the 3rd house (paradoxical signature).

The God consciousness of sharing, caring and inclusion to guide Souls back to Natural Law was rejected by Rajneesh in this particular lifetime. The evolutionary intention in these dynamics was to lead the Soul into right relationships with others whereby his communication skills, teaching methods, thinking processes, creativity, self-expression, power and will could shine as an expression of Truth and Light. This means eliminating deception from consciousness through right speech and language, and aligning with a spiritual belief system that is based on truth, knowledge and Natural Laws. In time, the Soul will learn to make his universe God's universe where he can selflessly play a communicative role to teach others.

With the North Node of Neptune in the 3rd house, the current life Neptune in Virgo ruled by Mercury, and Mercury Capricorn 7th skipped steps, the resolution is to harness the 3rd house/Mercurial energies, consistently focus on emotional self-reliance in order to regain balance, transform the way he relates to others to express equality (rather than domination/submission), and above all, return to the natural consciousness, the original root of the Soul, through the Natural Law of sharing, caring and inclusion. With Venus Capricorn 8th ruling the South Node, the emphasis will be on new ways of relating (Venus/Mars new phase) and sexuality that can be expressed in a natural guilt-free and sacred way, not in a profane way. Due to the Natural Law of Karma wherein an action will have a proportionate reaction, the Soul of Rajneesh set himself up to be deceived by others, e.g. his disastrous karmic relationship with Sheela.

Ruler of North Node Neptune – Sun Sagittarius 7th

The ruler of the North Node of Neptune, Sun Sagittarius 7th, shows the dynamics through which the current life Neptune is consistently integrated thus releasing the continual state of tension brought in from the past. Sun Sagittarius 7th, the current life purpose, together with the North Node of Jupiter Cancer 2nd, portrays a clear picture of returning to Natural Laws, for survival purposes and to bring balance. The current life purpose as a spiritual teacher demanded equality, fairness and honesty, but this was not achieved due to deception, untruth, duplicity (Jupiter square Chiron

Taurus 12th, Jupiter inconjunct Saturn, Sun inconjunct Chiron), and a wound of delusion of being separate from Source exhibited in the behavior of a secret egocentric agenda which pointed the way to himself as the vehicle to salvation (Chiron square NN Neptune Leo). This was not the karmic signature of a true spiritual master, but rather one at the very height of a spiritual downfall brought about by extreme distortions.

Venus on the 12th house, Pisces MC/10th

In the context of Venus on the 12th house, posited in Capricorn 8th, and Pisces on the MC/10th, in terms of the totality of the Neptune archetype, the additional doors through which the archetype of deception manifested were through secret sexual liaisons based on voyeurism, deceiving partners and in turn being deceived by them. The magnitude of his deception that had reached the whole world brought upon himself a cataclysmic downfall from grace. Venus on the 12th is a repeating theme of extremes reached in a distorted relationship with Source itself, demanding 'surrender to Source,' which did not come about in this particular lifetime.

Conclusion

Rajneesh experienced a fall from grace because of intense spiritual delusions of grandeur and a secret egocentric agenda that pointed the way to himself as the vehicle to salvation. Since he was exposed as a fraud who perverted Natural Laws because of his own self-interest, we now know that he was really here to fulfill his own Soul's evolutionary intentions. There was a huge emphasis on paying his Saturnian karmic dues (Saturn exactly opposite Pluto), and having to learn some very harsh lessons around maturity, cooperation and taking personal responsibility for the consequences of his actions/choices: hence, the massive fall from grace was as an evolutionary necessity. As the mask was finally removed and his living a lie exposed as fraudulent, Pluto, his own Soul, would reveal the truth that was not in harmony with Natural Law, and eliminate (Pluto) the false doctrines to reveal the truth of his deception to the world. The deception was that he had created teachings of the Natural Truth, but in truth had lured his followers through a sexual vibration (PPP 8th), not a spiritual one. Rajneesh was a sexually-realized guru, not a God-realized one.

Comment from Moderator

A couple of other stories that I also remember about his are one wherein he had been given some sort of drug while reclined in his favorite 'dentist chair' that he had imported from somewhere because of his problems with his back. One of his personal bodyguards was present who reported this event later on in a book he wrote about Rajneesh because of his own disillusionment with him. While in a drug induced state reclining in this chair he reportedly said the words, "Thank God I do not have to pretend to be enlightened anymore."

Another one that I also remember took place during the filming of the movie *Ashram* by another 'devotee' who also became disillusioned and desired to expose this creep called Rajneesh. This was when he was 'selling tantra' to those who came to the ashram while it was still in India. Among many scenes, there is this one wherein some truly deranged man who had paid his money wanted to have 'tantra sex' with one of the women there who was, in fact, utterly repulsed by this man. She kept saying 'no, no' while at the same time this man forced himself, like a rape, upon her in order to have 'tantra sex.' She was shrieking while others simply looked on. While this was happening, the person making the film deftly went from the scene of this rape to a picture on the wall of the creep Rajneesh. Back and forth the camera went while she shrieked in total pain. The point being made about the reality of the 'Ashram.'

And I also remember JWG saying that because his counseling work took place in Seattle, Washington for many, many years that when the 'commune' collapsed for the reasons that it did that for a period of many months some of those who had become utterly disillusioned by the creep Rajneesh filled his office with their own horror stories.

EXAMPLE CHART B

Neptune and Deception

Neptune Sagittarius 5th house ruled by Jupiter Virgo 2nd

by Skywalker

- South Node of Neptune Aquarius 7th house
- Ruler of South Node of Neptune (Uranus for all people) Scorpio 5th
- North Node of Neptune Leo 1st
- Ruler of North Node of Neptune (Sun for all people), Sun Scorpio 5th conjunct Uranus and Mercury Rx
- 12th house Gemini/Cancer
- Pisces in the 8th/9th houses
- South Node of the Moon 8th house

Major relative natal aspects of Neptune to other planets

- Venus conjunct Neptune, new phase
- Saturn in Virgo in the 3rd house square Neptune, last quarter
- Uranus semi-sextile Neptune, balsamic
- Neptune conjunct the South Node of Uranus in Sagittarius in the 5th house, new phase

- Transiting Neptune in the 8th house, conjunct the South Node of the Moon, at the time of this assignment

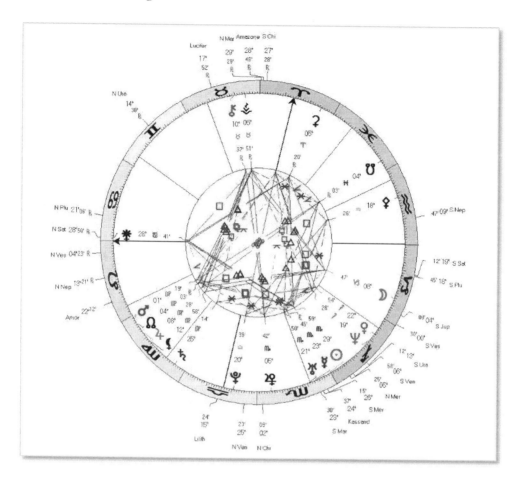

The South Node of Neptune is in Aquarius for every living Soul on the planet at this point in time and it correlates to our spiritual root, where our ultimate values come from and, what they are like, reflected in the Aquarian archetype, which correlates to our ultimate values of humanitarianism, individual freedom to be unique individuals, that make up a brotherhood or big human family, with ultimate values of inclusion and sharing, of supporting one another as in team work instead of the self-interest, competitiveness and exclusion we find in our world today. This South Node of Neptune placement correlates directly to a timeframe in which humans lived according to natural law, in a natural way. Those times and way of life are what is generally referred to as the Matriarchy. Most societies at those times, more or less 8000 years ago and before, were structured in a mother-dominated way, in which the male competitiveness and domination we experience today was minimal.

A time on Earth when humans lived in a way that was not detrimental to their environment or other living beings, no more than what was necessary for basic survival; when there was an adherence to truth as a way of life; and when all living beings on earth were respected as a life form in their own right, including the planet itself as a living organism. A time when humans shared resources and included one another in their pursuit of survival, knowledge, happiness, arts, evolution and so on. It probably wasn't perfect or without evil and suffering as these things are natural and have their place in our lives for evolution to proceed, to a certain point at least. Though, when natural laws and principles are violated on an exponentially increasing basis and frequency, then the suffering and destruction becomes as tragic as going from the beauty and intensely life supporting environment, like that of a tropical rain forest, to the death, destruction and years of radioactive contamination, of a place like Hiroshima at the time of World War II.

With the South Node of Neptune in the 7th in Aquarius, there can be memories of past lives wherein psychic trauma was experienced relative to these types of extreme imbalances, such as in some people going hungry their whole lives while others have gold toilets. Mental/psychic trauma due to violations of natural law, that are carried into this life – natal Neptune is in Sagittarius, conjunct the South Node of Uranus – reflect essentially a continuation of those ultimate values, connected to natural principles/natural law, and reflecting a desire to seek within Nature, or the inner self, in natural ways, for knowledge and spiritual or physical belonging. This in turn leads to a continuation of the psychic trauma experienced in the past, as the planet continues to be in a state of extreme imbalance relative to Nature and human living conditions, while the native simply cannot compute, understand, or truly integrate in such an individually disdaining, robotic, and sadly, what can be for many…an unjust, painful way of life.

The South Node of Neptune in Aquarius can correlate to mental trauma on a collective level, due to these and other dynamics. Souls who are aligned with natural principles who find themselves in environments that are in direct violation to those laws and principles, are at a higher risk of developing mental illnesses as they cannot integrate socially without going against those natural principles, which they know deep down to be the correct way to live their lives. It's no wonder that so many people have escapist tendencies of all sorts as they attempt to numb out the madness/pain of living against their own core human needs and ultimate sense of what is right and wrong. It's also not surprising that so many people in these times develop mental and emotional diseases. Diseases of all sorts that are 'treated' or more correctly, suppressed, with all sorts of chemical drugs which are often highly addictive or have dangerous implications for the health of the patient and are labelled and sold as medicine. Of course, this 'medicine' is making those in the pharmaceutical industries and some in the medical professions, a lot of profit as they DECEIVE the general population that they care and are working hard and honestly to treat people. Of course, there are many in the medical professions that do care too.

Amazingly, the pharmaceutical companies and their 'friends' in governments, other large and powerful organizations, banks and corporations that seek to profit and control others, lobby and manage to make natural cures and substances illegal or, simply make propaganda to discredit their effectiveness in treating illnesses. Basically, it's a vicious cycle of deception and profiting off human, animal and plant-life misery, by those who promote and maintain the distorted Patriarchal way of life. One main way humans have been deceiving one another in this past century is through the use of technological advancements that allow them to reach a vast amount of people via the use of radio, then television and now the internet, to brainwash and control the masses. This seems to be the South Node of Neptune in Aquarius and the North Node of Uranus which is in Gemini, expressed in a distorted way, correlating to the use of information, communication and technology such as computers, video cameras, and the world wide web, relative to the South Nodes of Pluto, Saturn and Jupiter in Capricorn (i.e. the patriarchy), and to the [current] transit of Pluto in Capricorn, to keep the general population under increasingly tighter surveillance and control. We are most probably also headed for a worldwide society that is run by computers with artificial intelligence, programmed by those in the shadows who have the power.

Something interesting to note is that in ancient Matriarchal times there was no notion of time as we have today and, still today in some tribes there is no time as a measuring system as there is in most of the 'civilized' world. On the other hand, there is no personal property in some tribes that, with the absence of modern time measurements, creates a totally different way for the people in those tribes, of experiencing their environment and interacting with it. Personally-owned land or the ability to accumulate land and pass it along to their children/heirs are not dynamics of such ways of life. This in turn leads to these native tribes only using what they need and little more of Earth's natural resources and, without artificial time plus capitalist values, the people in those tribes live without the stress of needing to be on time, against the clock, simply to make ends meet. There is a natural time, the time it takes to get from point A to point B, but not the stress of having to go to the office every day at 8:00 am for the next 8 hours or be home at noon sharp for lunch. They will have NATURAL RHYTHMS as their timing will be connected to their NATURAL ENVIRONMENT and not a distorted man-made division of the days, weeks, months and years. Because of this, they are actually much healthier and their awareness and emotional bodies are not filled with stressful thoughts and anxiety, as most people in the modern world experience on a regular basis. Even children in our modern societies experience much more stress and anxiety than is natural or necessary.

Just to note how disconnected from Nature we are in this day and age, I'd like to note that we have a calendar that was created to facilitate the collection of taxes and has nothing to do with the real planetary cycles. It's my understanding that the Mayan calendar of 13 months, consisting of 28 days each month, is accurate or more naturally accurate than what we have now, as it reflects the lunar cycles and the female menstrual cycle. Our current calendar and similar un-natural human implementations, in order to control or profit, are the very essence of distorting that which is natural and true, which then in turn leads to people all over the planet deceiving primarily themselves, and then others, in order to survive or live with security and material wealth as a way to live comfortably.

The problem is that most of the people born after the 'patriarchal take-over' and living in the world today, do not question their reality or how it is structured, and consequently ASSUME that the way humans attempt to live, as separate and superior to nature and out of sync with their natural rhythms and cycles, is normal, or has always been that way, or is just human nature or some other rationalization. The list of deluded excuses and clichés is as vast as the ignorance of the masses alive today. All this to say that this dynamic is where a lot of the DECEPTION in present human inter-relating originated. Some people even believe that humans are an evil cancer destroying the Earth, and while it's true that we most surely can and do act as a cancer, we do not necessarily have to do so. It's man-made brainwashing/deception of the masses that leads people to believe in such ideas.

With Venus being the ruler of the 4th house, occupied by Libra, and being conjunct Neptune in the 5th, with Pisces occupying the 8th and 9th houses, relative to the dynamics just described and the need for the majority to compete with one another for basic survival and material comfort, the individual can experience deception within the home, or family environment from a very young age and see it as a kind of norm or prerequisite for survival, relative to the sharing of resources or even satisfying their own emotional needs. With this combination, deception relative to the use and distribution of shared resources can be an everyday reality. It can all basically be so distorted in the family environment, just as in the society of birth, that it's business as usual for people to purposely lie to one another about a multitude of things and deceive one another as a natural way to respond to an unnatural way of life and familial/social power structures. It can become a method for a person in a weaker position to survive or get what they want or need. With this combination, it can be present within the family of birth, and the native, while very young, can pick up this behavior from a parent or others in the family.

With Taurus occupying part of the 10th house and on the 11th house cusp, and Venus conjunct Neptune in the 5th, some of these dynamics of deception can be experienced with parents, role models and friends and acquaintances or later in life with people in their professions. Someone with a Pisces South Node of the Moon and all these planetary combinations can be very naive and trusting of all of humanity and even all living things, thus becoming easy prey for those who wish to use him/her for some reason or steal from them. Actually, with the Lunar South Node in the 8th in Pisces, Venus conjunct Neptune/5th, people would of just needed to ask for whatever they wanted as the native with this combination would probably be happy to provide what others needed if he/she were in a position to provide the help others needed. In turn, the individual with these symbols may have no real sense of personal boundaries and may also be the one to use others or their resources as a kind of God/naturally given right.

With the South Node of Neptune in the 7th house, one can 'see' archetypically, through the lens of Astrology, that the past search for ultimate meaning of this individualized Soul, has been relative to the act of giving and receiving in personal relationships. This involves giving and receiving on an equal basis, that leads to each person in the relationship having his or her projected needs met through the involvement, thus leading to a sense of balance. Libra, the 7th house and the outer expression of Venus, all correlate to our desire and need for balance and equality between us and the other or others. This combination reflects a Soul who, in the past, had potentially developed, to a point at least, the ultimate values of sharing/inclusion, and attempted to give to others what they needed in any way possible, even through self-sacrifice. Or, that others gave to this Soul in ways that could be sacrificial to their own personal needs, in order to fulfill the needs of the 7th house South Node of Neptune Soul, in a spirit of good faith.

These dynamics would be idealized to the point of projecting them onto friends and acquaintances or, on a larger scale, to the whole of humanity, the animal and plant kingdom or, for some, even outer space beings/aliens or inner space entities. Due to this, with Aquarius in the mix, the Soul can be easily deceived as it sees the whole of existence as connected and benevolent and every other life or consciousness a potential friend. On the flip side, once the Soul is deceived and disillusioned with others in general, it can become good at deception by identifying with what individuals and the masses desire, value and identify with. This, plus the acute sensitivity to the needs of others, and this Soul's inherent abilities to 'listen' to the other, plus its own desire for self-preservation and survival, can lead to becoming good at deception itself.

With Aquarius on the 7th house combined with the South Node of Neptune, it shows that the Soul has desired to be free and, at the same time, has engaged with others in relationships in order to develop a detached sense of objective awareness of its own core needs and to learn about the core needs of those who were in relationship with this Soul and humanity at large, in order for each one to express their unique individuality to the fullest (South Node ruler Uranus in the 5th). The South Node of Neptune in Aquarius is a position that we all share and it correlates to the ultimate sense of community and brotherhood we humans shared during the times of the Matriarchy, or to ultimate values that are deep within our psyches because it just seems right, because it is. It shows that although we were inter-connected, we were also allowed or encouraged or desired to express our own uniqueness and our own individuality (Aquarius) was sacred and highly valued (Neptune). This, in most likelihood, because through individual evolution and objective awareness, humans were able to develop tools (technological advances for those times) and/or different viewpoints and experiments that had the effect of helping the whole social circle or tribe survive and evolve and, because human and animal nature is meant to be free, just as true love comes freely.

What this placement shows, in the highest sense, is that this Soul has experienced or desired to experience total union with another or others in natural ways, that led to deep experiences of losing personal boundaries and merging emotionally, mentally, physically and spiritually with others, as a way of experiencing and expressing divine love, bliss and deep unity with another, possibly in the hope of feeling united with Universal or Source energy or to simply transcend limitations of time/space reality by feeling special feelings with another.

In a distorted sense, it shows that the Soul acting in a spirit of self-interest, may have deceived others in order to have its own projected needs met. This, in turn, sets up the dynamics Rad described about creating karma relative to deceiving others and others, in turn, then deceiving the Soul in similar ways. It can correlate to an addiction to relationships and the belief that life without a partner is boring or that without a relationship one cannot be complete or even evolve in some cases. It can, in turn, lead to the individualized Soul creating the delusion/self-deception that it needs others in all sorts of exaggerated ways in order to evolve, grow and have a sense of meaning and belonging. This, in turn, can lead to the individual deceiving others in many ways in order to relate and have its projected needs met. Others who are living their own delusions and self-deceptions can also deceive the individual and use him/her for their own needs of a similar nature.

The end result are situations in which the deception is exposed for what it is, but generally the dynamic of deception will be 'swept under the carpet' or suppressed in some way by the consciousness of the one doing the deceiving, as it knows deep within itself that it's naturally wrong to deceive others, leading to natural guilt but, as Rad said, finds rationalizations in order to justify its behavior. The one being deceived creates assumptions that the other will not abuse their confidence or deceive them, thus falls into the deception due to a lack of discrimination and/or lack of experience of these dynamics and how they operate in Earth's current reality. Then the deceived can either rebel against these types of behavior or imitate and treat others according to the same dynamics if necessary for survival or to achieve some sort of goal of a personal nature.

Jupiter in Virgo in the 2nd house conjunct the North Node, new phase, and Mars balsamic, shows that in the highest sense, the individual will value honesty, integrity and courage and act instinctively in ways that reflect values of ongoing searches for personal meaning and truth in a direct way, that lead to a personal sense of inner value and self-worth. With Neptune being ruled by Jupiter in Virgo in the 2nd, the individual can value the little things in life and value being of service to others, instead of looking for ways to profit too much for him/herself. With Jupiter in this configuration, the person will value honesty and simplicity too much to be able to feel good from within if he/she deceives others unnecessarily, for profit or to get ahead in unnecessary ways. On the flip side, if the person is living in a victimized or distorted state, in which a healthy perspective is lost, the individual may cheat others in a big way (Jupiter) and not even realize it fully in order to make money.

His/her security needs for survival may be highly exaggerated to the point of having an insatiable appetite for material wealth, food or sexual pleasure, leading the individual to deceive others in order to satisfy his/her insatiable appetite. In this quest for satisfaction, he or she may become a great sales man/woman and cheat others or exaggerate the value of what he/she sells, the importance or quality of the goods, never be satisfied with any profit margins and simply be extremely greedy, as nothing is ever enough to fill up the inner void that planets in Virgo can feel, until there is an alignment with truth and the perspective becomes a healthy one. Jupiter can exaggerate the survival needs of the 2nd house and Mars conjunct Jupiter can be wasteful of resources or literally burn them as, with this aspect, one can feel that there is always more and the balsamic nature of the conjunction can translate into a belief that the universe will provide for the individual, no matter what happens.

With both planets on the North Node, it means that these dynamics have been worked on in past lives and specifically the life just prior to the current one. Indicating that the native can come into this life with certain values very well defined, and in this life he/she is meant to continue developing the values of survival through service and develop honesty as a personality trait. Also, these dynamics and attitudes will be natural for this individual and highly rewarding as he/she develops them further. With Jupiter on the North Node of the Moon and trine the Moon in the 6th house, it will also be a re-stating of the Soul's desire to develop itself and its values and ability to survive, in ways connected to nature, that reflect natural law (Jupiter).

The Moon in the 6th in Capricorn, trine Mars, the North Node, Jupiter and sextile the South Node in Pisces in the 8th, and in a grand trine to Chiron in Taurus in the 10th, can correlate to natural methods that this Soul will use to heal itself and others that are worked on in a consistent way, on a constant basis, as the Soul desires to perfect and humble the Ego. Some methods may be through the daily practice of Yoga or Martial Arts or similar practices that through dedication and a step by step process, humble the ego in various ways, in order to learn about patience, as things have their 'due process' dedication, effort and devotion. The sextile from the Moon to the South Node in Pisces, relative to Neptune and deception, indicates that the Soul, through the Ego (Moon), can be open to, or will likely at key points, experience very deep humbling and transformative experiences in its search for healing and its spiritual evolution, as it ultimately values truth and searches for it with passion, Neptune in Sagittarius in the 5th.

The ruler of the South Node of Neptune (Uranus) in the 5th in Scorpio, conjunct the Sun and Mercury, shows a desire in the past to penetrate (Scorpio) to the very core of illusions that created trauma in the first place and to live life in a truly creative and empowered way (5th house). It shows that this Soul may have been in positions of authority within a tribal community in the past and that there is a potential for the Soul to have used and possibly abused its influence or status in order to attract the opposite sex and satisfy its needs. It also shows that the Soul, because of the Sun's conjunction to Uranus, will have memories deep within itself that directly correlate to traumas of abuses of power and trust (Scorpio). The Sun conjunct Uranus and Mercury in this context, correlate to the Soul's desire to shed light (Sun) upon these past traumatic experiences/memories and to mentally and empirically formulate concepts in order to understand them (Mercury) to eventually liberate from these traumatic memories (Uranus). With Uranus in the 5th house there will be, in this life, a need to liberate from the need to be acknowledged as special and unique or superior to others so the Soul can free itself of such illusive dynamics.

Mercury is also the ruler of the North Node of the Moon in this incarnation and is conjunct the ruler of the South Node of Neptune, Uranus, which is also conjunct the ruler of the North Node of Neptune, the Sun. The nodal rulers of Neptune being in conjunction, reflect the ongoing continuation of past life dynamics, to be lived in new ways. With the North Node of the Moon in Virgo in the 2nd house there is a need for humility in this lifetime, and Mercury is conjunct the ruler of the 2nd house, the Sun and is in the 5th, indicating a need to use and develop one's talents in ways that will lead to self-sufficiency. With Mercury Rx conjunct the Sun and Uranus, the Soul will reject, in this context and lifetime, anything that is not relevant to its evolutionary intentions/needs to actualize itself and rebel against Patriarchal distortions.

With both the South and North Nodal rulers of Neptune in Scorpio, conjunct the ruler of the Lunar North Node (Mercury) in the 5th house and the Lunar North Node being in Virgo in the 2nd house, relative to personal evolution and the need for humility, correlates to the need to purge (Scorpio) the Soul of past delusions of grandeur that lead to emotional, mental, physical and spiritual trauma. With the North Node in the 2nd house it shows that relative to all these potential dynamics of deception, that by being totally self-sufficient and working on the individual's self-value, by developing talents and abilities, to learn that the value is in the effort and through learning to use discrimination and extreme personal honesty, he/she will minimize the need to deceive others and minimize the ability for others to deceive this individual Soul and Ego in return.

With the North Node of Neptune in Leo in the 1st house, it shows that a new cycle relative to how the Soul actualizes itself or acts on behalf of its ultimate ideals and values, must be initiated in this life. Relative to the Sun's conjunction to the ruler of the North Node of the Moon, Mercury, it shows the possible need to break free from dependencies on others and relationships in general to find its own sense of purpose, sustainability, and what is true and right by the use of its powers of discrimination. It shows that courage is necessary to simply be who one is (Leo North Node and Nodal rulers in the 5th). The fact that it loops back to the 5th house but in Scorpio, shows that an attitude of no B.S. is necessary in order to achieve these goals of inner clarity relative to deception and self-deception, and to confront and eliminate any internal or external dishonesties that limit a true, creative expression of the self. These symbols reflect a need to be FREE from within to be able to initiate a brand new creative cycle.

The ruler of the North Node of Neptune conjunct the ruler of its South Node, both new phase in the 5th, reflects the need to initiate this new cycle in order to live relationships (7th house South Node of Neptune) in new ways as this will be how the individual will be able to express him/herself to a higher potential. It reflects a need to believe in one's self and in one's dreams or to actually have dreams. Ultimately, this Neptune placement asks for faith in the self to break free and express one's self to the maximum potential. Neptune, in the end for all of us, is about faith and its unique combination in each of our natal charts combined with our desire to have faith, can show us in what area we will need to surrender to a higher power. In this case, with all these aspects, relative to natal Neptune also in the 5th, it seems to be able to surrender to the fact that the Source is the ultimate creator in one's life and to have the faith to just go (1st house) in whichever direction it feels directed to go, without the fear of being alone or fearing not succeeding to live up to its own high ideals or whatever parts of it that wants to be in control, Saturn and Pluto, mostly does to hold it back.

With Gemini on the 12th house cusp with the rest of it occupied by Cancer and, Virgo on the 3rd house cusp, relative to deceptive dynamics in the current life, there is a need to dissolve any form of communication and connections to others that lead to deceptive dynamics. Since Cancer is also on the 12th, it shows that any form of emotional victimization of the self and the Ego's excessive security needs are to be dissolved in order for deceptive tendencies to be replaced with honest communication of a mental and emotional nature. Cancer on the 12th can show that the individual can use crying as a form of deception too.

With Natal Neptune conjunct the South Node of Uranus, both in Sagittarius, we can see that this Soul's search for ultimate meaning and connection to the divine will be through natural law and the pursuit of truth and freedom, and the understanding of cosmological belief systems and the breaking down/dissolving of the separation between these systems such as in religions or personal philosophies. It shows that this connection to natural law and metaphysics is not new to this Soul and that there is a re-living or re-aligning with knowledge and principles of those times. Shamanism, Metaphysical, Esoteric and Hermetic knowledge are all possible areas of interest in the current lifetime as a way to re-connect to these ancient principles that are deep within the Soul's memories. Due to the conjunction being new phase, there is a re-stating of the need for freedom for this Soul to pursue these types of experiences that lead to real knowledge connected to nature and natural law.

Natal Venus/Neptune in Sagittarius in the 5th, relative to the South Node of Neptune in Aquarius in the 7th, and square Saturn in Virgo in the 3rd house, correlates, in an ideal expression, to the Soul's desire for new types of relationships in which the divine is experienced and expressed without restrictions. A desire to relate with transcendental qualities/values that can defy the laws of physics, or relate on a Soul level with others based on pure feelings and unconditional love. In Sagittarius in the 5th house there can be a need for total freedom to be whatever one truly is without restrictions to self-expression or expansive search for truth, ultimate meaning of existence and connection to the cosmos. This can lead to a desire for a multitude of relationships at the same time or one after another in an indiscriminate way, which can be confusing to the individual as he/she is judged or criticized by those in the environment, due to going against what is socially expected behavior, or by getting negative reactions from those in relationship with him/her due to a lack of boundaries.

There may also be confusion as to who the individual truly wants to be with or if he/she wants to be in a committed relationship at all, due to the need for freedom and the desire for constant expansion. In order to deal with the confusion and not hurt others or not assume the true nature of the attractions to others, the individual may hide his/her real feelings about these dynamics, with the consequence of deceiving others intentionally or unintentionally. With Venus square Saturn and conjunct Neptune, the individual may act like a child without any maturity and manipulate others in any way he or she feels. With Saturn in this aspect, there is a need to learn about emotional maturity and self-reliance and not do whatever it takes to get whatever one wants, including the use of deception. Venus and Neptune square Saturn can also have a crisis in what to believe and not believe in the partners or others, therefore acting in underhanded ways that deceive others who relate with him/her as there can be a lack of trust in people due to painful past disillusionments of being deceived him/herself.

There is also a possibility to deceive others, as the individual can be so sensitive to criticism and judgment from society in general, those in the environment or even siblings and people one communicates and interacts with (Saturn in the 3rd house in Virgo), with a Pisces South Node of the Moon in the 8th. This sensitivity can lead the individual to try and hide his/her inner nature and emotional vulnerabilities in order to not be judged or persecuted by others. The fear of persecution and judgment can be a fear that is in the memory of the Soul due to past lives of speaking one's truth whether it fit into the mainstream ideals of the times or not. Due to these dynamics and the fear of persecution, whether real or not, plus the extreme emotional sensitivity of the Pisces South Node of the Moon in the 8th, the individual can use emotional deception when dealing with others in the environment, as a survival/defensive mechanism or just not to be overwhelmed emotionally and psychologically by others who are energy leeches or simply too intense in some way which has the result of affecting the individual in ways that are detrimental to his/her health (Pisces South Node relative to the Moon in the 6th house).

Another concept that is connected to Neptune and can be considered a form of deception is evasion. A native with these symbols can relate to others by constantly evading them in various ways in order to avoid being judged or leeched or simply to maintain his or her privacy. This is done by passively allowing others to believe whatever they want, by being vague or by using one's sensitivity to be 'two steps ahead,' such as in not making eye contact or not allowing certain themes in conversations to be addressed. With all these symbols in the 5th house, the native can be quite domineering and tend to know how to lead conversations and manipulate communication to go in the desired direction. Other possibilities for deception relative to the combination of these Astrological symbols are relative to one's creative or other abilities which can be totally exaggerated. Relative to children, someone can deceive their child to protect them or to use them in some way; the individual may have no boundaries and get women pregnant in extramarital affairs if a male and deceive whoever is necessary to maintain the child is kept a secret. If a woman, she may give birth to a child that is from an affair and deceive her husband and family by acting as if it's the husband's child. Some could live double lives and have two homes and families and deceive everyone, while someone else could have a long-term extra marital affair with a lover or be married and always have someone on the side or, possibly, another who doesn't get in a real relationship but ends up with married or committed people who can't really give them what they need, and end up by generally deceiving themselves and their lover's partner.

Others can deceive relative to the desire for fun and games and possibly gambling, when the native doesn't admit to having a gambling problem and depletes resources that were vital for the family or business. Others simply might not take life seriously and thus deceive others on a continual basis as they live life as a game and see no need for honesty, at least until they are the ones being deceived. In the 5th house, Neptune can also deceive others about all sorts of things simply in order to receive the attention they crave, such as in the "Peter and the wolf" archetype, including exaggerations of their personal stories (Sagittarius) and dramatizations, which are lesser forms of deceptive behavior and can be generally inoffensive but still dishonest and deceptive.

Another core issue relative to potential deception in a Patriarchal society is relative to sexuality. With all these symbols, the Soul can have an intense sexual nature that may or may not be well accepted by the parents/family while growing up or by society in general when an adult and therefore hide its highly sexual nature, leading the individual to have hidden or secret involvements with partners that may not be well accepted by the family or others in the environment, thus leading to the individual deceiving the family or others, in order to relate and have his/her needs satisfied without being judged. Due to intense sexual needs, coupled with the need for freedom, the individual can also use others and deceive them by using people sexually and moving along to the next thrill or adventure. Of course, in turn, others can do the same to the individual. Another potentiality relative to sexuality and deception could be a homosexual who hides his/her sexual orientation from others simply not to be judged or criticized. Some could go as far as having a heterosexual marriage in order to maintain appearances, thus deceiving all others including the marriage partner.

In sexual expression, Neptune in the 5th relative to its South Node in the 7th, the individual may pretend to enjoy him/herself in order to please the partner even if he or she is not experiencing pleasure as in when a woman fakes an orgasm in order for the sexual act to be over without hurting the feelings of the partner, or when a man or woman over-compliment the partner or their performance in order to make them feel good or secure. Some forms of deception are lighter than others, but still deceptive and painful when the truth is found out. In a more extreme sense, relative to these dynamics and with Pisces on the 8th with the South Node there, one could go as far as marrying for money and deceive others and one's self emotionally, to the point of almost believing in that relationship for financial security, status and power.

With Neptune in the 5th there can also be drug/alcohol/substance abuse problems due to the native desiring to simply have fun and party like there is no tomorrow, especially in Sagittarius, which in turn can lead to the individual deceiving others in various ways, such as in not admitting to the problem in the first place and pretending to be fine. Such as in stealing or, through underhanded ways to generate money to support the drug and party addiction which can lead to very deceptive behavior, even to the point of stealing from friends and family.

All sorts of addictive behavior is possible with Neptune and how it's configured in this example, from sexual addiction to drugs or relationship… anything that ultimate meaning can be projected upon or the desire to be larger than life or simply because of escapist tendencies, due to an extreme sensitivity to a harsh reality. With such dynamics, Saturn square Neptune, one could be exposed to the streets and could have to learn to get 'street wise' and most probably be deceived and learn to deceive in return, even if just not to be deceived, as a defensive tactic. And, last but not least, the deception of authorities in various ways when one doesn't respect the boundaries and restrictions imposed on one's self by not following the rules and breaking the law in various ways.

Transiting Neptune in the 8th house, conjunct the South Node of the Moon at the time of this assignment, relative to deception, correlates to the need to confront and dissolve a sense of victimization relative to all 8th house dynamics that then, in turn, leads to the individual Soul deceiving itself and others. It is an opportunity to become conscious and aware of dynamics that are preventing a direct perception of truth in any area of life that deception or illusions may be operating. It's a time in which a dissolution of past life egocentric structures and emotional behaviors that are not serving the Soul's purpose any longer can and should be dissolved once and for all.

A time for healing old wounds from past lives carried into and continued to be experienced in this life. A time for forgiving all others for past traumas relative to emotional and psychological abuses of power and betrayals of trust, including forgiving the self for these same reasons and/or releasing guilt that may have accumulated in the emotional body for having hurt others, intentionally or unintentionally. A time to let go of excessive financial security needs, sexual distortions, separating desires that are not in accordance with one's spiritual development and any and all addictions/escapist tendencies that may have been developed in this life or carried over from other lives. A time that can potentially indicate, depending on the native, a desire to unite and merge with the Source Of Creation in such a way as to be able to experience the Source directly, in ways that can prove to the individual Soul and/or others, the deepest possible truths about itself and existence.

EXAMPLE CHART C

Neptune and Deception

Neptune: To Deceive or to be Deceived and Why?

by Kristin

As a result of a response by Rad to a question regarding the Soul's awareness of deception, I chose to focus primarily on deception that occurs at the Advanced Stages of Evolution. Rad writes:

> Deception, being deceived, deceiving, or both, can occur within the egocentric consciousness of the Soul as well as in its subconscious or individuated unconsciousness. As the Soul naturally evolves through the four natural evolutionary states the level or degree of what the Soul is conscious of increases, and that which is unconscious or subconscious decreases. Thus, as the Soul evolves there does come a time in which the Soul is utterly conscious of its own totality in such a way that it's consciousness has no boundary between what it is conscious of, and that which it is not. The Soul has liberated, Uranus, itself from this division within consciousness that most Souls have.

> As the Soul naturally evolves through the four evolutionary states, again, correlates to what degree the Soul is consciously aware of anything including deception, and the underlying causes or reasons of why deception is occurring in the first place.

Even though a Soul may be conscious of its totality in the later stages of evolution, this will not necessarily prevent deception by another, in fact the chances for deception increases the more one evolves. What also occurs as the Soul advances is that, due to their consciousness being wide open, they are also able to see the true potential of another Soul. The Soul in question may show up with the intention, Scorpio, to evolve and to make the necessary changes, but when the temptations of old patterns re-surface, as they always do for any Soul as they will always be tested, there is no guarantee that the Soul won't repeat those patterns of deception.

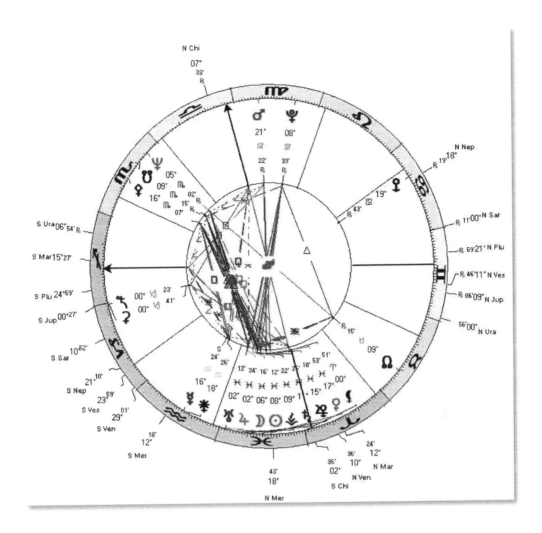

JESUS

Pisces Moon conjunct the Sun, Jupiter, Saturn, Uranus,
and Venus – all in Pisces

South Node in Scorpio conjunct Neptune which trines the Pisces stellium

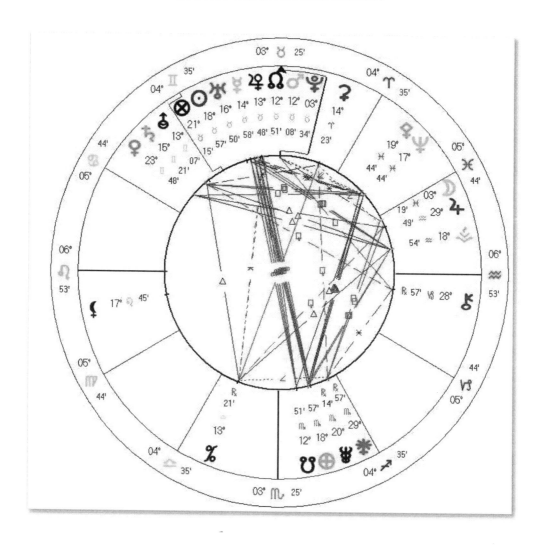

YUKTESWAR

Pisces Moon in the 7th

South Node in Scorpio trine Neptune in Pisces in the 8th

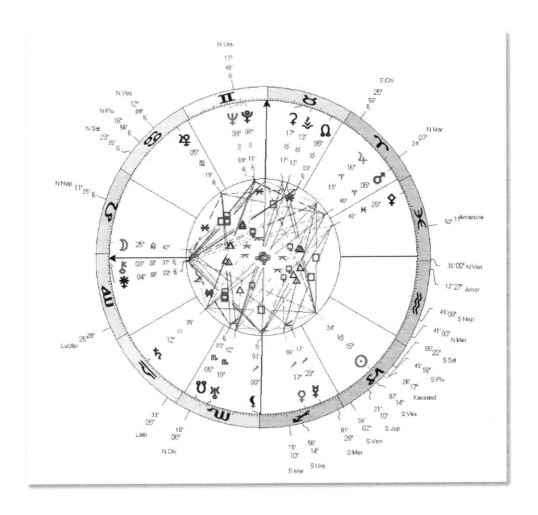

YOGANANDA

Moon in the 12th

South Node in Scorpio conjunct Uranus in Scorpio

Neptune conjunct Pluto

Venus, ruler of his North Node, in the 4th

Mercury, ruler of his Pluto/Neptune conjunction in Gemini, in the 4th

Mars in the 8th, a Scorpio house

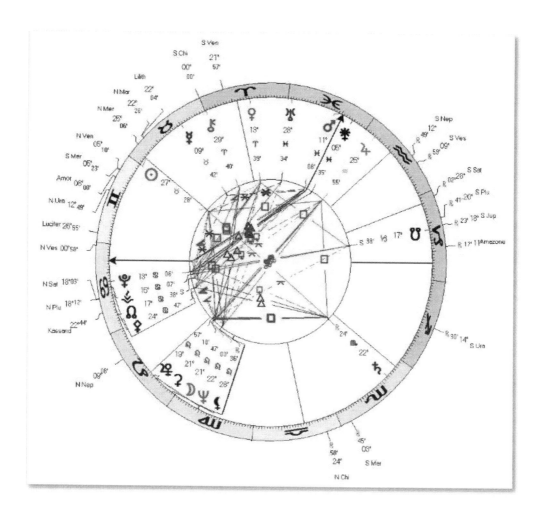

KRIYANANDA

Neptune conjunct Moon

Cancer Ascendant

Pluto in Cancer trining Mars in Pisces

Sun in the 12th

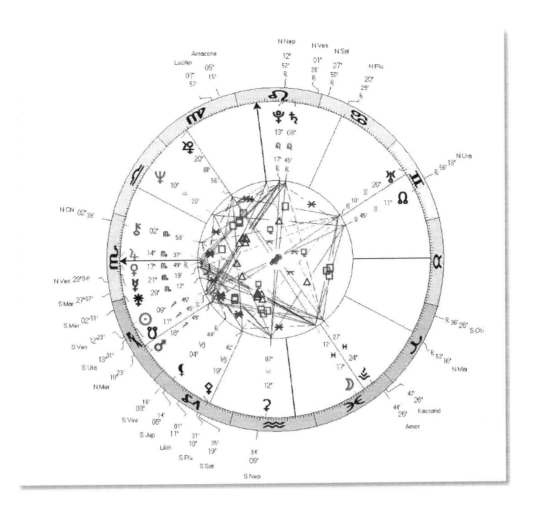

JEFFREY WOLF GREEN

Pisces Moon in the 4th

Neptune trine North Node

Jupiter, ruler of his South Node in Sagittarius, in the 12th in Scorpio

Scorpio Ascendant

Venus in Scorpio

Mercury, ruler of the North Node, in Scorpio

Pluto/Saturn making a balsamic conjunction

It is natural law that the more evolved Soul will inevitably re-meet Souls that have betrayed or deceived them in past lives in order to give them another chance to right the ship, to right the error of their ways. The image of extending the hand down the mountain comes in strong here. The other challenge as a Soul evolves into more advanced stages of evolution is their role to expose, Scorpio, the impurities in another. Even if a Soul in question shows up ready to evolve, most often than not it may require many lifetimes for the Soul to rise to the evolutionary occasion. Once they interface with their own limits, what they first were open to look at in themselves, is commonly turned around and projections are made onto the teacher, blame becomes the name of the game. This is the chance, and thus the risk any advanced Soul must take.

The advanced Soul will be able to see clearly all the broken roads that led up to this point, where the searching Soul turned left instead of turning right, and the temptations that brought them down. The advanced Soul would also see where the Soul had sacrificed itself for the truth and for what was right and just, the times and the turns where real progress had been made. The potential it sees won't be an illusion but a clear picture of what is possible. So whenever a searching Soul has a pure desire to see themselves honestly and with lidless eyes, the advanced Soul has no choice but to give them another chance. I remember JWG saying, "Even if only one Soul makes it after an attempt to help and heal countless others, it will be worth it."

As the Soul advances, there will inevitably be a preponderance of water shown in the chart as I shared in an earlier post in research I was doing looking at Neptune similarities as well as the compelling synastry in the five charts of JWG, Kriyananda, Yogananda, Yukteswar and Jesus. Because evolution occurs through the emotional body, heart, Soul, Spirit, the natural water trinity via Cancer, Scorpio, Pisces, there would be a common theme of strong water, especially Scorpio and Pisces in the advanced stages of evolution as "the river always finds the path of least resistance, the river always finds its way back to the sea," a metaphor for the Soul merging back with God. This would also reflect the liberated consciousness that Rad wrote about, the consciousness without borders or boundaries.

Examples of the Prominent Water

JWG   Pisces Moon in the 4th
Neptune trine North Node
Jupiter, ruler of his South Node in Sagittarius, in the 12th in Scorpio
Scorpio Ascendant
Venus in Scorpio
Mercury, ruler of the North Node, in Scorpio
Pluto/Saturn making a balsamic conjunction

Kriyananda   Neptune conjunct Moon
Cancer Ascendant
Pluto in Cancer trining Mars in Pisces
Sun in the 12th

Yogananda   Moon in the 12th
South Node in Scorpio conjunct Uranus in Scorpio
Neptune conjunct Pluto
Venus, ruler of his North Node, in the 4th
Mercury, ruler of Pluto/Neptune conjunction in Gemini, in the 4th
Mars in the 8th, a Scorpio house

Yukteswar   Pisces Moon in the 7th
South Node in Scorpio trine Neptune in Pisces in the 8th

Jesus   Pisces Moon conjunct Sun-Jupiter-Saturn-Uranus-Venus in Pisces
South Node Scorpio conjunct Neptune trine the Pisces stellium

Let's take the story of Judas for example. We know that Jesus has South Node in Scorpio with Neptune conjunct the South Node in the 11th house. The ruler, Pluto in the 9th in Virgo opposes a choir of planets in Pisces in the 3rd. Jesus was deceived by others he thought were of like mind, those he thought were 'in his camp' which caused him great disillusionment and trauma in times prior to the life of Christ. This was clearly a theme that was being carried through from past lives.

Judas was a disillusioned disciple who betrayed Jesus as he took a bribe for money to turn Jesus in which then led to his crucifixion. Beyond personal greed, Judas did this because he doubted Jesus. He felt himself already somewhat superior to the other disciples and Jesus had put him in charge of the moneybox, which may have boosted his ego. He doubted Jesus on the one hand because of his own sense of superiority and yet he also believed him at the same time. This flip-flop of uncertainty caused him to 'go for the money.' Following his deception, the reality of the magnitude of this betrayal devastated Judas for he knew in his Soul that Jesus was pure, that his teachings were true and that he really was the 'real deal,' so Judas hung himself out of guilt.

Venus, also ruling money, is the lower octave of Neptune and reflects the shadow side of Venus, the greed and the extent of just how low people will go for their own self-interest and survival. It has been written that Jesus saw the betrayal before it happened but he could not interfere with the path, the choice-making and ultimately the karma that would play out for Judas — an example here of a consciousness in Jesus without borders or boundaries.

Jesus said, "It is easier for a camel to go through the eye of a needle, than for a rich man to enter into the kingdom of God." (Matthew 19:24)

It would be essential for any form of deep Spiritual work to occur for a Soul to have a strong Neptune/Pisces influence represented in the chart as the Soul's consciousness would need to be open and without borders. A Soul with this kind of lens would show them not only the potential for what is possible for growth in another but also all they wish they did not have to see.

Another phenomenon that occurs within those of an evolved consciousness is that the Soul is gifted and granted this universal screen of wisdom, seeing through the ages, yet they are limited in what they are able to share for if this knowledge is shared with a Soul who is not 'ready,' this could interrupt their evolution. So they must hold back information, so to speak, for the growing Soul must come to these truths on their own.

The responsibility shouldered at this stage and the truth seen that must be contained is immense and JWG has shared being a lonely experience. The reality that no one can possibly understand what it feels like for the movie screen to continue to play even when he wants to turn it off.

The crazy and delusional PROJECTIONS that are made, like arrows to the heart, inevitably occurs as the Soul advances into 3rd Stage Spiritual. This also reflects the DECEPTION by others, as searching Souls are attracted to the more evolved Souls and tend to want 'what they have' or tend to want to get a piece of them.

In the advanced stages, these teachers are teaching whomever exactly what they need in any given moment even when it could be 'interpreted' in the way it was never intended, doing what needs to be done no matter what, which then leads to projections when a Soul hears something they do not want to hear, even if it is for their own good and necessary for their evolution.

It may appear as if the searching Soul is aligning with the teacher along the way but if it is all stripped down, in more cases than not, these Souls in search of the truth and the light may actually be doing it for reasons of self-interest, money and their own personal needs and agendas.

In extreme cases, this can lead to deception and it is more common than people realize. These signatures in various degrees of advanced stages of evolution can be seen with Venus (lower octave of Neptune) in stress to Neptune, also 7th house-Aquarius/ Uranus/11th.

Other Souls Using Advanced Stage Souls for their Own Ends

JWG   Pisces Moon square the Nodes
South Node 1st / North Node 7th
Ruler of Pisces Moon, Neptune in Libra 11th
– ruler Venus Retrograde rising in Scorpio

Kriyananda Venus in Aries in the 11th square the Nodes
– ruler Mars in Pisces – ruler Neptune conjunct the Moon in Leo

Yogananda Neptune conjunct North Node opposite Venus

Yukteswar Venus square Neptune in Pisces

Jesus   Neptune in Pisces square Venus
Pluto/Mars opposing Venus

Trauma Signatures as a Result of Deception

JWG   Neptune in Libra in the 11th
– ruler Venus Rx in Scorpio square Pluto/Saturn/NN of Neptune as
  well as South Node of Neptune in Aquarius
Uranus opposing Mars and squaring Pisces Moon in the 4th

Kriyananda Venus in Aries in the 11th square the Nodes – ruler Mars in Pisces
– ruler Neptune conjunct the Moon in Leo inconjunct Uranus in
  Pisces

Yogananda Uranus conjunct the South Node in Scorpio which squares South
Node of Neptune in Aquarius and North Node of Neptune in Leo

Yukteswar Nodes of Neptune, South Node Aquarius/North Node Leo squares
his Lunar Nodes as well as Uranus
Uranus conjunct Sun, Mercury, North Node, Mars

Jesus   South Node in Scorpio conjunct Neptune in Scorpio in the 11th
– ruler Pluto opposing Uranus in Pisces
Uranus conjunct Jupiter, Moon, Sun, and Saturn in Pisces

Having strong water signatures and being advanced on the wheel is a blessing and a curse. It is a blessing because it involves a more open consciousness, open to the universal pulse and to personally and naturally know/experience 'God' in a more personal and intimate way, but it also creates a bigger target for others to deceive. The brighter the light the greater the shadow suggesting more of the dark will be attracted to that light therefore pulling in more Souls with ulterior motives.

Souls using People's Ideas for their Own Agendas and Deceiving Others as they do using the Name of God as Justification for their Actions

Consider someone with an 8th house Pluto who wants to feel power by association.

> They have necessarily desired to transform their limitations by forming relationships to anything that symbolized what they needed or desired in order to evolve beyond their personal limitations.
>
> (JWG)

They would be attracted to a teacher who reflects this power and then feel powerful themselves by absorbing these teachings. Take it a step further and put their Neptune in the 10th in Scorpio which squares the South Node of Neptune in the 1st and North Node of Neptune in the 7th, this would then reflect a Soul who claims to feel called forth to put these teachings on the planet, to not respect the natural boundaries from which these teachings came and be totally swept away by their own illusion of who they think they are. They may potentially deceive the very Soul from where these teachings originated, with the rationalization that "God told them to do so," becoming essentially parasites to whatever will make them feel more powerful. There is a limit to what their Souls have the capacity to accomplish and create and so they attach to others who do have it. They often do it "all for the money," Venus, all for the recognition and personal fame.

When they are exposed, the deceivers then see themselves as the victim for they do not have the capacity to see themselves clearly or capable of owning actual motivations for if they do, their world will fall apart. So to save themselves, they claim, it was all 'in the name of God.' Many 8th house Pluto Souls have had prior lives where the rug has been pulled out from beneath them perhaps due to over investing themselves or an over-dependency on another for power, so to put Neptune in Scorpio in the 10th squaring the Nodes of Neptune would make the tendency for deception even greater as they consciously or unconsciously seek revenge.

The evolutionary intention for this Soul in looking at the polarity of Pluto being in the 2nd as well as the polarity of Neptune in Scorpio being in Taurus in the 4th, would equal emotional and financial self-reliance, doing something they can call their own, something that does not require the dependency of another versus parasitic practices in order to feel powerful. It would be critical in the end for this Soul to take responsibility for the reality they created or they will continue to create scenarios where they are kicked to the curb and thrown back upon themselves any time they try and lean on the power symbol for empowerment and personal gain.

There have been a handful of cases in JWG's story as ideas were taken, swiped and stolen by Souls and claimed as their own in other lifetimes. This theme carried through into this life. His South Node of Neptune is in Aquarius, Astrology, in the 3rd, North Node of Neptune in Leo in the 9th conjunct his Pluto and his Saturn. The ruler of JWG's South Node of Neptune in Aquarius is Uranus, in his 8th house opposing his Mars and squaring his Pisces Moon. This Neptune nodal axis is also squared by his Jupiter in the 12th, Scorpio Ascendant, Venus and Mercury all in Scorpio in combination reflecting many lifetimes of betrayal, even being killed for the teachings and truths of genius he brought to this planet, losing his life due to jealousy or people wanting to take him 'out of the game.'

With North Node of Neptune conjunct his Pluto in the 9th, the deception followed by crushing disillusionment was not just a theme from the past but a theme that trailed him into his future even to the point of certain Souls admitting having the desire to 'kill him' because of jealousy or wishing they were him, because of his capacity. The ruler of his North Node of Neptune in Leo is the Sun. His Sun in Sagittarius squares Moon in Pisces, ruler Neptune in Libra in the 11th, trauma. I remember him saying, no matter how many times it happens, the deception and the betrayal, it always feels like the first time. This is a common feeling for anyone with a strong Piscean, Neptunian signature.

For Yogananda, it was in his death where the greatest deception occurred. He wanted Kriya initiation to be always free and he wanted his teachings via books, including correspondence courses to be available to all without anyone owning a copyright. SRF claimed they had a copyright on his work so the organization could make money, South Node in Scorpio with Uranus, squaring Nodes of Neptune, also ruler Pluto is exactly conjunct Neptune to the degree in Gemini in the 10th, being deceived by the organization because of their agenda. Yogananda's Nodes of Neptune, South Node of Neptune in Aquarius in the 6th, and the North Node of Neptune in the 11th house are squaring his own Lunar South Node in the 3rd in Scorpio and his North Node in the 9th in Taurus. The Nodes of Neptune also square Uranus, the ruler of his South Node of Neptune, in his 3rd house.

SRF tried to take Ananda to court over the fact that they had been publishing Yogananda's material, which was Yogananda's wish for all to be able to disseminate the material, and during the court proceedings it came out that SRF never had any copyright at all to anything of Yogananda's for the reason stated above. I was recently listening to an audio of Yogananda and he shared that he never received a salary from SRF, everything that he had was given to him along the way, nothing was in his name. Everything that was given, he shared. This reflecting the highest expression of

Neptune, Unconditional giving and un-attachment to the material world, Pluto conjunct Neptune in Gemini in the 10th, ruler Mercury conjunct Venus in Sagittarius in the 4th, a Soul who honors natural laws of giving and sharing.

It is so common any time either a genius or a highly evolved Soul surfaces for people wanting to piggyback or take a coat tail ride on their Soul, and to spin whatever they have learned and make it their own. You can see this clearly in the chart of Carl Jung, 3rd stage individuated, with his Neptune in Taurus in the 3rd squaring the Nodes of Neptune. Also, Venus the ruler of his natal Neptune, which also rules his South Node in Libra in the 8th are clear symbols for betrayal by others. The theme of others stealing his ideas and trying to make them their own or morphing them into something else also applies here, which is why he was quoted saying, "I am so glad I am not a Jungian." It reminds me of the game of telephone where by the time the message or the teachings makes it all the way through a line of people it comes out discombobulated and not at all the way it was intended, as a result the teachings become distorted and diffused.

On a more evolved note, I wanted to add one of my favorite teachings from *The Autobiography of a Yogi* where Yogananda shares an exchange he is having with his guru Yukteswar relating to the theme of expectation, reflected in the archetype of Venus, the lower octave of Neptune. No Soul is perfect in the human form and although being a deceiver does not occur in the far advanced stages of evolution as their Souls are aligned with God and conscious of their own Soul's totality, there still can be choices made in the human form that may lead to disappointment or the concern for disappointment of others.

Yogananda Master I must have disappointed you by my abrupt departure from my duties here; I thought you might be angry with me.

Yukteswar Wrath springs from thwarted desires. I do not expect anything from others, so their actions cannot be in opposition to mine. I would not use you for my own ends. I am happy in your own true happiness.

Yogananda Sir, one hears of divine love in a vague way but today I am indeed having a concrete example of it from your angelic self! In the world even a father does not forgive his son if he leaves his parents business without warning. But you show not the slightest vexation, though you must have been put to great inconvenience by my leaving many unfinished tasks I left behind.

We looked in each other's eyes where tears were shining. A blissful wave engulfed me; I was conscious that the Lord in the form of my guru was expanding the limited ardors of my heart to vast reaches of cosmic love.

This is something for all Souls to aspire to experience, to be free of expectation, and an example of the upside of Neptune, unconditional love. This reflects an evolved example of a complete inner state of self-reliance. Yukteswar has Pluto, Mars, North Node, Mercury, Uranus and the Sun in Taurus. Also a Soul who is centered in the sea at all times, versus centered in the wave, reflected with the South Node in Scorpio in the 4th trining Neptune in Pisces in the 8th, and Neptune sextiling his strong 10th house Taurus stellium.

EXAMPLE CHART D

Neptune and Deception

Aleister Crowley

by Cat

I decided to use Aleister Crowley in order to investigate how Neptune and the Pisces archetype operate in a chart in relation to deception. Crowley was a well-known occultist, writer, poet, astrologer, painter and philosopher, among other things. In early 20th-century England, Crowley was known as "the wickedest man in the world." Crowley is primarily known for his occult writings and teachings. He founded a religion known as Thelema, which was adopted by the Ordo Templi Orientis (O.T.O.) and the magical order Argenteum Astrum, the Order of the Silver Star. Crowley was a controversial member of the Hermetic Order of the Golden Dawn as well.

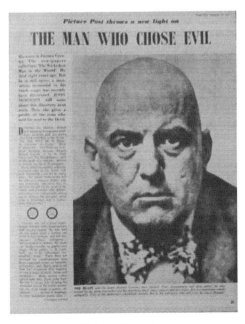

Aleister Crowley

In order to understand Crowley, and why he was considered to be the "the wickedest man in the world," one must take into consideration the time in which he lived. Crowley was born and raised during the Victorian era in England. This was a 'prudish' time in which the expression of emotion and sexuality was publically repressed. Homosexuality and prostitution were both considered to be capital offenses. It was a time in which Evangelical Christianity was very popular. During this period, there was a cultural shift away from rationalism and towards romanticism and mysticism as well. Both spiritualism and occultism grew to be very popular in Crowley's lifetime. The year of his birth was the same year that gave birth to Theosophy. Crowley also lived through both World War I and World War II.

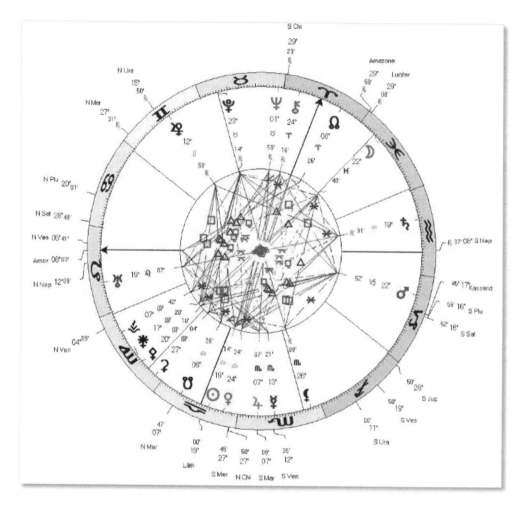

CROWLEY

Crowley was born with:

- Saturn in Aquarius in opposition to Uranus in Leo
- Saturn in his 7th House
- Uranus in his 1st House

- 10th House Neptune is part of a t-square, being opposition Venus in Libra in the 4th House and square Mars in Capricorn in the 6th House
- Pisces is on his 8th House cusp
- Pluto is in his 11th House

It's no surprise that Crowley's lifestyle was considered to be shocking and immoral during the era in which he lived. He was sexually promiscuous, having affairs with members of both sexes, and known to have been involved with prostitutes with whom he engaged in sadomasochistic sexual practices. In addition, he was a drug addict and practiced and promoted sex magic. Many believed him to be a Satanist. Based upon his lifestyle and behavior, I think he was a 2nd stage individuated Soul, rebelling against Victorian era morality and Evangelical Christian beliefs.

Crowley believed himself to be a religious and spiritual being. He was "a systematic and scientific explorer of religious practices, techniques, and doctrines." As such, he performed devotional exercises to Satan as well as to Jesus Christ and the Virgin Mary, to various deities from the Egyptian and Hindu pantheons, to Jehovah as well as to Allah, and to the divine personifications that are unique to the system of Thelema. At one time or another Crowley was an Atheist, a Polytheist, a Monotheist, and a Pantheist, a Satanist and a Christian, a Hindu Yogi, a Hebrew Cabalist, a Muslim Mystic, a Buddhist, and a Pagan. In 1904, he became the Prophet of the New Aeon and the founder of the religious, magical, and philosophical movement called Thelema, through his reception of Liber AL vel Legis, the Book of the Law.

Today it is believed that Crowley was a British Intelligence officer who used the occult to mask his role as a secret agent, or spy. In his book *Secret Agent 666: Aleister Crowley, British Intelligence and the Occult*, Richard B. Spence cites information found in documents from British, American, French and Italian archives to argue that Crowley "was a patriotic Englishman who endured years of public humiliation to mask his role as a secret agent." Crowley is believed to have played a major role in the sinking of the Lusitania, a plot to overthrow the government of Spain, the thwarting of Irish and Indian nationalist conspiracies, and the 1941 flight of Rudolf Hess.

There are two major versions of Crowley's chart floating around. One is calculated for 11:30 pm and comes from *Astrology, Aleister and Aeon* by Charles Kipp. The other is calculated for 11:42 pm. This time is a rectification calculated by Crowley himself. The major differences being whether his Moon is involved in a Yod or a Grand Trine configuration. Being that Crowley has strong Pisces/Scorpio energy (deception/manipulation), I decided to go with the original 11:30 pm version. Crowley's Neptune is in the 10th House, which correlates to one's career or sociological role. Right off the bat, we can see that Crowley was born with the potential to deceive both himself and others through his career or sociological role. One of the many hats Crowley wore was that of an astrologer; I decided to look up his interpretation of Neptune in the 10th House, thinking that it might be autobiographical. According to Crowley:

The native may have brilliant ideas in regard to his business. He will carry them out with great vigor, but only for a time. Then he will forget all about it, only to begin again later on. As business depends so largely upon application, the effect is on the whole, unfortunate. There is also to be considered a good deal of risk from the nature of the business itself. This is likely to be of a queer and unusual character, and there will be many loopholes for fraud; also it is to be presumed that it may be a little difficult at times to keep track of the business. Profits will be irregular and uncertain. There will be a number of bad debts; and the business may also suffer from the occurrence of apparently trivial circumstances, totally unconnected with it. There does not seem to be much risk of a definite smash. The indications are rather those of vicissitudes. The native may feel inclined, again and again, to give it up for something steadier but he will find it hard to relinquish it.

Was he alluding to his career as an occultist, or to being a British spy? Notice the phrase, ". . . and there will be many loopholes for fraud." In either case, Crowley acknowledges that deception or fraud played a role in his career.

Crowley has Pisces on the 8th House cusp, ruled by Neptune in Taurus in the 10th House opposition Jupiter in Scorpio in the 4th House. Here the Pisces archetype meets the Scorpio archetype manifesting in the 10th House of career, the 8th house of sex and intimate others, and the 4th house of home, family and emotional security. There is a potential for deception in each of these areas. This deception may involve the occult, mysticism, psychology, manipulation, sexual practices, drugs, alcohol, or anything considered as being taboo.

In his book, Spence offers a good example:

> Crowley was an adept amateur psychologist, had an uncanny ability to influence people and probably utilized hypnotic suggestion in his undercover work. The other thing he made good use of was drugs. In New York, he carried out very detailed studies on the effects of mescaline (peyote). He would invite various friends over for dinner, fix them curry and dose the food with mescaline. Then he observed and took notes on their behavior. Mescaline was later used by intelligence agencies for experiments in behavior modification and mind control.

Turning to his decision to publicly label himself as 'the Beast' or '666,' Crowley has Leo on the Ascendant, and is known to have loved to call attention to himself. 'The Beat, 666' is what his mother, who was frustrated with his waywardness, called him as a youth. Was it his intention to deceive others by using this name?

Crowley has Cancer on the 12th House cusp, ruled by the Moon in Pisces in the 9th House, trine Mercury in Scorpio in the 4th House and sextile Pluto in the 11th House. Both the Moon and Pluto are quincunx Venus in Libra in the 4th House forming a Yod. Crowley had an emotional need and desire to spiritualize his life by aligning himself with some type of transcendental belief system that would allow him to see or experience himself as an extension of the Source. In addition, the potential to deceive himself in relation to his religious and spiritual beliefs was strong.

It is apparent, through his writings, that Crowley believed himself to possess great occult powers. In April 1904, he wrote *Liber Al vel Legis* or *The Book of the Law*, a book that proclaims that humanity was entering a new Aeon and that Crowley would serve as its prophet. In addition, it introduced a 'supreme moral law' known as "Do what thou shalt be the whole of the law," stating that people should learn to live in tune with their 'true will.' This book and its philosophy later became the foundation of Thelema, a new religion created by Crowley.

Crowley claimed that this book was dictated to him by an entity named Aiwass during his honeymoon in Cairo, Egypt, in April 1904. Transiting Neptune was conjunct his 12th House cusp at this time. It is interesting to note that he and his bride were masquerading (deception) as a prince and princess during their stay in Cairo. On March 18th, 1904, the couple visited a museum in Cairo, in order to view a mortuary statue known as the *Stele of Ankh-ef-en-Khonsu*. It is reported that Crowley was astounded as the exhibit's identification number was 666, the number of the beast, which he likely deceived himself into believing was some kind of sign.

With transiting Neptune conjunct his 12th House cusp, trine his natal Mercury in Scorpio in the 4th House and sextile his Neptune in Taurus in his 10th House, and transiting Uranus conjunct his 6th House cusp (opposition transiting Neptune on the 12th House cusp) trine his natal Neptune, and transiting Venus and Mars both conjunct his natal Neptune, in April 1904, Crowley penned *Liber Al vel Legis* or *The Book of the Law*. He claimed that Aiwass, his guardian angel, dictated it to him and assured his readers that it was not the product of automatic writing, but rather a voice he had heard and originally thought was the god, Horus. Crowley declared this book to be the equivalent of the Christian Bible.

Crowley wrote,

> For these reasons and many more I am certain – I, the Beast, whose number is six hundred and sixty six – that this third chapter of The Book of Law is nothing less than the authentic Word, the Word of the Aeon, the Truth about Nature at this time . . . I must be crucified . . ., but, being lifted up, I will draw the whole world unto me; and men shall worship me, the Beast, Six Hundred and Sixty Six, celebrating to me their Midnight Mass . . . their God in man is offered to me, The Beast, their God.

In April 1904, Crowley became a delusional cult leader, like many before and after him, such as Joseph Smith (Mormonism), L. Ron Hubbard (Scientology) and Mary Eddy Baker (Christian Science) to name a few. He believed himself to be a prophet and justified his immoral lifestyle via *The Law of Thelema* which he deceived himself into believing was a form of higher law. This self-deceit freed him from the emotional burden of Christian guilt. With his natal Chiron in Aries conjunct his natal Neptune in Taurus in the 10th House, this guilt was his deepest wound, which he was attempting to heal in both himself and others, via this massive delusion.

With his Pluto in the 11th House, Crowley gravitated towards like-minded people. His Pluto is sextile natal Neptune in Pisces in the 9th House. He is known to have associated with others who were seeking esoteric knowledge. These are the very people he introduced to his new religion and who helped spread it to other like-minded groups of people throughout the world.

If anyone had the time to read all of his works and study his life via the many biographies written about him, Crowley turns out to be a fascinating study in relation to Neptune and the Pisces archetype. Here we have only scratched the surface. Who was he? A delusional occultist who believed himself to be the prophet of a new religion, or a master spy purposely creating a cover for himself? Maybe a little of both?

One reviewer writes,

> An ancient, mystical, noble, and lofty tradition--namely Rosicrucianism--was infiltrated by the likes of Crowley, for all the wrong reasons. Here was a man whose primary goals were personal pleasure, money, power, and influence at any cost . . . seekers are cautioned to remember that the British government at that time was purposely infiltrating so-called "secret societies" because many influential scholars, artists, politicians, noblemen, and even royals were themselves involved in mystical societies and Rosicrucianism, in its various manifestations. The Brits' goal was information at any price. Crowley, using occult societies as his cover, did spy work far and wide for decades. Be assured, this man is NOT to be taken as a true representative of Rosicrucianism, and in many occult circles, even at the time, was considered a Black Magician.

There is apparently a lot of evidence documenting Crowley's activities as a British spy who traveled around the world on various intelligence assignments, using sex, drugs and magic as his guise. It's way too much to get into here, but if true, proves him to be a master of deception.

Crowley's Pluto, Moon and Venus form a Yod. Pluto in the 11th House sextile the Moon in Pisces in the 8th House, indicates that Crowley's intention and desire was to break free of crystallized and outmoded forms of self-definition by eliminating all external dependencies and learn to become emotionally secure from within. These lessons took place in the realm of sexuality, intimate relationships, the occult, and anything else deemed to be taboo at the time. The potential to deceive himself by believing that his doings in these areas were spiritual was immense. Crowley claimed to have had his first significant mystical experience while on a holiday in Stockholm in December 1896. Several of his biographers point out that this was the same time as his first bisexual encounter. He may have confused or deceived himself into believing that this sexual experience was a mystical experience.

According to JWG,

> The meaning of the inconjunct is to realign your sense of personal identity or ego with a higher will or ego called God, and until you do so you have a crisis equaling the inability to manifest what you sense is a possibility or purpose for your life. The nature of an inconjunct is to teach humility at an egocentric level. The way it teaches the humility is to experience a sense of powerlessness or a core sense of inferiority in which you do not feel you're quite ready or good enough to do what your higher mind is suggesting that you can do; and until the conscious linkage is made with a higher power (we can call that God), you are blocked.

Venus is the apex planet, correlating to one's relationship with oneself and others, as well as one's values and meaning in life. Venus is in Libra in the 4th House, indicating that this would play out on a very emotional and unconscious level, through his relationships with groups and associations that were based upon mystical or occult beliefs and philosophies.

In *Magick in Theory and Practice*, Crowley writes,

> My former work has been misunderstood, and its scope limited by my use of technical terms. It has attracted only too many dilettante and eccentrics, weaklings seeking in "Magic" an escape from reality. I myself was first consciously drawn to the subject in this way.

Is it possible that Crowley's escapades were merely a form of self-deception that served to cover up deep unconscious feelings of inferiority? Did feelings of inferiority and powerlessness inspire him to rectify his chart, ridding himself of this Yod and replacing it with a Grand Trine?

Crowley was blocked from being recognized and acknowledged as the great spiritual leader or genius that he perceived himself to be. Instead he was labeled as a Satanist or Black Magician, both of which he denied being.

Spy or mystic, Crowley spent his lifetime mastering the fine art of deception. He was blocked from being recognized as either a spiritual leader or a master spy in his lifetime. Much of his work has only been recognized as something other than Black Magic and Satanism since his passing. Reading about his life and some of his writings has left me in a Neptunian cloud of confusion in relation to who and what he really was. It is easy to see how anyone, including Crowley himself, can easily be deceived into thinking or believing he was this or that.

EXAMPLE CHART E

Neptune and Deception

L. Ron Hubbard

by Ari Moshe

L. Ron Hubbard

Basic EA Signatures

- Pluto in Gemini in the 7th squaring Sun Mercury in Pisces in the 3rd
- South Node in Scorpio in the 11th
- Jupiter, ruled by Pluto in Gemini in 7th
- Pluto is the ruler of the 12th house
- Pisces rules 3rd house

- Neptune is retrograde in Cancer in the 7th house squared with Venus the ruler of the North Node in Aries in the 4th

- The South Node of Neptune is in Aquarius in the 2nd house square the Lunar Nodal Axis

- The North Node of Neptune is in Leo in the 8th house.

- Lucifer is in Taurus in the 5th

- South Node of Lucifer is in Leo in the 8th square the nodal axis of the Moon

- A developing skipped step of Mars and Uranus in Capricorn in the 2nd house squaring the Nodal Axis

- Uranus is the ruler of the South Node of Neptune also in the 2nd house

- Natal Neptune is in opposition to that Mars and Uranus

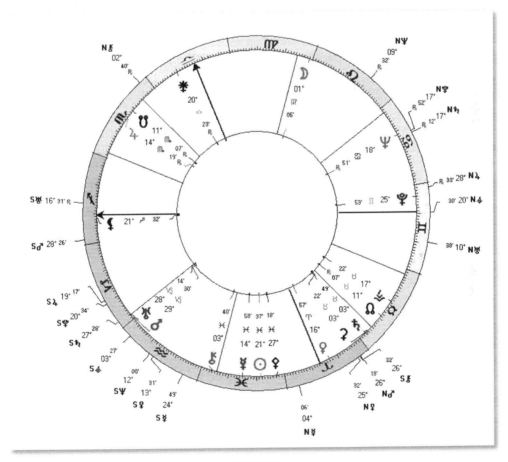

HUBBARD

I'm going to focus both on how this Soul created such widespread deception as well as how his deception affected other people.

There is among the masses a great proclivity to become persuaded and convinced of almost anything. This is because for many Souls the emotional assumptions of goodness in others are simultaneous to a lack of trust in one's direct connection with the Divine. This lack of trusting one's connection leads almost most Souls to be wooed by anyone or anything that offers some sort of inspiration, higher meaning or promise of salvation.

When we find a Soul on the dark side who is acutely aware of human psychology, how to manipulate it, and is concerned only with his own massive gain of power, then we have a Soul that is capable of persuading lots of people to do and become exactly what he wants them to be.

This Soul Hubbard has learned how to appear to other people, how to talk, how to pick just the right words in order to effect a relationship of dependency in which he becomes the one with the power (Pluto in Gemini in the 7th). The square of that Pluto to Gemini in the 3rd with Neptune ruling that in Cancer in the 7th implies that this Soul has known how to speak to other people, to communicate just the right 'logical' constructions of reality to sound completely coherent according to what other people were needing to hear at the time. This made his words and the salvation they offered a deeply safe place to many people who felt that he was a savior and a person to come home to: Cancer in the 7th. His profound capacity to relate to the core of the human experience and to speak about it in ways that all kinds of people can understand is implied in these signatures.

His South Node is in Scorpio in the 11th: he has manipulated groups of people to wield his own power – the rulership by that Pluto in the 7th squaring Pisces in the 3rd indicates just how he did that as described above. With Neptune retrograde ruling all the Pisces in the 3rd, prior to this life he had employed great duplicity and manipulative listening skills in order to get people under his wing. What he promised was power in a distorted 11th house sense: freedom from the limiting conditions of the human experience, psychic skills, telekinesis. He created a cult wherein the people of that cult that considered themselves more liberated, more intelligent and smarter than all the other humans who were still 'programmed.' He claimed that the Scientology process of auditing actually raises one's IQ one point per hour of auditing.

Neptune trines the South Node and his Mercury and Sun in Pisces in the 3rd further emphasizing the great skill of this Soul and how well developed his capacity for deceit has already been prior to his incarnation as Hubbard.

Pluto rules the South Node with Jupiter and also rules the 12th house. Prior to this life, he has had the aspiration to master his mind and understanding of human psychology in order to harness and deepen his own power. He has made himself a de-facto god (Scorpio on the 12th house) by aligning himself with all kinds of symbols of power. He projected that image of being god-like in his relationships: Pluto in the 7th ruling the 12th, Neptune in the 7th.

His North Node in Taurus in the 5th with Venus in Aries in the 4th squaring Neptune in the 7th points to the immense stamina and self-interest this Soul must have had in order to have established the life that he did for himself. It requires one hell of a sense of delusional self-importance/self-worth to construct such a grand life built entirely around manipulation of others, including his own children (4th house Aries, Neptune in Cancer), all for the purposes of his own self gain and glory.

The South Node of Neptune is in Aquarius squaring the Nodes. The bottom line history of this Soul's deceitful nature has been through granting his own self the right to determine how he wished to live – no matter what that looked like – and using the power of mind control (Aquarius relative to Scorpio in the 11th) to brainwash groups of people to give him their money. Scientology was started on the prime basis of a 'genius' (Aquarius) idea on how to make a lot of money (2nd house).

Uranus rules that South Node and is in Capricorn in the 2nd in a new phase conjunction with Mars, approaching a square to the Nodes. He built a very large estate based on the resources he acquired from his followers, from the cult of Scientology. He was on a mission to become wealthy and he succeeded. He also constructed a story about how human beings were seeded with essences that were muddled up by an evil alien named Xenu. Since humans existed, their essences have been 'unconscious.' Scientology processing can make everyone 'clear' and free from the very old alien invasive influence that all humans are subject to.

This theme of 'cleansing' reflects the Virgo/Pisces axis in this Soul's chart in the sense of how he deluded others to follow him on the promise of his own messianic version of salvation. This salvation was based on the core premise that there is something inherently 'wrong' with humans in the first place that needs cleansing (Virgo). Of course, this Soul had Virgo ruling the 9th house: cosmology linking the need to atone or 'cleanse' from something that is dirty and unnatural. Mercury ruling that in the 3rd house with Pisces: he just made these stories up with his imagination.

South Node of Neptune in Aquarius in the 2nd squaring the South Node in Scorpio in the 11th: Alien species seeding a form of intelligence on this planet as a sort of root species that has genetically spread to all groups of humans – and that only a special group of people can be cured of: those who join Scientology (for a massive fee).

This Soul also had Chiron in Pisces in the 2nd house which was in a full phase inconjunct with its ruler, Neptune in Cancer in the 7th. Both Neptune and Chiron trine the South Node. He created great wounding for others by offering himself as a savior to others who were suffering from low self-esteem, and lack of confidence. He made himself a God-like figure who can save and heal them of their issues. Of course, this was just a ploy of self-interest, and he actually depleted people of their self-worth and resources by way of using their weaknesses to further his own gain. This lead to great disillusionment for MANY Souls when they realized that he was a chronic liar. All this points to a core sense of inadequacy within this Soul that over time he learned to overcompensate for.

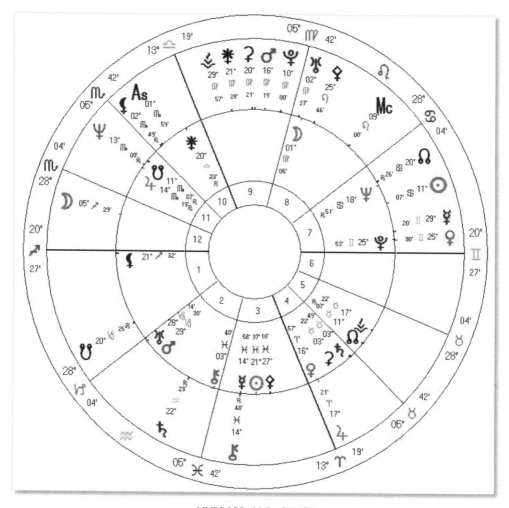

HUBBARD AND CRUISE

He was emotionally immature and needed to have his way, otherwise he would get angry and psychologically manipulative – Venus inconjunct Jupiter/South Node in Scorpio in the 11th. He would present himself as having been taken advantage of quite often whenever other people tried to actually get their own needs met. (Relative to Venus in Aries in 4th in a disseminating square to Neptune in the 7th, he wanted others to be dependent upon him). In such cases, his wrathful selfishness would come out and he would do the kind of thing that people who are identified with the darker aspects of life are generally expected to do: he would poke at other people's greatest weaknesses with blackmail and threats. He did most of this indirectly (11th house). He even did this to his own son. He wanted total control and when his own son (who inherited his same name) began speaking out, he was sued by his father's wife and was threatened and blackmailed and ultimately signed an agreement in a legal settlement.

What I appreciate about this chart is how strongly the mutable archetypes come together to exemplify what Rad spoke about lying and deceit. Hubbard had a Sagittarius Ascendant ruled by Jupiter on the South Node in Scorpio – both of which trine Neptune in Cancer in the 7th. He knew how to lie, to convince others and manipulate people with his magnanimous capacity to explain the truth in deeply convincing and intellectually adept objective scientific terms (Jupiter Scorpio in the 11th) – while that truth itself was nothing other than him drawing upon a bunch of other already well-established scientific constructs and formulating them in such a way as to present exactly what he wanted to present in order to persuade others to join his cult.

He communicated such truths by constructing and putting together 'facts' that were really not facts at all – but to the ignorant mind may as well be truth. His Mercury and Jupiter were in a full phase trine: he knew how to lie well and was quite skillful at duplicitous story telling. This aspect also means he totally KNEW what he was doing. His utter lack of moral concern enabled him to say anything to anyone in order to actualize his own motives. In this sense, he was incredibly successful at deceiving others.

> We are extending to you the precious gift of freedom and
> immortality—factually, honestly. (Hubbard)

Personal sharing: I recall 10 years ago or so I stopped a couple of times in a New York city subway to test out the e-meter which is a device used in Scientology that supposedly 'measures' stress on a subconscious level. I held the metal rods and was asked a bunch of questions by some auditors. This was the general dialog:

> Do you have a sibling that caused you problems at any point? Ok, think about this sibling. Well, this meter is indicating that there is strong psychological impediments from the past. Would you like to clear yourself of this? There is a way…

I have a Mercury/Jupiter conjunction both in a balsamic phase conjunction with Neptune in Sagittarius in the 4th. Pisces Descendant also squares my Nodal Axis. I have definitely held the emotional assumption that people are inherently concerned for the well-being of one another and have wanted to trust what others tell me is true. These signatures for me have implied a lack of discrimination relative to what kind of information I allow myself to take in or not take in – and how other people's constructs have shaped my sense of identity. I did not get very far with those folks, though the appeal of their offer to help me was quite alluring as I was perpetually seeking some sort of higher guidance at that time.

Here's a great quote from Wikipedia that exemplifies the deceitful nature of this Soul:

> After returning from Alaska, Hubbard applied to join the United States Navy. His Congressman, Warren G. Magnuson, wrote to President Roosevelt to recommend Hubbard as "a gentleman of reputation" who was "a respected explorer" and had "marine masters papers for more types of vessels than any other man in the United States." Hubbard was described as "a key figure" in writing organizations, "making him politically potent nationally." The Congressman concluded: "Anything you can do for Mr Hubbard will be appreciated."

> His friend Robert MacDonald Ford, by now a State Representative for Washington, sent a letter of recommendation describing Hubbard as "one of the most brilliant men I have ever known." Hubbard was said by Scientologists to be "a powerful influence" in the Northwest and to be "well known in many parts of the world and has considerable influence in the Caribbean and Alaska." The letter declared "for courage and ability I cannot too strongly recommend him." Ford later said that Hubbard had written the letter himself: "I do not know why Ron wanted a letter. I just gave him a letterhead and said, 'Hell, you're the writer, you write it!'

Thought I'd also share this because it stands out: Tom Cruise is a member of the Church of Scientology. His Neptune is conjunct the South Node and Jupiter of Hubbard: being convinced and persuaded to become more powerful. Interestingly Hubbard's own Neptune is right on Cruise's North Node as well.

CHAPTER SIX

NEPTUNE AND THE GOD COMPLEX

Introduction

One of the archetypes of Neptune correlates to what we can call the 'god complex' wherein the egocentric structure of the Soul can inflate itself, like blowing air into a balloon, to the point of giving itself delusions of egocentric grandeur wherein it convinces itself that it has a 'mission' from on high to bring to the world at large in general, and to specific communities of people specifically. This is what the German philosopher Nietzsche called 'Zarathustra's' or super-humans.

These Souls thus consider themselves as above and beyond most other humans who are, through implication, inferior to their inner delusions of being superior. These types will then construct an inner language within themselves, delusional, in which they convince themselves that they have some ultimate or superior mission to accomplish that is to benefit the whole in general, and their specific communities of people in which they have focused their personal MISSION FROM ON HIGH upon. These communities of people can be anything: the world of art, music, politics, astrology, technologies of all kinds, and so on. And, again, these types of Souls create a language within themselves that reflects these delusions of grandeur, the god complex. Such language can be things like "I am a 'being of light' who desires to be in communion with other 'beings of light,'" or "God has told me to do the following," or "My authority comes from God," and so on.

Of course, human history is full of these types in all fields of endeavor. Insane asylums house Souls who have convinced themselves that they are God or variations of God. And these types of Souls all too often use God as their ultimate rationale for doing what they do: from the serial killer, political figures, religious figures, to all kinds of unseen humans in their ordinary lives. In other words, in worlds large and small the egos of these types of Souls can operate in this way. And when they are confronted by anyone who does not agree with their egocentric delusions of grandeur by way of the god complex they will try to attack and destroy. They all too often create the psychology as a result of the god complex of being a victim to forces of 'persecution' that they convince themselves are trying to destroy whatever their delusional mission from God is about. All too often, they then delude themselves into thinking that 'no one understands me.' When they feel victimized in this way they will then, all too often, resort to creating imaginary realities that are projected onto those forces or others who they judged as to be undermining their god complex, their mission from on high.

Such Souls all too often have a deep inner sense of powerlessness, of being 'nothing,' of an inner existential void, of inferiority that then compensates for this by way of blowing into the ego balloon these delusions of egocentric grandeur. In turn, this then manifests as a deep Soul desire to be recognized for just how wonderful and special they are.

In lesser degrees, any Soul can become intoxicated with itself after some degree of external recognition for something that it has done. The musician who is suddenly famous, the artist, the writer, the actor, the banker, etc. etc. that can then lead to ego inflations. In so doing, they then become superior to others. This is a natural 'temptation' that can occur to a Soul and the ego it creates where temptation as an archetype is Scorpio, 8th house, and Pluto which forms a natural trine to Pisces, the 12th House, and Neptune. When this happens such a Soul and its ego will, at some point, create the necessary crisis that has the intended effect of humiliating the ego to remind the Soul that God is the Origin Of All Things: not the Soul and its pathetic ego.

This temptation of the Soul to glorify itself through its egocentric structure is further symbolized with the North Node of Neptune being in Leo for all Souls on Earth. One of the core archetypes of Leo is to creatively actualize and give purpose to the current life of the Soul. It is ruled by the Sun, which of course is the center of our galaxy. So we can then symbolically see that the temptation of the Soul to glorify itself, to consider itself special, to have some degree of the god complex is reflected in this North Node of Neptune being in Leo. The Soul and its ego then considers itself to be the center of all things in which the rest of life is nothing more than props in its personal play: life. Props to be used for its own purposes, which are rooted in the god complex in some way. Thus, to become some kind of icon in its own way. Such Souls have forgotten that our galaxy is of course only a tiny part of the totality of the entire Universe: the South Node of Neptune being in Aquarius for us all.

A Soul that is truly God inspired, who is in alignment with the inner godhead, will never desire to draw attention to itself, its ego. Such a Soul will always deflect any kind of acclaim back to God and/or others who may have helped in whatever it is that has drawn attention to the Soul/ego for what it has done. Such Souls manifest a sincere and real humility because they are inwardly defined by much larger wholes than themselves, wholes in which they are only one part. Not THE part, but one part. One of the stories I remember about JWG is that so many people wanted to project some kind of 'guru' status upon him wherever he went or was. One of the things he would do in order to stop this was to smoke cigarettes. When he would deliberately light up a cigarette in front of such people he said you could literally see these projections become instantly deflated which, he confided, he took some degree of actual glee in.

As he often said, Souls that actually 'have it' do not want it or even realize that which they have, and Souls that do not have it want it in such a way as wanting to put neon lights around their names: the god-complex. Egocentric delusions of grandeur.

Beyond the individual, this god complex can manifest in whole groupings of people, communities, as well as whole countries where such countries or communities hold some kind of conception of 'God' that is the ONLY CORRECT conception of God. When this is then linked to the human Soul's need to feel secure, where security is a function of self-consistency, we can now understand how 'God' has been used to purposefully destroy other humans, other communities, as well as whole countries. And this is done, always, IN THE NAME OF GOD. 'God' now becomes a WEAPON OF DESTRUCTION. We will go into this further later on.

For now, we will focus on the individual Soul. When this archetype of Neptune, the god complex, is activated, it will manifest through the house and sign of the natal Neptune, and the aspects that it is making to other planets. In the past, prior lives, it can be seen through the South Node of Neptune by house and sign locality, and the placement of its planetary ruler by its own house and sign, and the aspects that it is making to other planets. When this archetype is active, the North Node of Neptune by house, sign, and the location of its planetary ruler will correlate to the future directions of this god complex that are integrated and given purpose in the context of the current life.

Questions and Answers

(Q) Does racism correlate with Capricorn/Saturn/10th and, if it does, could you explain why?

(A) Yes it does. First, the races of people and their skin colors are reflected in the pigmentation of their skin where skin correlates to Saturn, the 10th House, and Capricorn. That pigmentation is caused by a hormone called melanin. This hormone correlates to Neptune, Pisces, and the 12th house that is then co-ruled with Saturn, Capricorn and the 10th House.

An underlying dynamic in all people is one of needing to feel secure: Cancer, Moon, the 4th House. A core dynamic in most humans is to feel secure. To be secure for most people is to be self-consistent. Each race can then feel threatened by other races because each race of people correlate with their own uniqueness defined by that race. That uniqueness in turn creates a psychological and emotional sense of being different as judged, Capricorn, the 10th House, and Saturn, by each race towards all other races. Each race does this. That unique difference then creates a psychological/

emotional sense of being insecure by the sheer presence of other races as judged from within each race towards other races. Those unique and inherent differences then creates a sense of insecurity within race because of the differences of the races.

This then becomes the basis of racism that needs to stamp out the differences of the races in order to feel secure within its own race, its own SKIN. When this natural difference among the races is then further combined with whatever the cosmologies are, their DEFINITIONS OF GOD, this underlying dynamic of insecurity becomes magnified to the point of psychological extremity within those that commit racism. An evil example of this would be Hitler and the Jews. Hitler's Pluto was conjunct his Neptune in the 8th, South Node in Capricorn in the 3rd, which was then ruled by his Saturn in Leo in the 10th. So he made scapegoats of the Jews because of their race, which was then used to fuel his delusions of egocentric grandeur, the God complex, by way of the Nationalism that he created for the German race of people who were considered superior by him, and the German people themselves by extension. In turn, this then created the rationalizations for the wholesale persecution of the Jews, Gypsies, and all others who were considered to be the undesirables where undesirables were created and judged against the standard of 'Arian' perfection.

Lost in racism is the fact that all humans are created by the same SOURCE.

(Q) I read in the EA Glossary that compensation is a Jupiter/Sagittarius/9th dynamic but I'm not seeing why, also relative to the compensation aspect of the God complex. Why Jupiter? I would have thought it could be a Libra dynamic as, for example, a parent who has three kids and loves one more, but tries to re-balance the giving to the other two kids by compensating in various ways.

I also dreamed this night that you were typing with me online, and you told me that the grandmother correlated with Cancer. Thought I'd share that, plus it fits in the realm of Neptune!

(A) Compensation correlates with Jupiter, Sagittarius, and the 9th House because it is linked with the mutable grand cross of Virgo, Pisces, and Gemini. Relative to Virgo, this correlates to any Soul that can feel lack, for example, or being inferior, or a deep inner sense of emptiness, an existential inner void, and so on that then, relative to the Sagittarius, Jupiter, and the 9th House, it compensates for. Compensation can manifest in many ways of course. So this is why the connection then to the 'god complex' and Neptune, Pisces, and the 12th House.

The web of extended family members such as grandmothers, cousins, grandfathers, etc., correlate to Aquarius, the 11th House, and Uranus. Why? Because extended family members are one-step removed from the immediacy of the family which of course is Cancer, the Moon, and the 4th House relative to its polarity Capricorn, Saturn, and the 10th House.

We indeed are writing together right now so in that respect your 'dream' was correct!

(Q) Relative to extended family, it doesn't seem possible to single out, in the chart for example, someone's sister's second child, or is there a way?

(A) Not that I know of.

(Q) And in the case that the person lives with the grandmother, she would then correlate to the Cancer/4th/Moon archetypes?

(A) Yes, but in combination with the Aquarius, 11th House, Uranus archetype where that would be the lead archetype in which the Cancer, etc., is then integrated within.

EXAMPLE CHART A

Neptune and the God Complex
Adolf Hitler

by Skywalker

Adolf Hitler

Adolf Hitler's chart was done in a great way by JWG in Pluto Vol. I. Anyone interested in an in-depth understanding of Hitler's chart should check it out.

Looking at it from a Neptunian point of view relative to his delusional God complex, I think he is a good example, as he was responsible for the death of more or less six million Jews and was also responsible for leading the world into World War II, in which around 50 million people worldwide lost their lives. He had no notion of the limits of what he could and could not do. Hitler had an extreme drive for power, he wanted to create a superhuman race, which he would lead and would go to any measure to achieve his objectives. He set up slave camps in the countries he invaded and exterminated whoever didn't fit the genetic purity he was seeking to create, including Germans with mental or genetic conditions.

Some quotes I found relative to Hitler's God complex:

> Do you realize that you are in the presence of the greatest German of all time?

> I am one of the hardest men Germany has had for decades, perhaps for centuries, equipped with the greatest authority of any German leader... but above all, I believe in my success. I believe in it unconditionally.

> No power on earth can shake the German Reich now, Divine Providence has willed it that I carry through the fulfillment of the Germanic task.

> I know how to keep my hold on people after I have passed on. I shall be the Fuehrer they look up at and go home to talk of and remember. My life shall not end in the mere form of death. It will, on the contrary, begin then.

- South Node of Neptune in the 4th with ruler, Uranus in the 12th in Libra

- Natal Neptune in the 8th

- North Node of Neptune in the 10th with ruler, the Sun in the 7th in Taurus

- Neptune in Gemini in balsamic conjunction to Pluto and both are in a wide inconjunct to the Moon in Capricorn in the 3rd which is conjunct Jupiter and the South Node of the Moon, opposite Chiron

- This conjunction is trine the Sun, Mars and Venus in Taurus in the 7th

- These planets in the 7th are also square Saturn in Leo in the 10th along with the North Node of Neptune which is conjunct Saturn

- Venus, which rules the Sun in Taurus, is Rx

- Uranus, the ruler of the South Node of Neptune is in Libra Rx

- Lucifer in Sagittarius in the 3rd house

- Pisces occupies most of the 5th house and is on the cusp of the 6th

- Virgo and Libra on the 12th

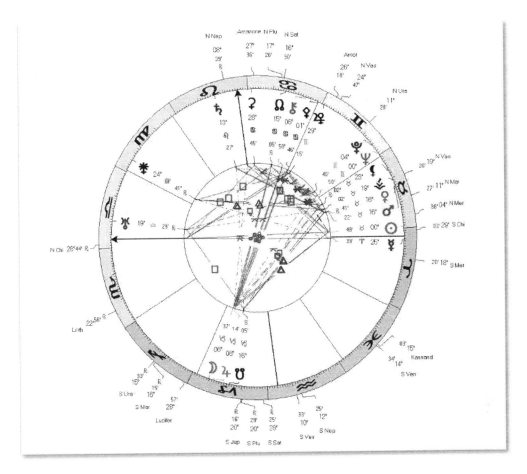

HITLER

Consensus 3 transitioning into Individuated 1

The first thing to look at in this chart would be Pluto in the 8th conjunct Neptune, both in Gemini which correlate to **his huge drive for POWER**. This conjunction shows he is culminating a series of lives in which he dreamt of acquiring a great deal of influence over others. It seems that these dynamics reached a peaking point in his Soul's separating desires. It seems like there were so many things coming to a close, that there were many lives that led up to the life of Hitler, and that these dynamics would not be continued in the lives he was to live after that one. Relative to the stellium with the Moon, Jupiter and the Moon's South Node in Capricorn and the ruler, Saturn in the 10th in Leo, conjunct the North Node of Neptune, we can see the fruition aspect of his mesmerizing ability to communicate and get his ideas across to the general public, an ability that he developed in a series of prior lives, relative to the Pluto/Neptune bottom line.

With these symbols it seems he was in positions of power in past lives and also lost power and authority as, within himself, he needed to learn the limits of personal power (Pluto 8th) and to learn personal humility, which can be seen by the inconjunct between the South Node of the Moon and Pluto. These dynamics coupled with the Nodal axis of the Moon squaring Uranus in the 12th in Libra and Pluto sesquiquadrate Uranus, reflects the shocks his Soul experienced in past lives from others, sometimes even others he was in close relationship with (Libra) due to them and society not accepting his strange ideas. The Moon and Jupiter conjunction, plus the Uranus sesquiquadrate to Pluto, form a de-facto yod pointing at Pluto, indicating the deep humiliation he would experience in the life of Hitler, as his Soul desired to humble itself. He had Lucifer in the 3rd in Sagittarius, trine Mercury in Aries in the 7th. Reflecting how easy it was for him to verbally distort the truth in such a big and convincing way, with the dynamic force Aries can have. With Mars conjunct Venus in the 7th, relative to Pluto/Neptune, he would have the fixed staying power that he did when giving his speeches plus the ability to tell people what they needed/wanted to hear (7th house).

It's clear that the evil influence of the asteroid Lucifer operated by way of his communicative abilities and that he saw himself as someone the country and possibly even the whole world needed, thus adding to his megalomania and God complex. Lucifer is in the 3rd house at the Galactic Center in Sagittarius. This seems to be the perfect symbol for a major distortion of Natural Law, and adds to the use of propaganda to influence others and their beliefs, relative to Pluto/Neptune and his desire for power.

To kill others is probably one of the worst things one can do on a karmic level and, in his case, to be responsible for the death of so many people and to believe in the right to do so is a huge distortion and delusion, reflecting his God complex.

Neptune and Pluto in the 8th in Gemini shows a desire for power and control over people's minds. It is said by some that he was very much into the occult, black magic, NLP, mind control and everything to do with hidden power, which could be used to influence others. It's also said that he was in direct contact with Aleister Crowley, a known occultist and Satanist. It's known that the Nazi's had all sorts of mind control experiments with all sorts of drugs (Neptune/8th) and many other technological or scientific experiments with the desire to get ahead, gain power and influence the minds of the masses, as well as attempting to develop an invincible army that could conquer Europe and maybe even the World. The desire for invincibility on a national level also reflects a desire for personal invincibility, as to him it must of meant to never be in a position of vulnerability or powerlessness again.

He rose to power through verbal, symbolic and written propaganda, with the intention to brainwash and influence the already susceptible German public. The Pluto/Neptune conjunction being balsamic, in the case of Hitler, seems to correlate with a culmination of a long time within his Soul history of desiring to achieve power over others, and thus would have some experience and be open to knowledge of a universal and transcendental nature. With these symbols it's possible that in his speeches or other attempts to gain influence, that he could of used rituals of some kind, subliminally influencing the general public or audience. He also used symbols such as the swastika and the famous Nazi salute with the arm in a very aggressive and domineering position, thus reflecting power. He wanted to convince the people they were capable of anything as a way to feed and continue pursuing the fantasy of unlimited power and expansion, of whatever he desired to conquer.

Saturn is the planet of judgment, and in order for people to feel secure with their way of life, they bind together by a set of defined rules, morals and regulations that makes them feel as if they are conducting themselves in the right way. Many will need to blame others for their own circumstances by finding scapegoats as a way to avoid self-judgment and taking responsibility for their actions. In this way, the ones pointing the finger at 'the boogey man' can justify whatever actions they may have taken or desired to take, since it serves the interest of their society and their attempt to maintain the status-quo. In the case of Hitler and Germany, JWG states that they needed to find a scapegoat to blame the problems the Nation was facing at that time and the perfect scapegoat were the Jews, who were financially successful, and other 'undesirables' who didn't fit into the social structure he wanted to create. With Saturn in Leo in the 10th ruling all that Capricorn energy in the 3rd, including Jupiter and its South Node, plus Lucifer in Sagittarius, it seems Hitler actually believed in his superior race ideas. He surely would of enjoyed being at the top of the pyramid with these symbols and the idea of conquering the world would have appealed to him.

The South Node of Neptune in the 4th and Uranus Rx in Libra 12th seems to correlate with an inner insecurity in relationships relative to rejection and lack of emotional care. With Venus Rx, the lower octave of Neptune, and the ruler of Uranus Rx conjunct Mars and square Saturn, there would be a difficulty in satisfying his sexual desires or even knowing how to act sexually and express himself as it was an area of difficulty from prior lives. There would be a fundamental fear of rejection and under-developed inter-relating skills. He would have to dissolve and heal traumas he endured in past lives relative to relationships and relative to the loss of his siblings and then his mother early on in the life of Hitler, which just added to his coldness. He seemed to have 'frozen emotions,' which would be normal after a lot of emotional trauma and repression.

With the South Nodes of Jupiter, Saturn and Pluto in the 3rd house conjunct his Capricorn stellium and square Uranus, relative to his 4th house South Node of Neptune, it seems that in many past lives he also lost the people who were close to him and ended up totally alone and disillusioned, possibly also due to betrayals (Uranus 12th Libra sesquisquare Pluto/Neptune 8th Gemini), leading in part to his insanity due to intense trauma. In the life of Hitler, with the 7th house Taurus stellium, he would go to extremes to maintain the relationships with the people he truly valued, as was the case with his niece who he forced to accompany him until she killed herself, or his mother whom he stood by until she died, and his one sister who survived. He made his sister change her name in order for her to be 'under cover' and thus to keep her alive, Taurus. The trine from Mars/Venus to the Capricorn Moon/Jupiter/South Node in the 3rd and all the South Nodes therein, leads me to think that his family were the only ones he truly trusted and, as a result, his Soul's evolutionary need to learn about self-reliance, as seen by the PPP in the 2nd, and the current life Sun in the very first degree of Taurus in the 7th, with Venus in Taurus, especially Rx, showing his Soul's desire for utter self-reliance, thus his Soul chose circumstances that would forcibly remove them and all attachments from his life.

Uranus in Libra in the 12th shows the sacrificing of groups of people, the Jewish people and other 'undesirables' in order for him to reach and maintain power relative to Pluto/Neptune in the 8th house and his desire for the genetic purity he sought to create, reflecting his God-like belief in his right to do anything he desired. All these symbols loop back to the 7th house as the planet that rules Pluto and Neptune in Gemini, Mercury, is in the 7th in Aries, and also the ruler of his North Node of Neptune, the Sun is in Taurus in the 7th. All of this when in square to Saturn in the 10th in Leo correlates with his desire to create the reality that he was the supreme authority and leader of the superior race he was to develop.

Thus, he demanded total respect from others. These symbols show how important others actually were for him, as he needed the feedback from others in general, to validate himself and his authority. He needed to associate with others who would promote or support in one way or another, the special feeling of being super-human. With the Moon/Jupiter/South Node conjunction ruled by Saturn in the 10th house, it shows that his emotional self and his actual self-image were all based on his status and ability to be superior to others and command them. If one sees his childhood photographs he is always controlled, very poised and seems to have an air of importance that is observable, as if though he is trying to project an image that shows strength and power.

With these symbols all turning back to the 10th house, we can see his conscious desire and efforts revolved around his ambitions and goals, and to control the lives of as many people as he could. That is one of the reasons he lost the war, because of his insatiable appetite for power (Pluto/Neptune/8th), relative to how his consciousness was structured with Saturn in Leo, reflecting his utter belief in his own authority. Saturn ruling the Moon, Jupiter, and the South Node, means he wanted to realize and manifest his authority, and in doing so, he over-estimated his true leadership abilities (Leo), and the limits of his power (Pluto/8th), leading to his 'fall from grace.' With the Sun and Mars in Taurus ruled by Venus Rx, also in Taurus, he would be so stubborn as to have the potential to challenge the Source of all of creation itself!

Besides the powerlessness and trauma he experienced in prior lives, he also came into this life into a very harsh family environment with a father who was severe and violent with him, adding to his lack of self-worth and feelings of rejection. All these dynamics contributed to the desire to compensate for the inner feelings of weakness and powerlessness that lead to the 'God complex' we are studying. It appears he also believed that, since he survived in certain situations while so many around him perished, at various points in his life, he had some sort of divine protection and was doing God's work.

These planetary combinations also correlate to deep frustration, anger and extreme cruelty, due to such a cold emotional nature that naturally leads to sexual inadequacy and possibly all sorts of sexual distortions due to emotional and sexual repression, partly caused by traumas relative to expectations he projected on others, and also his uptightness, due to a strongly defined sense of repressive morality, developed in prior lives as he gave in to patriarchal ways and further in the life of Hitler, with all that Capricorn Saturn and 10th house energy. The expectations and consequent disillusionment are seen with the South Node of Neptune in Aquarius in the 4th and natal Uranus Rx in Libra in the 12th. His emotional expectations may have simply been too strange or unique for those around him and they were not able to accept or nurture him emotionally. The intent would be for him to learn to be objective about his emotional needs in order to dissolve the traumas from past lives and the current life by forgiving himself and others.

With Uranus Rx in the 12th in Libra, it shows he could be internally rebelling from projected relationship needs on a subconscious level, in order not to suffer more traumas and violations of trust as these dynamics seem to be so deeply ingrained in his Soul's memory. With Neptune conjunct Pluto in the 8th house, in prior lives he would have experienced deep betrayals from others that led to him having the famous rug being pulled from under his feet. I suspect that he could have been subjected to extreme powerlessness in situations such as torture and possibly some sort of brainwashing himself in prior lives with this combination. JWG states he had been in a mental asylum and the symbols fit perfectly.

With the North Node of Neptune in the 10th house conjunct Saturn in Leo, relative to Neptune/Pluto in the 8th, his desire for power would be linked to his social role and he would feel he had a special purpose to accomplish in the life of Hitler. With the North Node of Neptune in the 10th, from a spiritual point of view, he could have been a leader for the common good if he had learnt forgiveness and to surrender to larger forces as seen by Uranus Rx in the 12th with the aspect to Pluto/Neptune. It seems to be a symbol correlating to a need to sacrifice his own individuality in order to serve the needs of others if necessary and, with the ruler of Uranus in Taurus in the 7th, he would have healed himself by learning to give to others. With the North Node of Neptune in Leo in the 10th and the ruler in the 7th in Taurus, he could have been a paternal figure for the nation by adopting values of inclusion instead of judging other races as inferior. He could have given to others what they needed and thus would have been doing the Source's work instead of leading the world into the biggest war ever.

The intended point of evolution was to develop a sense of purpose that could be tied to the national sense of purpose and regain for himself and the nation a creative way of life, with real dignity and respect. After World War I, Germany was not in a good place and his rise to power could have changed that if only he would of thought (Mercury 7th opposite Uranus) of all others to be as important as himself and looked for solutions that were for the benefit of all. Mercury is very important in this chart as it rules his Pluto/Neptune conjunction in the 8th and, by being in Aries in the 7th opposite Uranus, instead of listening and trying to satisfy the needs of others, he probably simply identified what he needed in order to rise to power and maintain power over others.

With Mercury in Aries in the 7th, relative to Pluto/Neptune/8th, we can see that he would desire to initiate contacts with others who could help him gain power. With that planetary combination, it shows that Hitler would go to any extreme, in an aggressive way to influence others. He would attempt to align himself with others who could help him reach his objectives. He would be domineering and use others in any way he desired and possibly agree with them in conversation, without even listening, just in order to get his way if necessary or simply always attempt to dominate verbally. With Venus Rx in Taurus in the 7th, it shows he should have really worked on his own inner relationship to himself and thus learned how to give to himself first and then to others.

The South Node of Chiron is in Aries in the 7th house, indicating deep wounds in his relationships that he carried into his life due to his confrontational nature and, with natal Chiron in Cancer on the North Node of the Moon, opposing the Moon itself, we can see that those wounds would be a real part of his emotional make up when dealing with others. There would be an inability to heal until he would go through an intentional and conscious healing process (Chiron). The North Node of Chiron in Libra, relative to its natal position, shows that to heal the wounds he had acquired over lifetimes, he needed to care for his own emotions and those of others, and in this way he would of initiated his own healing process, instead of going out the way he did.

The square between Uranus and the Nodes show that instead of being an emotional 'rock,' he would need objectivity to balance out his extreme emotions which would seem to range from total repression to intense rage and little in between, besides a zest and optimism related to his accomplishments and conquests.

With the North Node of the Moon in Cancer in the 9th house, conjunct Chiron which is opposite the Moon, relative to all the emotional repression in his life and past lives, he would have needed to learn to heal and expand his emotions and learn to be an emotionally nurturing and caring person. He could have done this by the use of writing (Moon in the 3rd) down his emotions and analyzing them in order to understand mentally where his emotional blocks were and how to release from them. He did end up by writing books but more about his political beliefs and anti-Semitic views. Another way would be simply to verbally communicate his feelings to people he trusted and who cared for him, to open up emotionally and allow himself to cry if necessary and access his feminine side, instead of having so many 'should's and should not's' blocking him from any form of healthy emotional expression.

I have the feeling that Hitler, deep down, actually hated himself (Scorpio 2nd, Pluto 8th, Venus square Saturn) due to past feelings of powerlessness and frustration, and due to his inability to satisfy his needs within relationships, in the life of Hitler and the lives prior. I read that four of his female partners actually committed suicide or attempted to, one of them being his niece, which he stated was the only woman he truly loved. I feel Hitler felt extremely victimized in past lives (Pluto/Neptune/8th plus Uranus/12th) and was already born with a degree of self-hatred and hatred of others, possibly also because of betrayals of trust and cycles of revenge, due to being totally rejected and misunderstood by others, carrying with him an utter and painful feeling of emptiness and probably a very considerable amount of natural guilt as well. With such a severe nature, he must have hurt many others in his Soul's journey. All this just added to his extremely cold and cruel emotional nature, and by way of compensation, to his God complex and delusional sense of grandeur, in the life of Hitler (Pisces 5th).

With the South Node of Neptune in Aquarius in the 4th house he would be coming from lives in which disillusionment led to deep emotional trauma, leaving him fractured and disconnected. With Uranus square the North Node of the Moon in Cancer there would be skipped steps relative to how he related to others due to his inner lack of emotional development and nurturing; he would essentially be very cold as a person due to the traumas endured in other lives and the life of Hitler. I am repeating myself here but there seems to be so much emotional trauma in the history of his Soul that it's worth mentioning. Then with him being a sore loser (Saturn square Mars/Venus relative to Pluto/8th) and channeling all his energy to his social position, he would simply repress all his emotional needs and self in order to carry out his agenda.

Impressively, Hitler had the North Nodes of Mercury, Venus and Mars all in Taurus in the 7th house with the Sun which rules the North Node of Neptune, indicating that the way for him to evolve those archetypes would be through the development of totally self-sufficient relationships, the development of his self-worth and his ability to survive by giving his life a sense of purpose and balance. All these symbols add to the fact his Pluto polarity point is in Sagittarius, in the 2nd house, further adding to his core evolutionary need to ground himself with values that were connected to natural law, to essentially learn what was right from a universal or natural point of view. With Pluto in Gemini and all its aspects, as is observable in the life of Hitler, he was a bit 'crazy' since relative to his intense drive for power, besides the entire trauma he experienced, he would have accumulated all sorts of information over many lives that would have the effect of confusing him on a very deep level. Thus, with all these symbols he would need to ground himself in actual truth (PPP

2nd/Sagittarius) and not just collect data that would serve to boost his power trip by using knowledge to influence and manipulate the minds of the collective. He would have to learn and respect the natural value of life, all of life. With Pluto/Neptune/8th/Gemini, it is also possible that others in positions of power used him and influenced his mind, in prior lives and in the life of Hitler, in order to achieve their own personal agendas while they stayed hidden in the shadows, and let him have the spotlight (Saturn/Leo10th). With Mercury in Aries in the 7th, ruling Pluto/Neptune, it is possible that there were key people such as Crowley or others that fed him with all sorts of ideas or served to stimulate his own dreams and ideas in a passionate way or manipulated him relative to their own agendas.

Mercury in this chart was a way to 'feed' the 8th house bottom line with contacts, information and ideas that could promote the ongoing desires emanating from Pluto. Being conjunct Neptune, it means that there was the desire within his Soul to metamorphose the nature of his dreams, ideals, delusions, in order to realign with actual ultimate reality.

With all that Capricorn energy, ruled by Saturn in Leo that in turn is ruled by the Sun in Taurus in the 7th house, relative to the North Node in Cancer in the 9th, conjunct Chiron, again, Hitler would have needed to soften up emotionally. He would have needed to learn to nurture himself and others with these symbols. Venus is the final ruler of these symbols and being Rx leads to a double signature corresponding to the need to turn inward to learn to relate to himself and satisfy his own emotional needs before being able to relate constructively with others. It seems to correlate in his particular case, to the need to acknowledge these dynamics within himself.

With the Moon conjunct the South Node, he would be reliving old emotional dynamics too, which in his case was a culmination of a cycle of emotional and egocentric development relative to his core evolutionary signature of Pluto/Neptune in the 8th to be all mighty, which led him to develop and refine a personality (Moon) that was highly focused on attaining all that he desired of a social and political nature, and in doing so, he totally repressed the feminine side of the self.

Even with Jupiter conjunct the Moon he wasn't an expansive and jovial type as it is in Capricorn, closing on the South Nodes of Jupiter Saturn and Pluto, which add to the fact that he was culminating so many dynamics within himself relative to his beliefs (Jupiter) which would be of a consensus and status-oriented nature. He would also be re-living dynamics that were very old in his Soul's history, meaning that his mind and thinking (Mercury) were potentially highly conditioned by patriarchal distortions and that his cold ruthless personality was also the result of many lives lived in a state of emotional and psychological repression, in order to focus his energy on his rise to power.

He did attain power in the life of Hitler but his core intentions were not pure enough and Pluto/Neptune/8th/Gemini was essentially metamorphosing the dreams and fantasies he had of attaining power, relative to the sense of victimization and powerlessness that was deep within his Soul, that lead to his God complex.

EXAMPLE CHART B

Neptune and the God Complex
Michael Bloomberg

by Cat

One of the archetypes of Neptune correlates to what we can call the 'god complex' wherein the egocentric structure of the Soul can inflate itself, like blowing air into a balloon, to the point of giving itself delusions of egocentric grandeur wherein it convinces itself that it has a 'mission' from on high to bring to the world at large in general, and to specific communities of people specifically. This is what the German philosopher Nietzsche called 'Zarathustra's' or super-humans. (Rad)

After thinking about this, I decided to use the chart of a powerful American businessperson, billionaire and politician to demonstrate the Neptune archetype manifesting as the 'god complex.' I wanted to use the chart of someone who I believe is well intentioned, but never the less, has a 'god complex.' My subject is Michael Bloomberg.

Michael Bloomberg

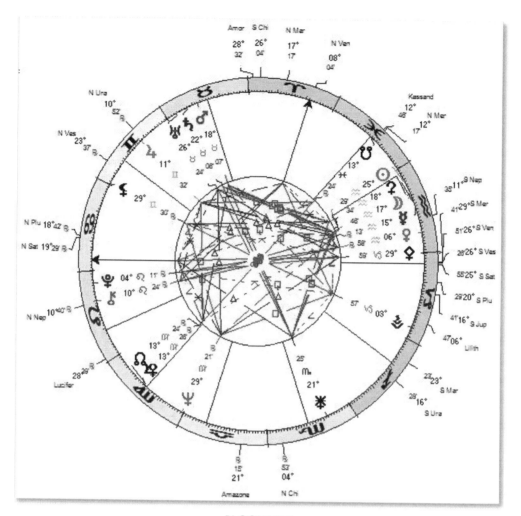

BLOOMBERG

According to his bio, Michael Bloomberg is a ruthless competitor with a hot temper. He is also said to be very compassionate and "deeply serious about the social responsibilities of wealth and privilege." Although he gives over $100 million a year to charity, his critics call him pompous and egocentric. In addition, he has been criticized by many for some of his policies which some see as contributing to the creation of a 'nanny state.'

Outside of New York City, Bloomberg is best known for his attempt to ban the sale of supersized soft drinks. In an article titled, *From soda to guns: Michael Bloomberg's hubris, and the politics of prohibition*, Jeb Golinkin writes:

> Over the last decade, Mayor Bloomberg has transformed himself from a politician dedicated to protecting and empowering consumers to make healthier, better choices, into a self-absorbed lecturer hell-bent on forcing consumers to make the right choice.

Michael Scherer, who writes for Time magazine wrote:

> The cover story of this week's TIME magazine is about what
> Bloomberg will do next, with a clear focus on his enormous wealth
> and his determination to spend it down changing the world to fit his
> vision. We live now in a new age of mega-philanthropy, when newly
> minted billionaires have enormous powers to influence politics and
> how we live our lives.

Michael Bloomberg has Neptune in Virgo in the 3rd House, Pisces on the 9th House
cusp and Cancer, ruled by the Moon conjunct Mercury in Aquarius in the 7th House,
and Gemini on the 12th House cusp. The 'god complex' is a by-product of illusion
and delusion. Here we can see that Bloomberg's opinions, beliefs and point of view,
as well as the information and data he bases them on, may be delusional or nothing
but illusion at best. In other words, when presented with information, he is only
going to acknowledge that which supports his beliefs, ideas and point of view, and
discount or ignore anything that doesn't. He will look at facts and data and imagine
them to support his ideas and beliefs whether they really do or not. In addition, he
initiates relationships with like-minded others who support his views.

Writing about Bloomberg's attempts to ban guns, Golinkin writes:

> Bloomberg, surrounded by people with similar views, appears to
> have fallen victim to the same echo-chamber effect that left so many
> conservatives utterly confused when Barack Obama crushed Mitt
> Romney in November. When you only talk to people who agree with
> you, it becomes easy to mistake your own view for the view of the
> majority of Americans. As a result, Bloomberg has used his position
> and his public profile to castigate anyone who has ever even
> considered opposing the gun control measures he has proposed.

With Neptune in Virgo and Mercury in Aquarius conjunct the 12th House ruler
(Moon in Aquarius) in the 7th House, Bloomberg is an idealist whose demands for
perfection are somewhat unrealistic. He is a visionary thinker who spends his time
and energy thinking about, and imagining, how he can improve the world or
society. He is very opinionated, tends to be out of touch with his emotions, and has
a very specific vision, or view, of how society can be improved and works toward
making these improvements. He is the type of person who likely thinks. "Everything
would be perfect if everyone would just do as I say."

With his Mercury in Aquarius, ruler of the 12th House, conjunct the Moon in
Aquarius in the 7th House, Bloomberg doesn't care for the status-quo, and is not
afraid to speak up against the norm. For the most part, he initiates relationships with
others who share his point of view and speaks up against those who do not. As he
told Time magazine, "A lot of elected officials are afraid to back controversial things.

I'm not afraid of that," he said. "You're not going to hurt my business, and if you are, I do not care. I take great pride in being willing to stand up."

With Pisces on the 9th House Cusp, ruled by Neptune in Virgo in the 3rd House trine Saturn and Uranus in the 11th House, Bloomberg has no problem imagining that his beliefs, moral values and point of view should be enacted into law, especially in relation to issues that pertain to health and the well-being of others. He has attempted to initiate and enact laws that reflect his own personal values and vision of how things should be onto the public with little regard for their freedom to make their own decisions and choices. He seems to believe that the public's welfare is his responsibility and attempts to radically change the system to reflect the way he believes things should be. With Neptune trine Saturn in the 11th House, Bloomberg is under the illusion that he is superior to most others. Although he may not express this in his one-on-one relationships with others, he projects it onto the collective believing that idealistic and radical change will occur in the world if they follow his lead and way of doing things.

Jeb Golinkin writes:

> It all started so well. From his first day in office, Bloomberg dedicated real effort to using laws to improve public health. In 2002, Bloomberg banned public smoking in the city's bars and restaurants. In 2005, he made New York the first city in America to pass a trans-fat ban. Then, in 2008, Bloomberg took the very reasonable and important step of forcing fast food restaurants to post calorie counts on menus.
>
> In 2010, though, Bloomberg shifted from protecting and empowering consumers to coercing them. He lobbied to ban the use of food stamps to purchase sodas and he urged state legislatures to make it more expensive for consumers to purchase sodas by taxing sodas with sugar. In 2011, the mayor banned smoking in most outdoor areas. Whereas providing people with calorie counts gave people the information to make better decisions, the soda tax proposal aimed to punish "bad" decisions. Similarly, where the indoor smoking ban sought to protect "captive audiences" from immediate exposure to secondhand smoke, the outdoor smoking ban aimed to make it harder for people who choose to smoke to actually do so.

After mentioning the Big Gulp Ban, Golinkin continues:

> Telling people they cannot do bad things is more efficient than arming them with the information to make good choices. But

citizens view the two types of legislation very differently, and the further the mayor's legislative agenda moved along the spectrum of coercion, the more the public has begun to wonder whether the mayor was helping them or imposing his preferences upon them.

Bloomberg's Pluto is in Leo in the 1st House sextile Neptune in Virgo in the 3rd House. In addition, the North Node of Neptune is in his 1st house as well. At a core level, he likely feels very insecure and powerless, as well as very special. In order to mask this inner sense of insecurity and powerlessness, he has developed an inflated ego. With the North Node of Neptune in the 1st, the temptation of the Soul to glorify itself is very strong.

Neptune's South Node is in Aquarius in the 7th House and its ruler, Uranus, is conjunct Saturn in the 11th House. In prior lives, Bloomberg was likely a leader of a group of people whom he was responsible for. Having been such a leader in the past, and having Neptune's North Node in Leo in the 1st House in this life, as well as his ascendant and Pluto in Leo in the 1st, it's really no surprise that he has a 'god complex.' He likely has a karmic history of enacting laws and deciding how people should act and behave as it was his responsibility to do so in the past. Neptune's North Node Ruler is the Sun in the 8th House. Here we see that he would be under the illusion that it's his purpose to coerce others into doing things his way.

EXAMPLE CHART C

Neptune and the God Complex
Shabbatai Tzvi

by Ari Moshe

I would like to talk about a very interesting historical figure that exemplifies the archetype of "God complex" or "Messiah complex." This is a man from the 17th century named Shabbatai Tzvi.

Quote from Wikipedia:

In the 17th century, among European Jewry, there was great anticipation of the possibility of a Messiah. In many Jewish communities, the messiah is regarded as an individual that would represent God's plan for salvation: to take all the Jewish people back to their homeland where the Temple would be rebuilt and the "days of old" would be restored.

This collective sense of hope is of course a natural Neptunian dynamic: the collective dream that one day something external (like a messiah) will show up and make everything better. Such projections alleviate the collective from any personal responsibility as it places both the cause of suffering and the alleviation from suffering in something that is beyond personal control.

Shabbatai Tzvi

The yearning for a savior will of course bring forth various individuals that will consider themselves to be a savior that would appeal to those who are calling out for it. The yearning of the Soul to find God outside of itself implicitly creates the expectation for something or someone to magically save the day. This leads to the personal abnegation of one's direct relationship with Source which results in things like disillusionment and anger. The story of Shabbatai Tzvi depicts all of this as this Soul amassed quite a following in his lifetime.

I do not have the birth time of Shabbatai Tzvi, however there are some basic themes in his chart which are consistent and clear regardless, and on which I focus upon here. Rad wrote:

> So we can then symbolically see that the temptation of the Soul to glorify itself, to consider itself special, to have some degree of the god complex is reflected in this North Node of Neptune being in Leo. The Soul and its ego then considers itself to be the center of all things in which the rest of life is nothing more than props in its personal play: life. Props to be used for its own purposes, which are rooted in the god complex in some way. Thus, to become some kind of icon in its own way. Such Souls have forgotten that our galaxy is of course only a tiny part of the totality of the entire Universe: the South Node of Neptune being in Aquarius for us all.

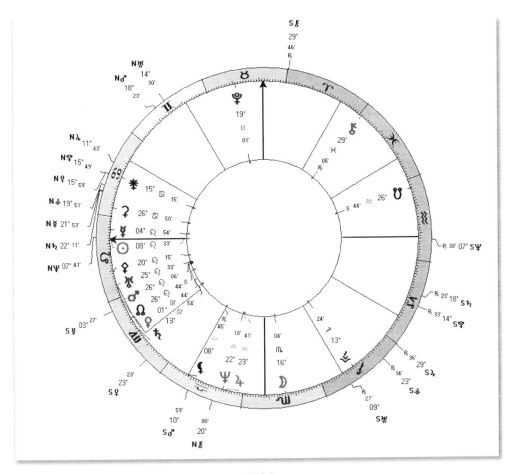

TZVI

Shabbatai Tzvi had Chiron in Pisces in a full phase inconjunct with the North Node in Leo. That right there strongly exemplifies the delusions of grandeur and self-importance within this Soul: to project his own divine importance into the collective sphere and the subsequent wounding that has created for others. The deep Chironic wound within this Soul relates to an inner sense of feeling totally small and meaningless, of not being "somebody." This lead to the need for this Soul to overcompensate: Chiron and Neptune ruling that Chiron with Jupiter.

Shabbatai Tzvi had his own Sun in Leo with Mercury conjunct the North Node of Neptune: special purpose to be a light of salvation for the masses. He also believed he had a divine prophesy to fulfill (Jupiter conjunct Neptune) which he was sure to express to the entire world. He had Pluto in Taurus squaring the Nodes in a first quarter square with the North Node in Leo which is ruled by the Sun and takes us back to the North Node of Neptune in Leo. The Resolution Node is the South Node in Aquarius. This implies that this Soul's inner karmic work was to ultimately humble the inflated sense of importance and be one among many: not the center of many. The evolutionary potential of this Soul was clearly to be in service to the masses, rather than becoming the center of them.

The ruler of the South Node is Uranus which is conjunct Mars and the North Node of the Moon in Leo. That nodal configuration implies that it was karmically quite difficult for this Soul to get out of the trap of being someone special (ruler of South Node conjunct North Node in Leo, ruled by Sun in Leo). This also implies he has created this immense momentum before – to stand out of the crowd a lead a group of people on a special revolutionary purpose, Mars Uranus.

Eventually he and his followers were placed in cherem (excommunication: Uranus) creating massive trauma and further polarization for many of the Souls that followed him. Shabbatai Tzvi declared himself as Messiah on the Jewish new year of 1665 just when Mars was in Leo in the middle of his Leo stellium, opposite transiting Uranus, Chiron and Jupiter in Aquarius.

I'm appreciating this chart because it really focuses on the Nodes of Neptune so intimately woven with the Nodal Axis of the Moon and their rulers. His messianic persona (Neptune Libra: becoming a savior to fit other people's imagined need for a savior) appealed to the minority groups of Jewish people nearly all over the world who were perpetually living in a context of anti-Semitism and persecution. He rallied a sense of activism and purpose for so many Jews.

Eventually Shabattai was forced to either convert to Islam or be killed. He converted and so did many of his followers. Until he died, this Soul consistently adopted a story to fit his changing circumstances in such a way that there was always a "divine" justification for why he was doing whatever he may have been doing at that time. This particular form of duplicitous speech and deceit is indicated through his Mercury in Leo on the North Node of Neptune: always creating some sort of grandiose logical explanation that serves to promote his own specialness, no matter what the circumstances. It emphasizes the delusion of life being a grand stage to play on as one wishes.

This Soul would justify anything he chose to do as de-facto perfect no matter what it was that he did. He did not separate his own individuality with that of a higher power or inspiration.

(Q)   What's unclear to me is if he was actually totally deluded in believing in his own Messiah complex, or if he was being intensely, consciously deceitful. Rad, do you have any insight on that?

(A)   He deluded himself into 'believing' that he was the messiah, yet, at the same time, knew that he was not. So he was at once consciously deceitful yet, at the same time, deluding himself into 'believing' that he was not: a paradox.

CHAPTER SEVEN

NEPTUNE AND DREAMS

Introduction

Neptune, Pisces, and the 12th House correlate to the phenomena of dreams that occurs within the consciousness of the Soul while sleeping. Thus, the phenomena of sleep itself correlates with these archetypes.

Why sleep at all? Why does the consciousness of the Soul need to sleep? The reason is that consciousness in human form is constantly bombarded by all kinds of stimuli on any given day … this stimuli of all kinds of circumstances that the Soul has created, as well as the internal stimuli that goes on at all times by way of thoughts, emotions, inner dialogues and analyses, and so on.

In combination, these stimuli overwhelm consciousness that manifests as feeling increasingly tired. Thus, the Soul needs sleep in order to regenerate itself by way of a relaxed state of consciousness that sleep induces.

Yet, even in the sleep state, the Soul will create what we call 'dreams' within consciousness. The question then becomes, why dream at all? The answer to that question is found by way of examining the three natural types of dreams that are caused within consciousness by the Soul.

(1) The most common types of dreams are non-sensible. These are the types of dreams that mean nothing at all. These types of dreams are the result of all the different types of stimuli that the Soul encounters on any given day. These types of dreams then are a natural way for the Soul to cleanse itself, to repair itself, and to regenerate itself by way of these types of dreams. In essence, the Soul is releasing the results of all the types of stimuli that it encounters on any given day.

(2) Past life dreams. There are two types of past life dreams:

   (a) Dreams that occur over and over, in which a core dynamic that has been caused in prior lives is experienced in a variety of ways on a repeated basis. The images the Soul creates in these types of dreams can be varied and yet that core theme or dynamic from prior lives is replayed over and over. These types of past life dreams occur to the Soul because whatever those dynamics are from the past that are causing these types of dreams has not been resolved. Thus, the Soul causes these types of dreams not only for the self-knowledge they are intended to create, but to also try to resolve those past life dynamics in this way.

(b) A dream that is about a singular past life. In other words 'dreaming' about an actual past life that has occurred for the Soul. These types of dreams will almost always be very dark in nature, not dark in the sense of something ugly, but dark by way of the luminance of the dream itself: it's like looking to see something through a shadow. The reason the Soul can have such a dream is that the very nature of the life that the past life is about will have some direct bearing on the current life being lived.

(3) Super-conscious dreams. Super-conscious dreams are 'dreams' that the Soul can create wherein the Soul is 'transported' to other planes of astral existence such as the astral plane. The Soul will find itself, experience itself, in this other plane of existence in which some kind of super knowledge, transcendent, is given or imparted to the Soul by an entity that is inhabiting that plane of existence. These types of dreams are extremely bright in their luminescence. These types of dreams create an incredible sense of emotional, Soul, well-being while in the dream itself. And, typically, when the Soul then becomes awake, it will either have the ability to recall this dream in total detail or, at minimum, a knowing that it has been 'somewhere else' in which something very important took place. In either case, the Soul upon wakening will have the feeling of a deep depressive moment or moments that can last for some time until the Soul moves into its daily routine for a period of time.

At times, by way of the past life type dreams and/or the super-conscious dreams, when the Soul awakens it does not immediately remember who it is in the context of the current life egocentric structure created for that life that equals the identity for that life. When this happens a typical inner reaction upon waking is "Who am I, and where am I?"

All dreams emanate from the brain stem or the primary brain, which correlates to Pluto, Mars, and the Moon. The 'seat' of the Soul in fact is within the primary brain, or brain stem. The mid-brain by way of the limbic system, Neptune, correlates to our emotional responses or reactions to the dreams. So we can now see the natural trinity that correlates to dreams as symbolized by Pluto, Scorpio, the 8th House; Neptune, Pisces, and the 12th House; and Cancer, the Moon, and the 4th House. By way of the natural interaction of the primary brain through which dreams manifest and the mid-brain and its limbic system, which is pure emotion, we can now understand that when we dream our inner reactions to them occur within the emotional body, the natural trinity. This is intentional by way of the Soul because, in the end, the liberation of the Soul takes place within the emotional body.

The Soul gets its most rest, renewal, by not dreaming at all. When the Soul does not dream this is called absolute sleep. Absolute sleep correlates with Neptune, Pisces, and the 12th House.

Questions and Answers

(Q) Why is it that some people dream in great detail and others do not? For example, if someone ONLY HAS random feeling, imagery and content, what JWG used to call junk dreams, where the Soul is just throwing off all the stimulus from the day, does this say anything about their stage of evolution?

(A) No.

(Q) Could it be true that someone is working through unresolved past live stuff in their dreams but when they wake up, they have zero memory of what went on in the night?

(A) Yes. The working out of the unresolved past life stuff is occurring at a subliminal level: the sub-conscious or, in Jungian terms, the individuated unconscious.

(Q) I assume that for someone to have a super-conscious dream they would need to be at a certain stage of evolution. Is that true?

(A) No.

(Q) Is not the pineal gland also involved in dream activity through secreting melatonin?

(A) Melatonin is the hormone that induces sleep. It also operates in such a way as to have the emotional responses or reactions to the dreams themselves that, again, manifest instinctually from the primary brain or brain stem: the seat of the Soul itself. Melatonin can also give 'color' to dreams.

(Q) Why can it be so difficult at times to remember any dreams for a long period of time, let's say, months, and then at other times, dreams are remembered during a period of time?

(A) There can be many causes for this. Within all the possible causes, there will be one common denominator for this: need. If the Soul is needing to remember or not remember, it will or it won't. So the underlying issue is to determine or figure out what that need is about.

(Q) What could be the reason to be in a dream and then experiencing or perhaps just 'dreaming' that one is pulled between waking up at two different places, from one to the other and back several times, as if one had different yet simultaneous identities/lives where one could wake up at?

(A) This can be an indicator of the Soul creating more than one life at a time.

(Q) Can memories or prior lives that are dreamed be memories of others or of the collective?

(A) No.

(Q) Why could one dream to be on an inhabited 'planet' experiencing a major cataclysm of the whole planet? … or on a giant starship carrying the population of a whole, devastated planet being rescued?

(A) This sort of dream reflects 'content' that the Soul has taken in from various sources that then manifests as dreams of this nature.

(Q) I was wondering if you could speak about dreams wherein one has a dream, or series of dreams, about one's individual future. Is there any different astrological correlations with dreams of this nature? These types of dreams can be symbolic or filled with specific symbolism; there can be a specific emotional presence or theme that is recurring, and also, there can be individuals from the past or who have passed on, who can show up to show a vision of the future. Those are just some types of things that could occur in these types of dreams.

(A) The astrological symbolism of such dreams of course correlates with Uranus. The reoccurring nature of them will generally correlate too and symbolize the Soul's desires, or intentions, to actualize, at some point, that future that is symbolized within these types of dreams in some way that will be assisted in one way or the other by important others.

(Q) "Melatonin is the hormone that induces sleep. It also operates in such a way as to have the emotional responses or reactions to the dreams themselves that, again, manifest instinctually from the primary brain or brain stem: the seat of the Soul itself. Melatonin can also give 'color' to dreams." Is this the role of the pineal gland and melatonin in spiritualization of consciousness?

(A) As the Soul naturally evolves and the consciousness within it expands in ever widening concentric circles reflecting that expansion, melatonin is the hormone secreted from the pineal in direct proportion to that expansion. The determinant for this is desire itself within the Soul. So the more desire the Soul has to expand its consciousness in its ultimate evolutionary journey to return Home to its Source the more the pineal gland secrets this hormone.

(Q) Also, do all Soul desires emanate from the brain stem? Or do they also/only emanate from the chakras that are associated with the different types of desires?

(A) The seat of the Soul for all Souls is the brain stem.

(Q) What is that part of us that seems to be constructed only out of fear and has its own sense of self? I have spoken to others who had the same experience of meeting their "shadow side" too. Maybe the dark side of the Moon or part of Pluto and its resistance?

(A) All fears come from and are enmeshed within the emotional body that the Soul has from within itself. These fears are caused by experiences that the Soul has had at some point and thus constituent emotional memories. It is not uncommon for a Soul to be fragmented from within itself when such emotional memories, and the fears attendant to them, have been severe. When this happens that fragmentation can then cause what you said about having their 'own sense of self.' That sense of 'self' of course are other life identities or egos that the Soul has created in other lives.

This can also occur in the context of a current life when the Soul creates experiences that have such an emotional impact that any fears generated from that can themselves become buried within the consciousness of the Soul as it seeks to contain or repress, Saturn, those experiences/emotions/and the fears that come from them. This is coming from the Soul. Any resistance, Pluto, from accessing and dealing with the emotions that have come from these kinds of experiences, and the fears they create, has its own reasons. This of course can be a very complex dynamic in which the Soul will actually have to DESIRE to unlock. Until such a desire manifests from the Soul, these types of fears generated from the emotional memory of whatever the experiences have been that are responsible for them, will remain. Thus, a seeming 'life of their own.'

(Q) Why would a Soul be fearful of anything once it has realized that God has created it and everything is just experience to progress towards the Source?

(A) Because the Soul is the source of what it has created for ITSELF coming through its own evolutionary times/lifetimes. Thus, any 'future' that the Soul can 'imagine' when linked with unresolved emotional traumas/memories/fears can be PROJECTED into that imagined future.

(Q) Does this also mean that Souls are mostly unaware of their own nature of being a Soul and part of the Source even in the astral realms, until they reach a certain level of evolution? That they are born as kind of "baby Souls" and then gain self-awareness?

(A) Yes.

(Q) I'd like to ask a little about how JWG learnt Astrology in his dreams and how it was a way for him to do God's work. I think it fits really well in the realm of Neptune and I am also personally interested in this. If there is anything you would like to share that could also be beneficial to this discussion, I would appreciate it.

(A) In the early part of JWG'S life, he often said he 'hated' things like astrology. As it turned out, one of the personal lessons for him was to confront his hatreds of whatever including astrology. He wanted to be a reclusive monk in his life. He was living in a monastery, at the time of his second Jupiter return, when he first had a dream wherein he was 'informed' that his life destiny was to be in the world of astrology.

Of course, he was stunned senseless at this dream. At some point, he inwardly asked to be taught astrology, as he knew nothing of it. So for a period of time he then had dream after dream that taught him the correlative nature of astrology to human beings. Along the way, wherever he lived in the world, he would do charts for free in order to apply that which was being received in dreams.

This went on for a period of years until his first Saturn return. On that very day, which was a Sunday as it turned out, he was walking the streets of Seattle, Washington. He noticed a little astrology store that had one bookcase. He looked into the window and the owner spotted him. She opened the door and asked him to come in. This led to a conversation wherein that owner asked him to be the astrology teacher for that store.

Shortly after this is when he had his famous dream wherein the entire EA paradigm was downloaded into him: the entire first book that he wrote in detail. This dream came from the guru of Yogananda whom JWG was very committed to, Yukteswar. Interestingly, Yogananda also very much 'hated' or disliked astrology. Yet Yukteswar was very much involved with astrology, especially what we could call 'galactic astrology.'

As we have learned in this thread, one of the correlations of Neptune is dreams, and the different kinds of dreams we can have including 'super-conscious' dreams. JWG had his Moon in Pisces at 17 degrees. This was exactly Yukteswar's Neptune and Pallas. Yogananda has his Pluto conjunct Neptune, which was conjunct JWG's North Node in Gemini. The ruler of JWG's South Node was Jupiter in Scorpio in his 12th. This was Yukteswar's South Node as well as Yogananda's who also had Uranus on his South Node. Uranus: astrology. This is also the South Node of Jesus which is also conjunct his own Neptune. As an aside, JWG also had a difficult childhood, without going into any detail. He mentioned that one of the ways he got through it was with the mother of Jesus, Mary. She would come to him in 'dreams' then and nurture him in that way. The asteroid 'Mary' is also exactly conjunct JWG's Moon at 17 Pisces.

So we can see through the lens of EA these incredible connections. Again, he wanted to be, as he often said, 'invisible' to the world, to just be a simple monk. Yet he was taught, inwardly, that to do so in that life was to be 'selfish,' a spiritual narcissist really. He was shown in his inner communions that his path was to go into the world and help others in their own desires to go 'home' to their Source: God. To give, and to give without any expectation of reward. Just to give. His North Node was in his 7th House. This is where the astrology came in, but a specific astrology that was to be called Evolutionary Astrology: the language of the Soul. His North Node is also conjunct his natal Uranus in Gemini in the 8th. The symbolism is perfect for what he did in his life.

(Q)   Why Astrology as a vehicle to do the Source's work?

(A)   My answer to that would be specific to EA, not astrology in general. The reason being that EA, as JWG often said, 'is the language of the Soul.' The whole orientation, its bottom line, that JWG taught was rooted in the ultimate origin of the Soul, as well as everything else in the Manifest Creation. Thus, the teaching in EA, which mirrors the teaching of Buddha that was rooted in his own enlightenment, about the nature of desire: the dual nature of. Thus, in the context of EA, the language of the Soul that is rooted in this duality of desires wherein the desire for the Soul to return 'home' to its Originator. So the EA that was 'downloaded' into JWG's dream that came from the guru of Yogananda, Yukteswar, is about the long evolutionary journey of the Soul as defined by desires.

So the EA astrology uses the paradigm of EA to understand the Natural Law of cause and effect that is set in motion by desires to help a client understand the 'why' of her or his life, their own evolutionary journey that leads right back to the Source itself. This is also why JWG called those who do this work "Soul workers" who use the language of the Soul through the prism of EA to help others understand the nature of their own Souls.

(Q)   ". . . communicating with Souls in other planes of existence that are no longer in a physical body, telepathic communions . . ." When people dream, do they always communicate in this way? By reading the mind (no sound in the dream), only telepathic communions? Or does this only happen in certain type of dreams?

(A)   This only happens in what JWG called 'super-conscious' dreams.

CHAPTER EIGHT

NEPTUNE: INSTABILITY OF THE CONSCIOUSNESS OF THE SOUL

Introduction

So now we can add to our ongoing understanding of the totality of the archetypes that correlate with Neptune, Pisces, and the 12th House the potential for the consciousness of the Soul to manifest various neuroses, psychoses, schizophrenia, multiple personality disorders, and total insanity.

When the inherent structural nature of consciousness, which correlates to Saturn, Capricorn, and the 10th House, becomes fractured, the structural integrity that keeps the consciousness stable becomes unstable. The stable nature of the consciousness defined through its inherent structure correlates to the inherent proportions of the physiology of the brain. When this physiology changes in its proportions then the nature of the consciousness changes relative to its inherent design. Neptune, Pisces, and the 12th House specifically correlate to the balance or imbalances of the various physiological substances within the brain. These potential imbalances can be from relatively slight to extreme.

The causative factor in the proportions of the various physiologies within the brain of course is the Soul. Thus, the conditions that the Soul creates for itself coming through its evolutionary time, which reflects its desires, and the consequences of those desires, causes the specific physiology within the brain in each life.

Pluto, Scorpio, and the 8th House correlate to the primary brain. As we just learned, this is where our dreams manifest from. The nature of most dreams seem non-sensical where all kinds of images manifest in a non-structured way. They seem to have a life of their own where the 'dreamer' of the dreams feels unable to change them. The dreams appear or 'seem' to be in charge of the dreamer: a hapless witness who at once is observing and experiencing the emotional effects of the dreams themselves.

When the Soul becomes fractured for whatever reasons, this fracturing will create some degree of trauma. The nature of the trauma(s) then becomes the causative factor in the nature of the dream images. The physiology of these then alters the natural physiological balances of all the various substances within the brain. In turn, this can then lead, in varying degrees, to various neuroses, psychoses, schizophrenia, multiple personality disorders, and total insanity, wherein the egocentric structure that the Soul has created in whatever current life becomes overwhelmed by the unconscious content that then manifests in these ways: like 'dreams' that become the 'reality,' Saturn, for the Soul itself.

It is as if the primary brain that, again, is the seat of the Soul that contains within itself all prior life memories, is pounding on Saturn's door in such a way as to overwhelm that structural control of consciousness in its natural or inherent state. Thus, the inner imagery that comes from this primary brain interacts with the mid brain, Neptune, by way of the limbic system. Here, again, we have the secretion of physiological substances that directly correlate to and trigger emotions. So now we can see that the Soul is reacting to itself by way of the images manifesting from it that have an emotional reaction that now begin to overwhelm the natural or inherent structural nature of the brain by way of the natural proportions of the various physiological substances that keep it that way.

In essence, Saturn correlates to the natural boundary within consciousness that separates the unconscious content of the Soul and its current life reality that is defined by the egocentric structure that the Soul has created for that life. This is the natural structural nature of consciousness. And this is deliberate by way of the Soul, and the Creator of the Soul, so that the Soul can focus on the life at hand, and the intentions for that life which of course reflects its ongoing evolutionary journey. Thus, a natural evolutionary progression can occur for the Soul in a natural way.

When the natural proportions of the various physiological substances within the brain become altered for the reasons we now can understand, this then causes the Soul to IMAGINE, Neptune, 'realities,' Saturn, where what is being imagined by way of the various neuroses, psychoses, schizophrenia, and total insanity is being caused by memories from this or other lives that is projected from within the consciousness of the Soul into its current life circumstances. Again, this can range from being relatively mild to extreme. In all cases, there is an imbalance of the inherent total physiology of the brain. This is why, for example, these conditions of consciousness, in the times we now live in, are treated with drugs, physiological substances, whose intent of course is to stabilize the consciousness within the brain that is being caused by the Soul itself.

From an EA point of view, when any of these conditions occur from within the consciousness of the Soul it is necessary to determine the 'why' of it in order to understand it. This, as we know, is one of the great wonders of EA for it allows the

EA astrologer to play a role that is similar to a detective. An EA detective! Thus, an understanding of the core EA paradigm can provide exactly this understanding because of its detective nature: cause and effect.

Within that EA paradigm there will almost always be a signature that correlates with these altered states of consciousness wherein the inherent physiological substances within the brain are out of balance in some way. This signature can be seen in many ways but the archetype of Neptune, Pisces, and the 12th House will always be indicated by, typically, stressful aspects: squares to Neptune, t-squares to Neptune, oppositions to Neptune, or planets in the 12th House, to the ruler of the 12th House, or to the Nodal Axis of Neptune…can all correlate to this signature.

Questions and Answers

(Q) If the Soul is fractured/traumatized and thus leads to dreams and images that then alter the physiology of the brain in a way that alters a person's structural sense of reality and leads to psychosis, it seems to be a way for the Soul to heal and integrate the fracture itself, and taking chemicals to re-balance the physiology of the brain would seem to counter that intention to heal, by simply treating the symptoms and not addressing the root cause for the psychosis. Is this correct?

(A) I do not think so because in a psychotic state the Soul is now detached, removed, from objective reality in general, and thus the Soul's capacity to objectify itself in that psychotic state. Without an ability to objectify, there really is no ability to heal by way of the causes that has created that psychotic state. Thus, the drugs that are used are meant to stabilize the consciousness of the Soul so that such objectification can take place. For example, the guy who first started the great group *Pink Floyd*, Syd Barrett, had a psychotic break at one point in which he was then hospitalized, and given the drugs to stabilize him. In time, that is what happened, and he was then able, presumably, to carry on with his life because of being able to objectify what had happened to him. In turn, this led to decisions he made for the rest of his life in which he remained stable.

(Q) The chart I found for Syd Barrett is a rectification.

(A) Rectified charts are just guess work in the end remembering that one of the great weaknesses of astrology is to be able to justify and rationalize just about anything relative to symbols used to do so. So if you want to do his chart then simply do a noon chart wherein the heart of your analysis is based on the planets themselves, the signs they are in, and the aspects they make to other planets.

(Q) I have a question regarding the ego, Soul and fear. Where does that fear actually originate? Is it in the Soul itself due to being separate from the Source or in the ego? It seems to be in the Soul itself as the ego has to be a reflection of the Soul or parts of it but I have experienced within myself, while in a very deep meditative state, a kind of fragment of myself that was part of my consciousness. This part of my consciousness was totally fear-based and had a mind of its own or its own ego and was operative below the threshold of conscious perception. It was a huge realization when I discovered that this part of my own self was controlling me via fear and when it was discovered it kind of smiled and lost its power over me. I am not sure what part of us this is. Do you know what I am referring to and what it is?

(A) Everything emanates from the Soul. The ego only reflects that which takes place within the Soul. Fear is an EMOTION. Thus, the emotion of fear, whatever the causes of specific fears maybe, can overwhelm the intellectual body/capacity of the Soul to 'reason' with whatever the fear may be. This is possible of course and fears can be released by way of reasoning. But when the fears are deep and unresolved, especially when linked with traumas that are themselves unresolved, no amount of reasoning will displace those fears. The result is then what is called post-traumatic stress disorder.

(Q) Why would a Soul create a mental illness? What is the purpose of it?

(A) There are so many potential causes for psychological illness in which the 'purpose' of it can only be understood by first understanding that cause or causes.

(Q) If one did not have access to stabilizing medicines, then is the intention of the Soul to just wait it out, until it heals itself, over lifetimes?

(A) The Soul chooses the conditions of any given life for the reasons that are reflected in its own unique evolutionary journey through time. For a Soul to choose to be born into conditions in which there are no stabilizing medicines for whatever psychological illness it has will have its own reasons and causes as to the 'why' of that choice.

(Q) Are there ways the Soul can heal without medicine?

(A) Yes, of course. And that will always be linked with a Soul that DESIRES to understand the causes of the psychological illness that it has. Thus, such a desire then requires the Soul to 'objectify' itself in order to understand those causes wherein such objectification detaches the Soul from its emotional body so that that which needs to be looked into in this way can be seen. In the end, all Souls are responsible for that which they create.

(Q) Is it correct that certain disturbances, imbalances, traumas or memories held within the Soul could manifest such an illness?

(A) Yes.

(Q) Is there some reason why a Soul would remain in this kind of dissociated state of limbo if they didn't have the power to heal or objectify it?

(A) Yes, there are reasons for everything.

(Q) Will each Soul manifest an illness like this at some stage in the evolutionary journey?

(A) No.

(Q) I just don't get it.

(A) The getting of it is to understand that the Source Of All Things has set in motion the natural laws of free choice and desires as determinants in the evolutionary journey of all Souls. When natural laws are perverted through the choice making of Souls this automatically 'disturbs' the natural balance of all Creation where that balance is a function of all the natural laws interacting with one another in a natural way. When that is changed through the perversion to those laws, this natural balance is then disturbed. Thus, that disturbance is then reflected in all the possible ways any Soul itself can become 'disturbed' to the point of manifesting the various psychological states we call neuroses, psychoses, schizophrenia, dissociative personality disorders, and so on.

As an EA exercise, it may be useful for us to examine now the birth charts of Souls who have been diagnosed with the various conditions of neurosis, psychosis, schizophrenia, or total insanity. Once the signature becomes apparent in those charts, it then becomes a matter of trying to understand the evolutionary and/or karmic causes of that condition.

EXAMPLE CHART A

Neptune: Instability of the Consciousness of the Soul
Virginia Woolf

3rd stage Individuated

by Cat

As an experience, madness is terrific I can assure you, and not to be sniffed at; and in its lava I still find most of the things I write about. It shoots out of one everything shaped, final, not in mere driblets as sanity does. And the six months - not three - that I lay in bed taught me a good deal about what is called oneself. Indeed I was almost crippled when I came back to the world, unable to move a foot in terror after that discipline. Think - not one moment's freedom from doctor's discipline - perfectly strange - conventional men; 'You shan't read this' and 'You shan't write a word' and 'You shall lie still and drink milk' - for six months. (Virginia Woolf)

Virginia Woolf was a prolific stream of consciousness writer who was diagnosed as suffering from "manic depressive psychosis," which is a mental illness now known as Bipolar Disorder. When someone suffers from Bipolar Disorder, he or she swings between two mutually exclusive states: one, a severe, disabling depression, and the other, a highly energized enthusiasm. During the enthusiastic state, the individual may get little sleep and can be highly creative, productive and full of ideas. During the depression phase, he or she feels immobilized, worthless and despairing to the point of suicide.

Virginia Woolf

After completing her last novel, *Between the Acts*, Woolf fell into a state of depression and on March 28, 1941, put on an overcoat, filled her pockets with stones, and walked into a river and drowned herself. She left a note to her husband that began,

Dearest, I feel certain that I am going mad again. I feel we can't go through another of those terrible times. And I shan't recover this time. I begin to hear voices, and I can't concentrate. So I am doing what seems the best thing to do . . .

Karmic Axis

Virginia Woolf's Pluto is in Taurus in the 12th House conjunct the South Node in Gemini, ruled by Mercury in Aquarius in the 10th House. Pluto is conjunct Chiron in Taurus in the 12th House. Pluto conjunct the South Node indicates one of three conditions: an evolutionary and karmic reliving condition due to a failure to deal with, or successfully resolve, the issues described by the house and sign; a karmic fruition condition; a life in which both of the first two conditions are in effect. Woolf has stressful and non-stressful aspects to Pluto indicating that she was reliving past conditions as well as experiencing karmic fruition.

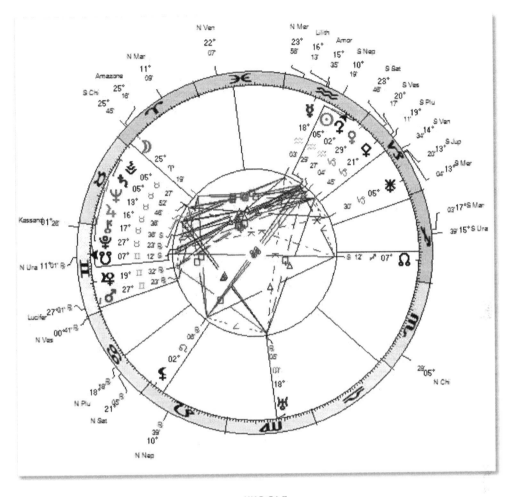

WOOLF

Woolf's prior evolutionary intention and desire has been to align herself with some type of transcendental belief system in order to realize the unity of all Creation, and to see or experience her individuality as an extension of the Source of Creation. In addition, there has been a need and desire to withdraw within herself and internalize her conscious focus in order to discover her own needs and values from within herself. She has been learning how to identify her own personal resources in order to find value and ultimate meaning in her life.

The South Node in Gemini in the 12th House is ruled by Mercury in Aquarius in the 10th House. In order to actualize her Soul's intention and desire in previous lives, Woolf has been gathering information in order to understand who and what she is as well as her place in the grand scheme of things. Self-contemplation and reflection have helped her break free from pre-existing conditions and emotional dynamics that have been limiting her growth in prior lives.

Pluto's Polarity Point is in Scorpio and the North Node is in Sagittarius in the 6th House ruled by Jupiter in Taurus in the 12th House. Woolf's current evolutionary intention and desire is to explore the deepest depths of her being and develop specific and practical methods or techniques through which she can consciously examine and analyze herself. This is necessary in order for her to adjust, change or eliminate any inner dynamics that are creating blockages. In order to actualize this desire, there is a need for some type of practical work that is useful to others and is a reflection of her own need to understand life, and herself, in a cosmological, metaphysical, philosophical or religious context.

Woolf was a self-proclaimed atheist, as well as a natural mystic, possessing an ecstatic consciousness and an awareness of the ultimate reality.

> If life has a base that it stands upon, if it is a bowl that one fills and fills and fills---then my bowl without a doubt stands upon this memory. It is of hearing the waves breaking, one, two, one, two, and sending a splash of water over the beach; and then breaking, one, two, one, two, behind a yellow blind. It is of hearing the blind draw its little acorn across the floor as the wind blew the blind out. It is of lying and hearing this splash and seeing this light, and feeling, it is almost impossible that I should be here; of feeling the purest ecstasy I can conceive. (*Moments of Being*, Virginia Woolf)

Neptune/Pisces/12th House Archetype

- Saturn, Neptune, Jupiter, Chiron and Pluto form a stellium in Taurus in the 12th House

- South Node in Gemini in the 12th House

- 12th House is ruled by Venus in Capricorn in the 9th House

- Pisces is on the 11th House Cusp

- Neptune is in Taurus in the 12th House square the Sun in Aquarius in the 9th House; square Mercury in Aquarius in the 10th House; semi-square Mars in Gemini in the 1st House; and trine Uranus in Virgo in the 5th House

Anatomically, the Pisces archetype correlates to melatonin which is a hormone secreted by the pineal gland in the brain. In addition to regulating sleep cycles and other biological functions, melatonin facilitates spiritual development as its function within the consciousness is to dissolve any and all barriers that the ego has created that are preventing Soul consciousness. In addition, the Pisces archetype correlates with mental disorders that are characterized by an inability to distinguish the difference between illusions/delusions and reality. These disorders are caused by chemical imbalances in the brain that range from slight to extreme.

In addition to important biological tasks, melatonin is responsible for the awakening of kundalini energy. It is possible for kundalini energy to be awakened in both spiritual seekers and those who do not consider themselves to be on a spiritual path. Should this energy be awakened in someone who is unaware of what is happening, he or she can easily become overwhelmed, fragmented, fearful, confused and/or disoriented by the influx of stimuli.

With a preponderance of planets conjunct Neptune in the 12th House, and all of the other planets in her chart, with the exception of Mars, aspecting these 12th house planets, it is very possible that Woolf's brain chemistry may have been out of balance, producing an excessive amount of melatonin triggering the awakening of kundalini leading to spiritual emergencies at various points in her life.

> A spiritual emergency can be defined as a critical and experientially difficult stage of a profound psychological transformation that involves one's entire being. This is a crisis point within the transformational process of spiritual emergence. It may take the form of non-ordinary states of consciousness and may involve unusual thoughts, intense emotions, visions and other sensory changes, as well as various physical manifestations. These episodes can often revolve around spiritual themes. (Spiritual Emergency on Blogger)

Woolf lived in an age in which transpersonal psychology had yet to be developed. She was diagnosed as being manic-depressive (bipolar) and treated with barbiturates and bed rest. It is possible that what was diagnosed and treated as manic-depression may have actually been part of the spiritualization process.

Woolf cycled between states of mania and depression throughout her life. She would first experience a state of mania, followed by a state of depression. Manic psychosis correlates to Uranus and depressive psychosis to Saturn. Woolf's Uranus is in the 5th House in Virgo trine her Neptune in Taurus in the 12th House. Her Saturn is conjunct Neptune in Taurus in the 12th House.

According to her husband, at the early stages of her mania, "She talked almost without stopping for two or three days, paying no attention to anyone in the room or anything said to her . . . Then gradually it became completely incoherent, a mere jumble of dissociated words." As this phase progressed, she began to see friends and family members as her enemies. She became abusive and assaulted them. She refused to eat or drink. She imagined that birds were speaking to her in Greek. Voices in her head told her to do wild things.

- Saturn is in Taurus in the 12th house and is part of a stellium along with Neptune, Jupiter, Pluto, Chiron and the South Node

- Pluto is inconjunct the Moon in Aries

- Jupiter is square Mercury in Aquarius in the 10th House

Saturn correlates to manic depression while Jupiter square Mercury correlates to bipolar or manic-depressive psychological conditions. Jupiter correlates to the right-brain, while Mercury correlates to the left-brain. When these two planets are square they can create what Jeffrey Wolf Green refers to as:

> . . . a maze of competing thoughts and perspectives, resulting in the drive to 'collect' even more information which complicates things further in the form of clarity leading to confusion and vice-versa... If Saturn is involved, this is the specific archetype for manic-depression or a progressive psychology of self-defeat.

Green goes on to point out that stressful dynamics between the rulers of the 10th House and the 4th House correlate to a bipolar condition as well. Woolf's Uranus (10th House Ruler) and Sun (4th House Ruler) are sesquiquadrate. In addition, Jupiter and Saturn are in a stressful phasal relationship, that being a loose balsamic conjunction.

So here we have a manic-depressive archetypal soup with the Neptune/Pisces/12th House archetype being the main ingredient. Themes of liberation, boundaries, emotions, ego, self, identity, dreams, imagination, illusion, disillusionment, delusion, spirituality, distant memories, inner resources, creativity, writing, mysticism, "reality," so on and so forth, come together competing for expression.

> The very act of writing represents at times an attempt to escape the real world, or at other times a sort of coming to terms with herself, with her past, memories, longings, fears. Thus, to Woolf writing became a therapy, a means of exploring the existential labyrinth, a way of finding some equilibrium between swings of mood, an exploration of her inner states in the hope of finding a way out of this labyrinth. 'It is this writing that gives me my proportions,' writes Woolf in her diary, pointing out the fact that the written word is her own way of defeating madness which she defines as 'not having a sense of proportions.' (Cristina Nicolae)

Uranus correlates to one's long-term memories, which includes memories from past lives. Woolf's Uranus is trine her Neptune indicating an ability to tap into memories belonging to the collective or universal conscious as well as her own personal memories. The Soul's purpose in bringing these memories into consciousness is to enable the individual to liberate themselves from any blockages these memories are causing.

In her autobiographical essay, *A Sketch of the Past*, Woolf explains that her novel, *To the Lighthouse* came out "in a great, apparently involuntary, rush … Blowing bubbles out of a pipe gives the feeling of the rapid crowd of ideas and scenes which blew out of my mind." She did not feel that these thoughts were her own, but rather came from somewhere else, "My lips seemed syllabling of their own accord as I walked. What blew the bubbles? … I have no notion."

In the case of someone suffering from manic psychosis, like Woolf, this can be a very intense experience as memory after memory spews into conscious awareness overwhelming the individual. In addition, it can be a very creatively active time, especially when trine Neptune as it allows the imagination a channel of expression.

In Woolf's case this liberating, or deconditioning, process occurs in the realm of her 5th House ruled by her Sun in Aquarius in the 9th House. These memories are released into consciousness for her to examine and analyze (Virgo) by giving them concrete form through artistic expression, which in her case with Uranus quincunx Mercury in Aquarius in the 10th House, was through creative writing. With her Sun in the 9th House, the creative purpose being the expression of spiritual, metaphysical, religious, cosmological or religious themes.

In *The Flight of Mind*, Thomas Caramagno writes,

> Woolf recognized that the manic state stimulated her already rich imagination to create and project fictions that had little basis in reality but that explained (or at least embodied, if obscurely) her experienced moods.

In contrast, a state of severe depressive psychosis would often follow "when reality would hit the morning after one of these mystical, even joyful visions." (McMillen)

In 1932, she wrote in a letter: "My own brain is to me the most unaccountable of machinery—always buzzing, humming, soaring, diving and then buried in mud. And why? What's this passion for?"

Once again, with the strong Neptune/Pisces/12th House signatures in Woolf's chart, her brain likely produced a great deal of melatonin. According to JWG,

> When one consciously begins the journey to truly spiritualize, melatonin is increased within the brain/consciousness in order to dissolve the apparent boundary between the current ego and the Soul. As this occurs, the Soul then becomes increasingly aware,

consciously, of the Source Of All Things: actual inner 'cosmic' consciousness in varying degrees of realization – the Ultimate, the Absolute. As a result of this, when the consciousness is then 'snapped' back to 'normal' reality – life on earth with all that that means and implies – the contrast that one's consciousness is then presented with causes, for many, a transiting state of depression. This depression is caused by the inner knowledge that one must complete whatever the current life is about – the gravity of time and space, mortality, the baggage of the 'body,' the baggage of the totality of what the life is about.

If an individual is not tuned into this spiritualizing process, the melatonin production can become a causative factor in all kinds of neuroses and psychoses.

Referring to her manic-depressive states, Thomas Caramagno writes,

> In her early years, starting at age thirteen, she would alternate from one to the other during her most severe attacks, but just before her suicide was the only time when the severe psychotic depression hit her without the elevated state of mania.

Re-experiencing the Past

We need to remember that Woolf's South Node is part of her 12th House stellium and is conjunct Pluto. In addition to having past life memories burst forth into her consciousness, Woolf had to relive many of them, literally and in her mind through the characters she created in her novels (Pluto/South Node square Mercury in the 10th). With Neptune being an important part of this stellium, sorting out what was real from what was imagination was difficult. In addition, there were no boundaries; they all seemed to dissolve.

> Woolf's psychotic episodes made it hard to separate her thoughts from others' (e.g. hearing voices or, famously, birds singing in Greek), or to be sure of what was real. She was at times violent, delusional, and incoherent. Given her assertion that the life of the mind was the only "real" life, the grip on what she called reality must have felt tenuous. (Richard E. Cytowic)

Woolf's 12th House stellium begins with Saturn at 5 degrees Taurus and ends with Pluto at 27 degrees Taurus. Taking orbs into consideration, every degree of Taurus is involved in this stellium. Whenever a transiting planet aspected any one of the points or planets in her 12th House, all of them joined the play. If you think about it, all 30 degrees are covered by this stellium meaning this stellium and everything it represents was always activated to one degree or another by every planet.

Note that her 12th house stellium does not include any personal planets. (She does not have any planets in Pisces either.) Jupiter, Saturn, Neptune, Pluto, Chiron and Saturn are all here along with the South Node. The only outer planet missing is Uranus, which is in her 5th house, the area in which she channels her creativity as well as her 12th House energies. In simplistic terms, Jupiter in the 12th House brings a love of solitude and a need to be alone. Saturn brings depression and a fear that existence is random and meaningless. Neptune allows her access to the unconscious, as well as the collective unconscious. In addition, it gives life to her inner world and imagination. Pluto in the 12th is the power of creative visualization. The South Node is the past, which is to be re-experienced or re-lived due to its relationship to Pluto (conjunction). Chiron here correlates to emotional wounds from the past. In addition, Chiron in the 12th House correlates with a wounding lingering in the unconscious mind related to a fracture in one's relationship with the Source, or God.

Woolf's Mars forms an exact balsamic semi-sextile with Pluto and her South Node. Mars is in Gemini in the 1st house and describes how Pluto's desires manifest in her life. If you recall, her current evolutionary intention and desire is to explore the deepest depths of her being and develop specific and practical methods or techniques through which she can consciously examine and analyze herself. With Mars in Gemini in the 1st House, she would tend towards independent thinking, questioning everything, and create her own mental constructs independent of what others have taught her to believe. There's a desire to break free from past patterns and create new patterns of being and expressing her individuality. This involves re-living her past and coming face to face with past life memories as the South Node, Chiron, Jupiter, Saturn and Neptune are all part of this equation due to their relationship to Pluto in the 12th House. If you think about this, and everything we have covered up to this point, hers was a "heavy" life. This is especially so with Saturn being part of this equation.

> Meditating on the self-represented a permanent challenge and need to Virginia Woolf in both life and art. Analyzed from this perspective, the characters that animate the world she imagines/remembers are to be seen as reflections/representations of her own search for selfhood, a quest for self-understanding in fact, for it is through writing that Woolf frees herself and keeps a sense of proportions in drawing the boundary between real and unreal, sanity and insanity, life and death. (Cristina Nicolae)

In *Dynamics of the Unconscious*, Liz Green defines depression as:

> . . . an inverted or indirect statement of unexpressed destructive emotions . . . Depression is concerned not only with destructive feelings, but also with separateness and separation, and therefore with mourning, even though there may be no apparent external cause for grief.

With her Saturn in the 12th House conjunct Neptune, it is no surprise that her thoughts and unconscious memories were dark. At the root of her psychosis is an awareness of separateness and of being separated from the Source. This in turn is the cause of her unexpressed destructive emotions, which are in turn caused by a sense of disillusionment.

Saturn, Neptune and Jupiter conjunct in the 12th House create a problem in which Woolf's intuition and imagination are at odds with "reality," resulting in an utter sense of disillusionment. In addition, Saturn conjunct Jupiter correlates to consensus religion while Jupiter conjunct Neptune correlates to intuition, Natural Law and the transcendent impulse.

In an essay about Thoreau, Woolf writes,

> The Transcendentalist movement, like most movements of vigor, represented the effort of one or two remarkable people to shake off the old clothes which had become uncomfortable to them and fit themselves more closely to what now appeared to them to be the realities . . .

implying that this belief system did not resonate with her either as she saw all "realities" to be nothing but illusion.

In *The Waves*, Woolf writes,

> I observed with disillusioned clarity the despicable nonentity of the street; its porches; its window curtains; the drab clothes, the cupidity and complacency of shopping women; and old men taking the air in comforters; the caution of people crossing; the universal determination to go on living, when really, fools and gulls that you are, I said, any slate may fly from a roof, any car may swerve, for there is neither rhyme nor reason when a drunk man staggers about with a club in his hand - that is all.

Woolf's novel *Orlando* is evidence that she perceived life as nothing but illusion and disillusionment. The main character, Orlando begins life in Elizabethan England as a young nobleman. He lives 300 years becoming a contemporary of Woolf's in 1928. She writes in one place, ". . . not only had he had every experience that life has to offer, but had seen the worthlessness of them all. Love and ambition, women and poets were all equally vain."

In another place, she writes:

Illusions are to the Soul what atmosphere is to the earth. Roll up that tender air and the plant dies, the color fades. The earth we walk on is a parched cinder. It is marl we tread and fiery cobbles scorch our feet. By the truth we are undone. Life is a dream. 'Tis waking that kills us. He who robs us of our dreams robs us of our life . . .

In the end, after living hundreds of years, Orlando realizes that he/she is composed of hundreds of selves and experiences, which together combine to form the person he/she is at the present moment.

Once one becomes conscious that life is but an illusion, and does not have a belief system in place to help him or her cope with this ultimate reality, he or she is likely to experience mental problems once the disillusionment sets in. Having actualized her North Node she withdrew within in order to examine and analyze herself, wrote her findings down in the form of novels, essays, letters and diary entries, sharing it with the world.

Woolf was not allowed to write during her breakdowns. She was heavily sedated with barbiturates and force-fed. In *Mrs. Dalloway*, Woolf writes about this experience from the perspective of a character who is a World War I vet suffering from post-traumatic syndrome. Like Woolf, he isolates himself, hears birds singing in Greek and ultimately dies from suicide.

In a note she left for her husband before she died, she wrote:

I feel certain that I am going mad again. I feel we can't go through another of those terrible times. And I shan't recover this time. I do not think two people could have been happier 'til this terrible disease came.

EXAMPLE CHART B

Neptune: Instability of the Consciousness of the Soul
Syd Barrett

Entering the 3rd stage Individuated by a hair

by Kristin

Astrological signatures for SCHIZOPHRENIA

(While no birth time was found, all the themes can still be seen within the planets and their relationships to one another.)

- South Node of Neptune in Aquarius opposing Pluto in Leo inconjunct Venus in Capricorn

- Neptune in Libra square the Nodes

- Neptune in Libra square Venus/South Node of Venus in Capricorn

- Uranus, ruler of South Node of Neptune, is Rx in Gemini

- Uranus Rx, ruler of South Node of Neptune is conjunct North Node of Uranus and opposes South Node Uranus

- North Node of Neptune in Leo is conjunct Pluto

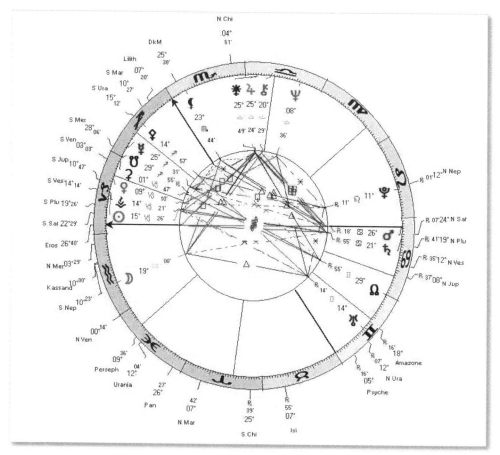

BARRETT

Syd Barrett, a founding member of the band *Pink Floyd* and one of the most legendary rock stars to develop a mental illness, believed to have suffered from schizophrenia according to band members, close friends and mental health professionals. Along with the sheer stress and pressure from his career, this condition was triggered by significant drug use; he was using a wide array of street drugs that were "taken by the shovelful," especially LSD. However, it is believed that the LSD simply compounded an already existing condition.

Syd suffered from a highly stressful early life as his father died a month before his 16th birthday. In his late teens and early twenties, when schizophrenia usually starts in men, Syd began to show the progressions of symptoms that typically define the brain disorder such as odd thoughts, odd behavior and then later psychosis, delusions and vision, bizarre actions, paranoia, disorganized thinking, catatonia and social withdrawal.

Syd Barrett

As the disorder progressed, Syd's personality and social skills changed. For example, the band members talked about how he would stare into space or stare at them as if he was looking right through them. At a concert in San Francisco, he chose to detune his guitar until his strings fell off. Other nights he would simply stand on stage in a catatonic stupor and play the same note over and over. A music magazine once reported that he stood on stage and played the same note, middle C, for the entire duration of the concert.

The alarm bells really began to ring when he locked up his girlfriend for three days, occasionally shoving rations of biscuits under the door. There are symbols suggesting this could well be a re-live as well as he may have been captured himself, Moon in Aquarius conjunct the South Node of Neptune inconjunct a retrograde Saturn/Mars in Cancer. This Moon is also sesquisquare Neptune in Libra. But through the symbols, this also suggests it was his karma of his own doing from a prior time with Pluto in Leo, inconjunct the Sun, its ruler, and opposing his Moon in Aquarius. This Moon is also inconjunct a retrograde Saturn and Mars in Cancer suggesting he was in charge and in control of the pain and trauma he caused others. These symbols reflect extremities on both sides of the trauma equation due to the karma for his own actions. Some of the leftover instincts would still surface. "On one occasion, I had to pull him off Lindsay (Barrett's girlfriend at the time) because he was beating her over the head with a mandolin" (Watkinson & Anderson 2001). Some groupies had locked Syd up in the linen cupboard (which may have mirrored his own cell in another time) when he was on a bad trip which would have only re-activated the trauma from the past. The symbols seen with Neptune in Libra squaring Venus in Capricorn/South Node of Venus in Capricorn suggests surviving in extreme conditions, perhaps small spaces where he was either captured or in hiding with little or nothing to eat. These same stress points to the Moon in Aquarius as well as the South Node of Neptune could also symbolize being forced to watch his own family being tortured and murdered, Pluto in Leo, ruler Sun opposing Mars Rx and Saturn Rx conjunct in Cancer inconjunct Moon and South Node of Neptune in Aquarius.

The flip flopping life from torturer to being tortured is seen with:

- Neptune in Libra squaring Venus/South Node of Venus in Capricorn

- Ruler Saturn Rx is conjunct Mars which opposes the Sun in Capricorn, and forms a yod, inconjuncting the South Node and Mercury in Sagittarius on one side and inconjuncting the Moon in Aquarius on the other side

- Neptune squares the Nodes

- South Node in Sagittarius ruled by Jupiter in Libra (extremes)

The Question Becomes WHY?

Through Geodetics, it shows Barrett having a history in Eastern Europe in the region of Bosnia, Serbia, Croatia, Macedonia and Albania in the quad of the Cancer, Capricorn, Aries, Libra axis that is strongly pronounced in his chart. What we know from this region is that these countries for centuries have been at war due to religious differences as well as harboring an historical hatred for the neighboring races. All of these bordering countries have been at war with one another and even though at times because of proximity and survival they may have needed to learn to live 'together' or near one another, there were so many emotional trip wires that could set either side off at any time.

One wrong move and all would have been blown out of proportion; civil war could have started over something as simple as someone mocking another from the other side. Any Soul born into this cultural experience, who is raised in these environmental settings, would quickly learn who was who, every thought would be colored and ultimately these harsh lines of division would condition every groove in the Soul as this accumulation of violence and brutality builds upon itself life after life. You can see this playing out in Syd's chart with:

- South Node in Sagittarius conjunct Mercury, ruler Jupiter in Libra (extreme) which squares a Saturn Rx conjunct Mars Rx in Cancer

- Saturn/Mars retrograde also opposes his Capricorn Sun, the ruler of his Pluto in Leo

- Also Saturn Rx/Mars Rx form a t-square with Chiron in Libra and the South Node of Chiron in Aries Rx

An example of how this would play out for any culture would be with the intention or desire for ethnic cleansing. Ethnic cleansing is the systematic forced removal of ethnic or religious groups from a given territory with the intent of creating a territory inhabited by people of a homogeneous or pure ethnicity, religion, culture, and history. The forces applied may be various forms of forced migration (deportation, population transfer), as well as mass murder.

All as a result of either feeling that they are of a superior race or else justifying acts of brutality and bloodshed in the name of God, Neptune, their God 'told them' to purge the impure, equaling anyone that was not 'one of us.' Syd's chart suggests violence against other cultures as well as women and children, which explains the haunting look and the horror in his eyes. Being raised in a culture with practices and beliefs such as these conditions and energizes the instinct to defend and if necessary to blow away anyone who crosses the line or threatens their people. Individual villages would even go so far as killing their own if there were signs of their people going to the other side for any reason.

Syd may also have fallen in love with the enemy and there would have been any number of extreme consequences for this if discovered. You can also see within these signatures falling in love with his captor and this dynamic may very well have been playing out when he locked up his girlfriend for three days and fed her rations of food under the door.

The signatures for Schizophrenia are seen with:

- Neptune in Libra (extreme) square the Nodes
- Neptune square Venus/South Node Venus in Capricorn
- Neptune is also inconjunct the Moon in Aquarius and the South Node of Neptune
- South Node of Neptune in Aquarius opposing Pluto in Leo inconjunct Venus in Capricorn
- Neptune in Libra square Venus/South Node of Venus in Capricorn
- Uranus, ruler of South Node of Neptune, is Rx in Gemini
- Uranus Rx, ruler of South Node of Neptune, is conjunct North Node of Uranus and opposes South Node of Uranus
- North Node of Neptune in Leo is conjunct Pluto

The primary reason for this fracturing exists in the fact that there would be no way for him to put together in his brain what occurred in the past, the bloodshed and the violence and to have it make sense, so much so, it would have created an inner insanity as if his Soul was constantly at war, being forced to re-live the scenes of horror from his past.

Drugs was a way of trying to get away from himself but it had a way of unlocking the past.

Guilt

His Soul carries an un-reconcilable guilt for being the torturer, sexual, physical and otherwise:

- Saturn Rx/Mars Rx inconjunct the South Node and Mercury in Sagittarius and forming an inconjunct to Moon in Aquarius in Cancer

- Saturn Rx and Mars Rx also t-square Chiron in Libra and South Node of Chiron in Aries.

These acts occurred as a result of being born into a society or culture, part of a heritage, Saturn Rx and Mars Rx in Cancer opposing a Sun in Capricorn, ruler of Pluto in Leo, where they were raised with the belief that they were the superior religion or race, the extreme and harsh judgments where cruelty and brutality of others occurred as a result.

Syd's South Node in Sagittarius with Mercury in Sagittarius, ruler Jupiter in Libra (extreme), is linked with beliefs, and reflects an aggravation or exaggeration of this theme with Jupiter squaring Saturn Rx and Mars Rx in Cancer reflecting the war symbols, fighting and defending his homeland and doing whatever necessary to extinguish people from neighboring lands that were not 'one of them.' Being that Mars and Saturn are both retrograde suggests in the life of Syd Barrett his Soul would always be inwardly re-living the past and emotionally forced to shoulder the guilt for the lives of other Souls he was responsible for destroying. The Mars Rx reflecting an inversion of the instinct for war and so this energy boomerangs and the war is lived within. Even though he was often described as looking like 'no one was home,' this was in part due to the aftershock of the trauma created but also this inner hell his Soul had to continue to experience. Band member Waters, without overly admitting it, wrote these lyrics of Barrett, "Now there's a look in your eye, like black holes in the sky." Taking it a step further one might write, "I can see all the GHOSTS in your eyes."

I Can't Quiet these Voices in my Head

Rad writes:

> They seem to have a life of their own where the 'dreamer' of the dreams feels unable to change them. The dreams appear or 'seem' to be in charge of the dreamer: a hapless witness who at once is observing and experiencing the emotional effects of the dreams themselves.

Pluto, brain, in Leo, inconjunct Sun in Capricorn, opposes Saturn Rx and Mars Rx. Primary brain is where the dreams manifest- natural trine, Scorpio, Pisces.

North Node of Neptune is exactly conjunct his Pluto, the past karma still catching up with him creating a hysteria, forced to watch with lidless eyes and open ears. Mercury in Sagittarius conjunct his South Node in Sagittarius, ruler Jupiter square Saturn Rx conjunct Mars Rx in Cancer which opposes his Sun in Capricorn. The Sun, together with Venus in Capricorn square Neptune in Libra. Left over voices and left over screams and scenes of bloodshed and pain, and in some cases sexual torture that he was responsible for partaking in. No doubt, the same occurred to him in return. He may very well have been on the receiving end of this torture, sexual and otherwise, as a man or a woman in another life as well with all the gender switch signatures, seen with:

- Pluto in Leo, ruler Sun in Capricorn conjunct Venus in Capricorn conjunct South Node of Venus in Capricorn conjunct South Node in Sagittarius, ruler Jupiter in Libra

- Also the Sun in Capricorn is opposing the ruler Saturn in Cancer Rx which is conjunct Mars in Cancer Rx.

He keeps looking back INTO THE PAST:

- Lucifer is 24 Gemini conjunct his North Node

- The ruler Mercury is conjunct the South Node in Sagittarius and is inconjunct the Saturn Rx/Mars Rx in Cancer

An example of one story that may have played out. In the movie *In the Land of Blood and Honey*, produced by Angelina Jolie, based on a true story, takes place during the war in Bosnia where a Serbian soldier had been in love with a Bosnian woman and she becomes a prisoner in the camp he oversees. The end is most shocking as his love and loyalty to her turns dark because of his tie to his culture, his religion and his people. She is setting up a flat for them to be together and he returns only to shoot her in the head:

- Saturn Rx conjunct Mars Rx opposing Sun in Capricorn, ruler of his Pluto in Leo

- Also Saturn Rx conjunct Mars Rx inconjunct the Moon in Aquarius/South Node of Neptune in Aquarius, ruler Uranus Rx inconjunct Venus in Capricorn

- Uranus Rx is conjunct North Node of Uranus Rx and opposes South Node of Uranus in Sagittarius

An Attempt to Repent

In a life prior to Syd's most recent life, there are symbols reflecting an intent to repent as he chose a life as a monk although it may not have been fully played out:

- His South Node of Venus is in Capricorn and conjunct his natal Venus, also in Capricorn, as well as his South Node in Sagittarius

- These symbols square Neptune in Libra

- Also, Pluto in Leo is forming an inconjunct to his natal Venus and South Node of Venus.

He may have lost his focus and been swept away by love. In a movie I recently watched called *Before the Rain*, a Macedonian monk offers an Albanian girl on the run protection as the Christians hunt for her saying she murdered one of their own. The young Macedonian monk and the Albanian girl ultimately run away together. They get caught by her family but in that moment his life is spared because she explains that he saved her life but when he walks on she runs after him and she is hit in the back by her own brother, murdered before his very own eyes by her family. More heartbreak and trauma as another Soul that he loves is brutally extinguished.

How could being raised in these cultures not taint the Soul? How could this ultimately not cause a Soul to go insane, experiencing the back and forth of this violence and irrational rage, forever torturing others and forever being tortured in return? There would be no way for Syd to reconcile any of it – a prisoner of his own guilt and grief.

Syd Barrett

Dark Side of the Moon

by Pink Floyd

I'm afraid of day and night
I'm breaking into thousand pieces
Hands are touching me, again and again
And I can't defeat myself
Is this only a dream?
Please tell me why!

It's the dark side of the moon
When I see your face in black

Every night, destroying my dreams
I'm crying and try to escape
Cause the pain is unbearable
When you close
The door behind you
I stay alone with my shattered
Dreams and all the pain

It's the dark side of the moon
When I see your face in black

I'm trying to walk away
But I know that you're coming back

And it will happen in the most
Beautiful parts of my dreams
And everything will start again
And I ask you why?

I'm trying to walk away
But I know that you're coming back

It's the dark side of the moon
When I see your face in black

EXAMPLE CHART C

Neptune: Instability of the Consciousness of the Soul

Female – Early 40's – 1st Individuated

by Skywalker

Relevant Planetary Configurations

- Pluto in Libra in the 4th house

- Venus in Leo in the 3rd house

- South Node of the Moon in Cancer in the 2nd house

- North Node of the Moon in Capricorn in the 8th house

- Moon conjunct Saturn balsamic in the 12th house

- Neptune in the 6th house in Sagittarius

- South Node of Neptune in the 8th house in Aquarius

- North Node of Neptune in the 2nd house in Leo

- Uranus in the 5th house in Libra

- Sun in the 4th house in Libra

Aspects

- Sun conjunct Pluto balsamic

- Pluto in Libra conjunct Mars late Virgo balsamic

- Jupiter in Capricorn in the 7th square Mars, Pluto and the Sun

- Moon conjunct Saturn balsamic

- Moon opposite Neptune

- Uranus square the Nodal Axis, South Node is the resolution Node

- Mercury conjunct Uranus balsamic

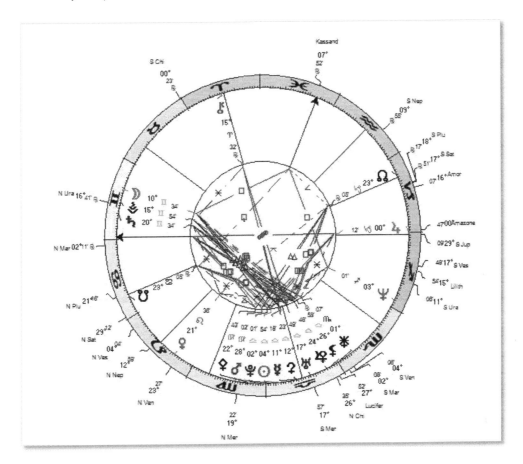

Bipolar Disorder aka Manic Depression

Bipolar Disorder is an emotional/psychological disorder where the person flip-flops in their emotional expression, experiencing one extreme and then the other side of the pole, to go from intense joy and well-being, to deep suffering and depression on a cyclical basis. The person can feel as if they are out of control and insane, that their emotions are too strong for them and end up being scared of the intensity of what they feel. When on the positive side of the emotional experience they can be extremely creative and giving, and when on the depressive side they can experience a very dark or gloomy reality that can very often lead to suicidal thoughts and/or impulses and possibly actions, as a way to end their suffering. It is a debilitating condition and many cannot live "normal" productive lives and take care of themselves. In extreme cases, they may become suicidal as they lose perspective and figure it's the only way out.

Pluto in the 4th house in Libra seems to be the perfect symbol for the Soul being the root cause for the extreme emotional imbalances, correlating to Bipolar Disorder, carried over from past lives of emotional extremes that manifest via potential chemical imbalances in the physiology of the brain in the current life, through stress to the limbic system since it correlates to the Moon, Neptune and Pluto.

This Soul has desired in the past to experience its emotional and vulnerable side with Pluto in the 4th house. This Pluto placement indicates that the desire has been and is to experience life from an emotional perspective, to understand and experience the whole spectrum of emotions and what it is to be an emotional being with sensitivities and vulnerable security needs. Essentially, to learn about emotional security by being secure from within. Further, by being in Libra it shows that she is part of a generation that brings with it the lessons of balance in relationships. Balance between what one gives and receives, between what the individual needs and the other needs and, balance between the individual life and the life of the partner.

With these signatures there seems to be the desire within the Soul to grow and begin a new cycle relative to emotional expression within relationships as shown by natal Pluto being in the 4th house in Libra, indicating a new cycle has recently been initiated in the past which led up to the current life circumstances. With the balsamic conjunction to Mars and the Sun, this planetary configuration indicates that there is a culmination of a long evolutionary progression that will come to a close in the current life as all the circumstances that need to be finished will be experienced whether the person wants to complete the cycle or not. Any form of resistance to this culminating of the cycle of growth and development will be crushed by the evolutionary pressure emanating from her own Soul. That is why in her current life the circumstances have become so intense as we will see by where she is at the present moment in her life by looking at the transits.

As the Soul has been learning and will continue to learn about emotions and inner security, this is where her karmic challenges will present themselves primarily. People with 4th house Pluto's tend to constantly try and find a sense of security and can depend on others for that, especially when in Libra where their needs can be projected onto others in general, but especially those in the family environment or close friends and partners.

What the Soul is trying to do from an evolutionary perspective is to balance out the emotions by being self-secure from within, thus minimizing dependencies and projections onto others which, in the past or in the current life, led to situations of abandonment, betrayals of confidence from those closest and/or to situations in which others were unable to nurture the child's emotional or even physical needs. In extreme cases, the child may experience intense emotional, psychological or physical abuses within the family environment. These potential abuses and abandonment issues, which of course lead to deep wounds within the emotional body, are part of the evolutionary intent to learn about self-determination, a sense of responsibility and maturity. Over a period of time, the Soul and Ego will get tired of being needy and vulnerable, of being insecure or dependent on others in order to satisfy its needs.

By accommodating to circumstances in which the Soul feels secure it can create situations of stagnation and attempt to cling to limiting circumstances or people just in order to feel a sense of consistency which will create evolutionary pressure as the Soul simultaneously desires growth. This evolutionary pressure, if not dealt with by conscious actions towards a metamorphosis of the existing limitations that are preventing emotional growth, will lead to the famous rug being pulled from under the feet of the individual in key periods in his/her life. These emotional cataclysms are the direct result of the resistance to the subconscious desire emanating from the Soul to grow beyond whatever is causing its insecurity and can cause deep fears relative to emotional expression in general as the experiences can be so intense.

The dual desire nature of the Soul is reflected, on the one hand, in the desire to maintain what is perceived as consistent and secure and, on the other hand, the desire to grow beyond whatever it is that is perceived as secure as it is also perceived by the Soul as a limiting factor in some essential way that is at the same time an impediment to its growth. With this combination, Pluto in Libra emotional projections will be channeled towards the parents and certain key people that were symbols of security and were consistent with the child and certain key relationships with others and animals, if present in the environment that, at key evolutionary periods could be forcibly removed or change in their emotional support for the child which would force the child to turn back in on herself for a sense of inner security.

With the conjunction to Mars and the Sun there can be intense confrontations with others even to the point of violence if the sense of security were to be threatened. Emotional outbursts of anger can be a learnt reaction in childhood from others in the environment or a reaction to the environment itself. With this planetary combination, there can also be a genetic predisposition within the family of origin for emotional extremes and other types of personality disorders that, would simply add to others in her environment being unable to nurture her, as she would have to learn emotional nurturing and maturity on her own.

With the South Node in Cancer in the 2nd house and the ruler of both of the Moon's Nodes in the 12th, this can indicate a hiding signature where the child or individual goes to a secret or sacred place where he or she feels secure and isolated/hidden from any potential dangers or threats to her security and survival. This was her tendency as a young child and then she developed escapist tendencies as a teenager with substance abuse which continued as she used medication for the same escapist reasons but justifiable because they were prescribed by doctors.

Within these symbols we also have four indicators of a potential gender switch which in combination with direct observation, leads me to think that this Soul has most probably, very recently switched from male to female. I also considered the possibility of the Soul preparing for a gender switch due to the balsamic conjunction between the Moon and Saturn but, through observation, it would seem more likely that she has just begun to switch from male to female. This can be a prime indication of hormonal imbalances as the Soul does not feel quite at home (4th house) within the current physical structure that contains it because of the novelty and the natural time it takes to adapt to a new gender. These hormonal imbalances reflect the Soul not feeling comfortable in its own skin, which can lead to many psychological and behavioral problems as the individual has a hard time fitting in and relating to others based on what he/she feels inside.

These dynamics can essentially lead to a sense of insecurity and sometimes alienation from others, due to a difficulty in relating to her own self in the current gender. These dynamics can correlate with a negative self-image as the individual does not feel very much like the others she compares herself to (Libra). Negative emotions due to a sense of abandonment and possible abuse can also compound on the negative self-image and when in a depressive mode of expression, can be very hard to deal with on a moment to moment basis, as the person is essentially focusing on the nature of their emotions in order to penetrate to the core of what is causing discomfort. They cyclically go through emotional deaths and rebirths that renew them from the inside out but are also very painful experiences.

With the South Node of the Moon in Cancer in the 2nd house there has been in the past a desire to ground the self and learn all these lessons of self-reliance and emotional stability, to learn to develop the nurturing side of life. In this life, she is very loving of animals and nature; she is very empathic, kind and generous towards others in need and has no sense of discrimination regarding whom she be-friends. This is seen astrologically through the ruler of both Nodes in the 12th house in Gemini, Jupiter in the 7th square the Libra stellium and Neptune in the 6th, where she essentially sees others who are suffering and in need of help and care as part of her family too, as others she can identify with and relate to since they all share something in common, suffering and alienation from the consensus based society which leaves them crippled in some way.

With Neptune in the 6th house opposite the Moon, relative to the 8th house South Node of Neptune and relative to Pluto's bottom line need to learn security from within, the Soul has in the past had shocks and disillusioned itself with others in relation to issues of power, trust, and shared resources. The Soul has potential fractures due to these past traumas, which can of course be repeated in this life. These traumas are in part due to excessive expectations projected onto others to serve her own personal needs. With Uranus, which rules the South Node of Neptune in the 5th house, the Soul can have memories of being special and part of a prestigious family or some similar dynamic that leads to a sense of feeling important and superior to others and, thus naturally deserves to be treated in this life as a 'princess.'

These projected expectations in turn also set up the Soul and Ego for further trauma and shocks in the current life as the need to be acknowledged as special goes unsatisfied. The evolutionary need is to liberate from the projection upon others to be acknowledged as special with Uranus in the 5th in Libra and, in her specific case, there was also a very interesting dynamic as she projected the ultimate meaning of her existence, at one point in her life, on the desire to have a child. This desire was unfilled for a very long time as she was unable to conceive until one day it just happened, to her surprise, Uranus in the 5th house. This child and the need to care for it tested her inner strength (Uranus 5th square the Nodes in the 2nd/8th) as she was in a difficult position to nurture the child due to her own difficulty in nurturing herself.

This child and the need to nurture it reflect the nature of her skipped steps in this life, where she possibly abandoned or was simply unable to nurture herself or a child in a recent past life. She has been flip flopping between the 2nd and 8th house dynamics in relation to her ability to nurture herself and others, potentially translating to an inability to generate resources and the ability to maintain her subsistence and that of her offspring or extended family. The Resolution Node being the South Node of the Moon in Cancer in the 2nd house reflects the need to continue developing her inner value and self-esteem, to ground the emotional body in order to achieve the emotional and psychological stability her Soul desires. By stabilizing the emotions on a consistent basis (Cancer/2nd house) and grounding herself, she would in fact be working on her skipped steps by being emotionally stable enough to generate resources for herself and her family and would be in a psychological state of inner strength and independence which would allow her to nurture her child in a positive way.

With the ruler of the Moon's Nodes being conjunct in a balsamic phasal relationship in the 12th house, it can correlate to the fact that she has potentially had mental illnesses or personality disorders in past lives and is potentially re-living conditions and circumstances that were left incomplete. There are a lot of culminating aspects in this chart meaning that in this life she will be finishing off a cycle that is impeding her from proceeding with the new evolutionary cycle relative to the Pluto in the 4th in Libra bottom line. With both planetary rulers in the 12th house in a balsamic conjunction, she can have a deep-rooted inner sensation of being stuck and not able to build in the directions she would desire on an egocentric level, as there would be dynamics from prior lives that were still not totally culminated. Dynamics relative to her personal emotional and egocentric structural development and maturation as seen by the Moon and Saturn, relative to the Moon's Nodes and to Pluto in the 4th house bottom line desire to experience and learn about emotional security and balanced relationships, including the relationship to herself.

There can be a need to surrender to forces beyond her control and simply accept life and death as it is, to stop creating crisis based on a sense of victimization and confusion, to simplify her life by accepting responsibility for her own emotions and/or life circumstances. With the Nodal rulers of the Moon in the 12th and especially being the Moon and Saturn opposing Neptune, there can be an innate tendency to have escapist tendencies, which in her case led to substance abuse from a young age. These escapist tendencies were simply a way to deal with her own emotions which, in part, are quite underdeveloped due to a tendency to escape from overwhelming emotional challenges, that can also be a learned reaction from others in the family or, due to trauma in past lives and, possibly early on in the current life.

With Uranus square the Nodal axis of the Moon and the current life Moon in the 12th, it seems that the substances would be a way to numb herself out and also to gain some form of objective awareness through the numbing out emotions with substances or medical pharmaceuticals, which would allow for emotional detachment in order to objectify her emotions and process them in a logical way, leading her to communicate them or write them down, which she did quite frequently, to the point of developing a talent for creative and dramatic writing. She has natal Venus in Leo in the 3rd house which is also close to the North Node of Neptune which is in the 2nd house but approaching the cusp of the 3rd house.

The North Node of Neptune in the 2nd house in Leo with Venus in the 3rd, in addition to her Moon/Saturn in the 12th in Gemini, can correlate to her ability to heal herself and others via her creative communication skills such as writing, possibly even song writing as the North Node of Neptune in Leo is in the 2nd house and this can correlate to music. Music can be a way for her and others in general with emotional problems, to help express positive emotions in a way that can be truly invigorating. She did and does enjoy music very much and it gives her a sense of healthy joyful expression. Pluto in the 4th plus the Nodal conditions and rulers in this chart all point to a highly empathic Soul with a sense of unity between all beings and a deep desire for peace and harmony. With Venus in Leo in the 3rd and the Sun in Libra in the 4th, one can see how the nature of her emotional expression would be highly dramatic and subjective and also desire to receive feedback therefore, would develop a very strong sense of humor in which the tendency would be to exaggerate and shock others who had consensus morals, by being provocative. This can be seen with the square that Jupiter is making from the 7th house in Capricorn to the Libra stellium in the 4th. I feel her shocking sense of humor was to make others laugh and also a way for her to challenge her own and society's patriarchal beliefs, Jupiter in Capricorn in the 7th.

Neptune in the 6th house opposing the Moon in the 12th, is a symbol for the need to learn about humility as it shows a deep desire from within her own Soul to heal herself of the past disillusionments that led to trauma in the first place (South Node of Neptune in Aquarius in the 8th/Uranus 5th, relative to Pluto in the 4th) and to be of service to others in some way that can give her life a sense of ultimate meaning.

Remembering the Pluto in the 4th bottom line and the fact that so many dynamics are culminating within her own Soul journey, plus the highly possible recent gender switch, relative to Neptune in the 6th house, we can see the huge potential for physiological imbalances within the brain itself, conditioning emotional responses through the creation of an extremely sensitive Ego in the current life. The Moon/Saturn in the 12th opposite Neptune and Pluto in the 4th chemical imbalance can be between Serotonin, Noradrenaline and Dopamine but in my understanding the current medical view is flawed in the sense that they blame the chemical imbalance for the disorder when it seems to be rooted in the Soul itself. This aspect correlates with the fact that her doctors medicated her heavily in order to treat the chemical imbalances but that in the end it was always a failed effort and disillusionment, as that form of treating is not an effective treatment. It actually seems like she was deceived by the doctors, who were probably deluded themselves and therefore she was a money making machine for the pharmaceutical companies making her "medicine" as the doctors convinced of their own delusions, convinced her that she would have to take these chemicals for the rest of her life.

With Pluto in the 4th in Libra, the security needs that are projected onto others would be met with everything but what she needed, which would be to learn to balance herself out from within in a step-by-step process with a commitment to develop techniques in order to gain emotional stability. We can see this with the PPP in the 10th house in Aries, ruled by Mars in Virgo, which is conjunct Pluto itself and by the Moon and Saturn in the 12th.

Neptune in Sagittarius in the 6th and Jupiter in Capricorn in the 7th, her beliefs about her health were conditioned by her doctors and those she was in close relationship with, further it shows that her beliefs would possibly be introduced by those she would be close to and that they would generally be of a consensus nature, even in the individuated stage as she also adopted some traditional postures and attitudes in relationships. With the Moon and Saturn Balsamic in the 12th in Gemini which rule the Nodes of the Moon, she would be surrendering to the beliefs of others as Saturn is what rules Jupiter in Capricorn and by being in the 12th in Gemini she could actually be quite confused herself as to what to actually think. She could do her own research and end up confused with too much conflicting information and just surrender to what others were saying.

In addition, due to her need to learn about emotional maturity, her family, which was and continues to be highly supportive of her situation, are unable and powerless themselves to do anything to help her. Further, she would overwhelm her inner circuits as there is so much 3rd house and Gemini energy in this chart, along with Neptune opposing the planets in Gemini and Mercury conjunct Uranus, basically stressing or overwhelming the nervous system because of such intense emotions and further by the use of substances and pharmaceutical drugs.

All of these dynamics lead to a very strong sense of futility in the depressive cycles of the Bipolar experience which can then add to the sense of victimization and powerless to pick herself up, thus creating a vicious cycle of numbing herself with medication as that's what the doctor prescribed.

With the North Node of the Moon in the 8th in Capricorn, she would need to penetrate to the core of her own psychology with self determination to uncover the reasons for having such a disorder. She would need to go deep within and dissolve all accumulated opinions and conflicting information gathered from others (Moon-Saturn/Gemini/12th) and try and find ultimate meaning in her existence by aligning her life with a higher purpose. Basically, she would have to turn to God or the Universal in one way or another to try and make sense and understand why she was going through such a difficult experience in this life. One way she could do this would be through doing some form of service or charity work for others who were in a worse situation than she was. This form of service (Neptune 6th) could have the effect of minimizing her own tendencies towards victimization and give her a healthy sense of purpose through service to others. Neptune in the 6th plus Uranus in the 5th and the Moon/Saturn in the 12th, are all symbols for the need to learn humility as the special sense of purpose carried over from past lives of being treated as special are limiting the evolutionary intentions of the Soul to learn about self-determination and emotional maturity, as shown by the Pluto polarity point in the 10th house in Aries.

Relative to the Pluto bottom line and the need to learn emotional consistency and self-determination and the natural resistance that Pluto and its dual desire nature express, we can see resistance to the evolutionary intent to grow that is directly linked to the manner in which the disease is dealt with. On the one hand, there is the desire to heal and therefore she went to the doctor but, on the other hand, the acceptance of the doctor's ways of dealing with the Bipolar disorder in general leads to a sense of victimization which disempowers the individual and turns them into a source of income for the company that sells them the medication. Surrendering to the disorder in such a way creates a situation of non-growth in which the Soul feels stuck because through the Ego and the constant health crisis and sense of victimization (Moon/Neptune placements and aspects), it would essentially be hiding behind the disease in order to resist the evolutionary intentions to mature emotionally and take responsibility for the emotions and life in general.

Pluto is an unconscious force and prime mover, as we know, which is one reason why it's so hard for any one of us to become aware of the need to change and also to have the courage to change as the need arises. In the 4th house it's a double whammy or intensified dynamics relative to insecurity, where the Soul never really feels secure, because ultimately it knows that the consistency it desires is not possible since no one survives life in the end. The only way that a 4th house Pluto individual can truly find a lasting sense of security is by turning inwards to the Universal, the Source or God in some form. Everything else will only provide temporary security but the development of the Pluto polarity point will help build confidence in him/herself as the individual manages to achieve set goals by the force of his/her will and effort and thus minimize insecurities.

At the present moment she is actually fighting off cancers which have been spreading and are very hard to contain ever since she had Pluto in Capricorn and Saturn in Scorpio form a Yod to her Moon at 10 degrees Gemini in the 12th house. She has been in intense crisis ever since that time and has been trying all sorts of new and experimental drugs in which the side effects were simply too hard to take, therefore she stopped and is doing chemotherapy even though she and most doctors do not really believe that she can heal and recover. She and her family are hoping to get a few more years so that she can see her son grow up a little more, the only problem is that the medical treatment she has been getting seems to be accelerating her condition.

I also have the impression that her cancers are the consequence of her own negative emotional cycles that have always been suppressed because of the way she and her doctors decided to deal with the disorder, which was simply through the constant suppression of symptoms through the use of a huge assortment of chemical drugs. These drugs in combination with the negative emotions that don't find a positive expression, in my opinion, lead to cancer. The cancer is a result of years of accumulated self-destructive energy and emotions, which translate into cells that mutate (Pluto) and destroy the body. Also with the current Uranus/Pluto square aspecting her Mercury in Libra, her Chiron in Aries and transiting Neptune which just squared natal Neptune and is approaching her natal MC, she might finally be disillusioned with the consensus based medical establishment and simply wish to free herself from the opinions of others such as doctors who, in the end didn't help her as much as she thought they could.

The Yod aspect with Pluto and Saturn pointing at the Moon, indicated a time of intense humbling for the Egocentric structure of this Soul, in addition transiting Neptune was forming an inconjunct to her Sun, adding to these dynamics of total surrender to the humbling experience. She was and is still experiencing the karmic results of years of giving away her responsibility to others, which, in turn led to crisis, and a sense of futility and victimization on a cyclical basis.

At the same time, her desire to survive and be there a little longer for her child is showing and reflecting a sincere desire to complete her evolutionary path, to develop self-determination and maturity and is, at the same time, working on her skipped step with the Nodal axis of the Moon in the 2nd/8th houses and Uranus in the 5th, as she attempts to survive as long as possible for the benefit of her child to have a mother for as long as possible. She seems to know deep down that the value is in the effort and has been truly trying her best.

Fortunately, she has also had tremendous support from her family, especially her grandparents and parents and even her ex stepfather who is extremely dedicated to supporting her. They all do their very best to provide comfort and anything else she or her child may need. I feel this unwavering support is a need she has deep down in her own Soul that she desired to experience in order to understand that she truly was loved to the best of others' abilities, even if life doesn't seem fair at times (Libra).

EXAMPLE CHART D

Neptune: Instability of the Consciousness of the Soul
EA Analysis of Marilyn Monroe's Bipolar Disorder

by Linda

Marilyn Monroe

- South Node of Neptune Aquarius 6th
- Ruler of South Node of Neptune: Uranus Pisces 8th
- Current life Neptune Leo 1st
- Ruler of Neptune: Sun Gemini 11th
- North Node of Neptune Leo 1st
- Ruler of North Node of Neptune: Sun Gemini 11th

Although never officially diagnosed, many studies of Marilyn Monroe's life predominantly reach agreement that she had the mental illness known as Bipolar Disorder (or manic depression). This disorder manifests as elevated or agitated moods known as mania, alternating with episodes of depression. These fluctuating episodes greatly impaired Marilyn's ability to function in ordinary life. Later in her life, one of her psychiatrists commented on the severity of Marilyn's condition: "Marilyn is a very sick girl." Another syndrome she was thought to have was Histrionic Personality Disorder, classed as a mental disorder, and characterized by enduring maladaptive patterns of behavior, cognition and emotion such as a high need for attention, inappropriate seductive behavior, and excessively strong emotions.

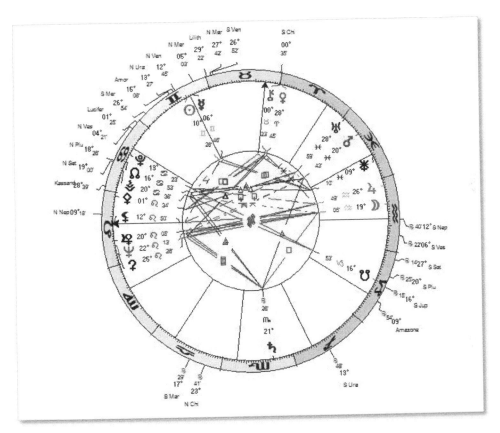

MONROE

Marilyn's Pluto Cancer 12th shows that the Soul was learning the evolutionary lesson of internal security. The sickness stored within the Soul originated in the emotional body and correlated to many past lives of not receiving sufficient nurturing or appreciation, emotional rejection/non-responsiveness of a parent, an emotionally dominating parent who was abusive, cruel and vindictive, a lack of trust based on being let down by people in whom she had become overly dependent, sexual abuse by a parent, not being fed enough food as a baby, or being neglected as a baby. She was an emotional wreck!

In the current life, she had been rejected by her mother, a paranoid schizophrenic, who had lived in a psychiatric hospital most of her life. She also had had an absent father (Saturn Scorpio 4th Rx). The Soul lesson was to break free from excessive attachment to external sources of security. Therefore, many of these experiences of emotional neglect and neediness repeated themselves in the current life in order that the necessary changes and evolutionary lessons could be realized. Marilyn would constantly be forced back in upon herself to examine the inner dynamics that created each emotional crisis. Being what many considered the 'epitome of femininity,' it is likely that Marilyn had been a female for many lifetimes seeking to unite the anima/animus.

With Pluto in the 12th house, the emotional depth of the Soul was profound. There was a deep desire to heal the emotional body. The emotional make-up was extremely intense, sensitive, touchy and moody. She expected her displaced emotional needs to be met by others in a childlike way. To feel secure required a bottomless pit of emotional nurturing. For Marilyn, the two distinct emotional cycles – withdrawal because emotion was manifesting from the subconscious realms, and becoming animated due to processing the emotions – became extremely distorted and had resulted in mental disorders in the current life. This past life karmic pattern was unresolved within the deeper unconscious. The Soul in the current life had to deal with the unfinished business of seeking to understand these dynamics and make changes. With Pluto/North Node in the 12th house, there was a need to release the suppression of the emotional body and learn to let go and surrender. There was a need to completely cut the psychic umbilical cord with the past.

With the South Node Capricorn 6th, the past life impact of insufficient nurturing created a suppressive pattern that manifested as episodes of depression. Stored in the Soul was deep pain, severing and fracture of the emotional body: CRISIS held in the emotional body. It is possible the Soul had alternated between playing the masochist and the sadist. In the role of masochist, she subconsciously felt that she was being punished, was at fault, felt bad, felt judged, felt like a victim that attracted cruelty, abuse and anger, and that she deserved pain, humiliation and suffering. The sadistic pathology correlated to past life occurrences of cruelty, anger and guilt that had been suppressed. Suppressed anger is one cause of depression. Many lifetimes of suffering judgment, persecution and emotional suppression resulted in severely distorting the emotional body and creating a very negative self-image or self-worth (2nd house Virgo).

The ruler of the South Node, Saturn Scorpio 4th, shows that the sickness of the Soul that had resulted in the Bipolar Disorder originated from the suppression of emotions and hysteria. Frightened at the depth of her own emotional needs and vulnerability, she desperately clung to the past, to what is known and familiar, in a Cancer-like way, repeating the cycles of animation/withdrawal, and the extreme emotional highs alternating with bouts of depression. Her immense emotional depths were both a blessing and a curse. She was plagued with feelings of being abandoned and betrayed by those whom she had trusted. Any form of emotional rejection would trigger the implosion of hysteria and a nervous collapse would result.

Ruler of the North Node Cancer 12th, Moon Aquarius 7th conjunct Jupiter (a double signature of trauma) would exaggerate the emotional responses. When she was happy, she was REALLY happy. When she was sad, she was REALLY sad. And since the nature of the Moon correlates to moment-to-moment experience, one moment she would be happy, and the very next moment she would be sad. No doubt, there was extreme sensitivity to what others thought of her. Whatever dynamics were imbalanced would be projected out onto the partner and reflected back to her through the partner. She did not feel comfortable without a partner, yet the Soul created three divorces in order to force the necessary evolutionary lesson of internal security by cutting the symbiotic chords between herself and her partners.

Marilyn's disorders were treated with drugs as well as psychotherapy in order to stabilize the consciousness. An important relationship was the patient/psychotherapist relationship in which she could learn to view objectively her emotional needs in a detached manner. The long experience with psychotherapy would allow the unconscious to be brought towards the conscious awareness with flashes of insight that would lead to self-revelation and healing. In this way, the self-image (Cancer) could be renewed and strengthened.

Moon opposite Neptune re-emphasized the intense extremes of imbalance: the swinging from hot to cold, which would take her deeper into the depression. Moon square Saturn shows the suppression and distortion of the natural emotional body alternating with emotional outbursts like a child, the lesson being emotional maturity. With Moon conjunct Jupiter she was learning about the "natural" healthy expression of emotions.

With Mars Pisces 8th, there had been past life sadistic sexual abuse, probably by the father, memories of imprisonment, and the psychology of hiding. She reverted to obsessive sexual manipulation of others in order to get the emotional sustenance that she craved. The puckering of the lips: could they be the lips of a baby seeking milk? There was also deep anger stored in the Soul due to the sadomasochistic pathology.

Neptune Leo 1st, conjunct its own South Node, symbolized the Soul's intention in this life to confront and evolve beyond the existing limitations of the past. This was not easy since Neptune forms a t-square with Saturn Scorpio 4th (ruler of South Node) and the Moon Aquarius 7th (ruler of North Node) showing the inherent dynamic tension in the structure of the Soul's consciousness. With Neptune in Leo conjunct the Ascendant, the disorder played out as a lack of control of impulses, high need for attention, making loud and inappropriate appearances, inappropriately seductive behavior, excessive need for approval, craving stimulation, and persistent manipulative behavior to achieve personal needs.

With the South Node of Neptune Aquarius and the Moon's South Node Capricorn both in the 6th house, the trauma pattern from past lives was like a tight knot within the Soul's consciousness. The South Node of Neptune Aquarius at the very end of the 6th house correlates to where the Soul left off in the last lifetime, that is, bringing to culmination the pathology of sadomasochism and guilt/atonement dynamics. The Soul, tying up many loose ends, re-traumatized as it moved from one crisis to the other.

Ruler of South Node of Neptune Aquarius, Uranus Pisces 8th (culminating degree), correlates to bringing to closure a series of past lives where the Soul had experienced betrayal (real or imagined), abandonment, loss and violations of trust through family relationships (Pluto Cancer). Marilyn's three major relationships correlated to tying up and resolving past life karma with key partners. The Soul sought deep psychological understanding in order to evolve beyond the limitations of the crystallized patterns of the past. Uranus Pisces 8th reflects a Soul desire to understand the consequences of its desires that had caused the mental illness.

With the North Node of Neptune in Leo 12th, there had been escapism, substance abuse, excessive fantasy, sexual provocativeness, disillusionment, and loss of meaning. She suffered with nightmares and insomnia, haunted by dreams with past life content. To escape the pain she would retreat into a fantasy world, fashioning her sense of separate self into international stardom to reach a legendary iconic status (Venus Aries 9th conjunct the MC).

Ruler of both Neptune and the North Node of Neptune Leo, Sun Gemini 11th correlates to the Soul's purpose in the current life to bring in new information that would allow a detachment and objectification of the emotional dynamics, and act as a stabilizer or integrator, in order to focus on the purpose of its life lessons. Marilyn died at the age of 36, the autopsy recording cause of death as acute barbiturate poisoning resulting from probable suicide.

The intention of the North Node Cancer conjunct Pluto (no Pluto polarity point) was to continue to learn inner security. How? By learning to "balance" her emotional responses by taking an objective view of them (Cancer ruled by Moon Aquarius 7th), by giving herself the emotional "space" to find emotional detachment, and encouraging relationships with others who could appreciate her unique individuality. How does she change the pattern? By learning balance, creating balance and space between self and others, and surrendering to peace. How does the Soul heal? By opening up to the Universal, developing the feminine (Vesta conjunct North Node-Pluto), and opening up HEALTHY emotions in a balanced way.

CHAPTER NINE

NEPTUNE: THE COLLECTIVE CONSCIOUSNESS AND UNCONSCIOUS

Introduction

W e have come a long way now in our development and understanding of the archetypes of Neptune, Pisces, and the 12th House. What I want to do now is to share with you a very important part of these archetypes, which, to me, has been severely underdeveloped in the world of astrology in general. These archetypes concern the collective unconscious, and the collective consciousness.

We have now correlated Neptune, the 12th House, and Pisces to the consciousness of the Soul in general, and the nature of the consciousness within any given individual Soul. If we remember that consciousness always assumes and manifests relative to the nature of the form that it exists within, then we can understand that the totality of all the dynamics existent in any given Soul determines the 'form' through which its consciousness will manifest. Within this state of consciousness, we must also apply the effect of the collective unconsciousness, Neptune, the 12th House, and Pisces upon the current state of consciousness for any Soul. The collective unconscious correlates to the TOTALITY OF THE ENTIRE HISTORY OF THE HUMAN ORGANISM TO DATE: THE CURRENT MOMENT. At the same time, we need to apply the effects of the collective consciousness to the individual state of Soul consciousness in such a way as to understand how the effects of collective consciousness shapes and defines the individual state of consciousness. The collective consciousness simply means the TOTALITY OF ALL HUMAN'S EVENTS THAT ARE TAKING PLACE AT ANY POINT IN TIME TO EACH INDIVIDUAL.

Within the consciousness of the human organism is an awareness of the totality, the immensity, of the Manifest Creation: of something much larger than any one part of that Manifest Creation. This awareness, of course, is the causative factor, the determinant, for human consciousness to understand in some way exactly the cause of that Manifest Creation. This need to understand this cause then becomes the determinant of creating some kind of cosmology that can explain it. As a result, whatever the agreed upon cause is of that Manifest Creation, at any point in time in the human evolutionary journey, conditions the nature of the individual Soul consciousness.

This agreed upon, collective, cosmology thus becomes the CORE STRUCTURE OF THE INDIVIDUAL AND COLLECTIVE CONSCIOUSNESS AT ANY POINT IN TIME. This core structure, in turn, thus conditions every other dynamic within the totality of the collective and individual Soul consciousness itself: its emotions, its mental structures, and its sexuality. Thus, the inner relationship of the collective and individual Soul to whatever the Source of the Manifest Creation is as reflected in the specific cosmologies of any group of humans at any point in time AND PLACE. Thus, however, the collective and individual consciousness of the Soul DEFINES the Source of the Manifest Creation, and is exactly how that Source will be experienced. From the point of view of Natural Laws that were set in motion by the Source Of All Things, it of course is entirely possible for consciousness of each individual Soul to be in some kind or form of 'communion' with its own Source.

This communion or desire to KNOW the very origin of all things, the origin of the Soul itself, is intrinsic to the consciousness of the Soul. This desire to know is not dependent on any external source for that knowing. This desire to know, the actual natural truth of the Creation, can be known by any Soul by way of the Natural Laws that allow it to do so. Those natural laws start with the natural law of the breath. The inhaling and exhaling breaths correlate to the natural laws of cause and effect, thus the natural law of duality. This natural law thus correlates to thought and counter-thought, of the ongoing manifestation of phenomenal reality that is rooted in this natural law of cause and effect. Yet, this inhaling and exhaling breath can also be suspended: a state of breathlessness. In this natural state of breathlessness, the consciousness of the Soul is thus temporally free from the natural law of duality. In this natural breathless state, the consciousness of the Soul expands from within itself allowing it to perceive the very nature of the manifested Creation by way of all the natural laws that are responsible for it. Consciousness can inwardly expand to the point of being able to perceive the actual manifestation of the manifest and the un-manifest from which that manifests.

All Souls, by birthright, have this natural capacity: IT IS 'HARD WIRED' IN THE SOUL BY ITS CREATOR. And what is perceived in this naturally breathless state is identical to all Souls who are able to arrive at such a state. In essence, a universal truth that is not dependent on any invented cosmology by humans that is agreed upon to be true when, in actual reality, it is not.

These invented cosmologies began when the human organism shifted from nomadic ways of living to settled communalities in which foraging in order to survive was progressively replaced by growing crops and raising animals for clothing and food. The very first 'conception' for what we now call God began exactly at that time. Before then humans lived in accordance with Natural Laws which they were dependent upon for their very existence. Their world was one of nature spirits of all sorts that did not have a perceived Source or cause.

The South Node of Neptune being in Aquarius for all humans on the planet today directly correlates with the time in which humans began to live in farming type communities, of when cosmologies were invented to explain the nature of phenomenal reality. The concept of 'God' began that progressively was defined by humans in all kinds of ways that had nothing to do with the ACTUAL Source Of All Things.

So we can see by way of the South Node being in Aquarius how the collective conscious/unconsciousness from that time until now has affected the individual consciousness of each Soul by way of the various man-made religions and cosmologies that have defined 'God' in all the ways that it has been. One of the archetypes that Aquarius correlates to is one of PROJECTION. This of course is a reflection of the fact that the Manifest Creation itself is a projection from the Source Of All Things. Thus, the consciousness the Soul projects its desire for understanding and ultimate meaning upon the phenomenal nature of the Creation. Such projections are the basis of what philosophies and religions from the East called Maya or illusion: life is nothing but a dream. Relative to the fact that the human life form is a social form of life this then is the determinant of needing a consensus in order to bind the whole together in a state of security which is the basis of 'collective agreement' about what 'reality' is and is not. So it then becomes totally possible for the human life form to create a reality based on projections that has nothing to do with actual or ultimate reality.

The bottom line in this is that any invented religion and cosmology that is not NATURALLY TRUE has caused all kinds of traumas, Aquarius, to the collective and individual Souls that has been brought forwards since that time until now. As we all know, religion has been one of the primary causes of wars between peoples in which one religion attempts to dominate/eliminate any other religion that it feels threatened by. And, of course, this is always justified, rationalized, because each religion is the 'right' religion, the 'right' God. Thus, we have the whole extermination of people, genocides, terrorism, car bombs, human sacrifices to the avenging God, 'witch' burnings, torture, etc., etc., in "the name of God.' And each group, Aquarius, Uranus, the 11th House within the totality of humanity has their own race, or their own version of 'god,' of their own religions/cosmologies, that is USED AGAINST any other group of people or race as a weapon to punish, eliminate, control, or dominate because that version of god and the religion/cosmology that follows that is the RIGHT ONE.

With the North Node of Neptune being in Leo for all Souls, we can see how the idea of 'god,' the creator, is at the heart of all of Creation: Leo. We can also see how each of these invented religions and gods is the 'right' one and all others wrong. We can now understand the root of all religions: "God created man in its own image." We can now see how so many Souls use the language of God to justify that which they do: 'In the name of God.' And we can see, because of this, just how illusory this is, illusions that are considered to be 'real.' We can also see, however, how the core desire in all Souls to know that which has Created them is also true. So the issue then becomes to inwardly KNOW the real and actual nature of what humans call God, and the true Source Of All Things, versus all the invented/projected religions, cosmologies, and 'gods' that have nothing to do with the true nature of the Creator and what It has created. And we can know which Souls actually represent in some way the actual nature of the natural truths, of the Natural Laws, and of the real and Natural Source Of All Things.

So focusing on an individual birth chart, we can see where and how the impact/effect of the collective unconscious on any given Soul by way of the placement of the South Node of Neptune by house, with its ruler, Uranus, also by house, sign, and the aspects to it. Inherent to the Aquarius archetype is the desire to individuate from and within all other human beings in general, the very nature of the society that the Soul is born into, and the immediate peer group that it belongs to. Thus, the impact of all of these groups, and the collective unconscious ignite this desire to individuate. The South Node of Neptune by house, the location of its planetary ruler by its own house, sign, and aspects to it correlate to how this was done in the lives leading to the current life.

The natal location of the current life Neptune by house, sign, and aspects to it correlate to how the collective unconscious impacts on the individual's Soul consciousness in such a way as to stimulate and ignite the desire to individuate from it, and, in turn, how this will impact on the current state of the collective consciousness.

And the North Node of Neptune by its own house, and the aspects to it, correlate to how the Soul will actualize, give purpose to, and integrate both the current life Neptune relative to its past which is, again, symbolized by the South Node of Neptune.

Questions and Answers

(Q) I am not sure I am getting exactly how this works. Do you think you could give a short example of how to work on this?

(A) Here is a simple example that hopefully will help in understanding how to apply the archetypes that we are discussing:

So let's put the South Node of Neptune that is in Aquarius in the 3rd House, its ruler Uranus in Gemini in the 8th House, the natal Neptune in Libra in the 11th House, and the Leo North Node of Neptune in the 9th with its ruler, the Sun, in Sagittarius in the 2nd House. The evolutionary stage will be 2nd Individuated.

Here we can see that this Soul has been progressively rebelling against all the ideas, and the opinions they generate, of the collective consciousness/unconscious in order to individuate itself by way of desiring to know that which can actually be known by way of various ways of personal investigation: this is the relationship between the 3rd and the 8th House in our example.

The desire of the Soul has been to orientate to knowledge that can be proven by way of these personal investigations: 8th House. Coming into the current life with the Neptune in the 11th House, in this evolutionary context, the Soul is inwardly feeling like an outsider relative to the social milieu, and its various groupings of people within the total context of humanity itself. It feels itself to be an outsider because of all the ideas/opinions that most consider or cherish to be true. From the inner perch of being an outsider, the Soul is then observing how whole groupings of people are organized relative to what and how they think. The ongoing effect of the collective unconscious/consciousness continues to be used by this Soul by way of rebelling against any ideas/opinions that cannot be directly provable by way of personal investigations.

This Soul will only form relationships, Neptune in Libra, within the context of the country that it is born into to others who also feel radically different than the consensus, others who are standing on the outskirts of society, others who question everything, others who demand some kind of proof of what is actually real versus that which is simply belief that is considered to be real.

With the North Node of Neptune in the 9th House, and ruled by a Sagittarius Sun in the 2nd, the Soul is beginning to desire to understand, just beginning because of the 2nd stage individuated, the Natural Laws that are responsible for Creation itself. Within these symbols, the Soul will progressively be shifting its consciousness from a left-brain orientation to phenomenal reality to the right-brain. From the liner to the nonlinear. In essence, to begin the process of conceptual understanding of the whole versus a linear approach that builds the whole in that way.

In this way, the Soul is evolving from a consciousness of total rebellion of all ideas — this is not real, this is bullshit, this a lie, and so on — to a consciousness that is just beginning to replace that existing orientation to one wherein it desires to know that which can actually be known via proof relative to an understanding of the conceptual whole of Creation by way of the Natural Laws that are the very structure of that Creation.

This evolution of the Soul's consciousness is thus changing its own inner relationship to itself: the Sagittarius Sun in the 2nd House. In so changing its inner relationship to itself, it is simultaneously changing its own inner magnetism, its own inner vibration that in turn will change the Soul's relationships to others in general, those in its life specifically, and, finally, to the Soul's relationship with the collective itself: the world in which it lives.

As the Soul evolves in this way it will, as a next evolutionary step, desire to help others understand that which itself has come to understand about the nature of what is true, and what is not, what is real, and what is not. This will at first manifest in very limited ways by way of its personal relationships that will finally evolve into being able to actualize sociological roles, Neptune in the 11th House, the evolution of the South Node of Neptune being in Aquarius, in which the Soul, by way of those roles, will progressively help increasing numbers of people to understand the actual truths of themselves, the truths of humans beings, of how and why societies form and organize in the ways that they do.

Relative to the evolutionary stage of development, as the Soul begins to move into the 3rd individuated, the Soul will naturally desire to be able to 'teach' this in one way or another: the North Node of Neptune in the 9th relative to its ruler the Sun being in Sagittarius. The vehicle of teaching will thus serve the Soul's desire and need to reintegrate itself progressively into the world in general, and its country of origin specifically. In this way, that which the Soul teaches will impact on the very nature of the collective consciousness.

Tying this together with another archetype that we have discussed in our thread, this Soul could be receiving, and thus inwardly hearing, the 'whispers' for what we call God that is encouraging the Soul to do just that.

Much more could be said relative to these symbols, i.e. a series of prior lifetimes in which the Soul itself has been attacked and persecuted for its own individual/unique ideas that challenged the existing consensus and thus their security, others who have been attacked or punished in some way for the same reasons, but I am trying to purposefully keep it simple so that, hopefully, we can all understand how to apply the archetypes of what we have been discussing in our last segment. If it doesn't, or you or others need another example, or have questions about the example used here, just ask.

(Q) I am thinking about Neptune in relation to Darwin and the collective unconscious/conscious. I feel like as far as a symbol of what sort of collective unconscious and collective conscious was impacting Darwin at the time, I at least have some solid ideas already. What I am not sure I am clearly understanding or not is how Saturn is functioning as a filter to his awareness of the collective unconscious and conscious since it is in a close balsamic conjunction to Neptune (then it is also in square to the Pisces Pluto-Mercury-Ceres). Does it mean that both the collective unconscious and conscious could flood the structure of his consciousness at times and at least on a subconscious level he would have access to the information he could perceive and communicate?

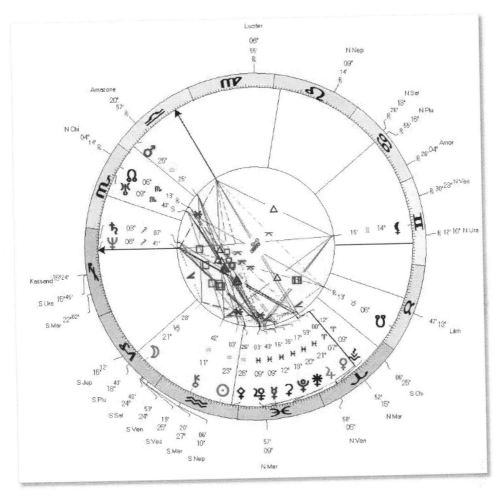

DARWIN

(A)   Yes, and by any consciousness of any Soul, including Darwin, that 'flooding' into the individual consciousness of a Soul creates a natural physiological reaction to this that, in turn, affects the natural individuation process that exists in all Souls. In essence, that physiological reaction affects the overall proportions of the physiology of the brain in such a way as to 'individualize' the brain of any given Soul. This natural process of any Soul's desire to individuate from the collective of all Souls then reflects the individual ongoing evolutionary journey of each Soul. The individual evolutionary journey of any given Soul becomes the DETERMINANT of how that individual Soul is thus ORIENTATED to the collective unconscious/consciousness.

(Q) One point about the collective conscious for example, I feel with the Saturn-Neptune he was very tuned into it, as the example that Wallace was working on the exact same idea at the same time attests. Or would it be more of a filter, blocking his conscious access to collective unconscious memories and perceptions to a large extent more so than allowing a large amount of the collective to filter through?

(A) The filter, as you put it, of his Saturn/Neptune conjunction operates in such a way that his Soul unconsciously 'tuned into' the parts of the collective unconscious that was/is linked to the desire in all humans to understand their origins: Saturn/Neptune in Sagittarius in the 12th House that is then squaring all those Pisces planets in his 3rd including the very nature of his own Soul structure. With his Soul structure thus attuned, this then set in motion the physiological reactions within his brain that allowed him to individuate in exactly the way that he did. And, in so doing, affect the ongoing understanding of all humans relative to their origins: his effect upon the existing nature of the collective consciousness of that time which has been progressively receding into the collective unconscious as the collective consciousness accepts the truths he realized relative to the natural laws of evolution for all forms of life.

(Q) I get the idea that Saturn is involved with his internal criticism, and no doubt the "psycho-pathological masochism" aspect of his Neptune archetype. Or, is it the idea that all of this is happening at the same time?

(A) It is all happening at the same time within his Soul.

(Q) I feel I would like to understand and apply the collective unconscious/consciousness dimension of the Neptune archetype. If it is ok, I'm briefly posting what I've done to date, so I can ask if it is on the right track.

(A) Sure, go ahead.

(Q) With Neptune in the 12th House Sagittarius, this reflects the natural unity within consciousness, and within the collective unconscious, experienced in natural times before patriarchy – Saturn conjunct – of the whole of Nature and the Manifest Creation. Thus, there is a theme of 'Paradise lost' because of Neptune's South Node ruler being Uranus in Scorpio in the 11th House, this Uranus ruling the 3rd House which contains all the Pisces intercepted and Pluto, this reflecting various types of traumas of an individual and collective nature, leading to a questioning about the underlying natural laws which are the basis of such collective experiences; within this, a questioning about the nature of 'evil,' not necessarily evil only in a metaphysical or proper sense, but also the questioning about how that which does not work, that which falls, fails, breaks down, or dies, as a part of a 'fallen' Nature is contemplated and is a part within a larger scheme.

With the South Node of Neptune in the 2nd House conjunct Chiron and Uranus in Scorpio in the 11th House, types of collective traumas include episodes of extinction of large groups or humanity in general. Thus, the questioning being also triggered by the survival instinct. With Uranus being in the 11th House Scorpio, relative to Neptune in the 12th House, and Pisces intercepted within the 3rd House, this questioning has led to ways on understanding based on duality, or in a fragmentation of forces interacting within Creation, in various ways along many lifetimes. Thus, different dualistic cosmologies, as cosmologies in which Creation is not created by God, but by some 'fallen' god or demiurge.

Also, there is a dual orientation and response to the collective unconscious/consciousness dimensions, because on one side there is a permeating orientation to unite with these contents – Neptune 12th House, all the Pisces – and also a need to detach and individuate from these same contents – Uranus 11th House, Aquarius on the 3rd House cusp – in order to understand objectively what the underlying Natural laws are, in contrast with beliefs and invented cosmologies about the nature of Creation, the nature of those forces, etc.

Both dual orientations are based at their core on desires to know the origin of everything, either directly, or through formalization and creation of explanations and systems that give account of the known. This last aspect has also been connected with desires to 'unite' with social forms and structures, social contexts in which teachings about Nature were very attuned to actual reality or made ultimate sense to Darwin's Soul.

The duality has also been a source of intense polarization of forces within those cosmologies his Soul has gravitated to in the past, and from which the Soul has needed to individuate. This individuation would then lead into a form of Pantheism, in which, through the intuition of Spirit within matter, matter is recovered in some ways.

The intention in place with Neptune in Sagittarius within the 12th House and Pluto and the Pisces planets within the 3rd House, would be to know and realize exactly what is true and what is not true, in how Nature works, and to dissolve prior beliefs, assumptions and opinions which permeate the collective unconscious/consciousness and which have been adhered to in the Soul's past.

Within the conflict between desires to unite with and osmose belief systems which explain the nature of things, and the desires to detach and liberate from these systems in order to have direct experience, the intention – however conditioned by other desires in the birth chart as we have seen – would be based on desires to find shortcuts, to get to know quicker, by recurring to the pre-existing knowledge forms, knowledge put together by others within the collective, in order to test these knowledge forms through intellectual experimentation, with the risk however of confusion or over-identification with knowledge which is not actual knowledge.

(A) Yes, you are very much on the right understanding and approach relative to the relationship of Darwin's Soul to the collective unconsciousness/consciousness and his own individuation from it. His individuation from it, over many, many lifetimes, finally led to the life of his Soul being Darwin who then radically altered, Uranus the ruler of his South Node of Neptune being in Scorpio in the 11th, how the human species understood their own origins relative to the Natural Law of evolution. Thus, this one singular Soul affecting the very nature of the collective consciousness, his North Node of Neptune being in Leo in the 9th which is ruled by his Aquarius Sun in the 2nd, in such a way that the understandings that he taught the human organism through his 'radical' book called the *The Origin of Species* will stand for all time.

(Q) I wonder if the 'flood' of the contents of the collective unconscious/consciousness occur at a physiological level by an increased release of oxytocin, like an oxytocin rush?

Oxytocin is considered to be connected with social bonding, and social defense. Also, "there is some evidence that oxytocin promotes ethnocentric behavior, incorporating the trust and empathy of in-groups with their suspicion and rejection of outsiders" (Wikipedia). The collective unconscious has divisions in it that correspond to the collective unconscious of the race, the country, or the tribe. It seems like these types of group-identification, i.e. "this is my tribe, and 'we' are different from that other tribe" existed/exists in natural humans under natural law. Thus, it looks like a natural function of oxytocin would be promoting identification and bonding with one's own group? Thus oxytocin would be directly involved in individuation, i.e. becoming a minority through association with a more defined group as compared with a larger group, in order to progressively become a group of one. Both dynamics involved, i.e. bonding with a smaller group and differentiating from a larger group, seem to be dependent on oxytocin.

(A) The collective unconscious/consciousness includes the totality of all humanity. Of course, within that, there are all kinds of groupings of humans by race, geography, time/place, and so on. Each of these has their own histories, as do all existing groups of humans in every possible way humans can group themselves sociologically. Oxytocin is one of the physiological substances that correlates with this in terms of the Soul/ego identifying with specific groups that they are born into, and reflect the heritage of whatever group. This is much more about a sociological/identity function than one of orientating the Soul to the totality of the collective consciousness/unconsciousness. Melatonin, a hormone, has much more to do with this than oxytocin. Oxytocin would more specifically correlate with Uranus because of this whereas melatonin specifically correlates with Neptune.

All of this goes into the collective consciousness/unconsciousness that any Soul lives within, at any point in time. Each Soul has a natural individuation desire relative to the totality of humanity, and the totality of whatever specific group of humans it is born into. That desire is universal in all humans: it is a Natural Law. That desire also reflects the ongoing evolutionary progression of any Soul with its own history leading to whatever current life.

When that interfaces with the collective consciousness/unconscious this naturally affects and determines the total physiological response within the brain in such a way as to orientate that brain, and the Soul consciousness with it, to the collective in general, and its specific groups of humans that it has chosen to be born into specifically. Thus orientated, the Soul individuates from that in such a way as to progress on its own intended evolutionary journey that then, of itself, affects the collective consciousness in some way. For most, that is quite minimal on an individual level yet each individual does add to the whole. In rare cases, like Darwin, that individuation process then affects and reflects how, at times, any one Soul can have such a revolutionary effect on collective consciousness so that the collective itself can evolve.

EXAMPLE CHART A

Neptune: The Collective Consciousness and Unconscious

Edgar Cayce

by Cat

Edgar Cayce

The term "collective unconscious" was coined by Carl Jung in order to distinguish this part of the mind from the personal unconscious, or subconscious mind. The collective unconscious is also known as the universal unconscious. It contains all knowledge since the beginning of time, including every thought, idea, feeling, deed, intention, desire, event or experience that has ever occurred at any time in the history of creation. The collective unconscious is also known by other names including the *Akashic Records*, or *The Book of Life*. Each and every Soul has its own personal book or record, which is but a page in the larger book, which contains them all, the collective unconscious.

(1) Natal Location of Current Life Neptune by House, Sign, and Aspects

This correlates to how the collective unconscious impacts on the individual's Soul consciousness in such a way as to stimulate and ignite the desire to individuate from it, and, in turn, how this will impact on the current state of the collective consciousness.

- Neptune conjunct the Moon in Taurus and Chiron in Aries in the 9th House
- Neptune semi-square Venus in Pisces in the 7th House
- Neptune trine Mars and Jupiter in Capricorn in the 5th House

Edgar Cayce was one of the world's best-known psychics (Moon/Neptune). He was also a medium and a channel. Cayce spent 43 years of his adult life accessing the *Akashic Records* of individual Souls and those of the world in general. Cayce claimed there were two sources of information from which he derived the information given in his readings. The first was the subconscious mind of the individual and the second was the *Akashic Records*, or collective unconscious. I believe that Edgar Cayce was 3rd Stage Spiritual.

With Neptune conjunct Chiron in Aries in the 9th House semi-square Saturn in Pisces in the 7th House, Cayce had the ability to tune into the physical bodies of other people and accurately diagnose their medical symptoms. He was also able to prescribe remedies to cure their ailments. When beginning a reading for an individual, Cayce would begin by saying, "We have before us the records of the entity now known or called _____." He would describe the individual's state in complex biological and medical terms that he could neither remember nor comprehend upon awakening from his trance.

In addition to these individual readings, Cayce also brought back information about the nature of reality. He answered questions about health, illness, astrology, reincarnation, karma, war, ancient civilizations, the Bible, the life of Jesus and his previous incarnations, as well as many other topics.

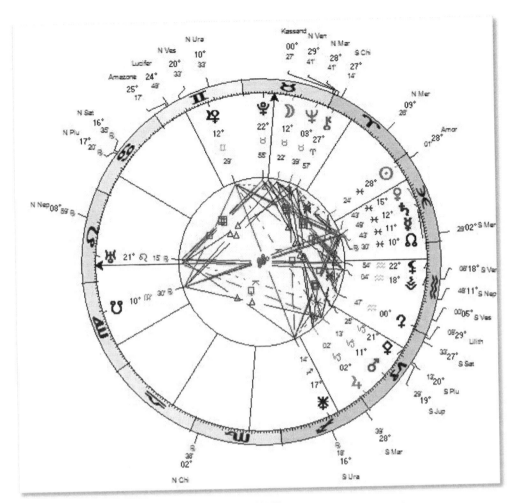

CAYCE

In Reading 294-19 Report File from A.R.E. (Association for Research and Enlightenment, Inc.), Cayce describes what it was like when he journeyed beyond his own subconscious mind and into the realm of the collective unconscious:

> I see myself as a tiny dot out of my physical body, which lies inert before me. I find myself oppressed by darkness and there is a feeling of terrific loneliness. Suddenly, I am conscious of a white beam of light. As this tiny dot, I move upward following the light, knowing that I must follow it or be lost.
>
> As I move along this path of light I gradually become conscious of various levels upon which there is movement. Upon the first levels there are vague, horrible shapes, grotesque forms such as one sees in nightmares. Passing on, there begin to appear on either side misshapen forms of human beings with some part of the body

magnified. Again there is change and I become conscious of gray-hooded forms moving downward. Gradually, these become lighter in color. Then the direction changes and these forms move upward and the color of the robes grows rapidly lighter.

Next, there begin to appear on either side vague outlines of houses, walls, trees, etc., but everything is motionless. As I pass on, there is more light and movement in what appear to be normal cities and towns. With the growth of movement I become conscious of sounds, at first indistinct rumblings, then music, laughter, and singing of birds. There is more and more light, the colors become very beautiful, and there is the sound of wonderful music. The houses are left behind, ahead there is only a blending of sound and color. Quite suddenly I come upon a hall of records. It is a hall without walls, without ceiling, but I am conscious of seeing an old man who hands me a large book, a record of the individual for whom I seek information.

With his Sun, Venus, Saturn, and Mercury in Pisces, ruled by Neptune conjunct the Moon in Taurus and Chiron in Aries in the 9th House, and Pluto sextile the Sun and quintile Mercury and Saturn in Pisces in the 7th house, Cayce's other worldly journeys and power of creative visualization made a huge impact upon others for generations to come. This in turn had a huge impact upon the collective unconscious.

While tuned into the collective unconscious, Cayce learned a new interpretation of the Bible. According to Cayce, the Bible is the symbolic account of the fall and restoration of the human Soul to its divine origins. Genesis is a symbolic story describing humanity's fall from heaven and paradise, while Revelations is the symbolic story of humanity's restoration to heaven and paradise.

Cayce was also introduced to a new way of understanding the relationship between God and humanity, relative to the cultural religious beliefs of his day and age. He learned, and shared, that human beings have three levels of awareness: the conscious mind, the subconscious mind and the super-conscious mind. He revealed that an important goal in everyone's life should be to awaken the super-conscious mind within themselves and attain at-one-ment with God. This super-conscious mind being the collective unconscious, which is also known as the Universal Mind, Christ Consciousness, Buddha Consciousness, Brahman, God, Allah, the Higher Self, so on and so forth.

As we have seen, with his Neptune in Taurus in the 9th House, Edgar Cayce was able to journey to other realms within the collective unconscious. What he learned here, he brought back to "earth" and by sharing this information with others, he had a huge impact upon that very same collective unconscious.

Note that with his Moon in Taurus in the 9th House, religion played a large role in Cayce's life. Cayce was a fundamentalist Christian who was raised on strict 19th century Bible tradition and taught Sunday School for many years. With his 9th House Moon square Uranus in Leo in the 1st House, he is said to have suffered a great deal of mental and emotional shock when he discovered that the subconscious information he passed along to others while in a trance "declared the ancient mystic religions to be true and acclaimed Jesus as their crowning glory."

According to Kevin Williams:

> . . . the body of work that Cayce presented to others while in a state of trance can be described as "a 'Christianized' version of the mystery religions of ancient Egypt, Chaldea, Persia, India, and Greece. It fits Christ into the mystical tradition of one God for all people, and places Christ in his proper place, at the apex of the philosophical structure – the capstone of the pyramid."

> Edgar Cayce only had a 7th grade education and a fundamentalist Christian upbringing. He knew nothing of the subjects he spoke of while in a trace. It is said that he spoke at length about Christian Gnosticism. The Gnostic writings that are available today were not discovered until well after Cayce's death.

> Cayce affirmed that Christian Gnosticism is the type of Christianity that was taught by Jesus. Much of the information from Cayce has solved some of the greatest mysteries of humanity, some of which were later validated after the discoveries of the Dead Sea Scrolls and the early Christian writings discovered in Egypt.

Again, with Uranus square his 9th House Taurus Moon, discovering that this type of knowledge was coming from within himself, was a shocking and traumatic experience for Cayce. In addition, while in a state of trance, he focused on issues such as the evolution of man, reincarnation, past civilizations, as well as predictions of future events. This was all quite stressful for a fundamentalist Christian to acknowledge as true and accurate.

(2) Where and How the Collective Unconscious has Impacted or Affected a Soul

> Inherent to the Aquarius archetype is the desire to individuate from and within all other human beings in general, the very nature of the society that the Soul is born into, and the immediate peer group that it belongs to. Thus, the impact of all of these groups, and the collective unconscious ignite this desire to individuate. The South

Node of Neptune by house, the location of its planetary ruler by its own house, sign, and aspects to it correlate how this was done in the lives leading to the current life. (Rad)

- South Node of Neptune is 12 degrees Aquarius in the 6th House ruled by Uranus Rx in Leo in the 1st House
- Uranus is bi-quintile the Sun in Pisces in the 8th House, square the Moon in Taurus in the 9th House and square Pluto in Taurus in the 10th House

With Uranus Rx in Leo in the 1st House square his Moon in Taurus in the 9th House, which is conjunct Neptune, Edgar Cayce was able to "remember" several of his own past life identities by accessing the *Akashic Records* or collective unconscious. These past life memories (Uranus) of his various past life identities (1st House) reveal that he was King Asapha, Ra Ta (the messenger angel at Sodom), Uhjltd, Xenon, Pythagoras, Armitidides, Lucius of Cyrene, Arawak (an Indian), John Bainbridge I, John Bainbridge II, and Ralph Dahl (Civil War Soldier). Due to his ability to access the collective unconscious, Cayce was able to share quite a bit of information about his experiences as each of these past life egos.

Like everyone, these past life characters were affected by the collective unconscious, and in turn contributed additional information and memories to the collective unconscious as well.

With the South Node of Neptune at 12 degrees Aquarius in the 6th House, the collective past life ego of Cayce has been focused on serving others and on issues related to health, hygiene and care of the body. The Soul has desired that its past life egos be different, or unique, from others who were also healers or who served others via the healing arts as well. With the South Node ruler Uranus falling in Leo in the 1st House, Cayce's past life personas, or identities were unique and different from others in the societies and cultures he was part of (Uranus in 1st) as well as powerful and sometimes regal personalities (Uranus/Leo/1st). In addition, with Uranus square the Moon in Taurus in the 9th House, these past life characters were capable of tapping into the collective conscious and possessed psychic abilities similar to those of Cayce. Uranus is also square Pluto in the 10th House, which correlates to the Soul's past intention and desire to use these abilities in relation to his career or social role.

Cayce is said to have been Ra Ta (the messenger angel at Sodom). According to Cayce's readings, Ra-Ta was born in a less-civilized area, ruled by the tribe of "Zu," somewhere in ancient Sumeria. He was a very unusual child (Uranus/Leo/1st) in that he had pale white skin and blue eyes. Most Sumerians had dark complexions and dark hair. It is said that tribal elders were very spooked by him. In addition, his mother did not have a husband, something that was frowned upon in their culture. She blamed the Gods for making her pregnant. (Sun in Pisces = missing father;

Neptune conjunct Moon = delusional mother.) The elders ordered that Ra-Ta and his mother be banished from the land (Uranus in Leo square Moon in Taurus).

As Ra-Ta grew up and matured, it became obvious that he had prophetic abilities (Uranus square Moon/Neptune 9th) and could channel very accurate psychic information. When he was 21, he predicted that earth changes would destroy the land in which he was living and the neighboring land of Atlantis. He determined that the safest place to be was in Egypt.

> When the Earth's poles shifted, Egypt would be the balance-point for their movement. Ra-Ta communicated this prophecy to the King's son Arart, and a pioneering group of 900 people led by Arart with Ra Ta as their spiritual leader made the journey from Turkey to Egypt. After a long and arduous journey, they arrived in the Egyptian city of Luz. Initially there was mistrust and scrutiny, but eventually the Egyptians accepted the Atlanteans and exalted them. Arart was proclaimed King and Ra-Ta was accepted as their high priest. Over a period of time, spiritual and moral reforms were instituted by Ra-Ta and he became beloved by the people. He built temples for self-healing and transformation, and was able to perform many miraculous acts. (Divine Cosmos)

There is a lot more information about the Life of Ra-Ta but it's beyond the scope of this assignment to go into all of the details. With Uranus in Leo in the 1st square Pluto in Taurus in the 10th House, it is no surprise that he experienced a sudden fall from grace. With Neptune semi-square Venus in Pisces in the 7th House, Ra-Ta made enemies with various others who kept their dislike of him hidden. Having instituted a moral code that included loyalty in marriage and communal living (Jupiter in Capricorn in the 5th trine quintile Venus/Saturn/Mercury in Pisces in the 7th semi-square Neptune in the 9th), Ra-Ta created more than a few powerful, hidden enemies who sought to bring him down. They conspired against him and tricked (Mercury) him into breaking his own law. He was then banished once again.

It is said that ". . . wherever Ra Ta lived he carried his blessings with him, and the banishment only helped to further his Soul evolution." It is said that during his banishment, Ra-Ta met an earlier incarnation of the Soul known as Hermes Trismegistus who the Egyptians hailed as "the scribe of the Gods" as he had prophetic dreams and could look "forward and backward" in time. Hermes and Ra Ta were closely associated, and Cayce referred to Hermes as "the heart and the tongue of Ra."

Ra-Ta was eventually called back to Egypt and his banishment lifted. During this period the pyramids were constructed. Cayce credits Hermes as the architect and Ra-Ta as the second most significant collaborator. He claims, "By some esoteric means, the stones were levitated and set in place."

Going back to the 6th House archetype (South Node of Neptune in the 6th House), Cayce also incarnated as Lucius of Cyrene, who is mentioned twice in the New Testament. According to Catholic Online, Lucius was Bishop of Cyrene in Ptolemais, Africa. He was one of the prophets and doctors mentioned in Acts.

According to the A.R.E.:

> The Gospel of Luke, Chapter 10, verses 1 to 20, introduces readers of the Bible to the group of Seventy disciples who were sent out in pairs by Jesus to preach, heal, and advise the local residents of His pending arrival in their area. Lucius was one of Jesus' disciples in this group. There is speculation that Lucius was "Luke," who Paul refers to as "Beloved Physician," author of the Gospel of Luke in the New Testament, but in one reading Cayce states that Lucius was a nephew of Luke, not Luke himself.

In any case, both Luke and Lucius were physicians and healers.

Again, with the South Node of Neptune in Aquarius in the 6th House, Lucius was "disregarded and questioned by those who were of the Jewish faith who were the close followers of the Master" due to his Greek and Roman parentage. The reason for this was because if he had been chosen as one of the Apostles, "there would have been a puffing up." His true purpose in meeting Jesus and becoming one of the seventy was to "grow" through "lessons gained through" these experiences (6th House - self-improvement).

Cayce also incarnated as Pythagoras, the Greek philosopher and mathematician, who taught that the Soul was immortal and merely resides in the body, survives death and goes through a series of rebirths until the Soul is purified. Pythagoras is one of the great teachers in recorded history. He is said to have remembered all the details of his past lives and could even listen to the "harmony of the spheres" or the vibration of the planets orbiting in the solar system.

Cayce's South Node of Neptune in Aquarius in the 6th House is sextile Jupiter in Capricorn in the 5th House trine Moon/Neptune/Chiron in Taurus in the 9th House square the North Node ruler Uranus in Leo in the 1st House. Together these symbols correlate to an ability to tap into the collective unconscious and give structure and form to what is learned, as well as an ability to grasp mathematics (Uranus/Aquarius) and teach (Jupiter/9th/Chiron) others.

Although Cayce appears to have had many "glamorous" lives in which he was endowed with psychic and healing powers, he also experienced several lives in which he expressed the other side of Neptune. In 18th and 19th century America, Cayce reincarnated two times as a man named John Bainbridge who was a gambler and a womanizer. It is said that Bainbridge's escapist behavior was so strong that he drowned the first time and felt a need to return and do this particular life over, even taking the same name as before. At the end of this second life, he redeemed himself by giving the last of his food to a starving child. In doing so, he saved the child's life while sacrificing his own. According to the Cayce Readings, such a selfless act of love alleviated a great deal of the karma that he had accumulated as Bainbridge.

Uranus in Leo in the 1st square Moon/Neptune in the 9th trine Jupiter in the 5th and semi-square Venus in Pisces in the 7th sextile Mars in the 5th correlate to an escapist adventurer with a penchant for gambling and romance. Of course, his Pisces stellium in the 7th house correlates with self-sacrifice for the well-being of others. With Neptune's South Node in the 6th House semi-sextile this stellium, the self-sacrifice serves to purify the Soul. I believe that these lives as Bainbridge were necessary in order to evolve from 2nd Stage Spiritual to 3rd Stage. This was accomplished when Bainbridge sacrificed his life by giving his food to the child.

These are just a few examples that show how what we have learned about Neptune, its South Node and the South Node Ruler, in relation to past life experiences, seems to describe Cayce's past lives quite well. And we have only skimmed the surface.

(3) North Node of Neptune by its own House, Sign, and Aspects

This correlates to how the Soul will actualize, give purpose to, and integrate both the current life Neptune relative to its past which is, again, symbolized by the South Node of Neptune.

Cayce's North Node of Neptune is 8 degrees Leo in the 12th House. This shows that Cayce would apply all of the psychic skills he developed in previous lives in his current life as Edgar Cayce in order to continue accessing the collective unconscious and channeling metaphysical and health related information to mankind. Leo is ruled by the Sun in Pisces in the 8th House. Cayce's creative purpose was to use his psychic energies and abilities to tap into the collective unconscious in order to answer essential questions pertaining to life and death and the mysteries of life and the afterlife.

With Neptune's North Node ruler being the Sun in Pisces in the 8th House, there is a desire for union with a superior being, as well as a desire for oneness and unity. In addition, there is an ability to tune-in to others and the collective unconscious. The occult, hidden mysteries, intuition, healing, transformation, psychology and death are all themes tied to this purpose. Cayce's creative purpose was to enlighten people about these topics. In doing so, he helped people learn how to heal their bodies and what the cause behind their "dis-ease" was. He also helped people deal with grief. In addition, he revealed a lot of metaphysical information about the history of humankind, the evolution of the Soul and other metaphysical realities that have been forgotten over the course of time. Cayce is now known as the "Father of Holistic

Medicine" and one of the most prolific psychics of all time. Just about everything he brought into the collective awareness was recycled information derived from the collective unconscious.

Aspects to the Sun in Pisces in the 8th House are:

- Semi-square the Moon in Taurus in the 9th House
- Square Jupiter in Capricorn in the 5th House
- Bi-quintile Uranus in Leo in the 1st House
- Sextile Pluto in Taurus in the 10th House
- Semi-sextile Chiron in Aries in the 9th House

These are all the same archetypes that have been in play in the past. The sextile to Pluto in the 10th House shows that Cayce's creative purpose would also be the greatest sociological role he would play in his life. The semi-sextile with Chiron in Aries in the 9th House shows he would instinctually teach people how to heal themselves. In addition, it may have been part of his purpose to reconcile the Christianity of his day with Natural Law.

(4) Psychic Abilities

In addition to everything discussed above, the North Node of the Moon is Pisces in the 7th House and part of the stellium that includes Mercury, Saturn, and Venus. Venus rules Taurus with the Moon, Neptune and Pluto in Taurus which correlate to his psychic abilities and the past intention and desire of his Soul, as well as his sociological role/career. In addition, Saturn rules his 6th House, showing he was determined to do this work, which was his way of serving God or the Source. His Saturn is conjunct Mercury giving him the discipline needed to control his mind. This control is necessary in order to go in and out of a trance state at will.

In Reading 254-2, Cayce was questioned, and provided answers to these questions, about his own Soul. This psychic reading was given by Edgar Cayce in Selma, Alabama, on March 19, 1919:

> We have the body here - we have had it before. In this state the conscious mind is under subjugation of the subconscious or Soul mind. The information obtained and given by this body is obtained through the power of mind over mind, or power of mind over physical matter, or obtained by the suggestion as given to the active part of the subconscious mind. It obtains its information from that which it has gathered, either from other subconscious minds - put in touch with the power of the suggestion of the mind controlling the

speaking faculties of this body, or from minds that have passed into the Beyond, which leave their impressions and are brought in touch by the power of the suggestion. What is known to one subconscious mind or Soul is known to another, whether conscious of the fact or not. The subjugation of the conscious mind putting the subconscious in action in this manner or in one of the other of the manners as described, this body obtains its information when in the subconscious state.

As to the forces of this body, the psychical is obtained through action of Uranus and of Neptune, always it has been to this body and always will, just outside the action of fire-arms, yet ever within them, just saved financially and spiritually by the action of great amount of water - the body should live close to the sea, should always have done so. The body is strange to other bodies in all of its actions, in the psychical life, in all of its ideas as expressed in the spiritual life as to its position on all matters pertaining to political, religious or economic positions. This body will either be very rich or very poor.

(Q)   Is there any other information that this body should have now?

(A)   The body should keep close in touch with the spiritual side of life; with sincerity to the spiritual side of life, if he is to be successful, mentally, physically, psychically and financially.

Here we see that Cayce himself, while channeling the collective conscious, names Uranus, the ruler of Neptune's South Node, and Neptune itself, as the source of his psychic abilities. He states they have always been this source, and always will be.

EXAMPLE CHART B

Neptune: The Collective Consciousness and Unconscious
Professor Carl Jung

by Linda

- Natal Neptune 3.03 deg Taurus 3rd house

- South Node of Neptune 10.43 deg Aquarius 1st

- South Node ruler, Uranus 14.48 deg Leo 7th (conjunct North Node of Neptune)

- North Node of Neptune 10.13 deg Leo 7th

- North Node ruler, Sun 3.19 deg Leo 7th (conjunct North Node of Neptune)

Carl Jung

The Collective Unconscious - so far as we can say anything about it at all - appears to consist of mythological motifs or primordial images, for which reason the myths of all nations are its real exponents. In fact, the whole of mythology could be taken as a sort of projection of the Collective Unconscious... We can therefore study the Collective Unconscious in two ways, either in mythology or in the analysis of the individual. (Jung)

Carl Gustav Jung was a Swiss psychiatrist and psychotherapist who founded analytical psychology. Jung's interest in philosophy and the occult led many to view him as a mystic, although his ambition was to be seen as a man of science. He was a prolific writer, with many of his works not published until after his death. Jung loved nature, chose to live by the sea, and developed an early interest in plants, animals and stones. Around the age of 10 he became aware that God's image was not only reflected in man, but in all of nature reflected through the cosmos. As pointed out on Wikipedia, Jung created some of the best-known psychological concepts, including:

- **Archetypes** [which are also studied in astrology; some developed by Jung are Mother, Rebirth, Spirit, Trickster]

- **Collective Unconscious** (the part of the unconscious that contains memories and ideas inherited from our ancestors). Jung agreed with Freud's model of the unconscious, what Jung called the "personal unconscious," but he also proposed the existence of a second, far deeper form of the unconscious underlying the personal one. This was the Collective Unconscious.

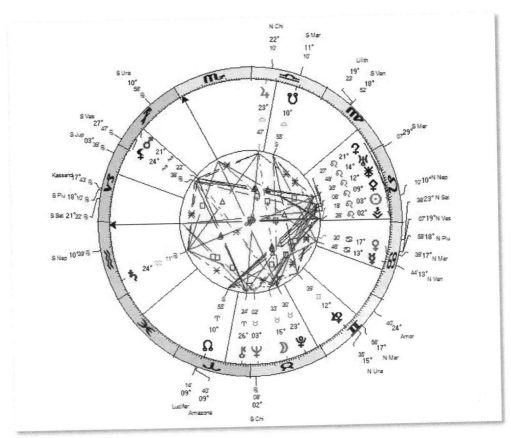

JUNG

- **Individuation** [Uranus, Aquarius, 11th house, Planetary Nodes of Uranus] – a process of transformation whereby the personal and Collective Unconscious are brought into consciousness (by means of dreams for example) to be assimilated into the whole personality. It is a completely natural process necessary for the integration of the psyche to take place, creates advances in humane values, and understanding of human nature and the universe.

- **Shadow** [Saturnian judgment, Plutonian darkness, Neptunian false persona] and **Anima/Animus** [masculine and feminine, relationship dynamics]. Jung considered that the 'shadow' and the 'anima/animus' differed from other archetypes because their content is more directly related to the individual's personal situation, and less to the Collective Unconscious.

- **Persona** [Moon, Moon's Nodes, ego, self-image, egocentric structure]. The persona appears as a consciously created personality or identity fashioned out of part of the collective psyche. The persona, Jung argued, is a mask for the "collective psyche," a mask that "pretends" individuality, so that both self and others believe in that identity, even if it is really no more than a well-played role

261

through which the collective psyche is expressed. Jung regarded the "persona-mask" as a complicated system, which mediates between individual consciousness and the social community: it is "a compromise between the individual and society as to what a man should appear to be."

> In addition to our immediate consciousness, which is of a thoroughly personal nature and which we believe to be the only empirical psyche (even if we tack on the personal unconscious as an appendix), there exists a second psychic system of a collective, universal, and impersonal nature which is identical in all individuals. This Collective Unconscious does not develop individually but is inherited. It consists of pre-existent forms, the archetypes, which can only become conscious secondarily and which give definite form to certain psychic contents. (Jung)

The hypothesis of the Collective Unconscious at first was limited to denoting the state of repressed or forgotten contents, and, for Freud, the unconscious was of an exclusively personal nature. This personal layer of the unconscious is undoubtedly personal and is called the "personal unconscious" (containing complexes, the personal side of psychic life). But this personal unconscious rests upon a deeper layer that is called the "Collective Unconscious." The term "collective" was chosen by Yung because this part of the unconscious is not individual but Universal. In contrast to the personal psyche, the Collective Unconscious has contents and modes of behavior that are more or less the same everywhere and in all individuals. It is identical in all humans and thus constitutes a common psychic substratum that is present in everyone.

> The Collective Unconscious is content of consciousness that pertains to the entire human species. It resides within each human body. The collective conscious is the totality of all thoughts and vibrations existing at any moment in time, on the conscious level. We each tune into these through Neptune, and osmose them into ourselves through Scorpio. The impact of totality alters our perceptions and personal realities. (Rad)

The contents of the Collective Unconscious are known as "archetypes." Primitive tribal lore modified the archetypes: they are no longer contents of the unconscious, but have already been changed into conscious formulas taught according to tradition, generally in the form of esoteric teaching. This is a typical means of expression for the transmission of collective contents originally derived from the unconscious. There is a considerable difference between the "archetype" and the historical formula that has evolved. Each archetype of unconscious content, by being perceived, took on the psychic dimensions of the individual consciousness in which it happened to appear.

I would place Jung in the 3rd stage Individuated moving into the 1st stage Spiritual because of his work with the Collective Unconscious. Within the Soul of Jung, as within the Soul of every human, was an awareness of the totality and immensity of the big picture of manifest creation. He had a deep desire to know intrinsically the origin of all things, as well as the origin of the Soul itself. His strong need to understand creation via the vast collection of information in many past lives – Pluto Taurus 3rd – was the basis of creating current life cosmologies that could explain it – Pluto polarity point Scorpio 9th ruled by Pluto itself.

The following signature:

- Neptune Taurus 3rd
- Pisces in the 2nd house
- 12th house Capricorn ruled by Saturn Aquarius 1st

. . . gave him the capacity to be able to tune into the Collective Unconscious and the collective conscious, and to osmose them into himself through the Pluto polarity point Scorpio 9th.

Specifically through the following aspects:

- Saturn Aquarius 1st (ruler of his 12th house)
- Saturn's opposition to Uranus
- Saturn conjunct South Node of Neptune
- Saturn opposite North Node of Neptune
- Saturn last quarter square Pluto (exact)
- Moon square Saturn

. . . he was able to study the structural nature of consciousness itself. This meant understanding the natural boundaries between the conscious and the unconsciousness, with these progressive levels made up of:

- **Egocentric Structure** – the subjective awareness of the individual, created by the Soul (Moon, Cancer, 4th house, Moon's Nodes)

- **Individuated Unconsciousness** of the Soul – the totality of a Soul's dynamics/memories for all lives it has ever lived, unique to that Soul (Uranus, Aquarius, 11th house, Nodes of Uranus)

- **Collective Consciousness** – the totality of all thoughts/vibrations existing at any moment in time, on a conscious level (Neptune, Pisces, 12th house, Nodes of Neptune)

- **Collective Unconsciousness** – the content of consciousness that pertains to the entire human species, residing within each human (Neptune, Pisces, 12th house, Nodes of Neptune)

Jung's ability to study all of these levels of consciousness correlated to his Moon Taurus 3rd being the Final Dispositor of the Chart (along with the Sun Leo 7th). He also understood that the natural boundary of Saturn in relation to the structural nature of consciousness could change the individual's perception of its identity from ego to its timeless identity: the Soul (Pluto). The spiritual evolution of Yung enabled him to perceive himself as not separate from anything, but in fact interrelated to everything (the unconscious). This can be summed up through the ruler of his Pluto-Moon-Neptune Taurus 3rd ruled by Venus Cancer 6th: an x-ray vision, an eye for detail, a desire to be of service, a caring and nurturing nature, and the ability and determination to undertake rigorous scientific work.

Pluto Paradigm

Due to the structure of the Soul – Pluto Taurus 3rd – Jung naturally gravitated to the collection of data by way of deductive logic, and this began with university studies in medicine, psychiatry, psychology and pathology – and of course, this had been the Soul's purpose for many past lives. This Soul intention (Pluto Taurus 3rd ruled by Venus) was supported by South Node Libra 8th (also ruled by Venus, amplifying the Natural Law of "giving, sharing and inclusion") – the desire to absorb and merge with powerful sources, symbols, people and systems of knowledge, a desire to probe into the mysterious of life and death, a natural psychoanalytical ability, and the desire to SHARE these psychological findings with others in order to be of service to others, the Collective of Souls – and with both of these facilitated by Venus Cancer 6th (ruler also of Neptune) the Soul had a desire to be of service to others through self-analysis, while at the same time developing emotional security because of the detailed information collected. Venus is ruled by the Moon Taurus 3rd, the integrator between the egocentric structure of the past (South Node) and the evolutionary forward of the potential future (North Node).

Neptune, Pisces, and the 12th House

Neptune, Pisces and the 12th house correlates to the nature of consciousness. These dynamics determined the form through which Jung's consciousness would manifest in the current life: Neptune Taurus 3rd describes a consciousness that was constantly on the move collecting and disseminating information and knowledge; Pisces on the cusp of the 2nd house defined a mystical, religious nature or relationship with the Divine (the Collective Unconscious) that brought a sense of emotional and physical security; and Saturn ruling the 12th house – Jung's social purpose, his explorations into the human mind, the unconscious, and the actual "structure" of consciousness, and how his individual Soul consciousness conditioned the collective of his time, and how his individual Soul consciousness was conditioned by the collective cosmologies of his time.

Neptune Taurus 3rd

Neptune Taurus 3rd in opposition to Jupiter Libra 9th demanded that Professor Jung enter the social sphere where he could develop his discoveries, cosmologies, and search for truth, especially the theory of the Collective Unconscious. Furthermore, with Sun Leo 7th and the North Node Neptune Leo 7th it was imperative that he share this life purpose with others. Gradually, as Yung individuated from the Collective Unconscious, the statements made in his many writings and books (deductive logic Pluto Taurus 3rd) were reformulated into an established stable core of theory (inductive logic, intuition, psychology, Pluto polarity point Scorpio 9th) thus impacting the state of the collective consciousness.

Neptune Taurus 3rd in the same house as Pluto, the Soul, emphasized Jung's mind and intellect, and especially his inner messages to himself that had a direct bearing on his self-image – ruler Venus Cancer 6th. It is revealed that Jung not always felt ready or good enough, and perhaps explains why he saw the human psyche as "by nature religious" and made this religiousness the focus of his explorations, an example being his creation of long monographs on the symbolism of the self in the Christian aeon (saviors, and doctrine of universal reconciliation), Gnosis and Christian Mysticism. Pluto 3rd forming a yod with Jupiter Libra 9th and Mars Sagittarius 11th describes a Soul that had experienced ongoing intellectual crises from which he desired to liberate and individuate from forms of distorted information and untruths in order that universal truths could be restored. Due to the Virgoan archetype of "self-humiliation" represented in the yod, Yung never felt satisfied, and this desire motivated him toward continuous self-improvement. Having produced many collected works, he could easily have been a workaholic, self-sacrificing himself in order to establish his theories (Pluto Taurus 3rd). Suffering the deep emptiness of existential void, he could have compensated for this inner emptiness by always being busy.

In general, the Neptune archetype resonates with the Age of Pisces just ending. Within the Pisces Age, and during Jung's life, was the underlying cause of the sadomasochistic distortion of life being the religious foundations of the patriarchal culture. Jung's work on himself and his patients convinced him that life has a spiritual purpose beyond material goals. "Our main task," he believed, "is to discover and fulfill our deep innate potential." Based on his study of Christianity, Hinduism, Buddhism, Gnosticism, Taoism, and other traditions (Pluto polarity point Scorpio 9th), Jung believed that this journey of transformation, which he called individuation, is at the mystical heart of all religions. Because of the Collective Unconscious that everyone is tuned into, Jung was affected by this cultural conditioning, along with everyone else. Jung warned that the collective shadow as well as our own personal shadow has a very powerful influence on the choices we make. The impact of WWI, the Depression, and inequality of the sexes no doubt had an influential effect upon him.

South Node Neptune Aquarius 1st

With the South Node of Neptune Aquarius 1st the Soul resonated with the past Astrological Ages of Aries, Aquarius and Pisces, and specifically correlated to the time when humans began living in farming communities when cosmologies were invented to explain the nature of phenomenal reality. "Projections" of individual Souls and groups took place in order to understand the phenomenal nature of creation. The past contents of the unconscious had already been changed into conscious formulas passed down through tradition, religion and esoteric teachings, being the transmission of the collective contents originally derived from the unconscious becoming altered by becoming conscious.

"Projection" of the Soul's desire for understanding and ultimate meaning upon the phenomenal nature of creation became the basis for those philosophies and religions. It then became necessary for the Soul to decondition and liberate from these past realities that had nothing to do with actual reality. Invented religions and cosmologies from those Ages past that were not naturally true and that had caused all kinds of traumas (Aquarius) to the Soul (and to the collective) were brought forwards into the current life of Jung. In order to break free of concepts of God, philosophies, religions, and past realities that had nothing to do with the actual Source, the Soul of Jung had followed the new path of the 'instinctual archetype' existing in the unconscious mind (South Node of Neptune Aquarius 1st). Resonating with the Age of Aries comprising religious notions of a war-like God, and cosmologies that had been used against other groups as a weapon to punish, eliminate, dominate and control, Yung probably had a courageous and competitive spirit, but needed to dissolve (through disillusionment) many illusions (religious concepts) in relation to what held ultimate meaning in his individualized consciousness.

Ruler of South Node Neptune – Uranus Leo 7th

- Ruler of the South Node of Neptune, Uranus Leo 7th conjunct the North Node of Neptune Leo
- Saturn opposite Uranus
- Moon square Uranus
- Uranus square Pluto
- Uranus trine North Node Aries 2nd
- Uranus trine South Node of Uranus Sagittarius 10th

Jung drew upon the "collective memory" of the "Collective Unconscious" (applying to all humans) via his own "individuated unconscious" (unique content of the Soul in relation to all past lives) in order to liberate from and become free of the past.

Jung drew upon the long-term memories of the current life and past lives in order to access "thought forms" at key evolutionary stages. The long term memories that bound the Soul to the past which had provided a sense of security and familiarity, interfaced with the new thought forms or repeating messages that would actualize the evolutionary forward in order to liberate from that past. Acting upon these new message would allow the Soul to make gigantic evolutionary leaps (accelerated evolution). The thought forms that appeared of their own accord that then led to the process of conscious thinking (Mercury Cancer 6th, lower octave of Uranus) allowed Jung to understand the meaning of the messages arising from his individuated unconscious that was connected to the Collective Unconscious, hence evolution was effected, breaking free from the past intellectual framework, and developing new ideologies more in line with Natural Law (Pluto polarity point Scorpio 9th, Jupiter Libra 9th, Mars Sagittarius 11th), and defined through the egocentric structure: North Node Aries 2nd ruled by Mars Sagittarius 11th, with those reinstated Natural Laws giving his life more value, purpose and meaning.

> Astrology is of particular interest to the psychologist, since it contains a sort of psychological experience, which we call projection - this means that we find the psychological facts as it were in the constellations. This originally gave rise to the idea that these factors derive from the stars, whereas they are merely in a relation of synchronicity with them. I admit that this is a very curious fact, which throws a peculiar light on the structure of the human mind. (Jung)

Astrology had a significant impact on the formation of Jung's theories. Through his study of mythology, he came to understand the correlation between astrology and myth. This understanding helped him to formulate his theories on archetypes, a critical underpinning in his understanding of the human psyche. Astrology also was critical in the composition of his understanding of personality types. With his theory on synchronicity, Jung tied the universal symbols, including astrological symbols, which he called archetypes, directly to the workings of the human mind while circumventing the need to show a direct causal connection.

North Node Neptune Leo 7th

The South Node of Neptune in Aquarius reflected the original matriarchal roots of the current and future desires in the Soul of Jung to spiritualize consciousness, thus signifying accelerated evolution to restore the Natural Law of "giving, sharing, and inclusion" (North Node of Neptune Leo 7th). Due to the patriarchy, this Natural Law became perverted to self-interest and exclusion, which caused humans or groups to compete with others relative to the survival instinct, leading to dominance and submission (7th). Thus, the North Node of Neptune Leo 7th served as the vehicle for the evolutionary future to manifest, integrated in each moment by new information correlating to Neptune Taurus 3rd. The North Node Neptune Leo 7th was linked with unconscious expectations that were projected upon others in relationships, and extremities such as an inability to reach a balanced state of giving and receiving. The North Node of Neptune generated delusions and fantasies when ultimate meaning had been "projected" externally within relationships. Balance was gained in Jung's relationship with the Divine which, in his world, correlated to the Collective Unconscious, and in which Jung found an immense creative intellectual purpose (5th house ruled by Mercury).

Ruler of North Node Neptune Leo – Sun Leo 7th

Via the archetype of South Node Neptune and natal Neptune, the North Node Neptune represented the evolutionary forward of bringing balance to past life ideas of God being at the heart of all creation (Leo). With his Sun Leo opposite the Aquarius Ascendant, Jung had to deal with extreme swings between his own individuation and the sublimation of his individuated consciousness into the collective (Aquarius). Sun square Neptune was another symbol of dissolution of personal untruths, and the reinstatement of balance through a surrender of the personal will to a Higher Will. Evolution toward balance would allow the Soul of Jung to evolve beyond the illusory contents of his individuated unconscious – invented religions, gods that are "right," "God creating man in its own image," as well as puffed up images of himself. However, this archetype also showed Jung how he could "know" that which had created him. So for Yung, that meant a lifetime of exploration, study and service, that was to become the vehicle by which to disseminate his psychological/spiritual knowledge to others.

Conclusion

- Jung's evolutionary journey was to meet the Self (Egocentric Structure, Individuated Unconscious), and at the same time to meet the Divine (Collective Unconscious, Neptune).

- Jung shared with others true aspects of the Source (Collective Unconscious, Neptune) thus liberating his Individuated Unconscious (Uranus) beyond all the invented and projected religions and cosmologies cast down through centuries.

- Jung's explorations and discoveries into the "structure" of Consciousness impacted upon his own Soul in such a way as to effect accelerated evolution.

- Jung's own accelerated evolution via his life work accelerated the evolution of the Collective Conscious of his time, imprinting upon it his own unique brand of individuality (Individuated Unconscious).

- The accelerated evolutionary journey of the Soul in the lifetime of Carl Jung also impacted upon the Collective Unconsciousness in such a way as to indelibly stamp upon it his own uniquely evolved Individuated Unconsciousness in order to evolve the bigger picture of the Collective Unconsciousness itself.

EXAMPLE CHART C

Neptune: The Collective Consciousness and Unconscious
Rachel Maddow

by Kristin

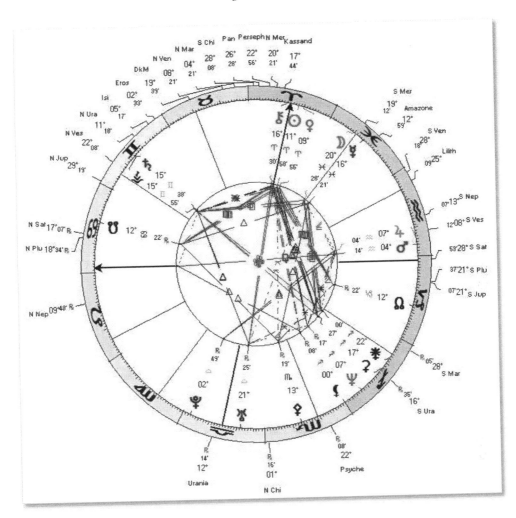

MADDOW

The collective unconscious impacts on the individual's Soul consciousness in such a way as to stimulate and ignite the desire to individuate from it and, in turn, the Soul will impact on the current state of the collective consciousness. (Rad)

We are all individual creations from God, each one of us uniquely designed to express our individuality in the world. Similar to waves separating from the sea, we are Souls emerging and traveling in a separating motion with full intentions to actualize the desires born out of our being, but as we enter a superstructure in a society that separates and excludes versus invites and includes, so many Souls' unique design becomes diffused and repressed.

Countless combinations of realities will have a way of coloring and conditioning the naturalness and the original intention set forth by the Soul as we all have the South Nodes of Pluto, Saturn and Jupiter in Capricorn. It takes great courage to walk in the shoes that were designed to fit us as we have all been subjected to patriarchal influences, and very few Souls have been able to maintain the purity of their natural design, rebelling at all costs. However, even underneath the armor of protection, the many skins that Souls have collected over time, the individual make up exists and is a piece to the cosmic puzzle. Each one of us influenced by the totality of the whole and, as a result, ignited with the desire to actively express our individual selves in order for the puzzle pieces in the collective to fit.

The chart I chose is one of a Soul who has done her fair share of rebelling, persecuted harshly as a result of expressing her own unique individuality, ridiculed and raped by the system, locked up, maimed, tortured, killed 'for her words,' you name it, simply for trying to be who she is, which led to lifetimes of hiding behind this natural design. South Node in Cancer in the 12th, ruler Moon in Pisces 9th with Mercury 8th, squaring South Node of Uranus Rx in Sagittarius opposing Saturn in Gemini in the 11th, this squares her Moon, chart ruler, in Pisces, as well as Mercury. However, in this life, she is back on her horse, Neptune in Sagittarius in the 5th trining a 9th house Sun, the ruler of her North Node of Neptune in the 1st, testing the very edges of those waters, as a daily spot light serves to help restore her sense of self, providing sound for that instrument called her voice, as she gives others the courage to "come out, come out, wherever and whoever you are."

Journalist Rachel Maddow – 3rd Stage Individuated

Maddow is the first openly gay anchor to host a major prime-time news program in the United States. She has a degree in public policy from Stanford and holds a doctorate in politics from Oxford University. For Rachel, it would have been essential, especially not only being a woman in a man's world, but a gay woman, to earn the social stripes necessary in the form of degrees from schools of this rank and caliber in order to be given even the slightest consideration to be taken seriously and viewed capable and credible to do what she came here to do, to deliver news, words of truth, to the nation and the world.

All it would take to ignite her desire to influence public policy and to use her voice for change is to experience the lies and the injustices that pervade the world of politics, fueling her desire and natural need to help restore a greater balance for a democratic nation versus a country being driven by the top few percent, who also happen to be primarily men. She has been rebelling against mainstream doctrine as long as she has been on this plane of existence; her intention is to challenge backward thinkers, mainstream herd state mentality. Maddow was destined for the world stage and her greatest attributes include not only her supreme intelligence, rumored IQ of 135, but the sheer speed at which her mind works, which is always driven by her search for the hard, cold truth:

- Neptune in Sagittarius in the 5th sextiling South Node of Neptune in Aquarius in the 7th conjunct Mars/Jupiter in Aquarius
- Ruler Uranus Rx in Libra in the 4th trine Saturn Rx in Gemini in the 11th
- Natal Neptune in Sagittarius forms a Grand Trine to her North Node of Neptune in Leo in the 1st and her Sun/Venus balsamic conjunction in Aries in the 9th
- The Sun being the ruler of her North Node of Neptune.

Nothing means more to her than the truth, no matter what it looks like. The pain and trauma of the collective unconscious as a result of countries colliding and subgroups within cultures finding themselves polarized due to opposing beliefs, political, religious and otherwise, has driven her to search and uncover, to speak up and do what she can to promote more awareness about the root cause for the unrest. Nothing drives her more than being able to expose the facts, Pallas Rx in Scorpio in the 4th trine her Mercury/Moon in Pisces in the 8th/9th and trine South Node in Cancer in the 12th, for justice sake, for fairness for all.

- South Node of Neptune in Aquarius in the 7th is conjunct Jupiter and Mars in Aquarius
- Mars rules her 9th house Sun and Venus
- Uranus, the ruler of her South Node of Neptune in Aquarius is in Libra in the 4th and is retrograde
- Uranus forms an inconjunct to her 9th house Pisces Moon
- Rachel's natal Neptune is also in Sagittarius, truth again, in her 5th house, and is trining her 9th house Sun and Venus forming a balsamic conjunction

What is felt beneath her keen awareness and unparalleled ability to cut to the chase and carve out the facts is a palpable compassion for those who suffer at the hands of the heavy hitters. Her Moon in Pisces in the 9th is conjunct Mercury in Pisces in the 8th and they both square Saturn in Gemini in the 11th reflecting the trauma from the judgments and rigid mind sets of the mainstream world, a world she has never fit into. She has never fit in, in any form, nor was she meant to, so she could represent those Souls seeded on the outskirts:

- Her South Node of Neptune is in Aquarius in the 7th conjunct Jupiter and Mars in Aquarius
- The ruler is Uranus retrograde in the 4th in Libra opposing her Sun, MC and Chiron in the 10th in Aries.

For lifetimes she has been born into families and tribes that were more on the fringes of society, except for perhaps lifetimes as of late due to her Soul hiding behind and within families that allowed her to appear 'normal,' giving her a foundation of sorts to prepare for a life where she can launch herself into the world on a fair playing ground, where she could fairly earn her way to the top. In this life, she was in full compensation mode in high school, sporting blonde highlights and pearls (photo attached). Maddow has stated that her family is "very, very Catholic," and she grew up in a very conservative community:

- Saturn in Gemini in the 11th opposing Neptune Rx in Sagittarius in the 5th and square Moon in Pisces in the 9th

- Also, her South Node in Cancer is conjunct North Nodes of Pluto and Saturn in Capricorn in the 12th and square her Uranus Rx in the 4th in Libra, the ruler of her South Node of Neptune in Aquarius in the 7th

When hiding is in place, often times Souls will be born into families that reflect the extremity of their nature in order to force them out of hiding, and so it did. Rachel could only hold that cover for so long as in her freshman year at Stanford, at the age of 17, she was ousted by the college newspaper when an interview with her was published before she could tell her parents. An unconscious or perhaps conscious rebellion towards authority figures. Surprisingly enough, there was only one other female student at the entire university, which happens to be in the so-called alternative San Francisco area, who was openly gay, so Rachel decided to announce her sexual orientation, written in her own words on the inside of all the bathroom stalls at the school. As a result, the school newspaper wanted to do an interview. She asked that they not release the story until she told her parents over the weekend but someone anonymously sent her parents the article before she arrived. Her parents' greatest concern was that, due to their conservative faith, they believed that being a lesbian was a 'sin' and their concern that she would 'go to hell.' Uranus, the ruler of her South Node of Neptune is Rx in Libra in her 4th.

This reflects being a role model for being different, having the courage to lead the way when no one else will, coming out of her own closet and creating shocks if necessary. It also connects to her actions to support others like her, serving as what Jeffrey used to call, plucking piano wires, like a radio signal being sent out to others of similar desires and design, creating a resonance that carries a vibration to reach all of the other Souls like her, lesbians, androgynous types and the like, to strengthen their resolve. The life-changing event took place when transiting Uranus, ruler of her South Node of Neptune in Aquarius in the 7th was in Capricorn, conjunct her North Node and squaring her Venus/Sun, ruler of her North Node of Neptune, in Aries in the 9th. Transiting Saturn was in Capricorn and squaring her natal Uranus Rx in Libra in the 4th.

A Note on Retrogrades

Rachel's Uranus is Rx, which is the ruler of her South Node of Neptune in Aquarius in the 7th. All retrograde planets reflect an individuation process, as they mimic the energy of Uranus. With Uranus itself Rx, this exaggerates this theme and accentuates the focus with an acceleration along the lines of returning back to her alternative self. For Rachel it was similar to the analogy of pushing a beach ball under water, the further you push it down, and repress the natural expression, emotion, the harder it is to hold. That ball is going to dart up out of the water in some unexpected direction and with great speed. This is an example of what happened when Rachel 'ousted' herself, in an extreme and unexpected way. Detachment occurs in varying degrees with this signature and the clear visible DETACHMENT that she appears to have is because it removes her Soul from the emotional dynamics that have kept her bound to conditioning.

Her natural brilliance had her thinking way ahead of the game. Her mother has been quoted saying that she remembers Rachel at the age of four on the kitchen floor with the newspaper sprawled out in front of her. She has a mind for change and innovation and for bringing people together from all walks of life. She is queen diplomat, communicator, arbitrator, negotiator extraordinaire and her voice documents her findings with a proof that prevents the naysayers to question her position coupled with an objectivity that allows her to work hard to listen to what others are saying as well in order to give them a fair shot to speak their peace.

Maddow is a natural messenger, a storyteller and a speaker for the people, with a powerful handle of the language capable of delivering the news "with agenda and without hysteria":

- Pluto Rx in the 3rd trine South Node of Neptune in Aquarius
- Jupiter and Mars in the 7th
- Also, Pluto rules Pallas Rx in Scorpio in the 4th which trines Mercury/Moon (chart ruler) in Pisces

As an Aries, she has learned the art of being responsive versus reactive which allows her guests to remain at ease and open for productive exchanges and with Venus balsamic to her Sun in Aries trining Neptune in Sagittarius along with a South Node of Neptune in the 7th in Aquarius conjunct Jupiter, the ruler of her natal Neptune and conjunct Mars, the ruler of her natal Sun and Venus, she is able to see both sides to the story in any given situation but always finds a solid place to land once she has sussed out all things to consider. Her intuition is well honed and her instinct is fierce. She has been recognized and rewarded well for her ability to interrogate and investigate utilizing strategic questioning.

She leans with stories that stun and shock in order to induce greater awareness and to promote action in others. She represents everyone who is considered to be from a different walk of life. Not only is she a woman fighting to make it in a man's world, she is a lesbian, looking neither male or female but equally both in the same image, a truly androgynous Soul, seen with her South Node of Neptune in Aquarius conjunct Jupiter and Mars in Aquarius in the 7th trine a retrograde Pluto in Libra in the 3rd house.

Rachel Maddow – then and now

Maddow takes on the biggest stories of the day with lively debates with people from all sides and covers stories that at times no other show will cover, scouring every resource within reach to bring you the most extensive findings. She naturally, candidly exposes the truth, at times with an angle of humor, often the gallows kind, but she knows how to get her point across without mincing words, Scorpio style, with her Mercury in Pisces in the 8th. Maddow was destined for greatness in her field, natal Neptune in the 5th forming a Grand Trine with the North Node of Neptune in Leo in the 1st and her Sun/Venus in Aries in the 9th. She was given her own daily time slot on national news channel MSNBC in August 2008; she was only 35 years old. Jupiter, the ruler of her natal Neptune in Sagittarius, was retrograde in Capricorn and exactly conjunct her North Node in the 6th. The ruler, Saturn, was in Virgo and perfectly trining her North Node in Capricorn.

In addition, the transiting North Node was in Aquarius conjunct transiting Neptune in her 7th house, the ruler Uranus was retrograde in Pisces conjunct her Moon in the 9th. Her role to document stories around the world will only grow as her North Node of Neptune is in Leo in the 1st and forms a Grand Trine with her Sun/Venus balsamic conjunction in Aries in the 9th and her natal Neptune in the 5th in Sagittarius. A natural born leader to courageously take the lead, spear heading truth, out talking journalism, that turns heads and stops people in their tracks. She easily makes enemies from the middle to the far right but she knows that if she doesn't say something, then who will? She is often one step from crossing the line and she hovers there. As savvy as she may be, she also is limited by her speech to go for the jugular as the conservative corporations own her network, and these forced limitations hem her in, her survival and that microphone is on the line. These limits can be seen with Neptune in Sagittarius in the 5th, ruler of her Mercury/Moon in Pisces in the 8th/9th square Saturn in Gemini in the 11th.

Solid journalists consistently put themselves at risk when the truth exposed threatens the safety, livelihood or reputation of their target by tackling delicate stories that will inevitably set them off. She was designed with the mind of an informational/intuitive genius, where she see the bigger picture while synthesizing countless facts, coming up with the bottom line – like a Sherlock Holmes, a political investigator. Her mind works with ripping speed which also helps her respond to her guests during heated exchanges, she can pull from the inner annals of her memory bank which appears to happen as fast as pushing keys on a computer with her South Node of Neptune in Aquarius conjunct her Jupiter and Mars trine her 3rd house Pluto. As bright and 'mindful' as she is, she has heart, full on. Neptune in the 5th trining a Pisces Moon in the 9th. She cares most about helping people understand what is actually happening in the world, the truth being told especially if she can save a victim who has been unfairly singled out or persecuted. Why? Because she has been there, over and over, she has been there. Also because that is how she was designed. To find the missing piece, to uncover the hidden truth.

Maddow has dealt with cyclical depression since puberty. In a 2012 interview, she stated, "It doesn't take away from my joy or my work or my energy, but coping with depression is something that is part of the everyday way that I live and have lived for as long as I can remember." Most of her Soul energy is in her head, which can be the tendency for people with Pluto in the 3rd house. Also, her Mercury conjuncts Moon in Pisces and this squares Saturn retrograde in Gemini in the 11th. The depression would be a result of all she has battled for and lost, the weight of all the wrong doings of the world and all the innocents who have suffered. Her Pisces Moon and Mercury in Pisces would equal a very sensitive filter, open to the collective pain of the world, but its square to Saturn in Gemini in the 11th, does not allow her to emotionally integrate the magnitude of what she is feeling including the totality of her own trauma from other times, not to mention the challenges brought on in this life simply from being a gay woman in a patriarchal society. She will reach the roof of her own intellectual understanding in this life and there is a limit to what the mind can access, Mercury/Moon square Saturn in Gemini, and for her to evolve, the emotional gates must open, which will ultimately allow her to expand her reach and deepen her impact. However, to be a journalist, it requires an emotional distance to be in the trenches, in order to deliver the hard stories without attachment so a balance will inevitably need to be struck.

To put herself in the limelight is to subject herself to further attack, criticism, harsh judgments by the right wing and to be an open target for those who vehemently oppose her views. But for her, the verbal thorns appear not to touch her; she has heard it all before and has endured far more than what her attackers are dishing out. Just recently famous actor Alec Baldwin was fired from MSNBC for his homophobic rant, specifically negative comments toward Rachel. Baldwin was fired and his show canceled, proof that her influence is rubbing off on people who have the power to deliver appropriate justice. The attacks will continue, but she will continue to put herself out there, because she must. She does it for others, for the collective, South Node of Neptune in the 7th in Aquarius ruler Uranus Rx in Libra in the 4th. She does it for those who can't and she does it because at the end of the day, nothing is worth more to her than being exactly who she is and exposing lies and revealing the hidden truth. The people have a right to know.

EXAMPLE CHART D

Neptune: The Collective Consciousness and Unconscious
Mark Zuckerberg

by Skywalker

Mark Zuckerberg

- South Node of Neptune in Aquarius in the 5th house, ruler Uranus in Sagittarius in the 3rd house

- Natal Neptune in the 4th house in Capricorn

- North Node of Neptune in Leo in the 11th house, ruler Sun in the 9th house in Taurus

- Pluto in Scorpio in the 2nd house

- Pluto rules every planet but the Sun and Venus which are in the 8th house

All rulerships return back to the 2nd and 8th houses which contain most of the planets themselves; someone with so much money and emphasis on big business will usually have these houses highly emphasized, as is the case.

He is the world's youngest billionaire ever.

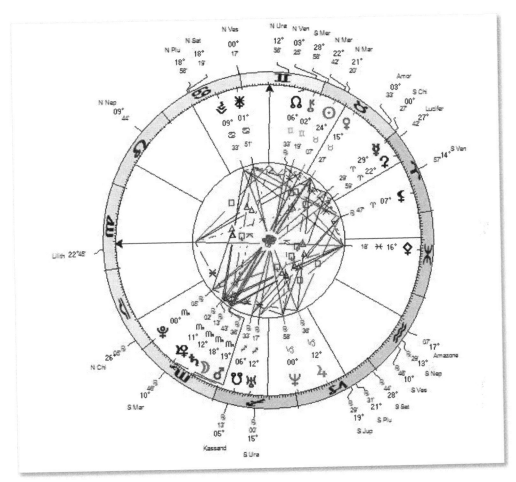

ZUCKERBERG

A couple of quotes by Mark Zuckerberg:

> At Facebook, we're inspired by technologies that have revolutionized how people spread and consume information. We often talk about inventions like the printing press and the television — by simply making communication more efficient, they led to a

complete transformation of many important parts of society. They gave more people a voice. They encouraged progress. They changed the way society was organized. They brought us closer together.

Helping a billion people connect is amazing, humbling and by far the thing I'm most proud of in my life.

Aquarius on the 6th house cusp with Uranus in the 3rd correlates to his desire to serve and "perfect" the world by the use of technology to link people and grant them access to information and education or other technological services he might have in mind or others of like mind might have shared with him.

He seems to be a great example of someone connected to the collective conscious/unconscious as he developed a computer program that was able to connect 1.3 billion people. This control over the flow of information gives him the ability to have an effect on the collective in not so subtle ways. The flow of information has rapidly increased, people are always connected and life is speeding up. People find their old classmates, meet people online as easily as in real life, create businesses and speak their minds to whomever they want. They connect to like-minded people and have faster access to new information and ideas that they wouldn't normally see. On the other hand, there is also the downside of the loss of privacy, people stalking one another and living each time more in the digital domain.

The Beginning of an Empire

January 2004 Transiting Uranus in the 6th house made its last trine to Pluto in the 2nd house which was in effect from the beginning of 2003. Pluto rules the 3rd house, correlating to the use of technology to gain access to information about his colleagues and to connect with them and connect them with one another. It also shows the creative aspect of this transit in which he was able to create something that would be of value with the programming skills he developed as Uranus transited the 6th house.

Transiting Neptune was also conjunct the South Node of Neptune at the founding of Facebook, indicating a new beginning relative to some of his past life dynamics, seemingly connected to information, communication and technology as seen by natal Uranus in the 3rd house. For that, he had to resume those past dynamics by creating the site, which would have an effect on the collective. The transiting Sun was also in Aquarius at that time, correlating to his focus on his creation and to the timing of his "invention." The transiting North Node of the Moon was conjunct Venus in the 8th house at the time of Facebook's launch; little did he know how much money Facebook would generate, or did he have those intentions all along? With Pluto in the 2nd with its aspects, I would say at least subconsciously the intentions were there to build something of value and profit from it. With these astrological symbols, he will not be the frivolous type and be interested in the long run.

Business as Usual

Jupiter, which rules his Uranus, is in Capricorn in the 4th house, trine Venus in Taurus in the 8th shows his self-righteousness in profiting off peoples' privacy and lives which, by accumulating and managing information/data of massive proportions, generates a lot of revenue.

He was accused of stealing the idea and code from other Harvard colleagues, Divya Narendra and twin brothers Tyler and Cameron Winklevoss, who had invited him to work on a project that was of a similar nature, but he ended up working on his own project, with the financial help of his best friend at the time, Eduardo Saverin, whose position in the company was later downplayed by Mark Zuckerberg himself. This was all seen as a betrayal by Eduardo who filed a lawsuit against Mark which settled out of court for shares of Facebook which ended up making him over 2 billion USD. The initial colleagues of Mark Zuckerberg also sued him and settled for around 65 Million USD.

All of this is to show that not all dealings were clear-cut and there are symbols of potential cut throat betrayals in this chart. Betrayals of this nature are very common in the world of big business and multinational corporations, where psychopaths are found in abundance. It's all just business folks! With all that Scorpio, 2nd and 8th house energy configured the way it is, there seems to be a history in his Soul's evolution of this type of phenomenon either as victim or perpetrator of intense betrayals that possibly led to entrapment or to the loss of resources and life itself. The square to the Nodal Axis of Neptune from the Scorpio stellium indicates the loss of his friend due to the "business as usual."

Privacy, Ya Whatever

The inconjunct between the Scorpio Saturn, Moon and Mars, to the MC in Gemini, also correlates to the dynamics of needing to commit to the value of keeping his word to the general public. Gemini and Scorpio have trust issues on an archetypal core level as Gemini doesn't commit too seriously and Scorpio is all about trust, and in order for there to be trust, Scorpio needs to know what it can count on and Gemini, being the sign of duplicity, many times cannot be counted on to commit to one thing and stick to its word. One way for the Scorpio archetype to deal with the Gemini archetype, is to count on the fact that one generally cannot count on Gemini to keep their word, and in this way the Scorpio archetype won't experience the rug being pulled from under its feet. In this sense, people naturally may not trust Facebook and Mark Zuckerberg to stick to his responsibilities relative to privacy and we can expect a certain degree of duplicity relative to his social or professional integrity as it relates to his values, through the inconjunct to the planets in the 2nd house.

Soul, Pluto Bottom Line

Relative to the Pluto bottom line desire for self-sufficiency and survival, in his social context and reality, this translated into making money. Pluto and Saturn together can translate into a huge drive for social success, as the Soul has potentially experienced intense traumas relative to the loss of resources, personal power/authority, social prestige or that which it valued most or even its own life. It can also reflect a Soul who has had a past of powerlessness in society due to extreme poverty, slavery or similar dynamics of not having enough or losing what he did have. A potential reason for loss could have been his lack of values in achieving these resources, whether in great quantities or simply enough to survive, which if gained through underhanded, greedy means, would lead to the evolutionary need to experience the loss of those very resources. There is also the possibility of having been in the power seat where this authority was somehow lost or abused due to a limited sense of personal values, which led to situations of stagnation that needed to be metamorphosed, in order for evolution to proceed.

Full Steam Ahead

The new phase conjunction shows a new cycle of development is underway between these planets and related psychological dynamics which, it seems to indicate, this life will be a continuation of a cycle he just began prior to the current life, in the sense that there will be the desire to move and push forward with his plans at all costs as the desires emanate strongly from within his own Soul. Within his Soul there is an intense driving energy for forward motion and growth (Pluto/Mars not in true conjunction but in new phase stage of development) which will be felt at the core of his being and channeled all the way through how he integrates his Soul's desires into his egocentric structure (Moon) which, in turn, is also highly connected to his social profession (Saturn) and life purpose as the Moon opposes the Sun. The Scorpio stellium in the 2nd house reveals these inner Soul dynamics he has experienced in his past lives which he is bringing forth in his current life as Mark Zuckerberg, CEO of Facebook and other technological corporations such as Internet.org, Instagram and What's App. With the South Node of the Moon in the 3rd house in Sagittarius, conjunct Uranus in a new phase aspect, he is re-living dynamics relative to knowledge and information and will be reliving these dynamics in new ways.

Knowledge Is Power

I'm impressed at how graphic and accurate this chart is at reflecting his life, and am constantly amazed (as are many others) at how accurate Evolutionary Astrology is at representing symbolically what the reality of a Soul is and has been, at least from archetypal/energetic/emotional points of view which, when complemented with actual facts from the person's life and the archetypes then adjusted to the evolutionary level of the Soul, gives such an accurate representation to those that are able to interpret the symbols. Anyway, it's obvious that being the owner of Facebook and the other tech companies he owns, he now has unprecedented access to information and knowledge that is worth a lot of money to a lot of people. These interested parties can range from simple investors to advertisers to governments or anyone in between. The amount of raw data that flows through the sites he owns and presides over is simply massive and, with the Scorpio stellium located in the 2nd house, there can be and obviously is, a voracious appetite for this type of power, an appetite which he has carried over from past lives.

Our goal was to type in a person's name and find out a bunch of information on them. (Zuckerberg)

With the South Node of the Moon conjunct Uranus in the 3rd house, this Soul has been interested in the free flow of information/knowledge of all sorts of things or about people themselves, also about freedom of speech, and in the right and ability to travel and be connected to others, potentially relative to the bottom line of survival and sustainability that Pluto and the Scorpio stellium represent in his Soul's history. Within the Uranus in Sagittarius in the 3rd house, ruled by Jupiter in the 4th house in Capricorn, we have potential symbols of someone who, in the past, desired to spread their beliefs of a philosophical or religious nature to others in such a way as to conquer the lands of others and expand his own territory.

I'm Special

Uranus for all of us is the ruler of the South Node of Neptune, which in Mark's chart is located in the 5th house in Aquarius. Relative to the collective conscious/unconscious, it reflects a past desire to be extremely creative, special, part of an elite group of powerful rulers and similar dynamics, which would get feedback, and a sense of specialness from the collective itself. He would desire to be regarded as a leader who was innovative and ahead of his time (Aquarius). He would have within his own Soul, memories of these or similar dynamics that would give him a sense of being special due to some unique gift, creative or intellectual talent or elite group which he was born into. It would also correlate to disillusionment due to the over-estimation of his own abilities and ultimately to humbling experiences, as Neptune, which correlates to the Source of all creation, is not really supportive of people acting in Godlike ways. With these symbols it's very possible he had, in his karmic past, various types of superiority complexes which possibly lead to developing God complexes too.

With the South Node of Neptune in the 5th house in Aquarius and Uranus in the 3rd in Sagittarius, remembering his evolutionary stage being in the middle of the individuated state of consciousness, means that he is at an evolutionary point in his Soul's journey in which he has already rebelled against all other thought forms, belief systems, dogmas, religions etc., that did not reflect his inherent individuality and therefore has already learned to integrate into the mainstream in a way that was 1, a true representation of his identity/personality and 2, in ways that could help some aspect of the collective itself evolve due to his objective ability to look at things in new ways thus, having the ability to think "out of the box" in ways that could contribute to a body of knowledge or field of activity.

Potential Traumas

With the South Node of Neptune in the 5th house, relative to his evolutionary station, we can see that his desire has been to totally express himself in ways that would be a true representation of who he was and in ways that could affect/direct/inspire the collective in whatever ways/directions he desired. These desires would be emanating primarily through Pluto's natal position and, in this case, we have the Scorpio stellium in the 2nd house, opposite Venus in the 8th in Taurus, in a square aspect to the South Node of Neptune in Aquarius in the 5th house. Amongst other things, it can correlate in the past to his lack of resources to complete a creative project, to support his children which then resulted in mental (Aquarius) and deep emotional (Scorpio) trauma or, to the desire to rule over others, in the case of him being in positions of great power and authority in the past, which then led to betrayals and potential losses of resources and even life itself. This is most probably one reason for him acquiring so much wealth in this life, the traumas he experienced in the past.

Powerful Past?

It's actually my own personal insight or illusive projection that this Soul has been in positions of great power and influence in the past. I meditated on him and focused on what I felt as I concentrated on him. In doing so I started to feel pain in various parts of my body and in my Navel Chakra as it triggered an image or memory of actually suffering at the hands of this Soul, and being in positions of powerlessness due to his policies or the way he ruled. I'm not sure if this was a true memory or a projection of my own mind but it seemed to me that he was possibly a Roman emperor, maybe even Julius Caesar. Even before that experience, I had the impression that in his Soul's history there were Greek and/or Roman chapters and he even looks Roman or Greek, to me at least. I don't have any reason to like or dislike him or even have any sort of opinion about him. I tend to trust my inner radar though and do believe that he was in a position of authority and power in which he possibly had influence over many others and, in this life, is re-living certain dynamics and re-creating his empire, but in different ways. These new ways will obviously be different from the medium to distant past, as humankind has evolved so much from a technological point of view in these past 150 years, which also had an immense impact on the collective conscious/unconscious.

Who he was doesn't really matter; what does matter are the dynamics that he is experiencing, why he is to experience them, what is connected to his Soul's evolutionary past, and how to evolve beyond his limitations in his present circumstantial reality. This is the gift of EA, to show the energetic imprint the Soul is born with, thus revealing the emotional/psychological dynamics of the past that lead up to the current life. In the end, the "why" is more important than "who" the Soul was on an egocentric level. The "why" is directly connected to the Soul's intentions and the determinant of the "who" that the Soul creates in each life. Being able to understand the astrological archetypes in their deepest possible expression and meaning will give a picture of the energetic or emotional imprints the Soul is here to experience. We are all energy configured in various unique ways although we share many similarities. We all have our unique consciousness and our nature is shown by Neptune and further by Saturn with how this consciousness is defined and experienced/materialized in the physical world, and to the other planets, which all have their unique functions in awareness/consciousness.

Power, Power and More Power

One thing that leads me to believe he was in such positions of power is the fact that prior to his first Saturn Return, he had already become so influential and financially rich with Facebook. As JWG taught us so brilliantly, the first Saturn Return is a period in which we will mostly be gravitating back to and recreating many dynamics of our karmic past. We are a composite of our past, present and potential future; the Saturn Return is a re-building of past life structures in order to relive and setup the conditions for our evolutionary progress to occur.

I can personally attest to the feeling I had at my Saturn Return when I finished a cycle relative to the work I was doing at the time in the music industry, it felt like it had all been done before and shortly after I moved on to other things such as Astrology which, since my North Node of the Moon has Mars, Jupiter and Urania conjunct, reflects the fact that I had already worked on this area prior to this life, at least to a certain extent and would continue in this life. It's interesting that after the Saturn Return was exactly when I felt the time with the music industry was something that was culminating and started to look in other directions.

All this to say that it seems to me that Mark Zuckerberg, by generating such influence and riches, was simply recreating his past structural reality (Saturn) in order to continue his evolutionary journey. This journey is very interesting astrologically as his chart is quite paradoxical due to Pluto being in Scorpio in the 2nd house with Venus in Taurus in the 8th house. This, to me, seems like a closed loop as both Venus and Pluto are in their own signs thus having no rulers and their expression being purer and limited to those houses and signs in which they are placed. So much of his life will be experienced within these two opposing archetypes and associated real life dynamics. These dynamics of course are related to power, survival, resources, issues pertaining to trust, merging with others in all sorts of ways, corporations, big business, and of course secrets related to personal privacy, which is a paramount concern in his life with Facebook and his other ventures.

The Architect

I'm here to build something for the long term; everything else is a distraction.
(Zuckerberg)

With Neptune in Capricorn in the 4th house, relative to the South Node of Neptune in Aquarius in the 5th house, and in the third individuated EA state, he is evolving from an awareness of the creative integration of his own unique self in idealistic ways, that can hopefully unite humanity in ways that can lead to the creation of a system that can be of greater security to all people. His consciousness is essentially connected to the material world; he is most probably a materialist in the sense that he believes in that which is tangible, provable, reliable, etc. According to his own words, he is an Atheist, not yet understanding the role of the prime Creator or Source Of All Things in the creation of existence.

He stated in an interview that he considers himself a builder and his desire is to build things that stand the test of time, essentially reflecting his creative streak carried over from the past as seen by the South Node of Neptune in the 5th house with natal Neptune now in the 4th in Capricorn. The architect, but not of a physical home where people can live, but the architect of a mental structure (Uranus 3rd) where all people can be connected and share information and ideas, ideas that he can "capture" relative to his bottom line Pluto in Scorpio with all that emphasis in Scorpio in the 2nd and 8th houses which translate to the desire to accumulate wealth as power and information as a means to have this power.

The Power of the Mind

With the Nodal axis of Neptune in the 5th and 11th houses and the Scorpio stellium square this axis, there is also the dynamic tension between his goals for the future of his creations (Facebook and other technological inventions) and the values he is here to metamorphose due to the huge amount of Scorpio energy in the 2nd house. There will be tension and potential crisis of what is important for him, his creations and empires, his wealth and status (as symbols for the potential to build and create), between these dynamics and his friends or those of like-mind or the power elite which he has become a part of, willingly or not, and what he would essentially like to implement in the world, that can have an effect on the collective conscious/unconscious and on the quality of life of people worldwide. He is essentially here to develop his internal security and value system to the maximum with these symbols and find out what is true for himself with the Nodal Axis of the Moon in the 3rd and 9th houses, and with Uranus on the South Node in the 3rd house. He will be evolving from an awareness of what is his special gift to the world and how to implement these gifts, to an awareness of how to let them go and simply go with the flow. He is also here to learn about emotional expression and to learn how to dissolve barriers preventing emotional expression with Neptune in the 4th house; to learn how to feel and be secure from within himself as being a part of the vastness of life.

With the North Node of Neptune in the 11th house in Leo and the Sun in Taurus opposite the Moon and Mars, he will be highly dedicated to his goals and be single-minded about how to implement them; he will be essentially fixed in his mode of expression, focused and have the desire to expand as much as possible. Within these symbols, he will desire to do things for humanity that are a reflection of his own values and creative ideas. Relative to the Scorpio/Taurus 8th and 2nd house emphasis, he will be intensely fixated on his desires, whatever they may be, to the point of obsession. He will also believe in economics and the economy.

With the North Node of Neptune in the 11th in Leo, he will need to learn to be more objective in order to implement his creative ideas and genius in the mainstream of the collective and, in order to do this, he will need to learn about total honesty, that which is a reflection of his true core values and what is essentially right for him, from his point of view. Further, with the South Node of the Moon in Gemini in the 3rd house, with Uranus conjunct, he will have liberated from the opinions of others in the past and in this life is initiating a new cycle relative to his beliefs and what he takes in from others in the form of opinions and ideas, etc. He seems to be in a state of fruition relative to the buildup of past lives of attempting to understand what is what, what is right and what is true; he must have accumulated a lot of information and is now liberating from an excessive left-brain approach.

Within these symbols and his fruition state, we also have the fact that he is a free thinker and doesn't condition himself by what others think or say, he potentially feels that on a mental level he is in a league of his own and has special gifts or talents he is here to share with the world at large. He is also in a fruition state relative to his intelligence and ability to stand back and see what others need in order to be more efficient. This is indicated by the reality that when he was just a child of 12 years of age, he developed a computer program that was for the purpose of helping his father communicate and connect with his secretary who sent him messages when clients arrived. His father was very supportive of his technological abilities and progression and hired a private tutor to give Mark programming lessons, further indicating his fruition state relative to information technology and the creative use of his mind potential (Uranus in the 3rd conjunct South Node of the Moon relative to the South Node of Neptune in the 5th).

Mercury is also significant as it rules the North Node of the Moon, his MC in Gemini and his Virgo Ascendant. Mercury in the 8th house at the very end of Aries is conjunct asteroid Lucifer, trine Neptune and opposite Pluto. The opposition to Pluto correlates to his immense ability to focus singlehandedly on an idea and to his drive to implement them to their completion, to make them reality as he desires to make his dreams reality through the trine to Neptune, of which he has the creative capacity plus intelligence to do so. The conjunction to Lucifer can indicate that through the information he acquires he can be pulled into the forces of evil by associating with people that are in some way also associated or influenced by dark forces. Lucifer/Mercury in Aries in the 8th house can be totally uninterested with the effects he has on others, and with how he uses information; how this information is achieved can be through dishonest trickster ways; he himself can be used by others who desire to use him as a means to benefit by the information he himself has access to, therefore making him a "victim" of the powers that use him for their own personal agendas. This symbol shows that there is potentially a lot more than meets the eye relative to the use of the information he has access to and the means he uses and has used in his Soul history to gain information that was quite probably with the intention of domineering others in various ways in his past.

Duplicity Can Backfire

Ruling the MC, Mercury, which in itself is a symbol for potential duplicity, means that he will use the Mercury function relative to information, communication and connections to others, in order to progress in the mainstream world he lives in and to use this information as a means to generate power for himself through making money. Ruling the Ascendant, the money he makes can equal freedom to act in any ways he feels or desires. Mercury here can also equate to the Soul's desire to dig deep within the psyche in order to understand what makes him tick so to speak and figure out who he really is. In the 8th in Aries, he will have the tendency to merge with others who can open doors for him and possibly invest in his ventures, especially with the opposition to Pluto which reflects the evolutionary intention of metamorphosing the way he uses his Mercury function itself.

Pluto/Mercury shows a desire within his Soul to eliminate outmoded ways of thinking, concepts or ideas he has that are no longer serving an evolutionary purpose for his Soul's growth. This can indicate that, at key periods in his life, he will experience intense confrontations with others in order to force him to let go of these outmoded and obsolete ways of using his logical mind; he may have the tendency to confront those who oppose him and will desire to dominate and pioneer in whatever field he chooses to operate in. Relative to the 2nd house Scorpio stellium, it will be obvious that these confrontations will be about that which he values, and in his life he has chosen to be in the area of big business as his Soul has identified what is of value to the collective conscious with the trine from Mercury to Neptune in Capricorn in the 4th house, money which equals power and security or the potential to act freely. The ability to act freely is very important and highly valued for this Soul as is shown by the amount of new phase conjunctions in the 2nd house and the ruler of his Ascendant, Mercury in Aries. Also, it's quite possible that in the current life he may feel somewhat entrapped by the very nature of the reality he has created, entrapped by those whom he must merge with, by the magnitude of his own business and technological ventures and by the commitments these require.

Others with whom he has had to unite with, in order to fulfill the 8th house desire to ground and own his power, may have ulterior motives of their own and therefore he may find himself serving the needs and desires of others who are more powerful than he is. Also, within his own Soul, there can be intense memories of the loss of life due to similar dynamics in which others turned on him because he was not interested in being a team player and desired to go his own way when he wasn't as powerful as he thought or believed. With that Scorpio stellium in the 2nd house, there are many potential scenarios of power struggles with others and, when we add Mercury in opposition in the 8th, conjunct Lucifer and trine Neptune, there can be many dynamics or experiences relative to deception, in order to gain power and influence, where he is either victim or perpetrator in alternate roles throughout his Soul's journey.

Better Be Honest

The yod from Pluto/Neptune to his Chiron in the 9th house, which is also conjunct his North Node in Gemini and in an applying conjunction to his Sun in Taurus, seems to reflect the need for truth and honesty at all costs relative to how he uses information and how he communicates. This is to be brought into conscious awareness as the Sun rules the current life purpose. Whenever he acts in ways that reflect duplicity and dishonesty, he will find himself in crisis situations just as he did at various times when he tweaked the Facebook program to reveal more information about people's privacy. He was pushing the limits of what information he could access and retrieve from others, which led to crisis of others revolting against his actions and forcing him to acknowledge these abuses of power and to apologize publicly for them, which he did on various occasions. Chiron's conjunction to the Sun shows that utter honesty is something he will need to integrate painstakingly into the current life as something important and of value to his life's purpose. It won't be enough to have power and money just for power's sake. Within his own Soul is the desire to heal from past abuses relative to information, honesty, duplicity, communication etc., that led to wounding himself and others, and with the Sun in Taurus in the 9th house, it can be achieved through the development of values based on truth and honesty and the value/preservation of Nature and life in general.

Creativity and Intelligence

South Node of Neptune in the 5th house, the Soul has desired to express its creativity in new and unique ways as viewed from the collective conscious/unconscious, and ways that reflected its core individuality. Within this dynamic, he would desire to be acknowledged as special for his accomplishments or creations, thus having a need for feedback to serve this purpose. He would also desire to be in charge of his own destiny, possibly above external authority of any kind and even be in charge of the destiny of others in society. With the ruler of Neptune's South Node, Uranus in Sagittarius in the 3rd house, there was the desire to gain knowledge and information in order to actualize the desire for creative self-actualization. This knowledge would allow him to develop his intelligence to a high level, to develop his rational mind and his intuitive mind at the same time, thus developing a certain degree of balance between both hemispheres in his brain. The type of knowledge he would be interested in would be that of technology, religion, travel, communication, all forms of education that could enhance his ability to impact on the collective via his new revolutionary ideas (Aquarius plus Uranus in the 3rd in Sagittarius). Further, he would be liberating from any ideas that didn't fit his own personal evolution and perspective or reflect his core values as seen in the Pluto 2nd house bottom line and desire to integrate into the collective his own unique and creative or individualized ideas and opinions.

Unity For All

With Neptune in Capricorn in the 4th house, he would come into this life idealistically desiring to dissolve any barriers that separate people from one another. He would desire for himself and others to feel at home in the world and connected to their environment; for this he would believe (Jupiter in Capricorn) in the system as a social structure that was able to satisfy the security needs of the collective. The new phase conjunction between Jupiter/Neptune shows there can be potential innocence in these beliefs as he pursues and acts upon them instinctively. This energy, to me, reflects his need for a personality with total integrity. Also potentially to wanting to be-friend the whole world as one big human family that is interconnected electronically, via his creative venture and invention or even "baby," Facebook. 5th house South Node of Neptune with natal Neptune in the 4th house in Capricorn.

Neptune in the 4th house relative to the South Node of Neptune in the 5th in Aquarius, his desire to connect the world through his social/economic/political influence and authority. Neptune in the 4th, self-image based on his own status and worldly influence, ability to build. Self-image intertwined directly with his social self-role and ambitions. Dreams of being the leader. Desire and dreams of ultimate security based on a perfect social system. Influence over the intimate personal lives of others coming from his past of having great power and authority. Possibly a creative genius in past lives due to South Node of Neptune in 5th in Aquarius which led to him desiring to help others in relation to living their lives more equally etc., which then led to the desire to give access to knowledge and education, religious education or the right to be free to choose their own religion or cosmological beliefs, or freedom to travel (Uranus in the 3rd in Sagittarius). In the current life with Neptune in Capricorn, relative to these past dynamics and evolutionary level of awareness, the Soul would desire to unify all countries and people under one socio/political/economic system, Capricorn, relative to the Scorpio stellium in the 2nd house.

Real Objectivity

With the Ruler of the North Node of Neptune in the 11th house in Leo, Mark Zuckerberg will develop/evolve his consciousness by learning to be objective about his own creative endeavors and ultimately desire to develop a life purpose that could serve the collective in order to help it transform and evolve. His spiritual evolution seems to be linked with the collective's need to learn how to develop the principle of living a life with purpose and creativity. The Sun, which rules the North Node of Neptune being in Taurus in the 9th house shows that he will need to develop an honest relationship to himself and the cosmos in order to relate to others in a positive, constructive way that can promote the spiritual evolution he and the collective desire and need. This placement, relative to the North Node of Neptune, shows that in order to help humanity evolve, he will need to value himself as a being that is connected to something larger than what his senses can perceive, that he will need to develop a deeper value system and connection to the world or universe, that he will ultimately find meaning in helping others in all sorts of socio/economic circumstances.

It's possible that in a distorted sense and expression, he may find himself amongst the power elite. This elite, if motivated by greed and self-interest, as many elite power groups are, will have the effect of shocking him and disillusioning him in order to set him back on the right track, as deep within his Soul is the desire for real values, for values of the deepest kind possible with the Scorpio/Taurus axis so highly emphasized relative to his EA station. In this evolutionary stage, the Soul is attempting to express its truest sense of individuality and will not bow down to the values of others; the Soul will progressively lose interest in all sorts of egocentric senses of grandeur as it approaches the 1st stage spiritual and, on the way, will begin to be extremely objective of its own egocentric needs that are not truly necessary anymore. The "I" in the equation will be rebelled against as the Soul is so objective and desires to improve, especially with a Virgo Ascendant. There will be a natural tendency to be self-conscious to the point of not liking the "I am," "I need," "I this and I that." Therefore, he will be developing humility in this stage of his evolution.

Information at the Touch of All Fingertips but at what Price?

Another dynamic relative to the collective conscious/unconscious is the fact that he has the desire to evolve it by giving internet access to as much of the world's population, even those who are very poor, for a very affordable price. This reflects the desire for a world system all interconnected as we have seen by his Neptune and Uranus placements plus the Sun in the 9th house in Taurus, plus it's good business for him and his 2nd/8th house bottom line subconscious and not so subconscious compulsion to generate income. It seems he is actually contributing to the speeding up of the flow of information that is shared between people, thus effecting the evolution of the collective conscious/unconscious by vastly augmenting the flow of digital information and accelerating it at an exponential rate. This is seen by his Uranus in the 3rd house relative to the South Node of Neptune in the 5th house via his creation of Facebook and other sites such as Internet.org, by the North Node of Neptune in the 11th house and the Sun which is its ruler in the 9th house of expansion and foreign lands which, relative to Neptune in the 4th house in Capricorn, is a way to implement his dreams of the system that connects people. Of course, the flip side of all this is the vast amount of power that he and others in similar situations such as Google or other corporations and Governments can have over people with highly efficient technologies at controlling the world's population for their own benefit. In this quote on Facebook from Julian Assange, the Wikileaks founder, he also mentions yahoo and Google as acting in similar ways. This RT.com news interview was videotaped and published on its site:

> Facebook in particular is the most appalling spying machine that has ever been invented. Here we have the world's most comprehensive database about people, their relationships, their names, their addresses, their locations and the communications with each other, their relatives, all sitting within the United States, all accessible to U.S. intelligence.

> Everyone should understand that when they add their friends to Facebook, they are doing free work for United States intelligence agencies in building this database for them.

What about the Future?

Relative to the collective conscious/unconscious and the evolution of consciousness itself for mankind in the present and near future, when people like Zuckerberg push for a technological advancement of these proportions, what will happen is that we will truly all be connected with one another and have information about everyone's personal lives and their Aunt, but this connection is via the internet, in contrast to the potential we all have to be connected with one another through our own inner nets. We humans have immense inner potential that is dumbed down due to the disconnected and distorted lifestyles we share. We are disconnected from our own truth in essence, from Nature, from God and from one another. We are relying each time more on technology and the internet to communicate with one another as we can see with the huge rise in smart phones, and in the near future will begin to merge man and machine, turning humankind into cyborgs. Cyborgs under the control of corporations such as Facebook or Google or Coca Cola. As man and the machine merge at an increasing rate, there will be, on the one hand in the collective conscious/unconscious, the desire to surrender to whatever is being implemented in society (Neptune in Pisces) as so many people simply feel overwhelmed by the reality on Earth at the present as experienced by the corporate takeover of the planet with Pluto in Capricorn.

The merging with the machine will accelerate to unimaginable proportions as Pluto enters Aquarius, unless the collective starts to wake up to what is happening via objective awareness, and we desire to evolve in more naturally oriented and united ways. By the time Uranus enters Gemini, the digital and technological advancements will be so great that children will possibly already have some sort of nano chips directly implemented into their brains in order to be connected to the internet from birth or even while still in the womb. I know it may sound like a stretch but mankind truly is merging with technology at a fast rate; just calculate how many hours on average we spend on a computer, tablet or smart phone as opposed to how disconnected we lived from all these technologies some 20 or 30 years ago. Facebook and other technologies that are in the hands of the corporations and other power elites around the globe, have the power to affect the collective in ways that have not been heard of before and are accelerating at an astonishing rate.

This also gives the collective the longing (Neptune) to return to simple ways of life, to return to that which is true and real from an ultimate point of view, as people get disillusioned with the emptiness of digital media and the ipod, iphone, ipad lifestyles, where the "I" is really a form of getting people to identify their egos with their "digital media and identities" in order for people to consume and therefore feed these corporations. One cannot smell a digital flower or make digital food and people will hopefully understand the trade-off of being sucked into this type of lifestyle when Nature and real life are the real deal and so much better for us. The North Node of Neptune in the 11th house in Leo in this chart example is ultimately about humanity and giving to humanity what it needs without any or minimal self-interest on his part. To spiritualize through liberating from delusions of grandeur, a need to be acknowledged as special as it moves away from the 5th house, and to use his creative potential for the benefit and evolution of Mankind as an integral part of Nature, respecting Natural law since the ruler, the Sun is in Taurus in the 9th house.

Evolution

Relative to his Pluto polarity point in Taurus in the 8th house, his Soul's intended evolutionary path is that of continuing to evolve his value system by penetrating to the core of his own Soul's attachments. Scorpio is all about evolution itself through metamorphosing its limitations based on subconscious security needs and its attachments, which need to be confronted as they limit the Soul's evolution. With this intense configuration, the Soul may have within itself a paradox. The paradox of desiring to move forward and grow, and the desire to stay fixed in its ways to the bitter end as it can be subconsciously insecure of change itself. In his case, it would seem to imply that for evolution to proceed, he would have to learn to give up on all he had, all the riches and all the power or at least willing to let go of all these things that were so important to him by finding out why he developed the desire to acquire so much, which can be out of fear in the first place. To analyze how the attachment to these things cause extreme pain and insecurity, the insecurity of loss.

Still got some Reviewing and Rebelling to do

All outer planets plus Mars are Rx. All Rx planets are either in the 2nd or 4th houses, indicating that in this life he will be reviewing dynamics relative to his personal security as an emotional and vulnerable individual in the material world. It correlates to his ultimate search for security from within and how this search will affect his core values. It correlates to how he will need to figure these things out for himself and will not allow himself to be too influenced by others in order to understand these dynamics.

Light and Darkness

With Lucifer on the Pluto Polarity Point, relative to the North Node of Neptune in Leo in the 11th house and the Pluto axis being square the Nodal axis of Neptune, it seems possible that he could channel the Source's light to the world by choosing, Pluto and all that Scorpio, to have the deepest values possible that promote LIFE as seen by the Sun which rules the North Node of Neptune, in Taurus in the 9th house. He could, in a flash of the Sources light, have an insight that would allow him to understand the bondage and karmic implications of making the wrong choices and adhering to greed and similar dynamics relative to power, and choose to put others before him with the polarity point of Lucifer in the 1st house in Libra, in order to serve humanity to the best of his creative and potential abilities (Leo/11th), while at the same time dissolving so much of the emotional repression that is in his emotional body as seen by Saturn on the Moon in Scorpio, Jupiter and Neptune in Capricorn in the 4th house and the South Nodes of Jupiter, Saturn and Pluto in the 4th house in Capricorn. These symbols reveal the potential for huge insecurities and an emotional nature that potentially is highly repressed and traumatized, which is in need of healing the wounds that the Patriarchal takeover of the planet has caused to his Soul. Further, we can see the trauma signature in recent past lives with Uranus on the South Node of the Moon and with the current life Moon square the Nodal Axis of Neptune in Aquarius. With Sagittarius on the cusp of the 4th house and Neptune/Jupiter in the 4th, it seems to reflect a desire to really open up emotionally in this life and free himself from feelings of guilt, insecurities or a negative self-image, in order to heal and simply be who he truly is.

To close, I'd like to say that this Soul seems to be in a powerful position to do great things in order to push the collective in the direction of the light, or to betray billions of people and have a spiritual downfall in which he succumbs to dark forces. Choose wisely and you will be rewarded with love, Mark Zuckerberg, loads of it!

Comment from Rad

Because of the Soul story of Zuckerberg that you have provided, I would like to share with you, and all those who read this, that in the recent prior life history of his Soul he was also Johannes Gutenberg.

Skywalker

Thank you so much for revealing who Zuckerberg was. It is so interesting that he was Johannes Gutenberg. For those who are reading and don't know who Gutenberg was, Wikipedia states:

> He was a German blacksmith, goldsmith, printer, and publisher who introduced printing to Europe. His invention of mechanical movable type printing started the Printing Revolution and is widely regarded as the most important event of the modern period. It played a key role in the development of the Renaissance, Reformation, the Age of Enlightenment, and the Scientific Revolution and laid the material basis for the modern knowledge-based economy and the spread of learning to the masses.

All of this fits in so well with his South Node of the Moon in the 3rd house, conjunct Uranus and how he is re-living conditions relative to the flow of information!

And here, relative to his Pluto in the 2nd house inconjunct Chiron and the North Node of the Moon (from Wikipedia):

> Sometime in 1456, there was a dispute between Gutenberg and Fust, and Fust demanded his money back, accusing Gutenberg of misusing the funds. Meanwhile the expenses of the Bible project had proliferated, and Gutenberg's debt now exceeded 20,000 guilders. Fust sued at the archbishop's court. A November 1455 legal document records that there was a partnership for a "project of the books," the funds for which Gutenberg had used for other purposes, according to Fust. The court decided in favor of Fust, giving him control over the Bible printing workshop and half of all printed Bibles.

(Q) For my own and the curiosity of others, was Mark Zuckerberg actually Roman or Greek and in positions of great power in his past?

Also, relative to his South Node/Uranus conjunction and him reliving dynamics relative to inventions, information, technology, communication etc. The life of Gutenberg was 700 years ago, and he is still living out similar dynamics. Would this be because there have been relatively few lives in between then and now, or is it just that evolution is so darn slow?

(A)   Yes, he did have former lives in Greece and Rome, and social positions of high power and status. You can see this through the prism of geodetics by way of his Mercury conjunct Lucifer in Aries in his 8th House, and his Neptune and Jupiter being in Capricorn in his 4th House. The Lucifer symbol in his context is quite interesting to ponder/consider relative to how his Soul has manifested from that time.

And, sadly yes, it's because evolution for most Souls is so darn slow.

CHAPTER TEN

NEPTUNE AND VICTIMIZATION

Introduction

One of the correlations of Neptune, Pisces, and the 12th House is one of victimization. There are two manifestations of this archetype:

(1) to feel victimized by some external source, and

(2) to victimize others through one's own actions which so often connects to a relative archetype: scapegoating.

A relative archetype that then correlates to this is one of persecution: being persecuted, or doing the persecuting.

When a Soul feels victimized, this typically occurs because it cannot understand and/or accept the responsibility in its own actions, actions that, at some point, have created the necessity of being victimized by another(s). This can be particularity difficult when those actions have taken place in another life, or lives, because most Souls do not have the evolved capacity to remember their own prior lives.

This is one of the wonderful things about EA because it allows for exactly that kind of understanding in order to accept the responsibilities in one's own actions even when those actions have taken place in another time and place.

When a Soul has felt victimized, is unable to accept/understand the responsibilities in their own actions, it can be very easy to victimize another(s). In essence, to blame others, scapegoat, others for that which the Soul is responsible. Thus, to project what is actually taking place within their own subconsciousness, Uranus, onto others and/or making up 'out of thin air' that have nothing to do with actual reality: delusions and illusions.

This, of course, can manifest as whole groups of people, countries too, attacking/persecuting/and victimizing other groups of people and/or whole countries. All too often, 'religion' is used in the 'name of God' as the justification in so doing. So we end up with evil creeps like Hitler, Pol-Pot, this religious group or that, attacking whole groups of people or races that are scapegoated, victimized, persecuted in order to mask their own actual realities and agendas that they are in denial of.

Sadly, human history from the time of the Patriarchy forwards is full of this, and is full of one human victimizing/persecuting/scapegoating another human. This happens in all dimensions and spheres of human interaction.

An extension of these archetypes of victimization/persecution/and scapegoating are the archetypes of masochism and sadism. Masochism is an archetype that is rooted in guilt, and the need to atone for that guilt. Thus, the Soul who is masochistic feels that the abuse that it attracts is DESERVED. Sadism is also rooted in guilt yet that guilt creates a deep inner anger that is projected onto others in sadistic ways: a deep need/desire to humiliate and abuse others FOR THAT WHICH IT IS RESPONSIBLE FOR. Masochists blame themselves for that which THEY ARE NOT RESPONSIBLE.

It is very important to understand that Neptune, Pisces, and the 12th House correlate to the 'potential' for masochism/sadism. In other words, it is within these archetypes. Yet, it is through the natural polarity of Virgo, the 6th House, and Mercury that triggers the potential within these archetypes to manifest as a reality. The archetypes of Virgo, Mercury, and the 6th House, among others, is one wherein the Soul creates various kinds of crises that, by their very nature, trigger the actualization of the potential contained in the Pisces, 12th House, and Neptune archetypes.

There is also a form of masochism that JWG called 'spiritual masochism,' which is very different from psychopathologic masochism. Spiritual masochism is the conscious act of sacrificing oneself on behalf of another or others so that by such an act of self-sacrifice another or others can benefit in some way. So we can have the extreme example of a Soul like Jesus hanging on the Cross and basically suffocating to death so that other Souls could benefit by this act of sacrifice; to a mother allowing one of her kidney's to be taken out, and given to another who could then live because of this act of sacrifice. These examples could be exampled in all kinds of ways.

Spiritual masochism thus correlates to a related archetype called martyrdom. Through the archetype of martyrdom, the Soul sacrifices itself for a cause that is larger than itself.

EXAMPLE CHART A

Neptune and Victimization
Oscar Pistorius – Summary of a Sadist
by Kristin

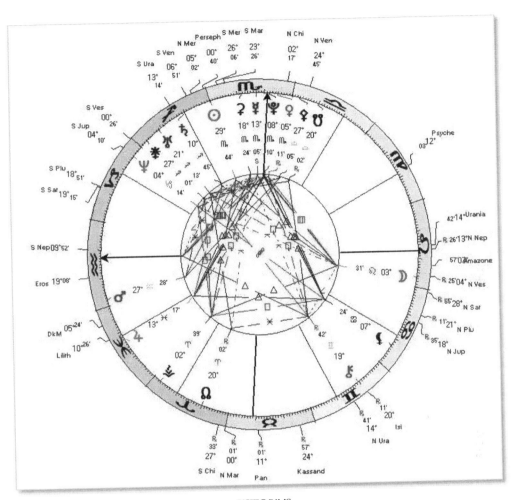

PISTORIUS

South African born Paralympian superstar Oscar Pistorius; lower legs were amputated when he was 11 months old as a result of being born without the fibula bone on both legs. He would never be able to walk so his parents had no other choice but to proceed with the procedure. The question becomes WHY was he born with the inability to walk. He says his life is about getting everything right in training and on the track in order to produce the perfect race. He is said to have a gentle manner but a forceful personality. He yearns for perfection. It's a word that he repeats again and again. He says:

You can only progress as well as your weakest link in training. Being a perfectionist is everything. If you skimp, you lose. With me, it's a mind-set, and I've always had it. I joke that if I toast bread, it has to be perfectly toasted. I suppose it's a bit OCD, but that's the way I am. I just do not like shortcuts. If I do something, it has to be done properly.

Crime of Passion:
Pistorius' Need for Control, Pathological Jealousy and Feelings of Inadequacy

On February 14, 2013, Oscar Pistorius was charged with the murder of his girlfriend, Reeva Steencamp, who he fatally shot in his own home in the early hours of the morning on Valentine's Day.

Reeva Steencamp and Oscar Pistorius

Oscar was a self-proclaimed perfectionist and a control freak, which can be seen with his Moon in Leo in the 6th, ruler Sun in Scorpio in the 10th conjunct South Nodes of Mars, Mercury, Venus. The Sadist permeates guilt, which creates a deep anger that is projected onto others in sadistic ways: a deep need/desire to humiliate, dominate and abuse others for that which he or she is responsible for creating. The potential for sadomasochism is seen in the 12th/Neptune with the trigger being the 6th house and, in his case, his South Node of Neptune is in the 12th, the North Node of Neptune is in the 6th with his Moon in Leo. Pistorius' Moon in Leo is there energizing emotional feelings of inadequacy. When Pistorius does not get his way, is not the star of the show and feels he is not the center of his partner's universe, the rage becomes unleashed, North Node in Aries in the 3rd, ruler Mars in Aquarius in the first squaring his Sun in Scorpio in the 10th, the Sun being the ruler of his 6th house Moon in Leo. Also, remembering that Mars is squaring his South Node of Mars in Scorpio in the 10th, COMBUST, or what Jeffrey would refer to as the hand grenade in the steel box.

Pistorius

The ruler of his South Node of Neptune is Uranus in Sagittarius in the 11th, trauma, which is sesquisquare his Moon in Leo in the 6th. Clearly, he was triggered that evening. His girlfriend may have told him something that triggered him that night in bed. They had only been dating a few months and she may have shared interests of hers or even sharings of her own past that may have triggered his pathological jealousy. The partner being honest about her sexual needs, Venus Rx balsamic to Pluto in Scorpio in the 9th, and they square his Moon in Leo in the 6th, sesquisquare Uranus in Sagittarius in the 11th, Uranus being the ruler of his South Node of Neptune in Aquarius in the 12th. His natal Neptune in Capricorn in the 11th squares Lucifer in Libra in the 8th; this Neptune refers to his natal Saturn in Sagittarius in the 11th, trauma caused to another because of truth-out talking. Also, Uranus, trauma, in Sagittarius, ruler Jupiter in Pisces in the 2nd, he claiming to be the victim, stating that on that night he thought there was an intruder in the bathroom, yet he kept firing through the bathroom door, even as he heard screams from a woman. In fact, a witness to the crime reported hearing a shot with a pause, then another shot with a pause and then bang bang again. This would not be someone firing at an intruder. He knew his girlfriend was on the other side of that door.

His North Node of Neptune is in Leo, ruled by the Sun in Scorpio in the 10th, the control freak that becomes sadistic. Jupiter in Pisces square Uranus, the ruler of his South Node of Neptune in the 12th as well as his Ascendant. Mars, the ruler of his North Node in Aries is in Aquarius in the 1st, fatally shooting her in the head, blowing out her brains, Uranus.

One may wonder why he was born without lower legs. Clearly this is karma for being a control freak, karma for taking his partner's 'out at the knees,' and taking another's life into his own hands, Jupiter is in Pisces in the 2nd forming a t-square to Saturn in Sagittarius in the 11th and Chiron in Gemini Rx in the 5th. There is a repeating theme of pathological jealousy that led to murder of his partner in other times, CRIMES of PASSION, South Node in Libra in the 9th, ruler Venus Rx balsamic to Pluto in Scorpio in the 9th conjunct North Node of Chiron. These symbols also square his Moon in Leo in the 6th sesquisquare Uranus in Sagittarius, Uranus being the ruler of his South Node of Neptune in Aquarius in the 12th. He undoubtedly has been down this road before where trauma was the result of his need for total control as well as feelings of inadequacy. So in order to gain control he regained it in the most extreme way possible by rendering his partner powerless, the person who was the source of his pain. He sets out to destroy the origin of his own perceived hurt. Being born without functioning lower legs is the karmic result of the trauma he has caused others due to his need for control and pathological jealousy within this, in an attempt to "slow him down." In essence, his Leo Moon was "cut down to size."

Pistorius and Steencamp

Within the same signatures of pathological jealousy are themes of pathological lying, in order for him to have total control in his relationships and allowing him to maintain his own double standards, South Node in Libra in the 9th, ruler Venus Rx which is balsamic to Pluto in Scorpio, square Moon in the 6th in Leo, ruler the Sun in Scorpio in the 10th: 10th house, Capricorn and Saturn connects with double standards and hypocrisy. These double standards are a result of his own duplicitous nature, "Do as I say, not as I do." Chiron is also in Gemini in the 5th, ruler Mercury station in Scorpio in the 10th forming a t-square with his Aquarius Ascendant and Leo Moon in the 6th. So he attracts a partner in this life with her own need for diversity, and when she is honest, he is ignited and unable to control his rage.

Reeva Steencamp reflects a repressed Amazon, a South African celebrity, attracting a great deal of attention. She was one of FHM magazine's 100 Sexiest Women in the World for the past two years, appeared in international and South African advertisements and was to make her debut as a celebrity contestant on the reality TV show *Tropika Island of Treasure* filmed in Jamaica. The freckled blonde, who appeared in scanty bikinis on magazine covers and sashayed down fashion ramps, was "continuously breaking the model stereotype." Steenkamp was known to be "the sweetest, kindest, just angelic Soul" and at the same time "a very inspiring individual, very passionate about speaking about women and empowerment." Not only was she drawing attention with her beauty, she was an intelligent activist with a law degree, campaigning against rape and violence against women.

She was going to wear black to protest the brutal rape and mutilation of a 17-year-old. But the glamorous South African celebrity was found dead in the home of Pistorius from four bullet wounds. So he attracted a repressed Amazon that was not going to be controlled. Her Amazon is conjunct his Moon in Leo. Note: Reeva's Mars was EXACTLY conjunct his Moon at 3 Leo. The sadist, Pistorius, is also a narcissist, expecting all things to revolve around him, Moon in Leo square Venus, expectations, just as the planets revolve around the Sun. He attracted someone that was getting all the attention from the world and her popularity was just picking up speed, he could not compete. He may have also been comparing her level of success with his own, feeling threatened by her light, her Mars in Leo on his Moon, and the attention she would be getting from other men, thus comparing himself to them and the projections that would then follow.

Transits on the Day of the Murder

- Pluto waning conjunction to his natal Neptune in Capricorn.

- Transiting Neptune was square his natal Neptune and forming an inconjunct to his Moon in Leo.

- Uranus, the chart ruler and the ruler of his South Node of Neptune, as well as the ruler of his North Node ruler, Mars in Aquarius, was in Aries and squaring his natal Neptune in the 11th.

- Saturn was conjunct his MC and station Mercury in Scorpio and forming a t-square to his Ascendant and transiting Venus in Aquarius and Moon/North Node of Neptune.

- Mars was in Pisces conjunct Mercury and Chiron, and squaring Saturn.

- Transiting Moon was in Aries, conjunct his North Node.

These transits for Pistorius become the ignition for his Soul to learn through extremes how to take responsibility for his own actions versus playing the victim.

In composite, together they have this trauma reflected in their chart with a South Node in Scorpio with Saturn in the 12th, ruler Pluto in Libra in the 11th balsamic to the Moon and Mercury in Libra. The Sun in Libra is also in a new phase to this stellium reflecting the opportunity for a new start for there is always an opportunity for anyone to make new choices at any point on the path. The Moon in Libra in the 11th is forming an exact inconjunct to the North Node in Taurus in the 6th, ruler Venus in Libra in the 11th is squaring Neptune in Capricorn in the 1st house, Neptune in Capricorn is sesquisquare Mars in Taurus in the 6th.

Steencamp's Amazon is 18 Scorpio, conjunct her Psyche (Soul) which is conjunct his Ceres, and conjunct his stationary Mercury in Scorpio in the 10th. Pistorius' Ceres, recovering something lost from the past, such as her life, is exactly 18 Scorpio, in his 10th. This is conjunct his Cupido and a stationary Mercury, which is her Amazon in Scorpio. These symbols square his Ascendant/Descendant and form a 9 degree square to his Mars in Aquarius in the 1st.

On the day of the murder, transiting Saturn conjunct the South Node in Scorpio in the 12th. The transiting North Node was exactly conjunct Saturn, nearly to the minute on the day of the murder. They have North Node conjunct Mars in Taurus in the 6th. The transiting South Node was exactly conjunct that point. The deadly past meets the deadly future.

In the recent court case that has been in session, Oscar Pistorius shows up in total denial of the reasons for this murder, convinced that his lies are true, South Node of Neptune in Uranus in the 12th, ruler Uranus in Sagittarius in the 11th, sesquisquare Moon in Leo in the 6th with the North Node of Neptune. He is putting on quite a performance, a drama queen at best, barfing in the courtroom every day, rocking like a baby, doing whatever he can to convince the judge and the court that he is a victim in his attempt for people to take pity on him.

It is not a coincidence that at the time of the trial, Mars is retrograde in Libra and is trining Reeva's North Node, sextiling her South Node and Neptune in Sagittarius. Maybe her Soul will get the justice she deserves. Retrograde Mars in Libra is also conjunct their composite Moon in Libra in the 11th, Retrograde Saturn is conjunct their composite Saturn and South Node in Scorpio. Uranus in Aries in their composite 5th is opposing their composite Sun in Libra in the 11th, the Sun being the ruler of their composite 9th, the house of truth.

For his Soul to have a chance, it starts with owning the truth, North Node in Aries in the 3rd, ruler Mars in the 1st, trine South Node in Libra in the 11th. But after these deadly events, unless he can finally be honest, versus living in denial and his investment in being a victim, and most importantly taking responsibility for what his Soul has created, he may come back without limbs at all.

EXAMPLE CHART B

Neptune and Victimization
Oscar Wilde
1854-1900
by Skywalker

Irish writer, play writer and poet who was persecuted in England for being homosexual and ended his life in exile in Paris, poor and pretty much alone, after being forced to two years of forced labor. He was an interesting character as he is so original and unique.

I believe he was individuated 3.

I have nothing to declare except my genius. (Oscar Wilde)

Oscar Wilde

In 1886, he had his first homosexual experience, with transiting Uranus conjunct Venus and later Saturn square Venus. Uranus then also squared his natal stellium in the 5th house in Capricorn which could have led to him initiating a liberating process from the values (Uranus/2nd) and the beliefs (Jupiter) he had acquired in his life up to then, which did not continue to reflect a true expression of his ongoing, evolving individuality. Included in this time frame for him, due to these transits, he was also redefining the way he was relating to himself and others, through experimentation with various forms of giving and receiving and experiencing love. Relative to Neptune being located on the cusp of the 7th house in Pisces, we can see the desire within his Soul to dissolve all barriers between himself and others in relationship to himself. To feel consumed by love and totally full, to merge as deeply as possible because of his Soul's desire for depth of feeling and emotion with another or others. This Neptune placement can also lead to all sorts of dynamics relative to projecting larger than life or godlike qualities onto partners, to see them as mythological figures, super heroes or extremely beautiful, beyond human and totally pure. Dreamlike to nightmarish qualities, and all the possible surrealism in between these two extremes, are possible dynamics with such a planetary configuration.

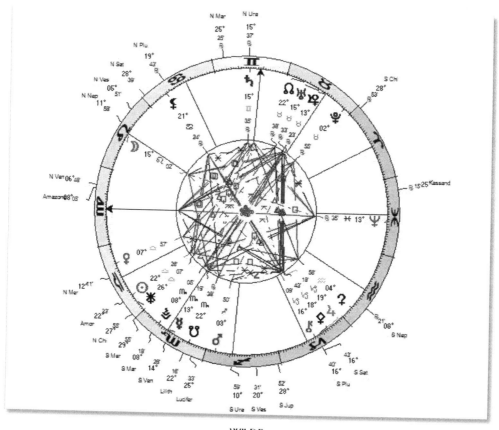

WILDE

The potential for victimization is also emphasized when such transcendent qualities can be falsely projected upon another, only to end in disillusionment when the partner is a disappointment or worse. He may have been used by others due to his willingness to see the beautiful side in them and not discriminate enough regarding whom he related to or how he related to others. The square between Saturn and Neptune indicates the judgment from society as his lack of boundaries and discretion in his same sex relationships got him into trouble with the law. By adding Mars in square aspect to Neptune, there can be even more of a lack of boundaries relative to his sexual desires and expression, confusion relative to which sex he actually really identified with, and by Mars being in Sagittarius in the 3rd house, it only adds to his expansive nature that didn't really know many boundaries or limitations to his own personal desire nature.

Soul Structure

- Pluto Rx in Taurus in the 8th house
- Venus in Libra in the 1st house
- South Node of the Moon in Scorpio in the 3rd house
- North Node of the Moon in Taurus in the 9th house

Within these symbols, we can see Oscar Wilde's Soul structure and past life experience has been relative to sexual dynamics, power and powerlessness, resources and values and the sharing of everything from sexual energy to material resources in order to survive and deepen his self-understanding.

With Pluto being Rx and ruled by Venus in the 1st house in Libra, square Jupiter in Capricorn in the 5th house, it reflects a past desire within his own Soul to break free from any restricting elements that blocked his expression. This Soul was learning primarily about self-worth, relationships and how it was connected to the larger society it was born into. In addition, it was rebelling against sexual morals and values that were defined by the consensus as is shown by Uranus conjunct the North Node of the Moon in the 9th house in Taurus. This conjunction being balsamic shows that the Soul of Oscar Wilde was closing a long evolutionary developmental process in which he was rebelling against what others considered ethical or non-ethical, he was rebelling in order to develop his own core individuality as a separate individual within a society, with his own values, natural gifts, talents and resources.

Pluto conjunct Uranus and both being in Taurus, with the North Node also conjunct Uranus, indicates the Soul's shift in sexual orientation as it desires to experience its sexuality in new ways. It shows that in the recent past, the Soul created egos/lives that would have initiated the process of relating to itself in new ways, thus redefining its self-image and way it would project relationship needs onto others. It would have probably already "come out of the closet" in recent past lives relative to being homosexual. This liberating from social expectations can further be seen by the ruler of the North Node of the Moon, Venus in Libra in the 1st house, where he broke free and initiated a new cycle in order to relate to himself and others in new ways, relative to the Pluto/Soul bottom line desire to gain self-knowledge/security through probing deeply into himself and discovering his true value.

> A man who does not think for himself does not think at all. (Wilde)

With Pluto in the 8th house ruling his South Node in Scorpio in the 3rd house, we can see the potential for his mind to be extremely deep and penetrating, especially with Mercury also in Scorpio in the 3rd house he would not be interested in B.S. We can see symbols for his obsessive-compulsive nature relative to sexual desires and gratification, to money and the ability to survive and to all things connected to secrets and knowledge as a form of power with the South Node, Lilith and Lucifer in the

3rd house. With these symbols, he would have already developed many mental and communicative abilities in past lives, therefore in the current life became a writer, relative to the massive creativity that is shown by his packed 5th house.

These symbols indicate the depth of his mind and the use of sarcasm in his verbal and written expression. He was extremely bright and witty and he knew how powerful the spoken or written word was with these planetary placements. He knew how to manipulate and how to get what he wanted or how to outsmart others simply by the use of language and his own wits. He even outwitted people in trial by the intelligent use of language, the second time he was taken to court. With these symbols, we can also see him being a "freak" as judged by the society he was in, also due to his provocative manner with Uranus on the North Node of the Moon and opposite Mercury, which rules the Ascendant.

No Money, No Honey

These symbols also show his financial dependency on others, especially his wife. He lived well over his means and loved to spend, loved beauty and expensive things and to spend money on his young boy lovers in extravagant ways. He also had to "buy" the affection his heart desired often and in this way was creating evolutionary pressure within his own Soul that would desire to free himself from relating dynamics in which he was relating to himself in ways that were not truly satisfactory.

He died alone and poor as apparently no one, not even Bosie, who was the lover who got him convicted (Bosie's father was the one who made the criminal complaint against Wilde), came to his financial rescue. Reflecting his own Soul's urge and desires to become self-sufficient, as those whom he trusted and loved, left him "in the gutter" in order to protect their own self-images as seen by society. With the Sun in the 2nd house in Libra, he would like the good things in life, he would be generous with those he valued and like to give them the good things in life, sometimes luxury items. Sometimes these offers were possibly in order for him to satisfy his own sexual desires by smothering or buying others in some way. This is seen by Venus being in Libra in the 1st house relative to Pluto in the 8th and as Venus also rules his Sun, he would be naturally very giving and amiable. He would be gracious and peaceful at heart with a desire for beauty in his life. With the Sun square Jupiter in the 5th house, he would naturally be led to excess, possibly to a kind of "folia" in regards to his own pleasures and he was known to be very extravagant in his life, always living above his means.

Arts, Aesthetics and Creativity

All art is at once surface and symbol. (Wilde)

With Venus so pronounced as the ruler of his Pluto, Sun, Venus and North Node of the Moon, plus the South Nodes of Pluto, Neptune and Saturn, and natal Chiron,

Pallas, Jupiter, Psyche, Ceres etc. in the 5th house, we can see the importance of creativity in this Soul's past and also so emphasized in the current life with the Sun in the 2nd house in Libra and of course Pluto itself in Taurus. He stated things like:

> The imagination imitates. It is the critical spirit that creates. (Wilde)

It was also part of his life purpose and evolutionary progress for him to develop his own sustainability through his art with the Sun in Libra in the 2nd house and Pluto in the 8th in Taurus. The skipped steps with the grand fixed cross and his Moon's Nodes and natal Moon correlate to this having been developed in past lives, the desire to sustain himself by doing things that reflected his own core individuality vs depending on others for his financial security or survival.

> Now Art should never try to be popular, the public should try to make itself artistic. (Wilde)

Oscar's Many Yods

Neptune is on the Descendent in Pisces inconjunct the Moon in Leo in the 12th house at the apex of a yod from Chiron, Pallas and Jupiter in the 5th house in Capricorn. He also has a yod pointing at the Capricorn planets in the 5th house and another yod pointing at Saturn in Gemini in the 10th house.

These three yods are also an indication of the downfall, persecution and utter humbling he experienced later in his life that led to his realization:

> One of the many lessons that one learns in prison is, that things are what they are and will be what they will be. (Wilde)

Neptune in action, in surrendering to the simple truth as it is. He was convicted in 1895 with Saturn opposite Pluto and Neptune on Saturn.

With the yod pointing to the Moon in the 12th house in Leo, relative to his heavy emphasis on the 5th house in his Soul's bigger picture and its inner sense of deep felt specialness, he would be in a lifetime in which a deep humbling process would be experienced that would aim at dissolving some of the sense of importance he would naturally have within his emotional makeup. This emotional makeup would be dissolved to a considerable degree with the experiences he had in the life of Oscar Wilde, and this would also be a way of resolving his skipped steps in which his sense of importance and lifestyle was potentially making him lazy on a very deep level, thus his Soul possibly created the experience of doing forced labor to break down and dissolve his ego. Uranus on the North Node of the Moon, relative to the Moon in the 12th house, correlates to the need to break free from his own old crystallized emotional structures and dynamics that didn't reflect his true self any more.

The yod pointing at his 5th house with Chiron at the apex reinforces the loss of his children which he loved and the consequent guilt and humbling process he may have experienced at the hands of a cold social system. This must have broken him and been an extremely humbling process, as he had to deal with the guilt of hurting and consequently losing his family due to his extravagances and his sexuality.

The yod pointing to the Moon in Leo also points to the loss of his children (Leo) because of the consensus values that he was not conforming to (Capricorn 5th house Jupiter, Chiron, Pallas) and due to his wife distancing herself and their children from him due to his conviction as seen by Neptune in Pisces on the cusp of the 7th house, which is also square Saturn in the 10th house. His loss of reputation with Saturn in the 10th house was caused by his lack of discrimination and care in his own relationships.

Then the yod from the 3rd and 5th houses to the 10th house Saturn, correlating to his social downfall due to the intrigues of others (his lover's father) who opposed his ways (Scorpio 3rd house), and the fact that he chose the same sex to enjoy himself with, which was then judged by society as immoral (Capricorn 5th house). The question I would like to ask and attempt to answer via Evolutionary Astrology is: Why would this Soul create circumstances that led to being persecuted as a way to evolve?

In the case of Oscar Wilde being persecuted for his sexuality, which in turn naturally led to a sense of victimization, I would say that it has to do with him learning within his own Soul's journey, all sorts of dynamics relative to his own self-worth. Souls who are persecuted can at times have the false belief that they deserve to be punished in some way for their transgressions. Conscious or not, they may carry guilt from this or other lives, which can set them up for some form of persecution, as they subconsciously put out a vibration that attracts persecutors in various forms. This is in order to atone for the guilt they carry and is a form of masochism. Masochists that subconsciously desire to suffer in order to atone for their sins, real or not.

Of course, there can also be natural guilt within any Soul and there normally is. In the case of Oscar Wilde, with the South Nodes of Saturn, Neptune and Pluto in the 5th house and the grand fixed cross, plus the yod pointing to the Moon and, Saturn square Neptune, it seems this life would be a "peak time" in which guilt from the past and current life would be purged.

Oscar Wilde had Neptune in the 6th house on the Descendent, relative to the South Node of Neptune in the 5th and the ruler, Uranus in the 9th house in Taurus, we can see that in the past he has desired to express himself creatively and in order for that to be accomplished he studied art forms, physical materials, nature and philosophical concepts deeply. Pleasure and self-gratification are dynamics that were also highly valued and actively pursued within this Soul's history. With the Nodal

Axis of the Moon square the Nodal axis of Neptune and the whole fixed grand cross with Pluto, Uranus, Mercury and Eros also being connected to this planetary configuration, we can see the potential for huge skipped steps within his Soul relative to these dynamics of various forms of pleasure and sexual gratification. This whole chart screams of crisis and a deep need to humble the Soul. Not that he was a bad and evil character, but he did seem to have reached a point of immense stagnation as symbolized by Pluto Rx in the 8th house and in the grand fixed cross with the South Node of Neptune etc., in which these desires to be special and for unlimited gratification have created a situation of non-growth for this Soul and in the life of Oscar Wilde created the necessary crisis and destruction of his self-image as seen by the three yods, especially the one involving the Moon in Leo in the 12th house.

In addition, with all the 5th house symbols configured the way they are, there can also be a high degree of narcissism and self-righteousness leading to indulgence and excess from way back in his Soul's past.

Pluto itself is Rx in the 8th house and is forming an inconjunct to Mars in Sagittarius in the 3rd house, indicating crisis in the current life, as taught by Jeffrey Wolf Green:

> You've already had the sense of inner power, you already know you can do it, but where the adjustment occurs, where the humility occurs, is that social circumstances will conspire in such a way as to block you until you make this linkage, until you learn to listen to that social sphere in such a way as how to integrate it on THEIR terms, not yours.

The persecution itself was therefore possibly caused by his Soul's design in order to grow beyond the pleasure seeking compulsions he had created within his own Soul for so long, in order to shock the Soul into an objective awareness of itself and its own core desires as reflected by Pluto in the 8th Rx and so close to Uranus which is also on the North Node of the Moon. The persecution, associated powerlessness, vulnerability and disintegration of his own life would help him develop objectivity into his own nature and into the limitations he was experiencing which, on a subconscious level were preventing growth. He also has the South Nodes of Venus and Mars in Scorpio in the 2nd house, adding to his desire to merge with others on extremely deep levels, having an intense romantic appetite and possibly going to extremes to satisfy his desires.

With the South Nodes of Saturn and Pluto in Capricorn in the 5th house, he could also have natural and man-made guilt relative to his sexual expression and orientation in past lives. He could have also created guilt relative to using whomever he desired for pleasure in many of his past lives, with these symbols relative to his 8th house Pluto and South Node of the Moon in Scorpio with Lucifer and Lilith conjunct. Lilith, South Node of the Moon and Lucifer in conjunction can also correlate to past life memories of sexual and intellectual rejection, experiences regarding suppressing his sexuality and his own femininity, and being deeply hurt by many potential betrayals in lives prior to the one we are analyzing or, himself also putting others through similar dynamics. It also correlates to him reliving these same dynamics in the current life.

He also had the Nodal Axis of Neptune in the 5th/11th houses square the Nodes of the Moon and the Moon itself in Leo in the 12th. There is this huge fixed cross with the South Nodes of Venus and Mars in the 2nd house adding to the depth of merging for money and pleasure and all the associated power dynamics and potential buildup of guilt over many lifetimes.

With the South Node of Neptune in the 5th with Eros included in this grand fixed cross we can also see the potential for no boundaries whatsoever relative to how he desired to enjoy himself, ruled by Uranus in the 9th house in Taurus, and so many planets having Venus in the 1st house as the final ruler, we can see that he would of done whatever he instinctively felt like doing in regards to intimate relationships and that he would have many attractions since there is so much of this energy in his Soul's past and makeup.

Within these symbols, we also see the provocative side of his nature, which also reflected in his lack of care in relation to him hiding his homosexuality, which he didn't seem to worry too much about. In those days, it was very bad to be seen as homosexual, something unnatural and immoral. In the Victorian days, even physical contact between men and women was only in private, women were very suppressed and English and European societies were very judgmental in general.

With all these symbols there is so much depth, so much passion, potential loss, betrayal, manipulation, abuse and desire for power and consequent guilt, that with the North Node of the Moon and Uranus conjunct, plus the North Node of Neptune in the 11th house, he would be learning to be objective about who he was, what made him tick, and what his needs were.

With the North Node of Neptune in the 11th relative to natal Neptune in the 6th but on the cusp of the 7th house, we can see that his desire to heal and deal with these issues is through purification (6th house) of masochism, excessive fantasies and romantic projections (Descendent).

CHART EXAMPLE C

Neptune and Victimization
King Henry VIII of England

by Cat

King Henry the 8th

One of the correlations of Neptune, Pisces, and the 12th House is one of victimization. There are two manifestations of this archetype:

(1) to feel victimized by some external source, and

(2) to victimize others through one's own actions which so often connects to a relative archetype: scapegoating.

King Henry the 8th had:

* Pisces on the 7th House Cusp ruled by Neptune in Sagittarius in the 4th House which is opposition Jupiter in Gemini the 10th House and square Mars in Virgo in the 1st House (t-Square)

* Neptune is also sextile Pluto in Libra in the 2nd House and trine Chiron in Taurus in the 9th House

During the reign of Henry VIII, between 1509 and 1547, an estimated 57,000 to 72,000 English subjects lost their heads or were otherwise brutally executed. It is said,

Henry would exact death to anyone who dared to complain or attest his will or who had incurred his displeasure, be it his close family, friends, acquaintances, employees and associates or even the normal every day commoner.

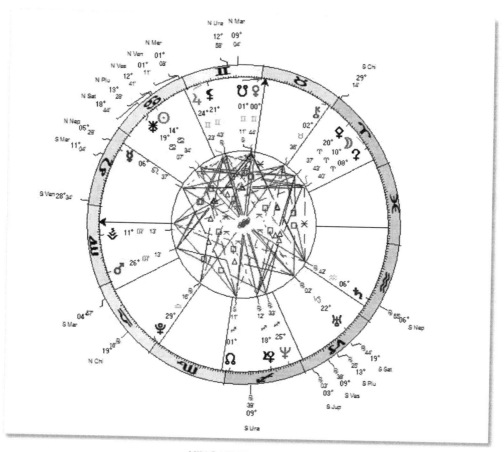

KING HENRY THE 8TH

Henry's Mars in Virgo in the 1st house is the apex planet of a t-square that includes Jupiter in Gemini in the 10th House and Neptune in Sagittarius in the 4th House. When Mars is the apex planet in a t-square, the individual is strong-willed and willing to meet any challenge without giving up. These challenges would primarily come through his role as king (10th House) and his family and domestic life (4th House). Religion and duplicity would be major themes, as well as victimization, scapegoating and sadism.

With Mars in the 1st House, Henry VIII instinctually resisted anyone or anything that restricted, or attempted to restrict, his freedom to do what he desired. He had a self-centered, narcissistic approach to life. He had a strong will and desire to establish his own authority. He would get angry whenever he felt he was being judged or controlled by an external authority. In addition, he had a need and desire for many kinds of sexual experiences with many different people. He was sexually willful, assertive and narcissistic. He instinctually formed quick attractions to others and pursued his interests with little regard for moral conventions (Mars square Jupiter in the 10th) or concern for his family (Mars square Neptune in the 4th).

Henry's Mars is in Virgo indicating a need and desire to create essential crises as a vehicle through which his Soul could actualize its core evolutionary intentions and desires. With Pluto Rx in Libra in the 2nd House, this has been to become self-reliant and self-sufficient, as well as learn to participate in relationships as an equal. In his "current" life as Henry VIII, the Soul's intention and desire was to confront his personal limitations by forcing him in upon himself in some way to examine the internal dynamics that were creating his life situations. In addition, the intent of this life was to teach him how to make his own decisions without depending on the opinions, advice or consent of another. At the same time, he was learning not to control, interfere with, define, or block his partner's need to make decisions. He was essentially here to learn to minimize his dependencies on others.

With his North Node in Sagittarius in the 4th House ruled by Jupiter in Gemini in the 10th House, he would have to learn to provide his own emotional security from within himself rather than deriving it from any external factor such as his parents, sociological role, lovers, wives, etc. In addition, he would have to learn to view and understand life from a cosmological, metaphysical, philosophical or religious context. His beliefs would have a huge impact on how he performed as King (his social function) and how he structured the society that he was in charge of.

The South Node is in Gemini in the 10th House indicating that in prior lives, he was learning to become socially responsible through the social functions he performed. He very likely occupied positions of power in his karmic past and learned how social systems work. He likely learned how to manipulate the system in order to get to the top. He needed and wanted to be in a position of control in society rather than allowing society to control him. He therefore collected all the facts, information and data needed to get ahead.

Mars is square both Jupiter in Gemini in the 10th House and Neptune in Sagittarius in the 4th House. Here we can see that Henry's will and desire to establish his own authority would bring religious controversy to both his homeland and abroad. When the Pope refused to grant Henry a divorce from his first wife, Catherine of Aragon, Henry became defiant and broke off relations with the church. Rather than submit to the Pope's authority, Henry declared himself the head of the Church of England in order to get the divorce he desired. This was the cause of internal religious strife, as well as external religious strife.

Pisces is on Henry's 7th House cusp. Here we see that the victimization archetype will be played out through a variety of relationships with a diversity of people throughout his life. Pisces is ruled by Neptune in Sagittarius in the 4th House indicating that many of these relationships are tied to his domestic relationships with foreigners. We have to remember that Henry's home and domestic relationships included his entire court, not just his family. These relationships included his wives, mistresses, foreign ambassadors, councilors, servants, so on and so forth. His domestic life essentially extended throughout Europe via these various relationships.

Pluto is quincunx Venus in Gemini in the 10th House. Henry had very idealistic and illusionary expectations of others and was sure to become disillusioned with each of his relationships at some point. With Venus in Gemini in the 10th, he was destined to have multiple Queens as well as multiple love interests. The inconjunct shows he had a great fear of disappointment. This disappointment manifested as a fear of not having sons and a male heir to the throne. So here we see he would enter into relationships with women in hopes that they would produce sons, and eventually become disillusioned when they failed to do so.

Venus is trine Uranus in Capricorn in the 5th House. Here we see that there would be sudden, unexpected and traumatic events in relation to his Queens (Venus in the 10th) and their children (Uranus in the 5th). Although Henry had a very conventional or traditional approach to love and romance, he was also inclined to revolt or rebel against conventionality as there was a strong desire to be free to do as he pleased in terms of his love life. In addition to his six Queens, Henry is known to have had several mistresses during his lifetime. As Uranus is trine Venus in the 10th, a few of his mistresses became wives.

With Mars in the 1st House square Jupiter in the 10th House and Neptune in Sagittarius in the 4th House, Henry was not about to let the Pope, the Catholic Church, or anyone else stand in the way when he decided he wanted to divorce his first wife, Catherine of Aragon. Henry and Catherine had several children but the only one to survive infancy was a daughter, Mary. After 16 years of marriage, it became clear to Henry that Catherine could not provide him with a son. In 1695, Henry decided he wanted a divorce. Not only did he want a divorce, but also he wanted it declared that his marriage had not been valid from the start. He convinced himself that he and Catherine did not have any sons because their marriage was lawless in the eyes of God. He based this on a Bible text from Leviticus 20:21 that stated, "If there is a man who takes his brother's wife, it is abhorrent; he has uncovered his brother's nakedness. They will be childless." Rather than acknowledging that his lack of sons might have anything to do with himself, he totally blamed Catherine, claiming he was being punished by God for marrying her, his brother's wife.

Mercury is in Leo in the 12th House. Along with Pisces on his 7th House and the Mars/Jupiter/Neptune T-Square, Henry blamed everyone but himself when the Pope refused to grant him a divorce. Keep in mind, Mars in the 1st House. Henry would get angry whenever he felt he was being judged or controlled by an external authority, in this case the Pope. His good friend and chief adviser, Cardinal Thomas Wolsey, Lord Chancellor of England became the first victim of Henry's anger and the first of many scapegoats.

> Wolsey's failure to secure the annulment is widely perceived to have directly caused his downfall and arrest...he was accused of treason and ordered to London...In great distress, he set out for the capital... He fell ill on the journey, and died at Leicester on 29 November 1530, around the age of 60. "Had I but served my god", the Cardinal said remorsefully, "with but half the zeal as I served my king, He would not in mine age have left me naked to mine enemies. (Living History Worldwide)

In July 1531:

- Transiting Neptune was in Pisces in the 7th House forming an exact square to Henry's natal Neptune in the 4th House

- Transiting Mars was conjunct his natal Moon in Aries in the 8th House

- Transiting Uranus was semi-sextile natal Mercury in the 12th House

- Mercury was transiting the 12th House

Henry separated from Catherine and began to live openly with Anne Boleyn. In January 1533, he married Anne in secret after learning she was pregnant.

In March 1533:

- Transiting Jupiter was conjunct natal Neptune in the 4th House and opposition natal Jupiter in the 10th House

- Transiting Pluto is trine Venus in Gemini in the 10th and sextile the North Node in Sagittarius in the 4th House

- Transiting Neptune in the 7th House was square natal Neptune in the 4th
    - quincunx natal Pluto in the 2nd House
    - sextile natal Uranus in Capricorn in the 5th
    - square natal Jupiter in the 10th
    - opposition natal Mars in the 1st

Henry gave up appealing for a divorce and broke with the Catholic Church. He declared himself the Supreme Head on Earth of the Church of England and had his marriage to Catherine declared null and void. An Act of Supremacy was issued along with an Oath of Succession. All government officials and subjects were expected to sign it. The Oath literally declared Henry's daughter Mary a bastard so that any children of Anne Boleyn would inherit the throne.

Henry, who had once been named Defender of the Faith by a pope, now claimed pope-like authority over the Church in England, which was thenceforth conceived as a distinct body answerable only to God, and to no man outside its national borders. This break with Rome was a revolutionary step for Henry to take, and it required firm support from Parliament and severe methods of enforcement by the government to secure it as reality. (SparkNote on Henry VIII)

Those who refused to sign the oath faced imprisonment and death. Sir Thomas More and Bishop John Fisher refused to take the Oath. Both were beheaded.

It wasn't long after he married Anne, that Henry became disillusioned with her. Anne had a miscarriage, which Henry perceived as betrayal on her part. He began to ask his advisers to find a way to leave her without having to return to Catherine. He also began an affair with a woman named Mary Sheldon.

In 1536:

- Transiting Jupiter in Pisces entered Henry's 7th house

- Transiting Mars was conjunct transiting Uranus in Henry's 11th House
  - sextile natal Mars in the 1st
  - semi-sextile natal Jupiter in the 10th
  - opposition natal Uranus in the 5th House
  - quincunx natal Neptune in the 4th House

Catherine passed away and Anne became pregnant again. Henry was involved in a jousting accident. "When news of this accident reached the queen, she was sent into shock and miscarried a male child that was about 15 weeks old, on the day of Catherine's funeral, 29 January 1536."

It wasn't long before Henry was claiming that Anne was a witch and seduced him. In late April or early May 1536, five men, including Anne's brother were arrested on charges of treasonable adultery. They were accused of having had sexual relations with the Queen. Anne was also arrested. She was charged with Treasonous adultery and incest. They were all sentenced to death. Anne was executed at 8 a.m., May 19, 1536.

Henry went on to marry Jane Seymour who gave birth to a son, the future Edward VI. Jane died two weeks later. Thomas Cromwell suggested that Henry marry Anne, the sister of Duke Wilhelm, of Cleves. Henry agreed but was upset and angry when he met her in person and discovered she was not the beauty he was led to believe she was.

"The King's anger at being forced to marry Anne of Cleves was the opportunity Cromwell's conservative opponents, most notably the Duke of Norfolk, needed to topple him" (Wikipedia). Cromwell was arrested June 10, 1540 and condemned to death without trial and beheaded on July 28, 1540. Henry married Katherine Howard the very same day. It wasn't long before Katherine had an affair. At first, Henry refused to believe the allegations. Once he was convinced of the reality of the affair, he flew into a rage and blamed his council for what happened. Katherine and two men that she had an affair with, one before her marriage to Henry, were all executed. Katherine was beheaded on February 13, 1542.

As we have seen, Henry didn't blink an eye when it came to victimizing those close to him. As far as having a son went, Henry always blamed the women in his life for not producing sons. He never once acknowledged that he might have had anything to do with it. Whenever anyone disagreed with him or refused to see things his way, he did away with them.

> Henry very often killed people not because they were guilty but because they were inconvenient. He used, of course, legal methods, but he did so with such frequency that Tudor historians routinely refer to 'judicial murder' for his reign: i.e. a court sentences someone to death not because they were guilty but because the king wanted them dead. (strangehistory.net)

With his Mars in Virgo in the 1st House, Henry was very self-centered and narcissistic. He was preoccupied with himself, power, prestige and vanity. He felt little if any empathy for others. He had no problem blaming others for whatever was wrong in his life and victimizing anyone who disagreed with him or crossed him in any way. In addition, he was somewhat of a sadist.

> Henry seems not to have attended the executions of those he knew. He was not a sadist in the normal sense. But he clearly enjoyed the knowledge that those around him were walking on eggshells that he had laid down: and that their survival and continued existence depended on his whim. (strangehistory.net)

Henry's wives and political associates got off easy compared to others who annoyed the King. When Father John Forrest of the Order of Observant Friars opposed Henry's marriage to Jane Seymour, Henry had him arrested and sentenced to be burned at the stake for heresy. He later changed his mind and sentenced him to life in prison. The Friar continued to oppose the King from his prison cell. When Henry got wind of this, he had him chained up and suspended over an open fire until he roasted to death. Those who complained about the severity of the execution were burned at the stake for criticizing a royal decision.

William Tynsdale, who translated the Bible into English, opposed Henry's divorce with Catherine Howard. After he was found and arrested, he was ordered to be tied to the stake, strangled and then burned.

> Sadism is also rooted in guilt yet that guilt creates a deep inner anger that is projected onto others in sadistic ways: a deep need/desire to humiliate and abuse others for that which it is responsible for. It is very important to understand that Neptune, Pisces, and the 12th House correlate to the 'potential' for masochism/sadism. In other words, it is within these archetypes. Yet, it is through the natural polarity of Virgo, the 6th House, and Mercury that triggers the potential within these archetypes to manifest as a reality. The archetypes of Virgo, Mercury, and the 6th House, among others, is one wherein the Soul creates various kinds of crises that, by their very nature, trigger the actualization of the potential contained in the Pisces, 12th House, and Neptune archetypes. (Rad)

Henry has Virgo on the Ascendant, Mercury in Leo in the 12th House, Aquarius on the 6th House cusp ruled by Uranus in Capricorn in the 5th House. As we can see, with Virgo on the Ascendant, victimization was part of Henry's identity. With Mercury in the 12th House, Henry believed his own illusions, fantasies and delusions. He could not distinguish between what was real and what was imagined. If he imagined that Anne Boleyn was a witch who put a spell on him, he really believed it, or came to believe it. Between having a mind that could not separate reality from fantasy and the trauma of suddenly losing child after child in infancy (Uranus in the 5th), it was not hard to trigger Henry's sadistic side. His Mars was in Virgo in the 1st House. This once again brings the Mars/Jupiter/Neptune t-square into play.

With Mars in Virgo in the 1st House, Henry's anger was guilt-based and a core part of his identity. Once he started having people killed, he could not stop. The guilt he felt from having executed one person created a great deal of inner anger, which he would project onto others. This usually resulting in the death of another, which in turn led to further guilt, and further anger. This anger then being projected out on another, or others, resulting in yet more death. This pattern kept repeating itself throughout his life.

CHAPTER ELEVEN

NEPTUNE AND OTHER ARCHETYPAL CORRELATIONS

Hope and Faith as Intrinsic to the Consciousness of the Soul, and Miracles

Consciousness as set in motion by the Source Of All Things that is defined by a Soul in human form contains the archetypes of hope and faith. Hope and faith are psychological dynamics that the Soul draws upon in the context of circumstances that are, by their nature, defeating or limiting to the Soul in some way, or when some kind of dead end is reached in which "all hope is lost" for any other outcome. In those kinds of circumstances, if the Soul was not able to draw upon these intrinsic dynamics to consciousness, hope and faith that leads the way through or out of those kinds of circumstances, the consequence would be wherein the Soul could feel so defeated, so futile, that this could cause the Soul to not want to continue on its life, its ongoing evolutionary journey through time: to feel utterly hopeless.

When a Soul becomes hopeless to alter or change anything in its life in general, or because of certain circumstances specifically, this simultaneously ignites futility, self-defeat – Capricorn, Saturn, and the 10th House – and loss of any desire to continue on with its life. In this state of hopelessness, the Soul also loses any capacity to have faith, a faith that somehow "things" can get better. The combination of hopelessness and a loss of faith can cause the Soul to lose any sense of meaning for its life: Neptune and its lower octave Venus. Without any sense of meaning, the Soul then becomes "lost as sea," so to speak. This can then ignite, through the natural triad of Pisces, Scorpio, and Cancer, the Soul to either 'escape' from the circumstances of its life, and/or to end its life outright by the act of suicide. Suicide correlates with Scorpio, Pluto, and the 8th House, and escapism is specific to Neptune, Pisces, and the 12th House. Escapism can have many forms including alcohol and drugs.

Escapism of course can then lead to another archetype of Neptune, Pisces, and the 12th House: addictions. Addictions can have many forms but all forms of addictions linked with escapism have one underlying cause: the desire/need to blunt the effects of actual reality: Saturn.

Hope and faith are also the determinants that can cause what the consciousness within the human Soul can perceive as "miracles." Miracles of course can be caused by the Source Of All Things Itself in which the very nature of the miracle can only be attributed to some "supernatural" force and/or what we call God. The history of human beings has many testimonies to this fact. These types of miracles can occur when one or more human beings appeal to, pray, for their idea of God to intervene in order to alter the circumstances as hand that otherwise seem "hopeless."

On the other hand, miracles can also be caused by the power that is inherent within the dynamics of faith and hope by human beings themselves. This is done through the power inherent in faith and hope, a power that when projected from the consciousness of the Soul creates an electro magnetism that then alters the nature of the circumstances that ignited the Soul in the first place to hope through faith, so as to alter that which needed to be altered or changed.

Healing Wounds of the Physical, Emotional, Mental Bodies, and the Soul itself

Neptune, Pisces, and the 12th House also correlate with the archetypes of healing, healing of some existing conditions whether they are on the physical level as in the body, the emotional level, the mental level, or for the Soul itself because of becoming so crushed through a diversity of possible causes.

Wounding of the Soul

"Wounds" which also correlate with the Neptune, Pisces, and 12 House archetypes can of course have many causes and many forms including terminal illnesses. In order for the Soul to be able to heal these various wounds, it is essential to identify the causes of whatever the wounds are. By identifying the causes, the remedies for those causes, the wounds, can then be determined.

If the wounds are physical in nature, some kind of problem in the physical body, then the Source Of All Things has placed within the Manifest Creation on our planet various substances in the forms of plants, minerals, foods, and other agents within Nature that can be used to treat these physical illnesses of the body.

Many of these natural substances are used by practitioners of medicine in the form of the potentized medicines that have been produced to also deal with physical illnesses. Humans have evolved to the point of also being able to create new "allopathic designs" that allow new drugs to be made to combat various ailments that have not been treatable before such designs were realized. In combination with the Scorpio, Pluto, and the 8th House, the triad with Neptune, Pisces, and the 12th House has allowed humans to evolve to the point of being able to surgically operate on the body in order to help it heal from various physical problems.

If the wounds are of a psychological/emotional nature to a Soul, Soul wounds, then the healing that can take place must, and can only, occur when the Soul in question is able to identify and accept the responsibility in their own actions that has been the cause or determinant of these types of wounds themselves. The effects, memories, of some wounds can never be changed of course. This is necessary so that the Soul will never do again, whatever it has done, that is responsible for whatever the wound has been.

The wounding of the Soul through its emotional body can be seen within the birth chart by way of the South Node of Neptune by house and sign, the aspects to it from other planets, the location of its planetary ruler by its own house/sign, and aspects to it, the natal placement of Neptune by its own house, sign, and aspects to it, where the sign Pisces is on a house cusp which then draws in the entire Neptune paradigm, the sign on the 12th House cusp, the location of its planetary ruler by its own house, sign, and aspects to it, and any planets that are within the 12th House, aspects to them, and the signs they naturally rule by way of the location of those signs within the birth chart.

Wounds can also be seen through the lower octave of Neptune: Venus. So in the same way we would examine the entirety of the Neptune paradigm, we must also examine the totality of the Venus paradigm in order to understand, in conjunction with the Neptune paradigm, all the potential sources, causes, of the wounds to the Soul that can occur through time: the history of the individual Soul's evolution through time.

Within this understanding, it is essential to remember that the vast majority of the wounds that can take place to the Soul occur because humans in general have perverted the Natural Law of giving, sharing, and inclusion. This Natural Law is in fact symbolized by these same two archetypes: Neptune and Venus, Pisces, Libra, and Taurus.

Once this perversion occurred, this Natural Law then manifested as self-interest and exclusion. The overall consciousness of humans in a collective sense, Neptune, Pisces, and the 12th House, devolved from the Natural Law of giving, sharing, and inclusion at the time of when humans went from being nomadic in nature to living in communities defined by farming and the raising of animals. This is when humans began to invent religions and cosmologies that progressively violated the Natural Laws that were set in motions by the Source Of All Things. The South Node of Neptune in Aquarius, which all humans have, correlates to exactly that time: from around 7,200 B.C.E. forwards.

Once this began, the collective consciousness of humans shifted their inner orientation from "we" to "I." In Natural Law, the "I" is understood within the context of "we" where "we" is the bottom line of how the individual understands itself. When this Natural Law is perverted, then the "I" is the bottom line within the collective consciousness. And when that happens, then all the wounds that can happen to an individual Soul and Souls within a group that has or can experience genocide as a sub-group of humans, occurs because of this perversion of the Natural Law of giving, sharing, and inclusion.

This inner shift to the "I" in collective consciousness is also, of course, responsible for the human organism being is a state of total imbalance to Nature itself. Balance as an archetype correlates with both Neptune, and its lower octave Venus. As a result, the human organism is in a state of collective consciousness wherein it dominates Nature in order to serve its own needs, which are defined, again, by self-interest and exclusion. So humans rape the Earth itself in every possible way, poison its atmosphere, and kill off or exterminate hundreds of life forms EVERY SINGLE DAY.

So when you look into the birth chart in order to understand all the wounds that can be seen relative to the paradigms of Neptune and Venus, just remember that the vast majority have occurred because of this violation of Natural Laws. When the focus shifts to the "I" as the bottom line that then equals self-interest and exclusion, then the understanding of how humans can wound themselves among themselves becomes self-evident.

Purity and Innocence that Manifests by being in Alignment with Natural Laws

When any given Soul is in fact in alignment with the Natural Laws of the Manifest Creation, then such a Soul is naturally pure, naturally 'innocent,' when understanding innocence is in relationship to the perversion of those Natural Laws. All Souls have at their essence these Natural Laws of the Creator. It is because of this that all Souls have an innate sense of what is right and wrong. It is because of this that all Souls have a natural conscience. This does not mean that all Souls are in fact 'conscious' of the Natural Laws by any means. Yet all Souls emanate from these Natural Laws. So, of course, Souls can be naturally shocked with these Natural Laws are violated whether they are conscious of the reasons that they are in fact shocked.

It is only when these Natural Laws are violated through the perversion of those laws BY HUMAN BEINGS that shocking events can take place: genocide, terrorism, gunman killing innocent people in whatever context, rape, abuse, and so on. When another naturally extends truth to another only to have that trust violated, and is then shocked that this occurred. And so on. The shock is in direct proportion to the innocence being violated to the nature of the event that generates the shock in the first place.

True Giving without Expectations of Reward
Tuning into the Actual Reality of Another or Others and thus Knowing What to Give, and What Not to Give

When a Soul is in such alignment with Natural Laws, it naturally wants to give: not take. And in that giving there is no expectation, Venus/Neptune, or receiving anything back. Thus, true giving. The true giver in this way is also a natural listener: Venus/Neptune. In this natural way of giving by way of listening, the Soul is then able to give to another(s) exactly what is needed. When what is naturally needed is given, then that which is given can be naturally received. By being in alignment with these Natural Laws, the Soul can also know when not to give and, in so doing, know that this is actually a form of actual giving.

When Natural Laws are violated, then this natural capacity to listen to another in order to know and understand not only their reality in general, but that which they need specifically, is perverted, wherein the Soul can only listen to another as it RELATES TO ITS OWN SELF-INTEREST. Thus, an artificial "filter" of listening that does not allow for a true or total tuning into the reality of another in order to know that other as they actually are. In turn, that which is given is given from the point of reference of self-interest. This is not true or natural giving.

Psychic Phenomena

Neptune, Pisces, and the 12th House also correlate with the archetypes wherein an individual consciousness of a Soul can be aware of various types of "psychic" phenomena that include premonitions; deja-vu type awareness; seeing the future in the form of visions that can be about the Soul itself, other Souls, or humanity itself; communicating with Souls in other planes of existence that are no longer in a physical body; telepathic communions; being able to read the mind of another(s); out of body experiences; and so on.

As an aside, it might be interesting to consider what the nature of a deja-vu is, given the fact that almost all Souls have independent of the degree of evolution. All Souls, prior to incarnating back into another life, receive a vision, like a movie, of what that life will be: its general contour. Thus, when the Soul encounters certain "scenes" that connect to that vision or movie in the context of the next life, they are then "remembered" as if THEY HAVE ALREADY BEEN THERE.

In Souls that have the various types of "psychic" phenomena occur, it will always correlate with, in some degree, elevated levels of melatonin in the brain. Melatonin, a hormone, is secreted from the pineal gland deep in the brain. Emotionally, this correlates with the degree of "sensitivity" that any Soul has within itself, and through extension to the degree of empathy a Soul can have for others. Sensitivity and empathy both correlate to Neptune, Pisces, and the 12th House. From the point of view of the consciousness of the Soul, melatonin correlates to expanding the degree of "awareness" that a Soul has relative to the totality of life itself. Thus, expanded awareness is the foundation for what we call psychic awareness in all of its forms. Astrologically, when a Soul has these psychic capacities in one degree or another, the Neptune paradigm will always be emphasized in some way: planets in Pisces, the 12th House, many aspects to Neptune, planets squaring the Nodal Axis of Neptune.

From an evolutionary astrologer's point of view, it is important to understand the "why" that any given Soul has that correlates with these expanded psychic capacities: the "why" correlating to the evolutionary needs of the Soul relative to its ongoing journey through time.

The Power of Imagination

Another archetype that we will focus on that correlates with Neptune, Pisces, and the 12th House is one of imagination. Imagination is an extremely powerful psychological dynamic that can have both constructive/positive effects and benefits to the Soul as well as destructive/negative ones. Think about the Source Of All Things setting in motion the Manifest Creation that was imagined within the consciousness of that Source. The "possibilities" that can be imagined by way of Creation into actual realities is only limited by imagination itself.

The root of all creativity lies in imagination. Inventions, art, writing, fantasies, the building of various forms, the structural nature of "reality" itself in every possible way stems from the imagination of the Source Of All Things. Thus, each conscious element of form within the total Creation that is Manifested, has the inherent capacity to imagine different realities in general, and different realities for itself as a life form that is conscious relative to the intelligence imbued within it.

For example, here on Earth all life forms have a consciousness that has intelligence within them. On this Earth, a core Natural Law for all life forms is one of being able to survive. All life forms interact with all other life forms in some way. In order to survive, the intelligence inherent to the consciousness of whatever life form must be able to imagine possibilities for itself that correlate with its survival needs. Intelligence thus linked with imagination gives life forms a way of actualizing that which is imagined.

The human life form, and the intelligent consciousness within it, has exactly the same capacity to imagine different realities, possibilities, and problem solving that correlate with its ongoing evolutionary needs as a species, as well as each individual Soul and its consciousness having the same capacity. In both, IT IS THE EVOLUTIONARY NEEDS THAT ARE THE DETERMINANTS OF THAT WHICH IS IMAGINED. This, of course, is also true for all other life forms that are conscious with an intelligence within that consciousness.

Of course, when the natural dynamic of imagination combines with other natural dynamics/archetypes within the totality of consciousness in human form, it can be both beneficial as well as not. For example, a Soul can "imagine" that which is not real yet consider that which is imagined as real. When combined with the dynamic of projection, for example, this can cause a Soul to project imagined realities onto others that have nothing to do with the actual realities of those others. Or a Soul can "imagine" that it has certain abilities or capacities that it does not actually have yet considers within itself that it does have. A Soul can imagine Creation stories that are not rooted in actual reality, yet the myths generated from such imagined Creation stories are considered to be reality instead of myths. A Soul can imagine that it is being attacked or persecuted when it is not, and so on and so forth. These are examples of the destructive use of imagination.

Conversely, a Soul may have a natural capacity to be a writer of short/fictionalized stories, who can then imagine realities created for itself if it takes action, effort, to actualize itself in this way. Thus, what can be imagined is within the realm of possibilities for that Soul, and this can then manifest as actual reality. This would be an example of the creative use of imagination that could be exampled in countless ways.

Imagination can also be a form of fantasies as well, wherein that which is fantasized about, fueled by imagination, is created and used by the Soul as a vehicle to create a counterpoint to the actual reality that it has created for itself. Thus, use of such imagined fantasies by the Soul is to create a kind of psychic release valve, like water boiling into steam that can depressurize the immediacy of the Soul's actual circumstantial life so that it can remain stable as much as possible in those immediate circumstances.

Conversely, the use of imagined fantasies, which will always be more free and vastly different than the actual circumstances of the Soul's life, can cause the Soul to suffer even more in those circumstances because of the Neptune/Venus archetype of comparing. So if the Soul then compares its actual reality to that which can be imagined/fantasized, this can have the opposite effect that leads to causing the Soul to suffer even more in the actual circumstances of its life.

In EA, one can determine the very nature of a Soul's imagination, of that which is imagined and why as this relates to possible future realities for the Soul, by way of understanding the totality of the Neptune paradigm in the birth chart: the North and South Nodes of Neptune by house locality, the placement of the planetary rulers of each by their own house/sign and aspects to them, where the sign Pisces is that draws into that house the entire Neptune paradigm, and of course the sign on the 12th House, the location of its planetary ruler with aspects to it, and any planets within the 12th House itself and the aspects that these planets are making to other planets as well as the signs that they naturally rule by way of the house cusps that they are on.

In the same way in EA, we can see through the totality of all those Neptunian signatures in the birth chart where the possibility of that which is imagined is entirely delusive in nature yet can be considered as real by the Soul.

Questions and Answers

(Q) Why does Pisces, Neptune and the 12th house correlate with wounds in general? Would it be that these archetypes correlate to all that is unresolved/unfinished within the Soul, to all the emotional and psychological baggage that has been suppressed, avoided, etc. which then represent unfinished business?

(A) Because they correlate with the TOTALITY of the emotional body that is symbolized in the natural trinity of Cancer, Moon, and the 4th House; Scorpio, Pluto, and the 8th House; and Pisces, Neptune and the 12th House. All wounds are registered in the emotional body relative to the specific kinds of wounds that take place through these related archetypes.

(Q) The question on despair/guilt and the desire to 'disappear' brought me to think about suicide and what astrological correlations between Capricorn, Saturn, 10th and Pisces, Neptune, 12th might there be?

(A) Suicide correlates to Pluto, the 8th House, and Scorpio.

(Q) How does the Chiron archetype fit into all this relative to wounds and Neptune?

(A) Again, Chiron as well as other archetypes correlate to specific kinds of wounds. Chiron, even though most do not know this, can also do the wounding as well as being wounded by others. Thus, its natal placement can correlate to how we wound others, but, of course, how others can wound the Soul. If a person had natal Chiron in Scorpio in the 12th, for example, this could correlate to a Soul who has blindly trusted others because of always seeing the good in whomever and, because of that blind trust of always seeing the good in another, becoming totally disillusioned when someone who has been trusted betrays or in some violates the trust extended. Others who use the Soul relative to their own agendas which the Soul never 'gets' because of the blind trust. And so on. Conversely, the Soul can wound others through misrepresenting themselves relative to some hidden agenda that demonstrates the real intent for being with them in the first place. And so on.

Chiron as an archetype can also WOUND ITSELF. The house, sign, and aspects to the natal position of Chiron would correlate to how a Soul can do just that.

(Q) Is it possible for a Soul to experience wounding related to a particular past life after that ego has passed on? For example, if the past life ego became a historical figure, and over the course of time its reputation was slandered and the masses believed the slander, would this affect the Soul?

(A) In varying degrees, depending on the evolutionary station of a Soul, yes.

(Q) Does pain correlate with Neptune?

It depends on the nature of the pain itself. From an emotional/psychological point of view, this would correlate with Scorpio, Pluto, and the 8th House, but of course this is part of the natural triad, trinity, with Neptune, Pisces, the 12th House, and Cancer, Moon, and the 4th House. Physical pain correlates with the lower octave of Pluto, the 8th House, and Scorpio: Aries, Mars, and the 1st House.

As was stated, the wounding of the Soul through its emotional body can be seen within the birth chart by way of the South Node of Neptune by house and sign, the aspects to it from other planets, the location of its planetary ruler by its own house and sign, and aspects to it; the natal placement of Neptune by its own house, sign, and aspects to it; where the sign Pisces is on a house cusp which then draws in the entire Neptune paradigm; the sign on the 12th House cusp, the location of its planetary ruler by its own house, sign, and aspects to it; and any planets that are within the 12th House, aspects to them, and the signs they naturally rule by way of the location of those signs within the birth chart.

Wounds can also be seen through the lower octave of Neptune: Venus. So in the same way that we examine the entirety of the Neptune paradigm, we must also examine the totality of the Venus paradigm in order to understand, in conjunction with the Neptune paradigm, all the potential sources, causes, of the wounds to the Soul that can occur through time: the history of the individual Soul's evolution through time.

So what I would like you to do is to focus on these two paradigms by way of any birth chart of your choosing in order to identify a core wounding is that chart. In other words, you do not have to do an entire EA analysis of ALL the wounds in that birth chart, just a core wound within the other wounds of that chart. Once identified, I would like you to see if you can determine in that Soul the actual cause that then led to that wound. This is one of the most vital ways we can help the clients that we have because almost all clients will want to talk about the wounds that they have in some way. So by helping them understand those actual causes is to help them heal those wounds. The self-awareness of the "cause" is that which allows the Soul to not only identify that cause but to actually do something about it that, if acted upon, will help eliminate the need to recreate that wound over and over.

(Q) I'd like to ask about Neptune's wounds for this assignment. Would they be only the wounds relative to Neptune's archetypal dynamics such as being disillusioned which then wounded the Soul, or other wounds relative to the other planets, which would be experienced or expressed via Neptune and potential imbalances, addictions, escapist tendencies, etc.?

(A) Wounds, as a general archetype, correlate to Neptune, Pisces, and the 12th House. Yet, as we know, there are all kinds/types of wounds that are specific to various archetypes, i.e. Scorpio, Pluto, and the 8th correlating, among other things, to betrayal, or abandonment. The underlying dynamics to focus upon is the necessity for any Soul to understand, and take responsibility for, the cause of whatever wounds so that as a result a healing can take place versus feeling like a victim.

(Q) I have read and studied the evolutionary stages, but do have doubts relative to determining if someone is in spiritual 1 moving to spiritual 2, or if they are beginning spiritual 3. It seems that in both stages 1 and 2, the Soul can be extremely devoted to God or some form of work for the benefit of others, and the main difference seems to be the inner reality and orientation. Does someone in spiritual 3 have total memory of their various past lives while in spiritual 1, these memories begin to progressively be remembered?

(A) Some of the hallmarks of the 1st Stage Spiritual are desiring to be of service to others; of orientating to various techniques or practices that will allow them to progressively expand the interior of their consciousness; of total humility of the Soul itself as it realizes just how small it actually is relative to the totality of Creation; of not feeling that it is actually ready to take on larger tasks by way of that service that is possible within the specific spiritual traditions that the Soul has chosen for itself; and, of being highly self-critical and self-effacing. In the beginning to middle part of this stage: of inconsistent practice of the methods, techniques, that are part of the spiritual tradition of choice; and, of always pointing to the teachers of their traditions and never to themselves.

Some of the hallmarks of the 3rd Stage Spiritual include positions within their traditions of choice that have them teaching increasing amounts of people about that tradition in which they themselves are inwardly knowledgeable of which means actual realization versus reciting of various practices. Within this rarely, if ever, saying the word "I" in relation to this but, rather, always teaching/talking about what is possible to know if one dedicates themselves to whatever the practices are of whatever spiritual tradition one is aligned with. As a result, the very nature of the "energy" that is emitted from such Souls is one of intense magnetism, a magnetism that comes from the inner knowing of the truths of that which they teach, a magnetism that attracts others in progressive amounts of people depending on just how far within the 3rd Stage Spiritual the Soul is. In the final stages, this equals Souls who are on the world stage, in many cases, or at least their teachings are.

Such Souls are the very essence of humility, naturally giving, naturally empathetic, always forgiving, always encouraging to keep on going in the efforts of one life no matter what. Typically, these Souls attract in increasing degrees, all kinds of projections from others who have no idea as to the actual nature, evolutionary, of these Souls because these Souls seem ever enigmatic to Souls of lesser evolutionary capacity.

Some of these Souls have great tasks in life, tasks that have the potential effect of affecting large amounts of people that are defined by the nature of the tasks themselves. And whatever those tasks may be are never a function of the desires within these types of Souls. The tasks themselves are given to these Souls by other Souls that are even more evolved than these Souls up to and including what we call God itself. This is when the Soul learns the difference between personal will versus Ultimate Will, of cooperating with what needs to be done versus personal likes and dislikes.

(Q)   Would negative projections from others occur only in 3rd stage Spiritual? I ask this as I have had my own share of these projections from others yet do not consider myself 3rd Spiritual.

Also, I'm interested in the ability to remember one's past lives, relative to EA stages, as the monk in the example chart that I am doing, didn't seem to remember them naturally. So is it correct to conclude that these past life memories and other abilities that are "transcendental" in nature are not totally dependent on EA level, but depend on karmic necessity?

(A)   No, projections from others upon another, of course, occurs to almost all humans. Yet, when a Soul reaches this state of evolution, it is the NATURE of those projections, and the reasons that they are made, that are specific to this state of evolution.

A hallmark of the 3rd Stage Spiritual as the Soul evolves from the 1st stages of it to its ultimate realization, starts with Souls that are able to remember the specific prior lives that are relevant to the current life being lived. That does not mean all of those lives, but a few of them in the beginning. As the Soul progressively evolves, it then is able to remember ever more as well as being able to "see" some specific prior lives of other Souls. In the final stage, the Soul is able to remember all its previous lives as well as all the previous lives of any other Soul.

So if the monk you are considering is not remembering too many of his prior lives, and yet you feel he is in the 3rd stage spiritual, then that would suggest that he is in the very beginning stages of it.

(Q) Thank you, I was under the impression that it was in Spiritual 1 that these memories would become apparent, that's why I was a bit confused. I'd also think that there are people who have some memories, and are not even in the spiritual stage, but have a specific purpose for a specific memory.

What I am not really getting is how a Soul in spiritual 1 can become intoxicated with itself when reaching Spiritual 2 since they feel so small and are but a tiny speck of sand in a big vast beach. I do not understand how the search and identification for ultimate truth and associated spiritual practices can lead to the delusional sense of grandeur if the Soul is so focused on truth and natural laws and has already identified itself as only a vehicle.

(A) Of course, it is possible for some Souls to have prior life memories in whatever EA condition they find themselves. And, yes, there are specific reasons that this would occur. However, this is not the general truth but a very limited truth for a very limited amount of humans.

In the 1st Stage Spiritual that leads to the 2nd, it is the very nature of whatever spiritual methods or techniques that were employed that have now led to a relative fruition of those methods and techniques. Thus, the Soul now becomes inwardly inflated by progressive degrees of cosmic consciousness as the inner consciousness expands. And it is this very inflation and expansion that the Soul can then delude itself relative to spiritual delusions of grandeur. In this way, the Soul can then begin to point to itself because of the inner expansion of its consciousness, which is perceiving deeper degrees of cosmic realization as to the nature of the Creation itself. It is as if the Soul becomes drunk on itself, intoxicated by its own realizations. Thus, patriarchal history become full of these "spiritual clowns" such as the Clare Prophets, Rajneeshes, etc. Not all Souls that move through the 2nd Stage Spiritual become, nor is it required they become, at such a gross level, clowns like that. Yet the over-identification of the Soul/ego with the nature of its inner realizations does occur in some way that then requires some adjustment in order for evolution to proceed. How that occurs, of course, is unique to each Soul, but occur it does.

(Q) I am confused about the delusion that happens in 2nd Stage Spiritual, if a Soul determines to be good, and only serve the good in one lifetime, like us learning EA, becoming aware of GOD/LOVE/LIGHT, and consciously desires to go back to GOD. How and why would a Soul be tricked again in a future lifetime? Can't we keep this realization in our memory? Even unconsciously, the memory that may help us to make choices to be good?

(A) Evolution is a very, very long process. As was mentioned before, the Soul in the 2nd Stage of Spiritual evolution can delude itself into believing that it is more evolved that it actually is. Within this, the momentum reflected in the ongoing desires to separate from the Source Of All Things generates a temptation for the Soul to glorify itself because of the degree of evolution that does exist within this stage of evolutionary development. As long as the Soul exists within the world of duality, every pure desire, such as the examples you used, is met with its opposite. And that opposite naturally exists, and because of its existence, be fueled by the forces of Evil, Lucifer, itself. Thus, history then becomes full of such Souls as Rajneesh, etc., etc.

Remember the closer any Soul becomes to its Source, the very existence of Evil, Lucifer, is threatened. And, because of this, the closer the Soul becomes to its Source, Evil will do all it can to keep that from happening. Thus, we end up with Souls like Jesus who often said, almost daily, "Satan, get behind me."

EXAMPLE CHART A

Neptune and Wounding of the Soul
Buddhist Monk
3rd stage Spiritual
by Skywalker

Neptune and its lower octave, Venus, both correlate to wounds that the Soul can experience and carry within the emotional body. The South Nodes of these planets correlate to wounds that the Soul has potentially experienced in the past thus, condition present and future experiences. The North Nodes of Venus and Neptune show how the Soul can grow out of the wounds by developing their personal relationship dynamics, including the relationship to itself (Venus) and, by developing its relationship to the divine, to God, the Source etc., through forgiveness and devotion, which leads to a dissolution of the emotional pain that is carried in the emotional body because of the wounds the Soul has accumulated (Neptune).

In the chart of Buddhist monk, Tsem Tulku Rinpoche, we have no recorded birth time so we will look at the planets in the signs and their aspects without the houses. I attached a photo of who he is in the current incarnation and also a photo of who he was in the most recent past life.

Wounds can correlate to any planet as they all correlate to specific wounds but Neptune correlates to the totality of the wounds that have built up within the emotional content of the Soul. In addition, Venus, the lower octave of Neptune correlates to further wounding we can experience, as these wounds will condition the way we feel about and relate to ourselves (Taurus), and condition our projected relationship needs, which we project onto others through the Libra archetype. In some cases, wounds can be so severe and extreme that they can make survival itself impossible. Survival in Evolutionary Astrology correlates with Taurus and the inner side of Venus.

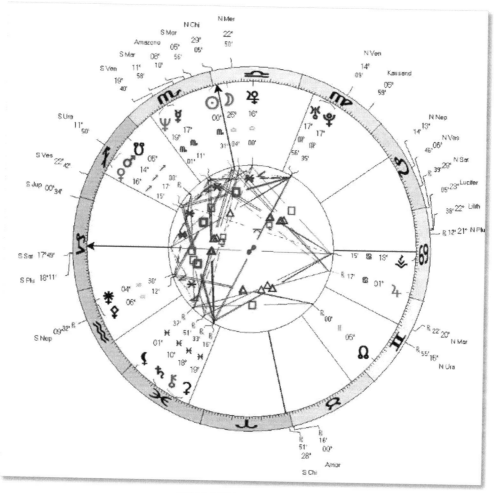

TSEM TULKU RINPOCHE

Neptune and Wounds

In the case of Tsem Tulku Rinpoche, he was an orphan who had an extremely difficult childhood full of violence and lies. The feeling of insecurity, fear, and lack of emotional nurturing and care were deeply felt and led to various attempts to leave his second foster home and even to commit suicide. He was also only told he was an orphan at the age of seven at his first Saturn square which also aspected his Pluto/Uranus conjunction and his South Node of the Moon along with Mars and Venus. At the time, he was introduced to his second foster family, he was told that they were his real parents, which was also another lie that ended up by hurting him deeply. Because of this, his ability to trust others was highly undermined. In the end, being physically abused at various points in his childhood, resulted in him leaving his second foster home with only $50 and his personal items, as he couldn't stand the way he lived anymore. He lived as a homeless person on the streets as he looked for a center to continue his studies in Buddhism, and went hungry many times in his lifetime.

Tsem Tulku Rinpoche
(current life)

Kentrul Rinpoche Thubten Lamsang
(most recent past life)

Soul Structure

Within his Soul structure, past and present, with Uranus conjunct Pluto in Virgo in a square with Mars/Venus and opposite Saturn, Chiron and Ceres all Rx, we can see a lot of evolutionary pressure to evolve at an accelerated pace in the current lifetime and to implement and materialize evolutionary lessons through extensive practice of various techniques in order to make these teachings part of his own structure and reality. Within these symbols, there is also a skipped step with Venus/Mars and the Nodes of the Moon in Sagittarius square the Pluto/Uranus opposite Saturn, Chiron Ceres. These skipped steps are relative to the practice of a religious system, to relationships with people within this system, and other personal relationships such as familial or personal relationships.

These relationships in the current life needed to be continued in order for his Soul to progress and pick up where it left off. The conjunction to the South Node of the Moon from Mars and Venus in Sagittarius show that Tsem Rinpoche has been relating to himself and others based on metaphysical principles and religious doctrines. With so much Sagittarius energy in this advanced stage of evolution, it's clear that he was relating and continues to relate to himself and others based on truth, honesty and natural laws. In his case, dedicating himself to Dharma. These symbols indicate that in the past, a new cycle had been initiated relative to how he related to others, to how he satisfied his needs, and how he acted upon his desire nature to perfect himself and evolve. We also see the conditioning and disciplined training with Saturn in Pisces and the need to further this training in the current life and how the lessons learned will be part of his evolving egocentric self in the current life, to be implemented at the North Node of the Moon and its relative archetypal dynamics. In this case, with the North Node of the Moon in Gemini and the ruler Mercury conjunct Neptune and trine the Pisces Saturn, Chiron and Ceres, we can see that his evolving self would actualize itself by communicating these teachings from the past and the present, to others, in order to further his own spiritual evolution.

To communicate and teach them as a way to heal the self and confront all limitations that limit a direct perception of universal truth as Mercury is conjunct Neptune in Scorpio. To teach the collective about reincarnation and evolution through Buddhism. In addition, Mercury being the ruler of his Pluto/Uranus conjunction in Virgo, would be the "river" through which he would be able to constantly work on his own Soul's evolution as a constant flow of studies and practices of various techniques. This work would be done by totally committing himself towards his spiritual practices and teachings to the point of total devotion for the benefit of others.

Where He's Coming From

With these symbols, relative to his evolutionary stage, we can see that he has practiced the Dharma extensively in his past lives and yet may be flip-flopping relative to how to follow his path in the way that would be most supportive to his evolutionary progress. With the South Node of the Moon in Sagittarius, and the skipped step signature he has, it seems to reflect the need to bring forward the direct knowledge (Sagittarius) he had acquired in the past and to bring it into his awareness in ways that could be logically understood, conceptualized, categorized and communicated to others, since he has the North Node of the Moon in Gemini. The skipped steps indicate that he has already taught natural law and metaphysical principles, such as the principles that are found in Buddhism.

With Venus and Mars conjunct, he could have been a champion for his causes, desiring to move forward with his pursuits and also have been passionate about some form of artistic expression. In his past life, he was a monk, and a choir singer in the life prior to that. He came into the current life with a natural love for music, which, in his teen years led to him clubbing and enjoying disco music yet his determination to spiritualize was so strong that he would come home after going out at night and continue his spiritual practices. So here we can see that he has been working at his spirituality and evolution for quite a long time and his skipped step signature reflects the fact he has flip-flopped between a high focus on his own meditations and understanding of metaphysical principles, the enjoyment of creative or artistic pursuits and the intended evolutionary path of passing this information/knowledge to others as a form of service and as a way to continue his own evolution. In other words, it seems he might have been flip-flopping within himself relative to the desire to stay in nature or secluded meditation, or to come out of his comfort zone and teach others in order to spread Buddhist principles.

The skipped step is 2 degrees out of orb but Venus and Mars are conjunct and Saturn is on the Pluto Polarity Point (PPP). Venus/Mars in a new phase conjunction on the South Node of the Moon, also new phase, is an indication that he is reliving certain dynamics in the current life but these dynamics will be experienced in new ways; such as the fact that, in the past, he was a choir singer, and in the current life, is so expressive, impulsive, and dramatic in the way he teaches and reaches out to people, bringing forth the Sagittarian qualities that were highly developed in his recent past lives. He is extremely dynamic with Venus/Mars on the South Node of the Moon, very playful and funny but serious and to the point, with a sense of sarcastic and penetrating humor due to the Scorpio Sun's life purpose of "getting to the point," by continually metamorphosing the way he expresses himself, in order to constantly be empowered and evolve. Saturn/Chiron/Ceres on the Pisces PPP and square the South Node/Venus/Mars conjunction can correlate to vows that monks naturally need to take that means they will be celibate. It can correlate to a certain suppression of natural desires that has already been in place from his past lives as a monk. It shows that there is potential for him to have had doubts in his past lives and present life whether to be a monk or not because of passions and relationship needs he may have had, and desires of a creative or artistic nature that would have to be given up or channeled in different ways.

Wounds, We All Have 'Em

Being a Buddhist monk doesn't equal being invincible or perfect and, although he had past lives in monasteries and devoted to spiritual practices, he still didn't have past life memories or an expanded awareness as to be able to understand the "why" of his current circumstantial reality and associated difficulties when he was still a child. At the first Saturn square to itself, there was deep wounding relative to his own core identity. When he found out at this young age that his family were not his real family, it was a traumatic experience that led to emotional and psychological wounding. Being an orphan and not knowing the truth about his own identity are two different types of wounds as the orphan's psychology can naturally lead to low self-esteem and feeling like an outsider or inferior to the real family members. The wounds relative to lies (Neptune conjunct Mercury) would create confusion and suspicion about the motives of others. He would become suspicious and fearful of believing in others and have a feeling of not knowing who his family members actually were. Of feeling extremely lonely and not knowing whom to trust, as what was once true suddenly was not; the people he once felt were his kin suddenly becoming strangers and, at the young age of seven, we can all imagine how traumatic such an experience can be. Further, with the way Venus is aspected, he wouldn't be able to be nurtured in ways that would help him develop a strong sense of self-value

(Venus) as he would be forced back upon himself for simple things such as food at many times in his childhood. These dynamics led to a child not valuing life and simply enduring it.

In addition, due to his high level of spiritual attainment in past lives, he wouldn't be able to relate to the values and desires that most people in his environment and family would be oriented towards such as the "American dream." Both of his foster families were not truly supportive of him and were abusive in their own ways; his second foster mother was a schizophrenic who was constantly violent with him, to the point of threatening to kill him in his sleep by stabbing him. Obviously, a child will have severe self-esteem issues and deep fears/insecurities due to the lack of nurturing and constant difficulty in surviving. These dynamics can create a natural sense of powerlessness and victimization, especially in a child who has little to no defense against adults with all the strength and authority to do as they please.

Looking at the South Node of Neptune, we see it is square the South Nodes of Mercury, Venus and Mars, which are all in Scorpio. Relative to wounds, it can correlate with past lives in which he was disillusioned with people in his relationships in general. The South Node of Neptune in Aquarius for all people on Earth can correlate with the disillusionment of mankind being dominated by elite groups as they distort the natural laws of inclusion and sharing, while they promote the capitalist way of life which, of course, is all about profiting and accumulating wealth/resources in order to live comfortably and to pass on resources through inheritances to the newer generations.

Capitalism and profit, to such a Soul, will be seen as ineffective and essentially anti-life itself, as the negative results to the planet are self-evident and irrefutable. Any Soul with a certain level of objectivity and awareness will be appalled at the distortion of the natural laws of giving, sharing and inclusion. It is a "cross" we all carry because of the way humans have lived and continue to live. So within his Soul memory, there can be wounds of betrayals because of these types of distortions of these natural laws, in which he expected others to share with him and was left in difficult situations in order to simply survive. Situations in which the loss of life was experienced because of these distortions or where he himself was the one acting in distorted ways thus, affecting others negatively.

With the South Nodes of Mercury, Venus and Mars all in Scorpio square the South Node of Neptune, we can see how there is disillusionment because of abuses of power and manipulation in personal relationships of many types in his Soul's past. We can see how physical, mental and emotional violence can be a past reality for this Soul as there may have been a lack of discrimination and boundaries in the way he related with others, leading to being trapped in situations with no way out, and leading to disease, poverty and many other potentially difficult and even dark situations. Of course, all these dynamics of abuse could have been experienced from both sides, both as victim and perpetrator. The square of the Nodes of these three planets to the Nodal axis of Neptune shows that, due to the distortion of the natural laws that define the ultimate values of all people of natural giving, inclusion and sharing, he experienced great emotional and psychological pain and suffering (Scorpio) that led to him being deeply emotionally wounded (Neptune).

Neptune in Scorpio is square its own Nodal Axis, reflecting a crisis relative to his faith and spiritual path which tested his faith in the current life by the difficult situations and experiences he had in his childhood. These painful experiences seem to be what catapulted him to be different from those around him, to relate in different ways and to have a different life path than the people in his family.

With Neptune square its own Nodes, there are also skipped steps relative to his spiritual evolution. In his current life, it's interesting that he had the opportunity to become an actor and was actually considering taking that route in life until his Guru told him that if he would become an actor, he would become rich and famous but, by being a monk, he would benefit more people. This reflects Neptune square its own Nodes, remembering that the North Node of Neptune is in Leo for all people and, Leo correlates to acting as it is a form of self-expression to "play roles." He chose to commit (Neptune in Scorpio) to his spiritual path. With his Sun in Scorpio at the very beginning, remembering it's the ruler of the North Node of Neptune and remembering that within his own Soul history there is a past of expression through music, we can understand his dynamic, dramatic and intense way of teaching Buddhism. In his younger days, he was extremely comical and expressive, very sarcastic in a funny way and straight to the point, like a true Scorpio Sun and Mercury. So, in essence, his Scorpio energy is all about deepening his commitment to Source energy through Buddhism, by teaching reincarnation, karma and dharma. In doing so, he is simply continuing his own evolutionary path and healing his own wounds because this Scorpio energy, relative to his evolutionary level, is very able to understand the WHY behind many of his experiences that led to trauma and wounds.

His root Guru, HH Kyabje Zong Rinpoche, died with transiting Saturn conjunct his natal Neptune in 1984; Chiron was conjunct his North Node of the Moon and Pluto was also inconjunct the North Node. This was a massive wound, which, in his own words, took him months or even years to recover. From his chart, we can see, with Saturn on Neptune, he was possibly left with no inspiration whatsoever to continue his spiritual development in the same way. He would have to find the strength to honor the commitments he had made towards his guru and towards his own spirituality. It was a test (Saturn) regarding his devotion and commitment, which he passed with flying colors, and thus initiated a new cycle of spiritual growth and development, through deepening his commitment to the goals he had set.

With Pluto/Uranus in Virgo in square aspect to the Venus/Mars/South Node and opposite Saturn/Chiron/Ceres, there can be masochistic dynamics in some of his former lives, in which there was a repression and/or suppression of his natural desires, in order to grow spiritually. There could have been strong criticism, judgments and even persecution with these symbols as the Soul has been focusing on its own purification in order to evolve. With these aspects, the Soul, in its past, will have all sorts of dynamics and experiences that led to a humbling of itself, through various types of difficult and painful experiences, in order to re-align with a destiny that is truly of service to the self and others. Pluto in Virgo is essentially about a desire nature that has been focused on evolving through the perfection of the self. In the world we live in, this many times will correlate to a Soul who is in need of total and painstaking honesty with itself and others, in order to correctly identify whatever it is that is in need of purification and healing.

Pluto/Uranus can essentially translate into a traumatized Soul because of so much criticism or persecution as the Soul itself has desired to atone for its failures, mistakes, shortcomings and "sins" as taught by the various moral codes of conduct from around the world, religious or social in nature, that naturally lead to guilt, natural or man-made, and the desire to atone for it.

Uranus, our individuating function, is the ruler of the South Node of Neptune for all of us. In his case, it's in Virgo, conjunct Pluto, the symbol for the Soul itself. This seems to be an indication of intense trauma this Soul has experienced in the past as the man-made distortions were experienced in ways that totally disillusioned this Soul, and is also an indication that these traumas are being brought into the current life, to be re-experienced and hopefully purged once and for all. Further, with the North Node of Venus conjunct Pluto and Uranus in Virgo, square the Nodal Axis of the Moon, Venus and Mars and opposite Saturn/Chiron/Ceres, it seems to indicate that in order to develop his self-worth and heal the wounds relative to relationships that correlate to Venus, he would have to revisit his past in key ways.

It's possible that some of the hardships he experienced were karmic debts he had accumulated from past lives, by hurting others because of survival needs or distorted values and/or selfish ways of life in which he hurt himself or others. The North Node of Venus being conjunct Pluto/Uranus shows that in order to evolve the relating dynamics within his Soul, he would need to go very deep within and heal his past, to purge and purify the way he related in order to be truly free from attachments to others, to repay karmic debts from his Soul's evolutionary past, and to continue his spiritual practices by persistent effort and constant humbling of the Soul.

The North Node of Venus is square Venus itself, indicating a skipped step relative to relationships and thus re-enforcing these dynamics that would be addressed in the current life, as the Soul needs to re-visit key dynamics of the past in order to resolve the skipped steps. The skipped steps may be because of a choice to be celibate in the current life and the recent lives prior, which led to him not fulfilling certain karmic dynamics with others from prior engagements.

Using the Wounds to Evolve

What we can see is a chart with a huge amount of dynamic tension as Venus is square its Nodal Axis, Neptune is square its Nodal axis too, the Pluto/Uranus, Saturn/Chiron/Ceres opposition and t-square to Venus and Mars, plus the fact the South Nodes of Mercury, Venus and Mars are all square the South Node of Neptune all correlate to a Soul that desires to grow immensely in the current life and also had the same desires to grow in recent previous lives. It's possible with these symbols that the desire for growth actually came from intense trauma and disillusionment with others and the distorted patriarchal way of life, which is in gross violation of the natural spirituality we are accustomed to deep within our Souls. With the South Nodes of Venus and Mars going from Scorpio to Sagittarius, it reflects the desire to go from abusive situations and dark places that are in direct contrast to these natural laws of sharing and inclusion, back to natural truths and ways of being and relating that are symbolized by Sagittarius as this sign correlates to the search for truth as we understand we are connected to something larger than just ourselves, to a planet in a solar system, in a galaxy and a universe and in the various vibrational planes.

It thus correlates with philosophy and cosmological belief systems such as Buddhism and organized religions. Therefore, it seems that this Soul has found in Buddhism a way to rapidly exhaust its separating desires through intense practice of Dharma which in turn has also led to him understanding the evolutionary need for his difficult circumstances in the current life and to even be thankful for them as he understands that they are, in part, what catapulted him to be so determined about his spiritual evolution.

With Neptune conjunct Mercury and Mercury being the ruler of his North Node of the Moon, Uranus and Pluto, plus the Pisces PPP, he would develop himself to his fullest potential by embracing a transcendental belief system and devoting himself to its teachings, in order to become capable of touching many others in the collective by his unique and controversial style of spreading/communicating these teachings.

In doing so, he would heal his wounds by understanding and learning about reincarnation, compassion, evolution and faith. These are all dynamics relative to his Neptune conjunct Mercury in Scorpio. In addition, with the Sun in Scorpio, being the ruler of the North Node of Neptune, in a grand trine to Jupiter and Saturn, shows his intense emotional approach or dramatic communication and ability to materialize that which he envisions, which he feels is possible, and also correlates to the immense healing that took place in his current life, as he worked through his emotions in an outstandingly dedicated way. He did this by taking responsibility and looking at the bright side at the same time, by not victimizing himself, and desiring to really understand the reasons for his wounds in order to heal them and live a life with true, ultimate meaning.

EXAMPLE CHART B

Neptune and Wounding of the Soul

Therese Neumann

3rd stage Spiritual

by Cat

Therese Neumann

Background

Therese Neumann was born on Good Friday, April 9, 1898 in Konnersreuth, Bavaria. She was a German Catholic mystic and stigmatic who was a member of the Third Order of St. Francis. A stigmata is a term used by Christians to describe marks, sores, or the location of pain on the body in locations that correspond to the crucifixion wounds of Jesus Christ. An individual bearing stigmata on his or her body is referred to as a stigmatic or stigmatist.

Therese Neumann began to experience stigmata in 1926. Her stigmata appeared every Friday for 32 years. She is documented as having bled from her hands, feet, side and forehead. She is said to have lost up to a half a liter of blood during these episodes. It is also reported that she didn't eat food or drink water for the entire 35 years that she was a stigmatic. All she consumed was communion wine and wafers. It has been reported that doctors established that her intestinal tract had withered. Neumann passed away in 1962.

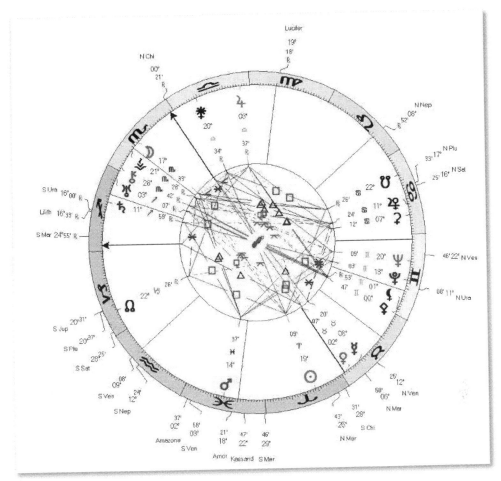

NEUMANN

Neumann, who was devoted to Therese of Lisieux, suffered from a number of physical ailments prior to becoming a stigmatic. On April 28, 1923, the day that Therese of Lisieux was beatified by the Pope, she miraculously regained her eyesight, after having been blind for a time. Two years later, on the day that Therese of Lisieux was canonized as a saint, she was miraculously cured of paralysis in her legs. She writes that a white light appeared and a voice asked her if she wanted to be healed, and after healing her said,

> Only through suffering can you best work out your desire and your vocation to be a victim, and thereby help the work of the priests. Through suffering you will gain more souls than through the most brilliant sermons.

Within a year, she had a vision of Christ in an olive garden. She writes,

He looked at me with a loving expression, and at that very moment I felt as if someone had pierced me through the heart with a sharp object, and then withdrawn it. I noticed that blood was flowing, and I felt this stabbing pain in my heart which, with the exception of Easter Week, has never left me completely.

She had similar visions every Friday as she experienced the passion of Christ and bled.

In 1935, Paramahansa Yogananda met with Neumann. He gives an account of his visit in *Autobiography of a Yogi* and attests to the genuineness of her visions. In regard to not eating or drinking, Neumann told him that one of the reasons she is here on Earth is to prove that man can live by God's invisible light alone.

According to Yogananda, Neumann had been Mary Magdalene in a past life and this life was intended to reassure Christians of the authenticity of Jesus' life and crucifixion as recorded in the New Testament:

As a helpless onlooker, I observe the whole Passion of Christ. Each week, from Thursday midnight until Friday afternoon at one o'clock, her wounds open and bleed; she loses ten pounds of her ordinary 121-pound weight. Suffering intensely in her sympathetic love, Therese yet looks forward joyously to these weekly visions of her Lord. I realized at once that her strange life is intended by God to reassure all Christians of the historical authenticity of Jesus' life and crucifixion as recorded in the New Testament, and to dramatically display the ever-living bond between the Galilean Master and his devotees.

Yogananda explains that Neumann was a jivan mukta, a free Soul, who enjoyed the highest state of nirvikalpa samadhi, which is union with God. Throughout her life, she served as a willing "victim" for the salvation of souls by taking onto her own body the karma of others.

Past Intention and Desire

- Pluto is conjunct Neptune in Gemini in the 6th House

- South Node is in Cancer in the 7th House ruled by the Moon in Scorpio in the 10th House.

- South Node, Moon and Mars in Pisces in the 2nd House create a grand trine

Therese Neumann's past intention and desire has been to serve both God and humanity by serving as a messenger of God. Over time, she has been learning lessons in humility, self-doubt, discrimination, purification, and self-improvement. Subconscious memories of past mistakes, or not doing things "right," have created a feeling of guilt within her Soul. There has been desire to atone for this guilt through suffering in service to others.

Pluto and Neptune form a balsamic conjunction indicating an attunement to the Divine and an understanding of herself in relation to the Divine. A long cycle in which her Soul has had a need and desire to realize the nature of illusions, delusions, dreams and ideals in relation to her desire to serve God and humanity is coming to a close. Her Soul is letting go of all that has come before in order to attune to God and begin a new evolutionary cycle.

In the past, Neumann spent lifetimes initiating emotionally based relationships with others in order to actualize her desire to serve God and others, atone for her guilt and realize the nature of illusions, delusions, dreams and ideals. She had a psychological need and desire to work with the public and make a powerful impact upon the world through her career or social role. She was driven to use her own inner resources in order to realize her dreams. She had an ability to sense the deepest underlying energies of those around her and tune into the collective needs of others. She was driven to sacrifice her own needs and desires in order to nurture and support others, as she was very kind and compassionate, as well as empathetic.

Current Intention and Desire

- Pluto's Polarity Point is in Sagittarius in the 12th House

- North Node is in Capricorn in the 1st House ruled by Saturn in Sagittarius in the 12th House

- North Node is square the Sun in Aries in the 1st House and septile Mars in Pisces in the 2nd House

Neumann's current intention and desire was to purge her ego of all impurities and allow the universal spirit to operate through her by aligning herself with a transcendent philosophy or metaphysical system that made sense to her on a gut level. In order to actualize these desires, she would use both her physical body and her ability to sense the deepest underlying energies of others to take the suffering of others upon herself. Through these selfless acts of self-sacrifice, she allowed the universal spirit to operate through her, giving her life meaning.

> She once took upon herself a throat disease that threatened the vocation of a young seminarian. She suffered this throat ailment for many years, until the day when the newly ordained seminarian, now a Priest, celebrated his first Mass. At that moment, the disease completely disappeared. Interestingly, the taking upon herself of this

throat disease coincided with the beginning of her perpetual fast from eating and drinking in 1922. (Mystics of the Church)

Therese Neumann's story is very deep, profound and complex. It would make a fascinating study, but our purpose here is to uncover her past life wounds, the wounds her Soul acquired along the way and were imprinted upon her emotional body.

Past Life Wounding of the Emotional Body

The wounding of the Soul through its emotional body can be seen within the birth chart by way of the South Node of Neptune by house and sign, the aspects to it from other planets, and the location of its planetary ruler by its own house/sign, and aspects to it; the natal placement of Neptune by its own house, sign, and aspects to it; where the sign Pisces is on a house cusp which then draws in the entire Neptune paradigm; the sign on the 12th House cusp, and the location of its planetary ruler by its own house, sign, and aspects to it; and any planets that are within the 12th House, aspects to them, and the signs they naturally rule by way of the location of those signs within the birth chart. (Rad)

In a nutshell, Neumann carries wounds within her emotional body that are related to lifetimes in which she served others as a religious teacher who was persecuted due to having revolutionary spiritual or religious beliefs and values.

- Neumann's South Node of Neptune is in Aquarius in the 2nd House ruled by Uranus in Sagittarius in the 11th House

- Uranus is quincunx Venus in Taurus in the 4th
  - sextile Jupiter in Libra in the 9th
  - conjunct Saturn Sagittarius 12th and Chiron in Scorpio in the 11th
  - and opposition Pluto in Gemini in the 6th House

Neumann's Soul experienced mental, spiritual and psychic trauma in the past, which has left scars (imprints) upon her emotional body. Neumann's religious or spiritual beliefs, as well as her overall view of reality, have been at odds with those of consensus society in her previous lives. She has experienced confrontation, ridicule and persecution from others due to having beliefs, morals and values that differed from those in the mainstream of the cultures and societies that she was a member. In addition, she has experienced traumatic events or circumstances, along with her peers or other groups of like-minded individuals, that resulted in group hysteria.

Most of the persecution and ridicule that Neumann experienced in her past was due to conflicts with authority figures and religious or legal institutions (Uranus conjunct Saturn in Sagittarius) whose patriarchal morals, rules and laws dictated the beliefs and behavior of those in consensus society. In some cases, she was persecuted, or not taken seriously, simply because she was a woman (Venus in Taurus in the 4th = gender issues).

The ridicule, persecution and confrontations were not only experienced at the hands of authority figures, but through her relationships with a diversity of different types of people (Jupiter in Libra in the 9th House) whose religious and spiritual beliefs were different from her own. Neumann carried wounds within her that were the result of the sudden fracturing or termination of relationships, intimate and otherwise, simply because in her view of reality, all human beings are equal and should be treated accordingly. This vision or point of view was not shared by consensus society and seeing one group of people dominate or take advantage of another was a traumatizing experience for her.

Neumann's Soul chose to be wounded in these ways, as it was her Soul's intention and desire to purify itself by eliminating all emotional, intellectual, physical and spiritual attachments that were preventing growth (Uranus opposition Pluto in Gemini in the 6th House). Neumann's Soul had a need and desire to experience trauma through crisis situations in order to force her to view reality from the perspective of those victimized by patriarchal society so that she could make inner adjustments and learn to serve and heal them through her work.

Neumann's greatest and deepest wounds (Uranus conjunct Chiron in Scorpio in the 11th House), which would enable her to heal and teach others, were the result of being persecuted, ridiculed or ostracized by those she trusted and were most intimate with, as well as her friends and groups of like-minded others. She experienced betrayal and abuse through these relationships, as well as death. She has witnessed the death of others with whom she was involved with, and has experienced sudden and untimely death herself.

- Neumann's Neptune is in Gemini in the 6th House conjunct Pluto in Gemini in the 6th House
  - quincunx the Moon in Scorpio in the 10th House
  - square Mars in Pisces in the 2nd House
  - opposition Saturn in Sagittarius in the 12th House
  - and rules Pisces on the 3rd House cusp

Neumann's Soul experienced emotional trauma in her past due to not being able to express herself, communicate, or deliver a message to those she served in some capacity. Either she was misunderstood, or people refused to listen to her or believe what she tried to express to them. This resulted in a great deal of emotional trauma and disillusionment on Neumann's part as it limited her ability to carry out her Soul's core intention and desire to serve God and humanity by serving as a messenger of God.

Neumann experienced limitation and oppression by those in authority, or the traditions of consensus society, in relation to her public life, career and social role in the past. She experienced crisis situations in which she was betrayed and abandoned by family members, along with having her public reputation damaged in some way. In addition, she is likely to have experience a fall from grace at some point in time. These experiences left her feeling powerless and depressed.

Neumann also found herself in situations in which she was taken advantage of by others which damaged her sense of self-worth. She has experienced lifetimes of poverty in which she had a difficult time sustaining herself. These experiences damaged her sense of self-worth as she may have been forced to sustain herself in a manner that went against her own personal value system. For example, she may have been a prostitute at some point in order to survive.

Neumann also has emotional wounds based upon feelings of emotional isolation and loneliness, coupled with irrational fears, related to her religious beliefs and religious dogma. She lived according to her own moral code and spiritual beliefs, which were at odds with the religious dogma of the times. She received little support from her parents and family who may have displayed a hostile attitude towards her personal beliefs. This lack of support left her feeling alone.

- Sagittarius on the 12th House cusp, ruled by Jupiter in Libra in the 9th House
  - semi-square Moon in Scorpio in the 11th
  - bi-quintile Mercury Taurus in the 4th
  - quincunx Venus in Taurus the 4th
  - sextile Uranus in Sagittarius in the 11th
  - trine Pluto in Gemini in the 6th House

Many of Neumann's past life emotional wounds were due to having religious or spiritual beliefs that resulted in persecution, ridicule, public shame and disgrace because they differed from the dogmatic religious beliefs of her culture and society. Neumann was involved in teaching and converting others over to the principles, laws, morals and spiritual beliefs in which she embraced. These were those of Natural Law and Christianity as originally taught by Jesus and were the basis of her emotional reality. Neumann suffered from emotional wounds related to some form of mass trauma and group hysteria involving themes of betrayal, rejection, abandonment, persecution, shock, death and destruction (Jupiter semi-square Moon in Scorpio in the 11th). These experiences left her with feelings of powerlessness, alienation, and hopelessness.

Neumann suffered from wounds to the individuation process, alienation, betrayal by her peers, shock, trauma, psychological fragmentation, group hysteria and loss of hope in the process of initiating and actualizing her Soul's desire to serve as a messenger of God. It's possible that she may have been a victim of the Inquisition at some point, or simply suffered from people refusing to listen to her and take her teachings seriously. No matter what the case, these experiences have left lingering scars within her emotional body.

- Saturn is in Sagittarius in the 12th House
    - square Mars in Pisces in the 2nd
    - conjunct Uranus in Sagittarius in the 11th
    - opposition Neptune in Gemini in the 6th House
    - opposition Pluto in Gemini in the 6th House
    - ruling Capricorn in the 1st

Again, Neumann suffered from religious persecution or judgment due to being a Christian and having Christian values. She experienced conflicts and confrontations with authority figures, religious institutions and those with traditional patriarchal values in general. Her desire to break free of tradition and the patriarchal morals, rules and laws of the times in which she lived resulted in persecution, alienation and feelings of isolation as her view of reality differed from that of the consensus societies she lived in. The wounds that resulted from these experiences left her with feelings of inferiority, humiliation, guilt, inadequacy, and generally not feeling good enough to be a messenger for God. These feelings of inferiority limited her ability to serve God and humanity as her Soul intended and desired.

In addition to feelings of inferiority, these past life wounds left Neumann's Soul feeling the pain of aloneness as she had clashed with civilized society, its institutions and traditions time and time again. She has suffered from violence, loss of social position, oppression, punishment, and has even experienced premature and violent death, due to her Soul's desire to serve God and humanity as a messenger of God.

- Neumann's Venus is in Taurus in the 4th House
    - quincunx Jupiter in Libra in the 9th House
    - quincunx Uranus in Sagittarius in the 11th House

This configuration is a yod, which is also known as "The Finger of God" and correlates to a feeling of destiny. A yod promotes a vision, or an awareness from on high, of something that the Soul is destined to do, whether the individual is consciously aware of this "mission" or not. In addition, yods are associated with dynamics involving crisis situations, as well as with health problems.

Venus correlates to past life wounds that are carried within the emotional body. Neumann's Venus in Taurus in the 4th House correlates to a past life wound that has left her feeling emotionally insecure due to having experienced some cataclysmic emotional event in the distant past. Her Soul carries emotional imprints and pre-existing emotional patterns within itself related to this past life wound.

- Venus is conjunct Mercury in Taurus in the 4th House
  - semi-square (balsamic) Mars in Pisces in the 2nd House
  - quincunx both Jupiter in Libra in the 9th House and Uranus in Sagittarius in the 11th House

Neumann's Soul has reached a point in its evolution in which it must now deal with old dynamics related to unresolved or incomplete matters from the past in order to bring them to closure. Past life dynamics related to Neumann's desire to communicate her spiritual values to others are stirred up with her reacting to them in old, well-known ways, which involve suffering and sacrifice.

Venus is the apex planet in a yod configuration in Neumann's chart. The apex planet describes something that needs to be adjusted or eliminated which, in Neumann's case, is the imprint of a past life wound from having experienced some cataclysmic emotional event.

Venus rules Libra, which is intercepted in the 9th house. This is an indication that Neumann has expanded her consciousness, in metaphysical terms, to the point that her intuition is very well developed and she no longer needs to develop this area any further. She is capable of experiencing visions, which allow her to adjust to the reality of another person.

- Venus is quincunx both Jupiter in Libra in the 9th House and Uranus in Sagittarius in the 11th House which are sextile one another

In order to fulfill her destiny, Neumann has developed an ability to remember past events, in the form of religious and historical visions, which serve to help her convince others that her own existing religious beliefs are true. It has been reported that Newman had many visions in which she was shown many details of the life of Jesus, from his birth to his resurrection.

> During these past seventeen years Therese has undergone many experiences which have convinced thousands of world visitors that she is gifted with unusual powers. Seated in a private prayer booth behind the Church altar, Therese has had visions of biblical events which coincide unquestionably with historical events. For instance, each Lenten period she passes with Christ through the Garden of

Gethsemane, through the trial presided over by Pontius Pilate, through the crucifixion, and later the resurrection. Hours after, she will describe her visions in detail, even to the pronunciation of Roman and Hebrew phrases spoken by lesser-known people, but identified by history. Any interrogator or educator, realizing her limited education, is convinced beyond a doubt as to the veracity of her story. (Ancestry.com)

The two quincunx aspects symbolize the challenges Neumann would face in relation to initiating and actualizing her special destiny. Venus and Uranus form a gibbous phase quincunx, which correlates to a state of sincere humility, which is the cause of individual limitations, while Venus and Jupiter form a full phase quincunx, which correlates to social limitations. In order to carry out her mission, Neumann would first have to make adjustments and improvements to herself in order to rid herself of a feeling of not being good enough to allow God to express through her, as well as learn to listen to others in order to integrate her special mission on society's terms.

Both the yod and the quincunx aspect correlate to health matters. Illness can serve to help one develop an awareness of what needs to be done in order to improve oneself and fulfill one's special destiny. This process occurs through crisis situations that serve to ultimately restructure or eliminate the way in which the Soul responds to the imprint of this past life wound, especially in relation to physical disease and illness, which is caused by this ancient emotional wound.

For the most part, those who have a yod in their chart have an intense and chaotic early life, which produces complicated and unfortunate experiences, which force the Soul to make the adjustments that are needed in order to bring the energy of the apex planet into focus. In the process, the individual begins to feel as though they have a special, predestined mission to fulfill. There may be repeating patterns and themes in the early life, which enforce specific lessons or highlight a specific path the Soul is to follow.

Neumann experienced several physical crises in her early life. On March 10, 1918:

- Transiting Pluto in Cancer in the 7th House was square natal Jupiter in Libra in the 9th House
  - quincunx natal Uranus in Sagittarius in the 11th House
  - and sextile natal Venus in the 4th House

Neumann's yod was activated at this time and she fell while putting out a fire. This fall resulted in a partial paralysis of the spine and severe leg cramps. Neumann forced herself to be as active as possible in spite of her handicaps. This resulted in several additional accidents and injuries. By March 1919, Neumann was totally blind. For seven years she was unable to walk or sit up in bed. It was during this time that "her spiritual life blossomed."

Therese Neumann Actualizes her Current Intention and Desire

Neumann was eventually healed of her physical wounds and ailments. These events are considered to be modern day miracles. Neumann spent the rest of her life experiencing visions and suffering in the name of Christ.

Teresa Neumann's life changed radically after her miraculous recovery from paralysis and total blindness at the age of 25. About a year later, she received the stigmata and began fasting, which lasted 36 years until her death. Her only nourishment was the Holy Eucharist and for this reason the Nazi authorities, during World War II, withdrew her food rationing card and gave her a double rationing of soap to wash her towels and clothing, because every Friday she would be drenched in Blood while she was in ecstasy, experiencing the Passion of Christ. Hitler was very fearful of Teresa.

To her people she spoke the words which were to become her theme of life: 'More souls are saved through suffering than by grand words of man. Through suffering I will devote my life to the glorifying of Christ's name.' A few days later the stigma of open wounds on her hands, head, feet, and heart, appeared with the pain from bleeding that appeared. She admitted to Father Naber at the time, that the pain was great, but announced her intention of abstaining from food and water for the remainder of her natural days.

With the war over, Therese hopes for a return of the German people to a Christian way of life. Though realizing the war guilt Germany will be held accountable for, she firmly believes that national differences become inconsequential where religion is concerned. The greatest lesson one can learn from seeing Therese Neumann is that Nazi ideology, however powerful, was incapable of overcoming the spiritual influence of the Christian religion. Hitler and Co. were no match for Jesus of Nazareth and his disciples. (therealpresence.org)

Was Therese Neumann Mary Magdalene?

Going back to the beginning, Yogananda stated that Therese Neumann was Mary Magdalene in a past life. This may well be, but Edgar Cayce, who was a contemporary of hers, did a reading for a woman who was also alive during Neumann's life, saying that she had been Mary Magdalene. So, who knows? The purpose of this assignment is to explore Neumann's wounds, not prove that she may have been Mary Magdalene. I tried to refrain from attempting to do so, and interpreted the chart without Mary Magdalene in mind. That said, after completing this assignment, I want to inject a little bit of information that does seem to tie it to Mary Magdalene.

Imagine having been one of Christ's closest companions and followers and watching him slowly die on the cross, feeling powerless to do anything about it. That would be a form of emotional trauma that one would carry with them for a very long time. Neumann re-experienced this every Friday for 32 years. Her Uranus in Libra is conjunct Chiron in Scorpio in the 11th House. Were these weekly visions and stigmatic experiences past life memories of her deepest wound, witnessing Christ die on the cross, re-surfacing on a weekly basis?

Neumann suffered from emotional wounds related to some form of mass trauma and group hysteria involving themes of betrayal, rejection, abandonment, persecution, shock, and death/resurrection (Jupiter semi-square Moon in Scorpio in the 11th). These experiences left her with feelings of powerlessness, alienation, and hopelessness." And then there are the wounds related to gender issues (Venus in Taurus in the 4th = gender issues) and emotional trauma due to not being able to express herself, communicate, or deliver a message to those she served in some capacity:

- Gemini in the 6th House conjunct Pluto in Gemini in the 6th House
  - quincunx the Moon in Scorpio in the 10th House
  - square Mars in Pisces in the 2nd House
  - opposition Saturn in Sagittarius in the 12th House
  - rules Pisces on the 3rd House cusp

And, her deepest wound – Uranus conjunct Chiron in Scorpio in the 11th House – being persecuted, ridiculed or ostracized by those she trusted and were most intimate with, as well as her friends and groups of like-minded others.

In the Introduction to *The Gospel of Mary of Magdalene: Jesus and the First Woman Apostle* Karen King writes:

> But the disciples do not go out joyfully to preach the gospel; instead controversy erupts. All the disciples except Mary have failed to comprehend the Savior's teaching. Rather than seek peace within, they are distraught, frightened that if they follow his commission to preach the gospel, they might share his agonizing fate. Mary steps in and comforts them and, at Peter's, relates teaching unknown to them that she had received from the Savior in a vision. The Savior had explained to her the nature of prophecy and the rise of the Soul to its final rest, describing how to win the battle against the wicked, illegitimate Powers that seek to keep the Soul entrapped in the world and ignorant of its true spiritual nature. But as she finishes her account, two of the disciples quite unexpectedly challenge her. Andrew objects that her teaching is strange and he refuses to believe

that it came from the Savior. Peter goes further, denying that Jesus would ever have given this kind of advanced teaching to a woman, or that Jesus could possibly have preferred her to them. Apparently when he asked her to speak, Peter had not expected such elevated teaching, and now he questions her character, implying that she has lied about having received special teaching in order to increase her stature among the disciples. Severely taken aback, Mary begins to cry at Peter's accusation. Levi comes quickly to her defense, pointing out to Peter that he is a notorious hothead and now he is treating Mary as though she were the enemy. We should be ashamed of ourselves, he admonishes them all; instead of arguing among ourselves, we should go out and preach the gospel as the Savior commanded us.

Unfortunately, there is little verifiable information about Mary Magdalene. There is a lot of propaganda. Almost everyone who knows anything about Mary Magdalene was taught that she was a prostitute. Neumann has Venus in Taurus and Mars in the 2nd house, so she may have been a prostitute at some point. I am not so sure that Mary Magdalene was a prostitute however. I think that church authorities made that up.

That is why I asked Rad if a Soul could be wounded from being slandered after they have passed on. But, it is possible that Mary Magdalene was a prostitute in her youth, and this is why Neumann (if she was Mary Magdalene) believed she was "not good enough" to serve as a messenger of God. Venus is the apex planet in a yod, symbolizing dynamics that need to be eliminated.

Neumann has a very complex chart. I could go on and on, but this is all speculation at this point.

EXAMPLE CHART C

Neptune and Wounding of the Soul
Lila and her Wound

3rd Stage Individuated moving into the 1st Stage Spiritual

by Linda

Love came, and became like blood in my body. It rushed through my veins and encircled my heart. Everywhere I looked, I saw one thing. Love's name written on my limbs, on my left palm, on my forehead, on the back of my neck, on my right big toe...Oh, my friend, all that you see of me is just a shell, and the rest belongs to love. (Rumi)

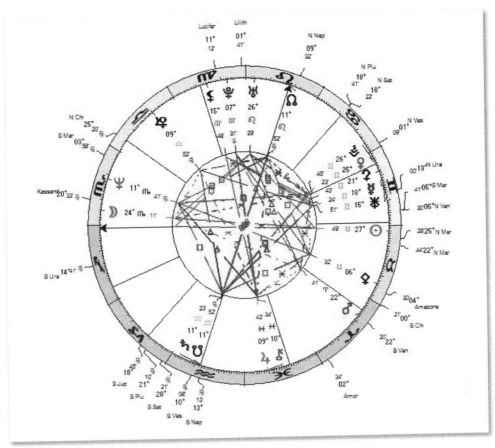

LILA

I have been given permission to examine the birth chart of a real person using the anonymous name of Lila (cusp of 3rd Individuated and 1st Spiritual). I will be focusing on her Neptune skipped steps signifying the root cause of one of the major wounds within the Soul. These skipped steps recently played out in a torrid relationship, which ended in betrayal and loss (Neptune Scorpio 12th).

The origin of the Soul's wounding goes back to the times of the transition from Matriarchy to Patriarchy when:

- the natural roles of men and women became distorted (South Node of Neptune Aquarius 4th, Pluto Virgo 10th);

- the 'sacred prostitute' role was created by men for women (Vesta Gemini 8th conjunct Venus);

- humans concocted man-made religions to explain the nature of Creation;

- humans relative to groups of humans became perverted to competition, artificial hierarchy, superiority/inferiority (triad of Gemini-Libra-Aquarius);

- nuclear families began to be formed where women were regarded as possessions of men; and

- the Natural Law of free choice became squashed.

The Matriarchy is a symbol for how humans have lived on this planet for the vast majority of time in accordance with the Natural Laws correlating to the feminine and masculine principles. With Pluto Virgo 10th and the South Node of Neptune Aquarius 4th, Lila is learning about past life choices and responsibilities that were made during the patriarchal transition relative to the male and female gender, gender assignment issues, masculine and feminine roles in relationship, judgments formed around 'rights and wrongs,' natural and man-made guilt, and their consequences that have led to the current life. With the North Node of Neptune Leo 9th, the Soul is learning that if her core beliefs are contrary to Natural Law, the way her life is interpreted and set up will reflect that distortion, therefore she is changing the effects of past crystallized man-made beliefs in order to return to intrinsic Natural Laws (Resolution North Node Leo 9th conjunct North Node of Neptune).

In the current life, I do believe Lila's skipped steps are in the process of being resolved! Lila understands that for evolution to proceed, her entire life is to be consistently integrated through the Resolution Node, the North Node Leo 9th, and its ruler Sun Taurus 6th. This means reinstating the Natural/Sacred Feminine (and Masculine), and learning how to be in natural intimate relationships (Neptune-Moon Scorpio 12th). I will demonstrate how the Feminine archetype in the Soul of Lila firstly became wounded and how she now has the opportunity for healing the wound of the Soul through the WATER archetype; evolution can only be effected through the emotions (Cancer-Scorpio-Pisces). The wounding of the Soul can be seen within the birth chart not only by way of the original wound of the Soul itself, Pluto Virgo 10th – sacred prostitute, servant/slave, subjugation of the Natural Feminine, judgment, persecution, suppression of Natural Laws, masochism, victimization – but also within the entire Neptune archetype:

(1) the South Node of Neptune 13.17 deg Aquarius in the 4th house, and its aspects;

(2) the location of South Node of Neptune's planetary ruler Uranus Leo 10th, and its aspects;

(3) the natal placement of Neptune Scorpio 12th, and its aspects;

(4) Pisces on the 5th house cusp;

(5) Libra on the 12th house cusp, the location of its planetary ruler Venus Gemini 8th, and its aspects;

(6) Planets within the 12th house – Neptune and Moon – and their aspects, and the signs they naturally rule.

NEPTUNE

(1) South Node of Neptune 13.17 deg Aquarius in the 4th house

- South Node of Neptune conjunct Moon's South Node
- South Node of Neptune conjunct Saturn Aquarius 3rd
- South Node of Neptune inconjunct Lucifer-Resolution Lilith Virgo 10th
- South Node of Neptune square Neptune Scorpio 12th
- South Node of Neptune trine Juno-Mercury-Ceres Gemini 7th

Background   The core wounding within the Soul has impacted the self-image, the subjective ego, and the "emotional body," within each egocentric personality created by the Soul. This emotional conditioning originated around 7,200 BCE, was carried through the patriarchal transition that began in 6600 BCE, and leads up to the current life (South Node Neptune conjunct Moon's South Node).

In previous lives, when the Natural Law of understanding the "I" in terms of "we" shifted to perversion, the "I" then became the bottom line within the collective consciousness. This bottom line dynamic in the Soul of Lila is naturally targeted by her Soul for its spiritual and evolutionary growth; therefore, the Leo archetype has been highlighted in the current life in many ways. The developmental stress associated with the past life and current life wounds of the Soul (Neptune square its own Nodes) came about as a result of being suddenly separated from her human family or group. This impacted upon the identity of the Soul and resulted in dissociation and becoming "a lost Soul."

The sense of, "Who I am," disconnected from the group, became confused and distorted (Neptune Scorpio 12th square Neptune's Nodes Aquarius/Leo, and square the Moon's Nodes Aquarius/Leo), with an evolutionary necessity to "TRULY KNOW WHO I AM" (North Node Leo 9th conjunct the MC) and what the ULTIMATE REALITY is truly about; to find her way home from being "lost at sea"; and to merge the individual "wave" (Soul) within the "ocean" (Source). The wound within the Soul then translated, on a collective level, to weak boundaries within her generation: the "I" in its relationship to the "we," and the "I" in its relationship to Source.

Her blind trust in others not only within the group, but also within the collective of Souls – always seeing the good in all Souls (Neptune double whammy in the 12th) – brought repetitive experiences of disillusionment when her trust was betrayed by them. This meant having to re-live and re-do the past life dynamics in order to change the past life pattern, and current life "reality" (Saturn conjunct South Node of Neptune in Aquarius, and Moon's South Node Aquarius 3rd Rx) by way of reformulating the intellectual structures according to Natural Laws.

Having to confront the "consensus" of opinion internally and externally, led to feelings of persecution and victimization when one or more others within any of her group associations did not agree with her spiritual ideas, the evolutionary intention of which is to "spiritualize her life." This judgment and persecution of the Soul that resulted in the wounding of the Soul is a replaying of the past life dynamics as she tried to recapture the sense of belonging to a family or group based on true caring and nurturing (South Node of Neptune Aquarius 4th). These traumatic experiences played out in her life and led to, in the words of Lila, dissociation:

> Dissociation. I actually realized on another level that my whole life – just being in the world – has been triggering dissociation experiences. I fall over and get back up again repeatedly. Just by being in the world, due to my sensitivity and fragility, I kept getting dissociated. Last year I was at my worst and it took 4 months to get back into my body. I want to work with healing whatever is behind the dissociation, the continual dissociation that has plagued me my whole life. This is the main issue that needs to be healed.

This karmic signature symbolizes re-aligning with the Natural Laws that correlate with the masculine and feminine principles as created by the Creator, and liberating from perversions of the Patriarchy in order to heal the Soul's emotional body. The core wound, originating on a basic emotional level, correlates with how Lila acknowledges herself or sees herself inwardly – a separate and unique ego with an identity. This sense of, "Who I am," is being re-identified through that which created it: the Soul; and through that which created the Soul: the Divine. The disturbance of the "emotional body" in the evolutionary journey of the Soul in general can be seen by way of the Water Trinity in Lila's chart:

EGO – Moon Scorpio 12th
SOUL – Pluto Virgo 10th
CREATOR – Neptune Scorpio 12th

And it is through these same water archetypes that evolution and healing will be effected. For Lila, the healing of the Soul comes by remembering her origins: Goddess; and thus consciously aligning her will and the choices she makes (Soul) with that Origin. In effect, she is realigning her Soul, and her personal will to a Higher Will.

Core wound A core wound in the emotional body is described by Lila's relationship to her mother in the current life. In ancient times, there were no nuclear families, but rather the biological mother was backed up by her group. With Jupiter Pisces 4th and Chiron Pisces 4th both opposite Pluto Virgo 10th, what wounding experiences occurred to Lila in past lives and in her early childhood affected her egocentric development? What beliefs were held by the mother that intermingled or were absorbed by the baby? We will never really know, however we are given a clue with Chiron conjunct Jupiter in the 4th house (and both opposite Pluto 10th): a symbol of wounding of excessive emotional proportions (Bipolar Disorder). Was the child able to break away to develop its own egocentric emotional security, or had it been smothered by the mother? With Chiron Pisces 4th, and Uranus ruling the 4th house, the emotional wounding and trauma signature is re-emphasized, as Lila shares:

> My birth was very traumatic. My mother was given a general anesthetic, episiotomy, and the labor was induced. I was a high forceps delivery and 'black and blue,' my cranium distorted. I slept for one week to recover from the trauma.

It is possible that in past lives Lila had created an unconscious de-facto goddess model out of mother and mother-types in general in order to survive (Jupiter rules 2nd house). The reason for this is the proclivity of the Soul to seek that which gives it a sense of security and familiarity, and this was very often connected to her relationships with women. Many of these past life relationships with women were culminating (Neptune-Moon Scorpio 12th) as Lila had osmosed what she needed from them, and let them go. Some of these relationships ended in betrayal, abandonment, loss and violations of trust, however, the understandings derived from these relationships served to expand her philosophical structures, and bring her closer to understanding her quest.

The psychic umbilical cord that tightly binds mother with child had never been cut, thus Lila's lifelong quest to liberate herself (South Node of Neptune Aquarius 4th) from the possessive mother archetype (backed by Pluto), and develop her own emotional self-security from within herself (Pluto polarity point Pisces 4th). For these karmic reasons, Lila has had to work on breaking free from the ties that bind her to her symbiotic family that keeps her desperately clinging on an unconscious level to the emotional connections that are known and familiar. For these karmic lessons to take effect, it was necessary for Lila to experience abandonment and rejection by, not only her own mother, and at times her own family, but many people throughout her life, leaving her to fall back upon herself in order to enforce the lesson of inner emotional security. With Mars Aries 5th, and Uranus Leo 10th, Lila recalls:

> A betrayal by my mother. At age 19, I told my mother that I thought I was pregnant. (It later turned out that I was not.) She reacted with a tirade of disapproval exclaiming that all she wanted for her daughters was that they would remain virgins until they were married. She ended by demanding I have an abortion because I had to, foremostly, think of my "father's position." I remember feeling as if a knife had been thrust through my heart in that moment.

To bring those skipped steps to light around my mother and the betrayal of the feminine, mother used to say, "Put the man first." She was always concerned for her own security and social standing which was dependent upon her husband (my father) and his success. I had an abortion at age 30. I had really wanted to have the child. Mother said, "You cannot be a single mother – you will have to have an abortion." I was abandoned by her. I begged for her support.

And what of Saturn that sits within just minutes of the IC, and conjunct the South Node of Neptune and the Moon's South Node? How did the role of father impact upon Lila's life and what 'ideas or messages' from past lives had Lila absorbed from the distorted masculine (Saturn 3rd)? What conditioning patterns did she have to re-live in order to liberate from the messages that had created her reality? Saturn and the South Node of Neptune square Neptune Scorpio 12th (ruler of Pluto 10th) meant having to identify and resolve the severe developmental stress that had impacted the Soul. It was necessary that Lila break free from her current life parental models that, in turn, had translated into distorted dynamics in the area of relationships, and specifically the feminine/masculine role models in relationships.

Not only has Lila had to deal with an alcoholic father, but has had to deal with her own addictions to coffee and tobacco (successfully quit!). These forms of escape are linked with an underlying cause to blunt the effects of actual reality (Saturn), to soften shocking and traumatic experiences, and cope with the developmental stress (overwhelming emotions) held within the subconscious memories of the emotional body (Aquarius 4th). She realized that these coping mechanisms – addictions – cause more stress in the long run.

In a key karmic relationship that recently took place, Lila had to deal with the unconscious patterns relative to patriarchal role models (South Node of Neptune inconjunct Lucifer-Resolution Lilith 10th). It took some time for the dynamics to come to consciousness in order that she make new choices for the future. With Chiron-Jupiter Pisces 4th opposite Pluto-Lucifer-Resolution Lilith 10th, Lila was wounded by the partner, over and over, until she finally dealt with the repeating messages to break free and liberate herself.

With Chiron-Jupiter square Mercury Gemini 7th, she learned to listen to the reality of the partner in order to understand his needs (in this case, for freedom and non-commitment), and to communicate and share her own needs. She learned to make new healthier decisions that would usher in a new cycle in her relationship dynamics.

With Neptune-Moon in Scorpio in the 12th house, Lila is not only learning about her personal dynamics, but also those of the "bigger picture."

The nature of the times and societies that we are living in promote the idea of collective "victimization." It is very easy to be a victim, and much harder to own or accept responsibility for our own action—to understand that the overall realities we create emanate from within ourselves according to our evolutionary and karmic requirements. (Jeffrey Wolf Green)

Healing Lila possesses an inherent faith and hope that when projected from the Soul creates an electro-magnetism that alters the nature of the circumstances created by her Soul. She has successfully been able to identify the causes of her wounds, accept the responsibility in her own actions, and find remedies for them. Through meditation, astrology, Buddhist philosophy, and Dharma practice, Lila has formed a body of knowledge pertaining to physical and ethical purification and transformation (Jupiter Pisces 4th opposite Pluto Virgo 10th). She regularly refashions her diet to incorporate natural healing substances – plants, minerals, nutrients, potentized medicines – to maintain the optimum health of her body. Not only has Lila been healing herself, she is able to pass on her knowledge, techniques and skills in order to help others. Understanding her own archetypal dynamics are always then translated to helping the wider group of Souls, as she restores her "natural feminine" role of "compassionate mother and nurturer" within the Universal.

(2) South Node of Neptune's planetary ruler Uranus Leo 10th

- Uranus t-square Moon Scorpio 12th and the Sun Taurus 6th
- Uranus sextile Venus Gemini 8th
- Uranus trine Mars Aries 5th

Background In past lives, the Soul battled with personal and collective authority. Uranus in Leo is a paradoxical signature: desiring to be a member of a group yet desiring to shine on a personal level. With Uranus ruling the South Node of Neptune 4th, she is able to liberate and reformulate the sense of "I" – the lost identity – to playing a role in the "we," her community. This has not been easy at all since she has experienced power struggles and scapegoating in her career and with family members (being treated as the "black sheep"). Not receiving validation for her contributions to society, in the way she would like, always leads to the transcendence of the ego into the Divine, purifying the techniques incorporated in her social role to help others, and self-improvement by way of the development of personal humility. Power struggles are reflective of distorted patriarchal dynamics involving inferiority/superiority, hierarchy, domination/submission, and pecking orders. The confusion and intensity of these dynamics have caused a major wound in the Soul: Bipolar Disorder. She has also battled with depression and suicidal thoughts (Uranus balsamic conjunct Pluto 10th) due to feelings of futility in relation to the future. She's had to develop her own self-authority and separate from the consensus view (10th).

Core wounding   The core wound of separation from the group extended into many lifetimes of struggling to feel accepted and validated by family and society. The Soul experience of being judged, shamed, persecuted and scapegoated by family, society or culture resulted in a hiding signature (Moon Scorpio 12th). A reaction to intense traumas that occurred in past lives caused Lila to create an outer reality below her actual state of Spiritual evolution. The Soul keeps being drawn back to the end of the 3rd Individuated stage to express the personal creativity of the "I" consciousness. This has been met with difficulties: rejection, scapegoating, or power struggles created by the Soul itself. She hides behind the mask of a somewhat conventional life (where she feels safe), yet the degree of depth and insight she exhibits goes well beyond the nature of her outer life. Carrying the burden of shame (10th), guilt and unworthiness (6th) extended a feeling of self-humiliation into her intimate relationship dynamics in which she is liberating herself from sadomasochism in terms of inequality between the sexes (Sun opposite Moon and both t-square Uranus).

Healing   Lila has had to liberate herself from the old role models of husband and wife. She has made new choices in picking potential partners, lovers and friends to those who offer support and validation. Hopefully she will find a supportive relationship, a spiritually aware partner who will not let her give her power away, and with whom she can safely express her natural innocence. She is in the process of healing past life trauma through her own efforts (self-healing) by finding new techniques to deal with trauma held in the emotional, mental and physical bodies (Sun Taurus 6th). Being a fully qualified and highly experienced Physiotherapist, the revolutionary yet simple new techniques that she has developed – movements, postures, exercises – are shared as a service to the community (Pluto Virgo 10th) and with the collective group of Souls (Moon Scorpio 12th).

Working with children

- 5th house ruled by Neptune
- Uranus Leo 10th
- Leo MC
- Leo North Node conjunct North Node of Neptune conjunct Moon's North Node

Lila recalls:

> There was an intensive period in my 40's when I worked exclusively with children. I came to understand the profound impact of birthing trauma that influences the developmental process of children – physically, emotionally, socially and mentally – and which affects learning ability and other life skill acquisitions and maturity.

When she is in alignment with true giving without expectations of reward (which is very often), she naturally wants to give: not take. Lila's personal egoic wound (4th) is then transmuted through the bottom line of the Soul (Scorpio), with true compassion flowing out to the collective (12th), and the Natural Law of caring, sharing and inclusion being restored. Lila's will (Scorpio) then becomes a beautiful expression of carrying out Divine Will through the natural water trinity (Cancer-Scorpio-Pisces). In this way, the center of gravity within the consciousness of the Soul (Pluto) becomes centered in the Goddess, thus changing the egocentric orientation (the original wound).

(3) Natal Neptune Scorpio 12th

- Neptune sextile Pluto
- Neptune square the Nodes (skipped steps)
- Neptune square Saturn
- Neptune t-square the Nodes of Neptune
- Neptune sextile Lucifer-Resolution Lilith
- Neptune inconjunct Eris
- Neptune trine Jupiter-Chiron

Skipped steps The Neptune paradigm is emphasized by Neptune skipped steps in addition to Neptune squaring its own Nodes. The 'why' of these expanded psychic capacities correlate to the evolutionary needs of the Soul as follows:

The South Node in Aquarius 3rd correlates to a desire within the Soul's egocentric consciousness to gather and disseminate information from groups to order logically the linear mind and her existence. The ruler, Uranus Leo 10th, indicates that the Soul desired to broadcast this information to society in her own unique way, and in her own unique societal function, in order to align with Divine Will reflective of the Natural Laws of giving, sharing and inclusion.

In past lives, the Soul had projected "ultimate meaning" (Neptune, Pisces, 12th) into a continual incoming flow of "ideas" from the environment (3rd) that led to creating experiences of fundamental disillusionment and unresolved Soul wounding when these sources of information proved to be false or inaccurate. According to Jeffrey Wolf Green:

> As a preexisting pattern of inner relatedness, the Venus in Gemini person hears an inner call for self-knowledge. This manifests as a deep inner restlessness, fueled by a constant inner dialogue within themselves. This inner dialogue poses a variety of questions leading to experiences of all kinds. The essence of these questions is defined by the inner question "Who am I?" which leads also to "Who are you?"

These disillusioning experiences occurred because the Soul discerned that the information gathered was patriarchally distorted in terms of Natural Law, and sparked the desire to analyze information coming in and discriminate its logic, truth and purity. This generated compulsive criticism of self, others and groups, in her continuous search for new ideas.

The Soul flip-flopped to other lives (North Node Leo 9th) in which it undertook a search for knowledge through spiritual teachers/teachings, gurus, consciousness-raising techniques, or other cultures. Because of the past experiences of fundamental disillusionment, the Soul became quite suspicious; therefore, she seeks out teachers and teachings that are trustworthy and pure according to her capacity for discernment.

The North Node Leo 9th – "Resolution Node" for the skipped steps – correlates to consistently aligning with spiritual/metaphysical systems that reflect the truth of Natural Laws. The ruler, Sun Taurus 6th, specifies a Soul desire to heal the physical, mental, and emotional bodies of self and others in order to fulfill the evolutionary desire to be of service and effect self-improvement. The Soul seeks to heal its disconnection from Goddess by means of its intuitive nature (energy going out, yang, teaching others). The expansion of the Soul's philosophical database in consistent alignment with Natural Laws will serve to heal the Neptune skipped steps.

The experience of disillusionment will be instrumental in shattering the crystallized "delusive" ideas in order to re-orientate to actual reality (Saturn conjunct Moon's South Node and the South Node of Neptune). With Neptune retrograde, there is an accelerated desire to throw off all things of a delusive nature thus emphasizing the process of disillusionment created by the Soul and bursting the bubble of its illusions, delusions, dreams, fantasies, false meanings, and its projection of ultimate meaning onto anything that has confused the Soul in the past as to what the Ultimate Reality is truly about.

Intimate relationship   A specific way the Neptune skipped steps and emotional wound of the Soul played out was in the area of intimate relationships (Scorpio) where the Soul was learning about the use/abuse of power (Neptune ruled by Pluto). With Pluto Virgo 10th, Lila had to deal with a karmic relationship brought in from the past in order to "tie up loose ends, and finally forgive." In this relationship, she gave over her authority to a male partner with a God-complex whom she had projected ultimate meaning onto, put up on a pedestal, and treated like a de-facto God. The relationship quickly turned into sadomasochism, betrayal, abandonment, loss, and violation of trust bringing a sense of unworthiness, humiliation and unloveability as Lila suffered on an emotional level (crying that would not stop, suicidal thoughts, bi polar flare ups, hiding signature) when the exposure of the truth of the partner's true motivations were revealed (Neptune sextile Lucifer 10th and inconjunct Eris 5th). At times Lila felt like a sexual slave as this seemed to be the only way she could feel loved or find acceptance in this relationship.

Driven by a sense of powerlessness and distorted ideas led to massive disillusionment when her illusions about this man were completely shattered. She experienced horrible betrayal and abandonment when the man whom she had loved so deeply and to whom she had committed herself suddenly changed his personality, leaving her to strengthen her emotional self-reliance without him. Lila began to fall apart and re-traumatize under all the stress of several failed attempts to reunite with the ex-partner as she erroneously believed that his confirmation of love for her would make her feel okay. Alternatively, she was also learning that she could not "save" him either; she could not "save the world," but rather, she needed to "save herself first." The Natural Truth was that she did not need his validation, but rather, needed to find that self-love first. The need for escapism through excessive fantasies of rekindling love were met by powerful disillusionment, fear and loss of meaning generated by her own Soul.

> When a Soul feels victimized, this typically occurs because it cannot understand and/or accept the responsibility in its own actions, actions that, at some point, have created the necessity of being victimized by another(s). This can be particularity difficult when those actions have taken place in another life, or lives, because most Souls do not have the evolved capacity to remember their own prior lives. (Rad)

Core wounding Soul memories of imprisonment (asylums), seclusion, monk, nun, persecution, psychology of hiding; being treated as a possession by the partner, sexual slave, secret sexual activities, sex with a stranger (Vesta Gemini 8th conjunct Venus).

Healing Knowing when to give, and when not to give to others (for self-preservation and to not deplete her psychic energies). To discern the truth of the fantasies she had created. To expand and align her philosophy about intimate relationships with Natural Laws. She is learning what it means to be in a "natural" relationship based on sharing, caring, equality and balance. To love herself and heal herself despite not receiving the love from another. To discriminate "unconditional" love versus "conditional" love. She is consistently focusing on expressing and restoring Natural Laws (Resolution Node Leo 9th): that which is natural within her nature and in life, and especially "the restoration of faith – that somehow things will get better." Alignment with the truth of Goddess has resulted in working tirelessly to heal and nurture others (PPP Pisces 4th), specifically through cooking for large groups of people in spiritual retreats. She is drawing upon the wellspring of Goddess energy to heal the Soul.

(4) Pisces on the 5th house cusp

Background Unconscious memories of sexual abuse in past lives; frustration around lack of acknowledgment; creating unrealistic or super-human abilities that she cannot live up to; held 'captive' in the drama of the king/queen relationship in which she became the victim.

Core wounding Pride becoming easily wounded; bottomless pit need for love and attention; creating illusions and fantasies around the male and the phallic symbol; crisis generated around personal will and Higher Will.

Healing Energy and warmth centered in the heart; showering others with benevolent attention; fulfilling a social purpose based on Natural Laws; expressing natural capacity for generosity and love; finding creative ways to satisfy her own needs without having to rely upon others for validation; creative expression in alignment with a Higher Will; understanding that EVERYTHING REVOLVES AROUND SOURCE, and not around herself; and understanding that her creativity is actually a channel from Source.

(5) Libra on the 12th house cusp and the location of its planetary ruler Venus Gemini 8th

- Venus sextile Uranus
- Venus yod with Moon and Mars

> But humanity advances; we advance because we can dream of Venus rising out of the Neptunian ocean of new possibilities. With Neptune, all things are possible; but troubles come to the person who deceives himself in confusing 'possibility' and 'actuality,' the dream and the reality, tomorrow (or some day after tomorrow!) and today. We can be so fascinated by the vision of Venus rising out of the sea as to rush into the sea, blind to the fact that water is not earth — and we drown. (Dane Rudhyar)

Here we can see how Lila had created illusions, fantasies and dreams around her intimate relationships. Being ruthlessly disrespected through sexual abuse, and never quite hearing the words she wanted to hear ("I love you" – Venus Gemini 8th, Saturn Aquarius 3rd) impacted the emotional body. Towards the end of Lila's disastrous relationship, she felt that, "All hope is lost." Blindly and innocently putting her faith into another because she saw the good in that person led to betrayal and violation of trust. Because of her blind trust, she was an easy target to be "used" by another who had a hidden sexual agenda. At that time, she had been unable to draw upon the intrinsic dynamics of consciousness – hope and faith. With 12th house planets, Moon and Neptune, ruled by Pluto 10th, futility, self-defeat, utter hopelessness, fear, and loss of faith caused the Soul to lose meaning to the point that she did not want to continue her life. She truly felt 'LOST AT SEA.' She shut herself away (hiding signature) trying to escape from the circumstances of her life.

Core wounding At the early stages of the relationship there had been denial of the emotional truth since she needed her fantasies and dreams around this man to be fulfilled. The bubble finally burst when she uncovered sexual secrets that would bring an end to the relationship. This brought on deep grief, a sense of betrayal, abandonment, loss, and pain so deep that she entertained suicidal thoughts to escape the agony (Neptune-Moon Scorpio 12th; Neptune Scorpio skipped steps; Neptune Scorpio square its own Nodes).

If the wounds are of a psychological/emotional nature to a Soul, Soul wounds, then the healing that can take place must, and can only, occur when the Soul in question is able to identify and accept the responsibility in their own actions that has been the cause or determinant of these types of wounds themselves.

Healing Rapid Soul healing started to take place when Lila was able to identify and accept the responsibility of her own actions: creating illusions and dreams around a partner. This led to unconditional love of self and others, forgiveness of self and others, and forgiveness and tolerance of her own and the other's perceived imperfections. Understanding the karmic necessity to heal her wounded Soul, she made the necessary adjustments by way of discerning what is real and what is not, to see the true reality of that past relationship. Learning the lessons, she now needed to make better choices for herself for the future.

With Libra on the 12th house cusp and ruled by Venus Gemini 8th, going down deep into her emotions, no matter how intense or hysterical or how long it would take … would lead to the phoenix rising from the ashes: a metamorphosis of limitations!

(6) Planets within the 12th house – Neptune and Moon – and the signs they naturally rule

- Moon's yod to Venus-Mars
- Moon square Uranus
- Cancer on the 9th house cusp
- Pisces on the 5th house cusp

The Soul has a high degree of sensitivity, empathy and expanded psychic awareness correlating with the hormone melatonin, and easily absorbs human suffering. With the Moon Scorpio 12th, the "personal" core wounding is experienced in conjunction with the "collective" wounding of the human family or group. The collective unconscious wounding impacts upon the individual while the individual's wounding impacts upon the collective. This creates a nature of psychic intrusion/extrusion of Lila's energies and motivations from/to others.

With the Moon forming a yod with Mars Aries 5th and Venus Gemini 8th, the area of love affairs and intimate relationships has undergone severe but necessary crisis. The Moon Scorpio 12th – ego, self-image – that which integrates the past with the future (the Nodes) – ruled by Pluto Virgo 10th – had built an ideal or fantasy around the masculine, the father, the partner, or authority. The Soul is having to evolve the distorted and obsolete 'ideas' (South Node 3rd) into 'truth' (North Node 9th), this also being the Resolution Node to the Neptune skipped steps. The Soul has had to re-align with the Natural Laws that correlate with the masculine and feminine principles as created by the Creator. Lila shares how she is releasing, processing, and transforming the dark emotions that arise from the depths of the unconscious (Moon Scorpio 12th, and Neptune Scorpio 12th):

> Shadow work. Currently I am aligning with female deities who keep appearing to me. What came up for me at a retreat: the Goddess of Darkness, Mara. When the Buddha sat under the Bodhi tree the night he became awakened, he was tempted by Mara the goddess of death, the evil one, the tempter. She summoned up all the demons to distract the Buddha from his path.

> 24/7 every day and in my dreams for 18 months, I can't deny or avoid or pretend that Mara hasn't been there, and I've had to develop a relationship with Mara and understand the knowledge/ information that Mara has brought to my attention because I had suppressed the shadow for so long.

> The work that reconnects me, to cope with the world, begins with gratitude, to acknowledge our grief and suffering and pain for the world, see the world with new eyes, and then move forward.

VENUS
Lower Octave of Neptune

Wounds can also be seen through the lower octave of Neptune: Venus. In the same way, we would examine the entirety of the Venus paradigm in order to understand, in conjunction with the Neptune paradigm, all the potential sources and causes of the wounds to the Soul. These are symbolized by:

(A) South Node of Venus 22.20 deg Aries in the 5th house

(B) South Node of Venus' planetary ruler Mercury Gemini 7th

(C) Natal Venus Gemini 8th

(D) Libra on the 12th house cusp

(E) Planets in 2nd and 7th houses

Healing the Emotional Wound of the Soul through Humility

(A) South Node of Venus 22.20 deg Aries in the 5th house

- South Node of Venus inconjunct Moon
- South Node of Venus trine Uranus
- South Node of Venus sextile Venus-Mercury-Ceres-Vesta

The sextile-sextile-trine pattern in connection with the yod to the Moon implies a feeling of destiny, and a trusting of the intuition so that when one approaches the "Y" in the road, one would know which road on the fork to take. The yod or "Finger of God" is like a telephone line where one receives messages/visions/knowing from God that, contrasted to normal reality, leads to perpetual complaints or crisis-making where none need to exist. The Moon is the area where the vision is meant to be expressed, and that means through action, one step at a time.

The Moon, as we read at the beginning of this assignment, correlates in Lila's chart to the original emotional wound of the Soul (4th) where the "I" has separated from the "we." To realize the path to perfection, the yod is emphasizing the necessity for humility from an egocentric point of view. So, in essence, the Soul of Lila will be healed through developing humility (Pluto Virgo 10th), and shifting the center of gravity from left-brain to right-brain, from deductive logic to inductive logic, from empirical to intuitive.

This yod seems to be a KEY pattern in resolving the whole chart since the Resolution Node, North Node Leo 9th, is imperative to shifting the focus to the intuitive brain where decisions and choices are guided and prompted by the Higher Self.

Healing the Emotional Wound of the Soul through Regaining Balance and Equality

(B) South Node of Venus' planetary ruler Mercury Gemini 7th

- Mercury conjunct Venus-Ceres-Juno
- Mercury sextile Mars
- Mercury square Jupiter
- Mercury trine Saturn
- Mercury square Chiron

From the 7th house, Mercury reaches out to Mars-Jupiter-Chiron-Saturn – emphasizing the importance of bringing balance and equality to communication, and really "listening" to the other – in order to begin a new evolutionary cycle of creatively redefining the entire intellectual framework.

Evolution and Healing through the Emotions

(C) Natal Venus Gemini 8th

- Venus sextile Mars-Uranus
- Venus inconjunct Moon

In addition to the yod, Venus (relationship dynamics) in a water house means that evolution of the Soul is effected through the emotions. Healing the emotional body comes via the dynamics in relationships – projected ultimate meaning, disillusionment, identifying reality and truth.

(D) Libra on the 12th house cusp

Additionally, Libra on the 12th house cusp means that Venus relationship dynamics (to self and others) in a water house makes evolution possible through the emotions.

(E) Planets in 2nd and 7th houses

- No planets in the 2nd house
- Juno-Mercury-Ceres in the 7th house
- Mercury's aspects (see above)
- Signs of their natural rulers being Taurus intercepted sign within the 6th house, and Gemini on the 7th house cusp

Healing of the Soul through Emotional and Physical Self-Reliance

Contributing to healing the Soul's emotional wound is Taurus (self-reliance) intercepted sign within the 6th house. With the Sun Taurus 6th opposite the apex of the Yod (Moon), Lila's lessons of inner emotional security, and humility, are greatly emphasized as the main healing for the Soul's wounds. This includes physical self-care and purification of the body and mind, the techniques that will allow her to be of service to others, and the development of self-security.

CONCLUSION

Lila has had to let the emotions really flow – and sometimes it seemed she would never stop crying – so that evolution could be effected, the wounds of the Soul healed, humility developed, and her consciousness spiritualized. Looking at Lila these days is like witnessing a miracle! There is a palpable light emanating from her whole being. Although not completely out of the woods, she has found hope, trust and faith again!

EXAMPLE CHART D

Neptune and Wounding of the Soul

Nelson Mandela

18 July 1918 – 5 December 2013

3rd stage Individuated

by Kristin

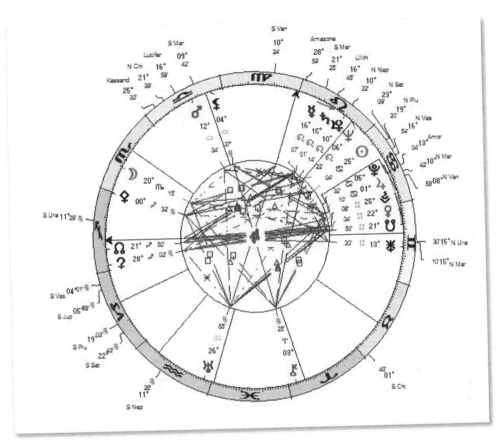

MANDELA

INEQUALITY and INJUSTICE

How far would you go to defend what was right? Would you put your life on the line? Would you be willing to die for it? Nelson Mandela in his mind had nothing to lose and everything to gain in risking everything for the sake of his country, in particular his native people who had suffered unjustly for lifetimes from the oppressive regime of the white supremacy:

- South Node in Gemini conjunct Venus in the 6th
  - ruler Mercury conjunct Saturn in Leo in the 9th
  - square Moon in Scorpio in the 12th

Mandela became actively involved in the anti-apartheid movement in his 20's and joined the African National Congress in 1942. For 20 years, he directed a campaign of peaceful, non-violent defiance against the South African government and its racist policies. Even though in his heart he knew that peace was the only way forward, 50 years of non-violence had gotten his people nowhere, only fewer rights and more repressive legislation. Mandela, who was formerly committed to nonviolent protest, began to believe that armed struggle was the only way to achieve change. He subsequently co-founded an armed offshoot of the ANC dedicated to sabotage and guerilla war tactics to end apartheid.

In 1961, Mandela orchestrated a three-day national workers' strike. He was arrested for leading the strike the following year, and was sentenced to five years in prison. In 1963, Mandela was brought to trial again. This time, he and 10 other ANC leaders were sentenced to life imprisonment for political offences, including sabotage. His Prisoner number was 46664, Lucifer conjuncts his Mars in Libra hence the 666, Mars forms a sesquisquare to Uranus in Aquarius in the 3rd, squaring his 12th house Scorpio Moon. It became a fight between man's law and God's law, known as 'natural law:' giving, sharing and inclusion, Venus on the South Node. Nelson Mandela was not going to go down easy, if at all:

- Saturn in Leo forms a new phase conjunction to Mercury in the 9th
  - ruler of his South Node conjunct Venus in Gemini in the 6th
  - squaring Moon in Scorpio in the 12th
  - the Moon being the ruler of his Jupiter which is forming a balsamic conjunction to Pluto in Cancer in the 7th
- Saturn/Mercury in Leo in the 9th trine North Node in Sagittarius in the 12th House

Themes of grave injustice and inequality specifically linked with white supremacy and the wounds caused therein are seen with Nelson Mandela's:

- South Node in Gemini in the 6th forming a tight conjunction to Venus
- Venus, ruler of his Mars in Libra conjuncts Lucifer in his 11th House, trauma, and forms a sesquisquare to Uranus in Aquarius, restating the collective trauma to his people
- Uranus also squares his Moon in Scorpio in the 12th, ruler Pluto, balsamic conjunction to Jupiter in the 7th

- Neptune is in Leo in the 8th, ruler Sun also in the 8th but in Cancer and the Sun inconjuncts his Uranus Rx in Aquarius

- Natal Neptune conjuncts his North Node of Neptune, and opposes his South Node of Neptune Rx which squares his Scorpio Moon in the 12th

- The Moon is the ruler of his Sun in the 8th, Pluto and Jupiter in Cancer in the 7th house

All of these signatures repeat a theme, that in combination reflect the depth of his wounds. He was a representative, a spokesperson and sacrificial symbol for the masses, for 'it takes one to know one,' who was beaten, burned, kicked down ridiculed and devalued simply because of the color of his skin:

- Saturn (skin) is in a new phase conjunction to Mercury in Leo in the 9th

- Mercury is the ruler of his South Node and Venus in Gemini in the 6th

- Saturn and Mercury also square his Moon in Scorpio in the 12th

- Moon being the ruler of his Sun in Cancer, the (black) African race, in the 8th House

Trauma/Emotional Wound Signatures

- South Node of Neptune in Aquarius opposing Saturn/Mercury, ruler of his South Node and Venus in Gemini

- South Node of Neptune in Aquarius, ruler Uranus in Aquarius square Moon in Scorpio in the 12th

- South Node of Neptune in Aquarius, ruler Uranus inconjunct Sun in Cancer in the 8th

- South Node of Neptune sesquisquare Mars in Libra in the 11th

- Neptune in Leo in the 8th conjunct North Node of Neptune square Moon in Scorpio in 12th

- Neptune in Leo in the 8th square Psyche in Scorpio

- Neptune in Leo in the 8th sesquisquare North Node in Sagittarius in the 12th and the Ascendant

- Venus conjunct the South Node in the 6th in Gemini, ruler Mercury new phase to Saturn in the 8th, square Scorpio Moon in the 12th

- Pluto in the 7th balsamic to Jupiter in a naturally Venus ruled house

- Pluto ruler of the Moon in Scorpio in the 12th and Jupiter ruler of the North Node in the 12th

- Pisces on the 4th house = homeland, ruler Neptune in Leo 8th sesquisquare North Node in Sagittarius

- Chiron Rx in Aries in the 4th square his Pluto and Jupiter conjunction in Cancer in the 7th

Nelson Mandela

After consecutive lifetimes being born into tribes who were the outcasts and the underdog, Mandela could not sit on his hands and watch on the sidelines. Not that he had not already lost his life time and time again for stepping into the ring, and in this life and years of imprisonment only fueled that fire of desire for justice even more. The wounds of trauma linked with mere survival in dire circumstances is extensive with his:

- South Node of Neptune Rx in Aquarius in the 2nd House

- The ruler Uranus is also in Aquarius, trauma restated, and is forming a sesquisquare to Mars in Libra in the 11th, an Aquarius house, reflecting devastation, dominance and cruelty of countless lives for many lifetimes of his tribe, his people/culture and race

- Mercury, ruler of his South Node/Venus in Gemini is conjunct Saturn in Leo in the 9th and his squaring his Scorpio Moon in the 12th

- Ruler of Saturn and Mercury in Leo is the Sun in Cancer in the 8th, rendered powerless by the system

These same signatures also reflects lifetimes in oppressive environments living as slaves. More powerful than the fear of death for Mandela was his desire for justice:

- South Node in Gemini conjunct Venus
  - ruler Mercury conjunct Saturn in Leo in the 9th
  - sextile Mars in Libra in the 11th
  - also square Moon in Scorpio in the 12th

An attempt to strip him of his power in his most recent life thereby putting more salt in the wound is restated again with his:

- Natal Neptune in Leo in the 8th conjunct his North Node of Neptune
  - ruler the Sun in Cancer forms an inconjunct to his North Node in Sagittarius in the 12th
  - ruler Jupiter forming a balsamic conjunction to Pluto in the 7th

This occurred because the powers that be knew he was not only an educated man but also a force to be reckoned with, so they used their rules and their court to lock him away. Nelson Mandela was incarcerated on Robben Island for 18 of his 27 years in prison. During this time, he contracted tuberculosis and, as a black political prisoner, received the lowest level of treatment from prison workers, mirroring prior lifetimes as a slave hand. However, while incarcerated, Mandela was able to earn a Bachelor of Law degree through a University of London correspondence program for he knew education is one's greatest weapon, North Node in Sagittarius in the 12th trine Saturn/Mercury in Leo in the 9th. In 1982, Mandela and other ANC leaders were moved to Pollsmoor Prison, allegedly to enable contact between them and the South African government. In 1985, President P.W. Botha offered Mandela's release in exchange for renouncing armed struggle; he rejected the offer because decades of non-violence had gotten his people nowhere.

For five more years, he sacrificed his own freedom and time with his loved ones in his fight for a balanced and fair system: Moon in Scorpio in the 12th square Saturn/Mercury ruler of his South Node and Venus in Gemini.

With increasing local and international pressure for his release, the government participated in several talks with Mandela over the ensuing years, but no deal was made. It wasn't until Botha suffered a stroke and was replaced by Frederik Willem de Klerk that Mandela's release was finally announced – on February 11, 1990. De Klerk also unbanned the ANC, removed restrictions on political groups and suspended executions.

Freedom Day ~ February 11, 1990

- Transiting Mars was forming a new phase conjunction to Uranus in Capricorn in Mandela's 1st House and was squaring his Mars in Libra in the 11th, freeing him from the system

- Transiting Jupiter was retrograde and making an exact return to his natal Jupiter, ruler of his North Node in the 12th, which is balsamic to Pluto in Cancer in the 7th

- The ruler, the Moon, is in Scorpio in the 12th, release from prison

Upon his release from prison, Nelson Mandela immediately urged foreign powers not to reduce their pressure on the South African government for constitutional reform. While he stated that he was committed to working toward peace, he declared that the ANC's armed struggle would continue until the black majority received the right to vote. In 1993, Mandela and South African President F.W. de Klerk were jointly awarded the Nobel Peace Prize for their efforts to dismantle the country's apartheid system ~ justice finally served and his people rewarded.

With Saturn new phase conjunction to Mercury in Leo in the 9th trine North Node in Sagittarius in the 12th, Mandela declared:

> I have walked a long walk to freedom. It has been a lonely road but it's not over yet. No one is born to hate another based on the color of their skin. People learn to hate, they can be taught to love, for love comes more naturally to the human heart.

He was willing to die for his people and spent 27 years behind bars sacrificing his life for the cause, North Node in the 12th in Sagittarius, ruler Jupiter balsamic to Pluto in the 7th. Mandela also said,

> We must surprise them with compassion, strength and generosity, all the things they denied us . . . During my lifetime I have dedicated myself to this struggle of the African people. I have fought against white domination, and I have fought against black domination. I have cherished the ideal of a democratic and free society in which all persons live together in harmony and with equal opportunities. It is an ideal which I hope to live for and to achieve. But if needs be, it is an ideal for which I am prepared to die.

- North Node in the 12th, ideal, in Sagittarius
  - ruler Jupiter balsamic to Pluto in the 7th in Cancer
  - ruler Moon in Scorpio in the 12th
- Also, Venus on the South Node in the 6th in Gemini
  - ruler Mercury conjunct Saturn in the 9th trine North Node in Sagittarius

Still so humble in his pursuit for freedom and justice for all, he says, "I was not a messiah, but an ordinary man, who became a leader because of extraordinary circumstances":

- South Node in Gemini in the 6th conjunct Venus
- Venus, ruler of his Mars in Libra in the 11th
- Also, North Node in Sagittarius in the 12th, messiah with an international impact.

He was called to a cause, larger than himself, considering himself to be merely a messenger:

- South Node conjunct Venus in Gemini in the 6th
    - ruler Mercury in Leo in the 9th
    - new phase conjunction to Saturn which trines his North Node in Sagittarius in the 12th House

From Prison to President

Nelson Mandela was elected South Africa's first black president in 1994 by a landslide.

As he entered his presidency he still preached this truth, "There is only one way forward and that is PEACE":

- North Node in Sagittarius in the 12th
    - ruler Jupiter making a balsamic conjunction to Pluto in Cancer in the 7th
- Venus in Gemini conjunct the South Node
-

South Africa is known as the Rainbow Nation because there exists an extraordinary diversity of races, tribes, creeds, languages and landscapes that characterize this country. There are 11 languages: English, Afrikaans and 9 ethnic tongues, Zulu and Xhosa are most common. The flag of the Republic of South Africa was adopted on April 27, 1994, at the beginning of the 1994 general election, to replace the flag that had been used since 1928. The new national flag was chosen to represent the new democracy. UNITY WITHIN THE DIVERSITY:

- Venus in Gemini conjunct the South Node in GEMINI
    - ruler Mercury new phase to Saturn in the 9th trine the North Node in Sagittarius

All paths lead to ONE.

"In order to become a nation, WE MUST ALL EXCEED OUR OWN EXPECTATIONS":

- Venus on the South Node in Gemini in the 6th
  - ruler Mars in Libra in the 11th
  - sextile Neptune in Leo, which is also conjunct the North Node of Neptune, in the 8th house of the Soul

Even when landing in a position of great power, he would not receive what he felt to be unnecessary payment for his work, especially as so many were going hungry. As president, he felt his salary was too high so he donated 1/3 of his income to charity, giving to those in need, Venus on the South Node in the 6th.

Sports Played a Role in Bringing the Nation Together

He encouraged black South Africans to get behind the previously hated national rugby team, the Springboks, as South Africa hosted the 1995 Rugby World Cup. After the Springboks won an epic final over New Zealand, Mandela presented the trophy to Captain Francois Pienaar, an Afrikaner, wearing a Springbok shirt with Pienaar's own number 6 on the back. This was widely seen as a major step in the reconciliation of white and black South Africans; as de Klerk later put it,

> Mandela won the hearts of millions of white rugby fans. Mandela's efforts at reconciliation assuaged the fears of whites, but also drew criticism from more militant blacks.

His estranged wife, Winnie, accused the ANC of being more interested in appeasing whites than in helping blacks. She could not find a way to his same page, a way of peace into the future, which also culminated this relationship, Venus conjuncts the South Node, as she harbored too much anger and resentment. But, as quoted by Mandela in the movie *Invictus*, "Forgiveness liberates the Soul, it removes fear. That's why it's such a powerful weapon." He said to all of his people, "If I can forgive after 27 years in prison, so can you?"

- North Node in Sagittarius in the 12th
- Neptune in Leo in the 8th conjunct North Node of Neptune
  - ruler Sun in the 8th trine Moon in Scorpio in the 12th House

Nelson found a way to bring his people together through sports, North Node in the 12th in Sagittarius, ruler Jupiter balsamic to Pluto in Cancer in the 7th. He helped to heal the WOUND of the nation, as they filled a stadium to cheer on their country; he brought them together as a nation, not just the 67,000 people in the stands but the 42 million others who watched. He showed them it was possible to be a GROUP of ONE, Venus on the South Node in Gemini, ruler Mars in Libra in the 11th. Symbolically they were all on the same playing field once again.

FRUITION Life ~ *Justice Realized!*

Venus forming an exact conjunction to the South Node in Gemini in the 6th reflects a life of fruition for the imbalance and injustice suffered for eons at the hands of the dominant race. This reflects the extremity and the duality and ultimately the fruition of this long-standing theme. His efforts paid off, Mars in Libra in the 11th is the ruler of his Venus on the South Node and sextile his Neptune in Leo in the 8th, a healing for himself and, according to him, more importantly for his people, could finally take place, for he was a father not only to his family but a father to many, a father to his nation. "I have a very large family, 42 million." Other symbols for FRUITION, a culmination of this wounding theme of injustice, is North Node in Sagittarius in the 12th forming a closing conjunction to his Ascendant in Sagittarius, ruler Jupiter balsamic conjunction to Pluto in the 7th in Cancer.

> THERE ARE COUNTLESS PEOPLE WHO WENT TO JAIL AND WHO AREN'T BITTER, BECAUSE THEY COULD SEE THAT THEIR SACRIFICES WERE NOT IN VAIN, AND THE IDEAS FOR WHICH WE LIVED AND SACRIFICED ARE ABOUT TO COME TO **FRUITION**. AND THAT REMOVES THE BITTERNESS FROM THEIR HEARTS. (Nelson Mandela)

This life of fruition would also include a culmination in certain key relationships that have repeated through time where infidelity on both sides occurred. He was guilty of his own infidelity and duplicity early on, Venus in Gemini on the South Node, and discovered his wife who stayed with him throughout his years in prison had been leading a double life even after his release. This was also a deep wound in him with his Scorpio Moon in the 12th, not only the betrayal of his wife but he was also such a well-known family man he felt 'abandoned' by his own family in ways, stating that they were going on with their own lives. The truth is, after years in captivity, what he needed most would have been never to have the ones he loved out of his sight, but they had all understandably gotten on with their lives and although there were visits, it would have never felt to be enough.

He survived both of his sons, something no parent should have to experience, his first son died in a car accident when he was in prison on Robben Island and his second son died of Aids in 2005. But perhaps even a greater heartbreak, a few years before his own death, the love of his life beloved great granddaughter 13 year old Zenani was taken when she was killed in a car crash from a drunk driver following a pre-tournament World Cup ceremony in which Mandela had energized an international buzz to bring his nation together. Inconsolably heartbroken, Mandela understandably pulled out of the World Cup Opening Ceremony. "It meant that a day the frail Mandela had long anticipated – his "rainbow nation" performing a new miracle under the world's gaze – became instead one of private grief and mourning":

- Moon in Scorpio in the 12th square Saturn and Mercury in Leo in the 9th
- Mercury the ruler of his South Node and Venus in Gemini in the 6th

No matter how hard he tried, he was faced with heartbreak until the bitter end.

Invictus
(Unconquered)

Out of the night that covers me,
Black as the Pit from pole to pole,
I thank whatever gods may be
For my unconquerable Soul.

In the fell clutch of circumstance
I have not winced nor cried aloud.
Under the bludgeonings of chance
My head is bloody, but unbowed.

Beyond this place of wrath and tears
Looms but the Horror of the shade,
And yet the menace of the years
Finds, and shall find, me unafraid.

It matters not how strait the gate,
How charged with punishments the scroll,
I am the master of my fate:
I am the captain of my Soul.

- Natal Neptune in Leo in the 8th conjunct North Node of Neptune in the 8th
  - ruler Sun in Cancer in the 8th which trines his 12th House Scorpio Moon

. . . can also reflect the healing of his people where he was able to empower his race and create a democracy that was more fairly balanced. With Saturn and Mercury the ruler of his South Node/Venus in Gemini trining the North Node in Sagittarius, his role served to influence the democracy of the world, a standard, within relative reason, that would prove to stand the test of time. These symbols also reflect a long hard-fought life where he needed to know that his efforts were not in vain, that true unity within the diversity would live on and on for his nation. Not only were wounds from lifetimes healed, the wound of the nation has also had a chance to heal. He lived well into his 90's, most importantly to share more moments with his family in attempt to make up for the 'lost time' in all those years being apart from the ones he loved:

- Moon in Scorpio square Saturn and Mercury
  - ruler of his South Node and Venus in Gemini in the 6th

He undoubtedly milked those years for all they were worth. May he rest in heaven and bathe in the timeless comfort found in the reunions with his loving family who have gone before him.

MAY HE, Finally, REST IN PEACE!

CHAPTER TWELVE

NEPTUNE AND VENUS ESSENTIAL NEEDS

A key to understanding essential relationship needs is to understand the inherent archetype in the horoscope between the 2nd, 7th, and 12th Houses. If you examine the inherent symmetry between these houses, you will notice that the 2nd and 12th Houses form inconjunctions to the 7th House, and the 2nd and 12th Houses are in a sextile relationship to each other. Thus, there is an inherent Finger of God (Yod) aspect pattern pointing to the 7th House. What does it mean that these houses are tied together in this way, and why should we utilize this archetype to understand the inner and outer relationship dynamics, including sexual dynamics, at all?

The answer is that the planet Venus naturally rules the signs Taurus and Libra, and that Neptune, the planetary co-ruler of Pisces, is the higher octave of Venus. Thus, since the natural zodiac has Taurus on the 2nd House, Libra on the 7th House, and Pisces on the 12th House, there exists this natural archetype that correlates to our relationship dynamics, including our sexual dynamics. So, the first step is to understand the nature of this archetype.

To understand this archetype is to understand the inherent nature of each of its components first.

The 2nd House, Taurus, and Venus

The first component we will examine is the 2nd House and Taurus. The core archetype that Taurus or the 2nd House correlate with is one of *survival* – one of the deepest instincts in all human beings. Within the human being, anatomically speaking, this instinct manifests from what is known as the primary brain, which regulates all the instinctual functions of the human being. The instinct to survive has many applications and manifestations. One of these manifestations is the instinct within the human species to perpetuate itself. Thus, Taurus and the 2nd House correlate with the sexual instinct to procreate the species within all of us. And, yes, the sexual instinct emanates from the primary brain.

The actual reason for the human species to procreate through the act of sexual intercourse, as opposed to asexual reproduction wherein a cell simply clones itself, is a biological act of survival. Because the main danger to the integrity of the human organism occurs through viruses, bacteria, and parasites, which mutate and evolve very quickly, it was and is essential that the human organism be able to evolve its own immune system in order to survive these types of assaults. In the case of asexual reproduction, the immune system remains static and fixed. To procreate the species through sexual intercourse is necessary because it allows for an ongoing evolution of the immune system through combining the genetic structures of two people into a third person. This constant evolution of the immune system thus allows for the survival of the human organism.

The immune system in astrology correlates with Neptune, Pisces, and the 12th House. The survival need of the species as a whole is reflected in each individual, and each individual determines the selection of a partner based on attraction. This natural selection is largely determined through a subconscious reaction to the secretion of pheromones, which emit a scent. This reaction will be either positive or negative, and thus serves as a basis of who has intercourse with who. Through this biological cue, we select partners who will produce offspring with an evolved immune system that is better able to defeat disease and infection. This, in turn, helps to guarantee the survival of the species. Pheromones are astrologically associated with Taurus, the 2nd House, and the inner side of Venus.

Another manifestation of the survival instinct is one of identifying what is *needed* in order to survive. This can have many applications, including identifying what resources we already have or possess in order to survive. This duality of what we already possess, combined with identifying what we need (i.e., what we do not already have) for survival to continue or be sustained thus generates the following paradoxical crisis for the human being.

On the one hand, identifying what we already have in order to survive correlates with the archetype inherent to Taurus or the 2nd House – the archetype of self-reliance, self-sustainment, and self-sufficiency. This archetype is one of inner awareness and focusing. On the other hand, identifying what is needed (that which we do not already have) for survival to continue correlates with the archetypal awareness within consciousness that looks outside of itself in order to gather or attract that which is needed. Long ago, the human being learned that it was much easier to survive individually by forming relationships to other human beings who could live together as an organized unit. Thus, the human being, in many ways, became dependent on other human beings for survival to occur. This is not to say that the human being cannot survive completely alone. Of course, this can be done. But how many people do you know of that live in absolute isolation, surviving only through their own capacity?

The paradoxical crisis of survival is rooted in that which is already possessed within the individual, and that which is perceived to be needed that is outside of the individual. Astrologically, this paradoxical crisis is reflected in the natural inconjunct between the 2nd and 7th Houses. It is also reflected in the inner nature of Venus (Taurus) and its outer or projected nature (Libra). Thus, psychologically speaking, it becomes the paradoxical crisis between the need for self-reliance, and our dependence on others (relationships) in order to survive – the procreational instinct combined with the awareness of what we do not currently have, and yet what is needed in order to survive.

Another manifestation of the instinct to survive is one of values. Why? Because whatever it is that correlates with what is needed in order to survive, or that which correlates with the resources that already exist in order for survival to occur, will be *highly valued*. And that which is valued will correlate with how much *meaning* we give to it. Thus, the 2nd House and Taurus correlate to the meaning that we give to life, in the broadest sense. In an immediate sense, the archetypes of Taurus and the 2nd House correlate with the meaning we give to *ourselves* and, through extension, the meaning we give to other people. This, of course, is dependent on how much we value both ourselves and others.

Astrologically speaking, the sign on the 2nd House cusp, the location of its planetary ruler by house and sign, plus the aspects that planet makes to other planets, will condition how the archetype of the 2nd House is oriented to and actualized by any individual. In addition, the location of the sign Taurus in the horoscope and its natural ruler Venus by its own house/sign, plus the aspects that it is making to other planets, will condition the archetypes inherent to those houses with the archetypes intrinsic to Taurus. In composite charts, these same principles apply to how the couple orients to actualizing these archetypes.

The 7th House, Libra, and Venus

The next component of this archetype is the 7th House and Libra. The core archetype of the 7th House and Libra is of the *initiation of relationships* with other human beings. The initiation of relationships has as its casual factor the projected need for survival that emanates from the 2nd House and Taurus. The projection of these needs from the 2nd House and Taurus to the 7th House and Libra occurs through the inconjunction that links these archetypes. Through the 7th House and Libra we initiate relationships with a diversity of people in order to discriminate (inconjunct) between those people who reflect what we need, versus those people who do not. Once the individual determines which people can best meet what it needs, needs that are now projected, the basis of expectations simultaneously occurs. That which we expect from other people, and they from us, in order for the projected needs of each to be met, is the causal factor for conditional giving, sharing, or love.

The inconjunction also teaches the human being that it must also learn to give to others in order to secure or receive what itself needs. In order to give others what they need, the human being must learn how to *listen*. Venus (the co-ruler of Libra and Taurus) correlates with the psychology of hearing, whereas Mercury rules the anatomy that exists within the ear. By learning how to listen, the human being learns how to objectify itself – to experience itself and others objectively. In this way, the human being is learning *equality*. The 7th House and Libra teach the human being to equally give and receive. When the balance of giving and receiving within relationships is disproportionate, a crisis (inconjunct) within the relationships will occur. The crisis created in this way is necessary in order for the relationships that we form to become adjusted. In this way, we achieve a state of balance, and the roles become equal.

The inconjunction between these archetypes will also create a crisis when the individual either becomes too dependent on others, or when others become too dependent on the individual. When excessive dependence occurs in this way, crisis occurs within the relationship in order for an adjustment to happen. The effect is to enforce actualization of the 2nd House and Taurus archetype of self-reliance.

The inconjunction that links the 2nd House and Taurus to the 7th House and Libra has another primary function – to define a person's individual identity. This occurs as a person compares or evaluates him or herself through interrelating with other people. In essence, it is through social interaction that people become aware of who they are as individuals. Through comparison and evaluation, people become aware of that which is unique and individual about themselves. In the same way, they also become aware of that which is unique and individual about other people. In this way, they become aware of their roles within the relationships that they form, and the function of the relationship.

The function of the relationship describes the reason for the relationship – the *purpose* of the relationship. The function, reason, and purpose of the relationship restates the expectations that we have for it, the roles that are created for those expectations to be met, and the relative dependence that is generated in order for the needs and expectations to be met.

In the individual chart, the sign on the 7th House cusp, the location of its planetary ruler by house and sign, along with the aspects that planet makes to other planets, will condition how the individual actualizes the 7th House archetype. In addition, the location of the sign of Libra in the chart, the house and sign locality of its ruler Venus, and Venus' aspects to other planets will condition the inherent archetypes of those houses relative to the archetypes of Libra and Venus.

In composite charts, the nature of the signs and houses that these archetypes are conditioned by, along with the sign and house locality of Venus and the aspects that it is making to other planets, will describe how the couple understands and actualizes the reason, function, and purpose for their relationship. The archetypes symbolized by the composite chart will reflect how each of the individual's needs (symbolized in their natal horoscopes) *combine* in a relationship. By combining the individual needs in a relationship, the needs of the relationship itself are symbolized by the sign on the composite 7th House cusp, the location of its planetary ruler, and the aspects that it is making to other planets. These symbols will correlate with the relationship's capacity to fulfill each individual's needs. In addition, these archetypes will show how the couple defines their roles within the relationship in order for their mutually projected needs to be met, along with the relative balance or imbalance in these roles. The inherent inconjunction between the 7th House sign and the 2nd House sign, and the locality of the planetary rulers for those signs by their own house and sign placement, will correlate with what types of crises could occur, and what the causes may be. This inconjunction also correlates to the creation of a crisis within the relationship when the relationship cannot meet the individual needs of one or both partners.

The 12th House, Pisces, and Neptune

The last component of the inherent archetype being discussed is the 12th House, Pisces, and Neptune. The core archetype here is one of *transcendence*. Transcendence of what? No less than the confines of time and space or place. This archetype reflects the desire in all human beings to search for or embrace an ultimate purpose or meaning for life itself. Anatomically, this desire or impulse emanates from the pineal gland within the brain. Astrologically, this gland correlates with Neptune. This gland secretes a hormone called melatonin. This hormone is responsible for many things including sleep, dreams, imagination, creativity, revelations from on high, insanity, and, from an evolutionary point of view, the spiritualization of consciousness. Psychologically, this archetype reflects the intention or motivation inherent within consciousness to search for the higher or ultimate meaning for the totality of what we call life. This is especially true when the human being experiences cataclysmic evolutionary or karmic events.

Because this archetype correlates with transcendence or the search for ultimate meaning or purpose, the linkage to the 7th House or Libra via the inconjunction correlates to the person's conscious or unconscious ideals that are projected into its relationship needs. This projection becomes the basis of idealistic expectations that we have in the relationships that we form – the desire for the "perfect" relationship. In addition, unless or until an individual truly acts upon the transcendent impulse for him or herself, this archetype explains why so many people unconsciously or consciously make their partners *de-facto* gods and goddesses. In essence, they project the ultimate meaning that the 12th House, Pisces, or Neptune correlates to upon the partner. When projected through the 7th House, Libra, or the projected nature of Venus (not the inner nature of Venus) in these ways, a crisis will result at some point. The nature of such a crisis is one of *disillusionment*. One realizes that the partner is not perfect, the partner is not a god or goddess, the projected ideals manifesting as unrealistic expectations not being realized, the partner is not who they seemed to be at the beginning of the relationship, and so on.

The crisis of disillusionment is necessary in order for the human being to readjust the focus within its consciousness. Instead of projecting the 12th House, Pisces, or Neptune's search for transcendence or ultimate meaning upon the partner, each of us, at some point, will focus and act upon this desire and need from within ourselves. The inherent sextile from the 12th House and Pisces to the 2nd House and Taurus correlates with the intention, evolutionarily speaking, within the Soul to relate to itself in a transcendent way, and to establish a relationship with the Ultimate Source Of All Things from within itself. Thus, that which is valued, and the meaning we give to that which is valued through the 2nd House or Taurus, changes. It changes from the temporal (time and space equaling the immediacy of what we need in order to survive) to that which is transcendent or ultimate. When this occurs, each of us will relate differently not only to ourselves, but also to other people.

Instead of trying to make our partners into gods and goddesses, we will realize that each human being has innate divinity within him or herself because all of us have been created by the Ultimate Source Of All Things. Instead of projecting our ultimate ideals upon a partner, we will actualize those ideals for ourselves. Instead of seeking our ultimate sense of meaning in our partners, we will discover this meaning from within ourselves by embracing a spiritual teaching or path. When the crisis of disillusionment manifests one too many times, the necessary adjustment that will lead to this shift of focus within our consciousness will create a vibrational shift in our emotional, mental and physical bodies.

The effect of this, in essence, will be that instead of projecting the search and desire for ultimate meaning outwards, the projection is now inward – toward self-reliance. The inner nature of Venus now actualizes its higher octave, Neptune, to create a vibrational shift from within the human being that will allow it to attract (Venus) other people who have achieved this shift for themselves. The shift is also reflected in the natural linkage between the 2nd and 12th Houses because of the natural planetary rulers of each being Venus and Neptune.

It must also be remembered that the 12th House, Pisces, and Neptune all correlate with the potential for sadomasochistic psychological behavior in relationships. The root of this, again, is reflected in the Garden of Eden myth, or any religious teaching that pretends that man is superior to woman, or that woman is the cause of man's spiritual downfall through the "temptation" of the flesh. In an individual's chart, the sign on the 12th House, the location of its planetary ruler by house and sign, and the aspects it makes to other planets will correlate with the ultimate ideals that he or she projects onto other people through the 7th House. The types of experiences that will lead to a necessary disillusionment in order to readjust the individual's focus will also be described in these symbols. Pisces and its ruling planet Neptune will condition the inherent archetypes of the houses and signs that they occupy. In composite charts, these same symbols will correlate with what ideals the relationship has for itself, what constitutes the sense of ultimate meaning for the relationship, how this is actualized, and what kinds of unconscious projections may occur in order to readjust the focus of the relationship.

CHAPTER THIRTEEN

NEPTUNE AND ITS LOWER OCTAVE VENUS

Introduction

At this point I would like to discuss the planet Venus in light of the astrological methods that correlate to the relationship we have with ourselves, the essential needs that we have and project onto others, and how and why we attract the types of relationships that we do.

As stated before, Venus has two natures – an inner nature, and an outer or projected nature. The inner nature of Venus correlates to how we are inwardly relating to ourselves, and how we go about uniting inwardly discordant aspects of our overall nature or personality. Within this archetype, Venus correlates to the psychology of *listening* – how we listen to ourselves, and, thus, how we listen to other people. Listening infers how and what we hear within ourselves, and how and what we hear from other people. Listening and hearing thus correlate to how we are inwardly relating to ourselves, and how we relate outwardly to other people. How we relate to (and thus feel about) ourselves generates an inner vibration or magnetism, which attracts others who reflect or symbolize our self-relationship. For example, if a person has Venus in Virgo and is inwardly relating to oneself in very self-critical ways, feels very inadequate, and is all too aware of their shortcomings, is it illogical to conclude that this person will attract others who are very critical towards this person? If this person is inwardly listening to oneself and hearing an ongoing inner dialogue that is self-critical, then is it illogical to conclude that he or she will listen to others and hear critical comments from them?

All of us are forever "out picturing," or projecting, our own inner reality in this way without realizing this one thing—that those whom we attract into our lives are symbols of our inner reality. We project outwards that which is a reflection of our inner reality. Would the Venus in Virgo person actually be able to accept the fact that by attracting those who were very critical of him or her that this was a projection or "out picturing" of how they were relating to themselves inwardly? That they needed this mirroring effect in order to learn about their inner reality? Typically, the answer would be no. The nature of the times and societies that we are living in promote the idea of collective "victimization." It is very easy to be a victim, and much harder to own or accept responsibility for our own action—to understand that the overall realities we create emanate from within ourselves according to our evolutionary and karmic requirements.

We must also remember, in terms of the time/space reality that we live within, that everything that we learn and understand occurs through polarity—night/day, yin/yang, Virgo/Pisces, etc. This is called learning through counterpoint awareness. So the Venus in Virgo person would be aware in some way of the polarity of Virgo (Pisces). He or she would inwardly "hear" the call and promise of Pisces. By hearing this call, the Venus in Virgo person must then actually listen to it in such a way as to apply what they are hearing. The polarity point correlates to the evolution of a pre-existing pattern (Venus in Virgo) to a new pattern (Venus embracing Pisces) which then allows for an evolution of the original imprint of Venus in Virgo. Again, this counterpoint learning reflects the law of the Trinity—from the original imprint to its polarity, which allows an evolution of the original imprint.

In the case of the Venus in Virgo person, this would mean that he or she would have to embrace the polarity of Pisces before they could attract others who were not so critical of them. In other words, they would have to change how they were inwardly relating to themselves before any external change could be expected. Until then, the Venus in Virgo person would typically complain about why they keep attracting very critical people into their lives, at the same time wistfully wondering why they would not be with someone who would just love them for who they were. In this case, the solution would simply be a matter of the person embracing the Piscean message, "I am trying my best; I resolve to be a little bit better each day; nothing on Earth is perfect; God is not perfect, but an evolving force just as I am." By applying what they are inwardly hearing, by listening to it, he or she would evolve into and embrace a compassion for themselves and others, which then allows for an entirely different attraction pattern to emerge. They would attract people who are loving and encouraging, who support this person's efforts to become a better person.

In understanding the role of Venus in the birth chart, it is very important to remember the four natural evolutionary conditions discussed earlier in the book. The four natural evolutionary conditions correlate to the natural conditioning at an archetypal level in consciousness. Venus in Virgo, as in other sign, manifests differently relative to the evolutionary condition of any given individual. In addition, by understanding the main karmic/evolutionary dynamic in the birth chart as symbolized by Pluto, its polarity point, and the South and North Nodes with their respective planetary rulers, you can then understand exactly how any planet will manifest in any birth chart. The point here is that no sign has just one meaning or orientation, but is an archetype that has a spectrum within it. Thus, by understanding the main karmic/evolutionary axis within the birth chart you will be able to understand what point within the total spectrum of any sign a planet is orientated to. It is also important to understand that the Venus function will be conditioned by other factors symbolized in the aspects to other planets. These aspects correlate, again, to a preexisting pattern at birth. Embracing the polarity point of the natal sign that Venus is in will automatically evolve or change these pre-existing patterns. In other words, the polarity point of Venus is the causal factor in changing the patterns shown in the planetary aspects.

A Note on Venus Retrograde

From a terrestrial view, the planet Venus goes into apparent retrograde motion every 542 days or so. Thus, it is retrograde the least amount of time of any planet in our solar system. Venus retrograde in a natal chart has very specific archetypal correlations that condition how we inwardly and outwardly relate to ourselves and other people. Consistent with the archetype of retrogradation in general, Venus retrograde correlates with a necessary rebellion or individuation of its function relative to our orientation to relationships. Thus, the Venus retrograde person will inherently rebel against the cultural conditioning of how we are expected to define ourselves in general, the meaning of life specifically, and how we are expected to be in our relationships: gender-specific roles, how children are meant to be raised, the purpose of relationship, and so on.

When Venus is retrograde at birth the individual consequently *internalizes* the Venus function. This means that such an individual is orientated to establishing an inner relationship with themselves as a primary focus in life. Consequently, there is a perpetual inner questioning of who they are, and what they need in order to actualize a life consistent with their individuality. By internalizing the Venus function, the individual is essentially defined through the Taurus side of Venus, versus the Libra side of Venus. There is a primary focus on self-sustainment, self-reliance, self-empowerment, and a desire and need to actualize individual values that correlate to the individual's sense of the meaning and purpose of his or her life. As a result, such people inwardly hear and respond to a very "different drummer." They create a very different inner vibration or magnetism that serves to attract others who are similarly vibrating or resonating, individuals who rebel against the "normal" way of living life according to the consensus of society in general, and the "normal" forms of relationship specifically.

Because of this deep internalization of the Venus function, the Venus retrograde person relates to others in a very different way. He or she is a deeply self-introspective individual that psychologists would classify as an introverted type. Being introverted, the Venus in retrograde person thus creates an aura or atmosphere around them in which there is a "buffer" that does not allow others to penetrate into their inner reality. As a result, the Venus retrograde person appears to be enigmatic or difficult to understand. This buffer creates a condition in which other people typically project onto the Venus retrograde person the realities that they represent, versus understanding their actual reality. Because this happens so often, it has the continuing effect of keeping the Venus retrograde person deeply withdrawn from the environment. This reaction to others' projections is a form of the survival instinct as embodied in the Taurus side of Venus.

In my work as a counseling astrologer, I have counseled over 15,000 clients to date, and I have observed that many Venus retrograde people naturally attract partners who have a strong Uranian emphasis in their natures, even if they do not have Venus retrograde themselves. Even in the consensus evolutionary state, which again correlates with generally seventy percent of the world population, the Venus retrograde person has either managed to uniquely define their relationship in some way so as to reflect the principle of individuation, or they have created a relationship dynamic in which they have deeply and silently withdrawn while "going through the motions" of the relationship itself. This deep inner withdrawal, when it occurs, serves the individuating function of Venus retrograde, for it creates a psychological condition of deep inner reflection, examination, and questioning that can and will be applied as some future point in such an individual's evolution. Furthermore, around twenty percent or so of the Venus retrograde individuals that I have counseled have had no relationships of an intimate nature whatsoever.

As a preexisting pattern, the Venus retrograde person has already learned, or is focused on learning, the polarity point or sign of the natal Venus in the birth chart. This is important to understand because the archetypal themes of Venus in the different signs or houses will be oriented to quite differently when Venus is retrograde. It is also important to understand that Venus retrograde individuals desire to continually grow or evolve within themselves. They are never comfortable with reaching a degree of comfort in their lives, and stopping their growth because of that comfort. As a result, when they are in a relationship, they desire a partner who also demands and needs to evolve and grow from within themselves. In addition, because the Venus retrograde person internalizes the Venus function (the Taurus side of Venus), they also desire a partner who is self-empowered, self-sustaining, and self-reliant. These qualities will be quite necessary in the partner if there is to be a successful relationship, since the Venus retrograde person typically is quite silent and withdrawn in relationships, and relates to their partner, or others generally, only as necessary. Thus, they need a partner who is self-secure, so that when these periods of silence occur the partner does not project onto them something that has nothing to do with them.

Karmically and evolutionarily speaking, the Venus retrograde person reflects a situation in which they are necessarily repeating or reliving past life relationship dynamics in the current life. The specific nature of those dynamics are reflected in the following indicators:

- The house and sign that retrograde Venus is in.
- The nature of the aspects that Venus is making to other planets.
- The nature of the planets that Venus is forming aspects to.
- The nature of the houses that these aspected planets are in.
- The nature of the houses that the signs Libra and Taurus occupy.

Venus retrograde also means that these people are karmically and evolutionarily determined to re-meet key people that they have known in other lifetimes in which something has not been finished or resolved. The intention is for final resolution of these circumstances in order for a new evolutionary cycle to begin. If you are a counseling astrologer, this point is necessary to understand because many people who have Venus retrograde can be quite frustrated because they seem to be in an ever-repeating loop of relationship dynamics with no way out. By helping such people understand the larger picture of why this is occurring, and that there will be a release from this requirement at some point, they can begin to come to terms with these karmic and evolutionary conditions in their lives.

At this point, I would like to provide a description of the general archetypal themes of Venus in its natal sign, which will correlate to the preexisting pattern of inner/outer relatedness. I will also address its polarity sign, which will allow these pre-existing patterns to evolve into a new way of inwardly relating to oneself. This, in turn, will change the types of people we attract into our lives. Please understand that these are general descriptions of Venus in specific signs that are not conditioned by any other factor such as aspects, the house that Venus is in natally, one of the four natural evolutionary conditions, or the specific evolutionary/karmic axis in the birth chart as symbolized the Pluto, its polarity point, or the South and North Nodes with their respective planetary rulers. These are all factors which must be considered for any complete and accurate analysis.

Venus in Aries

As a pre-existing pattern from birth, the Venus in Aries person will be quite narcissistic, self-orientated, and feel within themselves that they are quite special. Inwardly, they will instinctively feel that they have some undefined special destiny to fulfill which requires a fundamental independence in order to actualize it. Thus, in a relationship these people can never fully commit themselves to another person, always keeping a deep part of their inner self-isolated from the relationship. Cyclically, the Venus in Aries person can be extremely passionate and involved. They seem fully committed through displays of intense, 'passionate energy of a very creative nature which keep the relationship moving forward. On the other hand, the Venus in Aries person will cyclically withdraw this energy when they instinctively feel that they have become too involved, too caught up in the relationship in such a way that their need for independent actualization of their sense of a special destiny is threatened. The instinctual trigger for this cyclic withdrawal is when they feel that they have become too enmeshed with the other person. The other person will then feel totally deflated and confused, angry, and become intensely confrontational by way of projecting their own insecurities upon the Venus in Aries person.

Because these people feel inwardly that they are special, they need to be treated as special by other people. Conversely, they can make the person that they are with feel incredibly special, pumping the other person up with intense displays of love and energy. They are instinctively attracted to others who have a strong sense of self, who radiate a strong, passionate nature, who are as deeply self-orientated as themselves, and who have a strong sense of purpose in life. As a result, the relationships that the Venus in Aries person forms must have a sense of adventure, a continuing sense of ever-moving forwards in life. The Venus in Aries person will instinctively reject too much comfort, and established routines that lead to stagnation or boredom. Because Venus in Aries persons will attract others who are just as narcissistic as themselves, who can make them feel that they are the most special person that they have ever been with, yet also cyclically withdraw through their own fears of losing themselves in the relationship, they will cyclically lose their sense of self-confidence, and become deeply insecure. As this point, they can become extremely aggressive, confrontational, abusive, and project an intensity of displaced anger that is disproportionate to the actual circumstances that exist within the relationship. The problem here is that the Venus in Aries person operates instinctively and is essentially unaware that they create relationships in which everyone must serve them and their purposes in some way. Thus, they attract others who have this same orientation, and are reflections of their inner reality so that, at some point, the mirroring effect will produce self-knowledge.

Because Aries is a Mars-ruled sign, these people have a strong, passionate, and narcissistic sexual nature that generates an inner vibration that manifests as an animal kind of magnetism. This operates instinctively, not consciously, and the Venus in Aries person is unaware that they appear this way until others tell them. Consequently, others are sexually attracted to them without really knowing why. Physiologically, Venus in Aries people emit very strong pheromones that chemically excite people. Thus, others can be attracted to the Venus in Aries person as sexual objects through which they can act out their own sexual desires or natures. Such sexually narcissistic types of people are primarily orientated to acting out their sexual desires through the Venus in Aries person in a very self-centered way.

The Venus in Aries person is simply aware that their sexual energy is strong, yet it is unformed. From birth, they do not know who they are as sexual beings. Accordingly, they will experiment with different ways of being sexual with other people in order to discover, through experiences over time, what their basic sexual nature is, and what they need in order to actualize it. Thus, they will be attracted to others who also radiate a strong sexual nature. The Venus in Aries person instinctively uses their sexual nature as a way of securing the attention of another person that they are interested in, or as a way of sustaining an existing relationship. Conversely, relative to their cyclic withdrawal from an existing relationship, they will withhold their sexual energy, and stop being sexual with an existing partner. This is really a form of controlling the relationship so that their need for independence is not consumed in their fear of becoming enmeshed in the relationship. Venus in Aries will also use their sexual energy as a way of renewing the relationship, of bringing it back together, especially when major problems threaten to end the relationship outright. This pattern entirely depends on how much the Venus in Aries person wants to sustain the relationship for their own purposes.

In essence, the basic pattern of the Venus in Aries person is one of narcissistic self-involvement in which everything, including other people, must serve their own purposes for self-actualization. This naturally creates an emotional paradox linked with relationship. On one side of the paradox is their need for relationship, and on the other side of the paradox is their need for absolute independence. This paradox generates an instinctual fear of becoming too enmeshed in any relationship. Thus, it is very difficult for these people to remain committed to a relationship for long periods of time because their fundamental need is to be in control of their own destiny. They instinctively use other people for whatever their existing purposes or needs are, and others can use them in exactly the same way.

In evolutionary terms, the Venus in Aries person has embarked on a new cycle of personal development. Freedom is necessary in order to discover and actualize this new cycle. The key to actualizing this new cycle in a positive way is to embrace the sign Libra, because by embracing the individual needs of a partner or friend, and encouraging the independent actualization of those needs, they will then attract others who do this for them. Thus, their fear of losing their individuality, of not being able to have their own life because of their relationship, will no longer exist. By learning to give, rather than always creating relationships in which the other must serve their needs and purposes at all times, they will learn that they will be given to in ways that are free from subjective, ulterior, self-serving motives and agendas. In this way, they will learn role equality in relationship, and role interchangeability.

Venus in Taurus

As a preexisting pattern from birth, Venus in Taurus people have learned to deeply internalize themselves in order to understand who they are and what they need in order to have a sense of meaning in their lives. As a result, these individuals are quite introspective and self-possessed. They have learned, in the last analysis, that the only person that they can truly rely on is themselves. Thus, these people are more or less self-reliant and self-sustaining, and can be extremely resourceful and resilient in their ability to sustain themselves, even in the face of overwhelming problems or circumstances.

These people have learned to limit what they value relative to what life means to them. Thus, their sense of meaning, of what life means, determines what they value. Consequently, they can have a limited value system that is more or less fixed and static—one that works for them. In terms of relating to other people, these individuals tend to evaluate and hear others relative to their own value system. If there is no common thread between their value system and another's value system, then these people will generally be unable to relate. In other words, there is an inherent resistance to others whose values are different from their own, whose sense of what life means is at odds with their own. They simply "tune out" and do not hear what the other is saying. As a result of their intrinsic resistance to embracing other values, ideas, knowledge, or other forms of reality, these people tend to evolve or grow very slowly. In social situations as an example, Venus in Taurus people will typically remain silent and self-enclosed unless there is a commonality of values in which they can then relate to someone else. When there is a basis of relating to another through shared values, then the Venus in Taurus person can appear very warm, engaging, deep, intense, highly focused, and have an absorbing quality wherein others can feel drawn into their inner reality, which now appears magnetic and solid.

Whatever the Venus in Taurus person values, including other people who they have given meaning and value to, they will want to maintain and possess. It is very difficult for these people to give up or let go of anything that holds meaning and value to them because that correlates to their sense of purpose for living. In intimate relationships, as a result, Venus in Taurus people can be highly possessive of their partners, and attempt to limit what their partners do because of their fear of losing them. Because of this they can be quite controlling in covert and overt ways, the sense of ownership or possession of that which they value generating an emotional psychology of jealousy. Unless other astrological factors are indicated, this way of controlling or limiting their partners' activities manifests as psychological withdrawal and inner isolation from the partner. Vibrating inwardly in this way, Venus in Taurus people can also attract others who are very possessive of them, and who can also feel very threatened when they manifest any interest in other people. They can attract others who attempt to limit their own development, others who unconsciously expect them to be vicarious extensions of their own reality, to have no real life of their own, to be simply a prize possession like a trophy on the wall. Interestingly enough, when the Venus in Taurus person has projected value and meaning on such a partner they will allow themselves to be limited in this way even if it means limiting their own development. This means that the Venus in Taurus person has projected too much meaning and value into such a partner, because of their need for stability in life at all costs. Over time, when this occurs, the Venus in Taurus person will create a progressive build-up of resentment towards the partner, which can lead into very explosive confrontations. Conversely, if the Venus in Taurus person attempts to break free from the limits of a controlling and possessive partner, then that partner can manifest very explosive behavior, motivated by jealousy and the fear of losing them.

Venus in Taurus people will also have a very strong sexual instinct or nature. This is because part of the survival instinct in all forms of life, including human, is to procreate the species. Consequently, their sexual needs and desires are constant. Sexual energy, and the expression of it, correlates in a very strong way to their sense of meaning and relatedness of life itself. They have a strong, magnetic, earthy sexual energy that reflects a strong integration into their physical bodies. Whereas Venus in Aries desires strong, passionate, and relatively quick sexual expression, Venus in Taurus desires long, sustained, intense, and permeating sexual expression. This way serves to "ground" them, and serves as a way of releasing their cyclic build-up of internalized emotional and psychological energy. Sexuality will symbolize a great deal of meaning to them, and they find themselves thinking about sex a great deal of the time. It is very important for Venus in Taurus people to have a strong, positive, and ongoing sex life. When they do not, then their overall reality will seem negative and stagnated. Their psychology will be inwardly compressed and withdrawn, and their life force will be weak and heavy.

When this occurs, the Venus in Taurus person is forced to remember, or must come to understand, that the primary intention of Taurus is one of self-reliance and self-sustainment. As a result of this intention, the Venus in Taurus person can create periods of cycles in their life in which their sexual needs are not met, if those needs have become too dependent on another person. When this occurs, either the person that they are with appears to lose sexual interest in them, or there is no one in their life at certain times that they desire to be sexual with. In either case, the intention is for the Venus in Taurus person to take matters into their own hands, so to speak—to sustain themselves sexually through masturbation.

Many individuals with Venus in Taurus have a strong masturbatory instinct that manifests even when they are in a relationship with another. Sometimes this can create confusion for such individuals because of the fact that they are in a relationship with someone, yet still desire this form of sexual expression. The reason that this can occur, again, is because the primary intention in this symbolism is self-empowerment and self-sustainment. For others, this instinctual need can create confrontations with their partners when those partners feel threatened by this need. The partner can feel insecure and inadequate, especially when the Venus in Taurus person "isolates" oneself from the relationship in order to fulfill this need. Conversely, the Venus in Taurus person can attract partners who desire to masturbate even though they are in a relationship with them. The Venus in Taurus person can now feel threatened, inadequate, and so on. This condition will occur to the Venus in Taurus person for one of two reasons. Either they have become too possessive or too dependent on the partner, or they have attracted a partner who is also learning the Taurus lesson of self-empowerment, which dictates this need. Because of this, many people with this symbol have learned to incorporate sexual self-stimulation within their sexual dynamics with another person. For some with Venus in Taurus, masturbation has become an art form in which they have learned to create highly erotic rituals that involve various kinds of sexual symbols and "tools" that serve the intention of self-sustainment and self-empowerment. For some, depending on their evolutionary condition, this means that they have learned to use themselves as their own vehicle or symbol of metamorphic transformation. Some with Venus in Taurus will attract partners who will encourage them to learn to do this, partners who try to teach them about the power that exists within them.

Their sexual values and orientation are primary and basic. There is not too much of a desire or need to "experiment." The Venus in Taurus person will desire to sexually possess or own their partners, and they can attract partners who want to sexually possess and own them. Because there is such a high value given to sexuality, if they are with a partner who does not honor their need for monogamy, who has sex with someone else behind their backs, then their inner relatedness will suffer. They will feel insecure, unworthy, create a negative self-esteem, become withdrawn, and compare themselves to whatever qualities or traits that their partner has been attracted to in the "other person." Even though the Venus in Taurus person inherently desires monogamy, they can involve themselves in an "affair" when their partner is not monogamous with them. The motivation is one of vindictiveness, and also to rebuild a positive self-image through making themselves desirable to someone else.

In evolutionary terms, the Venus in Taurus person desires to stabilize him or herself. To do so, they have necessarily had to narrow their focus to that which is specific to their own life's purpose, and that which supports that purpose. Any other aspect of life in general that is not relevant to that purpose is "tuned out." This creates a "frog in the well" effect—the frog can only see the segment of the sky that is observable from the bottom of the well. The frog is stable at the bottom of its well. It can control and feel secure within that well. Accordingly, there is a compressed internalization leading to a highly subjective reality that defines a pre-existing pattern of inner and outer relatedness. This creates a block to growing, learning, and evolving beyond the parameters of the well. In a relationship, this can create a polarized state between the two people. For a positive evolution to proceed the Venus in Taurus person must embrace its polarity: Scorpio.

Essentially, this means that they must learn how to listen to other people in such a way as to objectively identify what motivates other people, and learn how other people are psychologically constructed. In this way, they will learn how to evaluate others objectively which will, in turn, allow them to evaluate their own inner/outer reality in an objective way. In order to do this, the Venus in Taurus person must learn to open up to the totality of reality that lies beyond the parameters of their own "frog in the well" reality. They will then remove the bottleneck of their own inwardly compressed reality, one that generates a fixity of subjective perception and interpretation of their own and others' behaviors, motivations, intentions, and what life mans in general. By learning how to listen to others objectively, to hear what others need and desire, and to support their development, they will attract others who do this for them, and who do not want to possess, control, or limit their own development.

Venus in Gemini

As a preexisting pattern of inner relatedness, the Venus in Gemini person hears an inner call for self-knowledge. This manifests as a deep inner restlessness, fueled by a constant inner dialogue within themselves. This inner dialogue poses a variety of questions leading to experiences of all kinds. The essence of these questions is defined by the inner question "Who am I?" which leads also to "Who are you?"

Venus in Gemini people relate to and understand themselves inwardly through a reactive process. This means that these individuals pose a variety of thought possibilities leading to potential experiences, and then react to these thought possibilities in such a way that the reaction itself produces self-awareness and self-knowledge. This is a perpetual process with the Venus in Gemini person, because Gemini as an archetype is mutable. The mutable archetype is one of unrestricted growth and perpetual expansion. Yet because we live in a time/space reality that is defined and understood through polarity, the process of expansion must, at some point, contract. Thus, Venus in Gemini people learn about themselves through cycles of contraction, which are induced as a reaction to excessive expansion. In the cycle of expansion, Venus in Gemini people are inwardly considering a diversity of thoughts in their desire to understand themselves, and life in general. These thoughts are induced by exposure to life itself: "What does this mean? What does that mean? By doing this, what will I discover? If I read this, what will I learn? If I talk to this person, or take that class, what will I discover?" and so on. By initiating experiences of kind, by bringing into themselves all kinds of information from all kinds of sources, they react inwardly to this relatively indiscriminate intake of information. "Do I really believe this? What does this really mean to me? How can I apply that?" becomes a perpetual inner dialogue that is restrictive in nature as a reaction to their desire for perpetual growth and expansion.

The rhythm between expansion and contraction is ever-shifting, yet always ongoing at an underlying level. Even though the cycles of inner/outer expansion and contraction are not predictable, there is always an underlying reactive dialogue that occurs within the Venus in Gemini person. Thus, these people may enter into a cycle in which they are seeking out all kinds of experiences, taking all kinds of classes, reading all kinds of books, seeing all kinds of movies, etc. This will then induce a cycle of contraction because they will reach the limit of such expansion. They simply become exhausted and fragmented because of too much intake of stimulus of this kind. When the cycle of contraction is induced in this way, the Venus in Gemini person necessarily assimilates the meaning of the different experiences they have created relative to their desire for knowledge. So, on the one hand, there is this reactive process occurring within them even during the cycle of expansion, and, on the other hand, they cyclically withdraw from the cycle of expansion because they simply become overwhelmed and exhausted. By withdrawing from external stimuli, they are able to assimilate what they have been exposing themselves to.

Because of their deep inner restlessness and intense inner curiosity to experience as much of themselves and life as possible, the Venus in Gemini person relates to other people in a very open, friendly way. They are naturally attracted to anyone who symbolizes new experiences or knowledge. Because they are open to all the possibilities of life, they are open to, and accepting of, the differences in all people. They are color-blind, so to speak. They are able to relate to people in a very free way that is relatively devoid of prejudice. Because of their own inner curiosity as to the possibilities of life itself, the Venus in Gemini person is very adept in being able to carry on conversations with other people. They ask good questions, and are able to communicate quite well. They are quite skilled at drawing other people out of themselves. They are versatile, quick, and quite witty.

Conversely, when these individuals are in a contraction cycle, they can be very reactive in their conversations with other people. The reactive process manifests as not completing their own sentences, or allowing another to complete their own sentences. When this occurs, the mutual reaction does not allow for either one to actually hear the other. Needing to contract and stabilize thus creates a resistance to any more intake of information. This reactive process, which is really a manifestation of the survival instinct intrinsic to the archetype of Venus via its natural rulership of Taurus, and thus the 2nd House.

The Venus in Gemini person understands their feelings through their mental body or process. Let us understand that feelings are different from emotions. Feelings are an immediate reaction to an existing stimulus, whereas emotions are a reaction to our feelings. Because Gemini is an Air archetype, people who have Venus in this sign relate to themselves inwardly through the nature of what they are thinking at any given moment. This process will induce a feeling reaction to the specific nature of what those thoughts are. In this way, they come to understand the nature of their feelings. On a projected basis, these individuals understand what and how another is feeling by approaching another through their intellect. In other words, they must engage someone's intellect or mental processes first in order to understand how that person is feeling about anything.

Sexually, the Venus in Gemini person values sexual openness in the sense of mentally entertaining all kinds of sexual possibilities. Again, they are naturally curious, and they do not want to preclude any possibility out of hand. They will (at least mentally) consider almost any sexual possibility. Some with Venus in Gemini will have a dual sexual nature that leads to bisexuality. Thus, they can be quite sexually versatile, playful, and "sporting" because of the implied adventure of being open to all sexual possibilities. There is also a particular attraction to oral forms of sexuality, and a strong mental orientation to the sexual act that induces a detachment from it. This is necessary for Venus in Gemini because it is through this kind of *de-facto* voyeurism that they learn about themselves as a sexual being, and learn about others as sexual beings. On the other hand, this kind of mental detachment can create sexual frustration because it is as if they are forever observing instead of being totally engaged at a purely emotional and physical level. It is as if they cannot get out of their heads, so to speak.

In evolutionary terms, the Venus in Gemini person desires to expand their consciousness in order to learn how to relate to themselves in a diversity of ways through the multiplicity of experience. The process of learning occurs through reactions to initiated experiences of an internal and external nature—thought and counter thought. For evolution to proceed, the Venus in Gemini person must embrace its polarity: Sagittarius. In essence, this means to continue the desire for expansion, to expand the inner and outer horizons of awareness, but in such a way that indiscriminate curiosity is replaced by conscious intention: "I want to learn this for this reason; I want to do that for this purpose; I am interested in learning this and will focus on it until I learn it thoroughly before learning something else; I am thinking about that because of this reason" and so on.

In addition, the Venus in Gemini person must progressively evolve away from externally acquired knowledge into the dynamic that the knowledge they are seeking is inwardly realized through the development of the intuition. They need to transfer the center of gravity in their consciousness from the left to right-brain. In this way, these individuals will learn to relate to themselves in a responsive way, versus a reactive way. They will create a deep inner center within themselves that is constant, versus an inner center that becomes cyclically fragmented. They will learn to listen to themselves in a different way, and thus how they listen to other people. In effect, they will learn to hear more deeply what is behind or within the actual spoken words and the thoughts that are occurring within their own consciousness. In this way, they will learn to communicate differently as they speak to the essence of what is being said, versus reacting to the specific nature of the words only. They will learn how to communicate their own essence in a very direct way versus a plurality of words that is trying to describe that essence.

Venus in Cancer

As a pre-existing pattern of inner relatedness the Venus in Cancer person comes into life fundamentally insecure. This insecurity is based on, and caused by, the nature of their inner emotional reality, which is like a tornado of different swirling emotional states that seem to come and go of their own volition, that seem to be beyond the control of the individual. Inwardly, as a result, the Venus in Cancer person feels that they are standing on ever-shifting sands. These people feel deeply insecure because the nature of their emotional state and the needs that these states create cannot be inwardly controlled. The inner cross-currents of different emotions converge and combine in ways that create moments in which they can feel stable and secure in one moment, and highly insecure and unstable in the next.

The intention of Souls who have Venus in Cancer has been, and is, to inwardly know and relate to themselves as emotional beings. The knowing of themselves through the ever-shifting cross-currents of different emotional states produces an inner confusion because of the different self-images that each emotional state induces. And each emotional state dictates needs that are motivated by the desire to feel secure, to feel safe, and to be stabilized. Inwardly, these individuals feel highly vulnerable and insecure. Typically, they relate to themselves from moment to moment. Each emotion (and the moods that they produce) defines their inner psychology on an ongoing basis. Inwardly, there is a fundamental desire to be taken care of, to be nurtured, by someone whom they can trust. There is a core desire for someone to help them feel stable, safe, and secure. The deep inner need for this is its own causal factor, generating the different emotional states in the first place.

The reason for this, typically, is that these individuals have missed a key step in their behavioral development as children. This step occurs around twenty months of age when the baby learns to internalize one or both parents in such a way that when the parent is not physically nearby or present, the baby still feels safe and secure. Missing this step becomes a causal factor leading to the displaced emotions of childhood manifesting in their adult life. These displaced emotions are essentially the emotions of a young child.

The root cause of this is that they bring forward from other lifetimes emotional imprints and pre-existing patterns that are defined by some cataclysmic emotional event in which their ability to feel inwardly secure has been severely compromised. Whatever the specific event was, it becomes a casual factor generating an inner abyss of emotional volatility and cross-currents of unpredictable emotional states. Even if they had parents who were loving, nurturing, and doing their very best to help them feel secure when they were a baby, it is never quite enough from the child's point of view. As adults, this same effect can occur even when they have loving and supporting people in their lives, for the same reasons. Even when the Venus in Cancer person is given the love, nurturing, and the stabilizing effect that they desire, it is never quite enough.

Venus in Cancer people have an inherent emotional expectation that is projected into their relationships in which others should somehow just know what they need without actually verbalizing what that need is. It is simply a deep, silent expectation. This is exactly what babies and small children do. They just naturally expect their needs to be identified and met by the parents. When this does not occur to the baby's satisfaction, they instinctively cry or scream in varying degrees of intensity. Similarly, the Venus in Cancer person, as an adult, silently expects their needs to be understood and met. When this does not occur, the unmet expectations produce emotional behaviors that can even shock the Venus in Cancer person themselves. These behaviors range from a deep, permeating silence in which the subconscious intent is to draw or pull someone into their emotional state in order for it to be identified and worked with, to extreme emotional displays that are driven or caused by displaced anger. The cause of this kind of extreme behavior, resembling a coiled spring that snaps under stress, is a build-up of emotional frustration. The emotional reaction is usually disproportionate to the event or circumstance that triggers it.

Because these people relate to themselves on an emotional basis, they naturally relate to others on an emotional basis. Because they are perpetually "hearing" or "listening" to their own inner emotional reality, they can naturally identify or "hear" another's emotional state, and the needs that any given emotional state generates, even when the other person is not verbalizing or actively projecting what that emotional state or reality is about. Venus in Cancer people have an inherent ability to emotionally empathize with other people, to silently tune in. When others are perceived to be in a state of emotional distress or need, the Venus in Cancer person naturally responds with very real emotional caring, wisdom, support, nurturing, and love. They will naturally encourage others to let out their emotions, and they will want to hold and embrace another who is in need. The very essence of their touch or holding is warm, consuming, and reassuring. This reflects their own need to be reassured through touch and holding.

More than words, the Venus in Cancer person responds to touch and holding because this is exactly how babies and small children are reassured when they are upset for whatever reason. For Venus in Cancer people, trust is established through touch, and through a silent emotional resonance with another that operates beyond the spoken word. This is very important to understand because of the Venus in Cancer person's inherent fear of being too vulnerable. Even verbalizing what they need, or are feeling, can be too vulnerable a situation for these people. In fact, the typical verbal response of these people when asked how they are doing, especially when some deep emotional state or need is causing a deep inner withdrawal from their environment, is "I'm fine" even when they obviously are not. This kind of response is instinctual, and is a form of the survival instinct relative to their fear of vulnerability and their fundamental distrust of most people. Thus, for those that are close to them and with whom there is a trust, the very best way to encourage them to come out of their emotional shell is through touch combined with soft, soothing words.

Sexually, Venus in Cancer desires and needs very strong touch, holding and kissing in order to feel sexually secure and trusting. Whereas Venus in Aries can simply get on with it, the Venus in Cancer person needs to be "warmed up" first. Inherently, these people desire and need to connect and merge the emotional energies or bodies first which then allows for a deep, permeating, and slow sexual merging to occur.

When this occurs, these people can feel very erotic and create erotic sexual environments that stimulate the emotional and sexual senses. But unless the Venus in Cancer person feels emotionally safe and secure, they will be sexually insecure. Some will be sexually immature, and can exhibit forms of sexual infantilism, such as wanting to be spanked, sexual pedophilia, a male preoccupation with breasts or nipples, a female preoccupation with the penis, impotence or frigidity, etc. When the Venus in Cancer person is in love and feels safe and secure, they can be very sexually giving and truly make their partners feel loved, safe, and secure.

For a positive evolution to proceed, the Venus in Cancer person must inwardly embrace its polarity: Capricorn. This means that they must learn how to minimize the projection of their external dependencies in order to feel emotionally secure, safe, and stable. They must learn that the security, safety, and stability that they are desiring exists within themselves. They must learn to become responsible for their own "emotional child." In order to do this, they must learn how to evolve their emotional consciousness in such a way as to be able to become aware of the specific causes or origins of any given emotional state that they find themselves in, versus just being caught up within it without knowing why. By doing so, they can develop emotional self-knowledge, which allows them to become emotionally responsible for themselves—to become emotional adults. They will empower themselves and minimize their projected needs, lose their fear of vulnerability, and thus learn how to relate with people in a much more straightforward and forthcoming way. In this way they will learn how to be in control of their emotions versus letting their emotions control them. They will attract others who encourage them to be responsible for themselves, and they will naturally encourage others to be responsible for themselves. Thereby, the "inner child" lives in a very positive and healthy way because it has now taken responsibility for its own actions.

Venus in Leo

As a pre-existing pattern, individuals with Venus in Leo have a very deep and intense inner focus that archetypally desires absolute creative self-actualization. Just as the Sun gives and sustains life in our solar system, these people have an inner wellspring of creative potential that allows them to sustain themselves. This "inner sun" is ever radiating and inexhaustible. Inwardly, they "hear" the call for creative self-actualization, and they give themselves the right to actualize themselves in any way they see fit. In this sense, they are the center of their own created universe and naturally expect all else to revolve around and support their desires for self-exploration and actualization. Whereas Venus in Aries manifests a primitive form of narcissism because it is so unformed and instinctual, Venus in Leo manifests a conscious narcissism because it is fully aware of its own creative potential.

Venus in Leo people expect others to understand how wonderful and special they are, and to tell them so. There is a fundamental need for positive and supportive feedback of their efforts for creative actualization however those efforts manifest.

When this feedback is not positive enough, or supportive enough, then the Venus in Leo person can inwardly feel unworthy and that the results of the efforts they are making are something less than what they had expected. Conversely, these people can shower others with very positive support and praise. This is very sincere and honest, yet is a reflection of their own inner expectation for others to do this for them. The only time that the Venus in Leo person does not favor another with such support and praise is when they interface with someone who is perceived to be a potential competitor in the same area that they are creatively actualizing themselves in. This can occur because, again, Venus in Leo people are the center of their own universe. Thus, someone who is perceived to be equal to or ahead of themselves changes their orientation to their own universe—they are not the "star" anymore.

Inwardly, Venus in Leo people relate to themselves as an unformed piece of clay that is waiting to be sculpted, a canvas waiting to be painted, an inner landscape desiring to be explored in all possible directions, or a universe waiting to be created. These people are literally "full of themselves." Within itself, Venus in Leo has no inner sense of limits whatsoever. Whatever they feel drawn to do they simply expect that they *can* do. The very deepest frustration occurs when they realize that there *are* limits to what they can accomplish or do. This evolutionarily necessary experience occurs in order to create a sense of humiliation of the ego. This must occur to counteract the Leo tendency to delusions of personal grandeur.

Within themselves, Venus in Leo people are quite optimistic, enthusiastic, and future orientated. They have a deep and positive feeling about themselves and life in general, and create many activities that lead to a sense of self-pleasuring and self-knowing. Generally, they simply feel good about themselves. They are deeply self-focused, and can focus on whatever is it is that they are trying to accomplish. The primary cause that creates a sense of brooding is when the Venus in Leo person feels inwardly blocked from being able to create, or when circumstances in their life are perceived to be thwarting or blocking their need for a necessary freedom or independence in order to creatively actualize. At worst, the Venus in Leo person can creatively actualize intense emotional tantrums and displays of a very melodramatic and negative nature.

In their external relatedness patterns, they have an inherent ability to make others feel really good about themselves, to "pump up" others, to provide positive motivation that encourages others to actualize whatever they are trying to accomplish, to make others feel "special," and to radiate a platonic kind of love that makes others feel embraced and regenerated just by being in their presence. This occurs because they themselves want to be heard and acknowledged by others. Thus, they have a great ability to hear where another is actually coming from, and to acknowledge this through validating and encouraging efforts at whatever it is that the person is focused on. Through positive feedback and support, they can help others focus on what they need in order to become more free and self-actualized. Conversely, when the Venus in Leo person is feeling inwardly blocked, or when they feel blocked by external circumstances, they can either totally withdraw from any kind of interaction with another, or become very spiteful and disdaining of another's efforts.

In their intimate relationships, the Venus in Leo person has a deep need to always keep the relationship in a kind of "love affair" situation. This is because the Venus in Leo person might as well die as be taken for granted. They need to be the sole focus of their partner's attention, and they desire to be considered special at all times. Their need to feel loved, and to be loved, is permeating desire that is never quite satisfied on an ongoing basis, though it can be satisfied on a momentary basis. As long as they feel that they are being loved and treated in the ways that they expect, they can also make their partners feel as if they are the very center of the universe. The Venus in Leo person must have creative independence that allows them to act on any desire that is based in self-actualization or discovery. Beyond the necessary independence, they also require a partner who encourages and supports their self-development. When this is extended by the partner, they will do exactly the same for them. The Venus in Leo individual is naturally a very powerful, self-directed, and self-motivated person who is strong willed and highly narcissistic. Thus, they will attract, and be attracted to, others who inwardly vibrate in the same way. The resulting relationship will be a highly self-indulgent one in which life can be lived to its fullest potential. The Venus in Leo person can be very generous. When they are in love, and feel loved, they can truly make another feel loved in ways that are quite unique.

When the Venus in Leo person feels that they are being taken for granted, or when their partner does not spend enough time with them, or when their partner feels that they are more important than the Venus in Leo person is, or when the partner is not monogamous, then the flip side of their Venus in Leo nature will manifest an intense emotional withdrawal that produces an inner vibration of disdain towards the partner. At this point they can become quite mean and cruel, and can completely belittle or humiliate the partner. They can manifest incredible emotional dramas of a melodramatic nature that are motivated by their need for attention, love, and recognition. They can create a life structure in which the other person is completely shut out. They can seek out love affairs with someone who will supply them with the love and attention that they need. And, of course, the Venus in Leo person can attract partners who manifest the very same behaviors when they feel that they are being taken for granted, etc. When this kind of degeneration occurs, the Venus in Leo person has become so self-absorbed that they simply couldn't care less about the feelings or needs of the partner, especially when the partner is perceived to be thwarting them in some way.

Sexually, Venus in Leo people have a natural love of the body and the sensuality that can manifest from it. Because of their strong narcissistic orientation, they can be intensely onanistic. It is as if they use their own sensuality and sexuality as a form of personal and symbolic self-actualization and metamorphosis. They view the body and sexuality as a kind of artwork in which they feel the inner freedom to create as they desire. At a body level, the Venus in Leo person emanates a vibration of strong sensuality, and a seductiveness that is natural yet consciously actualized. It is played with, so to speak. In relationship to another, they can be intensely passionate and consuming in their sexual expression when they feel good with the partner, or, conversely, totally withhold their sexuality when they do not. At this point, they will either satisfy themselves through different forms of autoerotic activities because of their strong sexual natures, or seek out "affairs" for the same purpose. Because of the principle of creative self-actualization, the Venus in Leo person is quite open to sexual adventures or experimentation of all kinds other than any form of sexual expression leading to a sense of humiliation or degradation. Venus in Leo desires monogamy, yet also enjoys sexual flirtations and innuendos since this feeds their need to feel special, important, and singled out.

For evolution to proceed, the Venus in Leo person must inwardly embrace its polarity: Aquarius. Essentially, this means that they must learn to objectify themselves versus perpetually living in a subjective reality that does not allow them to be experienced as equal to everyone else. For these people to fully and completely actualize themselves in the creative ways that they inwardly feel, they must learn to acknowledge the larger group, community, and society that they are living within, in such a way as to understand what that larger group needs. Once they understand that, they will be able to integrate themselves in very creative and unique ways within the larger group. But until they understand this larger framework in which they operate they can feel totally frustrated, because no one seems to acknowledge what special gifts and capacities they do have. In relationship, they must learn to give without that giving being motivated by their own need to be given to. They must learn to validate and acknowledge another's reality and needs without being told how wonderful and special that they are first, or in return. And they must learn to receive or accept feedback from other people even when this feedback conflicts with their own inner evaluations of themselves. In essence, they must learn that they are part of a very large universe, not the center of it. When this occurs, the Venus in Leo person will be always self-confident in a relaxed kind of way, versus having their self-confidence, and the positive self-image that this implies, dependent on others telling them how special they are.

Venus in Virgo

As a pre-existing pattern, the Venus in Virgo individual relates inwardly in very self-analytical and critical ways. In evolutionary terms, these individuals have been and are in a cycle wherein the desire and need has been one of personal self-improvement, and of an inner adjustment in how they have been inwardly and outwardly relating to themselves and others. The desire for personal improvement and adjustment reflects and implies that something has come before in which these people to not feel "right" or good about. Whatever this is, it implies guilt and the consequent need to atone for the guilt. Atonement caused by guilt correlates to a standard of judgment that, by its very nature, reinforces and causes the guilt itself. This standard of judgment is typically a belief system whose underpinnings are defined by a rigid set of rights and wrongs of a moralistic and religious nature, beliefs that essentially define the human being as something less than perfect when measured against a perfect God or world. The Venus in Virgo person uses this belief system to generate the desire and need for personal improvement and adjustment of how they have been inwardly and outwardly relating to themselves and other people.

Venus in Virgo individuals have usually had a series of prior lifetimes in which they have desired to deflate their excessively egocentric orientation to life, and lifetimes in which they have desired to remove all causes of personal delusions of grandeur. In addition, these individuals typically have desired, over a series of lifetimes, to align themselves with their *actual* inner reality as contrasted with any personal illusion or delusion of an egocentric nature that was previously considered to be real. Both desires generate an inner reality in which the Venus in Virgo person feels an excruciating inner aloneness, an inner emptiness, and an inner feeling of being very small. Whereas the Venus in Leo person feels inwardly to be godlike, the Venus in Virgo person feels like the proverbial grain of sand on an immense beach. Because of their need and desire to remove all forms of personal delusion and illusion, and the desire to deflate an excessive egocentric orientation to life, these individuals create an intensely self-critical and analytical consciousness of self that archetypally desires to humiliate itself at an egocentric level.

Consequently, these individuals have a negative feeling about themselves that creates the sense of never being good enough or perfect enough. This sense or feeling is reinforced, again, by a standard of beliefs in which the individual compares (comparison is a Venus function) itself to something that is more perfect and better than itself. This comparison function is also applied to other people whom the Venus in Virgo person respects in such a way as to be used to belittle him or herself. Because of this, the Venus in Virgo person can be very endearing to other people because they reflect and exhibit a very real humility that naturally deflects any excessive personal acclaim. In many cases, these individuals cannot accept or receive any acclaim or positive feedback whatsoever.

Because these individuals carry a conscious or unconscious guilt and desire to atone for that guilt, they create a form of personal masochism in which they must crucify themselves in some way. The pathology of masochism thus creates the inner and outer reality of crisis that can have many forms and applications. Crisis always leads to analysis, and analysis caused by crisis leads to self-knowledge for those individuals. The forms of personal crucifixion leading to crisis can manifest in a diversity of ways.

It can manifest as a deep inner abuse of oneself that manifests externally as being attracted to abusive people and relationships. It can manifest as perpetually submerging their own legitimate needs to the needs of other people. This reflects an inner feeling of guilt and the consequent thought that they do not deserve to be given to or acknowledged for what they need. It can manifest as all forms of self-undermining activities that lead to a sense of personal defeat and humiliation. It can lead to all forms of personal escape as a way of avoiding confronting the deep inner abyss of aloneness that they feel. It can be seen in the workaholic syndrome, keeping oneself compulsively busy, keeping the mind engaged in all kinds of superficial nonsense, the unconscious creation of one crisis after another in order to keep the left-brain engaged so that it can avoid peering into the inner emptiness, the manifestation of physical problems of all kinds, or excessive food intake (compensation for inner emptiness). A variation of this is the bulimic syndrome, which reflects the true complexity of this archetype in its most difficult applications or manifestations.

In essence, this condition reflects deep inner guilt and the need to atone for it—to expel it through the act of vomiting, relative to a negative self-image that feels empty and devoid of any inner meaning, which in turn causes the excessive intake of food in order to feel full. This is also a *de-facto* sexual act, because food intake is a sensation-oriented act that displaces the sense of inner emptiness through the intake of the food which is then "released." The releasing effect thus mimics a sexual orgasm of an intense nature, which in turn reinforces the guilt linked with the sexual act in the first place—sexuality being something less than "pure." Thus, the natural sexual desire is suppressed either through guilt or because of a fear of being "contaminated" by another person. The sublimation of this natural function can lead to not only the food problem as a form of compensation, but to any one of the above behaviors. Conversely, Venus in Virgo people can also involve themselves in indiscriminate sexuality, or being compulsively sexual, as a way of filling up the inner void.

Venus in Virgo people are plagued by a deep sense of inner doubt which is caused not only by the desire to deflate their egos, but also by the excessive inner analysis that creates a diversity of competing thoughts and perspectives. In turn, this can lead to an inner paralysis of their ability to take action as necessary. When these individuals consider some new project, or some new direction, or some new strategy leading to self-improvement, they will make these new ways seem so big and complicated that it reinforces their sense of personal inadequacy. Thus, they can defeat themselves before they even start. The way out of this self-defeating dynamic is to realize that the path to perfection, self-improvement, or the actualization of their abilities occurs one step at a time.

In their relatedness to other people, the Venus in Virgo person is quite self-effacing, humble, and ever ready to help another. They are natural givers. Because they have a deep inner pain born of too much crisis, they can naturally relate to the pain or problems of other people. Accordingly, these folks can be extremely good at helping other people solve their problems. The advice that they generate is practical and sound, but unfortunately, they are not so good at taking or applying the advice they give to others towards themselves.

Because of the inherent masochism that defines the Venus in Virgo individual, they do not feel that they deserve to be helped, but rather to be hurt, abused, taken advantage of, manipulated, deceived, criticized, or invalidated. They attract others who are emotionally crippled in some way. This is actually an "out picturing" or projection of the fact they themselves are emotionally wounded and deeply troubled. All too often, because of these dynamics, the Venus in Virgo person attracts others in intimate relationships who are very self-oriented, and who expect to be served and helped in a very unequal way. These types of partners typically deny the nature of their own emotional reality, and project those realities on the Venus in Virgo person. Of course, these projections are usually very critical and negatively judgmental, and play right in to the Venus in Virgo person's inner dynamic of self-doubt, guilt, and atonement.

All too often, these people sacrifice their own needs and purposes to their partners. They feel that this is the only way to maintain and sustain the relationship. Because of all of this, the Venus in Virgo person typically feels victimized by life in general, and other people specifically. Feeling victimized, they can create a consciousness in which they feel powerless to change the conditions of their life. Consequently, there is an ongoing dissatisfaction with their lives which manifests as either a silent, stoic, accepted suffering, or as an overt verbal manifestation that can wear on those in close proximity.

Sexually, the Venus in Virgo person is structured in such a way as to want to serve or please their partners. This is another form of personal sacrifice in which they experience vicarious sexual fulfillment through the sexual satisfaction of their partners. Unconsciously, the Venus in Virgo person can embody the archetype of the slave and master dynamic. Depending on other astrological considerations in the birth chart, the Venus in Virgo can either be the master who has learned a variety of sexual techniques and methods designed to induce intense stimulation in their "slave," or the slave who has no choice but to respond to the sexual will of the master. At worst, this can manifest as overt S&M-type sexual practices. Conversely, Venus in Virgo can also be asexual because of the deep, unconscious guilt association with the life of the senses and the body, and the fear of being "contaminated" in this way. The suppression of this natural function produces a sublimation manifesting in a nervous, uptight, anxiety-driven individual who is critical and judgmental to an extreme degree. As with Gemini, there is a strong mental orientation to the sexual act that produces an ongoing analysis of what is occurring when it is occurring that leads to self-knowledge. This mental, observational overlay to the sexual act produces its own frustration that can lead to being attracted to ever more intense forms of sexual stimulation as a way of getting out of their heads, and into their bodies. Venus in Virgo embodies the extremes, sexually speaking, from being asexual to absolute sexual immersion that has no limits whatsoever.

For evolution to proceed, the Venus in Virgo person must embrace their polarity: Pisces. This starts by understanding that the cause of the deep inner aloneness that they feel reflects an unresolved spiritual need. This individual must align inwardly with a spiritual system that promotes a direct inner connection to God. Once this inner connection is made, and practiced daily, the inner pit of aloneness will dissolve. This spiritual system must be defined through the principles of compassion and love, must be gentle and kind, and rooted in natural principles so that God is understood as an evolving-force instead of inherently perfect. In this way, the Venus in Virgo person can change their inner standards of judgment, dissolve the build-up of guilt and the need to atone for it, and allow for a deep self-acceptance based in the goal to be a little bit better each day. Negative self-feelings will change into positive ones, which will then allow the Venus in Virgo person to attract differently. Now they will attract others who are also compassionate and forgiving by nature, who are accepting and supportive instead of critical and judgmental, who will encourage them to develop their abilities and capacities, and who bring them the message that they are lovely people who do not need to be their own worst enemies anymore. In this way, they will learn that there are only solutions to life instead of life being just one big problem.

Venus in Libra

As a pre-existing pattern, individuals with Venus in Libra have learned to understand who they are as individuals through the initiation of all kinds of relationships with people who symbolize the diversity of life itself. Through the initiation of such relationships, the Venus in Libra person learns to evaluate who they are as individuals through comparison and contrast what which they are not: this person values this, that person values that, and so on. Thus, through relationships, these individuals learn about who they are as individuals through a counterpoint awareness that is defined by that which they are not.

One of the myths that many astrological authors and teachers support is that Libra, as an archetype, is inherently balanced. The reality is the Libra is *learning* balance. Archetypally, Libra is inherently defined through extremes—the opposite of balance. For those who have Venus in Libra this means that, by nature, they are cyclically driven between the extremes of too much social interaction, and the reactionary extreme of too much social isolation. The causal factor in this dynamic of extremes is based in the fact that Venus in Libra people are motivated to discover their sense of self through social interactions of all kinds. This typically leads to a situation or condition in which they become overwhelmed by the realities of those that they are socially interacting with. The Venus in Libra person thus cyclically becomes inwardly destabilized by losing the sense of self or inner centeredness. This causes the opposite dynamic to manifest—to cyclically isolate from all social interaction. This reaction occurs, obviously, in order for the individual to stabilize itself through such isolation. The individual then attempts to rebuild itself from within. This reactionary cycle is a reflection of the survival instinct

NEPTUNE: WHISPERS FROM ETERNITY

that is embodied in the Taurus side of Venus. Remembering that an inconjunct naturally exists between Taurus and Libra, these two extreme cycles are triggered because of this natural inconjunction. When excessive social interaction occurs, then the inconjunct manifests as an inner crisis leading to the cycle of withdrawal from such interaction. When excessive withdrawal from social interaction causes an inner implosion then the inconjunct manifests as an inner crisis causing the cycle of necessary social interaction to occur.

The archetype of Libra reflects a psychological condition in which the Venus in Libra person feels that they can only value themselves to the extent that other people value them. It creates a condition in which their sense of inner worth and meaning is linked to how much other people value and give meaning to them. Because it can be so extremely important that others value and give meaning to them, the Venus in Libra person all too often will reflect and support the reality of those that are important to them even though that reality is not the actual reality of the Venus in Libra person. In this way, they lose touch with their own reality. Thus, they can seem to be many different kinds of people depending on who they are immediately interacting with. It is for this reason the Venus in Libra person has been so typically characterized in the astrological cookbooks as a chameleon.

This chameleon effect also occurs for another reason. The archetype of Libra correlates to the principle of relativity. As Einstein pointed out, the only absolute is relativity itself. The Venus in Libra person inherently understands this principle in such a way as to be able to relate to the diversity of values and beliefs, and to the lifestyles they create. They can therefore support others in their lifestyles no matter how different they are. This is why they can seem like a chameleon to others who are more fixed in their relatedness patterns to others—Venus in Taurus, for example.

It is precisely for this reason that the Venus in Libra person can cyclically lose the sense of self. They can understand the relativity of all things so deeply that it creates an inner confusion of what to value, what to believe, and who they actually are. Whatever the existing reality may be for the Venus in Libra person, they are forever aware of other possibilities as symbolized and reflected in the lives of other people. This awareness of relativity can induce a very active imagination in which they feel what it would be like to live in this or that way, to try to feel what it would be like to live like that person, etc. This inner dynamic thus contributes to the questioning of who they are in a total sense. Because the inner sense of self is defined in relation to other people under Venus in Libra, these individuals all too often attempt to discover and actualize their individuality through the values and beliefs of other people.

The Libra archetype also correlates to the dynamics and principles of balance, equality, fair play, and justice. Venus in Libra people exhibit these principles strongly in their social interactions. Compromise and negotiation are the hallmarks of their social natures. They can also exhibit strong anger when their sense of justice, fair play, and equality are violated. For them, the axiom "treat others as you yourself want to be treated" is tattooed on their souls.

In intimate relationships, the Venus in Libra person desires and strives toward role equity and interchangeability. They value the psychology wherein each person in the relationship is equal to the other in every sense. They are exceptional listeners with the ability to hear and understand objectively the reality of their partners. As a result, they naturally expect to be treated in the same way, with the same respect. They are natural givers to other people in general, and to their intimate partner specifically. This is because Venus in Libra people have a need to be needed. This is caused, again, by their sense of self-worth being linked to the value that others give to them. Thus, to give is to be needed. To be needed is to be valued. To be valued is to have meaning for another. To have meaning for another is to have meaning for oneself.

Consequently, they naturally expect others to give to them even though many have an intrinsic difficulty in asking for what they need. For many, this occurs because they do not know what they need specifically, and for others there is an inherent fear of upsetting the relationship if they do ask for what they need. In both cases, not asking for what they need becomes a causal factor that undermines their desire for role equality and equity within the relationship.

A typical cause of these people's inability to ask for what they need is traceable to their childhood. Libra is archetypally square to Cancer and Capricorn. Generally, this promotes a situation where the Venus in Libra person grew up in a family in which their needs were not honored or embraced by one or both parents. Instead, one or both parents was always telling the child what they needed, and what was expected of them based on their *own* needs. When the child attempted to assert its own needs, the parents would not listen, and then reinforced their expectations. This effectively undermined the actual identity and authority of the child. Consequently, the child was made to feel insecure relative to its actual needs and desires, with a resulting fear of being negatively judged by others. Additionally, the child learned that love and acceptance would only be extended when and if he or she would conform to the expectations and needs of one or both parents. As a result, many individuals with Venus in Libra have learned to be reflections of other people's values, beliefs, and lifestyles. Consequently, the vibrational nature of Venus within the individual attracts partners who expect the Venus in Libra person to be extensions of their own realities.

Sexually, the Venus in Libra person is a natural giver who can be extremely sensitive to the needs, feelings, and desires of their partner. They harmonize instinctively with the vibrational nature of their partner, and reflect the sexual reality of their partner as a result. This occurs because the Venus in Libra's sense of self-worth, value, and meaning are deeply conditioned by how much value and meaning another extends to them. Thus, to give sexually to their partners means to harmonize with and reflect the partner's sexual desires and needs. In addition, the Venus in Libra person has a fundamental desire for love and acceptance that manifests as mirroring the partner's sexual reality. Consequently, their own specific sexual desires become undeveloped or submerged. For some, this will lead into experimenting with different sexual lifestyles as suggested to them by the different partners that they are with, or through relating to different people who reflect different sexual lifestyles. Many attract partners who expect the Venus in Libra person to act out the sexual desires that define their reality, not the reality of the Venus in Libra person themselves. When this occurs, the Venus in Libra person will progressively create a build-up of anger because their fundamental need and desire for role equality, interchangeability, and equity becomes violated. Anger then becomes a motivational force that leads to and creates sexual aggression.

On the one hand, this can be a very positive psychological development for the Venus in Libra person because it symbolizes that he or she is learning to ask for and seek out what they desire and need. In an existing relationship, this can manifest finally as sexual role equality, as the Venus in Libra person begins to initiate the sexual dynamics that reflect his or her own desires. If the existing relationship does not allow this, then the Venus in Libra person may use this anger to seek out other partners who will fulfill their sexual desires. On the other hand, this sudden assertion of their needs can also create a situation in which the partner becomes angry, and that anger creates extreme sexual intensity as the partner tries to reassert sexual control. It can also create a situation where the partner withholds their sexual energy from the Venus in Libra person who is now asserting or asking for what they need.

The Venus in Libra person will manifest a natural sexual grace and beauty. As a result, many become the symbol or vehicle on which others project their sexual fantasies on. This creates a deep frustration and anger in the Venus in Libra person because they want to be loved and accepted for who they are, not just because they are the basis of someone's projected fantasies. They need a partner who will encourage them to fulfill their own sexual natures and needs. They need a partner who has the capacity to awaken them through sensitive touch, and who has the capacity to create sensual atmospheres that induce an erotic response. The Venus in Libra person, evolutionarily speaking, is also balancing their inner anima/animus, seeking the integration of the inner male and female into a state of inner balance. This requires, as a result, a need to give and receive, to assert their own needs and listen to the needs of the partner. Sexual role equality will then follow. For some, this will lead to same-sex attraction or bisexuality.

For evolution to proceed, the Venus in Libra person must embrace its polarity: Aries. This means that they must learn to inwardly listen to themselves instead of always listening to other people. By learning how to listen to themselves, they will then learn how to assert and communicate their own inner reality. By so doing they will then learn how to remain inwardly centered in all social and intimate situations. By learning how to stay centered within themselves in social and intimate situations, they will achieve a state of inner balance in which they can embrace, understand, and support the realities of other people without excessively compromising or undermining their own. By learning how to listen to themselves, they will learn how to trust their instincts, and by learning how to trust their instincts they will learn whom they can trust, and whom they cannot. In addition, they will learn when to be socially interactive, and when not to, thus achieving a state of balance. In this way, they will attract people who encourage them to discover and actualize themselves, others who are not afraid of their need for independent self-actualization within a relationship.

Venus in Scorpio

As a pre-existing pattern, individuals with Venus in Scorpio have learned to inwardly relate to the depth of their Soul and inner life, through an intense self-examination that has focused on the nature of their motivations, intentions, fears, and desires. These individuals are psychologically orientated within themselves, and, consequently, towards other people. Why, why, why? defines the inner essence of what these individuals inwardly hear, and defines the essence of how they relate to other people. Inwardly, the Venus in Scorpio individual is like a compressed coiled spring that cyclically expands and contracts in such a way that each expansion/contraction leads to ever-deeper levels of self-knowledge of an emotional and psychological nature. The inner compression that is motivated by the necessity of self-knowledge produces a vibrational intensity that radiates from the Soul. The auric atmosphere that surrounds the Venus in Scorpio person, as a result, is one of a penetrating intensity that is able to evaluate the essence of any situation or person that he or she interacts with.

The intensity of the auric atmosphere that radiates from the Venus in Scorpio person is quite interesting in that it is analogous to the eye of the eagle. The eye of the eagle is uniquely structured to have the ability to focus on the large picture while at the same time telescopically zooming in on its point of focus. In the same way, the Venus in Scorpio person inwardly relates to his or her inner landscape, and simultaneously relates to the outer environment and other people.

Inwardly, they are forever monitoring their interior environment, their ongoing state of beingness, in a general way. Within this state of beingness, the Venus in Scorpio person will then zoom in on any given emotion, feeling, sensation, thought, inspiration, dream, or desire in order understand the causal factor, the "why" of its origin. Understanding the causal factor in this way thus leads to self-knowledge or understanding. When this is occurring, the Venus in Scorpio person deeply internalizes in such a way as to shut off the external environment. For those who do not understand how the Venus in Scorpio person inwardly relates to him or herself, this can be quite disconcerting.

The intensity of the internalized focus radiates outwardly in such a way as to cause others to feel generally threatened without necessarily knowing why. The reason for this effect is that the vibrational magnetism that is radiating from the Venus in

Scorpio individual magnetizes the Soul structures of others in such a way as to cause an instinctual response of insecurity. Most people are not accustomed to looking at themselves as deeply as the Venus in Scorpio person is. Thus, when others are in proximity to the auric atmosphere radiating from the Venus in Scorpio person, they are instinctively magnetized at a Soul level. This in turn causes their own survival instinct to be activated at an unconscious level because of the depth of the reaction that is created within them relative to the nature and structure of their own reality. It is as if contact with the Venus in Scorpio person causes them, for some unknown reason, to question who, why, and what they are. This effect is but a reflection of what is occurring within the Venus in Scorpio person at all times. The intensity of this effect on others is relative to how deeply compressed and withdrawn the Venus in Scorpio is within him or herself at any given moment. The inner intensity meter can range from one to ten!

Outwardly, the Venus in Scorpio person relates to the environment and others in the very same way. On the one hand, they deeply, quietly, and intensely survey and monitor the ongoing nature of their environment, and the people in it. This allows them to remain in a state of stability and security. This ongoing monitoring is absolutely necessary for the Venus in Scorpio person because every one of them is born into this life, as a pre-existing pattern, with fundamental fears of betrayal, loss, and abandonment. Thus, their survival instinct is intensely geared and conditioned by these fears. Accordingly, the generalized monitoring of their environment is highly attuned to the potential of any person, condition, or circumstance that may cause these instinctual fears to manifest as reality. When they detect any potential threat to themselves or those that they love and care for, the Venus in Scorpio person's eagle eye will zoom in and focus on that perceived threat with the intensity of a laser beam.

With their survival instinct conditioned in this way, the Venus in Scorpio person instantly evaluates any person, condition, or event that may constitute a threat. The pre-existing survival instinct in these individuals is oriented to preparation for any possible life situation or condition. This dynamic of evaluation and preparation is, again, conditioned by their inherent fears of loss, betrayal, or abandonment, and determines how they will respond to any person or life situation. This is why the Venus in Scorpio person appears to be defensive and distant in their initial interactions with others.

An evolutionary intention that all Venus in Scorpio people have had over many lifetimes is one in which their Souls have desired to remove all sources of external dependence. This intention has manifested because of the Scorpionic tendency to overly identify with, and give too much meaning to, any person, condition, or situation that allows them to feel safe and secure. Anything or anyone meeting these requirements will typically be attached to for as long as possible. When this rigid and fixed attachment becomes a casual factor inhibiting further growth and evolution, then a removal of that which is preventing the necessary growth has and will occur.

On an inner basis, this process of enforced removal will also manifest when the Venus in Scorpio person has become too fixed and rigid in their inner relatedness patterns within themselves. In other words, they will periodically eliminate what they feel they inwardly need in order to maintain a sense of meaning in their lives when those lead to a fixity of how they are relating to themselves.

This enforced removal occurs in order to induce necessary growth. Rarely does the Venus in Scorpio person consciously realize when they have projected too much meaning or intensity into a person, life condition, or inner dynamic that symbolizes security and safety to them. Thus, when that which they have overly identified with is removed from their lives, the psychological experience is one of intense loss, betrayal, or abandonment. The typical reaction is rage and anger, because the temptation when this occurs is to feel victimized (Scorpio is part of the natural triad between Cancer and Pisces). As a pre-existing pattern, many people with Venus in Scorpio are born with such anger.

The real issue, again, is that whatever the Venus in Scorpio person has focused on or determined that it needs for a sense of meaning, stability, and security to exist in their life has and can be rigidly held on to for too long. Because one of the underlying dynamics or laws of life in time/space realities is evolution, there is an inherent limit to the function and value of any given dynamic, condition, or relationship. Evolution is a function of metamorphosing limitations. Thus, when the Venus in Scorpio person has overly identified with something to the point of limiting his or her necessary evolutionary requirements, a removal of that which is limiting the growth will occur with or without the cooperation of the individual.

In their intimate relationships, the Venus in Scorpio person will naturally desire to probe the depths of those that they love. They are, again, naturally psychological. Thus, they will relate to their intimate others in terms of how and why they are psychologically and emotionally structured. They desire to know what motivates others, and what that person's intentions are for wanting to be part of their lives. Paradoxically, the Venus in Scorpio person desires to be with someone who can help him or her understand the depth of their own Souls, their fears, their needs, their desires, and yet simultaneously fear allowing anyone to get too close to them in this way. This fear, of course, is inherent because of the subconscious memories of loss, abandonment, and betrayal that have preceded the current life. Thus, the Venus in Scorpio person will "test" those that want to be close to or intimate with them. It is as if they require potential partners to prove their love or intentions before they will allow themselves to become open or available.

The Venus in Scorpio person desires to attract another who will help them understand the depths of their Souls, and will often attract others who desire him or her to do the same for them. All too often, as a result, the Venus in Scorpio person will attract others who will feel and expect that he or she can help them emotionally and psychologically heal and repair themselves. This dynamic can be very attractive to the Venus in Scorpio person because it creates an illusory sense of safety in which the partner appears to intensely need them. This dependency makes the Venus in Scorpio person feel safe, relative to the intensity of the expressed need. As a result of this, they will find themselves in the role of an emotional and psychological healer, which allows them to feel safe, yet simultaneously allows them to conceal their own deepest wounds and fears.

The Venus in Scorpio person can conceal their deepest fears and emotions in many ways because of their inherent fear of being vulnerable. This fear is, of course, a reflection of uncertainty regarding whom to trust, and trust issues in general. When this kind of dynamic is created, the Venus is Scorpio person not only undermines their own deepest desires and needs in a relationship, and the desire for another to understand the depths of their own wounds and needs, but it also creates the karmic danger of manipulating the other to keep them dependent. The potential manipulation can occur because of their ability to identify the deepest emotional wound in the other, and by identifying that wound present themselves as the only one who can help them heal it. Yet unconsciously the Venus in Scorpio person does not really want that wound to heal, because then the partner would not need them, and then the sense of security and safety in the relationship that the Venus in Scorpio person is dependent on would not exist.

When this is the operative dynamic in the Venus in Scorpio's intimate relationship, it is a reflection of the permeating insecurity that they are born with. Consequently, this dynamic generates many manipulative forms of control that can be as extremely overt as they are subtle. And much to the amazement and bewilderment of the Venus in Scorpio's sense of reality, they keep finding out that there is no security in this type of relationship. This occurs because the types of people that they attract will only sustain the relationship for the duration of the need that attracted them to these people in the first place. Thus, this dynamic only guarantees the experience of loss, abandonment, and the emotional interpretation of betrayal for the Venus in Scorpio individual. Rarely do they understand that it is their own emotional dynamics linked with the fear of loss that is the causal factor in this experience. And just as rarely do they understand that they themselves can be manipulated by these types of partners as the partners themselves desire to have their own needs met.

In essence, both partners will attempt to limit the growth of one another relative to the needs that they both have that brought them together in the first place. This becomes the casual factor in the psychological and emotional manipulations. And by trying to limit the dynamics in the relationship to only those that reflect the needs that brought them into the relationship, they will exhaust those dynamics to the point where no more growth can occur. When the resulting limit of no more growth occurs, then the causal factor is in place that leads to confrontations and the loss of the relationship, unless a desire manifests that allows for new dynamics and experiences to occur. Because of these dynamics, the Venus in Scorpio person can thus be extremely jealous, possessive, and controlling of their partner. They feel threatened by situations real or imagined that threaten their control, and the partners they attract can be of like mind.

Some individuals with Venus in Scorpio, especially those that have Venus retrograde, have skipped steps in evolutionary terms. The nature of those skipped steps is specific to emotional dynamics. The reasons for avoiding or denying the nature of their emotional dynamics can have many causes, and each birth chart that has this dynamic must be examined to understand the individual reasons. These individuals will create a life in which, through evolutionary necessity, they will be plunged into their emotional body and dynamics through intense emotional and sexual experiences. The nature of these experiences is typically based on deep violations of trust, emotional disillusionment, emotional betrayal, emotional abandonment, and, in some cases, sexual violations of one kind or another. They will typically attract people who are emotionally dishonest, manipulative, narcissistic, and who may be pathological liars.

The Venus in Scorpio person requires an intensity of emotional and psychological experiences in order to become aware of the depths of their own dynamics, motivations, intentions, desires, and needs. The need for intensity manifests as a deep emotional communion or discussion with the partner, as a deep and permeating sexual experience that ignites the sensation body, or as deep emotional confrontations or cataclysms that enforce the question *why* to manifest within their consciousness. Another form of intensity that can lead to the necessary awareness is one in which the Venus in Scorpio person is almost totally emotionally isolated, not allowing for anyone to penetrate their carefully constructed emotional flak jacket. This kind of withdrawal leads to an inner compression that will generate awareness at some point, usually when they become exhausted from such isolation.

Their need for intensity exists because intensity forces an awareness of that which is hidden or unconscious within them. When the Venus in Scorpio person feels that they need something for growth and self-discovery, they will focus on it intensely. They will attempt to totally absorb whatever they need in order to grow. Through absorption, an osmosis takes place in which they become that which they have identified with and formed a relationship to. In this way, they feel secure and actualize their own power because of their ability to penetrate to the essence of that whatever have identified with and formed a relationship to. Their challenge is to understand when to let go or to change their inner dynamics, life conditions, situations, or the emotional/psychological dynamics that are existing between themselves and their loved ones specifically, and others generally. When this understanding and the consequent behavior does not exist, then this becomes the casual factor in creating loss, confrontation, abandonment, or betrayal that is experienced in a variety of ways.

The intensity of these types of experiences will force, at some point, an inner awareness of why these kinds of experiences are happening. This awareness will lead to self-knowledge, and self-knowledge will hopefully lead to change. If not, then the dynamic of repetitive compulsion exists until the Venus in Scorpio person becomes exhausted through the experiences that the repetitive compulsion dictates. When they become exhausted in this way, the Venus in Scorpio person will then finally apply the knowledge learned relative to the question of why.

Sexually, the Venus in Scorpio person desires an intensity of physical and emotional sensation. There is a fundamental desire to merge and be absorbed into the entire essence of their partner, and thus themselves. The intensity of sexual energy, and its release, allows for a relaxing of the inner compression of their Soul. Generally speaking, they are deep, passionate lovers who need to be gently and intensely touched. They have a keen awareness of the power of touch, and can instinctively know just how vulnerable they can be in a sexual situation through the quality and nature of their partner's touch. The current status or overall nature of their own inner being will be reflected in their own touch. Touch is the one dynamic in which Venus in Scorpio people cannot hide or conceal themselves. When they feel safe enough to make love with their eyes open there is no greater level of sexual intensity that can manifest from an individual. They can be acutely aware of the various sensations going on in their partner's body and Soul, and harmonize with those sensations in order to deepen and intensify them. Their sexual energy is constant even though some may attempt to transmute it through various other focuses.

Venus in Scorpio people manifest a deep fascination with the mystery of sexual energy, for it symbolizes the mystery of life/death/re-birth. It represents a vehicle of self-discovery to be explored in every possible way. Some will have desires to explore what others call sexual taboos because of an inherent resistance to being limited to sexual social conventions. Some will have desires to use sexual energy as a way of transforming themselves and/or heal themselves and others. Thus, these types will be orientated to sexual rituals and methods whose specific intent is to heal and transform. Others can use sexual energy as a way of controlling their relationship. Still others can use this energy as a way of hurting, possessing, and dominating their partners. A variation of this is using sex magic to get back at other people whom they have felt wounded by in some way. All Venus in Scorpio people naturally desire commitment and monogamy from their partners in every way, including sexually. By nature, they are naturally monogamous and value the dynamic of commitment. Of course, other life or birth chart factors can alter this natural condition.

The Venus in Scorpio person inherently emanates an intense, if quiet, magnetism that can instinctively excites others sexually even if they are not attracted to the Venus in Scorpio person as a whole. The actual attraction is not specifically sexual even though it may feel that way. It is actually based on the inner intensity that manifests from the Venus in Scorpio person, and this vibrational intensity is unconsciously interpreted by others as something they need within themselves, even though what that specific need is can essentially be unconscious or undefined. Vibrational intensity in any form is always interpreted by people as the possibility of transformation even when that vibration creates a fear reaction. The nature of this vibration that emanates from the Venus in Scorpio person reflects their own Soul's intensity. Thus, this vibration naturally stimulates the Soul structures of others. And, for some, this will automatically stimulate the primary brain wherein lies our sexual instincts and desires. Generally, the Venus in Scorpio person is just being who they are, unaware of the intensity that is manifesting from them. At worst, however, some Venus in Scorpio people who observe others reacting to them in this way will begin to consciously manipulate their sexual energy in order to fulfill some sexual desire or need that is connected with power.

For evolution to proceed, the Venus in Scorpio person must embrace its polarity: Taurus. The essence of this lesson is to realize that every projected need they create is connected to some deep inner wound. The projection of the need is thus motivated by the desire for another to somehow repair this wound. Conversely, the intention in the Taurus polarity is to learn how to repair these wounds from within themselves. This will lead to a condition of self-empowerment, self-reliance, and self-sustainment that creates a deep and genuine state of inner security. Once this occurs, these individuals will relate to others in general, and their intimate partners specifically, in an entirely new way. Now they will encourage the independent actualization of their partner, and help motivate them to do this. Their partner will encourage them in exactly the same way. By changing their inner vibration in this way, they will attract differently. Thus, the dynamics of manipulation, control, betrayal, loss, and abandonment will disappear from their lives.

In addition, this lesson demands that they learn how to relate the nature of their emotional reality as it is without concealing it, altering it through misrepresentation, or representing it in oblique rather than direct ways. Until they learn how to do this, the Venus in Scorpio person will never have their greatest need and desire fulfilled— to have at least one other person in their life who totally understands who they are, how they are put together, and why they are put together this way. By learning how to do this they will simultaneously learn how to discriminate who should be in their life, and who should not be. By learning how to do this they will then learn how to identify the actual needs of their partner versus telling the partner what they need. And, of course, they can now attract another who reflects this very same psychological, emotional, and vibrational shift. The scorpion has now metamorphosed into the eagle via the Phoenix.

Venus in Sagittarius

As a pre-existing pattern, the Venus in Sagittarius person has a deep need to discover and actualize their own personal truth. This need is conditioned by the nature of that which confers a sense of meaning and purpose in their lives. That which constitutes value and meaning in their lives will in turn condition their orientation to, and thereby determine, the nature of their beliefs. And the nature of their beliefs will constitute the nature of their personal truth. In other words, the Venus in Sagittarius person must have a guiding philosophy of life in order to have a core sense of meaning and purpose.

Within this pattern, these people are committed to their ongoing personal evolution and growth. The Sagittarius archetype is defined through the archetypes of fire, mutability, and yang. These archetypes in combination create an inner energy that is defined through perpetual expansion. As a result, the Venus in Sagittarius person is fundamentally restless, and is committed to the value of the personal freedom to pursue any experience they deem necessary in order to discover and actualize themselves. The need for freedom permeates these people, and they generally will not tolerate any condition or constraint that inhibits their independence or freedom. When such conditions or constraints exist, the Venus in Sagittarius person will progressively feel an inner alienation from those conditions or constraints, and the psychology or alienation becomes a causal factor or determinant in separating, at least inwardly, from those conditions or constraints.

Inwardly, the Venus in Sagittarius person feels and knows that they are connected to something that is much larger than themselves. In a phenomenological sense, it is as if they instinctively know that there is a manifested Creation, and that there must be a universal truth or inherent laws and principles that can explain the nature of the Creation that appears phenomenal. Thus, there is a simultaneous need to understand not only their personal truth, but how that personal truth is connected to the Ultimate Truth that is the basis of the manifested creation. Connecting their personal truth to belief systems of a philosophical or religious nature that correlate to Ultimate truth thus becomes the core value, meaning, and purpose for their lives. Inwardly resonating and relating to themselves in this way will condition how they relate to other people. This conditioning function serves as a vehicle that allows them to discriminate who they will relate to in general, and who their intimate others will be specifically. In addition, the need for personal freedom and self-discovery also serves to condition with whom they will relate to in every way: generally and intimately.

The Venus in Sagittarius person is firmly centered in the right-brain. As a result, they relate to themselves in non-linear, image-based terms that are defined as ever increasing concentric circles that attempt to embrace the totality of life itself. This will reflect itself as a deep thirst for knowledge and experiences of a diverse nature that will in turn allow for the Venus in Sagittarius person to discover the underlying principles, archetypes, or dynamics that can explain the causal factors in what appears as diverse and contradictory. As a result, these people are highly intuitive, and have an inherent wisdom that is free from the constraints of linear, left-brain logic of a deductive nature. The inherent knowledge, wisdom, and intuitiveness of these people is a reflection of their capacity of inductive logic—the ability to grasp the whole first, which allows for the individual parts of that whole to reveal themselves in their own natural order.

Because their inner space is defined by ever-increasing concentric circles that attempt to embrace the whole of life, these individuals have an inner vibrancy that is buoyant, light, free, and enthusiastic. There is an innate capacity to see the famous light at the end of the tunnel, an ability to see the light within the dark. There is an inherent focus on solutions versus being caught up in problems, and there is a natural humor that embraces the vision of the absurd because of this. The Venus in Sagittarius person values the nature and function of humor as a vehicle that can lead to healing in a variety of ways, and in all kinds of conditions. They have the ability to laugh at themselves, and they have the ability to make others laugh at themselves, especially when others or themselves are taking themselves too seriously. They are very natural and spontaneous people, fun loving, and naturally project sincerity and honesty. The projection of sincerity and honesty is a reflection of their own desire for personal truth.

One of the inherent problems that the Venus in Sagittarius person has is a *generalization* of truth. They feel that their personal truth, or the truth reflected in their philosophical or religious belief system, is the truth for all. Belief systems of any kind determine how any of us interpret and give meaning to any kind of experience. The Venus in Sagittarius person typically hears and evaluates other people through the prism or filter of their own personal truths and beliefs. This can create a situation in their relationships with others where they always seem to be, or have to be, right. And when they are challenged or disagreed with, they all too often will attempt to convince and convert others to the validity of their particular point of view, much as a preacher in a pulpit attempts to convince others to the righteousness of his or her convictions. Accordingly, there are times in their relatedness patterns with others that the Venus in Sagittarius person can seem to be very insensitive, to the point of being extremely blunt. This can have the effect of hurting others' feelings even though this is not the conscious intention of these individuals.

This way of relating to others is a reflection of how they are inwardly relating to themselves. Again, the Venus in Sagittarius person's deepest sense of inner meaning and purpose are dependent on the nature of beliefs that allow for a personal connection to a larger whole—the Cosmos or God. The way this connection is understood or constructed becomes the basis of their truth at any moment in time, and constitutes their sense of meaning and purpose as a result. To have this challenged or questioned by anyone but themselves is to simultaneously create a loss of meaning and purpose. Thus, there is a deep need to defend those beliefs and convert others to them in order for the Venus in Sagittarius person to sustain their sense of values, purpose, and meaning. This is one of the forms that the survival instinct takes when Venus is in Sagittarius.

Another common problem that they have is one wherein they can exaggerate whatever their perceived problems are, exaggerate or embellish the retelling of an experience that they have had, or exaggerate the descriptions of others who may have violated them in some way. This can even manifest as the fabrication of total lies. At worst, the Venus in Sagittarius actually believes in their own lies to the extent that the lies become their actual truth, so to speak. The causal or operative dynamic that can cause this effect is based on the Sagittarian archetype of perpetually needing to expand in ever-increasing concentric circles. In effect, it is the principle of expansion that can cause exaggeration leading to outright lies. Within this causal factor is a little-known fact about the Venus in Sagittarius person—that within themselves they can feel deeply inadequate. The inner experience of inadequacy is caused by the natural linkage of Sagittarius to Virgo, Pisces, and Gemini—the natural mutable grand cross. The specific connection to inadequacy occurs through Virgo and Pisces, and the dynamic of exaggerations, embellishments, or total lies becomes magnified through Gemini. Sagittarius correlates to the dynamic of compensation in all its senses and manifestations. In this case, the Venus in Sagittarius person can compensate for their sense of personal inadequacy (which occurs through the Venus function of comparing oneself to others) by the creation of exaggerations, embellishments, or total lies. And because the Venus in Sagittarius person is innately sincere, natural, convincing, and has a gift for storytelling, it can be very difficult for others to know just when they are not telling the actual truth.

In their intimate relationships, the Venus in Sagittarius person is forever needing and trying to balance their need for independence within the context of their relationship. Because these people have an almost absolute need for perpetual growth within themselves, they need and desire an intimate other who is also committed to personal growth. This will then allow for the dynamics within the relationship to be defined by a mutual commitment to growth. In effect, these individuals need to be in a relationship in which there is an ongoing sense of adventure. The Venus in Sagittarius person will simply experience a deep alienation from their partner when the relationship has degenerated into a stale, static routine. They need a partner who can mirror and reflect their own reality of intellectual and philosophical pondering, a partner with whom they can interact in this way at an equal level. The Venus in Sagittarius person needs this kind of intellectual or philosophical stimulation, and to be periodically challenged by their partner through such types of discussions. When this occurs, they will have a tremendous amount of respect for their partner, and will sustain their enthusiasm for the relationship. When this does not occur, then they lose their respect for the partner and become progressively alienated.

Because of their fundamental restlessness, the Venus in Sagittarius person innately desires physical movement and travel. This restlessness, again, is a reflection of their need to explore the diversity of life in order to understand the underlying principles or dynamics that are the basis for the diversity in the first place. Thus, they require a partner who will allow them to travel alone without feeling threatened, or a partner who will travel with them so that the sense of discovery and adventure can be mutual. The best scenario, however, is one wherein their partners will allow them to travel alone sometimes, and to travel with them at other times.

By nature, the Venus in Sagittarius person needs levity, humor, lightness, and optimism to pervade their intimate relationship. If they are with a partner who is constantly too serious or withdrawn, this will also become a casual factor creating a state of alienation and withdrawal from such a partner. They will naturally encourage the independent actualization and needs of their partners, and will develop a deepening respect for their partners who independently actualize their own life purposes. They will not respect a partner who just wants to hang on to them without developing their own identity or life purpose, or a partner who attempts to restrict their need for necessary freedom and independence. In addition, the Venus in Sagittarius person is naturally spontaneous and extremely adaptable to life conditions and changes, and who values and needs this same quality in their partner. They are very natural people who couldn't care less about carefully constructed social personas—in fact, they have a disdain for such people. Honesty and truthfulness are extremely important to them, and they naturally desire a partner who is honest and truthful in every way. When they feel right about their partner and their relationship, the Venus in Sagittarius person can be very giving, attentive, passionate, and truly make the partner feel really loved. They will let the partner know just how much they are appreciated, and can naturally make their partner feel really good about themselves. Conversely, when they are feeling alienated and removed from the partner, they can be tactless in pointing out the deeper truths of a not-so-nice nature, with the effect of making the partner feel worthless and devastated.

Sexually, the Venus in Sagittarius person is quite ardent, giving, spontaneous, and natural. They can be quite playful, and are naturally open to sexual adventures of all kinds because of their need for a diversity of life experiences. This is important for them because, again, if their sexual life degenerates into a predictable routine, then the seed of restlessness will bloom into attractions to others who offer and reflect their need for adventure and growth. By nature, the Venus in Sagittarius person is not monogamous because of their need for unrestricted growth. It is not that they are incapable of being monogamous, but in order for this to occur they need a partner who is willing to sexually grow with them, one who is open to sexual spontaneity, who is sexually versatile, and who does not preclude any way of being sexual. The Venus in Sagittarius person requires the diversity of sexual experience as yet another way of knowing themselves totally.

For evolution to proceed the Venus in Sagittarius person must embrace its polarity: Gemini. In essence, this means that they must learn that their particular point of view, their truth, and their beliefs are relative, and not the only or absolute truth. Thus, when they are relating to others they must learn how to hear them in such a way as to be able to understand the actual reality as it exists for the other, versus interpreting what they are hearing through the filter of their own beliefs. In this way they will learn that "truth" is not only relative, but they will learn to let other people be "right" from the point of view of their own convictions and beliefs. As a result, they will learn how to be Socratic in their relatedness patterns with others versus indulging the inherent tendency to "convince and convert." The underlying pattern of inadequacy will then change. This, in turn, will negate the temptation to exaggerate, embellish, or lie. In addition, by learning how to listen to others in such a way as to embrace another's reality as it exists for them, they will learn how to communicate to others from the point of view of that person's reality versus always communicating from the point of view of their own reality. As a result, others will respond to them in an entirely different way because they will now have the feeling of being listened to and understood. Once this occurs, others will feel more equal to the Venus in Sagittarius person, versus being made to feel inferior because of the unevolved Sagittarian need to always be right. Once the feeling of equity is established in this way, others will be much more open to the beliefs, opinions, and points of view of the Venus in Sagittarius person. In this way, the natural teaching ability of these individuals can be received and applied. And the Venus in Sagittarius person will realize that others may just have something to teach him or her too!

Venus in Capricorn

As a pre-existing pattern, the Venus in Capricorn person has learned to be very cautious and controlled in how they express themselves and relate to other people. This external relatedness pattern is a reflection of how they have learned to inwardly relate to themselves: the Venus in Capricorn person has very deep feelings and needs that take time to surface into their conscious awareness. Even when they do surface these individuals require time to make sure, and feel secure, that what they are feeling, or are needing, is correct. Even then, they can be very slow to relate, share, or communicate these feelings and/or needs to others because of a pre-existing fear of rejection and/or false judgment. This pre-existing fear has occurred because these individuals have experienced rejection and/or wrong judgment all too often early in their life, from one or both of their biological parents.

The nature of Capricorn, as an archetype, correlates to the phenomena of time and space, and how time and space are structured or organized. It correlates to the phenomena of finitude or mortality, and to the nature of how collectives of people organize themselves into structured groups or societies with consensus-formed, manmade laws, regulations, norms, taboos, and customs. This in turn creates social expectations of how people should integrate and conduct themselves within the group or society (the expectation to conform) which, in turn, becomes the basis of social judgments. And when the expectation to conform to what the consensus expects does not occur, this becomes the basis of guilt.

In addition, Capricorn correlates to the structure and nature of consciousness in human form, to the nature of structure in any form, and to the use of form. It also points to the need to change the nature of structural form when that form has become counterproductive to necessary change—that is, when it has served its use and become crystallized. In psychological terms, Capricorn correlates to the function of conscious reflection, which allows for a simultaneous awareness of the overall state of our beingness and what we need to change, inwardly and outwardly, in order to grow. Because of Capricorn's correlation to time and space, finitude, and mortality, it also correlates to psycho-logical/emotional maturation, aging, defining the focus of our life via goals and ambitions, and the self-determination that this requires. Negatively speaking, this can produce the psychology of futility, pessimism, fatalism, and self-defeat.

The Venus in Capricorn person has typically been born into family structures in which the parental reality has been defined by the consensus of the society in which they live. Consequently, the parental reality has typically had a heavy undertone in which the child has been expected to conform to the parental value system. When the child deviated from these expectations to conform, he or she was made to feel guilty in covert or overt ways through the use of judgment. A related dynamic within the general pattern of expectation to conform to parental values is one wherein the parents have projected on the child a rigid code of conduct that the child is expected to adhere to even when the parents themselves do not. The cliché "Do as I say, not as I do" applies here. This creates the very real perception in the child of hypocrisy and double standards. Within this, the very way in which the parents related to themselves has typically been very rigid, controlled, emotionally distant, and perfunctory. There is a lack of spontaneity, and a lack of any real demonstrations of affection or love between them. Quite the contrary: the parents are generally very controlled in their emotional interrelatedness with one another. The nature of their relationship is commonly defined by predictable routine and order which each parent expects the other to adhere to and maintain. There is also a mutual fear of being too vulnerable with one another, and their sexual life is either blocked or distorted in some way. All of this has served to "imprint" the overall psychology and emotional reality of the Venus in Capricorn child.

As a result of this, the Venus in Capricorn individual learned as a child to deeply compress and protect their feelings. They learned that their needs could not be acknowledged, supported, or nurtured by their parents. As a result, they learned to either conceal or suppress their needs. This process of learning to control their emotional demonstrations is a reflection of the survival instinct. It is based on the situation in which the parents expected the Venus in Capricorn child to act almost like miniature adults, to shoulder many duties and responsibilities—in short, to control or suppress the normal behavior of the child. This undermines and stifles the child's true nature and activities.

Because there has been no real emotional support or nurturing relative to their actual needs and desires, there is a deep wellspring of insecurity that is born out of this type of parental environment. Thus, the normal emotions and needs of the child have become buried deep into the subconscious of many individuals who have Venus in Capricorn. These emotions and needs become psychologically displaced and surface later on in their adult life. This is important to understand because whatever any of us suppress, for whatever reasons, becomes distorted. Thus, the emotions and needs of these individuals have typically become distorted as adults because of the psychological displacement caused when they were children.

One of the displaced emotions that can surface in a distorted way concerns the nature of authority. Because of the typically authoritarian nature of the parental environment, the Venus in Capricorn person has had their own inner sense of authority fractured, suppressed, or crushed. As an adult, this displaced emotion can manifest in a few different ways depending on the overall nature of the person in question, as seen in the totality of their birth chart. For some, their underlying insecurity will manifest as a very timid, shy, reserved, and fearful way of relating to other people in general. In their intimate relationships, this type will typically attract controlling, dominating, willful, judgmental, hypocritical, and authoritarian individuals who more or less expect the Venus in Capricorn person to be vicarious extensions of their own reality and to be dependent on them. This type of Venus in Capricorn person would have had almost no sense of being emotionally nurtured as a child. Thus, this additional displaced emotion now manifests as wanting to be taken care of by this type of partner: to be dependent in order to feel safe and secure.

For others, this will manifest in an almost opposite way. These types have so thoroughly imprinted the nature of the authoritarian parental environment that they become very intense, authoritarian types who perpetually need to assert and project their own sense of authority in order to feel secure. The underlying insecurity that haunts all Venus in Capricorn individuals becomes compensated for in this way. As a result, these types are instinctively fearful of losing their authority, and will do almost anything to sustain it. To them, the end justifies the means. They will typically feel afraid of anyone else who has legitimate authority, and will generally challenge, or in some way attempt to undermine, the authority of such people in order to sustain their own. The means most commonly used are contrived and harsh negative judgments and pronouncements, and power plays in which they attempt to block or thwart the goals and ambitions of others. This type, even if they have no actual authority, will attempt to associate with others that do. Their sense of authority is thus created through vicarious association. In their general-relatedness patterns with others they will appear stoic, controlled, project an authoritarian stance, and attempt to control others through the use of judgment in one way or another. An example of this point could be the person who was the co-author of a book, who continuously reminded the other author that it was important to keep their names in the public eye in one way or another—the implied judgment being that if they did not, then no one would give them any interest or attention. On an inner basis, this type is emotionally frozen and fearful of their vulnerability.

In their intimate relationships, these types attract one of two types of partners. One type will be just as oriented to outward success, appearances, and social ambition as they are. Their inner life will be just as emotionally frozen as well. They may relate well through the commonality of their external goals and ambitions, yet their inner emotional relatedness will be slim to none. The other type will be just the opposite: a very emotionally needy individual who is essentially looking for a *de-facto* parent to be in relationship to. This type will be very dependent, and essentially attempt to live through the Venus in Capricorn's identity and reality. They will have no real life of their own, and subconsciously feel safe in being dominated and controlled. When this type of Venus in Capricorn attracts that kind of partner, it is really a reflection of their own subconscious desire to lose control, to be cared for, and to be nurtured more or less like a baby. Of course, they would never admit to this even though it is true. This subconscious desire reflects yet another form of the displaced emotions of childhood that were conditioned by living in the antithesis of a warm, caring, and supportive emotional environment.

Within all Venus in Capricorn individuals lies a very deep and reflective consciousness. To others, this can create the appearance of a withdrawn, quiet, reserved, conservative, and serious person. One of the potential causes for this reflective, inward-looking focus is the fact that many Venus in Capricorn people are born with an unresolved grief, or a grief that has been created in their early life, which is also unresolved as adults. As a result of this, the Venus in Capricorn person can seem as if they are in a perpetual or cyclic state of mourning. Their hearts seem to be burdened and sad. There can be many causes of this condition. The typical causes are childhoods in which there was not real love, caring, or nurturing; adult relationships that were devoid of any real emotional interaction, love, or support; the witnessing and experiencing of political or religious upheavals in which many people were hurt or destroyed; and/or political or environmental conditions in which great plagues, famine, or physical destitution occurred.

Another typical cause can be a situation where the Venus in Capricorn person was, or is, in a relationship lacking in any real inner relatedness with the partner and which, in turn, created an attraction to another who could or would give them what they needed. Yet, because the Venus in Capricorn person is inherently oriented to honoring their commitments based on their sense of obligation, duty, and being responsible, the attraction to another has been typically suppressed and not acted on. Thus, this creates a deep inner suffering leading to a state of grief or mourning. The results of whatever the causes have been have produced a more or less traumatized heart, and an emotional structure that lies deeply buried within these individuals. In the Anton Chekhov play *The Seagull* there was a character that was always dressed in black. A person asked her why she always dressed this way. Her answer was "because I am in mourning for my life!" This character symbolizes the heavy heart of Venus in Capricorn people until they are unlocked.

This is a rather sad state of affairs because, in reality, the Venus in Capricorn individual is a highly emotional person. Deep within themselves they are intrinsically warm, caring, nurturing, and sensual. Yet because they have learned to protect themselves due to the fear of being vulnerable and wrongly judged, and because their emotional body is essentially traumatized due to the above causes, it requires a very special kind of person to help them unlock their emotional nature. This kind of person must be very patient and gentle in encouraging the Venus in Capricorn person to access their feelings and needs. They must be the type of person who can help them understand the basis of what constitutes their own inner judgmental patterns, and to help them be free of those patterns. Within this, this type of person must have a deep understanding of the nature of societal and parental imprinting, and how it has caused the Venus in Capricorn person to conceal and suppress their natural emotional needs. They must be able to teach these individuals that it is necessary for them to learn how to relate, express, and communicate themselves freely and openly—to ask for what they need. This is essential, because all too often the Venus in Capricorn person silently expects that their partner should just know what they need without asking. In this way they recycle their sense of disappointment linked with childhood—the inner child's disappointment in its parents' unwillingness to give to it what it needed.

All of this must be done through positive reinforcement and non-judgment. Over time, this approach will help the Venus in Capricorn person hear differently. Instead of hearing and being over-sensitive to judgmental, critical, and authoritarian words which reflect the nature of their childhood imprinting, they will now hear words of acceptance, empowerment, and encouragement. They will hear that they are good and loving people who do not need to feel guilty for who they are. They will accept encouragement to define their own unique values, and to structure their life accordingly. They will begin to examine the nature of their conditioning patterns, and, in so doing, to be as free from those patterns as possible. Above all, the Venus in Capricorn person needs another who will hold and touch them so that the early lack of nurturing in their early environment can be healed as an adult. In fact, the key to unlocking the Venus in Capricorn person occurs through touch. Once they feel a sense of safety in this way, the Venus in Capricorn person will naturally begin to open up in a very slow and methodical way.

Once the Venus in Capricorn person is unlocked, their natural warmth, depth, and loving natures will be revealed. Instead of seeming forever reserved, serious, sad, fearful, and strangely old even when young, the opposite will occur—the inner child that resides deeply within will be set free. Now they will seem almost childlike in their emotional expressions, playful, and enthused instead of being morose and depressive. Instead of being controlled in their emotional relatedness with another, they will now be free to express their love and feelings as they occur. They will discover that their feelings and needs are deep, and they will learn that it is all right to have these deep feelings and needs. When this occurs, they will begin to radiate a deep and earthy sensuality that is magnetic and attractive to many people. Instead of walking with closed shoulders, head bowed, and protective clothing, they will now walk upright, head held high, dressing as they please. In their intimate relationships they will become very giving, supportive, loyal, warm and highly sexual.

Once the inner child is set free in this way the Venus in Capricorn person will begin life anew, no matter what age they are when this finally happens. At this point they will find themselves reflecting on the nature of their past. In this reflection they will develop a deep self-knowledge which will allow them redefine not only themselves, but the very nature of what we all call reality. In this way, they will redefine their sense of purpose relative to their role or function within society. And once this is done they will set themselves in motion to actualize this sense of purpose because of the inherent self-determination that they are born with.

Sexually speaking, the Venus in Capricorn person is naturally monogamous. They will naturally value the power of commitment. Conditioning patterns notwithstanding, the Venus in Capricorn person is naturally a deeply sexual archetype. By nature, they need to be "warmed up" through holding, touching, and kissing before actual intercourse. They need the act of sexual intercourse to be long and sustained. The depth of the Venus in Capricorn person's feelings can be ignited through the length of the sexual act. Because of the inherent tendency to withhold or suppress their feelings, needs, and emotions, the Venus in Capricorn person also desires sexual intensity. The degree of intensity directly corresponds to the unlocking of their feelings, needs, and emotions. They require fidelity from their partners because of the pre-existing pattern that creates a fragile and negative self-image. If their partner sleeps with someone else, then this will only add to the feeling that there must be something wrong with them. They require sexual integrity, honesty, and respect. If a partner attempts to sexually subjugate them, or to degrade them for any reason, the Venus in Capricorn person will feel intensely contaminated, dirty, and guilty. This will only add to, and deepen, their negative self-judgment.

When the Venus in Capricorn person is unlocked they discover that their sexual nature and need is constant. There is not much of a need for sexual experimentation. Straight, hard sex is their main orientation. Many will have an attraction to the anal canal as a source of sexual stimulation because, symbolically speaking, the anal canal represents that which we suppress in ourselves. Thus, when this area is stimulated sexually the Venus in Capricorn person is actually unlocking that which has been suppressed within them. Many will also have an oral sexual orientation as well. This typically occurs because of a breakdown in the early bonding process between mother and child linked with nursing. This breakdown thus creates a form of emotional arrest or displacement that manifests in their adult lives as an oral sexual orientation. The sexual intensity that the Venus in Capricorn requires can also uncover one of the deepest fears that they have: the fear of losing control, yet desiring to do so. The Venus in Capricorn person thus affected must learn that this fear is actually linked with the fear of being too vulnerable. Consequently, the sensitive lover will encourage them to "lose control" because real freedom and growth for the Venus in Capricorn person lies in their accessing the core of their emotions: that which is most vulnerable.

For the Venus in Capricorn person who remains locked, their sexual nature can be frozen to the point of being frigid or impotent. A lesser form of this is when the sexual act is simply reduced to a sense of perfunctory duty and obligation: the "grin and bear it" approach for women, and the woman as simply a sexual object for the man. For many, this will simply translate into no sexual activity whatsoever. This condition or state of affairs occurs when there is an unconscious or conscious association of guilt linked with the natural sexual needs and desires of the body and Soul.

For evolution to proceed, Venus in Capricorn must embrace its polarity: Cancer. In the last several years, ever since Neptune and Uranus began their transit through the sign Capricorn relative to Pluto transiting Scorpio, there has been a tremendous focus in the world of psychology to uncover and heal the inner wounded child. The natural polarity to Capricorn is Cancer. Archetypally speaking, the two signs that most perfectly correlate to this focus are Capricorn and Cancer. Thus, the Venus in Capricorn person must embrace Cancer in the sense of reflecting deeply on the nature of his or her psychological imprinting created by the nature of the parental environment, and, through extension, by the nature of the society that the Venus in Capricorn person has been born into. In this reflection the intention must be focused on how this imprinting or conditioning has shaped and defined the Venus in Capricorn's self-image. In essence, the evolutionary intention reflected through Cancer is to totally re-create a new self-image that is free from the shackles, chains, and conformity reflected in the imprinting and conditioning of the parental and societal environment. In this way they will not only feel different about themselves, but they will learn to "hear" differently from within themselves. Now they will learn that what they are hearing about their needs, emotions, and feelings are messages that reflect their need to heal the negative self-image created in childhood.

In this reflection, the Venus in Capricorn person will discover that they have become "emotionally arrested" at some point in their early life. This means that their emotional development and maturation became blocked or stopped at some point when they were children. They are living the wounded child syndrome. Thus, to evolve, these people need to go backward in order to go forward (the Cardinal archetype). In order to create a new self-image, Venus in Capricorn people must take themselves back to the time in which this wounding or emotional arrest took place. Through reflection they will discover childhood memories that house the causal factors of their emotional arrest. By focusing on those memories, these individuals will determine how their self-image in general and their emotional dynamics specifically were shaped and defined. In essence, it is from this time forward that these individuals must learn to "decondition" themselves in order to re-create a new self-image.

Once this deconditioning begins the Venus in Capricorn person will allow the inner Cancer archetype to live and thrive. They will learn to allow their feelings, needs, and emotions to be unearthed and set free—to remove all guilt associations linked with the very essence of their beingness. They will learn to relate their emotions, feelings, and needs in a free and non-restricted way. They will lose their fear of rejection and false judgment. They will learn the security that they have been looking for lies deeply within themselves. They will discover self-empowerment in this way. They will learn who to trust, and who not to trust. Those that will accept them, and encourage them to be who they are, will become those that they trust. They will learn to create a new self-image that will allow them to integrate into society in a new way, based on values that are consistent with their intrinsic individuality. In this way, the inner child will heal and be set free to become an adult who is self-secure, healed, and unafraid to be who they are.

Venus in Aquarius

As a pre-existing pattern, Venus in Aquarius individuals are and have been rebelling against, or liberating themselves from, common value systems and relationship forms as defined by the consensus of the society they live in. The causal factor that generates this rebellion is an emphasized feeling within the psychology of Venus in Aquarius people of being different—a sense of cultural alienation or estrangement. As a result of this archetype, these individuals learn about the nature of their individuality, the feeling of being different, through a process of elimination—an awareness of what they are not that precedes an ongoing awareness of who and what they are.

A perfect example on a collective level that illustrates this archetype was in the 1960s when Uranus was in Libra (naturally Venus ruled). At that time there was a massive rebellion among young people against the prevailing consensus social value system and the ways that society expected intimate or marriage-type relationships to be defined—namely, as role specific. The rebellion at a collective level created the slogan "free love" in which many of the young people began to experiment (Uranus) with different forms of relationship specifically, and a radical reformation of social, political, and economic values generally. This radical rebellion among the young people over time began to be integrated among the prevailing status-quo of society in such a way that society itself began to change at a mainstream level.

Even though the archetypal intent of Venus in Aquarius is to rebel against the prevailing consensus of the existing society, there are three reactions to this intention as reflected in the people who have it in their birth chart. The first reaction is one wherein there is an absolute rebellion against everything that the consensus symbolizes. This reaction will correlate to individuals who feel totally disconnected not only from the existing society and their parents, but also a total disconnection from their prevailing peer group. As a result, these individuals will stand as a group of one if necessary rather than conform to any expectation from any source. The second reaction will correlate to individuals who are also rebelling against the prevailing consensus, yet will form relationships to other individuals within the existing peer group who also feel just as alienated as they do. In this way, they join forces with this group of people who now stand apart from the consensus as a group. This estranged group now has a collective impact on the prevailing society in such a way as to change it in one way or another. Beyond the example cited above, Uranus moving through Libra in the 1960s, the "punk rockers" of the 1980s illustrates this point. The third reaction is a paradoxical one (Uranus directly correlates with the dynamic of paradoxes). In this reaction, these individuals rebel against not only the prevailing consensus, but also against their own peer group. This rebellion takes the form of trying to resurrect value systems, and ways of being in relationship, that comes from some other time in the collective past. An example of this phenomenon, is the movement among some young people of rebellion against having sex with anyone until marriage.

The causal factor that generates the necessary rebellion or liberation from the prevailing consensus of social values and the expectations that these values create in general, and the ways of being in relationship specifically, is *detachment*. Archetypically speaking, the evolutionary intention within the sign Aquarius is to objectify, in a non-emotional way, the nature of reality at any level that one focuses on. In order to objectify anything, the ego within consciousness must separate itself from its own subjective reality. For this to happen, detachment becomes necessary. When consciousness is in a detached and objectified state from its own egocentric reality it is then able understand the overall nature and structure of any dynamic in its totality: how the nature and structure of any dynamic came to be the way it is, and what is necessary for it to grow or evolve. This archetypal function within consciousness is necessary. If it did not exist, growth would not be possible. A state of absolute crystallization would occur.

The three possible ways that the Venus in Aquarius individual can react to the archetypal intent of liberation or rebellion from the prevailing consensus of social values and expectations, and the ways of being in relationship, will determine specific value associations and the meaning they generate. The specific value associations will thus determine or create the vibrational magnetism of attraction (Venus) that correlates to the types of people that the Venus in Aquarius person attracts into their life. This is the principle of like attracting like which leads to social groups of people. For Venus in Aquarius to have a sense of meaning and purpose in their lives, it becomes necessary to form social relationships with people of like mind. The commonality of shared values that this creates sustains their own individual values. In many ways, then, the Venus in Aquarius person is dependent on the commonality of shared values within specific social groups of people to have any individual sense of purpose and meaning. To be able to inwardly relate to themselves as an individual, to have individual meaning, is to be part of a larger social group. It is from this larger social group of shared values, and the meaning that these values create, that the Venus in Aquarius person will choose whom to be in intimate relationships with.

The type of Venus in Aquarius person who is in absolute rebellion against the consensus, including their peer group, will not be able to relate (Venus) to any existing social grouping of people. They will only be able to relate to other people on an individual basis—other people who are as socially alienated and as iconoclastic as themselves. If they are able to relate to any kind of social group, it is to the extreme radical edge whose values are aimed at completely overthrowing the existing system, including the consensus of their immediate peer group. The vibration of rebellion is extremely intense in these people, and this vibration will permeate their entire way of being, how they dress, appear, think, and relate themselves to others. The intensity of this vibration will naturally create an insecure and defensive reaction in all other people who are not like themselves. This occurs because the vibration and values of rebellion naturally challenge the security of all others who are aligned with social groups of one kind or another, the security dynamic being linked with others of like mind. This reaction is analogous to a group of yuppies sitting around a cocktail party table becoming happily drunk and, from stage left, someone throws a tarantula onto the cocktail party table. This type of Venus in Aquarius person is the tarantula.

This type will typically appear arrogant, superior, righteous, angry, iconoclastic, and intellectual. They will express themselves through some kind of radical or revolutionary mental construction of one sort or another. They stand apart from all others and project, overtly or covertly, critical atom bombs at anyone or anything that supports identifying with "the system" at any level, in any way. The very sense of meaning and value that they give to themselves is dependent on, and linked with, this almost absolute detachment from the social system. They can form friendships or alliances with other individuals who reflect this same psychological orientation to social reality. These friendships or alliances typically occur on a sporadic, moment-to-moment basis. And from this small amount of like-minded people they can choose or form intimate connections that may be just as sporadic and short-lived as their overall pattern linked with others at a friendship or alliance level.

Such a person is intimately attracted to those that are radically different. The sense or experience of passion is linked with intimacy being ignited because of the fact of being different, which ignites the natural curiosity of Venus in Aquarius. Because Aquarius as an archetype desires to know how whole systems are structured and put together, the curiosity function thus creates a Venus desire to know how the individual system of someone whom they are intimately attracted to is put together in such a way as to make them different. Inwardly resonating together in their individual differences born of rebellion thus stimulates this type of Venus in Aquarius passion for individual intimate relationships. Once the curiosity function has been satisfied, the passion may dissipate almost overnight. Thus, this type of Venus in Aquarius person typically goes through various intimate relationships that can only be sustained for small lengths of time. This type desires a fundamental freedom to explore and experiment with life as she or he sees fit. There is a rebellion against the idea of commitment in a relationship, which leads to a rebellion against the values associated with monogamy.

The second type of Venus in Aquarius people mentioned above is not quite so absolutist and isolated. They will relate to their immediate social peer group who are rebelling against the existing society, and the prevailing social values and ways of being in relationship that are expected by that society. A simple example of this dynamic, again, is the "punk rockers" of the late 1980s. From mainstream society's point of view, these individuals will appear to be social misfits—irresponsible, narcissistic, immature, and the causal factor in what used to be called the "generation gap." The group itself will be perceived by society as hurling the atom bombs of criticism, and the group will have the effect of creating insecurity within the consensus because of the challenge to the existing social values of the times.

Those within this group will perceive society at large as irrelevant and without meaning. Detaching from mainstream society, and the values that it promotes, thus creates a psychological perch on which this type of Venus in Aquarius person can also appear self-righteous, arrogant, superior, iconoclastic, rebellious, alienated, and angry. Yet this type needs and desires to be part of the immediacy of the peer group who, as a social grouping, is rebelling against mainstream society. Their sense of meaning and purpose is dependent on belonging to this type of social group. Each individual within the group can represent the group as an individual, yet that "individual" is a function and reflection of the group. What this means is that the individual who appears to be so different as perceived from the point of view of the consensus would not even exist unless there was a social grouping of these "individuals" in the first place. This is because their individual "rebellion" is dependent on other people who are also rebelling. If not for their supportive peer group, this type of Venus in Aquarius person would not have the inner courage to stand as a group of one if necessary (unlike the first type described above).

This is a very critical point to understand—that so many who identify in this way with their immediate peer group do not embody or reflect the archetype of rebellion or liberation in the sense that it actually defines their Souls as individuals. It can and does reflect their Souls on an immediate social grouping level relative to their peers. This type of social group at a peer level has occurred throughout time in all social systems, and is always embodied in the youth of the generation. And necessarily so, because this social grouping has the effect of changing, in some way, the existing consensus. In this sense, it is an evolutionary determinant that is part of the overall Creation from an intrinsic or natural point of view, operating from generation to generation. Because the majority of these individuals are not defined at an individual Soul level through the desire of individual liberation or rebellion from the consensus, this social group becomes assimilated or absorbed into the mainstream as they become older. The social causes or issues that were reflected in their youthful rebellion also become assimilated by the consensus. Inevitably, some change in the consensus occurs because of it. Thus, as this group becomes older, they begin to rebel against their own rebellion!. Another Uranian paradox. A modern example of this point is reflected in the "hippies" of the 1960s and early 1970s who became "yuppies" in the 1980s. Only a small few in this original group sustained the original rebellion reflected in the hippies as a whole.

This point is important to grasp for another reason, one that concerns the nature of the friendships that we form, and the values we define that create how we are in our intimate relationships. All of us go through the initial rebellion of youth in one way or another; rebelling against our parents' reality, and through extension the larger society in which we are born. Uranus changes signs every eight years. Each sign that Uranus is in correlates to what, why, and how each generation of youth rebels. For those who have Venus in Aquarius, this peer group bonding is especially emphasized, important, and necessary.

This is because they have an essential evolutionary lesson that concerns the nature of friendship, and the need to define their own sense of meaning and purpose. Through extension, this correlates to the need to define their own unique way of being in an intimate relationship. Thus, as this type of Venus in Aquarius becomes older, and begins to assimilate into the existing social system, they effectively rebel against the very rebellion that motivated them in youth as an extension of their immediate peer group. The friendships that were formed through the shared values of youth now become rebelled against unless those friends also begin to assimilate into the existing society. And the ones that do not rebel against the initial rebellion will rebel against those who do. The lesson of friendship is thus learned through what can be called *situational values*. If the values (and the meaning associated with those values) are relatively the same, then friendships are formed. Once they change, for whatever reasons, the existing friendships can be lost or broken in some way. The real issue here, and the lesson, becomes this: a true friend will always be a friend no matter what, and everyone else is an acquaintance.

By experiencing the disillusionment of broken or lost friendships, and by rebelling against the initial rebellion of youth defined through peer group association, this type of Venus in Aquarius person is learning to define their own unique value system, which is a function of their individual sense of meaning and purpose in life. They will learn to define their intimate relationship requirements, their essential needs, as a reflection of their overall sense of purpose and meaning in life. At best, this will create a relationship dynamic in which both individuals reflect an attitude of uniquely defining the relationship as an extension of each of their individualities.

The third type of Venus in Aquarius person mentioned above is also very much a rebel, in the sense of rebelling against not only their own peer group, but all people who live a contemporary lifestyle. They identify with value systems associated with another time—the past. They will appear very conservative, traditional, and iconoclastic and, as a result of this, will only form social or intimate relationships with those of like mind. This type is dependent on forming these small social alliances in order to have any individual sense of meaning, value or purpose. Thus, they will form a relatively small sub-strata within their own generation, and even smaller within the existing society. They will also advocate social causes or revolution linked with challenging the existing value system of society at large. They can seem or appear just as superior, arrogant, judgmental, and angry as the other two types of Venus in Aquarius people. The value system that they orientate to is generally very limited and rigid, and their attitude is typically one of a righteous authoritarian who has the self-created right to impose those values on all others.

In their intimate relationships, the Venus in Aquarius person is generally a good friend above all else. Most have the intrinsic ability to understand objectively the reality and individuality of their partner—to understand how and why their partner is the way that they are. As a result, they typically understand what their partner needs for their life to keep growing and evolving. And most can give their partner what they need in this sense. They are good listeners, and can reflect back to their partner exactly what they are hearing as the partner intends it. Thus, they can be exceptional at keeping the conversation moving forward in an ever-evolving way that leads to sudden insights and resolutions. They can also be very adept at posing questions, and leaving it at a question level in such a way that the one receiving the question creates a gestation within their own consciousness leading to the answer from within themselves.

By nature, the Venus in Aquarius person is not monogamous. As stated before, they need a basic freedom in order to manifest their cyclic or perpetual changes. There is an inherent rebellion against restriction in any form. Restrictions imply conditions. In love, the Venus in Aquarius person rebels against conditions that will restrict love and its expression. It can be just as easy for these people to find deep, sudden, and intense love with someone overnight as with someone for a lifetime. Thus their attraction function (Venus) can occur suddenly and unexpectedly. Again, they are attracted to that which stirs their curiosity, to that which appears different and unique. Others who vibrate in this way will stimulate the Venus in Aquarius individuals. This can create real problems in their relationships if they are not honest about this, and if their partner cannot live in this way. The Venus in Aquarius person needs freedom to engage and create many different kinds of social networks with different kinds of people.

Because of this, the Venus in Aquarius person needs a partner who is very secure within themselves. They require a partner who is willing to challenge the existing consensus of what life means in general, and how to be in relationships specifically. They need a partner who is willing to cyclically change the dynamics in the relationship, or to change as necessary. They require a partner who is intellectually sophisticated, and who can match or keep up with their own thinking process. This thinking process is typically eclectic in some way, and fast-moving. It can be very difficult for the Venus in Aquarius person to truly love or respect another if they do not intellectually respect them. There simply is a fundamental need to experiment with different values and ways of looking at life because, again, the Venus in Aquarius person learns about who they essentially are by becoming aware of what they are not. And they need a partner who can experiment with them in this way.

The Venus in Aquarius person has a deep, inner detachment from within themselves. This detachment primarily manifests on a feeling or emotional level. The evolutionary intention in this is to objectify their feelings, needs, and emotions in order to be aware of their causes. This leads to self-knowledge. In evolutionary terms, this symbol will always occur as a reaction to lifetimes in which the individual was lost to their emotions, feelings, and needs. This inner detachment can create the appearance within these people of not being totally integrated. This is an appearance only. For Aquarius, integration occurs through the vehicle of detachment. For those in intimate relationship to the Venus in Aquarius person, this detachment can be very frustrating when they do not understand its function or intention. In the middle of the deepest emotional crisis or turmoil the Venus in Aquarius person seems aloof and unmoved, somehow calm in the middle of the storm. Or when the partner now is pouring out his or her emotional guts to the Venus in Aquarius person they are met with nothing but cool, calm, detached, and objective feedback. Yet this is the function of Venus in Aquarius.

Of course, other chart factors can condition this. For instance, the Venus in Aquarius person can also have Mars conjunct Neptune in Libra in the Eighth House, which would create the opposite effect. In such a case, an absolute emotional/psychological empathy would result, mirroring the other person's emotional state. But the function of Venus in Aquarius is to learn how to objectify through detachment, so after the immediacy of the moment of this way of relating had passed, the Venus in Aquarius function would instinctively attempt to objectify what all the emotional/psychological dynamics were about, and the reasons for them.

The Venus in Aquarius person can also be very erratic and unpredictable in their life directions, the realities that their ever-shifting needs create, in their feeling and emotional states, and in their extreme cycles of communicating/not communicating. They can be just as unpredictable in their reactions to people, with sudden and unexpected behaviors that reflect these reactions. In these situations, the words that come from their mouths may be quite unexpected and upsetting. Again, this kind of unpredictability can be very difficult for others to understand, let alone tolerate and accept. Because of this, the Venus in Aquarius person is very quick on their feet, and can adapt to changing life conditions or social situations quite adeptly.

Sexually speaking, the Venus in Aquarius person will reflect the sexual values that are reflected in their immediate peer group—a group, again, that is rebelling against the existing sexual values of the consensus society that they are born into. Simply stated, if the existing consensus advocates free sex or non-monogamy, then this group as youth will rebel against this and promote monogamy. Conversely, if the existing consensus advocates monogamy, then this group as youth will rebel against this, and promote non-monogamy. The causal factor is simply the evolutionary determinant to rebel in order to effect necessary change within the existing consensus.

On the other hand, the Venus in Aquarius person is inherently defined by the need to experiment. Thus, many will engage in sexual experiments in order to discover who they naturally are through the process of elimination. Others will continue to sexually experiment simply because they find this exciting, based on the fact that what they are doing is "different." A few will experiment with sexual ways of being that can be quite bizarre if bizarre is understood from the point of view of what is considered as "normal." An example of this was a client of mine who claimed that she was having sexual intercourse with a disembodied spirit who was a prior life lover. For others, Venus in Aquarius can promote an asexual response to the sexual impulse that exists in all human beings. This is the type who is totally living in a mental reality devoid of, or detached from, their emotional dynamics. Physical or sexual living is considered by these types as somehow degenerative to their overall sense of purpose and meaning.

Most of these individuals have an observational awareness during the sexual act. It is as if they are watching themselves and their partners during the sexual act. This observational quality linked with detachment can create a deep knowledge of how sexual energy can be used, directed, or manipulated. On the one hand this can produce very adept sexual lovers who are extremely aware of everything that is going on in their partner. They know how to harmonize themselves with the feelings and sensations that are occurring within their partner. In this way they know how to keep those feelings and sensations moving ever-forward, which can lead to incredibly deep sexual responses. Some who have this capacity can actually help another become more sexually alive, free, and open. And a few who realize that they have this capacity will then use it as a form of power to create a dependency in their partner. A few of my clients who were oriented in this way could actually take another who was sexually frozen and turn them into sex machines, so to speak. On the other hand, this can create a deep frustration because the Venus in Aquarius can never really seem to fully engage in the sexual act. They are always observing. This frustration can then lead them into experimenting with different and more intense ways of being sexual so that a total engagement can take place. Yet, because of the very nature of Aquarius, this will never really happen even in the midst of the most intense sexual situation.

The sexual rhythm, the sexual need cycle of Venus in Aquarius people also is unpredictable. Within the archetype this runs the full range from no sex at all, to infrequent need, to moderate need, to average need, to total, constant need. The only time it is predictable is when certain types with Venus in Aquarius need it all the time! As stated before, the Venus in Aquarius person is inherently non-monogamous. This applies sexually as well. Sure, anyone can learn to be monogamous, including this type. For this type to be monogamous, though, they must have a partner that perfectly reflects their own sexual desires, and the reality that these desires create. And then be prepared for those desires to change! A simple curiosity with someone who appears different or unique can stimulate their sexual desire. This can be difficult for an existing partner because most of us want to be the sole focus of our lover's attention.

For evolution to proceed, the Venus in Aquarius person must embrace its opposite: Leo. The essence of this evolutionary lesson is for Venus in Aquarius people to learn how to separate themselves from the immediacy of their peer group in order to actualize their own unique and specific value systems. They need values, and the meaning that these values reflect, that are consistent with their own individuality. The intention within this is to creatively actualize their own unique sense of individual purpose within the larger social group, their generation, and, through extension, within society as a whole.

In order to do this, the Venus in Aquarius person must learn to use their intrinsic capacity for detachment to stand apart from their immediate peer group. By detaching in this way they can then intellectually objectify why the immediacy of their peer group is defined through the types of value associations that it is—namely, the evolutionary need to rebel against the preceding generation and the existing consensus. Within this detachment they can realize that any peer group automatically creates a psychological pressure to conform to its values, and the ways of being that those values dictate. Understanding this, the Venus in Aquarius person can then learn to objectify him or herself in such a way to question whether or not the values advocated through the peer group are truly consistent with its own individual reality. If they are not, then the challenge for the Venus in Aquarius person is to separate from this peer group in order to discover, through separation, just exactly what their own specific individuality is. In this way they will formulate their value systems, and creatively actualize a life that is consistent with those values. And, in this way, they will become more perfectly aligned and centered within their own individual reality.

Venus in Pisces

As a pre-existing pattern, the Venus in Pisces person has been learning to embrace, on an archetypal level, a transcendent value system in order to create a sense of ultimate meaning in their life. The evolutionary process leading to this need has been a series of lifetimes in which the individual has experienced a tremendous amount of personal and social disillusionment. This has created a sense of total meaninglessness associated with temporal values. Many individuals with Venus in Pisces have not consciously conceptualized or realized the archetypal intent, which is to embrace a transcendent, spiritual value system. This is important to understand because until they do, they will not have a clear and solid sense of who they are, and the experience of disillusionment will continue to occur.

For these individuals, the inner world is more or less like a giant movie in which a diversity of images, plots, scenarios, and possible realities swirl around in different combinations. Within this inner world the Venus in Pisces person instinctively imagines him or herself in these different roles, like an actor who assumes the identity of a specific character. By imagining and "trying on" these different images and identities, like different parts in a movie, the Venus in Pisces person tries to relate to the ones that *feel* most like him or herself. An additional cause that creates this need is rooted in a deep inner feeling of impurity, and the guilt that this implies. The guilt ignites an instinctual reaction of denial at an unconscious level. Thus, the individual will have a nebulous negative feeling about him or herself. These feelings are then compensated for through the Piscean imagination—by creating false identities linked with the movie-like nature of their inner world. This creates the psychological dynamic of "illusion as reality."

These inner dynamics are very problematic because the Venus in Pisces person knows at a core level that these different images and identities are not who they really are. Nevertheless, they will try to make them real, to convince themselves that they are real, by acting them out through external manifestation, just like an actor in a play or movie. They will manifest the appropriate clothes, hairstyles, home environment, types of possessions, and other factors that are symbolic of whatever the imagined identity is. Many individuals with Venus in Pisces actually succeed in convincing themselves that the artifact they have created is real. By externally manifesting the persona and the circumstances that reflect the inner imagination, it now seems tangible. They can point their finger to it and convince themselves and others because it obviously appears to exist.

A variation of this dynamic correlates to Venus in Pisces individuals who feel so inferior and weak, so without any personal power, so victimized by life itself, that they allow themselves to become vicarious extensions of someone else's reality. These people relate to themselves through the value systems, and the meaning that those values denote, of someone else. The Taurus side of Venus requires a personal effort to actualize and realize one's inherent values and resources of oneself. Venus in Pisces people can find it very difficult to make such an effort because they have no clear sense of themselves or of their inherent values and resources. Thus, the reverse of necessary effort occurs—laziness and a lack of any personal effort to define values that are consistent with who they intrinsically are. The old cliché "go with the flow" becomes the guiding motivation of these types of such people, and they go with the flow of someone else's reality because it can be easy to do. They do not have to take personal responsibility for themselves because they are essentially allowing themselves to be taken care of by someone else who is defining their reality for them.

In both cases, the Venus in Pisces person feels that they are either being punished for some undefined reason, or that they need to punish themselves for being something less than "pure." Punishment implies guilt with the consequent need to atone for the guilt, or to be angry because of the guilt. Some with Venus in Pisces will totally embody the atonement/guilt dynamic leading to the pathology of masochism. Some will totally embody the anger/guilt dynamic leading to the pathology of sadism. And some will embody both dynamics leading to the simultaneous pathology of sadomasochism. Such people will flip-flop between guilt and anger depending on whether the nature of the immediate circumstances is passive or aggressive.

The causal factor of these pathologies is rooted in the fact that the Venus in Pisces person has had at least one prior lifetime in which there has been a deep immersion into the religious conditioning of Judaic or Christian philosophies. As a result, there has been an acceptance within their consciousness that life on Earth requires suffering as a requirement to enter the "Kingdom of God." They have accepted that God is perfect, and everything else in the Creation is less than perfect. They have accepted the doctrine of original sin that presupposes that the Soul separated itself from God. They have accepted the doctrine that flesh and spirit are mutually antagonistic unless limited to the pro-creational act. They have accepted that one must submit to God's will, that God is an anthropological male who is superior to women, and that, through extension, men are superior to women.

The acceptance of these doctrines at some prior point in time has come to constitute an inner standard of judgment, which becomes the causal factor in a psychological pathology of sadism or masochism that is acted out in various ways and degrees of intensity. Some who have Venus in Pisces will continue to accept such religious doctrines because, again, they lack a clear image of who they actually are, and therefore cannot define a truly personal set of beliefs. Since the archetypal intent of Venus in Pisces is to embrace a transcendent value system, it thus becomes easy to "adopt" values and a belief system of a religious nature. This is yet another role to act out, in which they create a persona that reflects the essence of the religious doctrine in some way. The person in this role becomes very moralistic, constricted, and harshly judgmental of everyone else who is not in conformity to these doctrines. This orientation will ultimately lead to a state of absolute disillusionment and a state of inner emptiness, because these types of doctrines do not reflect the inherent truth of God.

For others who have Venus in Pisces, the opposite reaction to these doctrines will be manifested. These individuals will have rejected and rebelled against the doctrines at some point, and in this rebellion, triggered by anger over the nature of the doctrines, they would assume identities of an almost absolutely hedonistic way of living. Under this dynamic, the life of the Venus in Pisces person seems to be almost totally devoid of anything of a spiritual nature. The flesh and senses become glorified in one way or another, and/or values associated with materialism replace the values of spirituality. Some who react in this way may reflect a perfunctory acknowledgment of spirituality without actually living a life that is defined by spiritual or transcendent principles. This reaction will also lead to a state of disillusionment because of the ultimate emptiness that hedonistic and materialistic living eventually lead to.

Most people with Venus in Pisces create a synthesis or composite of these two extremes. On the one hand, they experience a vague feeling or acknowledgment of spiritual values that go more or less un-manifested. On the other hand, they create and attempt to manifest images of themselves that are based on the worldly values of the society they are born into. This dynamic can create the psychology in which these types feel that nothing is real, and the more real they try to make something the less real it becomes—even when there is "evidence" to support that reality. This reaction will also lead to progressive disillusionment, because the ultimate sense of meaning that the Venus in Pisces archetype requires cannot be found in this way.

The causal factor in the psychological experience of disillusionment in all of these reactions to the Venus in Pisces archetype is rooted in one simple truth: Until there is a conscious actualization of transcendent values and belief structures that reflect the ultimate meaning of life—the Natural and Inherent Truths of the Creation that exist of them-selves—the experience of disillusionment will continue. When realized and acted on, these values will constitute the core meaning for the Venus in Pisces person's inner and outer reality, and of how they inwardly and outwardly relate to themselves and others. Life will still seem like a movie, but this movie will be the movie of God, not the movies that are created by a disillusioned ego who attempts to find the meaning for its life in worldly forms that contain no essence.

The realization of God's movie will start with the realization that the idea of perfection is an illusion, since the only perfection possible is based on a Creation that remains un-manifested and unformed. It is only when that which is unformed and un-manifested has been manifested into the totality of all forms through a projected act of Creation by God that the idea of perfection occurs within consciousness. Once this is realized, manmade laws and man-made religions will give way to Natural law, allowing for an understanding that what we call God in simultaneously perfect and imperfect. The interaction of perfection and imperfection reflects the interaction of the un-manifested and the manifested. This simple truth is the causal factor in involution and evolution. In this way compassion, love, acceptance, and forgiveness of our imperfections will replace critical, harsh, and abusive judgments issued from manmade religious doctrines that attempt to artificially subjugate and control the natural spirit in the human being.

For those Venus in Pisces individuals who have committed themselves to spiritual values, and the lifestyle that those values correlate to, illusion considered as reality will relatively not exist. It will only continue to exist until an understanding of the Natural Laws that are inherent to the Manifested Creation are understood. For these people, the journey to that understanding is already under way. It is just a matter of time. Where they are in that journey will directly correlate to how they relate to themselves inwardly, and thus how they relate to others. This will run the full range from rabid fundamentalists who see their religion as the only true religion to the truly enlightened Soul who realizes that God has created many paths to the same goal. To arrive at this state of awareness, it is necessary at key points in the spiritual journey to achieve the dissolution of any "religious" or "spiritual" thought forms that do not allow for that realization and/or awareness. A perfect example of this point is found in the life of Edgar Cayce (who had Venus in Pisces). As a young man, he more or less reflected rigid Christian beliefs that included no doctrine of reincarnation—life was just once around. Yet in his Piscean trances and dreams he became aware of the existence of many of his own past lifetimes, as well as the prior lifetimes of many others, many of which could actually be documented in various ways. Thus, his trances and dreams had an effect of dissolving his belief and value structures, as defined in rigid Christian doctrine. Accordingly, he evolved further down the transcendental road leading to awareness and realization of the Ultimate Truth of Natural Laws that predate the human species.

Because of the transcendent impulse reflected in the Venus in Pisces archetype, all these individuals will be inherently idealistic. They will have ideals for themselves, and they will have ideals for how everything should be. The problem here is not the dynamic of ideals. The problem is with the expectations that are simultaneously linked with those ideals. Disillusionment occurs to many of the Venus in Pisces people because the expectations linked with the ideals are unrealized, defective, or not actualized in some way. Ideals also imply judgment when the perfection of the ideal is not realized. In essence, the Venus in Pisces person commonly has value systems, and the meaning associated with those values, that are rooted in all kinds of "should be's." This dynamic becomes the basis of all kinds in inner and outer judgments that these individuals pronounce on themselves and other people. All too often, these individuals subject themselves to various degrees of frustration and defeatism. They also cause frustrations for the people who are subjected to their unrealistic expectations. The lesson to be realized by the Venus in Pisces person is that the value is in the effort, and not necessarily in the outcome. They also need to realize that most people are doing the best that they can based on what they have to work with. Here again, compassion must replace unnecessary judgment.

All Venus in Pisces people are ultra-sensitive. They feel life in excruciating and exquisite ways. They are naturally emotionally empathetic to everyone and everything. Their psychic structures feel, and unconsciously osmose, the immediate and overall realities around them. As a result, they unconsciously duplicate the realities of those immediate to them, and the realities reflected in the collective consciousness. This, of course, can overwhelm the Venus in Pisces person who is not rooted in spiritual reality. It becomes its own causal factor in feeling confused, disoriented, feeling afraid for no reason, the inner sense of "losing it" or going crazy, or sudden uprisings of inexplicable emotional states. These effects are based in the transcendental intention of Venus in Pisces. It demands a progressive dissolving of anything that prevents direct connection to, and realization of, the Ultimate Truth. Since most individuals who have Venus in Pisces do not understand this dynamic, this situation causes the survival instinct intrinsic to Venus to manifest as a desire to almost totally shut down and withdraw from the external circumstances of their lives. This occurs cyclically, and helps them to re-stabilize themselves.

In their intimate relationships, the Venus in Pisces person is a naturally giving individual. They will always try to support their partner in whatever ways are required. They are good listeners who can identify with whatever the partner is saying. As a result, the partner feels as if they have been heard. They are highly sensitive and vulnerable people who reflect a natural kind of innocence and naiveté. They are in love with the idea of love, and, as a result, are highly romantic. Their romantic, dreamy nature lends itself to a high degree of imagination or fantasy that can become very creative. This creativity can manifest as creative problem solving, poetical abilities linked with metaphor and allegory, food preparation, colorful and decorative homes, musical ability, writing, a natural psychic capacity that just "tunes in" without knowing how or why, the way that they dress, etc.

Conversely, the intimate relationships that they form rarely if ever correlate to the "ideal" partner that they consciously and unconsciously desire. As a result, many will "settle for less" because it is the best that they think they can do. This dynamic becomes a causal factor in cycles of depression and meaninglessness, generating all kinds of escapist scenarios. At worst, this causes the Venus in Pisces person to become involved in all kinds of addictive and compulsive behavior. These activities can include indulgence in drugs and alcohol, constant and compulsive reading of books, excessive movie-going, compulsive clothes buying, eating disorders of one sort or another, compulsive sex, or the development of all kinds of phobias or various mental disorders. As an example, I had a client with Venus in Pisces who was married to a Protestant minister. She appeared to believe in the life of what a Protestant minister's wife "should be," yet secretly advertised herself as a "call girl" who would make house calls, so to speak.

For a relationship to be really positive and healthy, the Venus in Pisces person needs a partner who realizes that they are much, much more than what their constructed persona suggests, even if this is a spiritual persona. It is all too easy for the Venus in Pisces person to hide behind this carefully constructed persona because of the fear of being vulnerable, and because of their fear that no one who saw who they "really were" would want to love them. Yet for the Venus in Pisces person to attract such a partner, they must first accept who they are without unnecessary and artificial judgments that emanate from manmade moralities of a religious nature. Once this occurs, they can attract a partner who will embrace their totality and love them for who they are. Once the Venus in Pisces person realizes that they are being loved for who they are, they will let down their instinctual walls of self-protection. Their persona will collapse, and their hypersensitive natures can be freely expressed. The natural innocence that they embody will manifest in a childlike way. They will learn to receive and accept the love that they so desperately need. They will be loved for who they really are versus being related to, and only understood, through the persona that they create. In this way the shackles of a self-created frustration based in the feeling that no one knows who they are, or what they need, will be removed.

Sexually speaking, the Venus in Pisces person can run the gamut from sex only as a procreational act to a sex life in which they act out sexual scenes created in their imaginations. They can range from an absolute fear of feeling anything that their body creates via the senses to absolute immersion into the senses. Most Venus in Pisces people have a natural shyness about their bodies, at least when they are naked. By nature they are sexual givers who enjoy giving pleasure to their partners. As a result, they also must learn how to receive. Archetypally speaking, the Venus in Pisces person requires a very gentle approach to love-making. Touch, foreplay, romantic atmospheres, some wine or a few tokes of marijuana, music and candles set the stage for the Venus in Pisces person to become totally engaged. Sexual role playing and sexual fantasies of one kind or another become natural and psychologically healthy activities for the Venus in Pisces person when they have a feeling that their partner is honest, sincere, and without ulterior agendas or motives. Archetypally, the sexual act is "sacred" to the Venus in Pisces person—it is pure and clean in its natural state. For some, this will translate into employing sexual/spiritual doctrines and methods that have the intention of uniting with the divinity of their partner, and the ultimate divinity together.

For evolution to proceed, the Venus in Pisces person must embrace its opposite: Virgo. This means to create a highly introspective focus of self-analysis that will allow them to objectively discriminate between reality and illusion. In so doing they will be able to discern the actual condition and state of their inner beingness as it is. The intention in this polarity is to align the individual with their actual reality versus the illusions, delusions, and images that the Venus in Pisces individual creates and considers to be real because they exist in actual form. This is a very difficult intention to consciously grasp and work with, because it inevitably leads to great psychological pain. Disillusionment is one of the most difficult of all human experiences, and will always lead to anger in one way or another. Yet anger, which is an instinctual emotion, can be used in a positive way to motivate these individuals to always put the light of conscious awareness into their inner world so that images born of illusion no longer define their reality. In order to do this, it is necessary for the Venus in Pisces person to align themselves with some spiritual system that involves meditation in one form or another. Physical practices such as yoga, the "spiritual running" approach advocated by Sri Chinmoy, Tai Chi and so on are also excellent ways to accomplish this intention. Dream journaling, writing diaries, conversations with trusted friends who are natural psychologists that can help them understand their emotional/ psychological make-up, and a well-grounded type of work are all beneficial to actualizing this intention.

Now that we have completed our examination of the general themes that Venus correlates to in terms of our inner and outer relatedness patterns, and how these patterns attract the reflection of our own inner reality, I would like to say again that these are general themes that are not conditioned by any other factor, astrologically speaking. Every archetype in the birth chart, a planet in a sign for example, is conditioned by other planetary archetypes. These conditioning factors include aspects from other planets, the specific houses that the planet in question is in, and so on. It is imperative that the astrologer be able to integrate, synthesize, and interpolate all the conditioning factors in the birth chart to be truly competent and of positive service to another individual.

CHAPTER FOURTEEN

THE TRANSIT OF NEPTUNE

The bottom line in this transit is the ongoing evolutionary nature of the totality of all consciousness on Earth, and how this comes into the individual consciousness of the Soul. Each individual within the totality is affected in their own unique way relative to their total evolutionary conditions and, at the same time, experiencing what all other humans are experiencing in the world: the individual country where they live, and the specific groups of people in that country: whether it is Iraq, Rwanda, Ukraine, Samoa Island, etc.

All of these individual consciousnesses all add up to and correlate with the total amount of humans which creates the collective consciousness so that each individual Soul's consciousness is then simultaneously evolving at every moment in time as a REACTION to the collective consciousness! In turn, each individual Soul consciousness that is evolving according to its own evolutionary condition then affects the collective at any moment in time that then correlates to the evolutionary nature of the human race itself.

All of the archetypes that we have talked about that correlate with Neptune, Pisces, and the 12th House are occurring and interacting at every moment in time for each individual as well as the totality of all humans: the collective consciousness. The planetary rulers of the North and South Nodes of Neptune, Uranus and the Sun, correlate to additional archetypes that, in total, correlates to individual and collective dynamics that SERVE TO DEFINE THE NATURE OF EACH MOMENT THAT THE INDIVIDUAL AND THE COLLECTIVE IS CREATING AND EXPERIENCING.

As you, at this very moment, are reading these words, you are experiencing the 'world' around you as it is: all the events going on in the world, your country, your region, your city, your group or tribe of like-minded Souls, and your own individual Soul reality within all of this.

THIS IS YOUR LIVING EXPERIENCE OF NEPTUNE! THIS IS NEPTUNE'S CONSCIOUSNESS. RIGHT NOW, AND IN EVERY OTHER MOMENT IN TIME. THIS IS THE NATURAL TRIAD OF CONSCIOUSNESS SYMBOLIZED BY THE MOON, YOUR EGO; PLUTO, YOUR SOUL; AND NEPTUNE ITSELF: YOUR INDIVIDUALIZED CONSCIOUSNESS RELATIVE TO THE COLLECTIVE CONSCIOUSNESS OF ALL HUMANS.

With the transit of Neptune in Pisces the core issues for each individual, and thus the collective, correlate to that which is true, and that which is fiction where fiction is a function of projected beliefs that are only 'real' because they are 'believed' in. Remember the projection that occurs relative to Neptune manifests from its South Node being in Aquarius. Aquarius correlates with projection just as the Source Of All Things, Neptune, projected the manifest Creation in the first place. Thus, the individualized consciousness of each Soul as well as the collective of other Souls manifesting as groups of people of like-mind, whole races of humans, countries, regions within countries, all project beliefs that define the nature of individual and collective consciousness relative to the specific nature of whatever the beliefs are.

Pisces, the 12th House, and Neptune are part of the Mutable Cross that exists within it:

- Gemini, Mercury, and the 3rd House
- Virgo, Mercury, and the 6th House
- Sagittarius, Jupiter, and the 9th House
- Pisces, Neptune, and the 12th House

From the very beginning of time for the human species, the consciousness within it was aware, of course, of the massive sky at night that contains the whole of the universe with all the various stars and constellations within it. This natural awareness was coupled with the desire to understand the MEANING of this PROJECTED CREATION and the NATURAL LAWS that governed it. This then became the basis or cause of how human consciousness created natural knowledge of the phenomenal creation that it was part of, of how it thought, of how what it thought was communicated, of how progressive knowledge was analyzed and adjusted over time, and how all of this constituted what human consciousness was about. In essence, this was about acquiring KNOWLEDGE, natural knowledge, of the overall environment that contributed to the increasing understanding within the human being of what LIFE was and was not, and now natural knowledge was necessary in order for the survival of life to be sustained.

There were no beliefs of a cosmological nature at all until around 7,000 B.C.E. This is when the human organism began a shift from nomadic ways of living into a progressive stationary way of living that started with the learning of agriculture, and raising animals. This is when human beings began to PROJECT what the CAUSE OF LIFE was/is. This progressive projection manifested as cosmologies full of various 'gods' and 'goddesses' that governed various aspects or dimensions of human reality. Natural knowledge, natural laws, began to become displaced by BELIEFS. The 'spirits' within all of Nature were now made into divine deities.

As this progressed in time, these projections of 'divine' cosmologies among and within the consciousness of human begins in one group, area, territories, and races began to conflict with each other. This is when 'religious' wars began where religion became the first determinant of how the Neptunian consciousness of the Soul, Pluto, within it was conditioned by the very nature of the projected beliefs.

As a result, individuals and whole groups of humans everywhere can create a 'reality' that is defined by these projected beliefs whether those beliefs are actually true or not. Each individual can be influenced by the collective group consciousness in the form of behavioral contagion because, in the end, the human species is innately social in nature: like cows. Behavioral contagion specifically correlates with Aquarius, Uranus, and the 11th House.

The very nature of beliefs, whatever they are, conditions every other archetype within the totality of the consciousness of the Soul. Thus, beliefs condition what the Soul values and has meaning, of how it relates to other people, of how they form relationships to other individuals, Venus. Beliefs condition how the consciousness of the Soul thinks about life, of how it communicate what it thinks, of how it empirically puts together an intellectual framework that itself is a function of how life is 'interpreted': Mercury and Jupiter in combination. Beliefs condition what social groupings of people we form bonds and relationships with, Uranus, and conditions the very way we actualize and give purpose to our lives: Sun. Beliefs condition how humans understand the very nature of their own Souls. And so on.

When beliefs are then linked to various cosmologies, religions, they are then given the authority of GOD. Thus, when one group of people, or whole countries, have beliefs in God that differ from other beliefs in God, what God is and is not, what ethics and moralities that follow this, we then have conflicts between peoples, groups, and whole countries in which each feels threatened by the definitions of God that are different than their own.

Such conflicts create polarization between peoples, groups, and countries in which each feels that their definition and understanding of God is, of course, the RIGHT ONE. Thus, each person, group, or country then considers all others who do not agree in their definition of God to somehow be inferior, that they are 'godless,' that something is wrong with them.

All too often this then leads to conflicts and wars, terrorism, in which one person's, group, or country's God goes to war with another person's, group, or country's God. Insanely, this creates a situation where God is warring or fighting with itself as reflected in these differing definitions of God that are held by each person, group, or country. As a result, sadly, patriarchal history is full of religious wars that are fought on an endless basis in which many humans are crushed or destroyed in some way because of one group, person, or country needing to dominate another in order to feel that, in the end, their God has been the RIGHT GOD all along.

So we end up with unspeakable atrocities committed by human beings IN THE NAME OF GOD WHERE GOD IS USED AS A WEAPON to dominate and suppress any other person, group, or country whose definition of God differs from others. Genocides are created in this very way, and for this reason the most extreme forms of insanity, in the extreme OF THESE DELUSIONS.

So we can end up with a whole busload of people blown to smithereens, the detached arm of a little girl still holding her stuffy, the fingers still twitching, IN THE NAME OF GOD. We can end up with hundreds of girls being kidnapped from a school by a group who then proceeds to rape them all IN THE NAME OF GOD. We can end up with hijacked airplanes being flown into skyscrapers in which beyond the destruction of the buildings thousands die IN THE NAME OF GOD. We can end up with the political leaders in one country inventing lies that are presented as truths that are used to invade and destroy the sovereignty of another country IN THE NAME OF GOD. And so on.

Relative to the four natural states of evolution where the consensus state is roughly seventy percent of all humans, this then means that seventy percent of any population will desire to CONFORM with the consensus beliefs of whatever groups of people they find themselves in: countries, races, religions, and so on. As a result of this, we can then have the majority of peoples in various groups around our Earth who 'believe' in the projected 'realities' that they manifest whether they are actually true or not. Thus, whole populations and groups of people, Souls, can be living in an almost total state of delusion yet believe those delusions to be real. Such delusions are then reinforced within these various groups because such groups will rebel, Uranus/Aquarius, against any other group whose realities defined by their own projected beliefs differ from their own.

The sad fact is that human beings can literally make themselves believe anything. It is only limited by the power of imagination. All one has to do is open up any newspaper, visit the Internet, listen to television and the radio, tune into some random conversation going around oneself, etc., to know just how unhinged and 'crazy' human beings can make themselves relative to their beliefs. With Neptune transiting Pisces, this craziness of what people can make themselves believe accelerates and infuses the collective consciousness as a result. Since all human Souls are part of the collective consciousness, this can create a real feeling in Souls that remain grounded in that which is true versus not to feel like they themselves are going crazy. This can lead to a real sense of exasperation that affects the individual Soul consciousness to either try to do something about it and/or to desire to withdraw from the increasingly crazy world where white seems to be black, up seems to be down, and chaos seems to be just around the corner.

Differing beliefs within the collective consciousness of various groups of humans creates a psychological insecurity that is perceived as threatening to their need to be consistent in their delusive beliefs. So we end up with all kinds of groups of people who then desire to self-segregate from other groups in order to feel secure where security is dependent on the need to be self-consistent. To be self-consistent each group self-segregates in such a way as to reinforce TOGETHER their delusive projected beliefs.

These binding archetypes in the consciousness of the Soul thus can cause groups of people conflicting with one another where the nature of the conflicts can be as small as they can be large and traumatic. Human history from the time of around 7,200 B.C.E, the South Node of Aquarius, forwards is testimony enough to this fact. The most extreme examples of this correlate with genocides of one group attempting to exterminate another group of peoples.

At the time of this writing, the transit of Uranus, the planetary ruler of the South Node of Neptune, is in Aries. All over our Earth we have large and small conflicts, wars, and one group attempting to dominate into submission, Neptune in Pisces, other groups of people who differ in their own projected beliefs. The underlying issue, again, is the nature of beliefs that define the nature of the consciousness whether that is an individual, or whole groups of people. The Sun rules the North Node of Neptune in Leo. Thus, this gives 'purpose' to that which is believed in; it gives a way to actualize that purpose where that purpose is defined by the nature of the beliefs themselves, and for the individual and the group to integrate, Sun, their whole lives around.

With Pluto transiting in Capricorn as of this writing, we can now understand how all the different 'strata' or groups of each country's societies interacts within themselves as defined by the nature of the projected beliefs existing in all the different strata of whatever societies of peoples in whatever countries: Capricorn. Within this, we see yet again the specter of nationalism in almost all lands and how nationalism is used as propaganda, beliefs, to justify the actions of the leaders of various countries who are creating conflicts with other countries, and their populations of people.

This then applies to all kinds of human issues such as immigration issues, economic issues, educations issues, one country trying to dominate or take over another country, and so on. The events that lead to World War II started with Uranus in

Aries, and Pluto in Cancer: the natural polarity to Capricorn. As these initial events in the early 1930's led to the actual war as Uranus moved into Taurus, survival, and Pluto moved into Leo that led to the need to recreate the world after this war. And because of this war, it also led to the invention, Uranus/Aquarius of the atom bomb: Pluto. The 'belief' of the one who invented it, Oppenheimer, was that if he created such a weapon of massive destruction, that this would end all wars. Oppenheimer convinced himself, made himself believe, that GOD gave him this power to invent this atom bomb. Of course, his personal belief system came from India and focused on the God "Shiva": the power of destruction and creation.

When the USA dropped the bombs on Japan, the transiting Pluto was exactly conjunct its North Node. It not only changed the world, but also propelled that country into becoming what it became. Whole groups of people, countries, suddenly, South Node of Neptune in Aquarius, became realigned because of this new power caused by the invention of this weapon. The effect within the collective consciousness of all humans was unalterably changed.

We all know this recent history. It included the evil of Hitler that led to the genocide of the Jews, Gypsies, and all who were considered as 'undesirables.' And, again, it was the function of beliefs that was the fuel of collective and individual Soul consciousness that created these events.

In the 1820's, the transit of Neptune, with Uranus, were both in Capricorn. Remember Uranus is the natural ruler of Neptune's South Node in Aquarius. As an example of beliefs being used to justify one group of people, creating genocide on another group of people, this correlates with the 'Monroe Doctrine' and 'Manifest Destiny' that was used by the government of America to commit genocide upon its native population: the American Indians. Here again we see the specter of nationalism being used as the rationale as well as the artificial beliefs that the Caucasian people were far superior to brown-skinned American Indians.

That transit also correlated to the Industrial Revolution, which needed to occur for the human race because of the increasing amount of the human population that required a radical alteration of how humans organized themselves in order to meet the needs and demands of the increasing population of humans. A classic example of 'need being the mother of invention.' And what was then invented altered forever how the human race lived on this planet, and with one another.

And, as an example of how history can repeat itself, when Neptune was in Pisces the last time in conjunction with Uranus in Aries, this correlated with the CRIMEAN WAR.

So the underlying issue within this is whether that which is believed in actually true or not. Beliefs have many forms and types. From religious, cosmological, philosophical, political, economic, to human interactions of all kinds: family members, wives and husbands, lovers, friendships, employees and employers, to specific events where humans interact in some way.

When beliefs that are projected into any of these humans' dynamics that are not true, it will cause some kind of wounding to those who are the recipient of such projections. Those who have been wounded by such projected beliefs, in turn, can project back upon the source of their wounding with their own projected beliefs. This cycle can become un-ending. Within this is the fact that any Soul who projects beliefs of any kind that are not actually true is in reality wounding themselves. They wound themselves because they are believing in something that is not true. This type of wound is the wound of delayed evolution until the nature of the delusive belief(s) is pierced with the actual truth.

There always is an underlying truth to any given phenomenon. That underlying truth is not a function of beliefs because the truth does not require beliefs BECAUSE IT IS TRUE. When that which is actually true interfaces with delusive projected beliefs, that leads to a disillusionment that itself leads to a potential variety of reactions depending on the underlying and existing context of the individual Soul's overall reality, specific types of groups of people, races of people, and whole countries.

The Neptune archetype of disillusionment is necessary to counteract any delusion or illusion so that an alignment with what is actually true can occur. When such a realignment takes place, this then allows for an acceleration in the evolutionary intentions for each Soul, and its consciousness. To the extent that any Soul continues to blind themselves to the actual truth, to hang on to their delusions and illusions at all costs, which means to sustain their delusive sense of security that is defined by the need to be self-consistent, such a Soul is essentially *marking time* relative to their own ongoing evolution. The sense of psychological security and the need to be self-consistent correlates to Cancer, which is part of the natural triad with Scorpio and Pisces.

The opportunity that the transit of Neptune provides for all Souls is to become aware of that which is delusional and illusionary in our lives versus what the actual truth is. To become aware of the truth of something, despite how bitter that may be, or how revelatory it can also be, is to allow the evolution of the consciousness of the Soul to proceed. The realization of what is true about something does not always mean this occurs through the experience of disillusionment. The truth of something can be realized relative to something that the Soul has been wondering about, pondering about, or attempting to know in various activities like astronomy, some mystical need defined by a question, the motives of another, the reasons for this or that, and so on. The need to know the truth in this way for those types of reasons is also a key to accelerating the evolution of the Soul's consciousness.

If we remember that one of the core archetypes of Neptune is that which correlates with the need for meaning in our lives, including ultimate meaning, we can also see how it can correlate with meaninglessness. During the Neptune transit, this can correlate to a progressive inner sense of meaninglessness relative to something that had held real meaning, including ultimate meaning, up until the transit impacted on that. With the South Node of Neptune in Aquarius in mind, this starts with a progressive detachment that leads to dissolving of the prior meaning totality. As this occurs, the consciousness of the Soul can feel very adrift, out to sea, no land in site, floundering within a sense of meaninglessness that is not immediately replaced by anything.

The temptation when this occurs is to replace, immediately, that which is dissolving into meaninglessness with something, anything, that will recreate a sense of meaning for that which has been lost. Temptation, as an archetype, correlates with Pluto, Scorpio, and the 8th House which is, again, part of the natural trinity or triad with Neptune, Pisces, and the 12th House, and Cancer, the Moon, and the 4th House. This then correlates with a time frame in which the Soul must be very careful in terms of what it is choosing to do, that which will recreate the sense of meaning that was lost. This is a natural time in which the Soul by way of the 'inner whispers' from the Source Of All Things is being asked to have an essential 'faith' that what the next steps are to recreate that sense of lost meaning will be revealed or present itself in its own time.

The problem and issue for most Souls is that the actual whispers from the Source Of All Things that correlate with those steps is initially ever so faint. The whispers initially are sporadic as well. This is exactly where the temptation of the Soul asserts itself where whatever the temptations are that offer some 'quick fix' from the sense of meaningless, the sense of despair, of sorrow even, are all too often set into motion by the opposite of the Source Of All Things. That which we call Evil, or the Devil. The reason that this can occur is the very existence of what we call Evil, Lucifer; the Devil is dependent on Souls doing anything other than desiring to know their true Source, to replace that which is lost with something that directly leads the way back HOME where home is the Source Of All Things.

So the quick fix manifesting as this temptation or that can seem so attractive, so 'right,' that whatever it is, is the actual answer to the Soul's prayers or anguish. When any Soul makes choices to follow such quick fixes in the form of these types of temptations then, of course, the very thing that recreates the sense of meaning in order to replace the meaningless itself becomes a source of meaninglessness itself. Round and round the Soul will go until it realizes that it must be patient so that the original whispers that actually come from the Source Of All Things, whispers that actually reflect the individual consciousness of the Soul, its existing context, correlate with its own next evolutionary steps in some way, become ever louder, more frequent, and create a real sense of Soul meaning.

When the consciousness of the individual Soul responds in this way to that which has been dissolved into meaninglessness by making choices to act upon the whispers from the Source Of All Things, then this will lead to a true and real sense of meaning that will be sustained for some time, as well as allowing the Soul to actually evolve according to its own individual evolutionary journey.

Beyond the immediacy of whatever the circumstances that have led to the opportunity within the Neptune transit is to reflect, to turn inwards, in such a way as to have a determined intent to reflect in hindsight upon the Soul's entire life in order to become aware of any and all delusions, illusions, self-deceptions, being deceived by others, and deceiving others. Once identified, the next step is then to make the effort to understand the inner dynamics within the consciousness of the Soul that have been responsible for this. The self-knowledge that is thus gained and APPLIED allows the Soul to accelerate upon its own evolutionary path and trajectory.

This is why it is essential as Evolutionary Astrologers to understand the individual context of any Soul's reality: where it has been, where it is now, and where it intends to go. The entire Evolutionary Paradigm that exists in all birth charts for all Souls is that which allows us to understand this. It is the exact individual context of the consciousness of the Soul. So when trying to understand the Neptune transit in our or our clients' lives, it is essential to understand as deeply as possible the individual evolutionary journey for the Soul relative the Evolutionary Paradigm: the natal position of Pluto, its polarity point, the South Node of the Moon by its own house and sign, the location of its planetary ruler by its own house and sign, with aspects to all these points from other planets, the North Node of the Moon by its own house and sign, the location of its planetary ruler by its own house and sign, and all the aspects to these points from other planets.

Wherever the actual transit of Neptune in Pisces is, or whatever sign it can be in, relative to the house it is transiting must involve the understanding of the Evolutionary Paradigm. In addition, it is necessary to locate and understand the transits of the natural planetary rulers of Neptune's South and North Nodes: Uranus, and the Sun. All the archetypes that correlate to Neptune, as detailed in this book, as well as Uranus and the Sun, are active at any moment in time as symbolized by the location of the houses and signs that they are transiting.

Neptune correlates to:

o   that which needs to be dissolved in order for Soul growth to occur;

o   the nature of our existing delusions/illusions that exist that need to be confronted with actual reality so that evolution of the Soul can proceed by way of replacing them with the actual truth;

o where emotional and instability of the consciousness of the Soul can occur and for what reasons;

o how to heal that emotional and instability of the Soul, if it is existing;

o where we have been and are deceiving ourselves, and for what reasons;

o and/or how we have allowed ourselves to be deceived and for what reasons;

o where our Souls do not take responsibility for creating events and circumstances which leads to the feeling of being victimized;

o where we can be victimizing others by way of making others scapegoats for that which we, in the end, are responsible for;

o where the impact of the collective consciousness on our individual lives can be the most extreme leading to a feeling being out of control in our own lives;

o where the Soul can actually influence the existing state of the collective consciousness by way of its own actualization of its unique Soul consciousness and its capacities;

o AND WHERE THE WHISPERS FROM THE SOURCE OF ALL THINGS manifest within each individualized Soul consciousness that allows for a quickening of the evolutionary pace, if acted upon. Such whispers from eternity, God/ess, are the individualized messages that allow for an inner alignment of the individualized Soul consciousness WITH ITS SOURCE.

In conjunction with Neptune, the transiting Uranus (the planetary ruler of Neptune's South Node) correlates with the archetype of FREEDOM FROM THE KNOWN. Wherever this transit is by house and sign location, aspects that it is making to other planets, correlates simultaneously with the past of the Soul that is interfacing in each moment, Neptune, that then allows for a freedom of that known past by way of liberating from it. Liberating from it means to become inwardly aware, attuned, to messages, whispers, from the Source Of All Things wherein the nature of those messages is to not only leave the past behind, the parts of the past that are no longer necessary, for the ongoing evolutionary growth of the Soul itself. These whispers, messages, reflect and symbolize a revolutionizing of that past that metamorphose into the Soul's evolutionary future: to sustain the parts of the past, the inner dynamics that have caused it, that are still relevant to the Soul's evolving future with the messages that allow that future to manifest.

In combination with Neptune, these messages, whispers, directly correlate with the individual consciousness of the Soul: where it has been, where it is now, and where is going, as defined and symbolized by the EVOLUTIONARY PARADIGM itself. As such, the nature of the whispers and messages are directly linked with that unique nature of any given Soul. Uranus correlates with an acceleration of the evolutionary intentions of any given Soul when the messages, whispers, from the Source Of All Things become 'quickened' by way of Uranus. So the originally faint and relatively distant messages that correlate with Neptune become ever more conscious within the consciousness of the Soul by way of this quickening. The once distant billboard is now becoming ever closer.

Sometimes the nature of these messages and whispers demands a complete break from the past: a total letting go in order to start anew. Other times these messages and whispers simply demand that we add on to some existing reality that is in place, a reality that is still serving the evolutionary intentions of the Soul. In either case, a quickening of the evolutionary pace will take place. Sometimes these messages and whispers will seem to be very radical to the individualized consciousness of the Soul as compared to what the existing reality is. It is not uncommon for Souls to resist these messages and whispers, to detach from them, to create the rationalization that, indeed, they are too radical, that would require, if acted upon, total upsetting of their existing reality. In other words, the Soul can make itself feel insecure and ungrounded, Neptune, if it actually considered taking action of these messages. A typical reaction of this type manifests as, "Well, this is crazy, this is delusional," or "I will do this at some other time." In so doing, the Soul then creates a reality for itself that is essentially marking time in an evolutionary sense.

The natural quickening of the messages of Neptune to Uranus manifests wherein the messages and whispers become progressively repeating within the individualized consciousness of the Soul. This is intentional from the point of view of the Creator Of All Things. This is how God/ess attempts to get the ATTENTION OF THE SOUL ITSELF. These messages will now be a combination, a synthesis, of whatever the house and sign of the Neptune transit is taking place within, with the house and sign of the Uranus transit. Within this, the aspects that both planets are making to other natal planets, their own house and sign locations, will contribute to what the very nature is of these whispers and messages from eternity.

Again, these messages and whispers will become progressively repetitious: like a knocking on the door. Relative to the temptations of Evil, of Lucifer or the Devil, these repeating and progressively repetitious messages and whispers will be interfered with. This interference will manifest "sudden" ideas that seem to come from nowhere that create a real sense of Soul excitement in terms of how tempting they can be. Yet these types of Lucifer-induced messages do not have the ongoing repetitious nature of the actual messages and whispers from God/ess. They come, and they go. If a given Soul chooses to act upon them, they are inevitably met with some kind of traumatic event that pops the balloons of delusion being influenced by Lucifer itself. The intent, from Lucifer's point of view, is to keep the Soul ensnarled with delusions in such a way as to prevent the inner alignment of the Soul with its Maker by way of the whispers from eternity that the Maker is inducing in the individualized consciousness of the Soul.

There are, of course, times in the life of almost all Souls in which the very nature of the circumstances that it has created for itself ignites an inner feeling of hopelessness, of reaching a dead end with no way out, of desperation that can be so intense that they induce an inner feeling of hysteria, a sense of not being able to change or alter the circumstances themselves. At these times, many Souls inwardly or outwardly pray, or ask for some kind of divine or supernatural help from whatever the circumstances are that are causing this psychological state for the Soul. The Soul needs help, an intervention, to change that which can seem so hopeless and futile.

Many times, not always of course, if the Soul is sincere enough, and is not bound by some karmic determinant that requires that whatever the conditions are that are causing this inner psychology of the Soul, The Source Of All Things can in fact intervene to help change or create relief in some way from those conditions. When this happens, it seems to the Soul that some kind of miracle has taken place, that the answers to the prayers have been realized.

The North Node of Neptune in Leo, again, is ruled by the Sun. The Sun correlates to how we integrate the very purpose of our lives, of how we go about actualizing and integrating those purposes. Thus, the natal Sun in combination with the transiting Sun, both correlate to how the Soul is meant to integrate, actualize, and give purpose to the ongoing evolution of the Soul relative to all the archetypes of Neptune and Uranus that we have been discussing.

It should be clear, from the point of view of Evolutionary Astrology, that a total and complete understanding of the natal Evolutionary Paradigm serving as the foundation for the individualized consciousness of the Soul, needs to be understood. From that foundation, the Evolutionary Astrologer then understands how to understand and integrate the evolving, transiting, nature of this paradigm manifesting as the transits of Pluto, the North and South Nodes of the Moon, and the transits of their natural planetary rulers, but to now add to that foundation and context the understanding of the Neptune transit itself which includes the transits of the natural planetary rulers of its own North and South Nodes.

CHAPTER FIFTEEN

HOW YOU CAN NATURALLY KNOW GOD

When the Creator Of All Things set in motion the Manifest Creation, included in that was for the consciousness to KNOW its origin, its MAKER. In essence, this is actually 'hard wired' into the Soul by its Maker.

This natural way is provable and requires no allegiance to any religion, group, or philosophy. It does require 100% DESIRE in any individualized Soul consciousness to KNOW its Maker, the Origin of itself.

This natural way is rooted in the Natural Law of cause and effect. It is rooted in the Natural Law of the breath. The inhaling and exhaling breath is analogous to the law of cause and effect: inhale, exhale. Yet there is also a natural interval between the inhaling and exhaling breath. It is this natural interval that then correlates to a transcendence of the law of cause and effect: the interval correlating to infinity.

With the breath still, as Jesus and others said, one's whole being becomes full of Light: "When Thine Eye Is Single." And, indeed, it does. As the breath begins to shallow and suspend itself, the progressive perception of what has been called the 3rd eye begins. And that is perceived between the eyes, just above them in the forehead area. It is initially perceived as a circular outline that progresses into the perception of a circle. The outer circle is gold or yellow, the center of it is a deep blue, and in the middle there will be a five pointed White Star, or as the perception of a spinning galaxy of White, Blue and Gold that solidifies into a circle with the Gold on the outside of the circle, the blue in the middle, and then the White Star at its core.

In time, the Soul will remember, by BIRTH RIGHT, how to merge with the 3rd eye, the White Star. As this begins, progressive perceptions of what can be called true cosmic consciousness begins that allows for a state of SUPER-CONSCIOUSNESS. The final progression of this leads to the perception of where the Manifest Creation meets the un-manifested Creation. In essence, perceiving the very nature of Creation itself: God/ess.

This is provable and requires no belief at all. It only requires DESIRE TO KNOW THE MAKER OF ONE'S SOUL.

To know this for yourself is very simple. First, it is important to sit in such a way that your spine is vertical from the pelvic area up. Then center your entire attention, focused, on the point just above your eyebrows within your consciousness, with your eyes closed.

Then on your inhaling breath mentally affirm the number One. On your exhaling breath, mentally affirm the number Two.

The key and secret here is one of CONCENTRATION. Keep concentrating on the One and Two linked with your inhale and exhale. Of course, in the beginning, the left side of your brain will go nuts with all kinds of thoughts that attempt to undermine this, to distract, to follow. This is why the concentration is the vital key upon the One and Two.

Over time, and with sustained practice, the breath will progressively begin to shallow. As it does, so certain inner experiences will begin. For example, there will be an inner perception that the external world seems to be going into some kind of earthquake situation. Yet, if you open your eyes, then the Earth will in fact still be still. What this perception correlates to is a natural shifting in the CENTER OF GRAVITY FOR YOUR CONSCIOUSNESS.

That shifting correlates with a shift from the egocentric center of your consciousness to your Soul itself. This also corresponds to a molecular shift in the density of your body cells. They become lighter, less dense.

In time, this will progress to the initial perception of the 3rd eye which starts with a spinning galaxy that is blue, white, and yellow. In time, as the breath becomes ever more shallow, concentrating ever more on the One Two, this will consolidate into the 3rd eye wherein that circle of yellow, blue light is integrated around the white star.

This is when the breath suspends itself because of the concentration upon the One and the Two. This is when the INTERVAL between breaths occurs. Again, the breath, inhale and exhale, correlates to the world of duality, of cause and effect, of thought/counter thought. When the breath becomes suspended, this natural interval between the inhaling and exhaling breaths is realized. The interval can be understood to be that which correlates with INFINITY: the natural interval between One and

Two. The consciousness of the Soul is NOT DEPENDENT UPON THE PHYSICAL FORM THAT IT IS ENCASED WITHIN. THERE IS NOTHING TO FEAR, EVEN THOUGH THE EGO OF THE SOUL CAN FEAR 'LOSING CONTROL' AT THIS POINT.

This is when your Soul will remember, by birthright, how to penetrate or merge with the White Star. Everything that follows from there correlates to progressive perceptions of the Manifest Creation that will lead to the NATURAL LIMIT of the Soul's consciousness that is encased in the human form. And that limit, again, is when the perception of the Manifested Creation interfaces with the UN-MANIFESTED CREATION. This perception is the perception of Creation itself: God/ess. As this takes place, the Soul is then in a state of RAPTURE, OF WONDERMENT. The various truths of the Natural Laws that are the very basis of the Manifest Creation will then be progressively realized and understood. It is a natural state of enlightenment.

Yet, because the consciousness of the Soul is still living within the encasement of the human form, thus the time/space reality of duality, it is that which creates a RETURN to a 'normal' state of consciousness. Rapture and wonderment are soon replaced with a sense of depression upon this return to normal consciousness. Yet, because of that which has been directly experienced through perception, leading to realization, the consciousness of the Soul has been evolved. And this evolution that has occurred because of these realized perceptions in a super-conscious state is APPLIED to not only the individualized consciousness of the Soul who has realized this, but also given, NATURALLY, to others in all kinds of ways depending on the specific nature, the individualized context, of each Soul.

In the beginning of this practice, it is really important, in fact necessary, for you to allow at least forty-five minutes to an hour for it. And to do this consistently at least once a day. Your natural evolutionary capacity will then be the determinant at what pace you go. But, by birthright, if you practice faithfully, Neptune, for as long as it takes, this natural process of how to know your Origins, your Maker, God, will in fact take place.

GOD BLESS
AND GODSPEED

OTHER BOOKS ON EVOLUTIONARY ASTROLOGY

PLUTO: THE EVOLUTIONARY JOURNEY OF THE SOUL
(Volume I)
by Jeffrey Wolf Green

Pluto Vol. 1 first went into print in 1984 and has been in continuous print ever since, translated into many languages. It is one of the all-time best selling astrology books. This was the first book in the history of astrology to talk about the Soul and its evolution from life to life. It presented for the first time an actual astrological paradigm that could measure the ongoing evolution of the Soul, a paradigm tested by Jeffrey on over 30,000 clients/souls during his career. Through this work, Jeffrey founded the paradigm of Evolutionary Astrology. He first began lecturing on EA in 1978.

From the time this book exploded onto the scene, over two decades ago, it has continued to set a new pace for the evolution of astrology itself. Jeff Wolf Green's writing embodies everything you would expect from Pluto: intense, powerful, riveting, transformative and penetrating. A book that satiates both the desire for knowledge and the deep yearning for true understanding is a rare find indeed, and just as profound as the information included here, is the deep intuitive awakening it will bring to your own Soul. If you want to help yourself and assist others in conscious evolution, rather than simply waiting for it to happen, this book is the essential map for that journey!

PLUTO: THE SOUL'S EVOLUTION THROUGH RELATIONSHIPS
(Volume II)
by Jeffrey Wolf Green

The second volume details the Soul's evolutionary journey through relationships of all kinds, and the evolutionary and karmic purposes of such relationships. It discusses the various relationship types, i.e. Karmic, Soul mates, etc., as well as how to apply the EA paradigm in each individual chart to others whom we are in relationship to: synastry. Thus, the evolutionary and karmic background between two Souls can be understood as well as the current life intentions for the relationship itself.

The essential needs of any given Soul is discussed as well as the evolutionary and karmic reasons for those needs. A detailed explanation of Venus and Mars is presented in this context. Additionally, the evolution of a relationship with another(s) is detailed by way of the transiting nature of the core EA paradigm in each individual in the relationship that requires and creates an evolution within the relationship itself.

And, finally, the combined Soul in a relationship is focused upon by way of the composite Pluto, the combined Soul, that is seen through the composite chart of any two Souls. This will then correlate to the core evolutionary purpose of the relationship itself. In this chapter, the combined Pluto is presented relative to the natural states of evolution: the consensus, individuated, and spiritual states of evolution.

ESSAYS ON EVOLUTIONARY ASTROLOGY:
THE EVOLUTIONARY JOURNEY OF THE SOUL
by Jeffrey Wolf Green
Edited by Deva Green

Deva Green, Jeffrey Wolf Green's daughter, has put together a book that is a compilation of some of Jeffrey's old lectures that have not before appeared in book form. When Jeffrey Wolf Green retired and went into seclusion, he left his daughter Deva with everything that he had ever written which included drafts of various manuscripts which he had intended to publish at various points. This also included every audio tape, video, DVD, and transcript of his lectures delivered over a lengthy career. He also gave Deva his business and asked her to carry on with it. This book reflects her desire to continue to disseminate his work as widely as possible. Essays on Evolutionary Astrology: The Evolutionary Journey of the Soul, is a combination of transcribed lectures with parts of various manuscripts, most of which has never been in print before. It also includes a vital understanding OF ALL THE PLANETARY NODES IN THE BIRTH CHART.

EVOLUTIONARY ASTROLOGY:
PLUTO AND YOUR KARMIC MISSION
by Deva Green

Deva studied EA with her father for many years, from birth in fact. As a result, she is uniquely qualified to carry on his work, which she has been doing since his retirement. Her first book is an in-depth examination of all the core astrological principles that define the Evolutionary Journey of the Soul. Every aspect of the self, from our ambitions and motivations, to the Soul's evolutionary journey, can be traced back to Pluto. This powerful planet of transformation is the key to understanding the factors in your natal chart, ultimately revealing your karmic mission.

Inspired by Jeffrey Wolf Green's best selling, *Pluto, Volume I*, this groundbreaking astrology book offers clear, step-by-step instruction and practical application of his original work's methods. Pinpoint your Soul's evolutionary intention by locating Pluto in your natal chart. Gain insight into your psychological makeup, identify your Soul's evolutionary stage, and discover your true purpose in this life. Fascinating case studies of famous figures throughout history such as Richard Nixon and Nostradamus lend a vibrant and personal touch to the core principles of Evolutionary Astrology. As you master these techniques, you will reconnect with an evolving sense of purpose and actualize your potential for spiritual growth.

UNDERSTANDING KARMIC COMPLEXES:
Evolutionary Astrology and Regression Therapy
by Patricia Walsh

Patricia is both a graduate of Jeffrey Wolf Green's School of Evolutionary Astrology and a professional past-life regressionist. Patricia has written a groundbreaking book that bridges both disciplines. In it you will find actual past-life histories of individuals, gained through past-life regression techniques, that have the effect of 'proving' the methodology and paradigm of Evolutionary Astrology. It is exceptionally well written. It will help all who seek to understand the paradigm of Evolutionary Astrology learn to correlate the birth chart insights EA reveals with the actual life-to-life experiences that have shaped and conditioned the very nature of the lives that we live, past and present.

INSIGHTS INTO EVOLUTIONARY ASTROLOGY:
A Diverse Collection of Essays by Prominent Astrologers
Edited by Rose Marcus

Evolutionary astrology holds the key to life's most profound mysteries: Where does the Soul come from? How can we grow spiritually? What are our intended life lessons? Shedding new light on these vitally important questions, well-known astrologer Rose Marcus has compiled a collection of illuminating essays by today's foremost evolutionary astrologers, including Jeffrey Wolf Green.

Jeffrey Wolf Green, the world-renowned founder of this specialized field of study, begins the book with an exploration of the four natural evolutionary laws that propel Soul growth. Deva Green continues with a discussion of how Pluto drives our evolutionary growth, illustrated with case studies and charts of notable figures such as President Barack Obama.

Each contributor offers fascinating perspectives on Evolutionary Astrology and explores various aspects of Pluto's role in determining the Soul's evolving needs and desires. Contributors also explore Pluto's influence on the sexual and relationship characteristics of each zodiacal sign, the fulfillment of human potential, the dynamics between twins, past life regression, the interpretive importance of planetary nodes, and the cultural significance of Pluto entering Capricorn.

JEFFREY WOLF GREEN EVOLUTIONARY ASTROLOGY: URANUS: FREEDOM FROM THE KNOWN
(2014 Revised Edition)
by Jeffrey Wolf Green
Edited by Linda Jonson and The School of Evolutionary Astrology

Uranus: Freedom From the Known is based on a 6-hour workshop that was given in 1986 by Jeffrey Wolf Green, the founder of Evolutionary Astrology. It focuses primarily on the archetype of liberation from existing inner dynamics that are preventing the evolution of the Soul. Addressed in this book are the archetypes of trauma, individuation, liberation, and de-conditioning. These Uranian archetypes are always in dynamic tension with the Saturnian archetypes of individual and social conditioning. The dynamic tension between Saturn and Uranus is the primary theme of this book. It is the purpose of Uranus to try to shatter or break free from the conformity patterns that define one's sense of identity, in order to arrive at one's essential unique nature that is unconditioned.

Also covered are in-depth descriptions of trauma of the mental, emotional, physical and spiritual bodies correlating to the outer planets; Uranus retrograde, transits, aspects, synastry and composites; and the archetypal correlations of Uranus to anatomy, physiology, and the chakra system, making this one of the most comprehensive 'must-have' books on Uranus from an Evolutionary Astrology point of view.

This is a revised and expanded reprinting of the original book that was published in 1986.

JEFFREY WOLF GREEN EVOLUTIONARY ASTROLOGY: MEDICAL ASTROLOGY
Astrological Correlations to Anatomy, Physiology and the Chakra System
by Jeffrey Wolf Green
Edited by Linda Jonson and The School of Evolutionary Astrology

This is the most comprehensive book on Medical Astrology from the Jeffrey Wolf Green Evolutionary Astrology point of view. This book is derived from the medical information contained in Jeffrey's Evolutionary Astrology DVD course, and the message board for Jeffrey's School of Evolutionary Astrology. This book contains detailed correlations to the anatomy, physiology, and chakra system of the human body. It also has practice charts by those who participated in the medical thread on the EA message board so that this will help in understanding how to apply these correlations. The material contained in this book originates from Jeffrey Wolf Green, and has been augmented by way of the School of Evolutionary Astrology message board moderated by Rad Zecko.

JEFFREY WOLF GREEN EVOLUTIONARY ASTROLOGY: RELATIONSHIPS: OUR ESSENTIAL NEEDS

by Jeffrey Wolf Green

Edited by Linda Jonson and The School Of Evolutionary Astrology

In *Relationships: Our Essential Needs* the core archetypes are presented that correlate with how to understand the essential needs of any Soul in the context of the relationships that it forms with others in general, and its intimate others specifically.

The very first chapter presents an evolutionary astrology paradigm that needs to be deeply grasped in order to understand the inherent architecture within the consciousness of all our Souls that serves as the foundation upon which the root essential needs for any Soul exist.

The nature and function of Venus, the nature and function of Mars, the relationship between Pluto, the Soul, and its lower octave, Mars, and the phasal relationship of Mars and Venus are all intensely discussed and presented in order to understand the fuller picture of the essential needs that the Soul has within the relationships that it forms. The signs that both Mars and Venus are in are also presented in order for this understanding to be deepened.

The core or root evolutionary cause or intention for the Soul's relationship to another Soul is then discussed in the chapter, Pluto in the Composite Chart. This correlates to two Souls coming together in a relationship that symbolizes where the Souls have been together, the core evolutionary needs and intentions, prior to the current life as well as what the current life evolutionary reasons are in order for those two Souls to continue to evolve in their relationship.

Pluto is discussed in each house and sign with its corresponding polarities in each of the natural evolutionary stages of development: the consensus, individuated, and spiritual stages of evolution.

And, finally, the last chapter deals with one couple's evolutionary journey together that focuses on the entire core archetypes discussed throughout this book.

This book is based on an extraction from Pluto (Vol. II): The Soul's Evolution through Relationships. Specific chapters in that comprehensive book have been chosen for the purposes of this book, which is to help us understand the core and essential needs that we all have in the relationships that we form.

JEFFREY WOLF GREEN EVOLUTIONARY ASTROLOGY: EA GLOSSARY
(Updated 2014 Edition)
by Jeffrey Wolf Green
Compiled and Edited by Linda Jonson
and The School of Evolutionary Astrology

Incredible EA information, knowledge, wisdom and insight is skilfully woven into this second edition, condensing Jeffrey Wolf Green's four decades of world-renowned Pluto work into bite-sized info-packets. The EA Glossary is a well-researched, informative and illuminating compilation of key terms, topics and guiding principles used in Jeffrey Wolf Green's Evolutionary Astrology that affirms and expands upon the core EA paradigm taught in his books, *Pluto: The Evolutionary Journey of the Soul (Vol. 1)* and *Pluto: The Soul's Evolution through Relationships (Vol. 2)*. Compiled from extracts from the message board of the School of Evolutionary Astrology from March 2009 to October 2013, the EA Glossary provides indispensable study material for resourceful EA students and discerning members of the astrological community, in essence serving as a compass to help navigate into the depths of EA.

EVOLUTIONARY ASTROLOGY: A BEGINNERS GUIDE
by Ari Moshe Wolfe

This book is written for beginners as well as advanced astrology students who are new to the paradigm of Evolutionary Astrology as taught by Jeffrey Wolf Green. It is meant as an aid to those who are interested in studying the teachings of EA as taught by Jeffrey Wolf Green. The core teachings of this book are focused on understanding the nature of the Soul, and how to read the natal chart as a map that describes the reasons for the Soul's current incarnation – all from the point of view of the Soul's ongoing evolutionary journey from life to life.

UPCOMING BOOKS BY JEFFREY WOLF GREEN

Relationships: Our Essential Needs

Geodetic Equivalents

Lucifer and the Bearer of Light

The Planetary Method of Chart Interpretation

Saturn

All of these books are available from many sources but can be purchased as well from The School of Evolutionary Astrology website:

www.schoolofevolutionaryastrology.com

If you are interested in becoming a Certified Evolutionary Astrologer, there is a comprehensive DVD course available. This is based on the very first School that Jeffrey Wolf Green taught in Evolutionary Astrology.

For further information, please visit the website.

32512160R00273

Made in the USA
Lexington, KY
22 May 2014